GIORGIO AGAMBEN

A Critical Introduction

Leland de la Durantaye

STANFORD UNIVERSITY PRESS

STANFORD, CALIFORNIA

2009

Stanford University Press
Stanford, California

Printed in the United States of America on acid-free, archival-quality paper

Library of Congress Cataloging-in-Publication Data

De la Durantaye, Leland.
    Giorgio Agamben : a critical introduction / Leland de la Durantaye.
       p.   cm.
    Includes bibliographical references and index.
    ISBN 978-0-8047-6142-0 (cloth : alk. paper)
    ISBN 978-0-8047-6143-7 (pbk. : alk. paper)
       1. Agamben, Giorgio, 1942–   2. Philosophy, Italian—20th century.   I. Title.
B3611.A44D4   2009
195—dc22

                                                                    2008037590

080076335

For Katharina

"L'inferno dei viventi non è qualcosa che sarà; se ce n'è uno è quello che è già qui, l'inferno che abitiamo tutti i giorni, che formiamo stando insieme. Due modi ci sono per non soffrirne. Il primo riesce facile a molti: accettare l'inferno e diventarne parte fin al punto di non vederlo più. Il secondo è rischioso ed esige attenzione e apprendimento continui: cercare e saper riconoscere chi e cosa, in mezzo all'inferno, non è inferno, e farlo durare, e dargli spazio."

—ITALO CALVINO, *Le città invisibili*

Contents

is to invoke them where I felt it might lead to a better understanding of Agamben's thought. This engagement with secondary sources markedly increases as the book progresses for the simple reason that the critical literature on Agamben's early works is sparse and the critical literature on his later works is ample. For this same reason I have concentrated on summary and elucidation more in the chapters on lesser-known early works than in those on later ones, such as *Homo Sacer*, for which summaries are in rich supply.

The reader will not be long in noting that philological questions play a large role in this study. Paraphrasing Wittgenstein, Agamben has often argued that "philosophical problems become clearer if they are formulated as questions concerning the meaning of words" (P, 177 [273]; see also PP, 77). The idea that philosophical questions are inseparable from philological ones is central to this work, not only because the idea is Agamben's own, but also because of the many points of uncertainty surrounding even the most fundamental terms in his writing.

A final word on length: this book will seem long—and doubtless all the more so given that Agamben's books have, as a rule, been short; but they have also been many, and their concerns have been remarkably diverse—and it is to that diversity that this study responds.

GIORGIO AGAMBEN

Introduction: The Idea of Potentiality

The Idea of Vocation

In the summer of 1966, twenty-four-year-old Giorgio Agamben found himself in select company. He was one of five guests invited to one of the most singular seminars of the century. It took place in the village of Le Thor, in the south of France, and was presided over by the seventy-seven-year-old *éminence grise* of European philosophy, Martin Heidegger. Thirty-five years earlier Heidegger had already began to speculate that it was his "curious destiny" to be "a means for the awakening of philosophy in others" (Heidegger GA, 29–30.225). Like Socrates, he saw himself as a medium for ideas and a midwife for philosophy. Although he may have been wrong about many things in the years to follow, this was not one of them. By the 1960s, however, the midwife of such varied talents as Hannah Arendt, Emmanuel Lévinas, and Hans-Georg Gadamer had long ceased to teach in conventional settings. As a result of his membership in the Nazi party and his activities of the 1930s, he was banned from teaching by the Allied authority in 1945. Five years later he officially retired. Even at the insistence of such figures as Paul Celan, Heidegger refused to offer explanations or issue apologies for his actions, and, in his native Germany, he retreated ever more profoundly into his woodland hut in the Black Forest.

During these same years, however, his influence on the other side of the Rhine increased dramatically. Through the ambassadorial efforts of students such as Jean Beaufret, translations by Henry Corbin and Pierre Klossowski, and a host of impassioned, influential, and outspoken readers

from Sartre to Lacan, Heidegger became one of the most decisive influences on the intellectual life of postwar France. His host in the south of
France in 1966, however, was not a philosopher, psychoanalyst, translator,
or historian, but instead a poet—one of the finest of his generation, and
who had played a courageous part in the French Resistance. René Char
first came to know Heidegger during a conference held in Cerisy-la-Salle
(Normandy) in 1955 and was so taken by his reflections on poetic vocation
that he invited the aging philosopher to his home in the Vaucluse.[1] This
location became the setting for a series of small seminars in 1966, 1968, and
1969, which the young Agamben attended.

These seminars could not have been more classical, either in form or
content. The participants convened outside, seated in the shade of a syca-
more tree, to discuss philosophy's oldest mysteries—beginning with the
topic of the first seminar in 1966: the fragments of Heraclitus.[2] An ardent
hiker even at his advanced age, Heidegger lent a peripatetic element to the
seminar through the long walks on which he led the group. For Agamben,
the experience proved decisive. He described the seminars as much more
than a simple forum "in which one learns things" (LDV). They formed
instead what he called a *constellation:* a coming together of elements resulting in something truly unexpected. This unexpected thing was, simply,
philosophy. As he would later remark, it was during those seminars that,
for him, "philosophy became possible" (AC, ii).

The immediate result of this experience was what Agamben was
to call a new *vocation*. At the time he had been studying a subject that
lay far from his heart. Although he was an avid reader of literature and
philosophy, when he enrolled for university study he selected law. His experiences of that summer changed much, leading him not only to choose
philosophy over law, but to articulate an idea of vocation to match that
philosophy. In an essay published thirty years later, Agamben observed
that in Heidegger's ontology, "*Dasein* does not have a specific nature or a
preconstituted vocation"—and for himself and his own *Dasein* he seems to
have reached precisely the same conclusion (PP, 326).[3] Following the idea
Agamben forged that summer, "a true vocation is always the *revocation*
of an earlier vocation"—or as he said on another occasion, "an authentic
philosophical vocation is really nothing so much as the revocation of every
other vocation" (AC, iii, italics in original; UL, 16).[4]

At first sight, Agamben's definition of vocation looks a great deal like its opposite: the absence of vocation. The idea that a "true vocation" is actually the revocation of an earlier one does not mean simply seeing through the vanity of vocations, nor does it necessitate seeing vocations as vicious circles destined to be superseded by other vocations that in turn will prove equally unsatisfying. For Agamben, a "true" or "philosophical" vocation is not a revocation of one vocation for another vocation of the same nature, but instead a vocation without set tasks or fixed content. It is, in short, nothing other than the pure potentiality to think and to act.

For Agamben—and for his readers—this fine line between a meaningless paradox and a meaningful vocation is best understood in terms of writing. When asked about the beginning of his career Agamben once remarked that he started "like everyone else" by simply "wanting to write" (LDV). This uncertain desire—"wanting to write"—was, as he came to realize, not the desire "to write this or that specific work or novel" (LDV). It was, instead, something much vaster—something more "senseless and strange [*insensata e strana*]," but also "more profound" than any set goal or aim (LDV).

In a phrase that presents the central term of his philosophy, Agamben remarked that "wanting to write is the desire to experience potentiality" (LDV). The coming together of these two things—wanting to write and an experience of potentiality—is the common thread that links his diverse works.

One of Agamben's first publications is a poem from 1967 entitled "Clearings [*Radure*]." The title is an evocative and allusive one. Given the pride of place that Heidegger accorded in his late work to what he called the "clearing [*Lichtung*]"—an opening onto the site of primary and primordial meaning and being, for which his favorite metaphor was a forest clearing—it should come as little surprise that the twenty-five-year-old Agamben dedicated this poem to the teacher who, the previous summer, had helped him find his vocation. The second stanza of this poem begins, "Beauty is destiny [*Bellezza è destino*]", and continues with the following question:

Come può un uomo
fermarsi sulla sua strada e chiedere: questo
è il mio destino?

How can a man
stop on the street and ask: *this
is my destiny?*

This is a question that, in a remarkable variety of forms, Agamben has continued to ask. It points to three central aspects of his thought. The first is a thoroughgoing reflection on individual and collective vocations. The second aspect is the question, What activity or attribute, what potentiality or actuality, truly characterizes mankind, separating man from animal and the human from the inhuman? And the third is the sheer diversity of Agamben's writing.

Aristotle's Question

Henri Bergson once claimed that all philosophers have but one idea that is truly their own and that in their works—be they many or few—they seek to express (Bergson 1998, 122–23). In Agamben's philosophy we have no trouble finding such an idea. It is *potentiality.* Naming this idea, however, is a far cry from understanding it. As with Plato's *eidos,* Aristotle's *energeia,* Aquinas's *esse,* Descartes' *cogito,* Heidegger's *Ereignis,* and many similar terms, the first challenge to understanding Agamben's idea of potentiality stems from its very centrality.[5] By informing every other idea in that thinker's work, it becomes exceptionally difficult to define. A second challenge to an understanding of *potentiality* is the new and unexpected ways in which Agamben, like the other thinkers named above, employs it. Plato's *eidos* is an image and idea, but one that is singularly different from those of the philosophers who preceded him. *Cogito* means "I think," but the way in which Descartes conceived of this central fact was so new and so different from earlier declarations that it continues to resist easy description (though not, of course, easy citation). Closer to our times, the capital term of Heidegger's late philosophy, *Ereignis,* means, simply enough, "event," but the event or events it denotes bear little similarity to those with which we are familiar.

For Agamben's part, he makes no secret of the fact that the fundamental contours of his idea of potentiality are to be traced to none other than Aristotle. He has noted that "in both his metaphysics and his physics, Aristotle at once opposed and linked potentiality (*dynamis*) to actuality (*energeia*), and bequeathed this opposition to Western philosophy and science" (P, 177 [273], translation modified). As Aristotle's readers know, the relation of potentiality to actuality can be articulated in two modes. The first of these is easy to grasp: *the potentiality to be.* For a thing to be, it stands to reason that it must have first been possible (for if it had been *im*possible it could never have come to be). The second mode in which potentiality exists—which, as Agamben is careful to underline, "[Aristotle] calls 'the potentiality to not-be' (*dynamis me einai*) or also impotence (*adynamia*)" (CC, 35 [33])—requires more careful consideration. This "potentiality to not-be," or "impotence," is not to be understood as a privation, as an actual weakness or incapacity, for the reason that it is not to be understood in the context of actuality *at all.* It denotes the possibility for a thing *not* to pass into existence and thereby remain at the level of mere—or "pure"—potentiality.

At this point Agamben's reader might well wonder why he is so interested in a category without substance, a mode of potentiality that by definition never enters our actual sphere. Before answering this question we would do well first to ask why Aristotle was so interested in it. As Agamben points out, Aristotle discusses "the potentiality to not-be" with respect to "the supreme theme of metaphysics"—thought itself (CC, 36 [34]). Aristotle observed that if thought were only the potentiality to think this or that intelligible thing, it would by definition be less than its object. We think of an astounding variety of things, and yet thought is unquestionably more than the sum of the actual things of, or about, which it thinks. What is more, if thought were merely the sum of things of which it has thought, not only would it be inferior to its object, but it would also leave unexplained thought's most singular feature: its ability to reflect upon itself.

It was not only for the purposes of defining thought, however, that Aristotle was interested in potentiality. What it led him to focus on was nothing less than the question of what life is for—or alternately, what mankind is for. In the first book of the *Nicomachean Ethics,* Aristotle speaks, appropriately enough, of happiness. Of even such high matters as "honor, pleasure, and reason," he notes, "we choose them indeed for themselves (for if nothing resulted from them we should still choose each of them), but we choose them also for the sake of happiness, judging that through them we shall be happy" (1097a36–1097b6; Aristotle 1984, 1734). The relation of means to ends is different, however, as concerns happiness itself. As Aristotle observes, "no one chooses happiness for the sake of

these things, nor, in general, for anything other than itself" (1097a36–
1097b6; Aristotle 1984, 1734). Happiness is not sought as a means to an
end; it is its own end. Aristotle does not leave matters here, however, and
adds that "to say that happiness is the chief good seems a platitude, and
a clearer account of what it is is still desired." He then speculates, "this
might perhaps be given, if we could first ascertain the function of man"
(1097b23–1098a16; Aristotle 1984, 1735).

In order that the idea of happiness as its own end not remain at
the level of a platitude, man's essential vocation—or "function"—must be
ascertained, and to this end Aristotle marshals a set of examples. "For just
as for a flute-player, a sculptor, or any artist, and, in general, for all things
that have a function or activity, the good . . . is thought to reside in the
function," he remarks, "so would it seem to be for man, if he has a function. Have the carpenter, then, and the tanner certain functions or activities, and has man none? Is he naturally functionless?" (1097b23–1098a16;
Aristotle 1984, 1735). Carpenters and tanners have, of course, the vocations
of carpenter and tanner—but do they also, Aristotle asks, have a vocation
on another level—that of being human? To speak of such a vocation or
function is to assign a task—an essential and defining activity—to mankind as a whole, and it should come as no surprise that Aristotle pauses to
wonder whether mankind could indeed be said to have such a collective
vocation.

It is precisely this question that Agamben asks again and again in
his work and that is intimately bound to his idea of potentiality. He points
out that the question Aristotle asks—usually translated "Is man naturally
functionless?"—would be more accurately rendered "Is man born without
work [*senz'opera*] (*argos*)?" (PP, 365).[6] Aristotle points to the examples of
carpenters and tanners who in their capacities as such have specific and
defining work to do without which there would cease to be carpenters
or tanners—but would not, of course, cease to be men. What, Aristotle
then asks, of mankind as a whole? Do we have a specific task to complete, a select activity to exercise, set work we must do or works we must
accomplish?

Agamben's philosophy of potentiality evolves as an answer to this
question. In its simplest form, his response is *no*. For him, mankind has
no millennial or messianic task to complete, no divinely ordained work
that it must do, and no set function it must exercise. And it is this idea that
he presents in his discussions of potentiality and expresses through such

curious figures as Bartleby and such unfamiliar terms as *inoperativeness*. Just as, in his view, an authentic individual vocation is without determinate content—is more than merely "wanting to write this or that particular work"—so too is an authentic collective vocation. This does not, of course, mean that Agamben offers an apology for apathy, pessimism, or indifference to mankind's present or future; and he is careful to note that such "inoperativeness" must be understood with philosophical care. That mankind is "inoperative," as Agamben claims, does not mean that it is dysfunctional; it means only that it has no defined or definable function. "The vocabulary of inoperativeness [*inoperosità*]," to which the Greek term *argos* belongs, Agamben points out, "has in Greek no negative connotation whatsoever," and it was first in the works of Christian commentators on Aristotle that the "hypothesis of an essential inoperativeness [*un essenziale inoperosità*] of man" became unacceptable, and even "scandalous" (PP, 367). It is precisely this scandal that Agamben examines anew. In a chapter from *The Coming Community* entitled "Ethics," he writes, "the fact that must constitute the point of departure for any discourse on ethics is that there is no essence, no historical or spiritual vocation, no biological destiny that humans must enact or realize" (CC, 43 [39]). He continues: "This is the only reason why something like an ethics can exist, because it is clear that if humans were or had to be this or that substance, this or that destiny, no ethical experience would be possible—there would be only tasks to be done" (CC, 43 [39]).[7] On this level, where ontology and political philosophy converge, the idea of potentiality is the last thing but abstract or divorced from contemporary concerns. To answer Aristotle's question with a *no* is to see our past and present, our history and our philosophy, in a new, and strange, light. If we have no collective vocation, the question becomes, what, individually and collectively, we are to do. And it is this question that Agamben, from his first experiences of philosophical vocation in the 1960s to the present day, has endeavored to answer.

On Fame, Philosophy, and *Entwicklungsfähigkeit*

The one thing that every reader of this study will know about Agamben is that he is famous. With surprising speed his name has grown familiar in recent years, not only to specialists in the many fields in which he works—from classical philology to political philosophy—but also to those whose interests lie far from them. Nietzsche once described philosophical fame as the ability to influence even those who never read a line of one's work. Whatever he might think of such a definition, Agamben is well on his way to fulfilling its criterion. Precursors to his present fame were indeed glimpsed decades ago. In the wake of the publication of *Homo Sacer* in 1995, however, Agamben's intellectual star rose rapidly. Not only has that work been widely disseminated and discussed, praised, and attacked, but its central terms—such as *homo sacer* and *state of exception*—have become watchwords in a variety of political, philosophical, sociological, literary, and legal debates. Other key ideas from that work have migrated farther afield, such as, to choose a single example, the *bare life* that was selected as theme for the 2007 *Documenta 12* international art festival.

No writer gets to choose the influence that his or her works will exercise, and few have any success in curtailing uses they deem unpromising. Agamben is no exception in this regard. This is not, however, the end of the story of his newfound fame, nor does it mark the limit of the ways in which that fame should interest the serious student of his work. Agamben is a singular thinker, but many singular thinkers do not become famous during their lifetimes—or ever. Where, then, are the sources of Agamben's fame to be found? It is likely that his biography played at least some role. Private relationships with famous figures from Heidegger to Elsa Morante, from Pier Paolo Pasolini to Italo Calvino, are likely to attract interest, as are public acts such as Agamben's resignation from a post at New York University in protest of the revised Homeland Security Act of 2004.[8] Turning to a different class of external factors, there can be little doubt that some part of Agamben's current fame, like that of his countryman and friend Antonio Negri, was born of a coincidence of historical and political events. Just as Guy Debord's *Society of the Spectacle* gained greatly in notoriety thanks to the political uprisings that followed fast upon its publication in 1967, so too did Agamben's political writings—above all, *Homo Sacer*—in the wake of the attacks of September 11, the wars in Afghanistan and Iraq, and the ensuing states of emblematic exception in Abu Ghraib, Guantánamo Bay, and elsewhere. In retrospect, his discussions of sacrality and secularization, of stateless figures and states of exception, appear uncommonly prescient. To this prescience Agamben couples a provocative element that has not ceased to attract attention, and indeed it should come as no surprise that such declarations as "the concentration camp is the biopolitical paradigm of the modern age" have left few indifferent.

This cursory list of reasons for Agamben's growing fame is incomplete, but it nevertheless gives some idea of the converging factors involved, and which are ultimately as diverse as Agamben's readers. There is, however, a point that unites these elements and where fame relates to more philosophical matters. When asked what has drawn him to certain thinkers Agamben has consistently replied that it is their "capacity for development," for which he frequently employs Ludwig Feuerbach's term *Entwicklungsfähigkeit* (LSP, 45; see also LDV; DTP, 4; and SR, 8). As we saw earlier, Agamben's idea of vocation is an open one and finds an essential corollary in his idea of philosophy. He characterizes philosophy neither as a list of questions to answer nor as a set of methods to employ. Because philosophy is more than a body of ideas and doctrines, methods and forms, treatises and texts, it can be, for him, as little circumscribed as the desire to think, write, or act, and for this reason he will claim that "philosophy does not have a content purely its own" (DTP, 4). In one of his most recent books, *Signatura rerum* (2008), Agamben declares that "the genuinely philosophical element in any work, be it a work of art, one of science, or one of thought, is its capacity for being developed" (SR, 8).[9] Elsewhere, he similarly remarked that "the properly philosophical element in any work, be it a work of scholarship, of literature, or of art, is that which goes unsaid therein, and thereby possesses a possibility for development" (DTP, 4). For Agamben, the philosophical element—rich in potentiality—is that which, while present, goes unstated in a work and is thereby left for others to read between the lines and formulate in their own.

Given such a description of philosophy and potentiality, Agamben's account of his relationship to other more and less famous thinkers should come as little surprise. "In a certain sense," he has remarked, "I don't believe that I have ever done anything but cultivate the capacity for development contained in the authors important to me, be that author Benjamin or Caproni, Heidegger or Cavalcanti" (LSP, 45). Expanding on his related sense that "philosophy does not have a content purely its own," he said, "it seems to me that this principle defines my own method, and my manner of working. And not only with respect to the authors dear to me, and whose work I endeavor to continue, but also—in a manner that is more or less unconscious—with respect to myself. It is as though each completed work contained within it something that went unsaid and which demands to be taken up and developed" (DTP, 4).[10]

Whether or not such definitions prove interesting to the reader in their own right, they are of unquestionable assistance in understanding Agamben's relationship to the thinkers on whom he draws, as well as the relation of his works to one another. Of equal interest, however, is the model these definitions offer for the reading of Agamben's own works. An exhaustive knowledge of a topic is always to be preferred over a cursory one, but we indeed have only world enough and time for so much study. Whether the reader of this work has an extensive familiarity with Agamben's work or a fleeting one, there can be little question that the best way to approach it is with an eye for what can be developed therein and, thereby, with a sense of one's own potentiality for thought and action.

Homo Sacer and Continuity of Concern

Agamben makes amply clear that his *Homo Sacer* project has political aspirations. If this is the case, his readers might well wonder whether he is changing his field of focus. The topics of Agamben's earlier books ranged from aesthetics to iconography, historiography to philology, poetics to philosophy. While in its treatment of political questions *Homo Sacer* represents a departure, it is one that should not be overestimated. A bright light casts a dark shadow, and the notoriety of the *Homo Sacer* series has focused the majority of discussions of Agamben's work on that project.[11] In 2004 Stefano Franchi pointed to the "unfortunate side-effect" of the fame of *Homo Sacer*—that, "with rare exceptions, [Agamben's] work is mostly discussed within the context of *political analysis*" (Franchi 2004, 30, italics in original).[12] This effect is perhaps seen most clearly in a work that appeared the following year—the first book-length introduction to Agamben's work to be published in any language: Eva Geulen's *Giorgio Agamben zur Einführung* (An Introduction to Giorgio Agamben) (2005). Despite an announcement that she will have frequent recourse to "scarcely known earlier texts" by Agamben, even well-known ones tend to recede as Agamben's intellectual world is made to rotate tightly around the fragile figure of the *homo sacer* (Geulen 2005, 15). Geulen's analysis of that figure is insightful and original, but gives only a partial vision of Agamben's work as a whole, and his earlier books appear as nothing so much as preparations for the main event that is *Homo Sacer*. Geulen is a brilliant reader of *Homo Sacer*, but this brilliance leads her to see virtually everything Agamben has written through its lens. Equally telling in this respect is that the only two books exclusively on Agamben yet to appear in English—*Politics, Metaphysics, and Death: Essays on Giorgio Agamben's* Homo Sacer, edited by Andrew Norris (2005), and *Giorgio Agamben: Sovereignty and Life*, edited by Matthew Calarco and Steven DeCaroli (2007)—are both, as their titles show, dedicated to the *Homo Sacer* project.[13] A continuation of this tendency is seen in the the the fact that nowhere in the long introduction to a 2008 special issue of the journal *South Atlantic Quarterly* entitled "The Agamben Effect" is any book or essay prior to *Homo Sacer* even mentioned (see Ross 2008). It is indeed up to each reader to decide, if the need for such a decision is felt, which book is the finest—the fullest and most accomplished—in an author's oeuvre. The question of fame, however, is a different one, and *Homo Sacer*'s fame has often led to it being placed alone at the center of his thought.

Although *Homo Sacer*'s fame has played a large part in this process, it is not the only contributing factor. Agamben has not tended to present his work as a systematic whole or his books as parts of an overarching project. On the contrary, he has often characterized his writings as a set of responses to individual questions, as interventions in specific debates, and as treatments of authors important to him. The result has been that the work of linking his books to one another, as noted in the preface to this study, is left largely to the reader. Although *Homo Sacer* is indeed more directly concerned with political questions than any of Agamben's earlier books, and thereby begins something of a new arc in his intellectual trajectory, this is a change that is all too easy to overestimate. It is always tempting to locate "breaks" and "turns" in a philosopher's thought for the reason that they help make manageable distinctions and compose familiar narratives. The interests and issues of the *Homo Sacer* project are, at least in part, new ones; but alongside this novelty is an equally striking continuity and a remarkable reformulation of the concerns that have accompanied Agamben's work since his first publications nearly thirty years prior to it.

The Idea of Politics

Seventeen years before the publication of *Homo Sacer* Agamben lamented the loss of continuity between "poetry and politics" that earlier epochs had known and that was evident for him in such facts as that Aristotle's most ample treatment of music is found in his *Politics,* and that Plato dedicates an important part of his most quintessentially political dialogue, *The Republic,* to the arts (see IH, 147 [148]). A still more condensed instance of what Agamben saw in the past and wished for the future is found in his *Idea of Prose.* This least obviously political of his books contains a passage in which Agamben invokes "thought—that is, politics [*il pensiero—cioè la politica*]" (IP, 98 [84]). Agamben equates thought with politics here not because the limits of the political are of no importance to him, but because his idea of politics is vaster than the one to which his readers are accustomed. Politics is concerned with nothing less than the lives we lead and the forms our society takes, and for this reason Agamben refers in a recent installment of the *Homo Sacer* series to "that indefinable dimension we are accustomed to calling politics" (RG, 275).

Agamben has not been the only writer to find politics an indefinable dimension in his work. Some commentators have focused on uncertainties considering individual political concepts ranging from sovereignty to the subject to the state.[14] Others have made more sweeping judgments, such as Paolo Virno (2002), who, while stressing that Agamben is a remarkable philosopher, flatly declared that he is "a thinker with no political vocation" (54). Finding it telling that in the chapter from *Idea of Prose* entitled "The Idea of Politics" politics is nowhere mentioned, Oliver Marchart (2007) draws the conclusion that Agamben's idea of politics is a "politics without politics [*politiklosen Politik*]" (23). Marchart does not note for his reader that *every* chapter in *Idea of Prose* proceeds in this fashion with the idea named in each short chapter's title treated only indirectly therein ("The Idea of Communism," for instance, discusses pornography and "The Idea of Thought," punctuation marks). While this changes the force of Marchart's point, it does not remove the difficulty that led him to make it.

One response to the challenge of defining Agamben's idea of politics, and the concomitant problem of relating his early work on art to his later work on politics, has been to diagnose what a number of commentators have called an "aestheticization" of politics in his writing. J. M. Bernstein (2004) has called Agamben's approach in *Remnants of Auschwitz* an "aestheticization of [the concentration camp prisoner's] fate for the sake of a metaphysics of language" (14). A similar indictment is to be found in Mesnard and Kahan who find that Agamben's ethical and political reflections in that work stem from "an aesthetic position" (Mesnard and Kahan

2001, 126). The charges levelled by Bernstein, Mesnard, and Kahan are the most scathing that can be made, tantamount as they are to accusing Agamben of callous opportunism in his discussion of the most sensitive and painful of matters. Whether these charges are justified is something that we will look at in depth in Chapter Seven. For the moment, it is important to take note of this idea of an aestheticization of politics—as well as that this is not the only key in which it has been advanced. Benjamin Morgan (2007) has argued that Agamben's conceptions of the relations of means to ends and law to violence are fundamentally shaped by Kant's theory of aesthetic judgment and, thereby, that his idea of politics is one whose model is to be found in an idea of art. On a related note Arne de Boever (2006) has concluded that "Agamben's thought is crucially a *literary-political* thought. It is a literary thought that, in its political force, *cannot be articulated within the limits of political science.* Thus, it oscillates between the literary and the political and demands to be studied comparatively, across the disciplines" (159; italics in original). Whether or not De Boever is right in this claim, it should not be mistaken for a solution to the problem.

Like those who looked to *aesthetics* to define Agamen's idea of politics, Thomas Khurana (2007), in his own effort to do so, has turned to a field other than the political: *ethics.* He suggests that Agamben's work should be understood not as a "political project" so much as an "ethical turn," and that what Agamben proposes in works such as *Homo Sacer* is not a "political alternative" but an "ethical modification" (34–35). One of the advantages of such a view is the answer it offers to those frustrated by the absence of concrete political recommendations in Agamben's work (to which we will turn in Chapters Six, Seven, and Nine). Whether Khurana's claim is true in Agamben's terms is difficult to say—for a fundamental reason. That ethics and politics should not be treated as separate and distinct disciplines is one of the guiding ideas in Agamben's philosophy.

As we saw above, Agamben invoked "thought—that is, politics." The equation might seem strange, but for Agamben this is precisely the reason it needs to be stressed. What this remark highlights is that the realm delimited by politics is as complex and indeterminate as that of philosophy. This does not mean that politics is anything and everything one might choose to bring under its heading; but it does mean that, for Agamben, there are aspects of our lives that are informed by political conceptions and rich in political consequences we are inclined to neglect. For this reason Agamben will not simply ask, "What is politics?" but instead, "From where does our culture—both in mythic and in actual terms—derive its criteria for the political?" (RG, 283). How, in other words, have we arrived at our ideas of what belongs to the realm of politics and what does not? Aristotle charged Plato with insufficiently distinguishing the things of the *polis* (city-state) from those of the *oikos* (home). Agamben does not wish to conflate the two, but he does want to understand by what means things, ideas, and practices enter into what we call the political realm. Uncertainty concerning this question is precisely the reason he speaks in *Homo Sacer* of a neglected political vocation in urgent need of attention.

With these considerations in mind, what then, for Agamben, is politics, and what does it have to do with philosophy and potentiality? Politics is, as we saw, "thought," but this is not the only definition he gives. Elsewhere he refers to "politics as mankind's most authentic dimension [*dimensione più proprio dell'uomo*]" (RG, 11). This remark risks sounding hieratic or vague, but placed in the context of the considerations just noted, it is neither. For Agamben, politics is the entire realm of human action. As such, it is not a separate topic that only some may be interested in, or a separate realm that we may enter or exit at certain points in our lives. "That which poetry does for the potentiality of speech," Agamben writes, "politics and philosophy do for the potentiality of action" (RG, 275). As a result, thought is by nature political just as politics is by nature philosophical—and the two topics converge in his idea of potentiality.

Extreme Positions and Political Potential

The striking equation between politics and thought is not the only one of its sort to be found in Agamben's work. Elsewhere, he equates both thought and knowledge with potentiality. "Thought exists," he writes, "integrally in the mode of potentiality," and the same applies to *knowledge,* because "potential—or knowledge," he claims, "is the specifically human faculty of maintaining a relation with something which is lacking" (TDI, x; IH, 7 [xii]; translation modified). For this reason Agamben writes that "to think . . . means . . . to experience the pure potentiality of thought," as well as that an experience of potentiality is "the foundation of our rationality, our knowing and speaking being" (MWE, 9 [17], translation modified; DN, 112).

As any reading of Agamben's works reveals, no idea is so important for his thought as *potentiality*. His diverse reflections on that idea are conducted not merely for the purpose of performing arduous thought experiments or rendering tribute to the metaphysical subtleties of thinkers past. In *Idea of Prose* Agamben points to "the secret connections that link power [*potere*] and potentiality [*potenza*]," and these are connections he has continued to follow to the present day (IP, 51 [71], translation modified). "My concern," Agamben has stressed, "is not merely historiographical. I do not intend simply to restore currency to philosophical categories that are no longer in use. On the contrary, I think that the concept of potentiality has never ceased to function in the life and history of humanity, most notably that part of humanity that has grown and developed its *potentialities* to the point of imposing its *power* over the whole planet" (P, 177 [273], italics in original, translation modified).

For Agamben, the question of potentiality is intimately linked not only to the idea of politics we saw earlier, but also to concrete instances and institutions of political power. What is more, he contends that whether we are aware of them or not, our conceptions of potentiality condition our ideas of power and its limits. In the years when Agamben was beginning to publish his work, Arendt lamented that "the progresses made by science have nothing to do with the I-will; they follow their own inexorable laws, compelling us to do whatever we can, regardless of consequences." She then asked, in desperation, whether "the I-will and the I-can have parted company?" (Arendt 1970, 86). It is precisely such a failure to reflect on the difference between practical possibility and ethical actuality, on potential and possibility, that motivates much of Agamben's writing. As a result, he has characterized his goal as nothing less than "to bring the political out of its concealment [*occultamento*] and, at the same time, return thought to its practical calling [*vocazione practica*]" (HS, 4 [7]). This practical calling is one that he in turn links to a particular urgency: "the urgency of catastrophe" (HS, 12 [16]). The catastrophe in question is that the state of exception risks becoming the rule, that the exceptional abuses of power that our age has known threaten to become the norm—and that we accept them as such.

Walter Benjamin once wrote to Gretel Adorno, "My life like my thought moves by means of extreme positions" (Benjamin GB, IV, 440–441). There can be little doubt that Agamben's life and thought have proceeded by similar movements. Another student of Benjamin's who was drawn to extreme positions, Gretel's husband Theodor, presents a particular problem to his readers in this regard. As many of them have pointed out, they are often required to separate those statements he means quite literally and those that seem to have been made to shock them to attention. Although Agamben's positions might at times seem equally extreme, his manner of proceeding is different. He indeed makes surprising statements and presents provocative paradigms, but he does not appear to do so merely for the sake of surprise or provocation.

In a passage that there can be little doubt he meant to be read in all earnest, Theodor Adorno remarked, "There is something that all people, whether they admit it or not, know in their heart of hearts: that things could have been different, that that would have been possible. They could not only live without hunger and also probably without fear, but also freely. And yet at the same time—and all over the world—the social apparatus has become so hardened that what lies before them as a means of possible fulfillment presents itself as radically impossible" (Adorno and Bloch 1985, 353). Adorno's expression of the difficulty of grasping the means for radical change is echoed in Agamben's writing, and a similar imperative motivates the extreme positions he adopts. Whatever their differences, a fundamental idea they share is that the heart of the philosopher's vocation is found in the fact that so much that presents itself as "radically impossible" is not—and must not continue to be accepted as such.

In response to his denunciation of political states of affairs not only in his native Italy but also in China, France, Germany, Afghanistan, the Balkans, Iraq, and elsewhere around the globe, Agamben has found himself charged with advocating hopelessness. "People sometimes say that I am too pessimistic," he has remarked, "but this is something I have trouble understanding. . . . In fact, I am not in the slightest pessimistic, though I am, however, a bit mistrustful of exuberance" (UL, 18). About the extremity of certain states of legal exception, as well as about larger trends visible in phenomena ranging from the structure of the German concentration camps to contemporary bioethical debates, he has stressed, "I am not in the slightest interested in apocalyptic prophecies, but instead in the ways in which we might respond at the present time to the catastrophe in which we live" (UL, 18).[15]

These remarks exemplify two essential facets of Agamben's writing: the extremity of his diagnoses and his insistence that our desperate times call for redoubled energy. The political scene that Agamben sees stretched before him may be a dark one, but this is no cause for apocalyptic pronouncement and no cause for pessimism. On the contrary, it is, strangely enough, cause for *hope*. Paraphrasing Marx, Agamben has remarked that "the absolutely desperate state of affairs in the society in which I live fills me with hope," and it is this hope that motivates the extreme stances taken in his works (BM, 10).

There is indeed, as Adorno says, nothing more obvious than that to live without hunger or fear should be the common right of all. It is equally obvious that this is the furthest thing from the case. A point of agreement among contemporary political thinkers of the most diverse approaches— from Adorno to Habermas, Debord to Bourdieu, Deleuze to Negri, Althusser to Butler, Cixous to Luhmann, Foucault to Derrida, Baudrillard to Žižek—is that the means by which society controls its subjects are ever more difficult to perceive, and that the possibilities for change ever more difficult to identify. To follow a vocation at once philosophical and political is, for Agamben, to act and think on the basis of something we all know: that things in our world not only can but should be different. The task of the philosopher is then not only to realize that things *might* be different, but to conceive of how this *might* leave the realm of the conditional and enter the actual world of human affairs—not as abstract theory but as real potentiality.

Scholium I: The Inoperative

No single term in Agamben's writing is so easy to misunderstand as *inoperativeness* [*inoperosità*]. In an afterword to *The Coming Community* Agamben suggests that inoperativeness might form "the paradigm for the coming politics" (CC 93). The conferring of such a high political calling on this idea underlines its importance for Agamben but leaves his readers uncertain as to how such an inert-sounding thing might become a paradigm for political life. What is more, the English ear is quick to hear overtones of dysfunctionality here that seem far from the point.

The term that Agamben employs here is rich in associations, the most immediate of which is one to which he neither here nor elsewhere refers directly but to which many of his initial readers would have responded. To be "inoperative," it would seem, would be to refuse to be an operative part of the state's machinery, and thereby echoes a popular slogan employed by radical Italian workers' rights groups in the 1960s and 1970s: "Refuse to work!" This rallying cry was not made to advocate laziness or the carefree joys of a *dolce far niente,* and its point was by no means to reject work *per se.* In such movements, the idea of work retained its pride of place in the Marxist system of values. The motto "Refuse to work!" was instead a rejection of the conditions under which workers were being asked to work—an expression of the idea of a general strike, with its goal of forcing the powers that be to recognize the rights of an increasingly dissatisfied body of workers.[16] Although such a refusal to work is alluded to in Agamben's term, what he means by *inoperativeness* extends well beyond the political present and, as he makes clear, denotes far more than the practical possibilities available to a group of workers.

In the book that followed *The Coming Community,* Agamben gives a genealogy of the term *inoperativeness,* and the first thinker it leads him to is Georges Bataille. Neither in *Homo Sacer* nor in later treatments of the concept in *The Time That Remains* and *The Open* does Agamben make any secret of the fact that his conception of *inoperativeness* owes much to Bataille's *désoeuvrement,* in which the latter envisioned the most radical rejection of the utilitarian aims of modern society and progressive thought. It seemed to Bataille that society and its dominant modes of conceiving itself were increasingly focused on forming a homogenous body politic. *Désoeuvrement* was the name he gave his response to this totalizing tendency and it was through this that he sought forms of "negativity"—"negativity without employ"—that would escape reabsorption by a dialectic of historical progress.[17] Such negativity would be so radical and excessive that it would escape the forms of social control, as well as, on a philosophical level, the centripetal orbit of the Hegelian dialectic. In Bataille's own person and thought, *désoeuvrement* represented a commitment to inactivity and excess, a refusal to contribute to the work (the *oeuvre* or *oeuvres*) of his society. His search sent him into exoteric communities such as the Surrealists, *Contre-Attaque,* and the *College of Sociology,* as well as esoteric ones such as the infamous *Acéphale* group. It led him to plumb the possibilities of eroticism and ecstasy—experiences that he saw as capable of escaping or eluding a universalizing conception of individual and community experience. What Bataille glimpsed in such extenuated states of mind and body, which so fascinated readers from Blanchot and Lacan to Foucault and Derrida, was not only a glimmer of a possible communion, but also what he characterized as the revelatory experience of *désoeuvrement.*

Agamben's own "inoperativeness" or *désoeuvrement* (he frequently employs the French term) is of a similar nature but also represents a fundamental extension of the idea. It refers not only to a refusal to do the work of a coercive society, but also to something quite different—an ontological reflection on the modalities of being. In *Homo Sacer* Agamben writes that "the only coherent way to understand inoperativeness is to think of it as a generic mode of potentiality that is not exhausted (like individual action or collective action understood as the sum of individual actions) in a *transitus de potentia ad actum*" (HS, 62 [71]). Inoperativeness thus represents something not exhausted but inexhaustible—because it does not pass from the possible to the actual (*transitus de potentia ad actum*). This is an idea that Agamben is intrigued to find in Bataille but that he traces farther back—and to an unexpected place. Agamben claims that Bataille's *désoeuvrement* as well as those of other, similar figures (such as the *voyou désoeuvré* of Raymond Queneau and the "Shabbat of man" of Alexandre Kojève) were elements of "a posthistoric figure corresponding to an absence of a truly human work [*un'opera veramente umana*]" (PP, 366–67). In so doing he traces the idea back to Aristotle's considerations of happiness and of mankind's collective vocation.

What the term *inoperative* stresses is the other side of potentiality: the possibility that a thing might not come to pass. For Agamben, as for Aristotle, potentiality conceived of as merely the potential-to-be is but half the story. An idea of potentiality worthy of the name must also include a potentiality that does not pass into act, that is truly potential in the sense that it contains the possibility of not actualizing itself. It is for this reason that Agamben stresses both "the potential to be" and "the potential to not-be," because, in his words, "only a potentiality [*potenza*] that is capable of both potentiality and impotence [*impotenza*] is then supreme potentiality" (CC, 36 [34], translation modified).[18] For Agamben, not only is this second mode of potentiality not of less interest or importance than the first, but it also is absolutely necessary for understanding potentiality's "originary figure" (P, 182 [281]). For this reason Agamben finds that "politics is that which corresponds to the essential inoperativeness of mankind," and it is this idea that lies at the heart of much of his work (MWE, 140 [109], translation modified; see also RG, 274ff).

Scholium II: On Creation and Decreation

At the end of his film *The Decameron* (1971), Pasolini—a figure to whom Agamben was close (Agamben appears in another of Pasolini's films, *The Gospel of Saint Matthew*)—stands before the camera and poses a question to his viewer: "Why create a work when it is so beautiful simply to dream of one?"[19] Although personally addressing the audience is an unfamiliar gesture for a director, the question that Pasolini poses is not unfamiliar. As Romantic thinkers did not cease to stress, when seen from a certain perspective all works seem inevitably consigned to incompletion when compared with the fullness and intensity of their initial conception. Is not the potentiality figured in the imagination always richer than the actuality that follows, born as it is of the compromises that reality inevitably imposes? And if this is the case, why not revel in potentiality, as Pasolini suggests, rather than subject oneself to the travails of realization and the disappointments of actuality? The question was not so insoluble as to prevent Pasolini from creating works (like the one this speech closes), but it nevertheless played a part in their creation.

Pasolini was not the only figure close to Agamben who showed a special interest in this dynamic moment preceding the creative act. Calvino remarked in the preparatory notes for the Charles Eliot Norton lectures at Harvard University for 1985–86, which his untimely death prevented him from giving, "my point of departure will be . . . this moment so decisive for the reader—that of moving from unlimited and multiform potentiality towards something that does not yet exist and can only exist by encountering limits and rules" (Calvino 1993, 137). Before the passage to the act, before the realizing of possibilities and the actualizing of potentialities latent in the mind of the artist, the inspiration that lies at the origin of the work of art exists, for Calvino, in a state of "unlimited and multiform potentiality." Calvino evokes here a principle of potentiality that inheres in creation, and instead of seeing it through the customary optic of actuality, he adopts a less conventional lens, focusing on a moment that *precedes* creation, when an "unlimited and multiform potentiality" encounters "the limits and rules" that will give it shape. (It was his interest in such limits and rules that linked Calvino with the other members of the group of mathematicians and writers to which he belonged—OuLiPo). Is this "unlimited and multiform potentiality" evoked here by Calvino of the same nature as what his friend Agamben conceives under the sign of *potentiality*—and are the two expressions not in fact simply synonyms of *creation*? The answer to this question proves to be extraordinarily complex. Agamben does in fact speak of potentiality in terms of *creation*—but in a truly singular way. For him, *potentiality* is indeed to be understood in the context of creation, but seen from a strange side—one that he calls *decreation*.

In an essay on potentiality and creation written for an exhibit of Cy Twombly's works at the American Academy in Rome in 1998, Agamben evokes what he calls a "falling movement" in the moment of creative inspiration. Agamben isolates in Twombly's art what he calls, "a gesture where it is as if every ascension has been inverted and broken, almost on the threshold between doing and not-doing" (BCC, 5). Agamben then gives a name to this "threshold between doing and not-doing": *decreation*. "It is this point of *decreation* [*decreazione*]," he writes, "where the artist . . . no longer creates but decreates [*decrea*]" (BCC, 5, translation modified, italics added). In light of this remark, it indeed seems that Agamben conceives the idea of potentiality as an idea of *creation*, but its expression has been reversed as "*de*creation." What then does it mean for an artist to reach a point where he "no longer creates but decreates"? And what light does such a moment shed on Agamben's conception of potentiality?

Unlike *potentiality, decreation* is not a common term, and given both its sheer strangeness and the fact that Agamben does not define it, we would do well to try to circumscribe it more closely. Dictionaries prove little help in this regard. As concerns Agamben's language, the term does not appear in even the most capacious Italian dictionaries, and no entry is found in either the *Grande dizionario della lingua italiana* or the *Vocabolario della lingua italiana*. One does find it in the *Oxford English Dictionary,* defined as "diminution": "the undoing of creation; depriving of existence; annihilation." Are we then to understand Agamben's enigmatic *decreation* to be on the order of a *destruction*—as in the *Oxford English Dictionary*'s terms, a *diminution* or *annihilation;* as an "undoing of creation"? Is it instead like *deconstruction*: a way of examining by suspending a system or structure? And if it is neither of these things, how *are* we to understand it?

A clue to the term's meaning is to be found in an unlikely place. As a young man, Agamben wrote an unpublished dissertation on Simone Weil.[20] In the notebooks she left behind, with which Agamben was doubtless familiar, Weil repeatedly employs the strange term *decreation*.[21] She writes, "The self is only a shadow projected by sin and error which blocks

God's light," and the name she gives to her way of escaping from this shadow is *decreation* (Weil [1948] 1997, 81). This escape involves a dark, double movement. "We participate in the creation of the world," Weil writes, "by decreating ourselves" (Weil [1948] 1997, 171). For Weil, the question lay in *de*creating a false aspect of ourselves—an aspect that is the fruit of error and sin—to reach the source of creation. *Decreation* is the first step along this path.

Although it is likely that Agamben first encountered the term *decreation* in Weil's journals, the turn he gives to it is a novel one. His essay on Twombly is not the first time he employs this seemingly paradoxical term. It appears in the third and final section of "Bartleby, or On Contingency," entitled "The Experiment, or On Decreation." Continuing Leibniz's theological thought experiments, Agamben uses the term to approach an aspect of *potentiality* he found neglected in Leibniz's work. For Agamben, *decreation* is a "second creation in which God summons all his potential not to be, creating on the basis of a point of indifference between potentiality and impotentiality. The creation that is now fulfilled is neither a re-creation nor an eternal repetition; it is, rather, a decreation in which what happened and what did not happen are returned to their originary unity in the mind of God, while what could have not been but was becomes indistinguishable from what could have been but was not" (P, 270). *Decreation* is thus for Agamben not what it was for Weil. It does not involve shedding or *de*creating some inauthentic aspect of ourselves—an aspect that is the fruit of error and sin—so as to create. In Weil's hands, *decreation* is essentially dialectical—an antithetical moment that is part of the process of creation. For Agamben, however, it is something else—something that brings the contingent—"what could have been but was not"—into view.

To return, then, to Calvino's unlimited and multiform origin of creation, we might now offer an answer to the question posed earlier. There can be little doubt that for Agamben potentiality is a way of conceiving creation—but not under the sign of an actualized thing or a completed work. As Aristotle argued, potentiality truly understood is not only all that came to pass but also all that might have come to pass and did not. What Agamben strives to do through his evocation of *decreation* and *inoperativeness* is to conceive of *potentiality* not merely from the perspective of the completed work, from the perspective of the actual, but also in its own right.

Scholium III: Heidegger's Potential, or Creative Terminology

Agamben notes at one point that if the terms used in his discussion of potentiality seem strange, there is a good reason for this: "the vocabulary of potentiality has penetrated so deeply into us" that, for instance, when we read the discussion of potentiality in Aristotle's *On the Soul*, "what appears for the first time in these lines is a fundamental problem that has only rarely come to light as such in the course of Western thought" (P, 178 [275]). Because we lack simple and straightforward terms for discussing this second mode of potentiality—potentiality in what Agamben refers to as its pure state, potentiality independent of its actualization—we must plumb the resources of our language to express it.

On this point, Agamben's first philosophical master had remarked that "in accord with the entire history of Western humanity hitherto, and in accord with the interpretation of beings that sustains that history, we are all too accustomed to thinking purely and simply in terms of actualities, to interpreting in terms of the actual (as presence, *ousia*). For this reason we are still unprepared, we feel awkward and inadequate, when it comes to thinking *potentiality,* a kind of thinking that is always creative" (Heidegger 1984, 130, italics in original, translation modified).[22] In *Being and Time* this unpreparedness meant that new tools needed to be crafted, and led to what Heidegger called "the severity [*die Härte*] of my expressions"—a severity and strangeness that was to characterize all his writing (Heidegger 1993, 39).[23] Heidegger stressed not only the link between possibility and creation that so interested Agamben, but also how "unprepared" we are, how "awkward and inadequate" we feel "when it comes to thinking potentiality." This is something to which our language bears striking witness in that we often lack the terms, and even the tenses, to discuss such potentiality. To do so requires not just intelligence but also creativity, and it is precisely for this reason that Agamben summons unfamiliar terms such as *inoperative* and *decreation* to elucidate this second, shadowy mode of potentiality.

In *Homo Sacer* Agamben writes of the need to question and combat "the primacy of actuality over potentiality" (HS, 44 [51]). Agamben is not the first modern thinker to return to this Aristotelian problem and to move in its shadows. Heidegger sought to reverse this tendency, programmatically declaring in *Being and Time* that, "*potentiality* has primacy over actuality [*Höher als die Wirklichkeit steht die* Möglichkeit]" ([1927] 1993, 38, italics in original). One perfectly coherent way of viewing Heidegger's philosophical project is in fact as a reconception of *potentiality*. Heidegger defines the subject of his philosophy—*Dasein*—not through its *actuality* but through its *potentiality*, stating at numerous points that "*Dasein* is always and essentially its own possibility" (Heidegger 1996, 42). That this idea is not limited to the specific aims of *Being and Time* is witnessed elsewhere, such as in Heidegger's description of an "essential attentiveness to the possible" as characterizing both "original philosophy" and "great poetry" (Heidegger GA, 34.64). In an epilogue to his lecture "The Thing" entitled "A Letter to a Young Student," Heidegger stresses the need for thinking rigorously about what *potentiality* means: "Thinking, such as lies at the basis of the lecture ('The Thing'), is no mere representing of some existent thing. 'Being' is in no way identical with reality or with precisely determined actuality. . . . Even metaphysics already had, to a certain extent, an intimation of this fact in its doctrine of the modalities—which, to be sure, has hardly been understood—according to which possibility belongs to Being just as much as do actuality and necessity" (1971, 183).[24] For both Heidegger and Agamben, to think of the being that all beings share is to think not only of the sides it most readily presents to our everyday view—actuality and necessity—but also of the more elusive modalities of potentiality and contingency.

CHAPTER ONE

Art for Art's Sake: The Destruction
of Aesthetics and *The Man Without
Content*

Giorgio Agamben's first book,[1] *The Man Without Content,* bears a
title that raises many questions: Who is this man? Where has his content
gone? Does he want it back? And yet although this title might sound enigmatic, its subject is simple. *The Man Without Content* inquires into the nature and function of art. This is, however, no neutral inquiry. The book
does not engage in aesthetic inquiry for the sake of aesthetic inquiry, and
it is not written from the distanced perspective of a historian of ideas. It is
instead a response to what Agamben sees as an alarming state of contemporary affairs.

The Original Stature of the Work of Art

For Agamben, the nature and function of art in our culture has been
obscured. Art has come to resemble, in his words, "a planet that turns toward us only its dark side" (MWC, 43 [66], translation modified). With
the waning of the enlightening role that art had played for earlier eras, Agamben sees his goal as understanding *how* and *why* art's illuminating face
has turned away from us, and what we might do to see its return.

From the outset, his means are extreme:

Perhaps nothing is more urgent—if we really want to engage the problem of art
in our time—than a *destruction* [*distruzione*] of aesthetics that would, by clearing

away what is usually taken for granted, allow us to bring into question the very meaning of aesthetics as the systematic study of the work of art. The question, however, is whether the time is ripe for such a *destruction*, or whether instead the consequence of such an act would not be the loss of any possible horizon for the understanding of the work of art and the creation of an abyss in front of it that could be crossed only with a radical leap. But perhaps just such a loss and such an abyss are what we most need if we want the work of art to reacquire its original stature [*la sua statura originale*]. [MWC, 6 (16–17), italics in original, translation modified]

In his first book, Agamben's first call is for *destruction*. To effect this destruction he must traverse what he sees as the arid expanses of the formalizing discipline of *aesthetics*. Beyond these wastes, what he seeks is nothing less than the "original stature" of the work of art. However, if Agamben aspires to bring about a "destruction" that will help him understand both the "original stature" of the work of art and the "authentic sense" of the aesthetic project that was to circumscribe it, we might first ask what *sort* of destruction he is calling for. As is clear from the preceding passage, his tone is not that of Dionysian intoxication and what he is calling for is not merely anarchic. Although during these years he may have felt great affinity for such sulphurous artists from the past as Artaud and from the present as Pasolini, his manner and message are markedly different. The first hallmark of the destruction Agamben envisions is that it is singularly lucid. He aims to clear and clarify a field of inquiry, and the goal of such a procedure is clearly stated: understanding the original stature of the work of art.

Yet if Agamben's goal is so simple, why does he need such extreme measures—or at least such extreme language? The answer is that for him such "destruction" is necessary because the problem he isolates is not generally recognized as such. Art's having ceased to play a shaping role in our culture—its loss of an "authentic" or "original" status—has become, for Agamben, so accepted in our day and age that it does not attract special notice. In other words, the loss has become so complete that it is no longer even experienced as a loss. To make this absence felt, Agamben attempts to clear away that which has obscured our vision—and to this operation he gives the extreme name *destruction*.

The Structure of Destruction

Although Agamben's idea of *destruction* is unusual, it is not unprecedented. One of the things that Heidegger's philosophy first made possible for Agamben was precisely destruction. Heidegger entitled the programmatic sixth section of *Being and Time* "The Task of Destroying [*Destruktion*] the History of Ontology." There he writes, "If the question of Being is to have its own history rendered transparent, then our rigidified tradition must be loosened and its concealments dissipated. We understand this task as one in which by taking *the question of Being* as our guide, we are to *destroy* [*Destruktion*] the traditional content of ancient ontology so as to arrive at those primordial experiences through which we achieve our first ways of determining the nature of Being" (Heidegger 1993, 44 [22], italics in original, translation modified). In a lecture course from 1920–21 Heidegger had already noted that "the modern study of the history of religion can do much for phenomenology on the condition that it is submitted to a phenomenological *destruction* [Destruktion]" (Heidegger GS 60.78, italics in original). As Heidegger is careful to underline, the destruction for which he is calling is not just any destruction and should not be understood in a conventional sense. To begin with, its principal function is not negative. Heidegger is careful to point out in *Being and Time* that *Destruktion* is not meant in a merely "negative sense," and that on the contrary it is motivated by a "positive intention" (Heidegger 1993, 44, 45 [22, 23]). Heidegger asks that his destruction be understood as the clearing away of corrupted material so as to get at an untainted origin. To employ his favorite family of metaphors, it is the cleaning of the house of being.

The reason Heidegger saw a necessity for such extreme housekeeping—and the reason Agamben was so interested in it—was that philosophy's initial and most fundamental problem—that of the nature of the being that all individual beings share—had ceased to be considered a pressing philosophical problem *at all*—let alone *the* problem that should guide philosophy's steps. So grave had matters become, and so deep did this forgetfulness run, that Heidegger saw the problem that for the Greeks lay at the very center of philosophy—the true task of metaphysics, which he called "the wonder of wonders: that being is"—was now to be glimpsed only at philosophy's margins (Heidegger 1996, 261). This "forgetting of Being," as Heidegger called this loss of a sense for the largest question that philosophy might ask, was the first obstacle he saw lying before him, and it was in response to it that he called for the extreme measure of a "destruction of the history of ontology."[2]

How Heidegger envisioned this destruction that so influenced Agamben is best illustrated by his choice of words. German disposes of more than one word for what is rendered in both English and Italian as "destruction." Both *Zerstörung* and *Vernichtung* can mean the same thing as the English *destruction* or the Italian *distruzione*. Heidegger's Latinate alternative to these more common terms was the relatively rare substantive *Destruktion*. It is specially suited to his purposes in that what he outlines—both in this section of *Being and Time* and elsewhere in his work—is not a smashing to bits (what he would have called a *Zerstörung* or *Zersplitterung*) nor an annihilation or an eradication (what he might have called a *Vernichtung*). It is instead a sort of *irradiation* through which an underlying *structure* becomes visible in the process of being rendered inoperative. On this point Heidegger is perfectly clear as he writes, "destruction [*Destruktion*] does not mean here the destruction of demolition [*Zerstören*], but rather that of dismantling [*Abbauen*], of clearing away and laying aside" (Heidegger 1956, 53). He continues: "Destruction [*Destruktion*] means: opening our ears, making the way free for what addresses us in our tradition as the being beings share" (Heidegger 1956, 53). Heidegger's *Destruktion* is thus above all a taking-apart that, while rendering inoperative, also exposes a concealed *structure*. (As the term *Abbauen* indicates, the operative metaphorical register is architectural.) The difficulty of expressing this special process is what gave birth to *deconstruction*—the term Derrida coined to translate Heidegger's *Destruktion* and that came to play such a central role in his philosophy and its reception. This conceptual and linguistic difficulty that led Derrida to his celebrated neologism is the same one that the young Agamben responded to with his "destruction of aesthetics."

The goal of such destructions as those of Heidegger, Derrida, and Agamben is to reveal the concealed, to glimpse what has been so long viewed through what Coleridge called "the film of familiarity" that it is effectively hidden from view. The "destruction of Western metaphysics" for which Heidegger called aims, like Derrida's *deconstruction* and the "destruction of aesthetics," to return to the origins of philosophical thought and to uncover forgotten and fundamental ways of conceiving our world—way that have become buried in confusion and convention. Agamben's destruction of aesthetics is an attack that aspires not simply to topple aesthetics' towers, but also to glimpse, in their falling, the innermost forms and flaws of their construction.

Divine Madness

With the *how* of Agamben's inquiry clarified, we can turn to its *what*. One goal of *The Man Without Content* is indeed to regain a sense of art's original stature and structure—an *ontological* question. Another goal is to trace the progressive obscuring of this original space that art offered—a *historical* question. A third goal is the desire to restore art to its former status as a true shaper of actions and beliefs—a *programmatic* question. Agamben fuses these goals in his retelling of the history of Western art from the Greeks to the present.

A watershed moment in that history is recorded by Hegel, who in 1829 stated that "art no longer provides for the satisfaction of those spiritual and intellectual needs that earlier peoples and times found in art and in art alone." This conviction led Hegel to the extreme conclusion that "in all of these [cultural and spiritual] relations, art, in its highest vocation [*Bestimmung*], is for us a thing of the past"(Hegel 1970, 13.24–13.25). As had Heidegger before him, Agamben endeavors in his first work to take the full measure of Hegel's diagnosis.[3]

At first sight it has appeared to many that Hegel seriously misjudged the situation. Art, it seems, has not become "a thing of the past"—on the contrary, perhaps more than for any earlier age it is a thing of the present. Contemporary art stands at the center of our cultural stage, and there appears to be no lack of people seeking its satisfactions. Yet as Agamben well knows, this is not what Hegel is speaking of. What is at issue is not commercial value or cultural prestige but instead something more fundamental and more essential to the forms that cultures take and to the ideas they pursue. To better view the question Agamben takes a long historical step backward. As is well known, Plato recommended singular treatment for the artist in his ideal republic. Should an artist appear in that republic, he was to be paid the highest respects: he was to be anointed with myrrh, crowned, praised—and then led forth out of the city's gates. This was not because Plato lacked sensitivity to, or respect for, art and its audiences. On the contrary, his prescriptions seem to have stemmed from his very sensitivity. Following ancient rumor, Plato found his philosophical vocation in the same fashion as Agamben—by renouncing an earlier, poetic one. It is said that one day the young dramatic poet was traversing an Athenian square when he heard the voice of Socrates. He listened, and then went home, burned the tragedies he had been composing, and became a philosopher. Art had, in his view, such power that it could make the worse appear the better reason, and blur the lines that divided fact from fiction. For this reason, it was to be feared.[4]

Not only in Plato's day but also for millennia to come, in Western discussions of art it was the audience that was described as running a risk in the experience of the work of art—the same audience that was subject to what Plato called "divine madness." As Agamben's historical analysis in *The Man Without Content* demonstrates, one does not often find modern audiences subject to divine madness, and the passion that characterized the antique response to the work of art has largely disappeared from the contemporary stage. Audiences may come in equal numbers, but they come with much different ideas and expectations. To state the matter with maximal simplicity, they seem to have grown calmer and cooler. Be that as it may, the divine madness that was an integral part of the experience of the work of art has not simply disappeared. Instead, it has, in Agamben's words, "migrated." If a divine madness associated with the work of art is still to be found today, it is to be found not in the audience but in the *artist,* petrified by the terrifying whiteness of the blank page or struggling against violent forces roiling within. In modern times, it is no longer the purveyors but the *creators* of art who are subject to this divine frenzy, and one need only think of Hölderlin, Rimbaud, and Nietzsche for prominent instances. If the extremity of Van Gogh's self-mutilation is the exception rather than the rule, the idea of the modern artist doing battle with a lacerating force so as to emerge victorious with the completed work is not, and it is this historical "migration" that Agamben follows to inquire into art's original status and the means for regaining it.[5]

Art as Art

At this point in his investigation Agamben's question has become a simple one: What happened between Plato's and Hegel's equally profound reactions to the power of art? The answer Agamben offers is that what intervened is what he is seeking to "destroy": *aesthetics.* For Agamben, the discipline of aesthetics embodies this cooling of artistic passions. A chapter of *The Man Without Content* is titled "The Man of Taste and the Dialectic of the Divide." It makes programmatically clear that the doctrine of *taste* has brought about a division—or in Agamben's more extreme term, *laceration*—in our experience of the work of art. What is this laceration that Agamben associates with the man of taste? To answer this question and thereby understand the mystifying title of this chapter, we need to turn first to the title of the work of which it is a part. Who is this titular man without content? The answer is *the artist.* As Agamben tells his reader, "The artist is the man without content" (MWC 55 [83]). This designation, however, is by no means a denunciatory one. Agamben is not diagnosing a side-effect of art such as Diderot's *paradoxe du comédien,* where the actor is able to incarnate such a variety of characters because he has no single character of his own. Agamben's artist is a man without content not because of a psychological deficit but because of a historical development. He has not always been without content—he has been deprived of it by a historical shift, by the man of taste and the lacerating dialectic that he has developed.[6]

For Agamben—particularly in the essays leading up to the publication of *The Man Without Content*—the figure of Antonin Artaud is powerfully representative of this state of affairs. In an essay from 1966, the twenty-four-year-old Agamben evokes "this *impasse* in our culture which is the work of Antonin Artaud" (SG, 59). The idea of Artaud diagnosing and denouncing a desiccated vision of culture and standing at a turning point in the history of art is voiced by Agamben in another essay, from that same year, in which he sees the paradox of the work of art "reach its dead spot in the work of Artaud" (PB, 48).[7] In *The Theater and Its Double,* Artaud talks of "the senseless shrinking to which we have subjected our idea of culture" and gives a clear indication of blame: "What led us to lose our culture is the Western idea of art" (1964, 15, 16). Inspired by the indigenous cultures of Mexico (just as another figure important to Agamben, Aby Warburg, was inspired by the Hopi in the American southwest), Artaud proclaimed that "an authentic culture opposes to our disinterested [*désintéressée*] and inert idea of art one that is magical and violently egotist—that is, one that is interested [*intéressée*]" (1964, 17). This same primal passion and strident denunciation is found in another figure important to the young Agamben—Pasolini. Although Pasolini is nowhere cited in Agamben's first work, echoes of his violent criticism of Western culture and what he saw as its adulterated idea of art may be heard in its cardinal theme.[8]

With the rise of modern aesthetics the man of taste was asked to judge form independently of content, and thus a new distance—as well as a new division—was introduced into the experience of the work of art. The migration of divine madness from audience to artist that Agamben observes is a migration he traces to the introduction of the idea of *taste*. When this intangible sensibility, this new faculty, entered the intellectual scene in the seventeenth and eighteenth centuries (it was, as Agamben stresses, a concept quite foreign to earlier centuries), it brought with it wide-reaching implications (a point Agamben also stresses in his long entry on *taste* for the Einaudi *Encyclopedia*). The idea that Artaud was endeavoring to counter in his "interested" idea of art is that of Kant, who stressed "disinterested" judgment. In *The Critique of Judgment*, Kant defines taste as follows: "*Taste* is the ability to judge an object, or a way of presenting it, by means of a liking or disliking *devoid of all interest* [*ohne alles Interesse*]. The object of such a liking is called beautiful" (Kant [1987] 1999, 53 [302], italics in original). The dividing dialectic to which Agamben refers is one that, through its "indifference," opens a rift between art and its public. Looking at the break this "lacerating" dialectic introduced into the history of art, Agamben writes that "the original unity of the work of art has been shattered, leaving on the one side aesthetic judgment and on the other artistic subjectivity without content" (MWC, 36 [57–58], translation modified).[9] Here we have the heart of the division, and the heart of the problem that aesthetics represents for Agamben—as well as the rationale for its "destruction." In Agamben's view, a consequence of the rise of taste and the attendant discipline of aesthetics has been to distance form from content and audience from artist—and in so doing, to dissolve the original unity of the work of art. It is in this sense that Agamben speaks of a "migration that will take [the artist] from the lived texture of society to the hyperborean no-man's-land of aesthetics" (MWC 16 [29], translation modified). The exigencies of the doctrine of cool, reflective taste put into motion a process through which the connection of artist and audience to a common "lived texture" is lost. The call to refine and purify artistic judgment and to isolate a formal creative principle from a traditional body of cultural contents has pushed Agamben's artist north, forcing him to abandon along the way more and more of the contents of his culture and the tools of his craft.

This forced emigration of the artist is what, for Agamben, laid the historical basis for Hegel's prescient claim that art is a thing of the past, not in the sense that art has ceased to be produced and valued, but in that it has ceased to shape our culture—that it lives on in the present as a thing of the past.[10] In fact, it makes perfect sense for Hegel's *Lectures on Aesthetics* to announce that art is a thing of the past, for in Agamben's view it was precisely of the essence of the rise of taste and the discipline of aesthetics to effect such a change—to freeze art in its time, to make it a thing of our past with no living, shaping, original relation to our present. It is this assessment that led Agamben to quote a different declaration from Hegel's *Aesthetics*:

No content, no form, is any longer immediately identical with the inwardness, the nature, the unconscious substantial essence of the artist; every material may be indifferent to him if only it does not contradict the formal law of being simply beautiful and capable of artistic treatment. Today there is no material which stands in and for itself above this relativity, and even if one matter be raised above it, still there is at least no absolute need for its representation by *art*. [Hegel 1975a, 603; cited by Agamben in MWC, 36 (55–56)]

Taking a page from Heidegger's typography, Agamben then writes, "If we wanted to express this characteristic with a formula, we could write that critical judgment thinks art as a̶r̶t̶" (MWC, 42 [66]).[11]

Original Status

As Agamben points out, what has led us in modern times to "think art as a̶r̶t̶" is the loss of connection to the *origin* of the work of art and to its "original structure." "If one day a trial should be launched against criticism," writes Agamben, the accusation against which it would least be able to defend itself would be that of an insufficient self-criticism, of having "neglected to interrogate itself as to its own origins and its own meaning" (MWC, 46 [69], translation modified). What remains for criticism in the wake of this damage is to return to those origins. With its attack on the deleterious effects of what various contemporary critics have termed an "aesthetic ideology" or "ideology of the aesthetic," and on that ideology's according of a primary place to "disinterestedness," the first part of Agamben's inquiry resembles other critiques of this aesthetic heritage. His argument is at times close to Pierre Bourdieu's denunciation of the idea of taste and of the reckless accumulation of cultural capital in Kantian aesthetics, just as it is at other points close to Paul de Man's combating of an "aesthetic ideology" on the grounds that its claims to epistemological unity and purity are ultimately founded on linguistic mystifications. It is at this point, however, that Agamben diverges, turning to questions of artistic originality older and more fundamental than the rise of the discipline of aesthetics.

As a means toward returning to these origins, Agamben asks, "What does *originality* mean?" (MWC, 61 [91], italics in original). He begins his answer in negative fashion, designating all that originality is not, pointing out that the originality of the work of art is not limited to its being "authentic," "unique," or "different from all others." The originality he is aiming to understand transcends these more technical definitions, and his first positive indication of how he means to answer this question is the statement "Originality means proximity to the origin." By this token, an original work of art is so by virtue of "remain[ing] in perpetual proximity" to that origin (MWC, 61 [91]). It is clear from the context that just as Agamben was not thinking of the work's uniqueness, he is also not thinking either of a historical origin of art nestled or neglected somewhere in the far reaches of our Paleolithic past, or of the related search for a Darwinian explanation of the survival value that might accrue to a species or a culture that creates and values artistic activity. The origin in question does not point back to a remote past—and in fact does not point to the past at all. For Agamben, following the conceptions of both Heidegger and Benjamin, origin is not that which is dead and monumentalized in the past, but that which is dynamic and alive in the present.

Paradoxically enough, one of the things that has, in Agamben's view, made the origin of the work of art so difficult to understand is *originality* itself—or at least what is commonly understood as such. Agamben identifies what he calls a "dogma of originality": an atomizing movement brought about by the artist's separation from a common body of cultural material to be transmitted through the work of art. The price paid for this originality is a connection between artist and public, which led, in Agamben's analysis, to the voiding of the "common space" in which artists had formerly worked. For Agamben, "everything that in some way constituted the common space [*luogo comune*] in which the personalities of different artists met in a living unity in order then to assume, within the strictures of this common mold, their unmistakable physiognomy became a *commonplace* [*luogo comune*] in the pejorative sense" (MWC, 62 [93], emphasis in original). The English translator renders the passage well, but in doing so occludes the fact that the terms in question—*common space* and *commonplace*—are the same term, and the same space (*luogo comune*). This is not a lighthearted pun on Agamben's part; it is a historical diagnosis concerning the loss of "a living unity." The new status of the artist brought about by the rise of aesthetics and the spread of a conception of art in which common content and common creation are devalued is for Agamben one of the key steps toward our contemporary blindness to "the original structure of the work of art."

In modern times, the "split in the spiritual life of the artist" (MWC 62 [93]), the loss of common forms and of a common tradition—the migration into the arid spaces of disinterested aesthetics—has led, on the one hand, to such extreme artistic practices as those of pop art and, on the other, to Duchamp's "readymades."[12] In both cases, the changes wrought in the status of originality and artistic experience brought about singularly *critical* works of art pointing above all to this spiritual split.[13] For Agamben, only by understanding and assuming the consequences of the strangely divided status of the work of art in contemporary society is there any hope for escaping from what he calls "the swamp of aesthetics and technology" and for "restor[ing] the original dimension of mankind's poetic status" (MWC 67 [101], translation modified). *Aesthetics* and *technology* are presented as though they are working together, and there is a sense in which, for Agamben, they are. He does not feel the need to clarify for his readers that "technology" is not in any narrow sense to blame, and that he is using the term in a fashion similar to the way Heidegger did (most famously in his "The Question of Technology")—as a synonym for an insufficiently self-reflective rationality so focused on *what* it can do that it fails to ask *whether* it should be done. It is this same cold calculation of rational possibilities divorced (or alienated) from a lived relation to one's world that Agamben sees in the discipline of aesthetics.

The "original dimension" that Agamben opposes to these forces refers to an origin of a complex nature. The principal difficulty in understanding this dimension is that it points at once to an *ontological* and a *historical* origin. The originality in question is then not merely a flickering point on a historical horizon—be it ancient Greece or prehistoric Lascaux—but a cultural and conceptual space that we might all share and with which modern societies have progressively tended to lose touch.

Agamben's criticism is then a criticism of a historically observable philosophical problem, and his critique of aesthetics (and technology) is a critique of modern conceptions of rationality.

The motivation for this analysis is that what Agamben calls, in a grandiloquent phrase, "the poetic status of man on earth" has been lost from view. But what is this status and how are we to attain it? Are we all to become poets? Is Agamben evoking the dream of a complete generalization of the artistic process like that advocated by Andy Warhol? The answer to these latter two questions is clearly *no*. Agamben is not referring to a belletristic Eden to which we might all return, nor to a reactionary call for a society in which humanistic education has absolute pride of place. What he *is* referring to is something at once more sweeping and simpler. "What is certain," writes Agamben, "is that the work of art is no longer . . . the essential measure of man's dwelling on earth, which, precisely because it builds and makes possible the act of dwelling, has neither an autonomous sphere nor a particular identity, but is a compendium and reflection of the entire human world" (MWC, 33 [51]). For Agamben there was a time, at art's "Greek beginnings," when the artist was seen as the shaper of our cultural world, setting its limits and giving it form—a time when the artist still possessed "the wonderful and uncanny power of making the world appear, of *producing* being and the world in the work" (MWC, 34 [53], italics in original, translation modified). But art has lost this status and has consequently been driven into a no-man's-land of hyperrationalized and disinterested appreciation. In the age of aesthetics—the era of disinterested artistic judgment—art has been safely cordoned off, and the passion and fire of an authentic experience of the work of art has, in a strange historical turn, "migrated" from the public sphere to the artist's studio. Art continues to enjoy a certain prestige, but at the price of a "living unity" with its audience. This audience grants art cultural capital but does not experience it in a fashion that would allow it to play a fundamental and shaping role in their experience of the world. Art is certainly no longer the means through which they take "the measure of their world," and still less a "compendium and reflection of the entire human world."[14]

The great power that Agamben grants to the Greek beginnings of Western thought, as well as to the ideas of taking "the essential measure of man's dwelling on earth" and of the work of art "*producing* being and the world in the work" share a provenance of which we have already had several glimpses. The fundamental "dwelling" to which Agamben alludes here clearly evokes Heidegger's use of the term (in such seminal essays as "Building Dwelling Thinking"). Closer to Agamben's topic is Heidegger's account of art's vocation in "The Origin of the Work of Art": "Art is history in the essential sense that it founds history" (Heidegger GA, 5.65).[15] For Heidegger, art *is* and *founds* history in that it is in the work of art that the space of human experience first finds its terms, forms, and functions. In this sense, the origin of the work of art is the origin of experience, the origin of cultural forms and activities (such as history). Heidegger's origin of the work of art could quite literally not be more fundamental, for it carries with it the power of "producing being and the world in the work." This, for Heidegger as well as for Agamben, is the role that art played for the Greeks, and that it has ceased to play for us.[16]

Rhythm, Structure, and Structuralism

In light of these remarks, it should come as no surprise that a subsequent chapter of *The Man Without Content* bears the title "The Original Structure of the Work of Art." Turning from the idea of *origin* to that of *structure*, Agamben uses the latter term to guide the next stage of his inquiry. The chapter begins with a remark Hölderlin made during the years he spent sunk—or elevated—in madness that was taken down by the hand of a reverent visitor: "Everything is rhythm, the entire destiny of man is one heavenly rhythm, just as every work of art is one rhythm, and everything swings from the poetizing lips of the god" (cited in MWC, 94 [143]). Agamben takes this Delphic-sounding utterance seriously, examines it closely, and elects this "rhythm" to be his guiding thread in his search for an original structure of the work of art.

He begins by tracing the term *rhythm* back to Aristotle's *Physics,* where the latter employs it to define nothing less than *nature* itself. Closely examining Aristotle's terminological choice, Agamben concludes that for Aristotle "rhythm is *structure,* scheme, in opposition to elemental, inarticulate nature" (MWC, 95 [144], italics in original). "Understood from this perspective," he continues, "Hölderlin's sentence would mean that every work of art is a unique structure, and would therefore imply an interpretation of the original being of the work of art as . . . structure" (translation modified). This equation leads Agamben to the conclusion that the mystery of artistic *rhythm* is the same as the mystery of artistic *structure.* "If this is true," Agamben then says, "Hölderlin's statement would also point toward the path taken by contemporary criticism where—abandoning the terrain of traditional aesthetics—it seeks the 'structures' of the work of art" (MWC, 95 [144–145]).

For the reader in 1970 the reference would have been unmistakable. Structuralist thought was thriving—to note two representative examples, Roland Barthes's *S/Z* and Tzvetan Todorov's *The Fantastic: A Structural Approach to a Literary Genre* were both published that year—and few contemporary readers would have missed Agamben's reference.[17] Rather than turning to the leaders of this disparate school of thought—figures such as Althusser, Barthes, Derrida, Foucault, Lacan, and Levi-Strauss— Agamben wryly cites another and far older French source for a definition of *structure*: Lalande's dictionary of philosophy published in 1925. There Agamben finds the classical definition: "structure . . . is a whole that contains something more than the simple sum of its parts" (MWC, 95 [145]). "If we now observe more closely the use that contemporary criticism makes of this word [structure]," Agamben continues, again indirectly but clearly referring his readers to the structuralist and poststructuralist thought of the day, "we notice that there is in it a substantial ambiguity, such that 'structure' designates sometimes the prime and irreducible element of the object in question (its elemental structure), and sometimes what causes the ensemble to be what it is (that is, something more than the sum of its parts)" (MWC, 96–97 [145]). Aristotle had already noted an infinite regress in this way of thinking, and Agamben recalls it here. Revising Aristotle's criticism for modern times and use, Agamben likens structuralists to Pythagoreans who failed to heed the logical inconsistency pointed out to them. The Pythagoreans considered structure to be something more than the sum of its structured parts, but it was argued that they did so as if this fact were simply one more part of a structural whole, and thereby fell into an infinite regress in their speculations on structure. Agamben's sharp eye for analogy sees a parallel between the Pythagoreans of antiquity and the structuralists of his day. To indicate, however, that his goal is not to isolate shortcomings in the movement of thinkers who were then in vogue, Agamben specifies that "this ambiguity is not due to a simple imprecision or an arbitrariness on the part of the scholars who use the word *structure;* rather, it is the consequence of a difficulty already observed by Aristotle" (MWC, 96 [145]). The modern problem lying behind debates about structuralism are, for Agamben, ancient problems dealing with the difficult task of conceiving precisely that which he himself has set out to try to understand: the original structure of the work of art.

The difficulties of glimpsing this structure led Agamben back to poetic rhythm and the structures it scans. In an age of disinterested aesthetics that has schooled us in distance and indifference, we have, for him, lost touch with the aspect in the work of art that fundamentally shaped a people and a culture—the aspect of works of art that established, in the influential metaphorical commune of Heidegger's thought, a "dwelling," a "house," and a "habitation" in which man could experience the contents of his culture in an "original" way. "The original structure of the work of art is now obscured," writes Agamben, and "man risks losing not simply a piece of cultural wealth, however precious, and not even the privileged expression of his creative energy: it is the very space of his world, in which and only in which he can find himself as man and as being capable of action and knowledge" (MWC, 102 [154–55]). Aesthetics' dominant mode of conceiving "art as art" has led to the loss of art's role as that which guides the project of "taking the original measure of man" (MWC, 103 [155]). Agamben clearly sees structuralism as having led to much, but what it has *not* led to is any greater potential for recovering the original rhythm he is following.[18]

Danger and Rescue

As noted earlier, Agamben likens art to "a planet that turns toward us only its dark side." This standing in the shadow of art recalls the celebrated conclusion with which Adorno opens his *Aesthetic Theory*: "It has become a point of self-evidence that nothing that concerns art is any longer a matter of self-evidence [*Selbstverständlichkeit*], either in its relation to itself or in its relation to the whole, and not even in its right to exist [*ihr Existenzrecht*]" (Adorno GS 7.9). Agamben's indictment of our current vision and experience of art is no less extreme, and like Adorno he sees a glimmer of redemption emanating from the same art that is so imperiled. Concerning art and what is at stake in it, Adorno wrote elsewhere, "art means . . . to resist the course of a world that unceasingly holds a gun to mankind's chest" (Adorno GS, 11.413). Stendhal saw politics in a work of art as like a pistol fired during a concert.[19] For Adorno, the forces of a world order tending toward the totalitarian have taken the room and are holding hostages. To resist the turn that history is taking and that has all of humanity in its dark sights is the imperative his work follows—and that art offers privileged means of identifying. The global stakes that Agamben sets for art are no less in his first book, but his means of reaching them are different.

Agamben's man without content is, as he states, the artist. His analyses take his reader through the rise of aesthetics, the search for a concealed rhythm and structure, the idealization of originality, and the eclipse of origins. But despite this fluid succession of arguments, the reader might still ask what the real aim of his investigation is. Is the goal for the artist to reclaim these lost cultural contents? Agamben makes clear that the answer to this question is *no*. There is, however, another possibility. In 1955, Hannah Arendt wrote of how "present realities" seem to have brought about "a global present without a common past," which threatens to "render irrelevant all traditions and all particular past histories" (Arendt 1955, 84). In an essay entitled "Tradition and the Modern Age," from those same years, she wrote, "To most people today this culture looks like a field of ruins which, far from being able to claim any authority, can hardly command their interest. This fact may be deplorable, but implicit in it is the great chance to look upon the past with eyes undistracted by any tradition, with a directness which has disappeared from Occidental reading and hearing" (Arendt 1961, 28–29). Writing almost a decade later, Agamben sees an essentially unchanged state of affairs. In an unpublished letter from the same year as *The Man Without Content*, Agamben wrote to Arendt to express his admiration, stressing how "discovering your books represented a decisive experience [for me]," and this experience seems tied to a realization concerning not only a loss of tradition but also the unexpected possibility for change that this loss brought with it.[20]

In the final chapter of *The Man Without Content*, Agamben focuses on the idea of *tradition* and finds, as Arendt did before him, that "traditions and particular past histories" indeed seem to have been "rendered irrelevant." He notes that man has "lost his ability to appropriate his historical space, the concrete space of his action and knowledge" (MWC, 114 [171]). But just as the negative side of the diagnosis remains constant in the works of thinkers as diverse as Heidegger, Adorno, Arendt, and Agamben, so too does a positive potential—a "chance," as Arendt says, "to look upon the past with eyes undistracted by any tradition, with a *directness* which has disappeared from Occidental reading and hearing." To understand this chance for a new directness, Agamben hearkens back, however, to another, more artistic model.

Before control over the rhythms of his own thought left him, Hölderlin wrote in "Patmos" (Hölderlin 1969, 177):

Nah ist
Und schwer zu fassen der Gott
Wo aber Gefahr ist, wächst
Das Rettende auch.

Near
and hard to grasp is the God
Yet where there is danger, also grows
that which saves.

Hölderlin's location of rescue and redemption in immediate proximity to the danger to which they might respond is an intoxicating idea and has captivated many thinkers. For Agamben's first philosophical master it became an article of faith. In "The Question Concerning Technology," Heidegger interprets these same lines as saying, "In technology's essence grows concealed that which may redeem us from it" (Heidegger GA, 7.29). In the closing words of that same essay, Heidegger makes clear that this intimate proximity of danger and rescue is not limited to the question of technology. Making Hölderlin's principle his own, he writes that "the closer we come to the danger, the more brightly do the ways into the saving power begin to shine" (Heidegger GA, 7.36; 1993, 341). Adorno and Horkheimer, no friends of Heidegger or his ontology, also approvingly cite and elaborate on these same lines from Hölderlin's "Patmos" in their *Dialectic of Enlightenment* (see Adorno GS, 3.65ff).

This idea of urgency leads Heidegger, as it did others, to claim that philosophy at its highest is the product of dangerous times, and to write that "the question about the nature of something awakens at those times when that, whose nature is being questioned, has become obscured and confused, when at the same time the relationship of men to what is being questioned has become uncertain or has even been shattered" (Heidegger 1958, 43). In "What Are Poets For?" Heidegger offers yet another expression of this idea of redemption, going so far as to speculate that *only* where the danger grows is redemption to be sought: "Perhaps is any salvation that does not emerge from the site of danger but a further source of harm" (Heidegger GA, 5.296). What Heidegger sees in Hölderlin's poem, and finds reflected in the darkest corners of our contemporary landscape, is not only a faint hope but also a principle of dynamic reversibility: the greater the danger, the greater the potentiality for redemptive change.

Although in *The Man Without Content* Agamben does not cite either Hölderlin's poem or Heidegger's exegeses, their ideas of catastrophe and redemption could not more profoundly mark its conclusion. As early as 1966 Agamben evoked precisely this dynamic. In the course of discussing Artaud's theater and its unsettling double, Agamben paraphrases Hölderlin and praises Artaud's attempt to "transform an *impasse* into an escape route and to seek salvation where the danger is greatest" (SG, 68). This idea of the proximity of antidote to poison would prove as fundamental and as abiding an idea for Agamben as it was for Heidegger. Nineteen years later, Agamben addressed the idea directly, writing that "the capacity for dialectical reversal implicit in the affects of anguish and desperation . . . and that for Heidegger remained the custodians of the most extreme epochal hope, has today lost is prestige" (IP, 90–91 [74–75], translation modified); and in a book from 1998 he refers to "Hölderlin's principle often invoked by Heidegger, 'where there is danger, there grows the saving power'" (RA, 75 [69]). It is exactly this capacity for "dialectical reversal" that Agamben sees as neglected and that he is asking his reader to seek out.

To put things in the simplest possible terms, what has gone so wrong? The contemporary state of affairs seems to Agamben so dire because of a whole-scale loss of tradition—a loss of "living unity" between past and present, between artist and audience. What, then, is to become of tradition in the modern age? For both Arendt and Agamben, tradition not only enriches, not only gives content to a people and a place, but can also present itself as a burden, can also bend the backs and cloud the sight of those to whom it is handed down. As a result, this loss of common traditions that Arendt identifies brings with it the uneasy corollary of a new field of vision and a new possibility for what she calls "directness." In what might such directness, such new immediacy, consist is the final question Agamben endeavors to answer in his first book.

Construction and Destruction

As we have seen, there can be little doubt that Heidegger played the role of guide for Agamben. But as we have also seen, he was not alone in this role. No sooner had Agamben descended into this *terra aesthetica* than there appeared at his side a second guide: Walter Benjamin. In one of his own earliest writings, Benjamin identified, as would Agamben, an "indifference" at the heart of modern aesthetics, noting on a broader scale that "the term *scholarly study* [*Wissenschaft*] serves above all to conceal a deep-seated and well-vouched-for indifference [*eine tiefeingesessene, verbürgerte Indifferenz*]" (Benjamin GS, 2.76). To understand best how Benjamin guides the conceptual steps of the young Agamben traversing this *terra aesthetica,* however, we would do well to return to the concept of destruction discussed earlier.

Benjamin was no less interested than Heidegger in the liberating energies of *destruction,* and this interest had no less influence on Agamben than did Heidegger's. As Agamben noted later, one of the reasons that bringing the two thinkers into contact proved so fruitful for him was the degree to which they employed similar and even identical terms in radically different contexts and fashions (LDV). As Benjamin economically reminds his readers in his notes for a "theory of historical knowledge," "'construction' presupposes 'destruction [*Destruktion*]'" (1999, 470; GS 5.587). Seen in the light of Benjamin's other concerns, this seemingly commonplace remark acquires an uncommon intensity. As the title of one of his essays reflects, Benjamin was much interested in "The Destructive Character." And more singularly, the idea of *destruction* was for him tied to that of *criticism,* with the two conceptions even being at points equated, such as where Benjamin writes that "the destructive [*das destruktive*] or critical element in the writing of history comes into its own through the exploding of historical continuity" (Benjamin GS 1.1242). In his brilliant—and rejected—*Habilitationsschrift* (the work that every German academic then needed to complete, after the dissertation, to qualify for a professorship), the allegorical vision that Benjamin found embodied in neglected works of German Baroque drama was characterized by the manner in which it destroyed the unity of symbolic vision. For Benjamin, the open and avowed artificiality of allegorical art worked to destroy the harmonious context in which symbol and symbolized were imagined to merge mystically or grade imperceptibly into one another. In the studies of technological advances such as photography that Benjamin undertook in the years thereafter, the effect on the work of art in the age of mechanical reproduction was a "destruction" of that work's "aura." In his essay on the revolutionary energies harnessed by the Surrealists, Benjamin writes admiringly of how "the sphere of poetry [*Dichtung*] was here exploded from within" (Benjamin SW, 2.208; GS, 2.297). Yet it was in the "theory of historical knowledge" that Benjamin did not live to complete that his idea that "construction presupposed destruction" took on its full meaning.

In the sketched remarks found in the "Konvolut N" of his *Arcades Project*—remarks that Agamben stressed in 1986 "nearly fifty years later have lost nothing of their interest for the present" (AE, 8)—Benjamin again and again vigorously rejected "reconstructions" of the past. He makes it amply clear both there and in his *Theses on the Philosophy of History* that he is not interested in the past as such; he is not interested in "reconstructing" the experiences of more or less remote times and places. The task he assigns himself—that of the "historical materialist"—is to be distinguished from the reigning model of historiography in precisely this respect. In a manner like Emerson's, when the latter said that "books are for nothing but to inspire," or like Nietzsche's arguments concerning the use and misuse of history for life, Benjamin was interested not in history or tradition as such, but in whatever dynamic possibilities the past might offer the present.[21] For Benjamin, the typical historian of his day followed a "reconstructive" path, patiently trying to piece together historical documents and artifacts into a passable image—and for this reason not only failed to construct anything new but also failed to grasp the presuppositions implicit in such a view of history. The historical materialist, of which Benjamin saw himself as a pioneering type, sought something else: not to *reconstruct* a past that would in any event always remain inaccessible, but instead to *construct* a present. And for such a "construction," *destruction* was necessary.[22]

Tradition, Transmission, and the Work of Art

No thinker of his time was more sensitive to changes that the Western tradition was undergoing than Benjamin. It required, however, no great sensitivity to recognize the radical change in the status of *tradition* and traditional modes of historical transmission that was taking place during the first part of the twentieth century. For all of its complexity, this change is best characterized as a general erosion of tradition of the sort that Arendt noted. What was singular in Benjamin's response was his search for positive responses. Like Heidegger, Benjamin was a passionate and insightful reader of Hölderlin at a time when the latter was far from enjoying the fame and universal recognition he does today.[23] Benjamin once wrote that "in the writing of history, the strength of the destructive impulse will be proportional to the strength of the redemptive one" (Benjamin GS, 1.1242). Following his own version of Hölderlin's injunction, Benjamin sought a saving response to contemporary states of affairs—a response he adopted early and kept late, reminding his reader in his last work, the *Theses on the Philosophy of History*, that every moment of every day is "the narrow gateway through which the Messiah might enter" (Benjamin GS, 2.704).

Benjamin focused his sharp vision on the simplest cultural activities he could find in order to analyze this change in the status of tradition. "The Work of Art in the Age of Mechanical Reproduction" details an art without "aura"—a singular glow lost in an age in which the unique has been overshadowed by the reproduced. Benjamin found that such activities as *citation* and *collecting* amply revealed what he called a "destructive" force—a destruction of context effected by, for example, wrenching the citation or collected object from its original context and transposing it into another, essentially artificial one.[24] For Benjamin, such a displacement of statement or object from its context was possible only because the basis for the transmission of traditional words and things had begun to crumble. In an age in which traditions were critically endangered, art was subject to a similar "destructive" force; it too lost its original place, its common place or common space at the center of cultural life, and was set at a distance from which it could be observed with disinterested admiration—like a citation divorced from its content or an object isolated in the cabinet of its collector. Yet, surprisingly, for Benjamin it was through just such a "shaking [*Erschütterung*] of tradition" that the means for an eventual redemption were to be found (Benjamin GS, 2.478).

Following in Benjamin's footsteps, Agamben claims that "Baudelaire was the poet who had to face the dissolution of the authority of tradition in the new industrial society and therefore had to invent a new authority. He fulfilled this task by making the very intransmissibility of culture a new value" (MWC, 106 [160]). "The specific task of the modern artist" became then to reflect this alienation from traditional context, resulting in a work of art reflecting "the destruction of the transmissibility of culture" (MWC, 107 [161]). What Agamben saw as this "specific task" is illustrated by a passage from an essay written two years later (which would eventually become part two of Agamben's next book, *Stanzas*) in which he claims that "the greatness of Baudelaire with respect to the invasion of the commodity was that he responded to this invasion by transforming the work of art into a commodity and a fetish" (S, 42 [51]). Still fascinated by the difficult-to-locate role of Baudelaire, and following Benjamin's interpretation of "shock" as the fundamental experience in Baudelaire's poetry, Agamben wrote in his third book, "In Baudelaire, a man expropriated from experience exposes himself to the force of shock. Poetry responds to the expropriation of experience by converting this expropriation into a reason for surviving and making the inexperiencible [*inesperibile*] its normal condition" (IH, 41 [38]). The modern artist as exemplified by Baudelaire has a means—albeit a paradoxical one—of escape from the dissolution of the tradition in which earlier artists had worked and to which the modern artist no longer has access. That escape is, however, dearly bought: the artist must place at the center of that which is to be transmitted—the work of art—the very "destruction of the transmissibility of culture."

Aware of the difficulty involved in understanding the maneuver he attributes to Baudelaire, Agamben (MWC, 107–8 [162–63]) offers a clarifying explanation:

An inadequation, a gap between the act of transmission and the thing to be transmitted, and a valuing of the latter independently of the former appear only when tradition loses its vital force, and constitute the foundation of a characteristic phenomenon of nontraditional societies: the accumulation of culture. For contrary to what one might think at first sight, the breaking of tradition does not at all mean the loss or devaluation of the past: it is, rather, likely that only now the past can reveal itself with a weight and an influence it never had before. Loss of tradition means that the past has lost its transmissibility, and so long as no new way has been found to enter into a relation with it, it can only be the object of accumulation from now on. In this situation, then, man keeps his cultural heritage in its totality, and in fact the value of this heritage multiplies vertiginously. However, he loses the possibility of drawing from this heritage the criterion of his actions and his welfare, and thus the only concrete place in which he is able, by asking about his origins and his destiny, to found the present as the relation between past and future. For it is the transmissibility of culture that, by endowing culture with an immediately perceptible meaning and value, allows man to move freely toward the future without being hindered by the burden of the past. But when a culture loses its means of transmission, man is deprived of reference points and finds himself wedged between, on the one hand, a past that incessantly accumulates behind him and oppresses him with the multiplicity of its now-indecipherable contents, and on the other hand, a future that he does not yet possess and that does not throw any light on his struggle with the past.

In Agamben's historical estimation, the loss of a culture's "means of transmission" leaves mankind trapped between a past he can no longer relate to, and therefore can no longer use to orient and shape his existence, and a future of unlimited uncertainty. For Agamben, as for Benjamin and Arendt before him, man is trapped "between past and present" and the finding of "reference points" is of the greatest necessity. The problem thus posed by the work of art is "not simply a problem among the others that trouble our culture," because "only the work of art ensures a phantasmagorical survival" for this "accumulated culture" (MWC, 111 [167], translation modified).

Whereas at the beginning of the book Agamben called for a "destruction of aesthetics," by its end it is clear that he sees the discipline of aesthetics itself as founded on "destruction"—"the destruction of the transmissibility of culture . . . in which aesthetics is founded" (MWC, 111 [167]). Confronted with this problem, the artist—the modern man without content—can recover a measure of transmissibility for the work of art by reflecting this state of affairs. "In this way," writes Agamben, "at the limit of its aesthetic itinerary, art abolishes the gap between the thing to be transmitted and the act of transmission and approaches the mythic-traditional system, in which a perfect identity existed between the two terms" (MWC, 114 [171], translation modified). Such a perfect identity as that which prevailed in myth-based societies is indeed no longer to be had, and no longer to be wished for. But this return to near identity between thing to transmit and act of transmission that recalls mythic forms is to be effected, in Agamben's estimation, through a singular sacrifice: the thing to be transmitted—content—is sacrificed, so to speak, to the act of transmission—the work of art.[25]

The high priest of this sacrifice is not, however, Artaud or Baudelaire but instead Kafka. In an essay on the latter, Benjamin wrote, "Kafka possessed a rare skill for creating parables. Nevertheless, he made them such that they could never be exhaustively explained—he took, in fact, every possible precaution against their interpretation" (Benjamin GS, 2.422). For Benjamin, Kafka's gift for that most traditional form of cultural transmission—the parable—is to be seen, paradoxically, in that his parables do not reveal their meaning. Benjamin speaks of the two surest ways of misinterpreting Kafka's works as interpreting them as natural and interpreting them as supernatural (see Benjamin GS, 2.425). The summit of Kafka's parabolic genius was, for Benjamin, attested to by Kafka's ability to compose parables with no fixed meaning. The more the parables are pursued, the more their meanings recede; for Benjamin, their genius is in their inexhaustibility, and they thereby express something fundamental about both parables and their status in modern times. However curious this interpretation may seem, it was far from an isolated position. Adorno wrote that Kafka's parables "expressed themselves not through their expression but through their refusal, through their interruption," to which he adds, "each sentence says, 'interpret me,' and yet none will tolerate it" (Adorno GS, 10.255). Werner Hamacher writes of tradition as it appears in Kafka's work as "having no content, no longer having a gift to give beyond giving itself" (Hamacher 1998, 289). In starker terms, Guy Davenport has written that "signs and symbols have no claim on Kafka, who wrecks tradition rather than trust any part of it" (Davenport 1996, 5). Whatever Kafka's own innermost intention might be, the signs and symbols that so densely people his works have proven distinctive to his readers in never being subject to anything like a decisive interpretation. Writing of Kafka, Benjamin conjured the image of "the weight of riches piled on the backs of mankind"—but these are riches that can bring us no benefit because we lack the strength to shake them free and thereby lay hands on them. What we need, then, is "a destructive moment" so as to liberate ourselves from this weight (Benjamin GS, 2.478).

Following in the same vein, Agamben understands this inexhaustibility of interpretation in Kafka's works as a gesture of a singular order, and one with the greatest significance for the history of art. It is, for him, the continuation of the movement first sketched by Baudelaire: the sacrificing of the transmission of a given body or set of contents for the mere act of transmission. Without the fixed cultural coordinates of earlier ages at his disposal, Kafka set out on a radical path. Freed from the burdensome weight of cultural transmission, he found himself open for adventures of a radically new sort. The problem of man's having "lost his ability to appropriate . . . the concrete space of his action and knowledge" can, in Agamben's view, be remedied and this space recuperated through art's ability to "transform" man's suspension between past and future "into the very space in which he can take the original measure of his dwelling in the present and recover each time the meaning of his action"

(MWC, 114 [171–172]). By allowing man to envisage such a new relation to tradition, and by taking hold of the original space in which man takes his measure—in other words, by enabling a new relation of man to his content—Agamben envisions a possibility for the work of art to regain the shaping role it had long ceased to play.[26]

Of the last part of *The Man Without Content* Simon Jarvis astutely notes that "not merely the central thesis but also the approach, lexicon, and manner are strongly marked by Martin Heidegger's influence. What Agamben understands as the withering of the work of art's capacity to disclose a world could equally, as Hegel insisted, be thought of as its emancipation from fixed contexts and contents" (Jarvis 2000, 30). This is perfectly true, and it is also the point. Both Agamben and Jarvis agree that the work of art is freed from fixed contents; the only question is whether this is a good thing—for art as well as for the society that does not just value it, but is shaped by it.

The House in Flames

This last argumentative step brings Agamben to his conclusion. The final chapter of *The Man Without Content* is entitled "The Melancholy Angel." This angel is the angel of aesthetics, and like Benjamin's angel of history, it is a borrowed one. Whereas Benjamin's angel came to him from Klee's painting *Angelus Novus*,[27] Agamben found his in Dürer's *Melencolia I*. The wind has caught the wings of Benjamin's angel of history and is driving it relentlessly forward. Agamben's melancholy angel of aesthetics is in a different but equally desperate position; stranded in a land without wind, it is left to look disconsolately at tools of cultural activity that have lost their shaping function.

As we have seen, *The Man Without Content* aspires to return art to its original calling and its lost stature. In Agamben's next book he refers to a phrase from the troubadour poetry of the thirteenth century, "a joy that never ends," and says that it will "remain the always vital and luminous project against which our poetic culture will have to measure itself, if and when it succeeds in stepping backward and beyond itself toward its own origin" (S, 130 [155]). We can understand such a project and such an origin not as isolated in the reaches of a remote past but only as a dynamic possibility inhering in our present. The origin in question is not a completed state that then gave rise to a series of successive ones. Instead, it is a continuing potential for growth and change. In "The Origin of the Work of Art," origin is at issue because, as Heidegger says, "art is in its essence an origin" (Heidegger 1993, 202; Heidegger GA, 5.66). As in the reflections of both Wind and Benjamin, what is in question here is the means for art to play a shaping role in our culture—the role that despite its ever wider distribution it has ceased to play. At the end of this essay Heidegger wrote, "The question is . . . whether art can be an origin and therefore must be a step ahead, or whether it is to remain a mere addendum and then will only continue as a routine cultural phenomenon" (Heidegger 1993, 203; Heidegger GA, 5.66). Agamben was present at one of Heidegger's animated discussions with René Char about Rimbaud's statement that art will cease to set life's rhythm but will instead be "ahead of" it ("La Poésie ne rythmera plus l'action; elle sera en avant").[28] It is precisely such a decisive force in art—and in particular the privileged art of poetry—that Heidegger—and in his wake, Agamben—envisions. Art is not to play the role of a "routine cultural phenomenon" consumed as disinterested enjoyment but is instead to be a step ahead of life, shaping and guiding the way we experience it.

It is perfectly obvious that Agamben's first book is about art, but it is less immediately clear that it is also a book about *potentiality.* Agamben indeed discusses the passage from Aristotle that will remain at the center of his thought for four decades, but he does not use the term *potentiality* extensively, choosing instead an ontological vocabulary largely borrowed from Heidegger. Nevertheless, what interests Agamben in art is the potential it has lost, or that has gone unrecognized in it, which he works to reveal.

The Man Without Content begins with a call for destruction and ends in flames. "According to the principle by which it is only in the burning house that the fundamental architectural problem becomes visible for the first time," Agamben writes, "art, at the furthest point of its destiny, makes visible its original project" (MWC, 115 [172]). The book ends with this image—one that he silently adapts from Benjamin. At the end of the book that Agamben singles out as an unparalleled achievement in criticism—Benjamin says of the idea of the German *Trauerspiel,* "In the ruins of great buildings the idea of the plan speaks more impressively than in lesser buildings" (Benjamin 1977, 235). For Agamben, the house is not in ruins, it is in flames, and this house in flames is a figure for man's artistic being. For Agamben, the conflagration is not to be stopped but is to be learned from. Its destruction offers something of the greatest importance for constructions to come: it renders visible the "fundamental architectural problem" of aesthetics, and reveals for a luminous instant what Agamben sees as art's "original project"—a project whose name, in his books and essays to come, becomes "potentiality."[29]

Reception

In the Italy of 1970, Agamben's first book sparked relatively little response and in the years since has rarely been discussed in depth. It is an elegant and insightful, precocious and often profound work, but not a seminal one. Although much can be learned from it, students of the subjects it treats are likely to recognize its principle arguments in Nietzsche, Wind, Benjamin, and Heidegger, and the claim might easily be made that Agamben makes no major points not already found in Nietzsche's *Genealogy of Morals*, Wind's *Art and Anarchy,* or Heidegger's "The Origin of the Work of Art." However, *The Man Without Content* is not simply a treatment of the fate of the artist in the modern world. In Agamben's characteristically subtle fashion, it is also a reflection on being and becoming an artist—the work of a brilliant young man interested in creative as well as critical pursuits, and seeking his own answer to the problems his situation posed.

Scholium I: Benjamin and Heidegger, or
Poison and Antidote

We saw in this book's introduction that Agamben's discovery of philosophy's potentiality was born of his encounter with the person and works of Heidegger. Although this encounter was the beginning of a vocation, it was not the end of it. We saw earlier that Agamben noted it was his encounter with Heidegger that first "made philosophy possible." "That is the real interest of encounters," he continued, "in life as in thought: they serve to make life possible (or at times impossible). In any event, that is what happened with my meeting Heidegger—and at nearly the same time with my coming into contact with Benjamin's thought" (AC, ii–iii).

Although Agamben's discovery of Benjamin during these same years occurred purely through the medium of books, the encounter was neither less intense nor less decisive. Agamben relates that when he first read Benjamin in the summer of 1968, "it had the most immediate and astonishing effect on me," to which he added, "with no other author have I experienced such an uncanny affinity" (UIGA, 32). In characteristic fashion, Agamben paid tribute to this experience by drawing a parallel to Benjamin's life and works: "I seem to have experienced precisely what Benjamin himself did upon first reading Aragon's *Paysan de Paris,* where, after a few moments, he was forced to close the book because his heart had begun to beat so fast"(UIGA, 32).

"Every great work contains an element of darkness and poison," Agamben has remarked, "for which it does not always offer an antidote"— and to this general claim he added a specific illustration: "Benjamin was for me the antidote that allowed me to survive Heidegger" (AC, ii–iii). That this was not merely a passing thought expressed in one interview among many is attested to by his repeating it on a number of occasions, such as when he recently remarked that "perhaps Benjamin was the antidote that saved me from Heidegger" (DTP, 4).

Agamben does not say what, precisely, he found shadowy or poisonous in the work of his first philosophical master, and he says just as little about what redemptive element in Benjamin's thought helped him to survive Heidegger. Until after Heidegger's death in 1977 (seven years after the publication of *The Man Without Content*), relatively little was known about the philosopher's words and deeds of the early 1930s. Heidegger first spoke publicly about this period and his actions during it in an interview conducted in 1966 with *Der Spiegel* magazine in the same Black Forest hut where Celan had visited him. Following Heidegger's strict instructions, the interview was not published until after his death. The explanations given in the interview were partial ones, and it was not until the publication of a book entitled *Heidegger and Nazism,* written by another of Heidegger's students, Victor Farias, in 1987 that something of the full extent of Heidegger's professional involvement and personal investment in the Nazi Party became widely known.[30] It is far from certain, however, that Agamben saw this shadow and poison as purely—or even as primarily—political.

Benjamin's influence, and its complex relationship to the influence of Heidegger, is a topic to which we will return at a number of points in the following pages, but what bears noting here is what is already visible in Agamben's first work: its absolutely decisive nature. Just as he does at the end of *The Man Without Content,* Agamben continues to oppose and link the ideas and approaches of Heidegger and Benjamin.

Scholium II: The Potentiality of Art

In G. E. Lessing's play *Emilia Galotti* (1772), a painter named Conti asks his prince a question: "Do you think that Raphael would still have been the greatest painterly genius if by mischance he had been born without hands?" (Lessing 1985, 7.10). The prince finds it difficult to answer the painter's question—and with good reason. It is a question not only about where artistic creativity resides, about the relation between the potential and the actual, but also about performing the difficult task of conceiving of potentiality independently of actualization. The child Raphael may not yet be a painterly genius, but his potentiality for becoming one is not difficult to imagine. No necessity is involved, but the gift is there, ready to develop. But what of a more extreme case, such as the one Conti suggests, in which all such future realization is ruled out?

Lessing likely found his point of departure in Aristotle and in the latter's discussion of potentiality. At one point Aristotle chooses the figure of a sleeping geometer to illustrate dormant potentiality, which is to be distinguished from the type of potentiality in which an individual has no knowledge of geometry but possesses the mental capacities for learning it (see Aristotle 1984, 1141; 735a26). In *The Coming Community*, rather than referring to Lessing—or for that matter, to Aristotle's geometer—Agamben turns to a more modern artistic figure to make his point. "Every pianist necessarily has the potential [*potenza*] to play and the potential to not-play," Agamben writes. "Glenn Gould is, however, the only one who can *not* not-play, and directing his potentiality [*potenza*] not only to the act but also to his own impotence [*impotenza*], he plays, so to speak, with his potential to not-play" (CC, 36 [34], translation modified). Gould's musical genius is such that it accompanies him at every step; whether in the presence of a piano or not, whether playing or not, the potentiality to play remains richly and fully his. In other words, the artist is still an artist even when his instrument is absent, or when he, like Aristotle's geometer, sleeps. This is indeed self-evident, but it points to something that is less so: that we lack simple and straightforward terms for discussing potentiality in what Agamben refers to as its pure state—potentiality independent of its actualization—and that art, at the outset of Agamben's career, offers the most promising means for envisioning it.

CHAPTER TWO

A General Science of the Human:
Stanzas: Word and Phantasm in
Western Culture

The reader of Agamben's second book[1] might well wonder to what its title refers. The answer to this question is both simpler and more complex than it might first appear, and as is often the case with Agamben's writing, understanding the title proves to be an essential element in understanding the work. In both English and Italian, *stanzas* are divisions of verse—groups of lines numbering, as a rule, not less than four. Shakespeare, for instance, has a character in *Love's Labour's Lost* cry out, "Let me heare a staffe, a stanze, a verse," and it is clear enough that what he wants is a bit of poetry (IV.ii. 107). The reader who picks up Agamben's book and concludes that his title refers to divisions of verse would be right—but would also have grasped only half the matter. The poetic meaning of the word *stanzas* is not its only—or even its primary—meaning. This division in verse stems from a division in space. In Italian, a *stanza* is, simply enough, a "room"—and is familiar to many foreign eyes in the names of such celebrated ones as the Vatican's *Stanza della Segnatura,* decorated by Raphael. Agamben's book is indeed about poetry and its divisions, just as it is a book about rooms and the images that adorn them—but it is also a book about something entirely different.

An Ancient Enmity

"It is ultimately possible to accept that a novel may never actually re-count the story it has promised to tell," writes Agamben at *Stanzas'* outset, "but from a critical work one expects results—or at the very least, demon-strable theses" (xv [XI], translation modified). There is nothing surpris-ing in this claim, but there is something surprising in the turn Agamben gives to it. He follows this commonsensical observation with something that seems to run contrary to commonsense: a plea for granting critical works the same "absence of demonstrable theses" accorded creative ones. Agamben's reader must then ask why the author of a work of criticism would want it to be freed from such seemingly straightforward expecta-tions. This question lies at the heart of Agamben's novel enterprise, and its answer lies in one of the oldest disputes in Western culture.

For a problem to be treated—and solved—it must be recognized as a problem. Heidegger reviewed and revised the history of Western phi-losophy as the site of what he called a monumental "forgetting." For him, the problem that lay at the origin and heart of Greek philosophy—what he called "ontological difference," the difference between beings and the being they all share in one mysterious mode or another—had become so marginalized or, in his extreme formulation, "occluded," that this question that had been the most serious and central question that Greek philosophy at its inception was capable of posing had ceased to be consid-ered as a philosophical problem at all. He saw his philosophical vocation as remedying this state of affairs. In Heidegger's wake, Derrida saw his own philosophical vocation in a similar instance of a massive "forgetting" on the part of Western metaphysics—one to which even the farsighted Heidegger was, in his own opinion, not immune. Derrida's *logocentrism*—the denigration of writing in favor of speech and the consequent privileg-ing of an ineffable presence inhering in the spoken word that is absent from "fatherless" writing—was the name he chose for this other decisive, and millennial, case of "forgetting."[2]

In Agamben's own study of the history of Western metaphysics, he finds a similar act of "forgetting," which he, like Heidegger and Derrida before him, traces to a moment before Western metaphysics took its de-cisive turns of thought and phrase in Plato's dialogues. "Access to what is problematic" about the question of criticism, writes Agamben, "is barred by the *forgetting* of a scission stemming from the origin of our culture that is usually accepted as the most natural thing—that goes, so to speak, without saying—but in fact is the only thing truly worth interrogating. The scission in question is that between poetry and philosophy, between the word of poetry and the word of thought [*fra parola poetica e parola pensante*]" (S, xvii [XIII], translation modified, italics added). Agamben summarizes the resulting division as follows: "Poetry possesses its object without knowing it while philosophy knows its object without possessing it" (S, xvii [XIII]). Just as Heidegger began his inquiry by noting how the forgetting of ontological difference had become so pervasive in our culture that its operative distinction (between beings and the being they share) was accepted as "the most natural thing," requiring no special consideration, Agamben too notes how the "forgetting" of the strangeness and importance of a division held to separate philosophy and poetry has become so ingrained in our culture that it too has come to seem natural. The study of this ancient enmity between poetry and philosophy leads Agamben to the fundamental conceptions that Western thought has formed concerning the common topic of the different parts of his work: the subject and the object of knowledge.

Agamben's approach to this phenomenon, and the common theme of the diverse investigations that make up *Stanzas,* is the idea of the subject's *possession* of objects of knowledge. To achieve his ends Agamben must question what it means to possess an object and what it means to know one. This inquiry will lead him to call for "a science without object," not in the name of a narcissistic writing practice concerned with nothing but its own fluctuating inspirations, but for a "knowledge" capable of conceiving "possession" and "objects" in truly novel fashion. Linking the concerns of his first two books, Agamben asks in an encyclopedia entry on *taste* written during these same years, "Is a reconciliation possible between systematic study, which knows the truth but cannot enjoy it [*conosca la verità, ma non ne goda*], and taste, which enjoys beauty without being able to rationally account for it [*goda della bellezza, senza poterne dar ragione*]?" (G, 1020). This is the question that, by four separate routes, he tries to answer in *Stanzas.*

The Proximity of Poetry and Philosophy

Agamben begins *Stanzas* by arguing that criticism should not be seen as a positivistic discipline. "When the term *criticism* first appears in the vocabulary of Western philosophy," he observes, "it denotes inquiry into the limits of knowledge, into that which it is possible neither to pose nor grasp" (S, xv [XI], translation modified). It is in the name of criticism's original meaning and task that Agamben questions our modern insistence that it produce "demonstrable results." In Agamben's view, criticism should not be seen as the mere presentation of positive findings. Working as it does at the limits of what can be known, it must of necessity take on a richer, stranger, and more uncertain form. If criticism works at the limits of knowledge, it follows that any "results" it reaches will be shadowed by the unknowable that lies beyond them.

To locate better where Agamben sees "the limits of knowledge" that it was once the task of criticism to explore, he directs his reader's attention to the beginnings of Western thought. In *The Republic,* Plato refers to an "ancient enmity" opposing "philosophy and poetry" (*Republic* 607b–c). Well enough entrenched by Plato's time to already seem to him "ancient," this enmity went on, following Agamben, to shape other enmities—between truth and beauty, thought and language, criticism and creation. This ancient enmity, this division running down the middle of the humanities that its practitioners, despite their best and brilliant efforts, have been unable to bridge, is *Stanzas'* subject.

For the philosopher that Agamben became, poetry remained of fundamental importance, just as philosophy did for the poet he has remained. In response to a question about the continuity of his vocation, Agamben replied, "I indeed began by writing poems, but I don't believe I ever renounced that. On the contrary, it was as if I didn't really begin to write poems until philosophy entered my life"—to which he added a remark in German: "Poetry is something one can do only through philosophy."[3] As one might expect from someone with such a conception of the relation of form to content, and of philosophy to poetry, Agamben has remarked that "for me, reflecting on the forms thought takes has always been central, and I have never believed it possible for a thinker to evade this problem, as if thinking were somehow nothing more than simply expressing opinions that were more or less right concerning a given argument. Precisely this centrality of form makes for the proximity of poetry and philosophy" (UIGA, 33).

As we saw earlier, Agamben's first book was a treatise and followed a continuous line of argumentation, treating a single topic or question (that of the role of art and of the discipline of aesthetics that aspired to analyze it). Agamben's second book takes a different form. *Stanzas* is a collection of four long essays (two of which had already been published separately) treating four topics: melancholy, fetishism, images, and semi-ology.[4] Although in each essay only one of these topics guides Agamben's investigations, all of the others are present and play a role therein.[5] Each topic helps him approach a shimmering point where poetry and philoso-phy converge in a criticism worthy of its ancient heritage.

At the outset of *Stanzas*, Agamben presents a brief critical genealogy of the thinkers who came closest to this point of convergence. It extends from Alexandrian poet and philologist Philitas of Cos (fourth century BCE), with his indivisible blending of exegesis and invention, to the nineteenth-century Jena Circle's utopian project of a "universal progressive poetry" (see S, xv–xvi [xi–xii]). The latter group asked of a work of criticism that it, among other things, "include its own negation." Agamben suggests that two twentieth-century critics have managed to fulfill this seemingly paradoxical criterion. The first is Félix Fénéon, the French writer best known for the exceptional brevity of his works.[6] The second is an author already familiar to Agamben's readers, Walter Benjamin, and Agamben singles out his *The Origin of German Tragic Drama* in this regard. Later in *Stanzas* Agamben refers to this book as "surely the least popular of Benjamin's works, [yet] perhaps the only one in which he fulfilled his most profound intentions" (S, 139 [159]). In *One Way Street,* a creative work published the same year (1928) as his critical *Origin of German Tragic Drama*, Benjamin remarked that under the conditions in which he found himself living, "true literary activity" was not to be found in traditional literary outlets, and a similar intuition seems to have inspired Agamben's work during these years (Benjamin GS, 4.85).

After establishing this cursory pantheon of precursors, Agamben points to "a definite sign of the decline [*scadimento*] of this tradition."[7] This is, paradoxically, that there are "today . . . many who make claims to the 'creative' character of criticism" (S, xv–xvi [XI–XII], translation modified). Whereas this might seem like the very opposite—like a sign of not a fall but a rise—the character in question is creative only in ap-pearance. This is so much the case that for Agamben the "criticism of today"—that is, of 1977—is actually "a form of negativity" (S, xv–xvi [XI–XII]). As we saw in the last chapter, that so many modern works of art functioned as *critical* gestures—exemplified in the ironic display of Duchamp's readymades and in the indifferent surfaces of Warhol's pop art—much interested Agamben during the years in which he was writing his first critical works. That critics of the day made claims to the creative character of criticism was, following Agamben, not the result of criticism becoming more creative but, on the contrary, *of artistic creation becoming more critical.* As Agamben writes, because "art itself has renounced nearly all pretense to creativity," criticism has no difficulty identifying with it (S, xvi [XII], translation modified). The creative criticism that Agamben is asking his reader to envision is thus not one that would be deemed creative by the false standards of the day, but instead one that would be creative in a more fundamental sense. Agamben's aspiration is that such work would be both critical and creative at once, and thus not only restore criticism to its forgotten creative rights, but also liberate creative endeavors from the negative critical function that Agamben saw them increasingly inclined to adopt.

A Science Without Object

Agamben's aspiration in *Stanzas* is thus as clear as it is vast. What he is arguing for is a *creative criticism.* At first sight, this is a simple-enough plea. No one would advocate a narrow and uninspired assemblage of facts over a synthetic study combining creative insight with critical erudition. But Agamben's intention is not merely a difference of degree. If criticism is to be not the analysis and evaluation of creative works but instead creative work in its own right, what is to be its object? Criticism, as we have come to understand it, is the criticism *of* some thing—the analysis of some work or idea. If it is to be no longer the study of a creative product or act but instead such a product or act itself, what becomes of criticism's object? In other words, how does criticism proceed, and what, if anything, separates it from art?

It is at this point that Agamben calls for something equally surprising. He aspires to offer nothing less than a "critical foundation for the social sciences and the humanities" (S, xvi [XII], translation modified). What is more, this critical foundation is to be found in those same social sciences and humanities, simply subjected to more intense reflection. For Agamben, a sign of criticism's "decadence" is seen in the sharp disciplinary divisions that crisscross the social sciences and the humanities. As early as 1929, Heidegger—to whose memory *Stanzas* is dedicated—diagnosed what he saw as the "decadent multiplicity of disciplines" propped up by the "technical organization of universities," which led scholarly activity to lose touch with, and become "uprooted" from, its "essential origin [*Wesensgrund*]" (Heidegger GA, 9.104). In the year in which Agamben first encountered him, 1966, Heidegger saw "philosophy dissolving into individual disciplines such as psychology, logic, political science" (GA 16.674). If disciplinary divisions are to be granted less importance and if the field of critical speculation is to be widened, a danger, alluded to earlier, results: the loss of a distinct *object* of study. Yet Agamben presents this risk not as a problem but, surprisingly, as the solution to the problem of a common critical foundation. "If in the social sciences and the humanities subject and object come to be seen as identical," writes Agamben, "then the idea of a science without object [*una scienza senza oggetto*] is not a playful paradox but perhaps the most serious task conferred upon thought in our time" (S, xvi [XII], translation modified). Offering a critical foundation for the social sciences and the humanities is thus not a matter of "play" and "paradox"—to use the key terms of the poststructuralism of the period—but rather "the most serious task" with which thought finds itself confronted. We might then ask what is in need of correction: our conception of *knowledge* or our conception of its *object*? The answer that Agamben's book offers is categorical: both. "What is more and more frequently concealed by the endless sharpening of knives on behalf of a methodology with nothing left to cut—namely, the realization that the object to be grasped has ultimately eluded knowledge," Agamben writes, "is instead reasserted by criticism as its own specific character" (S, xvi [XII], translation modified). Criticism's "specific character" thus lies, for Agamben, in the realization that not only has criticism's object "eluded knowledge" in the past—a simple enough claim, and something that future efforts might remedy—but it also *will continue to do so* in the future. It is this elusive object of critical inquiry that leads Agamben through the varied terrains of *melancholy, fetishism, fantasy,* and *semiology* and brings him, at his book's close, to the polemical point that Plato saw separating philosophy and poetry.

The Melancholy Angel

At the close of *The Man Without Content* Agamben saw in Dürer's *Melencolia I* an emblem for the angel of art stranded between past and present with the tools of the creative trades strewn at its feet. Agamben saw in Dürer's image an allegorical emblem for the at once historical and ontological dilemma represented by the rise of aesthetics. In *Stanzas*, Agamben returns to Dürer's etching not as an emblem for some state of affairs that it might allegorically express, but in its own right and in its own melancholy context.

This first section of *Stanzas* is dedicated to understanding a *temperament*: the melancholic.[8] For millennia, melancholy was thought to be under the special influence of Saturn and, in Aristotle's wake, was associated with the activities of the scholar and the poet, as well as with the ascetic ideals of religious reflection. Agamben offers a rectification to this image through what he sees as the neglected figure of *love*. In Agamben's view, one element of the historical understanding of the melancholic temperament has been consistently missed by modern commentators. His study shows that the amorous and erotic component of the ancient discourse around melancholy has been neglected by even the most erudite commentators—including the authors of a *summa* on Dürer's iconological world—Klibansky, Panofsky, and Saxl.[9]

After tracing the genealogy of melancholy as mood and malady in Western thought, Agamben notes, "It is curious that this erotic constellation of melancholy should have so persistently escaped scholars who have attempted to trace the genealogy and meaning of Dürer's *Melencolia*. Any interpretation—whatever its ability to decipher one by one the figures inscribed in its field of vision—that fails to consider the fundamental relevance of black bile to the sphere of erotic desire is bound to be excluded from the mystery so emblematically fixed in Dürer's image" (S, 18 [23]). According to Agamben, without an understanding of this essential element of the cultural history of the melancholic temperament, its expression in such works as Dürer's remains a mystery. This is no minor matter as Agamben sees "the allegorical intention" of Dürer's work "entirely subtended [*sottesa*] to the space between Eros and its phantasms," and it is this at once melancholic and erotic space that he wishes to chart (S, 18 [23]). For Agamben, the melancholic, like the artist and the lover, has a special preoccupation with potentiality that he means to explore.

The adding of the amorous component helps Agamben to understand Dürer's singular work and rectifies a point of iconographical history. But this is not the only reason he goes to such philological and iconographical lengths to point out this lacuna. For Agamben, melancholy is not merely an affect; the space it moves broodingly across is the space of culture itself. "The topology of the unreal that melancholy charts," he writes, "is, at the same time, the topology of culture" (S, 26 [33]). In Agamben's analysis, by focusing on the potentialities and possibilities of the imagination, on its fantasies and phantasms, the melancholic distances him- or herself from the occupations of everyday life. A side effect of reflecting on the possible is that it makes the actual and the real seem suddenly distant. "The troubling alienation of the most familiar objects," writes Agamben, "is the price paid by the melancholic" (S, 26 [34]). Returning to the objects strewn across the lower section of Dürer's image he writes, "The compass, the sphere, the millstone, the hammer, the scales, and the straightedge, which the melancholic project has emptied of their habitual meaning . . . have no other significance than the space that they weave during the epiphany of the unattainable [*all'epifanie dell'inafferrabile*]" (S, 26 [35]). "The meditating angel," writes Agamben of Dürer's figure, "is not . . . the emblem of mankind's attempt, at the limit of an essential psychic risk, to give body to his own phantasies and to master in an artistic practice what would otherwise be impossible to be grasped or known" (S, 26 [34–35], translation modified). The question of possession and knowledge is thus formulated through a *phantasm*. Phantasy is not the purgatorial place of a melancholic imagination without relevance for more fundamental aspects of culture, but instead its most proper place.[10] This obscured phantastic and erotic space leads Agamben back to his point of departure—a space he sees as common to poetry and philosophy, as well as common to another dichotomy, that between *enjoyment* and *knowledge*. This phantasmatic space, glimpsed in an erotically charged conception of melancholy, is for him situated neither entirely in the subject nor entirely in the object, but instead in what he calls a "third area" between the two that forms the common theme of the different parts of his investigation.

In the next section of *Stanzas* Agamben leaves melancholy to the side and, so as to better delineate this "third space" that he locates "between subject and object," turns to marginal objects in liminal spheres. He examines fetishes, toys, and artworks in the age of their commodification, tracing them to the same phantasmatic "third space" first glimpsed in the ancient moods of the melancholic. Fetishism plays a central role here because of how it isolates its object in a curious space never clearly locatable in either the subject or the object. Building on Freud's analysis, Agamben continues: "The fetish confronts us with the paradox of an unattainable object that satisfies a human need precisely through its being unattainable" (S, 33 [41]). This structure is one that Agamben, turning from the psychological to the economical, finds in Marx's analyses of commodity fetishism: "The superimposition of the use-value corresponds, in fetishism, to the superimposition of a particular symbolic value on the normal use of the object. Just as the fetishist never succeeds in possessing the fetish wholly, because it is the sign of two contradictory realities, so the owner of a commodity will never be able to enjoy it simultaneously as both useful object and as value" (S, 37 [45]). Reflecting on London's Universal Exposition in 1851 and the Paris Exposition of 1867, Agamben sees that "the transfiguration of the commodity into *enchanted object* is the sign that the exchange-value is already beginning to eclipse the use-value of the commodity" (S, 38 [46], italics in original). He then turns, in a second analogy, to poets such as Baudelaire who embraced the psychological artifices of fetishism, as well as to psychologists such as D. W. Winnicott and his study of "transitional objects" (those first objects, such as a piece of bedding or a scrap of cloth, that the child isolates from the external world and appropriates as his own). Expanding on these analogies, Agamben states that the fetishized objects here in question resemble one another in that they "apparently properly belong neither to the internal and subjective nor to the external and objective spheres, but to something that Winnicott defined as 'the area of illusion,' in whose 'potential space' they will subsequently be able to situate themselves both in play and in cultural experience" (S, 59 [69]). This "area of illusion" then becomes one of many names for what Agamben is trying to grasp in *Stanzas*: the elusive "third area" or "potential space" "between subject and object."

The Idea of Philology

The third section of *Stanzas* approaches this "potential space" from a different side: through the idea of fantasy in thirteenth-century lyric poetry. It is preceded by the longest and most complex dedication in Agamben's oeuvre: "Manibus Aby Warburg et Robert Klein / 'Der liebe Gott steckt im Detail' / geniisque Henry Corbin et Jacques Lacan / 'C'est li miroërs perilleus'" (S, 61 [71]).

The dedication begins with a motto taken from the joined hands (*manibus*) of Aby Warburg and Robert Klein: "the dear God dwells in the details."[11] Agamben was intensely interested in Warburg and his motto, reflected not only in the year Agamben spent studying at the Warburg Institute (at the invitation of Frances Yates, who Agamben had come to know through Italo Calvino), but also in his citing of the motto in an essay from 1975, and in his indirect evocation of it in an essay from 1984 in which he speaks of "philological attention to details, in which, as it has been said, the dear Lord likes to hide himself" (UIGA, 32; P, 90 [125], 32 [15]). Warburg, a brilliant and eccentric art historian, used this expression as a personal motto of sorts and would often cite it to colleagues and coworkers at the Institute he founded in Hamburg.[12] What he used it to stress was the need for attentiveness to even the most minute details of a work, or of a life, in one's search for the most fundamental and far-reaching matters.

Warburg's at once playful and serious dictum recalls the approach of one of his many admirers—Benjamin—who for his part wrote that to approach the "truth-content" of a work required "the most precise immersion into the individual details of a given subject" (Benjamin GS, 1.208).[13] Years later, in his *Letter on Humanism,* Heidegger adopted a similar stance, writing that given "the current penury of the world," we need "less philosophy and more vigilant thought; less literature and more care for letters" (Heidegger 1949, 54). Such a care for letters marks Agamben's approach, and throughout *Stanzas* he displays the erudition and precision of a philologist, as well as the guiding sense that without a detailed investigation of image and word, true philosophical speculation is impossible. Elsewhere during these same years, he approaches the most fundamental insights of the poetry of Hölderlin and the philosophy of Heidegger through a philological analysis of the virtually untranslatable German term *Stimmung* (see "Vocazione e voce" in PP, 77–89); and in *The Time That Remains* he analyzes the Apostle Paul's messianism by glossing the first ten words, and only the first ten words, of the Letter to the Romans. To approach the fundamental dialectical kernel of the philosophies of Hegel and Heidegger, Agamben turns to a still smaller element: the Indo-European root "*se*" as it is reflected in these philosophers' terminologies (see "*Se:* Hegel's Absolute and Heidegger's *Ereignis,*" 1982, in P, 116–37 [163–90]). In a later essay on terminology and Derrida, Agamben remarks that "even a simple punctuation mark can acquire a terminological character" and proves it not only there but also in an essay on Deleuze in which the latter's use of colons and ellipses are shown to

reveal Deleuze's most fundamental intuitions about the idea of immanence (P, 208).[14] The correction of individual letters in transcriptions of
Benjamin's difficult handwriting has proved to be of great importance (as
we will see in a later chapter), and a still smaller detail to which Agamben
accords special attention forms the topic of the final, semiological section
of *Stanzas,* where Agamben analyzes the slash, or barrier (/), that Saussure
introduces between signifier and signified (see S, 137ff. [162ff.]).

In short, for Agamben, as for Warburg, the importance of philological attentiveness could hardly be greater. In Agamben's analysis of the
conceptual migration of *Stimmung* from a musical-acoustical sphere to a
psychological one, he wrote three years after *Stanzas* that "the history of
culture is often nothing other than the history of such displacements, of
such dislocations, and it is precisely for this reason that the interpretation
of certain categories and concepts of the past have often given rise to so
many misunderstandings" (PP, 78). Agamben finds a perfect example of
such in the case of *eros,* which began in archaic Greece as the name of a
theological figure—a god—only to evolve over time into a psychological
figure—that of *love* (see PP, 79). "In this migration," Agamben writes, "the
pantheon of Greek gods—or later, the Christian Trinity—is displaced,"
and "this theological *dislocation* is what we call *psychology*" (PP, 79, italics
in original). This mechanism—which Agamben simply calls "the history
of culture"—is what precise immersion into the details of a subject allows
us to understand. It is for this reason that the Provençal *amor* is a term
and concept of so much interest for Agamben, in *Stanzas* as well as in
earlier and later works. Agamben sees in it a watershed moment of such
historical displacement. The "project of a general science of the human,"
which Agamben describes his work as aiming toward during these years
of his career, must be conducted at the level of the letter—with all the
migrations, transformations, dislocations, and displacements of categories
and concepts implied therein (P, 101 [144]).

This is a movement, however, that goes both ways; not only must
the abstractions of philosophy take into account the details of philology,
but the descriptive disciplines must also open themselves to ontological
dimensions. In one of Agamben's early essays, written nearly ten years
before *Stanzas,* he speaks to precisely this point, proclaiming that "the
degree to which linguistics will open a semiological perspective to the
study of language will be conditioned by the extent to which it opens
itself to a more ample ontological dimension" (AL, 113–14). At various

points Agamben has spoken of the "temptation" he experienced to become a philologist (LDV). Of the period when he was writing *Stanzas* he notes, "It was during these years that I came closest to working as a philologist in the strict sense of the term, but it was also the period in which I began to see the limits of such an approach" (UIGA, 32). Of these limits he also remarked, "The philologist who wishes to follow his discipline to its limits is in need of philosophy and, as Nietzsche's experience shows us, must at a certain point become a philosopher" (UIGA, 32). It is for this reason that in *Stanzas* Agamben writes of how "Saussure represents . . . the extremely valuable case of a philologist who, caught in the net of language, felt . . . the insufficiency of philology, and who had to become a philosopher or succumb" to that insufficiency (S, 152 [182], translation modified). Simon Jarvis has reflected, "I am not sure that Agamben would wish to think of himself as a philosopher-philologist," but there is much in Agamben's work—and not only in *Stanzas*—that would incline the reader to think otherwise (Jarvis 2000, 30).

Agamben's conviction that it is only through the most careful and precise study of the details of a work that one can one reach its most fundamental conclusions was, as his dedication indicates, influenced by Warburg. The latter's famous attention to detail in text and image led to a series of remarkable discoveries. By examining the forms and gestures of early Renaissance art with unprecedented care, Warburg came to understand better the role that images from pagan antiquity played therein. As his peerless eye for detail led him to uncover subtle and surprising correspondences, he found his investigations leading him beyond the traditional confines of the history of art, and he began to form a special discipline. It was at this point that Robert Klein entered the picture—and Agamben's dedication. Klein, like Warburg, was an art historian specializing in the Renaissance, and he once remarked that the path-breaking Warburg was the founder of a discipline that, "in contrast to many others, exists but has no name" (Klein 1970, 224). What, then, is this science for which Warburg—a writer who possessed a rare gift for neologism—could find no name?

It was not for lack of trying that Warburg possessed no name for the discipline he pioneered. Early on in his studies it became clear to him that the initial designation, History of Art, would not suffice for his special purposes.[15] The reason for this was that Warburg's inquiries, though they were masterpieces of precise formal and stylistic exposition and explanation featuring remarkable feats of iconographical deduction (as in his deciphering of the cryptic astrological images at the Palazzo Schifanoia in Ferrara),[16] were only partially concerned with works of art in the way that the discipline of art history had come to view them. Central works of the Western canon such as Pollaiuolo's portraits or Botticelli's *Primavera* indeed interested Warburg passionately and served to guide his (extensive) research and (spare) writing. But what interested him still more than works of art seen through the lens of their formal and stylistic characteristics, and placed in a history of influences, were questions concerning the fundamental nature and function of images, and his detailed study led him beyond the confines of art history into sweeping ontological and anthropological speculations. Warburg soon came to occupy himself not only with works of art but also with images of all sorts—from antiquity to the present day, from the highest achievements in the visual arts to the lowest caricatures of the Reformation to the sports photography of his own day. Although he was a highly trained art historian capable of erudite disquisition on the most precise details of formal study or historical information—from Quattrocento Florentine dress to Babylonian symbology—Warburg's goal was to link art history to other fields of inquiry: to psychology, ethnology, anthropology, philology, philosophy, religion, and still other domains. Wind summarized Warburg's singular approach (in contradistinction to the reigning formalist approaches in the history of art of Heinrich Wölflin and Alois Riegl): "It was one of Warburg's basic convictions that any attempt to detach the image from its relation to religion and poetry, to cult and drama, is like cutting off its lifeblood" (Wind 1983, 25). This limiting aspect of the aesthetic (and formalist) tradition that Agamben so vehemently spoke out against in his first book expresses the same impatience that led Warburg to found a science that, though it existed, had no name.

Warburg never succeeded in naming this interdisciplinary discipline dedicated to the study of images and their cultural transmission (though he did come up with a series of promising candidates: the relatively straightforward and short-lived *history of culture,* followed by *psychology of human expression* and *history of the psyche,* then by *iconology of the interval* and the shorter and simpler *iconology*).[17] It should come as little surprise that Agamben repeatedly evokes Warburg in conjunction with thinkers such as Benjamin, Leo Spitzer, Claude Lévi-Strauss, and Émile Benveniste—thinkers working at the limits of their respective disciplines (philology,

stylistics, anthropology, and linguistics) and interested in the points at
which the most precise findings in those disciplines opened onto the broadest questions in the social sciences and the humanities (see P, 93).

Adopting Warburg's motto was a way for Agamben to call for careful reading and looking in his endeavors to bring together disparate areas
of inquiry—but there was also more to be heard therein. As the first part
of Agamben's dedication indicates, what Agamben is aspiring toward here
is not only vigilant attention to the minute details of texts and images
but also to break down the barriers that divide the different realms of the
social sciences and the humanities and thereby open the way for a "science without object" that could hope to become "a general science of the
human."[18]

Nachleben, or Culture

In Warburg's wake, Agamben then offers something absolutely fundamental: a definition of *culture.* "Every culture," he writes, "is essentially
a process of transmission and of *Nachleben*" (S, 112 [131]). The term *Nachleben* is one that Agamben leaves untranslated but that his English translator does not. The latter renders it as "afterlife." The notoriously difficult
to translate *Nachleben* indeed evokes a sort of afterlife and is composed of
words signifying "after" and "life" (*nach* meaning "after" and *Leben* meaning "life"). However, *Nachleben* does not designate "afterlife" in the way
in which we are accustomed to understanding it. It does not refer to the
afterlife in the sense of *another* life beyond this one, or of another world
beyond our own. Instead, it is continued life in this world, and for this
reason is more often translated as "survival." This makes the word sound
almost ghostly, and it is perhaps no wonder that the writer from whom
Agamben borrowed the term—Warburg—once described his writings as
"ghost stories for the very adult."[19]

Agamben leaves the term in German not only because of the difficulty of translating it, but also to direct his reader to the term that Warburg
used to denote the center of his interests: the "survival" or "continued life,"
the *Nachleben* of forms—of images, poses, postures, and gestures—in cultural artifacts and works of art over long periods. To borrow a title from
one of Warburg's friends and colleagues, Ernst Cassirer, what Warburg
was striving to formulate in his work was a *theory of symbolic forms.* The

reason Warburg did not choose a simpler term such as *form* and the reason Agamben does not do so in *Stanzas* when he seeks to define *culture* is that both thinkers are envisioning a more dynamic relation between past and present than the terms of art history or historiography are accustomed to expressing. Warburg used the term *Nachleben* for the same reason he spoke of the equally difficult to translate *Pathosformel* ("pathos formulae"): the point of his investigations was to understand the life and afterlife of images—to study images as "charged" with psychic energies or symbolic life.[20] The correlate of this conception was that images from our cultural past are not dead, gone, or extinguished; they are at most dormant and remain infused or "charged" with the energies that cultures have invested in them—a dynamic potential that they retain even when they lie forgotten for decades, centuries, or even longer. "In Warburg," Agamben writes, "precisely what might have appeared as an unconscious structure par excellence—the image—instead showed itself to be a decisively historical element, the very place of human cognitive activity in its vital confrontation with the past" (P, 102). In another essay, Agamben notes how Warburg "transformed the image . . . into a decisively historical and dynamic element" (MWE, 54 [49]). Warburg's largest aspiration was to understand and describe the energies inhering in a culture's images— energies that were, in his conception, stored in those images and that could lie waiting therein for centuries before being revived in the imagination of a new age (as happened during the Renaissance). It was this same energetic conception of cultural transmission that led Warburg to a series of neologisms coined to describe images invested with a particular psychological force or charge, which he alternately termed *engrams, dynamograms,* and *pathos formulae.* For Warburg, images were the history of culture in crystallized form, and he consequently found nothing so wrongheaded and limiting as the nationalistic and disciplinary divisions that had sprung up in the social sciences and the humanities of his day and that impeded the project of a comprehensive understanding of the psychological power and cultural meaning of images.

"European culture is, despite everything," Agamben stresses, "conservative, and it is conservative precisely to the extent that it is progressive and revolutionary" (S, 112 [131]). For Warburg and Agamben, Western culture is a "conservative" culture in the (literal) sense in that it tends to conserve its cultural forms—its signs, symbols, and images. This conservation, however, is the last thing but a neutral transmission of conventional forms and contents from generation to generation. European culture, although singularly dynamic in its valuations ("hot" in the terms of a thinker who was important for Agamben during those same years, Lévi-Strauss),[21] also shows a singular tendency to preserve or recycle its forms, even when they have disappeared from the main repertoire of a culture for years, decades, centuries, or in some cases, millennia. The durability of these forms and contents is what Warburg—and after him, Agamben—designated by the term *Nachleben*.

In later years, Antonio Negri (2003, 21) called Agamben "a Warburg of critical ontology," presumably both because he linked, in surprising and at times jarring ways, fundamental philosophical questions to precise philological ones stemming from other discourses and disciplines, and because of the exceptionally long historical half-life or afterlife he saw in figures from antiquity. When Agamben remarks that "historians of art and literature know that between the archaic and the modern there is a secret appointment," he is expressing an idea he shares not only with Benjamin but also with Warburg and that the latter imparted to a broad range of students from Wind to Panofsky, Curtius to Carlo Ginzburg, Gombrich to Horst Bredekamp (CCC, 23). At the heart of *Stanzas'* detailed analyses lies an overarching inquiry into the nature of culture and the process of its transmission. For those retrograde researchers who stood watch at the limits of the various disciplines of his day, Warburg coined a playful name—the "Guardians of Zion." Klein's observation about Warburg's inventiveness gives itself to the title of an essay Agamben wrote during these same years, "Aby Warburg and the Nameless Science" (1975), in which Agamben comes to the conclusion that "it is likely that such a science [as Warburg's] will have to remain nameless as long as its activity has not penetrated so deeply into our culture as to overcome the fatal divisions and false hierarchies separating not only the social sciences and the humanities from one another but also artworks from the *studia humaniora* and literary creation from science" (P, 100 [143], translation modified).[22] This should sound perfectly familiar to the reader of *Stanzas,* for it is precisely these "fatal divisions and false hierarchies" that, as we saw earlier, led Agamben to call for a "science without object." "It is to be hoped," Agamben remarks in *Stanzas*, "that in the context of a global approach [*approccio*] to culture similar to what Warburg envisioned," philology would learn to integrate the study of images into its methods (S, 72 [76]).[23] This is, however, only one step to be taken and one boundary to be crossed. Expanding on this hope, Agamben indicates the breadth of his ambitions for this nameless science by suggesting that "only a 'discipline of interdisciplinarity' is adequate to the interpretation of human phenomena" (S, 89 [102]). This same phrase, "discipline of interdisciplinarity," along with a "general science of the human," is found at the end of Agamben's next book, *Infancy and History*—as is reference to "a science as of yet without name," and thereby makes clear the interdisciplinary direction in which Agamben's thought is moving during these years (see IH, 147 [148], translation modified). *Stanzas* is an interdisciplinary book in that it calls on a wide array of methods and terms from the disciplines of philology, philosophy, iconography, iconology, and poetics. But it is interdisciplinary in still another way in that Agamben's aim is to overcome both the divisions that separate these individual disciplines and the more fundamental—and forgotten—divisions between poetry and philosophy, creation and criticism.

A Discipline of Interdisciplinarity

As the second half of the complex dedication given earlier indicates, Part 3 of *Stanzas* is not only about Warburg and his "discipline of interdisciplinarity"; it is also about the space of love as it is innovatively described in the poetry of the thirteenth century—particularly in *Le Roman de la Rose* (the perilous mirrors in question are from that work and form the pool into which Narcissus gazes).[24] What the genius of Corbin and Lacan (*geniisque Henry Corbin et Jacques Lacan*) encouraged Agamben to look into were the *miroërs perilleus,* the perilous mirrors of fantasy that reflect our own image. For Agamben, the innovative element of medieval descriptions of love is their focus on a dreamlike element. The classical world had little conception of a hallucinatory "image" suspended between lover and beloved. The perilous mirror here named is the pool of Narcissus—a pool that merges with the fountain of love and where a phantasmatic image becomes an integral part of conceptions of love. That this phantasmatic presence of the beloved was an uneasy one is seen in the ways in which figures from antiquity such as Narcissus and Pygmalion were taken up by medieval poets and reinterpreted. For this phantasmatic aspect of love to be fully understood in its now largely forgotten context, the scholar, following Agamben, needs to adopt a variety of approaches,

and Corbin and Lacan are honored for the invaluable assistance they offer in this regard. It is clear that both thinkers are representative members
of the "discipline of interdisciplinarity" he invokes. Agamben writes elsewhere, for instance, of how "the importance of Corbin's studies for the understanding of stilnovist lyric is yet another proof of the need for the social
sciences and the humanities to overcome division into specialized depart-
ments," and in an essay from 1982 he approvingly refers to Corbin's observations on religious phenomenology (see P, 127 [177], 145ff. [216ff.], translation modified).[25] Lacan's interdisciplinary approach is more well-known;
the psychoanalyst routinely integrated concepts borrowed from linguistic
theory, set theory, literary theory, mathematical topology, ontology, and
other fields into his psychological speculations.

Agamben's interdisciplinary study in *Stanzas* presents many insights
about heroic quests and loves, but its most profound lesson concerns the
"possession" and "enjoyment" they so often name and that they share with
criticism itself. "Like all authentic quests," Agamben writes, "criticism's
quest consists not in recovering [*ritrovare*] its own object, but in securing
the conditions of its inaccessibility" (S, xvi [XIII], translation modified).[26]
If this remark is to be taken seriously—and everything about the passage
in which it is found encourages this—Agamben, knight-errant of criticism, has embarked on a curious epistemological quest.

The plea for a new criticism evoked earlier is accompanied by the
observation with which we began: "When the term *criticism* first appears
in the vocabulary of Western philosophy it denotes inquiry into the limits
of knowledge, into that which it is possible neither to pose nor grasp." We
might wonder why Agamben places such stress on *grasping*, or rather, on
"that which it is possible neither to pose nor to grasp." As its title indicates, *Stanzas* is about a space—and a space like no other. This is not a
localizable "real" space but, as Agamben calls it, a "phantasmatic space,"
a "potential space"—which is, in fact, the space of thought. It is thus
located neither in the subject nor in the object, and as a result can never be
fully and finally grasped by a subject in the form of an object. The various
stanzas of the book are demonstrations of this singularly elusive idea.

"The split between poetry and philosophy," says Agamben, "testifies to the impossibility for Western culture of fully possessing the object
of knowledge (for the problem of knowledge is a problem of possession,
and every problem of possession is a problem of enjoyment, that is, of
language)" (S, xvii [XII]). The reader is faced here with problems and

presuppositions that are difficult to locate. Why, for instance, should the problem of knowledge be seen as a problem of enjoyment? Agamben focuses his attention, as we saw, on a division in language "between the word of poetry and the word of thought" and finds a new formulation for it in terms of a "possession" of an "object" of knowledge: "Poetry possesses its object without knowing it while philosophy knows its object without possessing it" (S, xvii [XIII]). The problem then is one not of assuring the conditions of possibility for *possession* of the objects of knowledge (as in Kant) but instead of conceiving them in a new light. For this reason it is perfectly coherent for Agamben to claim that "like all authentic quests, criticism's quest consists not in recovering its own object, but in securing the conditions of its inaccessibility." The idea evoked here, which will be at the center of Agamben's fifth book, *Idea of Prose,* is not one of the guardians of a disciplinary Zion keeping their treasures from a profane mass. It is instead a lesson about the limits of representation. In this lesson lie both the difficulty and novelty of *Stanzas* and, in the works to follow, Agamben's idea of potentiality. The division between philosopher and poet, between knowledge and pleasure, corresponds for Agamben to a division in language itself and is the reason for "the urgency for our culture of recovering the unity of its own divided word [*l'unità della propria parola spezzata*]" (S, xvii [XIV], translation modified). This recovery, however, is subject to the cryptic caveat noted earlier: recovery *not* in the form of possession.

Here we can at last see that the critical criterion that Agamben borrowed from the Jena circle—that a work of criticism should "contain its own negation"—was not advanced as a mere provocation. It corresponds instead to the most profound intention of this singular work. "What is secluded in the *stanza* of criticism," Agamben writes, "is nothing, but this nothing safeguards unappropriability [*l'inappropriabilità*] as its most precious good" (S, xvii [XIV], translation modified). To ask of a work that it contain its own negation is to ask it to ensure the *un*attainability of its object. That this is an aspiration consonant with the philosophy of the book's dedicatee bears noting. From *Being and Time* in 1927 to "The End of Philosophy and the Task of Thinking" in 1972, Heidegger made a distinction between a systematic rationality and what he calls, simply enough, "thinking." *Thinking,* as Heidegger understands and employs the term, is not the amassing of information and the cataloguing of elements—things he associates with the instrumental reason, bureaucratic control, and championing of technology that have brought about such ravages as the dropping of atomic bombs. Heidegger's *thinking*, like that which Agamben advances here in the name of a combined critical and creative discipline of interdisciplinarity, approaches its object in a far different fashion—one that stresses the fundamental *experience* of thought and does not measure its accomplishment by its stockpiling of objects of knowledge.

Although Agamben's reasons for championing a discipline of interdisciplinarity are easy to understand, the ends to which he puts them are not always easy to grasp. How are we to envisage this science without object, this critical quest whose goal is not the recovery of a lost object but the maintenance of the inviolability of that object? The logic of appropriation that Agamben adopted from the dedicatee of the book provides a different link with thinkers of his day—a link with a diverse group of French Heideggerians such as Derrida, Jean-Luc Nancy, and others whose principal conceptual question during these years was that of the logic of property, propriety, and appropriation in all its conceptual, psychological, and economic registers. Agamben's dialectic of subject and object, propriety and appropriation, possession and inviolability, pleasure and knowledge is best seen in such a light. Criticism's goal, following Agamben, is not to seize its object, not to secret it away in sacred confines, but instead to ensure the work's durable freedom. For Agamben, the much-desired bridging of the division between poetry and philosophy can be effected only if a fundamentally different conception of the goals of these disciplines is reached.

The End of the Quest

Between the title page and the preface of *Stanzas* is an image that the English translation neglects to include. Its caption is "*L'amore* (da Ori Appollinis Niliaci *De sacris Aegyptiorum notis.* Parisiis 1574)." Although the many other illustrations in the work are reproduced, this one is not—a fact all the more surprising in that Agamben refers to the image at several points in his text (see S xvii [XIII], xix [XVI], and 131 [152]). This introductory figure of love suggests much that is to come in the pages that follow, from the openings and closings of lyric poetry in the book's middle section to the Borromean knots of semiological analysis with which it ends.

At one point in *Stanzas,* glossing the poetics of the thirteenth-century lyric and its relation to contemporary psychological conceptions of phantasm, Agamben writes, "The phantasm generates desire, desire is translated into words, and the word [*la parola*] defines a space wherein the appropriation of what could otherwise not be appropriated or enjoyed is possible" (S, 129 [153]). In the love poetry that Agamben explicates for his readers, he sees how "desire, supported by a conception that constitutes the sole coherent attempt by Western thought to overcome the fracture of metaphysical presence, celebrates, perhaps for the last time in the history of Western poetry, its joyous and inexhaustible 'spiritual union' with its own object of love" (S, 130 [154–55], translation modified). The phrase "fracture of metaphysical presence" might for many readers call to mind Derrida's celebrated formulae and their following of a fault line between speech and writing. The fracture to which Agamben refers, however, runs along different lines—the same ones with which he began his book. He is referring to that which separates poetry from philosophy and criticism from creation, thanks to which "poetry possesses its object without knowing it while philosophy knows its object without possessing it" (S, xvii [XIII]). Here, through the figure of a phantasmatic and more than phantasmatic love, this fracture is overcome and an object is at once "known" and "possessed."

In an article composed during these same years, Agamben writes, "Only because truth and beauty are originally divided, only because thought can never fully and integrally possess its object, can there be love of knowledge—that is, philosophy" (G, 1020). Agamben reminds his reader that if truth and beauty, knowledge and enjoyment, were never separated, there could be no love of one for the other. In an early essay, he referred to philosophy and philology as "the two inseparable faces of the metaphysical project" (PS, 161). In the work that directly follows *Stanzas,* he calls for the placing of "critical philological disciplines on precisely the same level as poetry. Poetry and philology: poetry as philology and philology as poetry" (IH, 147 [148], translation modified). What Agamben is envisioning is not, of course, merely a matter of commissioning works of philology from poets or convincing philologists to try their hand at poetry, but instead, as Agamben says, "occupy[ing] a site in which the fracturing of the word which divides poetry from philosophy in Western culture becomes a conscious and problematic experience" (IH, 147 [148], translation modified). Such an experience is not the healing of this fracture or the end of criticism's quest; it is instead its beginning. Attempts to chart this terra incognita of the space common to word and image, the space of poetic phantasm and philosophical thought, are attempts to map a common space, a space that Agamben calls "third" in one of the essays because it does not simply correspond to subject or object, does not simply align itself with potentiality or actuality, and is thereby the truly common space of poetry and philosophy.

Stanzas is a work divided in a way in which its predecessor was not. Although its separate parts indeed relate to one another in the matters and manners discussed earlier, these are shifting relations and they make the unity of the project difficult to grasp elsewhere than in its preface. It should be noted as well that the book's underlying ambition—the founding of a "discipline of interdisciplinarity" or a "general science of the human"—is one that Agamben soon judged unrealizable and abandoned in his later works (though he has continued to reflect on the causes of this abandonment; see SR, 109–11; and SL, 4). In the Anglophone world, *Stanzas* has become one of Agamben's best-known works, but it is difficult to make a case for it as one of his finest. It has many remarkable insights and much originality, but the charge leveled at Agamben's work that its aims are vaguely stated applies to this book with more justice than either the one that preceded it or the ones immediately to follow—and only *Remnants of Auschwitz* will prove equally open to that criticism.

Scholium: On Erudition

One of the most common descriptions of Agamben's work, found in virtually every review and essay, is that it is "erudite." Even Agamben's harshest critics tend to begin by noting this erudition (before charging him with its misuse). There need be nothing surprising in this estimation. By virtually any standard, Agamben displays a depth and breadth of learning for which *erudition* is doubtless the best term.[27] But to describe Agamben as erudite is nevertheless a step away from understanding his relation to the material on which he draws.

In "Erudition et fétichisme," Eric Méchoulan asks, "What could Cassianus's *De institutis coenobiorum*, Beau Brummel's tie, Plato's *Cratylus*, Dürer's *Melencolia*, Baudelaire's 'Les Bijoux,' Grandville's *Les Petites Misères de la vie humaine*, Jean Renart's *Le Lai de l'ombre*, Alexander of Aphrodisias's *De sensu communi*, Cavalcanti's *Rimatori del dolce stil nuovo*, Arnaud de Villeneuve's *Praxis medicinalis*, and Saussure's *Cours de linguistique générale* have in common?" (Méchoulan 2006, 55). His answer is, "They share the same place: Giorgio Agamben's *Stanzas*. And it is erudition that brings them together" (55). Méchoulan goes on to specify that "these references do not remain outside of [Agamben's] investigation like neutral elements awaiting commentary," but instead are driving forces therein (55). Agamben's erudite references are so far from playing a merely supporting role for an overarching argument that Méchoulan sees "an almost surrealist poetry in the surprising juxtaposition of references in *Stanzas*" (56).

There is indeed something surprising, and even disorienting, about Agamben's range of reference—and not only in *Stanzas*. In *Infancy and History* we find a reflection on historiography alongside one on toys; in *Idea of Prose* an investigation into first philosophy is followed by one into pornography. *The Coming Community* links angelology with dialectical materialism and *The Open* moves from Rilke's poetry to the life cycles of tics. Part of the incendiary force of the *Homo Sacer* project can be found in Agamben's comparing figures from ancient Roman law with concentration camp prisoners, as well as his bringing together of figures normally kept far apart, such as underground anarchist Guy Debord and Nazi jurist Carl Schmitt. Earlier we saw Agamben stress the limitations of direct thematic treatment of certain questions as well as his desire to form a discipline of interdisciplinarity. The question of Agamben's erudition is thus also the question of his relation to the past and in this respect touches directly on the central question he raises in *Stanzas*—that of a truly creative criticism.

A Critique of the Dialectic: *Infancy and History: The Destruction of Experience*

Infancy and History is a puzzling as well as programmatic title. It can be best understood when we observe the manner in which the titular concerns of Agamben's third book are raised. *Infancy* and *history* correspond, for Agamben, to transcendental categories of human experience: *language* and *time*. Although as a conceptual pair *infancy* and *history* point to *language* and *time,* the question of their relationship to one another is nevertheless left open. In an essay from the same period as *Infancy and History* Agamben observes of a difficult passage in Benjamin's thought that "the comparison suggested in this passage between language and history, linguistic categories and historical categories, may seem surprising at first glance" (P, 48 [37]). The surprise he asks his readers to overcome with respect to the categories of Benjamin's thought is the same one his own readers must overcome in understanding such works as *Infancy and History.* What is most surprising about this book is the links it makes between linguistic categories and historical ones. Agamben's following of the two lines of inquiry named in his title will lead him to a point of luminous intersection that, in the years and books to follow, he will call *potentiality.*

To reach this luminous intersection where Agamben finds his key term and guiding idea, we must first follow the path he takes to get there. The subtitle of *Infancy and History* indicates an important step in that direction: *The Destruction of Experience.* After analyses of what he called in his first book a *destruction of aesthetics* and a *destruction of tradition*, another call for destruction might come as no surprise. But what is being destroyed here is vaster than the discipline of aesthetics or even the idea of tradition; it is *experience* itself. Whereas in Agamben's first two books the destructions at issue were ones for which he himself was calling, this destruction is one that he is trying to halt. Yet the reader might ask whether his concern is justified, whether the idea of a "destruction of experience" is to be taken seriously. For all the ravages that might be visited upon an individual or a culture, *experience*, it would seem, is precisely what cannot be destroyed. An experience can be vacuous or horrific; it can be traumatic, inauthentic, or forgotten; but does it not remain experience? Is it not the one thing that cannot be destroyed without extinguishing consciousness itself? Although it runs contrary to received opinion, Agamben's "destruction of experience" is not paradoxical in the sense of being incoherent. He chooses his extreme formulation to designate what he sees as a fundamental problem—a catastrophe confronting modern society.

Adorno's most elegant book begins with a blunt epigraph: *Das Leben lebt nicht* ("Life doesn't live"). It is meant to introduce his reader to the extreme stance he will adopt concerning the desperate situation about which he found himself writing. Life continues, but it has become so endangered, so corrupted and debased, by modern developments that for Adorno it scarcely seems deserving of the name. Agamben's vehement "destruction of experience" can be seen in a similar light. It as little means the extinguishing of consciousness as Adorno's epigraph refers to the end of human existence. It does indicate, however, a truly desperate state of affairs that must not, at any cost, be neglected.

Isolating the urgency that motivates Agamben's extreme formulation, however, is not the same thing as understanding it. The *experience* in question is direct, personal experience—that on which our culture places increasingly less emphasis. In this respect, the problem that Agamben is addressing could be seen as sociological, as a problem concerning social forms of knowledge and transmission like those anarchically attacked by Guy Debord and systematically studied by Pierre Bourdieu. This is indeed a phenomenon we see all around us, one that is easy enough to confirm and that has, if anything, become more pronounced in the three decades since *Infancy and History* was published. Our globalized world and networked age indeed often seem to find little place and still less time for firsthand experience, and clarity about what sort of knowledge corresponds to our continually growing wealth of information often seems in even shorter supply. It is to this radical devaluation of firsthand experience—the first-hand experience that formed the core of the social and intellectual lives of earlier ages—that Agamben directs his readers' attention, and it is this that leads him to a diagnosis as extreme as "the death of experience."

Experience: From Poverty to Destruction

The longest of the six chapters that make up the book, "Infancy and History: An Essay on the Destruction of Experience," begins with an announcement: "Every discussion of experience today should begin with the acknowledgement that it is no longer accessible" (IH, 13 [5], translation modified).[1] In militant tones, Agamben claims that modern man has been "expropriated [*espropriato*] of his experience" (13 [5]). That this expropriation will prove more than a passing concern is attested to by what Agamben has called in a recent work "the museification of the world [*la museificazione del mondo*]" (PR, 96). Expanding on the meaning of this formula, Agamben goes on to state that "everything today can become Museum [*Museo*], because this term simply names the exposition of an impossibility to use, to inhabit, and *to experience*" (PR, 96, italics added). This hard fact forms, following Agamben, "one of the few certainties regarding himself" that modern man possesses (IH, 13 [5]). The immediate source of this harsh claim seems to be Agamben's observations of modern life, but it is a claim not without precedent.

Early on in this chapter, Agamben cites at length a passage wherein Benjamin "as early as 1933 . . . diagnosed with precision the poverty of experience" that characterizes our culture (IH, 13 [5]). The analysis in question is from Benjamin's essay "Experience and Poverty."[2] There Benjamin speaks of the immediate aftermath of World War I:

Men returned from the front in silence . . . not richer but poorer in communicable experience [*an mitteilbarer Erfahrung*]. . . . And what poured out from the flood of war books ten years later was anything but the experience [*Erfahrung*] that is communicated orally. . . . For never had experience [*Erfahrung*] been contradicted more thoroughly: strategic experience contravened by positional warfare; economic experience by inflation; physical experience by hunger; moral experience by the ruling powers. A generation that had gone to school in horse-drawn streetcars now stood in the open amid a landscape in which nothing was the same except the clouds with, at its center, the thin, fragile human body caught in a force field of destructive torrents and explosions. [Benjamin SW 2.731–2.732 (GS 2.214), translation modified]

This diagnosis is one that Agamben will dramatically develop. Whereas Benjamin observed an impoverishment of experience in the wake of a cataclysmic war that changed every facet of Western culture, Agamben observes it in the most simple and banal of everyday activities.[3] "Today," he writes, "we know that the destruction of experience no longer necessitates a catastrophe, and that humdrum daily life in any city will suffice. For modern man's average day contains virtually nothing that can still be translated into experience" (IH, 13 [5]). Not only does Agamben generalize the time and place of this crisis in communicable experience, but he also takes Benjamin's diagnosis of a "*poverty* of experience" and radicalizes it as a "*destruction* of experience." What in Benjamin's analysis from 1933 was a scarcity and fragility becomes, nearly a half-century later, something more invasive, aggressive, and thorough.

Events and Experience

Tracing the genealogy of Agamben's choice of term still leaves us with the question of what he means by it? "Experience," Agamben claims, is to be found

not in reading the newspaper, with its abundance of unreachably remote bits of information, nor sitting in a traffic jam; not during the journey through the nether realms of the subway, nor in the demonstration that suddenly blocks the street; not in the cloud of tear gas slowly dispersing amid the buildings downtown, nor even in the rapid blasts of gunfire from who knows where; not in waiting at a business counter, nor in visiting the fantasyland of the supermarket, nor in those moments of silent proximity among strangers in elevators and buses. [IH, 13–14 (5–6), translation modified]

For Agamben it does not suffice to be active, to move about, to have encounters, to lose and acquire things, or even to witness more dramatic acts such as political resistance and violence in order to have *experience*. Wherever we turn, he claims, experience eludes us. "Modern man," Agamben writes, "makes his way home each evening wearied by a jumble of events, but however entertaining or tedious, unusual or commonplace, harrowing or pleasurable they are, none of them will have become experience" (IH,

14 [6]). How is it, we might ask, that we have *events* that fill our lives but no *experience* of them?

The Italian word that Agamben employs, *esperienze*, is a cognate to the English word *experience*. It derives from the same Latin root, *experientia,* meaning a traversing of a place or space, and thereby designating the results of such a passage. It covers roughly the same family of meanings as, and offers no problems of translation into, English. Nevertheless, it does present a problem of translation. As Agamben makes clear, the term he employs is borrowed from Benjamin, and it is here that the problem arises. Writing in German, Benjamin disposed of not one but two terms to designate what both Italian and English denote with a single word: *Erlebnis* and *Erfahrung. Erlebnis* is an *experience* in the sense of 'to have an experience,' something literally 'lived through,' reflected in the word's etymology (its root is *leben,* "to live"). In *As You Like It,* Jacques says, "I have gained my experience," and Rosalind replies, "And your experience has made you sad" (IV.i.ii–12). The experience that makes him sad, just like the experience that can make one wise or wicked, is expressed in German with an etymologically unrelated word—and it is this word that Benjamin systematically employs in "Poverty and Experience," "The Storyteller," and his other writings that treat this theme. To denote "living through" something, the word that Benjamin employs is *Erfahrung* (an excellent etymological match for *experience* in that it means literally "that which is traversed"). When Benjamin speaks of a "change in experience" or a "poverty of experience," he employs the term *Erfahrung* because it is *Erfahrung* that changes you, *Erfahrung* that affects you in a durable fashion, that you learn from and lean on, and that is handed down to you by tradition. (A clear illustration of this is found in the fact that in German one can know something not by *Erlebnis* but only by *Erfahrung*). With Benjamin's diction in mind, we can see in what sense Agamben speaks of a state of affairs rich in "significant *events*" (equivalent to Benjamin's *Erlebnisse*) yet devoid of "experience" (equivalent to his *Erfahrung*). Many things are indeed experienced in modern times—more than in earlier times, in fact—but these *events* do not coalesce into *experience* in the traditional sense of the term. To the richness of events corresponds a poverty of experience.

Of "today's man" Agamben then tells us, "His incapacity to have and communicate experiences is one of the few facts about himself of which he can be certain" (IH, 13 [5], translation modified). What is more, in our day "the destruction of experience" that Benjamin saw as a result of the ravages of World War I "no longer necessitates a catastrophe": "The peaceful everyday existence in a major city is, for this end, perfectly sufficient" (IH, 13 [5], translation modified). Agamben notes that experience is transmitted not by "the extraordinary" but by the "everyday," and that the ability to share and communicate everyday experience has been lost (IH, 13 [6]). We have, therefore, "events"—staggering quantities of them—but they are assimilated into no real "experience."

Barbarism

In a passage from "Experience and Poverty" that Agamben does not cite, Benjamin writes, "Poverty of experience [*Erfahrungsarmut*]: this should not be understood to mean that people are yearning for new experience. No, they long to free themselves from experience [*Erfahrung*]" (Benjamin SW, 2.734; GS, 2.218, translation modified). Benjamin claims that something has gone so terribly wrong in our culture that *experience*— a firsthand experience that seemed self-evident and inalterable to earlier generations—is threatened in an age that is traumatized by violence on an unprecedented scale and that is more and more reliant on new technologies and media. "Experience," Agamben writes, "has its necessary correlation not in knowledge, but in authority—that is to say, in the word and in the story" (IH, 14 [6], translation modified). As for Benjamin, the form of knowledge in question is one handed down in person: "the experience [*Erfahrung*] that is communicated orally" (Benjamin SW, 2.731–2.732 [GS 2.214]). One of Benjamin's cardinal concerns was the tracing of this loss of tradition to the stories a culture tells about itself, and how that culture transmits those stories from generation to generation. A great reader, and translator, of novels, Benjamin saw a sign of the loss of tradition and a decline in the art of oral storytelling in, precisely, the rise of the novel. "What distinguishes the novel from all other forms of prose—fairy tales, sagas, proverbs, drollery, jokes," Benjamin wrote, is that "its foundation . . . neither comes from nor flows into oral tradition" (Benjamin GS, 2.1286). The loss of an oral tradition is the loss of unmediated communication and sows the seeds for a weakening of this tradition. Earlier modes of traditional communication on which Benjamin focuses, such as the telling of stories, have been replaced in an age ever more dependent on a passive and distanced intake of information. Updating Benjamin's analysis, Agamben notes how "slogans" have replaced maxims and proverbs, how people have lost a sense for direct experience and chosen even in the presence of the most astounding monuments (such as the Alhambra) to document (photograph) them frantically in lieu of taking them in for themselves (see IH, 14 [7]). Indeed, any visit to one of the world's great museums will corroborate Agamben's claim. But the question as to what, if anything, might be done remains open.

In response to such a diagnosis, a first question is what should we do? For his part, Benjamin did not lose himself in pessimistic predictions or liberal doses of self-pity, and he does not encourage his readers to turn their backs on a corrupted civilization and seek solace in primitive cultures or the bosom of nature. In response to the dissolution of traditional experience he asks a simple question: If this living continuity with the past and its traditions has been lost, what is to be done now? What possibilities for *new* experience are open? "For what is the value of all our culture," Benjamin asks, "if it is divorced from experience [*Erfahrung*]?" (Benjamin SW, 2.732; GS, 2.215).[4] Benjamin's response to the situation is "barbarism." This is not the barbarism of anarchic violence or the destruction of tradition's treasures, and it has nothing of the Italian Futurists' call for the destruction of Europe's great museums (to make way for the radically new). Nor is it the barbarism that Benjamin will evoke years later in his *Theses on the Philosophy of History,* in the famous pronouncement that "there is no document of culture that is not also a document of barbarism" (Benjamin GS, 1.696). And it is also not the barbarism of a pure state of nature, of noble savages and primitive cultures not yet corrupted by telegraph, telephone, television, and the like. The barbarism evoked here is freedom from the weight of the past, the freedom from convention that is the rough province of the barbarian and that Agamben had evoked at the close of his first book in connection with Kafka's revaluation of tradition.

The loss of experience noted by Agamben in his third book is an extension of the loss of tradition examined in his first book. As in that earlier work, in *Infancy and History* his goal is not simply to underscore the darkness of our times. "The point is not to deplore this state of affairs," writes Agamben, "but to take note of it" (IH, 15 [7]). Paradoxically enough, the widespread refusal to experience things firsthand that Agamben diagnoses also harbors, for him, hope. "For perhaps at the heart of this seemingly senseless denial there lurks a grain of wisdom," writes Agamben, "in which we can glimpse the germinating seed of future experience" (IH, 15 [7]). In the midst of this dire state of affairs he again sees a radical possibility. His work then becomes "to prepare the ground in which this seed can mature" (IH, 15 [7]).

The Genealogy of Experience

At the start of *Infancy and History* Agamben speaks with a militant voice, but as early as the second part of its initial essay, he changes his tone and turns his attention to the history of ideas. "In a certain sense, the expropriation of experience [*l'espropriazione dell'esperienza*]," Agamben writes, "was implicit in the founding project of modern science" (IH, 17 [10], translation modified). Building on conceptions from one of the fathers of modern empirical science, Francis Bacon, Agamben states that "despite repeated claims to the contrary, modern science has its origins in an unprecedented mistrust of experience" (IH, 17 [11]). Agamben notes that in Bacon's terms "mere experience" was most often seen by early modern thinkers as a "dark wood" and a "labyrinth" (IH, 17 [11]). From Bacon to Galileo, the first steps toward modern science brought with them a denigration of "mere" experience and a mistrust of the senses. Agamben sees this nowhere so clearly crystallized as in the figure of Descartes and in the latter's radical doubt as to the veracity of the experience transmitted to the senses (in the form of his hypothesis of a *malin génie* set on deceiving us precisely through sensory experience).

The fruit of these first steps toward modern scientific thought and the corresponding casting into doubt of sense experience leads, in Agamben's genealogy, to a different history of the *subject* of experience. In medieval philosophy, the problem of thought was the relation of the *one*—conceived as a *general intellect* or *agent intellect* separate from individual sense experience—to the *many*—conceived as all those individual intellects who participate through thought in the larger intellect. With Descartes, the dialectic of the *one* and the *many* that was central to medieval philosophy was replaced by a dialectic of *subject* and *object*, and with it came a new status for *experience*.

One of the consequences of this change was that individual experience became what it had not been before—a fundamental epistemological problem—because it was first in the Cartesian framework that individual experience played a decisive role in the formation of the greatest certainties and the attainment of the highest knowledge. In the earlier conception—derived from Aristotle and codified by such figures as Aquinas and Avicenna—human knowledge and divine knowledge were separated by a gulf that was not to be bridged. Expressed differently, *knowledge* and *experience* pertained to two different and distinct realms. *Knowledge* was the realm of divine being, which one accessed not as an individual through individual *experience,* but instead by participating through thought and faith in a higher realm. "The great revolution in modern science," claims Agamben, "was less a matter of opposing experience to authority (the *argumentum ex re* against the *argumentum ex verbo,* which are not in fact irreconcilable) than of referring knowledge and experience to a single subject, which is none other than their conjunction at an abstract Archimedean point: the Cartesian *ego cogito*" (IH, 19 [13], translation modified).

The next cardinal point in the development of a modern conception of subjectivity and subjective experience is, for Agamben, one inaugurated by Kant. In Agamben's view, "the *Critique of Pure Reason* is the last place in Western metaphysics where the question of experience is accessible in its pure form—that is, without its contradictions being hidden. The original sin with which post-Kantian thought begins is the reunification of the transcendental subject and empirical consciousness in a single absolute subject" (IH, 32 [28], translation modified). The epistemological contradictions of the individual subject and of sensory experience that Descartes introduced into Western metaphysical speculation and that the brilliance of Kant brought into the starkest relief began with Hegel and his "absolute subject" to recede into the shadows. Hegel's masterful dialectic, with its "negation of experience" and "negation of the moment" in favor of a continually postponed future horizon of "absolute knowledge" and "absolute subjectivity," is for Agamben the beginning of the end of experience.

Agamben reminds his reader that Hegel's original title for *Phenomenology of Spirit* was *The Science of the Experience of Consciousness.* Of the Hegelian conception of subject and experience Agamben notes, "The fact that consciousness has a dialectical structure means that it can never grasp itself as an entirety, but is whole only in the total process of its becoming." He also notes that in Hegel's conception, "experience is . . . something which one can only undergo but never have" (IH, 34 [29]). This observation leads Agamben ever closer to a topic that will intensely interest him in the coming years and in his next book: the heritage of Hegel's dialectic and its recourse to "negativity." (The goal of Agamben's next book, *Language and Death,* will be to chart "the place and structure of negativity," as well as to understand its "original structure"; see also LD, xii [4], translation modified; and LD, xii [5]).[5] Hegel's dialectic brings with it, following Agamben, a "conception of the unappropriable [*inappropriabile*] and negative character of experience," as, in Agamben's paraphrase, Hegel's idea of the "Absolute" becomes "only at the end what it truly is" (IH, 34 [30], translation modified; see also LD, 100 [125]). Agamben then remarks, "The supremacy of the dialectic in our time, far beyond the limits of the Hegelian system, beginning with Engels' attempt to construct a dialectic of nature, has its roots in this conception of the negative and unattainable character of experience—that is, in an expropriation of experience" (IH, 34 [30]). The "expropriation" and consequent "destruction" of experience that Agamben referred to at the beginning of the book as a cultural phenomenon characteristic of our mediatized age is here historically traced back to the conceptual paradigm that gave rise to it. It is for this reason that Agamben later stresses the "urgent necessity" of "a critique of the dialectic" (IH, 34 [30]). Before we turn to this critique of the dialectic and to the critique of concepts of history and time that it will imply, we need first to address the other term in Agamben's title: *infancy.*

The Introduction of Infancy

In his survey of post-Hegelian attempts to conceive of the Cartesian subject and of a transcendental experience of subjectivity, Agamben turns his attention next to Dilthey and Bergson. He sees Husserl's *Lectures on Internal Time Consciousness* as broadening their approaches and building on their findings and, in doing so, representing a step forward in the analysis of the relation of experience to knowledge. According to Husserl, "we have no names" for our most fundamental experience: our experience of time (IH, 37 [33]). This observation leads Agamben to introduce a term that will prove decisive for him not only in this work but in many works to come: *infancy.* Agamben is led to this term via *experience.* "Does a mute experience exist?" he asks. "Does an *in-fancy* of experience exist?" (IH, 37 [33], italics in original, translation modified). As Agamben's hyphenation (in-fancy) stresses, the *infancy* in question is to be taken literally as the state of being without language (the Latin term *infantia* designates an inability to speak). Agamben's historical excursus thus serves to frame a question about experience and its impoverishment or destruction as a question about language.

"It is Kant's basing the problem of knowledge on a mathematical model that prevented him, as it did Husserl, from discerning the original place of transcendental subjectivity within language," claims Agamben, "and therefore from clearly tracing the boundaries separating the transcendental and the linguistic" (IH, 44 [41], translation modified). Basing his reflections on the linguistic analyses of Benveniste and, most centrally, on the latter's studies of pronouns, Agamben concludes that "subjectivity is nothing other than the speaker's capacity to posit him- or herself as an *ego,* and cannot in any way be defined through some wordless sense of being oneself, nor by deferral to some ineffable psychic experience of the *ego,* but only through a linguistic I transcending any possible experience" (IH, 45 [43]).[6]

Infancy is a term that, for Agamben, is intimately linked to *potentiality.* Unlike the potentiality of Aristotle's sleeping geometer, a child's countless possibilities or potentialities are yet to be developed and may or may not be realized. Agamben is interested in the potentiality of language, and the term *infancy* allows him to pose a question about potentiality independent of actualization. Agamben's systematic use of the term *infancy* began as early as part one of *Stanzas* (first published in abbreviated form in 1974). In a dense passage he says of the tools strewn at the feet of Dürer's representation of Melancholy that, "as the relics of a past on which is written the Edenic cipher [*la cifra edenica*] of infancy, these objects have captured forever a gleam of that which can be possessed only with the provision that it be lost forever" (S, 26 [35]). The relation of this idea to that of an "overcoming" of Western metaphysics, found in the philosophical projects of Marx, Nietzsche, Heidegger, and Derrida, is, for Agamben, linked to this idea of infancy. Writing in 1979 of *Infancy and History,* Agamben claims that "only if man is not the animal with logos, the animal that knows to speak [*che sa parlare*], but the infant animal . . . is it possible to enter into a region in which, perhaps for the first time, an overcoming of metaphysics becomes possible" (PS, 164–165). In an essay from 1980, Agamben relates his idea of infancy to the "originary infancy [*infanzia originaria*]" that he finds in what Hölderlin called *ursprüngliche Kindheit* (PP, 86). Discussions of *infancy* are found in both Agamben's fourth book, *Language and Death* (in the idea of man's "in-fantile dwelling . . . in language," LD, 92 [115]) and his fifth one, *The Idea of Prose* (which bears a chapter entitled "The Idea of Infancy"). Although Agamben gradually abandons the term *infancy* in favor of the more all-encompassing term *potentiality*, he remains interested in it and, in an effort to circumscribe a new conception of subjectivity written twenty years after *Infancy and History*, remarks, "Let us consider the individual living being, the 'infant' in the etymological sense, a being who cannot speak. What happens in him—and for him—in the moment he says 'I' and begins to speak?" (RA, 121 [112–13]). Later on in that work he states that "subjectivity and consciousness, in which our culture believed itself to have found its firmest foundation, rest on what is most precarious and fragile in the world: the event of speech" (RA, 122 [113]).

The term *infancy*, as Agamben understands and employs it, is thus meant both more and less literally than is usually understood. It denotes language's absence and thus, by extension, the period in human development before an individual has learned to speak. Agamben's separation of the word's two elements—*in-fancy*—serves to stress that what interests him is the privative element. In a preface written for the French translation of *Infancy and History*, he writes, "the in-fancy [*in-fanzia*] which is in question in this work is not a simple fact whose chronological place might be isolated, nor is it something like an age or a psychosomatic state" (IH, 4 [viii], translation modified).[7] If that which will be in question in his work "is not a simple fact whose chronological place might be isolated, nor is it something like an age or a psychosomatic state," what, the reader might ask, is there left for it to be?

Infancy, for Agamben, is an integral part of ourselves and the core of our experience. "Contrary to that which an antique tradition affirms," he writes, "man is not . . . 'the animal which has language' but instead the animal deprived of language and therefore obliged to receive it from elsewhere" (IH, 57 [60], translation modified). By this Agamben means that we are not born with the language or languages that will become our own and in which we will express our experiences; we must first learn language from outside. "Animals are not in fact denied language," Agamben writes. "On the contrary, they are always and absolutely language. In them *la voix sacrée de la terre ingénue* [the sacred voice of the unknowing earth]— which Mallarmé, hearing the chirp of a cricket, sets against the human voice as *une* and *non-décomposée* [one and indivisible]—knows no breaks or interruptions" (IH, 52 [50], translation modified). Animals are "always and absolutely language," in Agamben's formulation, because there is no distance or distinction between signifier and signified, no unmotivated relation between the semiotic (the level of the sign) and the semantic (the level of meaning) in their communications. Animals thus communicate *immediately*—that is, without the mediation of a sign system, and for this reason they are always and absolutely one with their language. Human speech, on the other hand, is acquired and, once it is, mediates our communication. We indeed achieve an inestimable gain in sophistication of communication, but at the price of immediacy.[8] As a result, we are aware of a disjunction that we can never directly formulate; the mediating effect of our language is not something we can every fully grasp. As Agamben remarked elsewhere, "To adopt an image from Wittgenstein, man exists in language like a fly trapped in a bottle: that which it cannot see is precisely that through which it sees the world" (UIGA, 33).

Because we are born infants—that is to say, incapable of articulate speech—we must learn language. We may be the speaking animal but we are also animals unlike any other in that we are born incapable of speech—or more precisely, *capable* of speech but not yet possessing it. This is something that might be expressed not just in terms of *privation* but also in terms of *potentiality*. The initial inarticulateness of the infant is also the sign of its capacity to say any manner of thing and speak any and all languages. It should come as little surprise that Agamben's student, translator, and editor Daniel Heller-Roazen, author of the finest analysis of Agamben's philosophical project, chooses as the starting point in his *Echolalias: On the Forgetting of Language* (2005) the fact that, "as everyone knows, children at first do not speak" (9). Following Roman Jakobson, Heller-Roazen goes on to note one of the consequences of this fact: that "no limits can be set on the phonic powers of the prattling child" (9). Actualizing linguistic capacity means leaving behind some of this undifferentiated potentiality, and for this reason Heller-Roazen writes, in an intuition kindred to Agamben's in *Infancy and History,* that "it is as if the acquisition of language were possible only through an act of oblivion, a kind of linguistic infantile amnesia. . . . Perhaps the loss of a limitless phonetic arsenal is the price a child must pay for the papers that grant him citizenship in the community of a single tongue" (11). It is for this reason that Agamben, like Heller-Roazen, sees in *infancy* the sign of the human and the center of our experience.

With this initial understanding of the idea of infancy in mind, we can see how, in this first part of *Infancy and History,* Agamben's interest has moved from a sociological critique (and denunciation) of contemporary experience and the place it holds in modern industrial societies to an ancient philosophical question concerning what defines the human. For Agamben, the essence of human experience is to be found in what he calls *infancy* and in leaving that infancy behind as an individual learns language. That which we are least able to express as we move beyond infancy is the nature of our experience of *time*—for which, as Husserl noted, "we have no names," and it is to this idea that Agamben then turns.

Time and History

As we saw earlier, Agamben announced the "urgent necessity" of "a critique of the dialectic," but we have not yet noted the reason he gives. His starting point is a simple observation: although Marx conceived of a revolutionary model of *history,* it was not accompanied by a correspondingly revolutionary model of *time.* The "traditional" conception of time employed by Marx was ill-suited to his revolutionary task "and thus diluted the Marxist concept of history"—becoming, in Agamben's words, "the hidden breach through which ideology snuck into the citadel of historical materialism" (IH, 91 [95], translation modified). "Even historical materialism," writes Agamben, employing the term that Benjamin gave to his approach (as opposed to the dialectical materialism of Adorno and the Frankfurt School), has "neglected to elaborate a concept of time worthy of its concept of history" (IH, 91 [95], translation modified). Agamben's critique of the dialectic will thus attempt to offer precisely such a revolutionary conception of time, and to give the Marxist conception of history the essential element it has lacked.

In *Infancy and History* Agamben offers a brief and lucid review of Western culture's dominant conceptions of time. "Every conception of history," Agamben observes, "is invariably accompanied by a certain experience of time that is implicit in it, conditions it, and thereby has to be elucidated" (IH, 91 [95]). Agamben even goes a step farther, claiming not only that every conception of history has a model of time proper to it but also that "every culture is first and foremost a particular experience of time, and no new culture is possible without an alteration in this experience." It is here, then, that historical analysis and revolutionary activity meet. What is at issue is nothing less than a "new culture" and the "revolutionary" politics that might bring it about. "The original task of a genuine revolution," Agamben claims, "is never merely to 'change the world,' but also to 'change time.'" Because "modern political thought has concentrated its attention on history and has not elaborated a corresponding concept of time," it is this crucial gap that Agamben will seek to fill (IH, 91 [95]).

Agamben's approach to the question of time is, naturally enough, through the idea of the *instant* and its relation to a *continuum*. Whatever the differences in various periods' and cultures' conceptions of time and its passage, the West has consistently considered time as a *continuum* made up of successively experienced *instants*. It is not rare to find critiques of what we do with the instants that form the continuum of our lives, but critiques of our actual conceptions of instant and continuum are relatively rare. Is not the reason for this fact that the time we experience as a continuum composed of instants is one of the most self-evident and unassailable aspects of our experience? To what might we oppose a dialectical conception of time in which each instant is succeeded by another and that together form a continuum of continuity and change? As we saw, Agamben defines culture as "first and foremost a particular experience of time." Although no one would dispute that conceptions of time vary from culture to culture and that our conception of time is so fundamental that it touches on every aspect of our experience, we might still wonder what radically new conception might be advanced that could strengthen Marxist reflection and achieve a new level of coherence and effectiveness. In short, is it possible to find and formulate a truly *revolutionary* conception of time? It is this question that *Infancy and History*, as well as a number of works to come, aspires to answer.

The Time of History

As does an earlier section of the book—the one that treated the question of *experience*—the section of *Infancy and History* that is dedicated to a new conception of time begins with a polemical and programmatic first section followed by a historical second section that is more sober in tone and philological in approach. Agamben begins with a characterization of the Greek conception of time as fundamentally cyclical, pointing to Pla-

to's famous assertion (in *Timaeus*) that "the creator of the world constructed a moving image of eternity," and Aristotle's development of this conception. "Western man's inability to master [*padroneggiare*] time, and his
consequent obsession with 'gaining' it and 'passing' it," writes Agamben,
"have their origins in this Greek concept of time as a quantified and infinite continuum of precise fleeting instants" (IH, 93 [98], translation modified). The seed for the dialectical continuum that snuck into the citadel of
historical materialism was thus, in Agamben's view, no recent intrusion; it
was sown at the very outset of Western philosophy. Agamben's tracing of
a seemingly modern phenomenon to its classical roots in ancient Greece
and Rome, first seen in *The Man Without Content,* is a characteristic gesture that recurs in many of his works—such as, to chose the most famous
example, in his analyses of biopolitics in *Homo Sacer.*

Agamben's historical survey proceeds from the Greek to the Christian
experience of time. To the classical circular or cyclical representation of
time Christian experience opposed a linear model with a trajectory moving "irreversibly from Creation to end" and with its "central point of reference in the incarnation of Christ" (IH, 94 [99]). The next turn is slow in
coming and is a secular one. Agamben traces "the modern conception of
time" to a "secularization of rectilinear, irreversible Christian time" (IH,
96 [100], translation modified). The secularization in question takes the
form of removing the goal and end of that temporal continuum, with
the result that we have acquired a notion of time "emptied of any other
meaning but that of a process structured in terms of before and after,"
which Agamben sees as "derived from the experience of manufacturing
work" and "sanctioned by modern mechanics" (IH, 96 [100], translation
modified).

Hegel famously said of an instant of time that it "is nothing other
than the passage of its being into nothingness" (quoted in IH, 97 [102]).
This "negation of a negation" is a fundamental aspect of the dialectic and
one of the central points on which Agamben seizes. "The dialectic," claims
Agamben, "is above all what makes possible the containment and unifica-
tion . . . of the continuum of negative fleeting instants" (IH, 98 [103]). In
such a conception, the instant ceases to be the site of either knowledge or
action and thereby leads to an important consequence. "Like time," writes
Agamben of this Hegelian conception, "whose essence is pure negation,
history can never be grasped in the instant, but only as a global process"
(IH, 99 [104], translation modified). With Marx, a fundamental change in

the conception of history was introduced, one in which *praxis*—concrete activity conceived in the concrete instance—is seen as decisive for how mankind conceives itself and defines human nature. However, as Agamben began by noting, "Marx did not elaborate a theory of time adequate to his idea of history"; and in Agamben's view, Marx's idea of history "cannot be reconciled with the Aristotelian and Hegelian conception of time as a continuous and infinite succession of precise instants" (IH, 99–100 [105], translation modified).

Agamben's historical survey from the Greeks to Marx shows that what remains constant in the varying conceptions of time—be they circular or linear—is the idea of the instant. "Any attempt to conceive of time differently must inevitably come into conflict with this concept," declares Agamben, "and a critique of the instant is the logical condition for a new experience of time" (IH, 100 [106]). Critiquing something so fundamental as our conception of time as a series of instants combining to form a continuum is no easy matter, and Agamben must use tools suited for such a critique. "The elements for a different conception of time," he claims, "lie scattered in the folds and shadows of the Western cultural tradition," but for precisely this reason they are not easy to recognize and assemble (IH, 100 [106], translation modified). Nevertheless, continues Agamben, "we need only to elucidate these so that they may emerge as the bearers of a message which is meant for us and which it is our task to verify" (IH, 100 [106]).

The Message Bearers

The first of these message bearers Agamben finds in Gnosticism and its conception of a time whose spatial representation, Agamben argues, would be a "broken line" (IH, 101 [106]). Because for the Gnostic the messianic instant is not awaited but has already occurred, "the time of Gnosticism . . . is an incoherent and nonhomogenous time whose truth is in the moment of abrupt interruption, when man suddenly realizes his own condition of being resurrected" (IH, 101 [106], translation modified).[9] A second element is found in the Stoics. In Agamben's view, "the Stoic posits the liberating experience of time as something neither objective nor removed from our control, but springing from the actions and decisions of man" (IH, 101 [107]).

The next two message bearers are more recent ones and already familiar to Agamben's readers:

It is certainly no accident that every time modern thought has come to reconceptualize time, it has inevitably had to begin with a critique of continuous, quantified time. Such a critique underlies both Benjamin's *Theses on the Philosophy of History* and Heidegger's incomplete analysis of temporality in *Being and Time*. This coincidence in two thinkers so far apart is a sign that the concept of time which has dominated Western culture for nearly two thousand years is on the wane. [IH, 102 (107–8)]

This conjuncture of interest is one that Agamben finds more than fortuitous. In his view, Heidegger's approach to the question of time opposes to a conception of continuous, quantified time an experience "at the center of which is no longer the precise, fleeting *instant* in linear time, but the *moment* of authentic decision in which *Dasein* experiences its own finiteness" (IH, 103 [109], translation modified). Heidegger was indeed intensely interested in such moments—and not only in *Being and Time*. In his lecture course for 1929–30, he announced that "the moment is nothing other than the *instant of decisiveness* in which the entire situation surrounding a mode of acting is opened" (Heidegger GA, 29–30.224, italics in original). In that same lecture course, in his long analysis of boredom, Heidegger writes, "The movement of time can only be broken through time itself, through that which is of time's essence and that we, following Kierkegaard, call the moment. The moment interrupts time's movement, and can do so because it is one of time's possibilities" (Heidegger GA, 29–30.226). Kierkegaard indeed often invoked such an "instant" or "moment" as the crux of his thought—the moment when God thunders into one's life and one is called to think and act anew—and it is in the wake of such a conception that Heidegger is reflecting. In another lecture course a few years later, Heidegger even spoke of a breaking or bursting of the continuum of time through a radical concentration on the fortuitous moment or instant (see Heidegger GA, 34.10).

Agamben's appealing to Benjamin for the purposes of developing a revolutionary politics is unlikely to surprise his readers, but the same is not true of his recourse to Heidegger. Benjamin's conceptions were openly, if at times cryptically, Marxist. Heidegger's most certainly were not—but neither were they opposed to it. As Agamben reminds his reader, Heidegger declared in his *Letter on Humanism,* to the surprise of many, that "the Marxist conception of history is superior to any other historiography" (IH, 103 [109]). Agamben pushes this proximity further in claiming that Heidegger's conception of "care [*Sorge*]" is "in no way opposed to the Marxist foundation of history in praxis" (IH, 103 [109]).

Yet it is not with this affect—care—that Agamben concludes, but with a different experience. "There exists for everyone," he writes, "an immediate and available experience on which a new concept of time could be founded" (IH, 104 [110], translation modified). This experience is *pleasure*. In the *Nicomachean Ethics*, Aristotle says of pleasure that it is "in each instant something whole and complete" (cited in IH, 104 [110], translation modified).[10] Agamben is quick to focus on the temporal conception that corresponds to such pleasure: "The dividing point through which [eternity and continuous linear time] relate is the instant as a discrete, elusive point. Against this conception, which dooms any attempt to master time, there must be opposed one whereby the true site of pleasure, as man's primary dimension, is neither precise, continuous time nor eternity, but history" (IH, 104 [110]). He continues:

For history is not, as the dominant ideology would have it, man's servitude to continuous linear time, but man's liberation from it: the time of history and the *kairos* in which man, by this initiative, grasps favorable opportunity and chooses his own freedom in the moment. Just as the full, discontinuous, finite, and complete time of pleasure must be set against the empty, continuous, and infinite time of vulgar historicism, so the chronological time of pseudo-history must be opposed by the kairological [*cairologico*] time of authentic history. . . . But a revolution from which there springs not a new chronology but a qualitative alteration of time (a *kairology* [cairologia]) would have the weightiest consequences and would alone be immune to absorption into the reflux of restoration. [IH, 105 (111), italics in original]

Progress and Revolution, or Empty, Homogenous Time

As we saw earlier, for Agamben, "every time modern thought has come to reconceptualize time, it has inevitably had to begin with a critique of continuous, quantified time," and "such a critique underlies" not only Heidegger's *Being and Time* but also Benjamin's *Theses on the Philosophy of History*. As is implicit in *Infancy and History* and as Agamben makes explicit in a later essay, for him there is a central idea in these dense theses: "the concept of messianic time" (P, 160 [252]).

This idea is one that Benjamin endeavored to express from his earliest works onward. "The Life of Students," from 1915, opens with the observation, "There is a conception of history that puts its faith in the infinite extent of time and thus distinguishes only the pace, or lack of it, with which people and epochs advance along the path of progress" (Benjamin GS, 2.75). That which is here criticized—a naive faith in the inevitability of historical progress—remained a constant concern for Benjamin and is on brilliant display in his final *Theses*. As his writings turned more and more toward a theory of historical knowledge, Benjamin's vision of historical time and historical consciousness came to be based on a "destruction" or "exploding" of the reigning "linear" view of history and a corresponding model of progress. In this same early essay, Benjamin wrote that "the elements of the final state [*des Endzustandes*] are not to be found in formless progressive tendencies but are instead deeply embedded in every present as the most endangered, discredited, and mocked creations and thoughts" (Benjamin GS, 2.75). Just as Benjamin pointed to out-of-the-way corners of our cultural past and present as places where the elements for a new conception were to be sought and found, so too did Agamben, claiming that the elements of a new conception of time were to be found in "the folds and shadows of the Western cultural tradition"—and not least in Benjamin's own works.

Throughout his *Theses*, Benjamin attacks an ideology of progress and its corresponding conception of time. In the preparatory notes he made for the *Theses* Benjamin wrote that "a conception of history liberated from the schema of progression in empty, homogenous time would finally return the destructive energies of historical materialism—so long deactivated—to the field of action" (Benjamin GS, 1.1240). The formula that Benjamin employs and Agamben adopts for the model of time that corresponds to this model of progress is "empty, homogenous time [*homogene und leere Zeit*]" (found in Theses 13, 14, and B; see Benjamin GS, 1.701–1.704). What is central about this new conception for which Benjamin is seeking to find terms is that it abandons a conception of infinite linear time for a more dynamic one that does not wait for an ideal state to be reached but instead takes decisive action to change the course of history. Its goal is to arrest the machine-like movement of a progressive ideology that has proved so easy for the conservative powers that be to manipulate. In an essay on surrealism written ten years earlier, Benjamin evoked the image of "an alarm clock that rings every minute for sixty seconds" (Benjamin SW, 218; GS, 2.310).[11] The dream from which he saw a revolutionary mankind needing to awaken is that of inevitable progress. In the most famous of the *Theses*, the one in which Benjamin introduces his iconic "angel of history," a storm drives that angel ceaselessly forward. "He would like to stop and stay," Benjamin notes, "to awaken the dead and to make whole what has been dashed to pieces, but a storm blows from paradise; it has got caught in his wings with such violence that the angel can no longer close them" (Benjamin GS, I.697). As Benjamin says at the end of his parable, "What we call progress is *this* storm" (Benjamin GS, 1.697, italics in original). This did not mean for Benjamin that things did not get better over time; it meant that simply assuming that they would, and that those in power would see to this come what may, was the most dangerous stance one could take. Attacking this reigning ideology of progress on the eve of World War II, Benjamin wrote, "The wonder occasioned by the fact that the things we are at present experiencing are 'still' possible in the twentieth century is by no means a philosophical wonder" (Benjamin GS, 1.697ff.; see also Benjamin GS, 5.570ff.). Benjamin's allusion here is not only to early Greek thought's locating the birth of philosophy in the experience of wonder, but also to the idea that a truly clear-sighted commentator cannot continue to fly the flag of progress with the same calm and faith as generations of intellectuals and politicians have done.

In the *Handexemplar* of Benjamin's *Theses* that was lost for decades after Benjamin's flight from Paris and that Agamben himself rediscovered in the *Bibliothèque Nationale,* there is an additional thesis. It is placed between the seventeenth and eighteenth theses and in it Benjamin remarks, "In his conception of the classless society, Marx secularized the conception of messianic time" (Benjamin GS, 7.783; see also Benjamin GS, 1.1231).[12] In an abbreviated historical survey Benjamin laments that social democrats took this idea and made of it an "ideal," and that Neo-Kantians made of it an "endless task" (Benjamin GS, 7.783; see also Benjamin GS, 1.1231). "With the classless society defined as an endless task," Benjamin writes, "empty and homogenous time become the antechamber in which one waited with more or less equanimity for the revolutionary situation to enter," and for Benjamin there is nothing so damaging for a revolutionary politics than such complacency (Benjamin GS, 7.783; see also Benjamin GS, 1.1231). In many respects, our world seems a fairer, safer, better, more humane world than that of one hundred or five hundred years ago. In other respects, there is room for caution and cause for prudence when employing those terms. Benjamin held progress to a justly high standard and saw too many lapses and too many dangers to warrant unwavering faith. Things may progress, but we must work, individually and collectively, to further that progress.

The Time of the Now

In the *Arcades Project,* Benjamin wrote that "the dialectician must have the winds of world history in his or her sails" (Benjamin GS, 5.591). For that dialectician, Benjamin added, "thinking means: setting sail. *How* they are set is important. Words are sails. How they are set makes of them concepts" (Benjamin GS, 5.591, italics in original). One of the most important as well as most enigmatic concepts that Benjamin employed to try to catch the winds of history in his conceptual sails was what he opposed to "empty, homogenous time" and called a "concept of the present as 'now-time [*Jetztzeit*]'" (Benjamin GS, 1.704; see also Benjamin GS, 1.702). In the fourteenth thesis, Benjamin wrote that "history is the object of a construction whose place is not that of homogenous, empty time but is instead filled with now-time [*von Jetztzeit erfüllte*]" (Benjamin GS, 1.701). The term that Benjamin chose to liberate the dynamic energies of revolutionary thought is an unusual one and, as a result, not easy to translate. In German, *Jetztzeit* usually means "contemporary times" or "the present time," and philosophers from Schopenhauer to Nietzsche to Heidegger used it as a derogatory term for the narrowly contemporary (that is, a superficial time focused only on the here and now, with no sense for the times of the past or those of the future). In Benjamin's hands, however, *Jetztzeit* is given a different valence and a new dynamism. "Now-time" is conceived of in the most literal possible sense as a conception of time focused on the radical opportunity that every moment brings with it— or to employ the terms of Agamben's approach, on the dynamic *instant* rather than on the progressive and normalizing *continuum.* Such a conception would grasp the present moment in and for all its revolutionary potential.

Agamben stressed the need to probe "the folds and shadows of the Western cultural tradition" for a critique of the instant, and one of his most important discoveries is found in Benjamin's final theses. In Benjamin's wake, Agamben adopted this model of a now-time, giving it the kindred name *kairology* and linking it to a "catastrophe" that he sees as ongoing (for more on both of these terms, see the scholia to this chapter). *Kairology* is best understood in opposition to *chronology*, and thirty years later Agamben returned to the former term so as to oppose it to the latter (see SR, 75). Like Benjamin, Agamben employs *catastrophe* not in the sense of *apocalypse* but instead in the sense of a *crisis* and the need for a decisive response to it. As we saw, Agamben has claimed, "I am not in the slightest interested in apocalyptic prophecies, but rather in the ways in which we might respond at the present time to the catastrophe in which we live" (UL, 18). That this response entails a reconceptualization of *time* is something that Agamben makes perfectly clear as he adds, "And the sole possibility we have to truly grasp the present is to conceive of it as end [*sie als das Ende zu denken*]" (UL, 18). The end in question is not the end of the world or the end of time but the idea of the end as a model or paradigm for a mode of thinking and living that is not waiting for dialectical completion or messianic fulfillment (an idea that will resurface later in his thought, and in this book, as the idea of the profane). Agamben also says that this time of the now as time of the end "was Benjamin's idea and his messianism is above all to be understood after this fashion" (UL, 18). Here we can clearly see what is so mystifying about Agamben's—and Benjamin's—recourse to the idea of the messianic, which we will return to at the end of this book. His idea is not of apocalypse but of *immediacy*; it is not waiting for the Messiah to come, it is acting as though He were already here. It is for this reason that Agamben will say not only, as we saw earlier, that the central idea in Benjamin's *Theses* is "messianic time," but also that "the paradigm for understanding the present is messianic time" (UL, 18). Here Agamben makes perfectly explicit that what is at issue is a paradigm— or model—for our action. To understand better this conception of time and its "messianic" elements, however, we must examine more closely the method that Benjamin—and after him Agamben—envisioned.[13]

Dialectical Method, or The Prince and the Frog

The chapter in *Infancy and History* that follows Agamben's call for a revolutionary conception of time, "The Prince and the Frog: The Question of Method in Adorno and Benjamin," might seem at first glance anecdotal—a sort of afterthought to the larger questions the book raises. When examined closely, however, it reveals what Agamben is endeavoring to adapt from Benjamin's idea of history, and why.

In modest philological fashion, this chapter begins with the texts that it will analyze and explicate: two long letters written in 1938. The first is from Adorno to Benjamin, acknowledging receipt of the latter's essay "The Paris of the Second Empire in Baudelaire" on behalf of the Institute for Social Research, which he helped to run and which was then located in New York. It expresses disappointment and offers trenchant criticism. The second letter is Benjamin's response sent from Paris to New York a month later. The essay on Baudelaire was of particular importance to both parties. The Institute for Social Research was then funding Benjamin's study, and Adorno had been hoping to bring his friend more closely in line with the methodological aims of the Institute. For Benjamin, the essay was to be nothing less than "a model in miniature" for the massive *Arcades Project* he had been at work on for nearly ten years.

After citing the two letters at length, Agamben carefully examines their arguments. To understand the debate more fully, however, we need to trace the story back a step farther than Agamben does. Benjamin had met with the Adornos (he was an old friend of Adorno's wife, Gretel) before the couple left for New York. The meeting took place in San Remo, and during it Benjamin and Adorno often spoke of ideas of *redemption* and the role they saw those ideas playing in their respective projects. Adorno was fascinated by Benjamin's gargantuan effort to capture the "physiognomy" and "phantasmagoria" of the nineteenth century through a disparate mass of documents centered around the paradigmatic Parisian arcades, and Benjamin was equally interested in Adorno's work-in-progress on Wagner. During these conversations and the letters that followed, the two thinkers explored the commonalities and differences of their conceptions of the role of the critic, as well as debating the meaning and importance of such categories as redemption.

In the works of both writers, *redemption* found itself in unlikely company. The term frequently appears in passages characterized by philosophical and sociological sophistication that seemed to leave little place for a concept and category that was, to all appearances, a religious one. For Adorno, *redemption* entered his philosophical picture in dialectical form and was shaped by a Marxist orthodoxy he held dear. It was something on the order of a dialectical horizon and its actual attainment was a matter not to be immediately contemplated. Benjamin's insistence on the term was every bit as central and intense, though more difficult to characterize. Whatever it was, Benjamin's use was not dialectical in the same fashion as Adorno's, and the latter came to view it as dwelling somewhere between the naively mystical (the messianic) and the naively historical (the anarchic). For Adorno, Benjamin's Marxism was becoming increasingly incoherent.

Where these tensions came to a head was in their conceptions of *materialism*. Adorno's problem with Benjamin's unorthodox recourse to Marx and his decidedly undialectical use of the term *redemption* was what he saw as its faulty or insufficient materialism. This vacillating, uncertain materialism that, in Adorno's view, Benjamin tried to accommodate to his other areas of interest—such as Jewish mysticism—did, in Adorno's view, a disservice to both materialism and Benjamin's other interests. They were, Adorno wrote, "intellectual tools whose movements your hand resists at every turn" (IH, 113 [119]).

Adorno's chastising of Benjamin for insufficient materialism led Benjamin to make a polemical distinction in his last writings between *dialectical materalism* of the sort practiced by Adorno and his own brand of materialism, which he called *historical materialism,* the enigmatic traits of which are sketched in his *Theses*.[14] For Benjamin, the historical materialist singles himself out for his refusal to think within the categories of continual progress and along the lines of a progressive model of history. In Benjamin's view, Adorno was not free from such faith in the progress of history (evidenced in his dialectical method), and Benjamin remained skeptical about the use Adorno made of "the categories of progressive and regressive" in his study of Wagner (see Adorno and Benjamin 1994, 337).

With this background in mind we can turn to Agamben's elucidation of this methodological exchange that is so charged with personal tension. Agamben begins his analysis by acknowledging the fundamental soundness of Adorno's critique. "At first sight," he writes, "the objections to Benjamin's essay that Adorno voices in his letter seem correct" (IH, 115 [122], translation modified). He carefully reads between the lines of

Adorno's letter the real charge it contains. Although he avoids saying this in so many words, Adorno finds Benjamin falling into nothing less than "vulgar materialism"—a materialism that, in Marxist orthodoxy, fails to give sufficient place to the all-important process of "mediation" between "structure and superstructure" (see IH, 115–116 [122–23]). Agamben makes clear that Adorno has good reason to make such objections and that "from Adorno's doctrinal point of view, his argument seems perfectly coherent" (IH, 117 [123], translation modified). Adorno is thus justified in the objections he makes, and although he does not refer directly to Engels' oft-cited letter in which the latter stressed that only "in the final instance" is production the determining historical factor in a cultural creation, Agamben points to the homology of the critique (see IH, 116 [123]). Adorno stresses the need for "universal mediation," refers to the "total social process," and sees both of these as necessary steps in the materialist dialectic—steps that Benjamin has either neglected or refused to take. This first part of Agamben's essay serves to stress the doctrinal soundness of Adorno's objections and the motivations behind his call for a more dialectically sound method.

After underlining the legitimacy of Adorno's objections, Agamben adds, "There remains only the problem that [Adorno's] critique is directed at a text which, as anyone who has read the essay in question will know, is perhaps the most illuminating analysis of a global cultural moment in the historical development of capitalism" (IH, 116 [123]). To this nonnegligible point Agamben adds the curious fact that in Adorno's letter a critique founded on such incontrovertible doctrinal bases employs strange rhetorical devices to achieve its end, and he finds it puzzling that Adorno "should have felt the need to borrow terminology that would seem more appropriate to the technical vocabulary of exorcism and ecclesiastical anathema than to a lucid philosophical refutation" (IH, 116 [123], translation modified). Agamben parses this difficulty by closely examining what Adorno sees under the headings "dialectics" and "mediation." Adorno's focus on the role of mediation leads him to tell Benjamin at one point in his letter, "[I will] express myself in as simple and Hegelian a manner as possible" (cited in IH, 117 [124]). Agamben astutely traces this allusion to Hegelian mediation to its source in *The Phenomenology of Spirit*. "The mediator interposing its good offices between structure and superstructure to safeguard materialism from vulgarity," writes Agamben, "is therefore Hegelian dialectical historicism"—which, adds Agamben, "like all go-betweens, is prompt in demanding its due. This due takes the form of renouncing the concrete grasp of each single event and each present instant of praxis in favor of deferral to the final instance of the total social process" (IH, 118 [125], translation modified).

To a certain extent, then, Hegel and his dialectic are at issue here, and Agamben sees Adorno as being fundamentally aligned with Hegel on this question. It is at this point that Agamben decisively enters the debate on materialist method via the category of causality—the *mediation* that materialist orthodoxy places between structure and superstructure. Agamben claims that the idea that structure (or material base) and super-structure stand in a relationship of cause and effect to one another is false and is in fact nothing less than a "scarecrow" (IH, 119 [126], translation modified). "Every causal interpretation of the relationship between mate-rial base and superstructure," writes Agamben, "is complicit with Western metaphysics and presupposes the division of reality into two distinct on-tological levels" (IH, 119 [126], translation modified). If this is so, then it would go against the driving idea behind Marx's materialism—the project of standing philosophy on its head and of merging theory and praxis into a single system. Agamben continues: "A materialism that conceived of economic factors as *causa prima* in the same sense in which the God of metaphysics is *causa sui* and first principle of all things would be only the obverse of metaphysics and not its overcoming" (IH, 119 [127], translation modified). Here again such a materialism would be unworthy of the task that Marx set for it. The materialism that Agamben argues is truly Marx's own is in a certain sense a materialism without mediation in the manner in which Hegel, Engels, and Adorno envisioned it.

The path left open for such a truly radical—and for Benjamin and Agamben, a truly Marxist—materialism would then be not one of dia-lectical mediation or causal determination between structure and super-structure, but one of *direct correspondence* or *unmediated identity* (IH, 120 [127], italics in original, translation modified). The experience of intense political engagement that Benjamin had at the side of Asja Lacis led him to new thinking about the relationship between theory and praxis, exem-plified in the promise made in a letter to Martin Buber that his work "will be devoid of all theory. . . . I want to write a description of Moscow at the present moment in which 'all factuality is already theory'" (Benjamin GS, IV.988).[15] Thus, for Agamben, "the only true materialism is one that radically abolishes this separation [between structure and superstructure] and sees in concrete historical reality not the sum of structure and superstructure but the unmediated unity of the two terms in the realm of praxis" (IH, 120 [127], translation modified). Although Adorno indeed compressed the Marxist distinction between theory and praxis to a remarkable extent—saying, for instance, that praxis is the "power source of theory" and that theory is "not only a part of the whole but also a moment of it; for if not, it would not be able to resist the spell of the whole"—he nevertheless kept them distinct from one another in a way that Benjamin and Agamben did not (Adorno GS, 10.780).

By direct reference to Marx (and by distancing himself from Engels' position) Agamben lays claim on Benjamin's behalf to a purer and more authentic Marxism than Adorno, and the Marxist orthodoxy to which he often adheres, employs. "If Marx is not concerned to specify the way in which the relationship between structure and superstructure is to be construed," writes Agamben, "and has no fear of being occasionally considered 'vulgar,' it is because an interpretation of this relationship in a causal sense is not even conceivable in Marxist terms—a fact which renders superfluous the dialectical interpretation intended to remedy this" (IH, 119 [127]). If Marx never feared "vulgar materialism," writes Agamben, it was because Marx's thought was operating with a fully different conception of praxis. Adorno felt he had to traverse what he called, citing Benjamin, the "icy wastes of abstraction" to arrive at his own conception of a "negative dialectic" (Müller-Doohm 2003, 661). Agamben's concern, however, is not with negativity or with a dialectic able to traverse such great distances of cold abstraction, but with the immediacy of historical reason and praxis he sees Benjamin take from Marx. Although it is in line with Hegel and the historiography that followed in his wake, Adorno's materialism is seen by Agamben as inconsistent with what in Marx's conception of history— and life—was most revolutionary: the materialism that would revolutionize philosophy and from which a new conception of causality would flow. Instead of defending Benjamin against Adorno on the grounds that it doesn't ultimately matter whether Benjamin was sufficiently materialist in his approach or not, as many critics have done, and instead of conceding to Adorno that he was the better Marxist but that Benjamin's idiosyncratic approach also has its own not-insignificant merits, Agamben takes a different tack. He philologically demonstrates that although Adorno may have been more dialectical than his correspondent, he was not more *materialist* in an authentically Marxist, and authentically revolutionary, sense.

By addressing the relation of theory and praxis through a seemingly incidental exchange of letters, Agamben approaches not only a question that lies at the center of the tradition of Marxist philosophy, but also one of the elements in Benjamin's thinking that has proved most durably mystifying. Adorno was indeed one of the first to raise the question of the relationship of theory to praxis in Benjamin's work, but he was far from the last. Scholem did the same and was disturbed by what he saw as Benjamin's proximity to conservative thinkers of his day. The anarchic note struck in certain of Benjamin's essays made the question still more difficult for his interpreters to decide on. In a much-read essay from 1972, Jürgen Habermas stressed what he characterized as dubiously conservative elements in Benjamin's thought, as well as what he termed "a highly mediated relation relative to political praxis"—a matter concerning which, following Habermas, "Benjamin did not manage to achieve sufficient clarity" (Habermas 1988, 118). Derrida, in what Agamben felt to be a fundamental misunderstanding, saw the arguments of "The Critique of Violence" as approaching figures employed in the Nazi Final Solution. Not a few readers have found Benjamin's remarks on violence and his enthusiasm for extreme and explosive charges and changes similarly disturbing. It is this highly charged field that Agamben subtly enters, through his analysis of Benjamin and Adorno's epistolary exchange, and that he endeavors to clarify.

In the thirteenth of his *Theses*, Benjamin explicitly attacks the reigning historiographical conception of progress of his day, claiming that the "empty, homogenous time" it posits demands a fundamental critique—"a critique of the concept of progress" (Benjamin GS, 1.701). Tellingly, it is precisely this thesis that Adorno singled out upon first receiving the text (more than a year after Benjamin's death). At this time, Adorno's collaborator Max Horkheimer was no longer living in New York (having moved to Pacific Palisades), and Adorno wrote to him with a summary of the contents of the *Theses*. "If I were to indicate a point where we diverge from Benjamin's theses," wrote Adorno, "I would point to the 13th. So certainly does the conformist view of history imply the conception of time as homogenous continuum, so little is it to be reduced to the experience of time" (letter from June 12, 1941; see Benjamin GS, 7.774). Still speaking of this same thesis, Adorno continues: "Benjamin seems to me here to be caught up in idealism," before conceding that, "there is something in the question of time as *sui generis*." For Benjamin, what is at issue is precisely and unabashedly an "experience of time," and Adorno is too sharp a reader not to see this. It is precisely this point that most deeply divides them—and that in turn lies at the center of Agamben's own reflections on the philosophy of history.

Given the chapter that precedes it in *Infancy and History* ("Time and History," with its kairological conception of time that would be adequate to the Marxist conception of history), it should come as no surprise that Agamben ends his chapter on Adorno and Benjamin with a final call for a new conception of time: "For the time has come to end the identification of history with a conception of time as a continuous linear process and, to this end, to understand that the dialectic is capable of being a historical category without needing to fall into linear time. It is not the dialectic that has to be adequate to a preexisting, vulgar conception of time; on the contrary, it is this conception of time that must be adequate to a dialectic that is truly freed of all 'abstractness'" (IH, 123 [131], translation modified). It is clear that the dialectic per se is not to be dismissed, but also that an appropriately radical conception of time should accompany the radical conception of history and praxis that is Marx's philosophical heritage.

This widened dialectical perspective can help Agamben's reader better understand the scope and aims of his third book. He sees experience endangered not only by the commodification and commercialization of everyday life, but also by guiding conceptions of history and progress. The polemical element in *Infancy and History* is targeted at dialectical conceptions of historiography, as well as at ideas of time attendant upon them and from which even Marx's radical revaluation of Western metaphysics did not manage to liberate itself. Here, as elsewhere, Agamben's calls should not, however, be mistaken for anarchic ones. What he advocates is not an Artaudian evacuation of meaning or a surrealist championing of the incomprehensible, but instead a reconceptualization of our place in history and our ideas on time, as well as the seizing of the possibilities open to us. Our perilous state of affairs brings with it a positive possibility, and the "destructive" project for which Agamben argues is to be conducted in the name of that possibility.

Scholium I: Benjamin's *Theses on the Philosophy of History*, or The Floodgates of Enthusiastic Misunderstanding

Shortly after Benjamin's death, what came to be called his *Theses on the Philosophy of History* were sent to his friend Bertolt Brecht.[16] Upon receiving them, the latter wrote in his journal, "One thinks with horror [*schrecken*][17] of how tiny the number is of those even in a position today to misunderstand such a work" (see Benjamin GS, 1.1228). Brecht was not the only writer to note how difficult it was to approach and understand Benjamin's fantastically condensed theses. In a letter to Max Horkheimer written in February 1940, Benjamin, writing in French, remarked that "the stripped-down character [*le caractère dépouillé*] that I had to give to the theses dissuades me from sending them to you as is" (Benjamin GS, 1.1225; this letter is one of a handful written to close German friends that Benjamin composed in French). In a letter to Gretel Adorno written a few months later, in April 1940, to accompany the *Theses* and that was never sent, Benjamin wrote, "In more than one sense is the text reduced" and "I do not even need to tell you that nothing lies further from my mind than the idea of publishing these notes (not to speak of doing so in the form you will find here) as they would open the floodgates to the most enthusiastic misunderstanding [*Sie würden dem enthusiastischen Mißverstandnis Tor und Tür öffnen*]" (GS, 1.1226, 1223).

In the wake of Benjamin's death five months later, this idea that lay furthest from his mind came to pass, and indeed, after a long period of inattention, these *Theses* have become the subject of no small measure of enthusiastic misunderstanding. So dense that they appear at points almost encrypted, they take up a mere eleven pages of the thousands in the seven thick volumes of Benjamin's complete works; but the wealth of enthusiasm, understanding, and misunderstanding to which they have given rise are without equal in his work, or perhaps that of any other modern theorist. They have, as their readers know, a lucid, stenographic power, as well as a rare emotional intensity. Benjamin wrote in the unsent letter to Gretel Adorno cited earlier that "the war and the constellation it brought with it led me to set down a few thoughts about which I can say that I have guarded them for some twenty years—indeed guarded them from myself" (GS, 1.1226). Benjamin wrote these "stripped-down" entries at the end of 1939 and the beginning of 1940, and the immediate impulse appears to have come from the Hitler-Stalin pact that was a cause of such shock and despair for so many communist intellectuals in Europe and elsewhere. Before fleeing Paris, Benjamin gave the *Theses* to Hannah Arendt, who was to take them to New York and pass them along to the Institute for Social Research, which had relocated from Frankfurt to New York. It was only after Benjamin's death that she was able to do so.

Benjamin's *Theses* were slow to attract interest. They were first published in the spring of 1942 by the Institute for Social Research (in a collection entitled *Walter Benjamin zum Gedächtnis*), but the publication run was extremely limited and the volume was never for sale in bookstores. The first major publication of the *Theses* was in the German journal *Die Neue Rundschau* upon Adorno's return to Germany in 1950 and was accompanied by Adorno's essay "Charakteristik Walter Benjamins." It bears recalling here that when Agamben began to write about Benjamin in the late 1960s and early 1970s, the latter's work was not yet particularly well known. When, however, Benjamin's work did at last begin to garner significant attention, his *Theses* were quickly seen as something of an intellectual testament. In the introduction that Adorno composed to accompany their initial publication, he called them precisely that: "the text has become a testament [*Der Text ist zum Vermächtnis geworden*]" (Benjamin GS, 1.1223–1.1224). In a letter from Scholem to Adorno from 1945, when the former had at last received the *Theses,* he concurred, although he complicated the expression by referring to them as "an encrypted testament [*ein Vermächtnis in Chiffern*]" (Benjamin GS, 7.780). Agamben clearly sees the *Theses* in this same posthumous light and repeatedly attempts to decrypt various passages therein. As we saw earlier, one way of approaching *Infancy and History* is as a gloss of the categories of historical experience, progress, time, and method presented in the *Theses*. This is true of a number of Agamben's other shorter and longer works as well. One way of understanding *The Time That Remains* is as a long, patient, and absolutely ingenious gloss of the first of Benjamin's *Theses* on the philosophy of history. *State of Exception* continues in this vein and, as we will see later, can be seen as, among other things, an equally ingenious gloss of Benjamin's eighth thesis.

Scholium II: The Now of Knowability

We saw in *Infancy and History* that Agamben spoke of "elements for a different conception of time" that he saw "laying scattered in the folds and shadows of the Western cultural tradition." He found such disparate elements in Aristotelian pleasure, in Stoic innovation, and in the reflections on time left behind by Heidegger and Benjamin. "We need only to elucidate these," Agamben continued, "so that they may emerge as the bearers of a message which is meant for us and which it is our task to verify" (IH, 100 [106]). Although it may not be immediately apparent, Agamben asks that this statement be understood quite literally. It is in fact the enunciation of the most singular of Agamben's methodological principles, which is as decisive as it is difficult to describe, and which applies not only to an idea of time but also to the time in which ideas are grasped.

In *Che cos'è il contemporaneo?* Agamben writes that historians of art and literature know that "between the archaic and the modern there is a secret appointment" (CCC, 23). Of *The Time That Remains* Agamben remarked, "I think that between Paul's Letter to the Romans and the present in which we live there is something that Benjamin called a secret appointment" (LAM, 51). In a more inductive vein he remarked elsewhere, "There is always a particular moment in which one can first truly understand something," and added, "Walter Benjamin called it the moment of knowability" (UL, 17). This comment tells us that Agamben, following Benjamin, rejects the idea that all texts are equally readable, equally understandable, at all moments of their history. In Agamben's view, *real* understanding—an understanding that would be more than the passive reception of a text, that would contain a dynamic element and a capacity for development—proceeds along different lines.

"Each now is the now of a particular knowability [*Jedes Jetzt ist das Jetzt einer bestimmten Erkennbarkeit*]," Benjamin wrote. "In it, truth is charged to the bursting point with time. (This explosion . . . coincides with the birth of authentic historical time, the time of truth)" (Benjamin 1999, 463; GS, 5.578, translation modified). Here and elsewhere, Benjamin could not have been more emphatic about the idea that the relationship between past and present in such a moment should not be understand along conventional timelines. "It is not that what is past casts its light on what is present," he says, "or that what is present sheds its light on what is past." Instead, he stresses the importance of a "now of knowability [*Jetzt der Erkennbarkeit*]," reflecting a less linear and more complex relationship of past to present. Every moment then "bears in the highest degree the imprint of the perilous critical moment upon which all reading is founded" (Benjamin 1999, 463; GS, 5.578, translation modified). Benjamin's is not a philological theory in a conventional sense, yet it is nonetheless a philological theory in the sense that it is concerned with methods of reading. (Benjamin employs in his notes the phrase "now of knowability" more or less synonymously with "now of legibility [*das Jetzt der Lesbarkeit*].") Here the decisive—and mysterious—element is fortuitous opportunity—or in other words, *kairos.* For Benjamin, "in reality there is not a single instant that does not bring *its* revolutionary opportunity with it. It wants only to be grasped as a specific one—namely as the opportunity for a completely new solution to a completely new task" (Benjamin GS, 7.783–7.784; italics in original; see also Benjamin GS, 1.1231). In the same vein Benjamin wrote, "The revolutionary thinker summons and validates the unique revolutionary opportunity of a given political situation. But the latter no less summons and validates the thinker himself through the moment's power to unlock a realm of the past that had up until that point remained closed" (Benjamin GS, 7.784).

Benjamin's most deeply felt, and least understood, philological conviction was thus that all documents of the past—be that past recent or remote—are *not* equally readable at all times. Because of the degree to which such a conception runs counter to orthodox philology, where the operative elements are erudition, application, intelligence, and patience, his view was not widely embraced. There is much that is singular about Agamben's development of Benjamin's thought, but nothing is so singular as this aspect. Agamben's approach can then be understood only if one bears in mind that it implies that a "historical index" mysteriously governs "the now of knowability" of a given text, which as Agamben makes clear is "the absolute opposite of the current principle according to which each work may become the object of infinite interpretations at any given moment" (TTR, 145 [134]). It is this principle, this *kairology,* that lends such urgency to Agamben's social, political, and ontological claims. The constant shifting of perspective effected by historical change closes and opens lines of historical sight. Axes that had been blocked for centuries or longer are liberated, and long-obscured elements suddenly come to the surface of the page. Every bit as central for *Infancy and History* as was his continuation of Benjamin's diagnosis of an impoverishment of experience is

Agamben's continuation of Benjamin's reflection on the pressing need for a radical reconceptualization of *time*. A corollary of the new conception of time that Agamben calls a kairology is a new conception of historical transmission. In a more recent work, Benjamin's "now of legibility"—or as he also called it, "now of knowability"—is seen by Agamben to form "a genuinely Benjaminian hermeneutic principle" that he has done his utmost to put into practice (TTR, 145 [134]).[18]

Following the idea that Benjamin advanced and Agamben adopted, there are times when the fortuitous encounter of text and reader allows for a lightning-like glimpse into the heart of a work—which allows the reader to decipher something that had long remained occluded. It is this moment that Benjamin described as "perilous" and on which he claimed that "all reading is founded." In his footsteps, Agamben is seeking to gather the elements not only of a kairology that is a radically different conception of time, a radically different conception of the relationship of *instant* to *continuum,* but also of a kairology of thought and reading themselves: a *kairology of historical transmission.*[19] The certainty of such encounters, of privileged possibilities of reading and understanding, cannot be methodically calculated or confirmed; yet, as Agamben stresses, they are "in no way arbitrary," born as they are of "a necessity" and "an exigence to which one cannot but respond" (CCC, 40). Such experiences are felt and contain a revolutionary element of faith, or expressed otherwise, a faith in revolutionary thought.

As the preceding has made clear, Agamben adopted Benjamin's idea of a "now of knowability" (or a "now of legibility"); but not only did he adopt Benjamin's idea, he also found the clearest instance of it in his own experience of reading Benjamin. In *The Time That Remains* Agamben says of Paul's letters and Benjamin's *Theses,* "I do not think it can be doubted that these two fundamental . . . texts . . . separated by almost two thousand years and both written in situations of radical crisis form a constellation . . . whose time of legibility has now come" (TTR, 145 [135], translation modified).[20] Even more explicitly, he remarks in his preface to the Italian edition of Benjamin's *Arcades Project,* "If it is true that the decisive moment in history is always under way, Benjamin's posthumous work has punctually arrived for its meeting" (AE, viii).

Scholium III: *Kairos*

The most striking neologism in *Infancy and History* is *kairology*. In the preceding discussion we saw its relation to models of time and history, but something of its own history also bears noting. Zeus fathered many children, but the youngest of these, according to Ion of Chios, was Kairos. The Greek word *kairos*, personified by the youthful god, has proved notoriously difficult to translate. No less able a Hellenist than Cicero claimed that it was simply untranslatable, and later commentators have been hard-pressed to find a single term to encompass all it expresses. Following context and circumstance, the translations arrived at have been "opportunity," "the proper or propitious moment," "occasion," "advantage," "the proper measure," and "proportion."

Although Agamben does not refer to this god or to depictions of him, the image of Kairos helps clarify Agamben's use of the term. Pausanias reports that there was an altar to Kairos at Olympia and that the god was portrayed there as a handsome, winged youth bearing scales that were about to tip. The tipping scales were interpreted as indicating that the moment of decision or moment of truth—the moment of favorable opportunity or *kairos*—was at hand. But *kairos* being at hand was not enough; one also had to grasp it. For this reason, the god had a singular hairstyle—long in the front and shaved in the back (he is sometimes depicted with his hair gathered into a forward-pointing ponytail of sorts, similar to that of a samurai).[21] The curious hairstyle was taken to say something about such decisive moments of truth. If one wanted to seize them, one needed to be ready and to do so as they arrived.

With this explanation of the figure corresponding to Agamben's neologism in mind, we might ask what sort of temporal model would correspond to such a figure. The model is clearly one of a moment of truth: a moment of decisive intervention that interrupts a continuum and changes the course of history. It is here that we can see how this "now-time" corresponds to what Agamben calls a *kairology* and to Benjamin's "*Jetztzeit* [now-time]." In a work written more than twenty years later he says of the latter that Benjamin "endows the term with the same qualities as those pertaining to the *ho nyn kairos* [time of the now] in Paul's paradigm of messianic time" (TTR, 143 [133]).[22]

Scholium IV: Dialectics at a Standstill, or
Means and Ends

Although Adorno singled out the thirteenth of the *Theses* as the one
that best defined his differences from Benjamin, Benjamin himself, in
a letter to Adorno's wife, Gretel, pointed to a different thesis as clarifying his intent: "I don't know to what degree their reading will surprise
you, or, what I would never wish for—confuse you. In any event, I'd like
to direct you especially to the 17th thesis. It will allow you to recognize
the concealed but consistent relation of these considerations to my earlier work" (Benjamin GS, 1.1226). The thesis in question explicitly distinguishes the method of the materialist historian from that of the historian whose addition of facts is used "to fill up the homogenous and empty
time" of traditional historiography (Benjamin GS, 1.702). "Thought involves not only the movement of thoughts," Benjamin writes, "but also
their freezing [*Stillstellung*]" (GS, 1.702). The method of the materialist
historian, he then adds, involves "a messianic freezing [*Stillstellung*] of
events—or expressed differently, a revolutionary opportunity in the fight
for the oppressed past" (GS, 1.703). How are we to understand this freezing of thoughts and events—and in what sense are we to understand it as
"messianic"? How does an arresting of the continuum of history represent
a "revolutionary opportunity" for all that in the past had been oppressed?
In light of the difficulty of these questions, it seems it was not without reason that Benjamin worried that this thesis might confuse its reader.

One way of approaching the matter is to ask, What would a method
look like that did not function dialectically, after the fashion of a Marxist
historiographical orthodoxy that Benjamin took to task, but instead abolished the separation between structure and superstructure and saw their
"unmediated unity" in "the realm of praxis"? The beginning of an answer
to this question is seen in the conception of a "time of the now" and the
"messianic freezing of events" it entails. To conceive of praxis and theory
as one is also to merge *means* with *ends,* and in this light it should come as
no surprise that Agamben entitled a later work *Means Without End* (1996).
"Means without end" is meant not in the sense of an inability to distinguish one from the other, but instead as a rejection of instrumentalized
rationality and of traditional models of historical causality. Agamben says
of the ideas expressed in Benjamin's "Epistemological-Critical Preface" to
his *Origin of German Tragic Drama* that they "imply a dialectic in which

origin and end are identified with one another and transform one another," and it is this same idea that he endeavors to express elsewhere (P, 59 [51], translation modified). To advance an idea of "means without end" is not to champion nonsense or anarchy. Instead, the title expresses precisely what Agamben calls for in *Infancy and History:* "a critique of the dialectic," a corrective to a dialectic that would see all means and moments as means and moments to a progressive end. The problem with this end is as simple as can be: it never occurs. It is pushed endlessly forward in the form of the dialectic whose end will confer on all earlier moments their sense and meaning by reference to the totality that will illuminate them, but that never comes. Agamben's critique of the dialectic in *Infancy and History,* as well as in subsequent works, is above all a critique of its conception of *teleology,* of a faith in historical progress that must, in the fullness of time, reach its *telos* and achieve an ideal state. Benjamin was responding to the teleological conception of history that he saw dominating nineteenth-century historiography, and in his wake Agamben attacked the idea of a redemptive day when all political and social losses will be restored and the people's sorrows will end.

After citing a passage from the *Phenomenology of Spirit* that begins with Hegel's declaration that "the True is the whole," Agamben outlines the role of the particular in the march of such a progressive historical dialectic. Glossing this central passage, he writes, "Since the absolute is 'consequence,' and 'only in the end is there truth,' each single concrete moment of the process is real only as 'pure negativity' which the magic wand of dialectical mediation will transform—in the end—into the positive. There is but a short step from this to declaring that every moment in history is merely *a means to an end*" (IH, 118 [125], italics added). To conceive of every moment as a means to an end is to conceive of the moments of life as negatives awaiting the magic wand of a progressive, dialectical model of history to come along to develop them—something that can happen only at the end of history's course, when "the True" that is "the whole" can bring them together. In the meantime—and the meantime, for Agamben, is all we have—they are but means to an end that we cannot glimpse and whose name (and alibi) is *progress.* It is for this reason that Agamben tries to do something exceptionally difficult: to conceive, following Benjamin, of a "dialectic" freed from all "abstractness" (IH, 123 [131]).

For Benjamin, the abstraction that entered the dialectic did so, as we saw, through a model of time as endless progress. To free it of this "abstractness" required a different model of time to replace it. In the passage cited earlier in which Agamben speaks of a "dialectic freed from all 'abstractness,'" he refers to the phrase "dialectics at a standstill" that Benjamin "left as a legacy to historical materialism, and with which it must sooner or later reckon" (IH, 123 [131]). No citation is given, but the enigmatic expression in question, "dialectics at a standstill," is found in notes on historical method written during the same period as the *Theses* and presented there in opposition to the idea of "empty, homogenous time" that was examined earlier (Benjamin GS, 5.578). It is precisely this conception that inspires the freezing of thought and action that, in the seventeenth thesis to which Benjamin pointed in his letter to Gretel Adorno, reveals the arc his work has traced.

Few phrases in Benjamin's writing are so puzzling as the "dialectics at a standstill" that Agamben claims Benjamin "left as a legacy to historical materialism, and with which it must sooner or later reckon." "Dialectics at a standstill"—and Benjamin's corollary conception, "the dialectical image," which is examined in Chapter Six—are presented as reflecting that "it is not that what is past casts its light on the what is present, or that what is present sheds its light on what is past"; instead, "what has been comes together in a flash with the now" (Benjamin 1999, 463; GS, 5.578). The question, however, might remain, Why should this be called dialectics *at all*? At first sight, Benjamin's expression seems a simple contradiction in terms. Whether it be the Platonic dialectic of a dialogue leading progressively toward illumination or a Hegelian dialectic of historical and spiritual actualization, the idea of the dialectic itself seems unequivocally to evoke something that takes place in and over time. "Freezing" or bringing it to a "standstill" would seem to spell its end—the end of the dialogue, the arresting of the process of actualization. The answer to this objection lies in how Benjamin uses the term. Although this use is strategic, it does not denote sabotaging the machine of the dialectic. The dialectic is never something grasped by Benjamin, or by Agamben, as simply to be destroyed or dismissed. However, classically dialectical conceptions of time and history, with their faith in inevitable progress toward a more just and spiritually integrated state—a faith that found its crowning expression in Hegel's philosophy, are in need of radical revision. The idea of continual progress in time is so stubborn a belief that it must be countered, for both thinkers, with radical measures.

Benjamin's "dialectics at a standstill" is part and parcel of his conception of messianic time—of time charged with what he calls messianic intensity. We will turn to the idea of the *messianic* in Chapter Ten of this book, but for the moment it suffices to stress that both Benjamin and Agamben employ the term in singular fashion. For them, a *messianic* idea of history is not one in which we wait for the Messiah to come, end history, and redeem humanity, but instead is a paradigm for historical time in which we act as though the Messiah is already here, or even has already come and gone. What is so difficult about Agamben's use of the term *messianic* is how radically it is to be distinguished from the *apocalyptic*. Agamben says that to understand "messianic time" as it is presented in Paul's letters "one must first distinguish messianic time from apocalyptic time, the time of the now from a time directed towards the future" (LAM, 51). To this he adds, "If I had to try to reduce the distinction to a formula, I would say that the messianic is not, as it is always understood, the end of time, but the time of the end" (LAM, 51). The model of time corresponding to this idea is one that no longer looks for its decisive moment in a more or less remote future, but instead finds it in every minute of every day, in this world and in this life; and it is through such expressions as "dialectics at a standstill" and "means without end" that the two thinkers aim to return our gaze from the distant future to the pressing present.

To bring the dialectic to a standstill is thus not to halt some singularity-negating process, the liberating of man from machine-like thought, but the creation of a revolutionary conception of history in which knowledge is situated not in an impossible future, but, through "exploding the continuum of history," right now.[23] The dialectic in question is at a standstill not because it has stalled, not because the winds of history have gone out of its sails or because anarchic activity has sabotaged its machinery. The standstill is brief—and opportune. It denotes the fortuitous moment, the favorable occasion to be grasped that, if it is, will prove rich with potential for a new—and very different—start.

CHAPTER FOUR

The Pure Potentiality of
Representation: *Idea of Prose*

Idea of Prose is composed of thirty-three short chapters.[1] Each poses the same question—that of "the pure potentiality of representation itself"—in novel fashion, and each bears a symmetrical title. Some address classical philosophical *topoi*, such as "The Idea of the Unique," "The Idea of Truth," "The Idea of Appearance," "The Idea of Thought," and "The Idea of Language." Others treat more personal matters like "The Idea of Love," "The Idea of Happiness," and "The Idea of Shame." Some invoke political concepts, such as "The Idea of Power," "The Idea of Justice," "The Idea of Peace," and "The Idea of Communism," while still others are concerned with religious conceptions like "The Idea of the Last Judgment."[2] Yet every one of these chapters is likely to surprise its reader for the reason that it does not address what is announced in its title—at least not directly. Few of the thirty-three chapters in *Idea of Prose* ever directly name the "idea" under whose heading they are written, and many seem to avoid not only the name but also the topic itself. "The Idea of Communism," for instance, discusses not the theory or practice of communism but, instead, pornography. "The Idea of Thought" discusses punctuation marks, and "The Idea of the Unique" multilingual poetry. "The Idea of the Muse" retraces Heidegger's pedagogical practices while "The Idea of Music" dedicates all but its closing lines to phenomenological analyses of affect. In every case, these "ideas" express more than what is stated here, and in every case they express something that Agamben finds fundamental about the idea. Upon study, they *do* in fact explore the idea they name, albeit never in direct, thematic fashion. The frustration of a reader turning to these "ideas" for solutions and finding what look far more like aporias would be easy to understand, but that same reader delving more deeply into the book is likely to see its indirection in a new light.

Idea of Prose begins with an "idea" unlike those that will follow it: "The Idea of the Work." Under this heading we find on the book's title page an anonymous engraving titled "Eros Raving on a Snail" (see IP, i [1]).[3] As with the image of knots that served as *Stanzas'* emblem, the reader is left to ponder the image's import and its relation to the book it opens. The image of Eros writhing atop a snail is a striking one and is hardly a common iconographical motif. Eros is more commonly depicted atop a dolphin, reinforcing the bracing speed of his desire, whereas a snail seems to move counter to the swiftness of his amorous designs. Although the engraving contains an iconographical paradox, it is also an image that can be deciphered. Like the image of a dolphin with an anchor wrapped around it that the Venetian publisher Aldo Manuzio chose as his emblem, "Eros Raving on a Snail" illustrates the Latin motto *festina lente,* "to make haste slowly." By placing the title "Idea of the Work" above this image Agamben gives not only an idea of the indirection to follow, but also of the sort of patient and imaginative attention he will ask of his readers.

This indirection begins, for Agamben, with an anecdote dating from 529 A.D. as the Emperor Justinian, acting on the advice of a group of anti-Hellenic advisors, decrees the closing of the Athenian Academy, thereby putting an official end to pagan philosophy and sending it into exile. In the company of six other Greek scholars, Damascius, the last head of the school founded by Plato, journeys to the court of the Persian king Khosrau Nushirvan. Once there, he delegates his philosophical duties at the Persian court to younger colleagues and goes into seclusion so as to devote his final years to a work entitled *Aporias and Solutions Concerning First Principles.*

As Agamben relates, the difficulty of Damascius' undertaking soon leads to frustration and despair. After three hundred days and as many nights of fruitless work—punctuated by despairing notes, preserved in his manuscript, such as "May God do as he please[s] with what I have just written"—he arrived at an aporia he could not overcome (see IP, 32 [10]). Agamben writes, "It is clear that that which is in question"—those "first principles" named in Damascius' title—"can never be thematized—not even as incomprehensible—and cannot be expressed even as inexpressible" (IP, 32–33 [10], translation modified). The aporia that followed pagan philosophy into this first exile and that is named here is one familiar to Agamben's readers from the two books that directly preceded it, *Stanzas* and *Language and Death:* that the limits of what can be understood and expressed are themselves incomprehensible and inexpressible—at least when presented directly.

The despondency that Damascius is said to have fallen into in his search for aporias and solutions concerning first principles was, however, transformed by the simplest of things:

Damascius lifted up his hand for a moment and looked down at the writing tablet on which he had been noting his thoughts. Suddenly he remembered the passage in the book on the soul in which the philosopher compared the potentiality of the intellect to a tablet on which nothing is written. How had he not thought of it sooner? [IP, 33–34 (11–12), translation modified]

The philosopher referred to here is Aristotle who, in his *On the Soul,* addresses the question of how we are to understand the mind's capacity for conceiving of things prior to, or independent of, their actually being thought. A simpler formulation of the same question is, How are we to conceive of the potential of thought? To clarify his conception, Aristotle employs a novel image. Even before it thinks of a given thing, Aristotle says, "what [the mind] thinks must be in it just as characters may be said to be on a writing tablet on which as yet nothing actually stands written" (430a; Aristotle 1984, 683).[4] Of all the questions Agamben treats in his works, this one—the relationship between the categories of potentiality and actuality—is the most central and the most abiding.[5] And of all the images he employs to illustrate this relationship, the writing tablet is the one to which he most often returns.

The same redemptively simple image that comes to Damascius in his hour of need liberates him from the aporia with which he is confronted and allows him to continue his work. It reminds him of something all too easily forgotten: "the ultimate limit that thought can reach is not a being, a place, or a thing, no matter how free from every and any quality, but instead its own absolute potentiality [*la propria assoluta potenza*], the pure potentiality of representation itself [*la pura potenza della rappresentazione stessa*]" (IP, 34 [12], translation modified). Aristotle's image of a writing tablet on which nothing has yet been written springs to the mind of Damascius and allows him to see "the glimmer of a beginning" (IP, 34 [12]).

After the introductory allegory of the aporias and solutions of Damascius, Agamben offers his thirty-three "ideas." Confronted with their indirection, one mode of proceeding is to identify and isolate the *exoteric* from the *esoteric*. Indeed, one perfectly legitimate way of characterizing these chapters would be to say they are divided between an *exoteric* content—that which they ostensibly discuss—and a more *esoteric* one that is named in their titles and to be read between their lines. In other words, the relation of title to content might be seen as *allegorical*. Benjamin called for a "philosophical understanding of allegory" (Benjamin GS, 1.138). Because allegory is an indirect and elusive mode, attaining such a philosophical understanding was no easy matter. From his masterful essays on Proust, Kafka, Baudelaire, and many others, with their tendency to rely less on classical argumentation than on flashes of insight expressed in arresting images, to his final and unfinished *Arcades Project*—an unparalleled experiment in indirection—the search for such a philosophical understanding of allegory is coupled with a strategic use of it. Benjamin's idea of allegory is not only a historical form, it is also an idea of form—one with profound affinities to the idea of prose practiced in Agamben's fifth book.

In connection to his idea of allegory, Benjamin wrote of his idea of the *fragment*. "The value of fragments of thought," he noted, "is the more decisive [they are] the less these fragments can be directly aligned with the fundamental conception under study. The brilliance of the representation depends on them just as that of a mosaic depends on the quality of the glass" (Benjamin GS 1.209). This allegorical approach and the fragmentary method it implies leads Benjamin to a curious methodological principle that could easily have served as *Idea of Prose*'s motto: "method is detour" (Benjamin GS, 1.209). Benjamin evokes here the literal meaning of *method* ("path") to highlight the virtues of indirection in certain philosophical undertakings. A true method of the sort he envisions must allow for many detours, which often risks becoming indistinguishable from a detour into the inessential. The fragments that fill Benjamin's books, such as his experimental prose work *One-Way Street,* try in ever-changing forms to follow this fine line between essential and inessential, method and detour. As noted earlier, immediately after the publication of *Idea of Prose* Agamben remarked of his work that, "for me, reflecting on the forms thought takes has always been central, and I have never believed it possible for a thinker to evade this problem, as if thinking were somehow nothing more than simply expressing opinions that were more or less right concerning a given argument. Precisely this centrality of form makes for the proximity of poetry and philosophy" (UIGA, 33). Benjamin began his *Origin of German Tragic Drama* with the declaration, "It is of the essence of philosophical writing to be continually confronted anew with the problem of representation," and *Idea of Prose* is just such a new confrontation with the problem of representation (Benjamin GS, 1.207). To recognize this characteristic of philosophical writing—that with every new effort it poses anew questions about representation—is to ask the question that Agamben follows in *Idea of Prose:* that of "the pure potentiality of representation."

Appropriate to an inquiry that begins by raising the question of "the pure potentiality of representation"—the question of the representation of thought and its limits—the book's contents and forms are unfamiliar and shifting. As we saw earlier, in *Stanzas* and in *Infancy and History* Agamben called for more creative forms of criticism. This call finds two responses in *Idea of Prose*. The first is the disappearance of many of the conventions of academic writing, such as footnotes and explicit links between sections. In Agamben's fourth book these conventions are abandoned in favor of a more experimental, fragmentary, and creative idea of prose—one that takes up in its form what *Stanzas* offered as its content: the overcoming of the "ancient enmity" that Plato saw separating philosophy from poetry. Agamben's work had shown since its beginning an impatience with certain academic conventions—what he refers to in a later essay as *coniunctivitis professoria*; but in *Idea of Prose* Agamben more completely abandons the academic forms of his earlier books (BPS, 115). This implicit critique is made explicit in an interview that closely followed the book's publication. "Notes, quotations marks, bibliographical references, see also's and the like," Agamben stated, "refer to a subject of knowledge ensconced like a ventriloquist behind the speaking subject"—and *Idea of Prose* makes clear that he wishes to avoid such ventriloquism (UIGA, 33). "For this reason," he notes, "today's academic prose is so often disappointing," with its separation of an "authentic experience of language" from "knowledge" (UIGA, 33).

To dismiss certain academic conventions does not, however, represent a radical break with the past. Instead, it forms a connection with different elements of that past. Asked in an interview to name, from a "methodological point of view," his intellectual masters, Agamben gave a surprising answer. "Rather than the names of masters," he said, "I would like to indicate two formal modals that have constantly inspired me: the medieval commentary and the brief and erudite notes of the great philologists of the nineteenth century" (LSP, 45). This inspiration and the brief and erudite form it takes is on proud display in *Idea of Prose*. Near the beginning of *Infancy and History* Agamben inserted a related formal model into his analysis: a "gloss" (see IH, 15ff. [7ff.]). Over the course of the book, as well as in such later ones as *Homo Sacer, The End of the Poem*, and *The Time That Remains, glosses* become a fundamental element in the organization of his works. The term *gloss* is not an abstruse one (many readers may recall James Joyce's exhortation to "wipe your glosses with what you know"), but its history and meaning are worth recalling. English and Italian derive the term from the Latin *glossa* (meaning a foreign or obscure word). A *gloss* thus denotes a term that demands explanation and, by extension, that explanation itself. It is, in other words, a point of terminological clarification; but in Agamben's hands, both in *Infancy and History* and in the works to follow, glosses are something more. At the end of *Infancy and History* Agamben cites as a sign of the crisis our culture is traversing "the loss of the commentary and the gloss as *creative* forms" (IH, 144 [144], italics added). This comment may sound surprising given that we are little inclined today to think of the *commentary* and *gloss* as having once been creative forms. Concerned as they are with terminological clarification, they seem to be quintessentially *non*creative. Agamben, however, sees other possibilities here—ones that he explores in *Idea of Prose*.

A Prisoner to Representations

Appropriately enough, the first of the "ideas" in *Idea of Prose* is "The Idea of Matter [*materia*]." Like the chapters to come, this one is brief and elliptical. It is composed of two paragraphs that treat seemingly distinct and unrelated themes: *language* and *death*. "For those who have had it," Agamben begins, "the decisive experience said to be so difficult to relate is not an experience at all. It is nothing other than the point at which we reach the limits of language" (IP, 37 [15], translation modified). As did *Infancy and History, Idea of Prose* thus opens with the question of *experience*. Instead of citing an "impoverishment," "decline," or "death" of experience seen in the light of the social and historical factors focused on in the earlier work, here the limits of experience are set by something else entirely: the limits of language. "There where language ends," writes Agamben, "is not where the unsayable [*indicibile*] begins, but rather the matter of language [*la materia della parola*]" (IP, 37 [15], translation modified). Two things named by the word *materia* are brought together in Agamben's expression: *matter* and *material*. *Matter* is meant here in the sense of both raw *material* and that which is at issue—the *matter* at hand. Agamben continues: "He who has never reached, as in a dream, that woodlike substance of language [*questa lignea sostanza della lingua*] that the ancients called *silva* remains, even when he is silent, a prisoner to representations" (IP, 37 [15], translation modified).[6] But what is this strange matter and how might it confine us to representations?

The second part of "The Idea of Matter" comes to a conclusion about *death* similar to the one the first part came to about *language*. As we saw earlier, he who *experiences* the limits of language (its "matter") ceases to be a prisoner to its representations. The second paragraph of this brief "idea," in a luminous recapitulation of the concerns of Agamben's previous book, turns from *language* to *death*. Those who have had near-death experiences, Agamben observes, were never truly dead, for if they had been they would never have been able to return. Nor, for that matter, are they liberated from the necessity of dying one day. "However," he writes, "they are freed from the representation of death" (IP, 37 [15], translation modified). In a bit of parabolic wisdom like much that follows in *Idea of Prose*, Agamben explains that "this is why, when asked about what happened to them, they have nothing to say about death, but they find, however, matter [*materia*] for many fascinating stories and fables about their life" (IP, 37 [15], translation modified). "The Idea of Matter" proves, then, to be about *potentiality*—the potentiality inhering in our language and that is the true matter of our lives. Aristotle remarks in *On the Soul* that "matter is potentiality," and it is this idea as much as any other that Agamben follows (412a17; Aristotle 1984, 656).

As we saw earlier, when asked to comment on his book Agamben spoke of an "authentic experience of language," of its connection to "knowledge," and of how the idea of prose that is found in much academic writing falsely separates these things. Among other things, *Idea of Prose* is then an attempt to avoid this separation. But how are we to view this unity of knowledge and language, and how are we to relate it to Agamben's ideas of prose and potentiality? In a preface written for the French translation of *Infancy and History* in 1989, Agamben offers something truly rare in his work: a *profession de foi*. "If for every author there exists a question which defines the *motivum* of his thought," he writes, "in both my written and unwritten books, I have stubbornly pursued only one train of thought: what is the meaning of 'there is language'; what is the meaning of 'I speak'?" (IH, 5 [x]).[7] This stubbornly pursued train of thought that moves through Agamben's writing is then given a name—a name that lends this preface its title: *experimentum linguae.*

What is this *experiment* or *experience* of language that Agamben evokes here? What is learned through such an *experiment* or gained from such an *experience* (both terms derive from the same Latin word, *experimentum*) of language?[8] Agamben defines *experimentum linguae* as an experience "in which what is experienced is language itself [*la lingua stessa*] . . . *without language experienced as this or that signifying proposition, but as the pure fact that one speaks, that language exists* [*del puro fatto che si parli, che vi sia linguaggio*]" (IH, 4–5 [ix–x], italics in original). As with what Benjamin enigmatically called "pure language [*reine Sprache*]," the question is how to understand—and "pursue"—a thought that seeks to inquire not into the meaning of specific propositions *in* language but instead into "the matter of language," into the "pure fact" that *there is language.* What is the nature of an experience "in which what is experienced is language itself"? What is to be understood in or experienced of a realm where, as Agamben describes it, "one can only encounter the pure exteriority of language [*la pura esteriorità della lingua*]" (IH, 6 [xi])? The only way to answer these questions is to look more closely at Agamben's ideas about the matter and experience of language and its relationship to his philosophy of potentiality.

It is against the background of this experience of language to which Agamben alludes that he isolates the *infancy* that played such a large role in the work he is looking back on eleven years later. "Infancy," writes Agamben in the same preface, "is an *experimentum linguae* of this kind—one in which the limits of language are sought not outside of language, in the direction of its referent, but in an experience of language as such [*un'esperienza di linguaggio come tale*], in its pure self-reference" (IH, 5 [x]). If this is the case, if this is the *infancy* in which Agamben is interested, the question remains as to how an experience of such a "pure exteriority of language" can lie at the outset of an inquiry, of how it can be its guiding thread rather than its endpoint. Phrased differently, how might such an experience constitute the *motivum* of his thought?[9]

The *profession de foi* quoted earlier is indeed something rare in Agamben's work, but it is not the only one of its kind. In a lecture given in Lisbon two years earlier he had offered another: "I could state the subject of my work as an attempt to understand the meaning of the verb *can* [*potere*]. What do I mean when I say 'I can, I cannot'?" (P, 177 [273]). The reader of these two *professions de foi* has ample reason to feel perplexed. Whereas in the French preface from 1989 Agamben declares that the question that has guided his work has been *What is the meaning of "there is language?" What is the meaning of "I speak"?* in the Lisbon lecture given two years earlier he claimed that "the subject of my work" is "an attempt to understand the verb *can.*" Does this divergence simply represent the most natural thing in the life of a philosopher: an evolution of interest? In other words, do the remarks represent a shifting of focus from a philosophy of *potentiality* to a philosophy of *language*? This would be a natural conclusion to draw were it not for Agamben's statement in a work from 1993 that philosophy, "in its deepest intuition," is "a construction of an experience of the possible as such" (P, 249). If this statement is not an evolution of concern, we might conclude that it is a contradiction born of a series of occasional essays. However, there also remains the possibility that we are confronted with something more complex: that these two *professions de foi* not only are compatible with one another, but complement one another. Might we not see these two driving questions behind Agamben's work—*What is the meaning of "I speak"?* and *What do I mean when I say "I can, I cannot"?*—as two expressions of a single question? More precisely, is it possible to understand the question *What is the meaning of "I speak"?* as a question about potentiality, as "an attempt to understand the verb *can*"? To do so would be to understand Agamben's infancy and the *experimentum linguae* he links with it as an experience of *pure potentiality*, and to do this would be to grasp the deep affinities between Agamben's idea of prose and his idea of knowledge.

Experimentum Linguae

Agamben's conception of philosophy—and of potentiality—is intimately linked not just to language, but to what he repeatedly calls an "experience of language." The question posed by Agamben's two *professions de foi* is, *What would it mean to see the two statements "I speak" and "I can" as expressing a single thing?* While to see human creativity as crystallized in even our most quotidian uses of language—what Wilhelm von Humboldt called "the infinite use of finite means"—is a provocative idea with a rich history stretching to present-day linguists such as Noam Chomsky, it is not, however, the one that Agamben is evoking here. We can see this in the fact that Agamben does not begin by evoking in his *experimentum linguae* a message of possibility ("I can") implied in every "I speak," but instead something more singular and strange. To attempt to answer the questions posed above, we must first understand what Agamben might mean by "the pure exteriority of language." This is not a common topic or term, but neither is it a totally isolated one. To the end of better understanding it, let us turn to a different *experimentum linguae*—that of another modern philosopher of language whose reflections developed from those of Heidegger and Benjamin and who, although he had no direct connection with Agamben, shares his idea of language to a remarkable extent: Paul de Man.

De Man's most famous as well as his most notorious attempt at effecting an experiment of the kind that Agamben describes is found in a talk on Benjamin's essay "The Task of the Translator" given at Cornell University in 1983. In this final period of de Man's work when he has abandoned the phenomenological dialectic of his earlier writing, he describes an experience of language reduced to something like its grammatical rudiments. In his efforts at deciphering what Benjamin called "pure language" he evokes an experience of language that is not an experience of this or that signifying proposition but, to borrow Agamben's formulation, of "the pure fact that one speaks, that language exists."

De Man states in this lecture that "Benjamin's language of pathos, language of historical pathos, language of the messianic, the pathos of exile and so on and so forth, really describes linguistic events which are by no means human. So that what he calls the pains of the original become structural deficiencies which are best analyzed in terms of the inhuman, dehumanized language of linguistics . . . one is impelled to read *reine Sprache* [pure language] as that which is the most sacred, which is the most divine, when in fact in Benjamin it means a language completely devoid of any kind of meaning function, *language which would be pure signifier, which would be completely devoid of any semantic function whatsoever*" (de Man 1986, 96–97, italics added). Speaking in "Reading and History" (contemporary to this lecture) of this same essay by Benjamin, de Man states that "the existential pathos [of Benjamin's text] is counterbalanced by the fact that these 'bottomless depths' of language are also its most manifest and ordinary grammatical dimensions" (de Man 1986, 62). What is for Benjamin couched in a language full of "messianic" experience is for de Man a radical experience of the privative, which he calls in this talk the "inhuman." Wishing to forestall misunderstanding, de Man says of this surprising figure that "the 'inhuman' is not some kind of mystery, or secret—it is linguistic structures, the play of linguistic tensions, linguistic events that occur, possibilities which are inherent in language—independently of any intent or any drive or any wish or any desire we might have" (1986, 96). It is clear that de Man would have found a more felicitous formula in a different privative construction, such as *a-human* or *nonhuman* (because the *inhuman* has become reserved for those things that are, in truth, all too human),[10] but this should not prevent us from trying to understand what he aimed to express through his impromptu expression (the talk is transcribed from a recording and, as de Man's spare notes indicate, he was speaking extemporaneously). What de Man is endeavoring to state here is what he sees as a tremendous expropriative force in language. In *Allegories of Reading* de Man writes, "We do not 'possess' language in the same way that we can be said to possess natural properties. It would be just as proper or improper to say that 'we' are a property of language as the reverse" (de Man 1979, 160). In the general sense that concerns us here, what this remark indicates is the common point that unites thinkers as diverse as de Man, Blanchot, Nancy, Derrida, Foucault, and Agamben, which is the inheritance of the Heideggerian dialectic of appropriation and propriety as a philosophical problem *concerning language*. It is in this light, then, that we can see that we would do better to understand the experience invoked by de Man under the sign of the *inhuman* as akin to what Paul Celan once referred to as "going beyond what is human, stepping to a real that is turned toward the human, but uncanny," and that is an experience of *language as such* (Celan 1986, 42–43; 1983, III.192; translation modified). Language is undoubtedly "turned toward the human," and this turning distinguishes man. In this sense, language is the last thing but inhuman, but it also does not remove that in language which is, while a "stepping to a real," "uncanny."

Despite the radical expropriative force conveyed by de Man's figure of the "inhuman," one finds another figure that expresses de Man's most personal *aporia* even more fully. In another of these late essays so often marked by a vertiginous concision, de Man states that "the bottom line, in Kant as well as Hegel, is *the prosaic materiality of the letter,* and no degree of obfuscation or ideology can transform this materiality into the phenomenal cognition of aesthetic judgment" (de Man 1996, 90, italics added). We are here confronted with an experience of "the pure exteriority of language" in the form of an experience of language's *materiality.* This materiality, which de Man elsewhere calls *inscription,* is language reduced to its graphic rudiments, materiality conceived as the materiality of an inscription. In short, it is an experience of language, to employ Agamben's description with which we began, "not as this or that signifying proposition, but as the pure fact that one speaks, that language exists." Like Agamben, de Man expresses, in another essay from this period, a desire for a greater concentration on such experiences among scholars, describing the "return to philology" for which he is calling as an "examination of the structures of language prior to the meaning it produces," thus conforming precisely to the experience described earlier—an experience of language "not as this or that signifying proposition" (de Man 1986, 24). Yet for de Man this experience of the "materiality" or matter of language is what blocks access to judgments of all sorts and prevents the certain and stable enunciation of presuppositions, propositions, and postulates that would form the bases for aesthetic and ethical precepts. This experience of the materiality of language, of language unveiled in all its chilling impersonality, removes, in de Man's final reflections, the epistemological foundations of language—and with it, those of aesthetics and ethics.

The Matter of Language

In Agamben's "The Idea of Matter" we find a passage that precisely mirrors this experience that de Man finds so devastating. "Where language ends," as we saw Agamben remark earlier, "is not where the unsayable begins, but rather the matter of language. He who has never reached, as in a dream, that woodlike substance of language that the ancients called *silva* remains, even when he is silent, a prisoner to representations." Here we are confronted with precisely the same experience of the materiality of language that we found in de Man—yet with a slight but decisive displacement.

For de Man, as with Agamben, where language "ends" it is indeed not the "unsayable" that begins but instead "the matter of language." What is more, whoever fails to conduct this radical *experimentum linguae* of "the matter of language" is destined to remain, for both thinkers, a "prisoner to representations," captive to the idea of an unsayable essence at the heart of language that one is consigned forever to strive after and never to reach. The two interpretations are thus identical in their essential coordinates. Agamben's essays "Language and History: Linguistic and Historical Categories in Benjamin's Thought" and "The Messiah and the Sovereign: The Problem of Law in Walter Benjamin" match de Man's in their lucid acceptance that Benjamin's concept of "pure language" sacrifices communication for communicativity—that "pure language" is a language that communicates no meaning other than itself and thus, in a sense, simply presents the matter of language. Both de Man's and Agamben's critiques of language, informed by experiences of the materiality of language akin to what Benjamin finds in translation—an experience of "the pure exteriority of language"—result in a recognition of the expropriative force of language. But it is at this point that the two critiques diverge.

In de Man's vision of language it is impossible to avoid becoming a "prisoner to representations" for any longer than the blink of an eye, and this experience of "the matter of language" marks, as we saw, the irrevocable endpoint or endgame of a reflection that must renounce any hope of offering a foundation for ethics or aesthetics. What lies beyond is only an endless cycle of forgetting and remembrance that de Man first finds in Nietzsche's speculations on language (most centrally his "On Truth and Lie in a Nonmoral Sense") and that offers neither issue nor hope. It is for this reason that this experience of the materiality of language is associated in de Man's late work with stuttering, loss, falling, failure, automatism, the "inhuman," and death.[11] Agamben's thinking on the *matter*—and the *potentiality*—of language proceeds differently. For him, this experience of language, this experience of what he calls elsewhere "the pure mediality of human communication," instead of engendering the disappearance of the human and the ethical in de Man's grammatical machinations of language, offers the foundation of an ethics and an aesthetics, transforming the *aporia* that "the matter of language" formed for de Man into a *euporia* (MWE, 117 [93]).

Before going farther, let us linger for a moment over this movement from *aporia* to *euporia,* from dead end to fortuitous outcome.[12] These terms of transition are themselves found in an essay by Agamben where, in discussing the role of terminology in the work of Derrida, he writes that "the aporias of self-reference . . . do not find their solution here; rather, they are dislocated and . . . transformed into *euporias*" (P, 217 (362), italics in original). To what does the "here" of this remark refer? It refers precisely to that which we have been considering—the *event of matter* or *experimentum linguae* (P, 217 [362]). This point is echoed in another context from these same years where Agamben writes that "not a hierarchy of types (like the one proposed by Russell that so irritated the young Wittgenstein) but only a theory of ideas is in a position to disentangle thought from the aporias of linguistic being (or better, to transform them into euporias)" (CC, 74 [60]). "The *experimentum linguae*," Agamben elaborates, "does not (as a common misunderstanding insists) authorize an interpretative practice directed toward the infinite deconstruction of a text, nor does it inaugurate a new formalism. Rather, *it marks the decisive event of matter, and in doing so opens onto an ethics*" (P, 219 [363], italics added). In *Remnants of Auschwitz,* Agamben writes, "Modern philosophy, which strips the transcendental subject of its anthropological and psychological attributes, reducing it to a pure 'I speak,' is not fully aware of the transformation this reduction effects with respect to the experience of language; it does not recognize the fact that language is thereby displaced onto an asemantic level [*un piano asemantico*] that can no longer be that of propositions" (RA 140 [130]). This "asemantic level" is none other than the matter of language, and on this level "without proposition" a new problem presents itself. It is clearly not enough simply to note the presence of such a dynamic reversibility, such a transition from *aporia* to *euporia.* We must also endeavor to understand how Agamben justifies the *possibility* of, the *potentiality* for, such a critical reversal. How is it then possible for an experience of language, an experience of the "matter of language" to "open onto an ethics"? As we saw earlier, Agamben fully recognizes the expropriative force of language—that which pulls statements loose from their epistemological foundation; and it is here, at last, that we can observe him effecting a slight but decisive displacement.

Ethics for Heretics, or On Eliminating
the Unsayable

In a talk from 1929 entitled "Lecture on Ethics" given at the invitation of the Heretics Society in Cambridge, Wittgenstein remarked, "I am tempted to say that the right expression in language for the miracle of the existence of the world, though it is not any proposition *in* language, is the existence of language itself" (Wittgenstein 1983, 43–44, italics in original). This conception of language and the formulation that Wittgenstein gave to it are important for Agamben.[13] This experience of "the miracle of the existence of the world," like the experiences of Agamben and de Man, is based on an experience of language—an experience of the mere fact that we speak rather than of an experience of something or other contained or expressed in a given statement or proposition.[14] In the closing words of this talk Wittgenstein states, "My whole tendency and I believe the tendency of all men who ever tried to write or talk Ethics or Religion was to run against the boundaries of language. *This running against the walls of our cage is perfectly, absolutely hopeless*" (1983, 44, italics added).

The displacement that Agamben effects in his theory of language—in his experiment on and experience of language—can be seen with particular clarity here. De Man's late work is in perfect agreement with Wittgenstein's assessment of the hopelessness of running up against the boundaries of language. Agamben, in his own fashion, concurs. Running up against the boundaries of language for Agamben, as for de Man and Wittgenstein, promises only disillusion and disappointment. The question lies in what else this lesson teaches and what other possibilities present themselves. What Agamben deduces is that resolving the aporias of language is not an option, that rendering all propositions transparent and unambiguous is impossible. But this is not tantamount to saying that only despair awaits those who proceed down this path. An escape from the prison of representations, from the aporias of language, will come not in the form of transparent language or unmediated truth but instead in our liberation from an idea of language's limits being like a cage, locking us in and closing us off from something better and brighter—some unsayable essence lying beyond our grasp.

As his idea of matter intimates, for Agamben the bars of such a cage are formed by precisely this idea of the *unsayable*. In a letter to Martin Buber from 1916, Benjamin wrote of his aspiration "to eliminate the unsayable from language" (Benjamin GB, 1.326).[15] This was obviously not to be done by pure poetic comprehensiveness—by saying all it was possible to say, leaving no subject taboo and no flower, leaf, or stone unnamed. Benjamin's youthful ambition is in fact not easy to grasp because the *unsayable* seems to be in no need of elimination—because it is already and by definition eliminated. What could we as speakers ever do to eliminate that which we could never hope to say in the first place? What Benjamin understands under the sign of this formula—"the crystalline and pure elimination of the unsayable in language"—is to eliminate from language something that in his view has no place there.[16] This was the idea that language bears in its folds something that for the moment remains unsayable but that, in a redemptive flash, could light up our darkness and remove all doubts, uncertainties, and enigmas from our world. The unsayable casts a shadow on the sayable, and this is what Benjamin—and in his wake, Agamben—wishes to eliminate.[17]

To *eliminate the unsayable* is thus to remove the idea of a secret hidden in language's folds, the idea of a blindingly full presence of thought, meaning, and being that our all-too-human language fails to reach. In the last lines of *Language and Death,* Agamben writes, "The *ethos,* humanity's own, is not something unspeakable or *sacer* that must remain unsaid in all praxis and human speech" (LD, 106 [133]). Benjamin wished to eliminate the unsayable precisely because it was unsayable. The means for effecting this—eliminating what was impossible to eliminate because it had never been present—lay in recognizing the idea of the unsayable for what it was: a mystification. In this conception, what hinders our efforts to understand our past and our present is the idea that the unsayable will somehow become sayable. In an essay published the same year as *Idea of Prose,* Agamben writes that "what is unsayable is not what language does not at all bear witness to but, rather, what language can only name" (P, 107 [151]). What Agamben thus seeks to demystify is the idea of some matter that lies beyond the limits of language and whose unsayable substance we might somehow reach. Although the analyses of de Man and Wittgenstein are, following Agamben's reasoning, perfectly correct in their coordinates, they stop one step short of their unrecognized goal. They make of the aporias of linguistic presupposition something unsayable—and thereby make a bondage of what should be a liberation. A more integral response to our language, following Agamben, would be to accept its limits and cease pining for an unsayable or sacred speech beyond the one we know. What one is left with after such an experience of, and experiment with, language is a vision of language as founded not on a transcendental presupposition, and not on the shifting forms of transitory presuppositions, but instead on what Agamben evocatively calls elsewhere in *Idea of Prose* "the innocence of language [*l'innocenza del linguaggio*]" (IP, 129 [117]). The innocence of language is this absence of presupposition experienced not as a lack or a loss but as, simply, our linguistic nature—as that which is truly common to all. This attitude is the one that Agamben will come to call a *profane* approach to language and life and that we will examine in more depth in this book's final chapter.

At the end of an essay entitled "Language," Heidegger remarks, "Nothing lies in advancing a new notion of language. Everything lies in learning to dwell in the speaking of language" (Heidegger GA, 12.30). What Agamben is advocating through his philosophy of language is perfectly in line with his former teacher's position and offers new means for its understanding. Agamben is not trying to offer a different vision of language than that with which other philosophers of language (such as de Man and Wittgenstein) operated. At issue for him instead is a different experience of the limits of language—in Heidegger's metaphorical register, a different way of *living* in language—and for this reason he places such stress on both the *experimental* and the *experiential* in his expression *experimentum linguae*.

In earlier chapters we saw Agamben's belief in the dynamic reversibility of desperate situations, and this belief is equally reflected here. In another chapter from *Idea of Prose*—"The Idea of the Last Judgment"—Agamben writes of how "the power of language must be turned back upon language itself. The eye must see its blind spot. The prison must imprison itself. Only then will the prisoners be able to leave" (IP, 99 [86], translation modified). This cryptic statement evokes not the traversing of language into some clearer empyrean of thought but the turning of the idea of the unsayable against language itself, because for Agamben what is truly unsayable is only language itself—that we have language. Once freed from the imprisoning idea of the unsayable, language need no longer seem to us a prison. We will be free to leave behind us an experience of language as negativity, punishment, curse, and constraint.[18] For Agamben, one is freer in a language that no longer bears a sphinx-like enigma in its hidden heart. It is for this reason that in *Idea of Prose* this same coming up against the limits of language is, in a poetic register, linked not, as in de Man, to figures of stuttering and silence but instead to the experience of nothing less than "inspiration" (IP, 60 [40]).

Such liberation has a political correlative that will slowly but surely move to the center of Agamben's thought. In a passage from his next book, *The Coming Community*—important here because it allows us to connect the earlier sociological reflections on language and experience of *Infancy and History* with the linguistic and ontological reflections of *Language and Death* and *Idea of Prose,* as well as with a spectrum of political paradigms that Agamben focuses on in such works as *Homo Sacer*—he writes, "Even more than economic necessity and technological development, what drives the nations of the earth toward a single common destiny is the alienation from linguistic being, the uprooting of all peoples from their vital dwelling in language [*dalla sua dimora vitale nella lingua*]" (CC, 83 [66]).[19] Here we have something that at first sight is highly enigmatic: a direct connection between an experience of linguistic alienation and an experience of political alienation. In the works and years to come, however, Agamben will strive to make precisely such connections, relating ontological and linguistic reflections to social and political problems.

With this widened perspective in mind, let us at last return to the question with which we began. In search of a first principle, Damascius' aporia becomes a *euporia* at the moment he realizes that what he had until then "believed he had been thinking of as the One, as the absolute Other of thought, was nothing other than the matter [*la materia*], the potentiality [*la potenza*] of thought" (IP, 34 [12], translation modified). Here we find *the matter of thought* in no respect opposed, but instead intimately and directly linked, to *the potentiality of thought.*[20] And it is here where "the matter of language" and "the potentiality of thought" converge so that we can at last answer the question posed at the outset of this chapter as to whether these two questions—What is the *matter of language?* and What is the *potentiality of thought?*—could be seen not only as compatible questions but also as the same question. The answer is *yes.*

The Idea of the Enigma

In its initial form in the first edition of *Idea of Prose,* "The Idea of the Enigma" begins, "We always and only are frightened by a single thing: the truth." This enigmatic declaration is followed by a qualification: "Or more precisely, the representation we form of it" (IP, 107 [96], translation modified). This "representation" we fear is not a given true thing that we might find horrible or unbearable (that we will die, for instance), nor is it the revelation of some individual fact or state of affairs that is terrifying or unbearable for our vision of ourselves (such as a truth about our past). The fear to which Agamben refers regards something more elusive: "the truth"—or more precisely, "the representation we form of it." This leads him to a fundamental conclusion: "The only true representation is one that also represents its distance from the truth" (IP, 107 [96], translation modified). Agamben's criterion for "the only true representation" is as reasonable as it is unfulfillable, and its corollary can be found in "The Idea of Truth" where Agamben refers to "the absence of any final object of knowledge" (IP, 56 [36]). An uncertainty principle applied to first philosophical principles is as impossible in practice as it is desirable in theory. We can indeed form representations of what we believe to be true, and we can conclude that our representations will never wholly coincide with what we believe to be the essence of that truth, but this is not something we can *represent*—at least not in any conventional manner.

"The Idea of the Enigma" is broken into numbered sections and the first of these ends with the remarks just cited. Without transition, as elsewhere in the book, the next section begins with another matter: an anecdote. It concerns the school referred to in the book's opening lines—Plato's Academy—and relates a lecture that the aging Plato is said to have given there. This lecture was eagerly anticipated by Plato's students because its title announced a revelation of the best and highest of all things and the expression of the very essence and heart of his philosophy: "The Good." At the appointed hour the auditors assembled, but what they heard was far from what they had expected. To the great consternation of an audience that was said to include Plato's brightest students and most ardent followers (including Aristotle), the master spoke not of the Good, the True, and the Beautiful but of *mathematics*—of numbers, lines, planes, and the movement of the stars. After a long examination of these technical matters, he offered a conclusion as brief as it was baffling: "the Good is the One" (see IP, 108 [96–97]).

Agamben lends a certain authority to this apocryphal incident. He does not attribute it to idle and unconfirmed gossip (that is, he does not say that it never happened), and he does not attribute it to mischief, bitterness, or senility on the part of the aging philosopher (that is, he does not say it happened but meant nothing for philosophy). Instead he sees the cryptic disjunction between title ("The Good") and content (mathematics) as absolutely central to what Plato had spent his life teaching. "In this fashion," Agamben writes, "Plato, who had always warned his students about the difficulties entailed in direct thematic treatment of problems, and who in his writings had willingly included fictions and stories, himself became for his students a myth and an enigma" (IP, 108 [96–97], translation modified). Following the subtle logic of *Idea of Prose,* this passage can be read as an indirect commentary on the indirect commentaries that make up the book. Just as Plato, father of the doctrine of ideas, announced that he would discuss "the Good" and then under that heading discussed mathematical procedures and principles without offering a thematic connection linking the two topics, Agamben's ideas purport to discuss one thing and proceed by discussing a seemingly unrelated matter.[21] The idea in question is that of representability, the same idea announced earlier where Agamben, discussing the first principles of Damascius, stated, "it is clear that that which is in question can never be thematized—not even as incomprehensible—and cannot be expressed even as inexpressible" (IP, 32–33 [10], translation modified).

Agamben claims that Plato's indirect methods served for his students as a "warning" against "thematic treatment" of questions. For Agamben, this approach is directly linked to a danger that Plato was well aware of: the danger of representations and the danger of the belief that a revelation will come that will be not a representation of a thing but rather the unmediated thing itself. This is the most fundamental and omnipresent idea in *Idea of Prose.*[22] Plato indeed appears to have seen a problem in direct thematic treatment of philosophical questions, and this was perhaps the reason he wrote not treatises offering such treatment of questions but instead dialogues that dramatized philosophical reflection. This was perhaps also the reason he did not shy away from including fictions such as the allegory of the cave or the myth of Atlantis in his works. It was in this sense too that the figure at the center of the dialogues, Socrates, claims to know nothing and to be a midwife for thought. Finally, it was perhaps for this reason that Aristotle said of Plato that he wrote neither in poetry nor in prose but, as Agamben recalls, in "their middle term" (see IP, 41 [21]).

This middle term was nothing other than an idea of prose, an idea that stressed the difficulty of expressing the nature of ideas, and the nature of things. In the book directly preceding *Idea of Prose,* Agamben had found in Heidegger, Hegel, Wittgenstein, and others what he called the "original connection of the problem of being with indication" (LD, 17 [25]). This expressed itself as "a fracture in the plane of language between showing and saying, indication and signification, that traverses the entire history of metaphysics and without which the ontological problem itself cannot be formulated" (LD, 18 [27], translation modified). Later in that work Agamben wrote that "perhaps neither poetry nor philosophy, neither *verse* nor *prose,* will ever be able to accomplish their millennial enterprise by themselves. Perhaps only a language in which the pure prose of philosophy would intervene at a certain point to break apart the verse of the poetic word, and in which the verse of poetry would intervene to bend the prose of philosophy into a ring, would be the true human language" (LD, 78 [98], italics in original). This remark allows us to follow the arc of investigation that leads from Agamben's focus on what divides philosophy from poetry in *Stanzas* to his focus on the limits and nature of our language in *Idea of Prose.* The problems of indication, signification, and representability that are directly treated in *Language and Death* are not different ones than those indirectly explored in *Idea of Prose.* In an essay on Plato published a year before *Idea of Prose,* Agamben claims that for Plato, "the thing itself is not a thing; it is the very sayability, the very openness at issue in language, which *is* language, and which, in language, we always presuppose and forget" (P, 35 [19], italics in original, translation modified).[23] In another essay published the same year entitled "The Idea of Language," Agamben interprets the concept of *revelation* in this light, claiming that "the meaning of revelation is that humans can reveal that which exists through language, but cannot reveal language itself" (P, 40 [26], translation modified). Agamben's enigmatic ideas—such as "The Idea of the Enigma"—are enigmatic for a clear reason—one having to do with language. The same is true even of his idea of the "idea." "The idea," he writes, "is not a word . . . nor is it a vision of an object outside language (there is no such object, no such unsayable thing); it is a *vision of language itself* " (P, 47 [35], italics in original). Agamben's ideas are meant, like Plato's emblematic lecture on "The Good," as a warning against direct "thematic treatment" of certain problems—particularly the most fundamental ones concerning the limits of language and life.

Benjamin once wrote that "a scholarly discipline that pretends to free itself from all that is esoteric is an illusion," and his writing bears witness to how true he remained to this maxim (Benjamin GS, 4.925). In the programmatic preface to his *Origin of German Tragic Drama,* Benjamin noted, "There is an esoteric element proper to philosophical method that it cannot discard or deny and that, were it to give way to, would destroy it" (Benjamin GS, 1.207). It is this idea more than any other that Agamben follows through such Benjaminian practices as the art of the fragment or the art of citing without quotation marks (which we will look at more closely in the first scholium to this chapter). Philosophical method customarily aims at the exoteric and the systematic, but for Benjamin as for Agamben, one of philosophy's most profound lessons—which is also a lesson about language—is that direct, exoteric, systematic treatment of ideas does not exhaust them. For this reason a special idea of representation and a special idea of prose are called for.[24]

To return to "The Idea of the Enigma," one of the few additions made to the text of the second Italian edition of *Idea of Prose* is a section placed at that chapter's outset. In it we find not only a statement of purpose for what was obliquely expressed in the other sections of this chapter, but also a statement of purpose for the book as a whole. "The most fundamental characteristic of the enigma," writes Agamben, "is that the expectation of mystery it gives rise to is in every case unavoidably disappointed for the reason that its solution consists precisely in showing that it was only in appearance an enigma" (IDP, 95). This is not because the enigma was a false enigma and might thereby be succeeded by a true one, but because a true enigma is insoluble. By definition its solution would reveal that it was not an enigma after all. Just as the reader enters *Idea of Prose* by traversing a "threshold"—the story of Damascius and his aporia—so too does he or she exit it. Unlike its predecessor, the threshold at the end of the work bears a title: "Kafka Defended Against His Interpreters." In light of the preceding, it should come as no surprise that the book nowhere names Kafka or any of his interpreters. It begins by noting that "the most diverse legends circulate about the inexplicable" (IP, 137 [127]). Agamben then tells a tale about "the current guardians of the Temple" (IP, 137 [127], translation modified). "The only content of the inexplicable—and in this lies the subtlety of the doctrine—consists in the command—truly inexplicable— 'Explain!' . . . Our illustrious fathers—the patriarchs—finding nothing to explain, searched their hearts for a way to express this mystery; but for the inexplicable they found no more fitting expression than explanation itself. The only way—they argued—to explain that there is nothing to explain is to give explanations. Any other stance, including silence, seizes on the inexplicable too clumsily: explanations alone leave it intact. . . . Emptied of their content, explanations thus fulfill their task. But at the point where explanations, by showing their emptiness, leave it be, the inexplicable itself is in jeopardy. Only the explanations were, in truth, inexplicable, and the legend was invented to explain them. What was not to be explained is perfectly contained in what no longer explains anything" (IP, 137–138 [127]).

Reaching the limits of language (the topic of the first section of "The Idea of Matter") or the limits of life (the topic of its second section) indicates for Agamben that the revelations we hope for can never come in the form of a message or a thing like other messages or things in our world. They can never present themselves as the discovery of this or that object or the hearing of this or that injunction. The idea here is that what occurs in revelatory experiences of whatever nature is never the revelation of this or that particular thing, which would be a thing like other things in the world, just as a vocation in the sense in which Agamben conceives it is never the vocation to do this or that single and particular thing. A true revelation is a revelation of possibilities, an opening of the field of possibility rather than its narrowing. It is, in other words, what Damascius saw unwritten on the wax tablet before him. What is revealed in such exceptional moments is that there is no final secret thing that we discover in this world. In an essay on Elsa Morante, Agamben discusses what she calls "the celebration of the hidden treasure" in her "*Canzone* of the Happy Few and Unhappy Many." Reading its closing lines, he comes to the conclusion that "the treasure is hidden not because someone or something buried or covered it over but because it is now exposed . . . in the absolute and despairing absence of all secrets" (EP, 108 [110]). This is something, however, to be *celebrated*—like Benjamin's idea of prose. Our state is—to choose a term to which Agamben increasingly turns in the books to follow—*profane*. This need not be experienced as an imprisonment, aporia, or loss, and on the contrary it can and should be viewed as an opportunity. Such realizations free us from waiting for a revelation and thereby leave the field of our activity open to new possibilities here and now.

In an essay on Benjamin written three years before the publication of *Idea of Prose*, Agamben cites the preparatory note for the *Theses on the Philosophy of History* in which Benjamin evokes his "idea of prose." Of an experience of language that would also be a "celebration" of it Benjamin says, "This is the idea of prose itself, which is understood by all humans just as the language of birds is understood by those born on Sunday" (Benjamin GS, 1.1239). Of this passage Agamben writes, "in a radiant abbreviation, Benjamin expressed therein one of his deepest intentions" (P, 49 [38], translation modified). This allows us to understand better why Agamben chose to title his book as he did. In this fragment Benjamin also writes that "the messianic world is the world of complete and integral actuality" (Benjamin GS, 1.1239; cited by Agamben in P, 48 [37]).[25] In such a world of "complete and integral actuality," Benjamin writes in another variant, "history is not written: it is celebrated as a festival. As a purified festival, however, it does not have the character of a ceremony and knows no hymns. Its language is a freed prose, a prose that has broken the chains of writing" (Benjamin GS, 1.1235). In this festivity without festival the division between sacred and profane no longer has any hold. It is without rite because there is nothing to divide sacred practice from profane life— from a life where all illuminations would be profane ones. Such a world no longer waits for any transcendental consecration or culmination, and what it celebrates it celebrates now. The language it employs is, from our perspective, an almost inconceivable one—a "freed prose" that has "broken the chains of writing."

In the meantime, there is study—but study conceived of in a new light. In one of the sections added to the second edition of *Idea of Prose,* "The Idea of Study," we read that "study is *per se* interminable. Whoever has spent long hours roaming among books when every fragment, every codex, every letter one comes across seems to open a new path, in turn quickly abandoned for a new encounter . . . knows not only that study can have no true end, but also that it desires none" (IDP, 45).[26] Agamben concludes, "This *festina lente*, this shuttling between bewilderment and lucidity, discovery and loss, passion and action is the rhythm of study" (IP, 64 [44], translation modified).

Scholium I: The Art of Citing
Without Quotation Marks

Like "The Idea of the Work" with which it begins, the *Idea of Prose* contains a number of images offering silent commentary on the surrounding material. The second Italian edition replaces some of these images and adds still others. Two of the most striking additions are images of Walter Benjamin. Neither is a photograph or drawing of the man himself—and neither, in fact, presents itself at first sight as having anything whatsoever to do with Benjamin. The first is a composite street map linking an outmoded Berlin with an equally dated Naples (see IDP, 65). In a radio interview, Agamben refers to experimenting with a scanner and linking "a lane in Berlin with a boulevard in Paris," as well as stressing to his interlocutors that Benjamin's description of Naples is among the finest ever written (see LDV). In linking these two crucial cities on Benjamin's intellectual itinerary, Agamben perhaps had in mind a passage from the *Berliner Chronik* in which Benjamin, writing to his son, noted that "for a long time—for years, in fact—I have toyed with the idea of representing the space of life—bios [*den Raum des Lebens—Bios*]—graphically, through the form of a map" (Benjamin GS, 6.466). The second of these images added to the later edition is the reproduction of a page of notes written on yellowed San Pellegrino stationary in Benjamin's cryptic and nearly illegible handwriting, recognizable not only by those who have seen Benjamin's difficult script, but also because it contains what appear to be drafts of Benjamin's essay "The Storyteller" (see IDP, 93).

These visual cues could not be more appropriate, for *Idea of Prose* owes a singular, if discreet, debt to Benjamin and to the variety of forms he explored in his work. As we saw earlier, *Idea of Prose*'s very title comes from a remark made by Benjamin in an unpublished fragment. Nowhere in the pages of *Idea of Prose* does Agamben note that his title is borrowed from Benjamin; this remark, however, seems to conform precisely to Benjamin's designs. It has not ceased to strike his readers that Benjamin had a singular relation to citation. He once wrote that the "craft of the critic" required a "theory of critical citation" (Benjamin GS, 6.171).[27] What does it mean to cite *critically*? To accompany his theory, Benjamin also developed a critical *practice* of citation. In his *One-Way Street,* he informed his readers that, "citations in my work are like armed thieves who emerge suddenly and rob leisurely strollers of their convictions" (Benjamin GS,

4.138). He thus uses citations strategically; they are part of the guerilla warfare he wages against the preconceived notions of his reader. In an essay on Karl Kraus, Benjamin singles him out for his diabolical skill in citation, and for his ability to make citations at once "save and punish" (Benjamin GS, 2.363ff.). But it is in a fragment from his *Arcades Project* that Benjamin makes his most puzzling claims about citation. There he stresses the necessity of cultivating "the art of citing without quotation marks" (Benjamin GS, 5.572).

There can be little doubt that for Benjamin "the art of citing without quotation marks" was a provocative formula with a provocative intent. There was an unquestionable measure of subversion in it, similar to that which Benjamin saw in surrealist *montage,* which in turn would inform the citational *détournement* of the Lettrists and Situationists. But appearances notwithstanding, it was not an apology for plagiarism or false citation, and even less was it a plea for philological laziness, an anarchic call for the death of the author or the termination of an author-function. Although Benjamin offers no further explanation of what he envisioned under the heading of this special art, it clearly involved a reconceptualization of *context* and *authority,* and has much in common with Agamben's diagnosis of contemporary academic prose as perfunctory and as having distanced itself from an authentic experience of language and its limits. Quoting an author or authority on a matter is a way of paying respect to their originality; but as Benjamin well knew and often observed, citing authorities can just as often be used to end a debate as to begin one.[28] To cite without quotation marks is to offer the idea without the imprimatur of an author or authority. This requires of the idea that it stand or fall on its own merits and not find automatic support from its lineage. Elsewhere in *The Arcades Project,* Benjamin compares citational footnotes to bills slipped under the garters of women for hire. His sensitivity to the less reputable sides of citation was particularly keen, and "the art of citing without quotation marks" was, for him, to be practiced in the name of a purer citation—one that could both "save" and "punish."

One of the ironies of the critical adulation with which Benjamin's works were belatedly met is how often he is cited as an authority. A reviewer of one of Agamben's more recent books claimed that "Agamben does not speak for himself, but is an imitator of voices [*Ein Stimmenimitator*] . . . every third remark of his in this volume is a more or less free parody of one from Walter Benjamin" (Kaube 2005, 41).[29] This remark shows a sensitivity to Agamben's sources but misses something fundamental about how they are used. Agamben's method of engaging with Benjamin is unique and complex, but it is not parodic. More than any other thinker of his generation, Agamben has taken seriously Benjamin's idea of citation without quotation marks. Not only did he dedicate a section of *The Time That Remains* to discussing the motives behind this singular art, but he has often practiced it himself—and nowhere more than in *Idea of Prose* (see TTR, 138ff. [128ff.]).

Scholium II: The Idea of Benjamin

Just as *Idea of Prose* can be divided into an *exoteric* and an *esoteric* content, so too can Agamben's passionate engagement with Benjamin. We saw earlier the absolutely decisive influence that Benjamin exercised on Agamben. This *exoteric* content is found in Agamben's philological work on Benjamin and has taken the most varied forms. As noted earlier, Agamben is not only one of Benjamin's most knowledgeable and insightful commentators, he also served for many years as editor of the Italian edition of Benjamin's complete works.[30] Beyond managing critical and editorial affairs, Agamben conducted the remarkable detective work of unearthing hitherto lost texts. As has often been noted, Benjamin's final works were subject to great travails on their way to print. The manuscripts and other materials that Benjamin left in his Paris apartment when he fled the city were confiscated by the German occupying force and then, through a curious error, filed with the archives of the *Pariser Tageszeitung*. In February 1945 the Gestapo ordered the destruction of this archive, but the workers sabotaged this attempt, thereby saving these materials (along with Benjamin's) from destruction (see Scholem 1983, 186ff.; Benjamin GS, 7.525). These archives were taken by the Russians and kept for fifteen years before being returned to Germany in 1960 and placed in a German Democratic Republic archive, first in Potsdam and then in Berlin. Only in 1983 and 1984 was access granted to scholars.

This was not, however, the only surprising discovery of its sort. A second recovery of lost material came about through Agamben's finding in the *Bibliothèque Nationale* an important set of papers that Benjamin had entrusted to Georges Bataille and that had gone missing, presumably separated from the papers that an aging Bataille helped Pierre Missac to find in order to send them to Adorno in America. Bataille believed that all of the papers Benjamin had left with him had been recovered, but Agamben's detailed study of the correspondence gave rise to doubts on this matter, and after a month of searching through the archives he at last discovered the missing manuscripts and papers in 1981.[31] These papers were not Agamben's only find. He also discovered typescripts saved by Benjamin's friend Herbert Belmore-Blumenthal in 1977; these remain in Agamben's possession, as does a *Handexemplar* of Benjamin's *Theses on the Philosophy of History*, "the origin of which," note the piqued editors of

Benjamin's complete works, "the person in possession of them [Agamben] guards in silence" (Benjamin GS, 7.526).[32]

Alongside this astonishing philological fieldwork (considering how many other detectives were on the case), Agamben has made important corrections to certain of Benjamin's texts already in print. The most remarkable of these concern a single letter each. One of them is found in *State of Exception*, where he shows that the German editors' emendation of the phrase *Es gibt eine barocke Eschatologie* ("there is a Baroque eschatology") to its opposite, *Es gibt keine barocke Eschatologie* ("there is no baroque eschatology"), was perfectly illegitimate and was an overhasty reaction to their inability to follow the difficult argument that Benjamin was making (see SE, 56 [73]). This philological attentiveness is on even more impressive display in *The Time That Remains* where, in glossing the suspension of the divisions that separate men (such as Jew / Gentile, circumcised / uncircumcised, married / single, and so forth), Agamben directs his reader's attention to a curious passage in the *Arcades Project* where Benjamin employs a singular metaphor for the division between what came before and what came after a given historical event. He describes it as being "like a line divided by the Apollonian incision [*wie eine Strecke, die nach dem apoll(i)nishcen Schnitt geteilt wird*]" (Benjamin GS, 5.588). Agamben points out that this comparison, as it stands in the German critical edition of Benjamin's works, makes no sense, for nowhere in Greek mythology is there reference to an "Apollonian incision." Benjamin's handwriting was notoriously difficult to decipher (to which any reader of facsimiles of Benjamin's manuscripts can attest). After examining the manuscript, Agamben suggested that although the illegible *i* is in fact an illegible *i,* the half-legible *o* is a half-legible *e.* Benjamin was not referring to the god Apollo—known for no notable division or cut—but to the painter Apelles (see TTR, 50 [52]). Agamben recalls Pliny the Elder's account of how Apelles paid a visit to fellow painter Protogenes and, on this occasion displaying the height of his painterly art, divided in two an incredibly fine line drawn by Protogenes—a discovery he used, as we will see later, to elucidate a matter lying at the center of Benjamin's—and his own—thought.[33]

In addition to providing these philological services both before and after *Idea of Prose*, Agamben has written and published erudite and insightful studies of specific questions and problems in Benjamin's works, such as "Walter Benjamin and the Demonic: Happiness and Historical

Redemption" and "Language and History: Linguistic and Historical Categories in Benjamin's Thought" (both collected in *Potentialities*). He has focused his exegeses on those conceptions that have been most resistant to understanding, such as the relationship of the historical to the linguistic, as well as such terms as the *messianic* and the *dialectical image*, and has employed classical philological argumentation to make his claims.[34] However, it is not only in the traditional modes of annotation, commentary, criticism, correction, and philological discovery that Agamben has engaged with Benjamin's thought. Alongside this *exoteric* engagement there is an equally important *esoteric* one in his works, and it is this engagement that is on such striking display in *Idea of Prose*.

Scholium III: Reading What Was Never Written

One of the strangest expressions in Agamben's writing is "reading what was never written" (see, for instance, P, 58 [50], and P, 158 [233]). Its strangeness stems from Walter Benjamin, who, although he was not its author, repeatedly employed it in the notes for his *Arcades Project*.[35] In the most revealing of his uses of the phrase, Benjamin writes that the "true historian" is he or she who reads "what has never been written" in "the book of life" (Benjamin GS, 1.1238). What task does Benjamin confide to the "true historian," and why is Agamben so interested in it? Do both men mean merely the effort to read between the lines, to read the subtext of texts—or is there something more they are seeking to express through this paradoxical injunction?

In *The End of Thought* Agamben writes, "We speak with the voice we do not have, and which has never been written," and although the citation from Benjamin is without quotation marks, Agamben does direct his reader to a source: "*Antigone*, 454" (FP, 5). When we turn to this passage we find Antigone saying to Creon, "I did not think anything which you proclaimed strong enough to let a mortal override the gods and their unwritten and unchanging laws" (*Antigone*, 454). However pivotal a moment this may be in the play, the reading of these unwritten and unchanging divine laws (as opposed to the changing mortal ones that Creon represents) does not seem to correspond to what Agamben has evoked elsewhere with this formula, concerned as it is with the divide between the mortal and the divine, and between private and public obligations. Elsewhere Agamben employs Benjamin's enigmatic phrase to speak of Aby Warburg's analyses of the frescoes in the Schifanoia palace as "reading what was never written" in those images (N, 67). As Agamben makes clear, Warburg is not reading into those images something not already present in them. He is instead looking and reading with more attention and erudition than anyone had in centuries, and is thereby able to solve the iconographic riddle the images had long posed. But when we turn from Warburg's pathbreaking iconographical study back to Agamben we see something more than merely insightful reading. In glossing what Warburg called the "dynamograms"—literally, signs charged with potentiality—found in those frescoes, Agamben says, "The heavenly constellations are, in this sense, the original text in which the imagination reads that which was never written" (N, 67). What, then, does this curious form of "reading" denote? Does it simply refer to laws unwritten because they belong not to the sphere of the *polis* (what Creon represents) but to the *oikos* (the unwritten laws of family honor and obligation that Antigone followed)? Is it reading in the extended sense that Benjamin might have given to his interest in occult pursuits such as astrology and graphology, and to his experiments with hashish and opium, whereby he tried to "read" that which was never written because it involves reading that which is inexpressible in language?

One answer is that Benjamin—and in his wake, Agamben—is aspiring to read not just words but, improbably enough, *gestures*. In the famously dense "On the Mimetic Capacity," Benjamin speaks of the translation of the mimetic capacity from the realm of dance, astrology, and the examination of the entrails of sacrificial animals—realms directly experienced through the senses—to what he calls the *insensible* realm of writing, which constitutes what he calls "the fullest archive of nonsensuous resemblance" (Benjamin GS, 2.213). Benjamin says of this "reading of what was never written" that "this reading is the oldest: the reading before all languages [*das Lesen vor aller Sprache*]" (Benjamin GS, 2.213). This oldest reading is not then a reading of a content communicated in language, but something much closer to a reading of the communicativity of language itself. The "reading before all language" is then "the reading of that which was never written" in that what has never been written and yet is read is precisely what cannot be written, or said, in language.

The answer to the question posed earlier as to what kind of reading Benjamin is invoking is then both simple and complex. To begin with, it is indeed not "reading" in any literal sense, but instead a form of thinking— a thinking about *potentiality*. To express this most fundamental problem, the "supreme theme of metaphysics," Aristotle evoked his wax tablet on which nothing had (yet) been written. Benjamin's enigmatic phrase—and in his wake, Agamben's citations of it—offers a paraphrase of Aristotle's image. To read what was never written is a way of reading the potentiality inhering in thought and life. Such images as Aristotle's wax tablet and such formulae as Benjamin's "reading what was never written" reflect how our thinking about potentiality is conditioned by actual circumstances. Of necessity we think of potentiality through some form of actuality, and this applies as well to reading as it does to other activities. But reading is always more than the mere processing of a page—the stocking, storing, and filing of units of fact or fiction. When we read, we assimilate both the actuality on the page in front of us and something more—what we ourselves bring to the reading table, the most general name of which is the potentiality of thought. To read what has never been written is thus to read in a creative fashion—the only sort of reading that, for Agamben, is truly worth our while.

Scholium IV: The Storyteller

One of the groups of Benjamin's manuscripts that Agamben recovered is notes for his famous essay "The Storyteller." Given the sort of book that *Idea of Prose* is, it should come as little surprise that Agamben chose to reproduce a page of those notes in it (see IDP, 93). This inclusion is apt not only because of the book's intimate connection to a number of ideas from Benjamin's works, but also because of the storytelling element that is at the fore of the work.

Of *Idea of Prose* Agamben later remarked, "I tried to resuscitate the resources of what Jolles called 'simple forms': the apology, the aphorism, the anecdote, the enigma, the fable" (UIGA, 32). What these short and simple forms have in common is their *narrative* element, and this is an element that Agamben employed with new energy in *Idea of Prose,* and that has remained a fundamental aspect of his writing in the years since. Agamben began an essay composed during the same period as *Idea of Prose* as follows: "During the winter of 1945, in the region of Nag-Hammadi (High Egypt), thirteen papyrus codices were fortuitously found by a group of fellahin, buried in the sand in an earthenware jar. The codices had belonged to a Gnostic library, transcribed in Coptic, which dated back to about the middle of the fourth century A.D. It was night, the fellahin, tired, sat down to rest. Suddenly the air grew colder, as happens in these regions. The fellahin tore the pages of three of these codices, covered with incomprehensible characters, and burnt them in order to heat water for their tea. . . . Passing from hand to hand, both the ten surviving codices and the fragments of the other three ended up on the desk of Togo Mina, director of the Coptic Museum in Cairo . . . " (AF, 1). The subsequent fate of these scrolls is well known, but of special interest for grasping the forms employed in *Idea of Prose* is the storytelling form that Agamben adopts here.

This is by no means a passing interest either in "simple forms" or in narrative approaches, and indeed many essays from these years could be added to the list of examples. Fifteen years later, *The Time That Remains* included a section on the proper understanding of *gossip* (as concerns the legends that have been handed down about the life of Paul); and the book that follows it, *The Open: Man and Animal,* begins in a distinctly narrative key: "In Milan's *Biblioteca Ambrosiana* there is to be found a copy of a Hebrew Bible dating from the thirteenth century and containing precious miniatures . . . " (O, 1 [9], translation modified). Still more recently, Agamben's essay "Nymphae" is dedicated to exploring Warburg's conception of the image but includes numerous narrative asides, such as the curious story of the idiosyncratic autodidact artist Henry Darger, related with such details as Darger's Chicago address and the precise date when his landlord entered his apartment and discovered the fantastical works he had left behind. Further instances would only belabor the point, but understanding Agamben's idea of prose, which is also his idea of a creative criticism envisioned in *Stanzas,* requires that his reader attend to these simple forms and the narratives that accompany them.

CHAPTER FIVE

From Spectacle to Shekinah:
The Coming Community

Asked in an interview following the publication of *Idea of Prose* whether there was a connection between his reflections on language and those on politics Agamben replied, "Yes, a powerful connection," and the reason he gave was as simple as it was sweeping: because "language is the common element that links all mankind" (UIGA, 33). It is this idea of a common element that links the works from *The Man Without Content* through *Idea of Prose* to the more explicitly political reflections of Agamben's next book, *The Coming Community*, and those, such as *Homo Sacer*, that will follow it.

Although it begins a new arc of political reflection, in both form and content, *The Coming Community* closely resembles the work that preceded it. The academic apparatus of Agamben's first four books (*The Man Without Content, Stanzas, Infancy and History*, and *Language and Death*)—their footnotes, bibliographical references, and explicit links between sections—are abandoned in favor of a more concentrated and fragmentary idea of prose.[1] There is, however, a fundamental difference between the two books. In subtle and indirect fashion, *Idea of Prose* illustrated something that only subtlety and indirection could illustrate: how easily direct thematic treatment of questions can miss their point, and how expectations of revelation can mislead us in our representations of first and final things. Whereas the earlier work offered "ideas," the later one offers something that Agamben will call, in this work and those to come, *paradigms*—and which will spark such controversy in *Homo*

Sacer and *Remnants of Auschwitz*. As Agamben reminds his reader in *The Coming Community,* the term *paradigm* simply means "example." Yet as he shows in both this work and later ones, exemplarity is never a simple matter. Of what, then, are the individual sections of his sixth book *examples* or *paradigms?* The answer is given in the work's title: *the coming community.*

The Idea of Community

The Coming Community was published in 1990 and thus in the immediate aftermath of the fall of the Berlin Wall. Unsurprisingly, its reflections on *community* are closely linked—to borrow a chapter title from Agamben's preceding book—to "The Idea of Communism." But *The Coming Community* is a response not merely to the geopolitical events of its day, but also to the continuation of a debate on the idea of community. At the center of this debate were the communal conceptions and experiences of Georges Bataille. In 1983, Agamben's friend Jean-Luc Nancy published an essay on those conceptions and experiences with a title borrowed from Bataille: "The Inoperative Community." That same year, Maurice Blanchot published a book-length response to Nancy's essay entitled *The Inavowable Community.* Blanchot's book bore an epigraph from Bataille—"The community of those who have no community"—and, taken alongside his title, it seemed to make a clear statement. The point of Blanchot's speculations was not to disavow the idea of community, but instead to find new forms for it.

Blanchot's *The Inavowable Community* sought to form a new idea of community by negating all those things that had hitherto been given as organizing principles for communities. The idea of community appears, at first sight, perfectly innocent, focused as it is on a commonality of experience and dedicated to bringing about the common goal of a common good. But Blanchot recalls for his readers the ideological uses to which it has been put and the catastrophic results that have ensued. To conceive of a new community that could take up the communist flag where it had been abandoned involved, for him, exploring "the apparently healthy [*saine*] origin of the most noxious [*malsain*] totalitarianism" (Blanchot 1983, 11).

Blanchot saw his departed friend Bataille's tortuous reflections on community—filled as they were with such qualifications as "negative," "impossible," "inoperative," and "inavowable"—as so important because they carried the clarity of desperation. In Bataille's wake, Blanchot aspired to sketch an idea of a community that would not be subject to being co-opted by totalitarian forces. It had seemed to Bataille that the only community that would be immune to this danger would be a community that offered no criteria for exclusion whatsoever. No criteria for exclusion meant, of course, no criteria for *in*clusion either, and here is where the difficulty and the strangeness of the project first became apparent. Whatever form it might take, it was clear that such a community could have no set requirements and no conditions for belonging.

Blanchot's book did not spell the end of this discussion, and three years later, in 1986, Nancy published an expansion of his earlier ideas on the question (in a book employing the same title as his initial essay, *The Inoperative Community*). As had Blanchot, Nancy chose not to focus on concrete analyses of individual communities in crisis—such as communist ones—in favor of attending to a global crisis in the very idea of community. The reigning Western conception of community seemed to Nancy able only to express itself as inexpressible (the inavowable community) or to display itself as dysfunctional (the inoperative community), and for this reason was in desperate need of reformulation. As had been his initial essay, Nancy's book was both diagnostic and deconstructive. In the most culturally prevalent ideas of community he found a pervasive nostalgia for a lost "original community" of one sort or another whose outline he endeavored to trace—and to deconstruct. "The lost or broken community," he wrote, "can be exemplified in all kinds of ways and by all kinds of paradigms: the natural family, the Athenian city, the Roman Republic, the first Christian community, corporations, communes, brotherhoods— it is always a matter of a lost age in which community was tightly woven and held together by harmonious bonds . . . born of of its own immanent unity, intimacy and autonomy" (Nancy 1991, 9). This nostalgic idea of an original community was, for Nancy, best expressed through a foreign term—the German word *Gemeinschaft,* with its focus on commonality of meaning and action. Opposed to this idea of community was what Nancy saw himself living in—a *Gesellschaft,* a "society" with its daily alienations and its gradual loss of common norms, values, and meaning.

The response that Nancy offered to contemporary society's alienated idea of community was an injunction to be wary of appeals to a lost "original community"—"whether this . . . is effectively retrospective or whether, disregarding the realities of the past, it constructs images of this past for the sake of an ideal or prospective vision" (Nancy 1991, 10). Such promised returns to an "original community," he was careful to stress, were most often made in the name of consolidating state power and neutralizing political dissent. Nancy also noted that this was not merely a modern problem. "We should be suspicious of this consciousness," he wrote, "because it seems to have accompanied the Western world from its very beginnings; at every moment in history, the Occident has rendered itself vulnerable to the nostalgia for a more archaic community that has disappeared" (Nancy 1991, 10). The political consequences of this nostalgia are, as Nancy is careful to point out, anything but negligible. Modern history is rich in cases where an appeal to an "original," "untainted," "integral," and fully "unified" community has been put to the darkest of ends— that same "apparently healthy origin of the most noxious totalitarianism" evoked by Blanchot. It is this part of our communities—a shared longing for a "lost" purity—that totalitarian political movements have used as a rationale for violently purging and purifying the body politic. For Nancy, as for Blanchot, our reigning Western conceptions of community are in need of fundamental revision because of how intimately they have become linked to ideas of national, racial, or religious unity and purity. If the idea of community, and a corresponding idea of communism, is to survive its present crisis, for both Blanchot and Nancy it is only on the condition that it discover new means for discussing what communities have in common.

It is against the backdrop formed by this debate that Agamben published his less despondently titled *The Coming Community*.[2] To a significant extent his starting point was the same as that of Blanchot and Nancy—just as it would be for works that appeared soon after it, such as Benedict Anderson's *Imagined Communities* (1993) and Derrida's *The Politics of Friendship* (1994). All of these thinkers began by noting that communities have always had criteria for belonging and have always organized themselves around these criteria—whether national, geographical, racial, religious, or other. Even when the conditions of belonging have been liberally formulated and flexibly interpreted, the result has nonetheless routinely involved exclusion and isolation, and sooner or later the purity of identity and the protection of real or symbolic resources has become a subject of violent contention. In the face of these facts, all these thinkers strove to formulate an idea of community that would be immune to hostile takeover, and all ran up against the theoretical and practical problem posed by a community without criteria for belonging.

Do all communities not need, if not a common enemy, at least a unifying point and a rallying cry so as to bond together as a community? Both Blanchot and Nancy—calling on the Heideggerian philosopheme *Mitsein* [being-together]—evoke a community that has in common "a possibility to *be together* [*une possibilité* d'être-ensemble]" (Blanchot 1983, 52, italics in original). This open and difficult-to-define being together would remain at the center of Nancy's reflections—most prominently in his *Being Singular Plural* (1996)—but would also remain exceptionally difficult to formulate in concrete terms. Is it possible to conceive of a community whose members share nothing but being? And if so, how does one form such a commonality? Like Blanchot and Nancy, Agamben proved equally interested in such a "being together," but he approached the question by a series of surprising routes.

Bataille's reflections on radical change in the idea of community were intimately linked to his ideas on Hegel's dialectic, and it should come as no surprise that Blanchot, Nancy, and Derrida also followed this fundamental thread. According to all three, Hegel replied to the communal question of the relation of individual part to political whole with the dialectic. Succeeding generations of philosophers, from Kierkegaard to the present, saw Hegel's conception of the relation of particular to universal, part to whole, as the hallmark of his genius and as a feat of philosophical brilliance that it seemed impossible to surpass—or escape from. In a poem written during his youth, Hegel proclaimed, "Let us throw the singularity into the fire!" For him, the role of negation was essential to the movement of his dialectic, and what was at once negated and subsumed in a larger unity was the singularity. Hegel's conception of negation was—as Agamben had illustrated in his fourth book, *Language and Death*, the subtitle of which was *The Place of Negativity*—as far as possible from a simple or static one. In Hegel's dialectic, the particularity—whether it be the instant in time that Agamben analyzed in *Infancy in History*, or an individual in society whom he would follow in *The Coming Community*—is at once "negated" and "sublated"—*aufgehoben*, to use Hegel's central expression. The part or particular is literally raised up as an example (*aufheben* means literally "to lift up") as well as suspended or annulled (the figurative meaning of *aufheben*). In this perspective, the exemplary part is of interest through and thanks to the whole it exemplifies. Throwing the singularity into the fire was, for Hegel, to live from the warmth of its transformation into something greater: universality. Hegel saw absolute particularity and absolute universality as perfectly compatible, and as mirroring one another. Although some indeed saw his dialectic as offering a way to conceive of what would otherwise be incoherent—the particular or singular—others saw in it something dangerous. Adorno, a perceptive and polemical reader of Hegel, wrote that "with cold-blooded decisiveness Hegel opted . . . for the liquidation of the singular [*die Liquidation des Besonderen*]," with the result that "nowhere in his thinking is the primacy of the whole over the part truly put into question" (Adorno GS, 4.15).For Adorno, this indictment of Hegel's metaphysics was also an indictment of his political theory. In his *Negative Dialectics* Adorno proclaimed that "a true preponderance of the particular would not be attainable except by changing the universal" (Adorno 1973, 313). It is at this point of philosophical convergence—where the particular and the universal would be "changed"—that Agamben begins *The Coming Community.*

For Agamben, the debate about the idea of community was at the same time a debate about ethics.[3] An ethics worthy of the name must strive to conceive how mankind might live together, how it might live in a community of common goals, aspirations, and conceptions that would not degenerate, as has so often been the case, into scenes of exclusion and violence. "There can be no true human community," wrote Agamben in an essay from 1984 that echoes remarks made by Blanchot and Nancy, "on the basis of a presupposition—be it a nation, a language, or even the a priori of communication of which hermeneutics speaks" (P, 47 [35]). It is this fundamental idea that became his focus six years later in *The Coming Community.* The goal that Agamben does not shy away from envisioning is the same one that Adorno had named—that of changing the relation of particular to universal—and the boldness with which he approaches the question distinguishes his writings on community from those that came before it. Although Agamben is not alone in facing an aporia in the idea of community, his *euporia*—his way out of this impasse—is truly unique.

Whatever

Given the preceding, it is not surprising that Agamben begins *The Coming Community* with the relationship of the singularity to the universal; but what is surprising is the unlikely term he employs: *whatever*. This indifferent-sounding word is taken not from teenage slang but instead from the austere vocabulary of scholastic philosophy, by translating the Latin *quodlibet*. "The Whatever [*Qualunque*] in question here," Agamben writes, "relates to singularity not in its indifference with respect to a common property (to a concept, for example: being red, being French, being Muslim), but only in its being *such as it is*" (CC, 1 [9], italics in original). The *whatever* with which Agamben thus begins is not indifference seen from the point of view of the universal, where all particularities are of indifferent importance with respect to the universal that gives them their meaning (the idea being that only universals provide us with the means of understanding particular cases, and without them we would find ourselves lost amid a world of nameless singularities). What Agamben uses this curious term to envision is instead singularity seen from an unfamiliar side—that of the singular. This would be the singularity seen as singularity or, in Agamben's deceptively simple formulation, "as it is." This is an idea of singularity not of indifferent importance but, on the contrary, conceived of in all its rich difference from other singularities—whatever they may be.

To truly think of something "as it is" represents, however, a daunting conceptual challenge, and it is to this challenge that Agamben replies in the pages that follow. It entails, as Agamben is quick to stress, not merely thinking of the singularity in terms of its predicates or properties—such as "being red," "being French," "being Muslim"—but to see beyond them so as to grasp the singularity itself. This is an eminently reasonable goal, for singularities are indeed always more than the sum of their abstract predicates. To think of a thing independent of, for instance, three of its most obvious predicates (such as "red," "French," and "Muslim") is not particularly difficult, but to think of it independent of any and all predicates is another matter. This conceptual difficulty is mirrored by a linguistic one. We may perceive the world in all of its rich and individual singularity, but to express it as such is another matter for the reason that our language is made of and from generalities. Agamben claims that when a singularity is conceived of not merely as a function of its predicates, "singularity is . . . freed from the false dilemma that obliges knowledge to choose between the ineffability of the individual and the intelligibility of the universal" (CC, 1 [9]). That a singularity would be caught between *ineffability* and *intelligibility* is easy to understand. A singularity is *ineffable* because what is singular about it is not shared with anything else—and for this reason it is nameless. It can become *intelligible* only by virtue of its parts and predicates. Although this idea is clear enough, why Agamben claims that it represents, in fact, "a false dilemma" remains open.

Singular Examples

Agamben's search to conceive of and express a singularity through a medium—language—whose essence is generality leads him from the scholastic *whatever* (*quodlibet*) to an at once extraordinary and everyday figure: that of the *example*. *The Coming Community* argues for the necessity of reconceptualizing the singularity and the need to find *paradigms*—exemplary figures and forms—through which to conceive a new relationship between part and whole, individuality and community, particularity and universality. "One concept that escapes the antinomy of the universal and the particular," Agamben writes, "has long been familiar to us: the example" (CC, 9 [13]). The *example* represents a way out of this antinomy because it is neither a singularity nor a universal. It is at once set apart as an example—a singularly representative instance—as well as included as an integral part of that of which it is an example. In this it belongs to both spheres and, for Agamben, offers a paradigm for envisioning a different relationship of particular to universal.

In a decisive step that will not only guide Agamben's thinking in this book but also provide the concealed link between it and his reflections on *the state of exception* in his next one, he argues that we should conceive of *singularities* precisely as we conceive of *examples*.[4] When envisioned after the fashion of an example, the singularity is no longer trapped in a dilemma forcing us to choose between ineffability and intelligibility. Instead of the dialectical opposition of particularity and universality, Agamben offers, via the figure of the example, a nondialectical relation in which the singularity or example is at once a member of, and excluded from, the set of things it exemplifies. *Examples* occupy a seemingly paradoxical relation to universality and particularity, but this does not prevent us from using them—and it is for this reason that Agamben suggests that "examples" are "exemplars [*gli esemplari*] of the coming community" (CC, 11 [14]). They are, however, not the only ones.

In the pages that follow, the *Coming Community* continues its search for *exemplars* or *paradigms* of this coming community. The remarkable breadth of Agamben's interests as well as his commitment to what he called in *Stanzas* "a discipline of interdisciplinarity" leads him far afield. He will draw not only from scholastic terminology but also from such disparate fields as linguistics, logic, set theory, theology, literature, and philosophy. He will turn from the fictional figures of Swiss writer Robert Walser to the real events in Tiananmen Square, from "tricksters" and "fakes" to the theological conundrums presented by the resurrected bodies of cannibals and the fate of children who die before being baptized.[5] But among all of these strange and singular "exemplars" of the coming community, one figure occupies a special place.

The Singular Scrivener

A reader turning to *The Coming Community*'s table of contents could not be blamed for thinking it was a book about indifference. Its first chapter is entitled "Whatever" and its last "Irreparable." The one at its midpoint would support this idea, named as it is after Herman Melville's hero of indifference, Bartleby. Such a reader's sense that *The Coming Community* is a book about indifference would not, in fact, be wholly wrong. It *is* indeed a book about indifference, but an indifference of a truly singular sort—and this can be seen nowhere so clearly as in its discussion of Melville's scrivener.

The chapter entitled "Bartleby" appears at first sight to be in strange company. Although it might conjure up indifference, it would seem to have little to do with the theological concepts named in other chapter titles—such as "From Limbo,"[6] "Halos," and "Shekinah"[7]—just as it would have little to do with the philosophical concepts named in still other chapter titles—such as "Principium individuationis"[8] and "Ethics." As with those terms, however, Agamben has chosen Bartleby for his exemplary potentiality.

When we think of Melville's scrivener and his haunting refrain, "I would prefer not to," it is difficult to imagine what might be paradigmatic about either his situation or his response to it. Agamben does not concern himself with philological, literary, or biographical questions, such as whether the story owes more to Poe or Dickens, or whether its enigmatic protagonist is based more on a friend of Melville's or on the author himself.[9] In fact, Agamben seems at first not to concern himself with the story at all. Turning to this chapter, we find something we have seen before: anything but what the title gave us to expect. As was the case for many of the chapters in *Idea of Prose*, the titular topic is first addressed in the chapter's final lines. In place of a discussion of Melville's enigmatic character, what we find is something else familiar from *Idea of Prose*: a discussion of Aristotle's categories of potentiality and actuality—the same categories he had employed the figure of the wax tablet to represent and that had helped Damascius come a little closer to "first principles." When Agamben at last turns from Aristotle and potentiality to Bartleby in the chapter's final lines, he tells us that "Bartleby, a scrivener [*uno scrivano*][10] who does not simply cease writing but 'prefers not to,' . . . writes nothing but his potentiality to not write [*la sua potenza di non scrivere*]" (CC, 37 [36], translation modified). But why should Agamben be interested in Bartleby and his preference for not writing, and what does it have to teach us about community?

Melville's tale famously closes with the cry, "Ah Bartleby! Ah humanity!" (Melville 1987, 45). For Agamben, Bartleby is a strange and solitary figure, but one who, if in singular fashion, is a figure for mankind. Although Agamben does not mention or even allude to the story's subtitle—"A Story of Wall Street"—he is clearly aware of it. Wall Street was initially the line that divided colonists from natives, the "civilized" from the "savage," and after the wall fell, what came to divide individuals was what Wall Street controlled: the flow of capital. Not only is Bartleby the instrument of a law that fails to dispense justice evenly and equally, but he also exercises his profession at the epicenter of capitalism—there where, in Marx's words, the "world's false prince" rules most mightily, and cruelly. At the foot, then, of this massive capitalist machine that legalizes inequality and injustice, Bartleby chooses civil disobedience, for his conditional is nothing if not civil and nothing if not disobedient. But his is no ordinary civil disobedience. Bartleby does not choose the pen over the sword and does not use the power of reason and rhetoric to denounce coercion and injustice. He does not, in fact, denounce anything. His civil disobedience, if it can even be called that, is a dual disobedience in that he not only prefers not to do what those around him do (copy out the law and, more generally, obey the conventions of the day), he also prefers not to provide what more and more around him demand: an explanation for his singular behavior. His reply is never more strident than the gentle conditional, "I would prefer not to," yet with it he doubly defies the powers that be, confounding and confusing those around him not only by not doing what is asked of him but also by not offering any explanation beyond his riddling reply. Some in the story take this as affectation, others see in it a laziness that demands discipline and a strong appeal to the American way and the capitalist work ethic. Yet no means suffice to force Bartleby to take up his pen.

It is this peculiar refusal that captivates Agamben. Not even Melville's narrator pretends to understand the reasons behind Bartleby's preferences. "But ere parting with the reader," he notes at the end of his tale, "let me say, that if this little narrative has sufficiently interested him to awaken curiosity as to who Bartleby was, and what manner of life he led prior to the present narrator's making his acquaintance, I can only reply, that in such curiosity I fully share, but am wholly unable to gratify it" (Melville 1987, 45). All the same, we might make educated guesses as to the cause of Bartleby's malaise. The life of a nineteenth-century scrivener (like the life of his creator) was not a joyful one, and reasons abound as to why an individual might find his work depressing or degrading and might then refuse to continue it. Perhaps it is the law he copies that leads to his despair, or perhaps it is his experience working as a clerk at the Dead Letter Office in Washington—where "on errands of life, these letters speed to death"— that sowed the seeds of his ultimate despair and his decision to have done with writing (Melville 1987, 45). But neither the narrator nor the reader knows for sure if it was sorting these stacks of letters secretly stamped *memento mori* that brought about Bartleby's final resignation—or if it was something else entirely.

Agamben is fascinated by the figure of Bartleby and *The Coming Community* is but one instance of this. He had already discussed Melville's scrivener in *Idea of Prose* and in the essay "Four Glosses for Kafka," published a year later, and placed him at the center of both a newspaper article entitled "Bartleby No Longer Writes" and a long essay on potentiality and contingency entitled "Bartleby, or On Contingency" (published with a companion piece also on Bartleby by Gilles Deleuze).[11] In all of these instances, Agamben eschews efforts to explain Bartleby's preferences through recourse to psychology.[12] Agamben's historical sights are often focused on distant points, and like Warburg before him he sees echoes and evocations of ancient figures in the most modern settings. In the case of Bartleby's suspended pen he sees an antique gesture—one with a distinctly Aristotelian lineage.

For Agamben, what Bartleby exemplifies is not only refusal of unacceptable conditions, not only civil disobedience, but also potentiality as we are least used to conceiving of it. We are indeed well accustomed to considering potentiality that converts itself into actuality, but things stand differently with a potentiality that remains potential. Aristotle asks how we are to conceive of a potentiality that never attains such actuality, and Agamben finds an answer to this millennial question in Bartleby's preferences, stressing that Bartleby "writes nothing but his potentiality to not write." The question remains, however, as to how we are to read such a writing. For Agamben, Melville's scrivener offers a singular answer to Aristotle's question by exemplifying not the potentiality *to do* or *to be*— the side of potentiality that is perfectly familiar to us—but the potentiality *not* to do or *not* to be.

In his companion piece to Agamben's essay, Deleuze stresses civil disobedience, and Bartleby is represented as a hero of "rhizomatic" resistance, a secret saboteur, a guerilla operative, unlocatable, unclassifiable by a state apparatus requiring fixed attributes and clear demands so as to subject citizens to its will. For Deleuze, Bartleby exemplifies an elusive response to a state's system of control based on identification, and his dogged refusals allow him to slip through the holes in its net. Bartleby shows Deleuze how one might be an effective outlaw in our hypersupervised world. This aspect of Bartleby's enigmatic character also interests and engages Agamben—but as the preceding remarks indicate, it is not the only one. The other level is best seen by recalling the figure that played so central a role in Agamben's early works: *infancy.*

The presence of the idea of *potentiality* in Agamben's work does not begin with his systematic use of the term. In his second book, *Stanzas,* the idea of potentiality is prefigured by the idea evoked therein of "the un-finished [*il non-finito*]," with its stress on the actual seen from the perspective of potentiality (S, 43, n. 2). In *Idea of Prose,* the term *latency* plays a similar role (see IP, 59 [39]). But it is in the term *infancy* that we find the most significant antecedent for *potentiality* in Agamben's work. This central concept, found in the title of Agamben's third book (*Infancy and History*) and to which a chapter of his fifth book (*Idea of Prose*) is dedicated, gradually disappears from his pages as it is replaced by *potentiality. Infancy* is supplanted, it appears, because it focuses on only one side of the potentiality that Agamben is endeavoring to formulate. This is most clearly seen in a distinction that Agamben finds important enough to stress in "Bartleby, or On Contingency," in what has thus far been the least understood chapter of *Homo Sacer* ("Potentiality and Law"), as well as in *The Coming Community*. In all three places Agamben turns to Avicenna's distinguishing of different types of potential intellect. One of these types is "material" potential intellect, which "resembles the condition of a child who may certainly one day learn to write but does not yet know anything about writing," and which thereby corresponds to Agamben's *infancy* (P, 246–247). This "material" potential intellect is distinguished by Avicenna—and following him, by Agamben—from "possible" potential intellect, wherein the child has begun to write but has not yet mastered it, as well as from another potential intellect: "a complete or perfect potentiality that belongs to the scribe who is in full possession of the art of writing in the moment in which he does not write," which corresponds to Bartleby's case (P, 246–247).[13] An *infant* cannot write or speak—yet. The child's linguistic potentiality is latent and may (but need not) be activated following the circumstances of its development. Bartleby is a related, if less heartening, figure. He "prefers not" to write—and means this quite literally. His situation is not that of an infant who cannot speak or write— what Avicenna called "material" potential intellect—for he has already activated this potentiality. Bartleby possesses the faculties of speech and writing—what Avicenna called "complete or perfect potentiality"—and has already shown himself quite capable in these domains. The mystery of the tale, and the source of Agamben's interest, is that Bartleby has chosen to remove himself from communal circulation, has chosen to cease employing his potentiality. Agamben calls on such a seemingly indifferent figure as Bartleby to represent pure potentiality because the latter stolidly refuses to convert his potentiality (to write) into act.

In *Infancy and History* Agamben stressed the exemplary value of a different short story that might help us clarify his interest in Bartleby. He wrote of Ludwig Tieck's "The Superfluity of Life" in light of the contemporary status of individual experience, "When humankind is deprived of effective experience and becomes subjected to the imposition of a form of experience as controlled and manipulated as a laboratory maze for rats—in other words, when the only possible experience is horror or lies—then the rejection of experience can provisionally constitute a legitimate defense" (IH, 16 [8], translation modified). To shut off, turn away, or tune out in such extreme circumstances is, for Agamben, a legitimate response—or in his words, "a legitimate defense." In a later interview Agamben links this idea to Arendt, noting that "Arendt once said that when everyone becomes unthinkingly carried away, those who *do* think find themselves unprotected and their refusal to join the others becomes itself a form of action" (AC, iii). In a chapter from *Means Without End* entitled "In This Exile," Agamben describes, for his own part, just such an experience. In *Infancy and History* he claims that in the face of the crisis of modern experience that he diagnoses, "anyone proposing to recover traditional experience today would encounter a paradoxical situation. For they would have to begin first of all with a cessation of experience, a suspension of knowledge" (IH, 23 [17]). Under extreme conditions the first step may not necessarily be direct and articulate resistance, but instead suspension or withdrawal. This is the path that Agamben sees Bartleby following, but it is only a part of what he sees. It is not only the *actual* choice of a given form of resistance or self-protection that so interests Agamben, but also the pure potentiality to which he testifies through the suspension of his participation.

Agamben's "Bartleby, or On Contingency" begins by noting that "as a scrivener, Bartleby belongs to a literary constellation" that includes Akaky Akakievich, Bouvard and Pécuchet, Simon Tanner, and Prince Myshkin—other masterful and mysterious literary copyists (see P, 243). "But Bartleby also belongs to a philosophical constellation," he adds, "and it may be that it alone contains the figure merely traced by the literary constellation to which Bartleby belongs" (P, 243). This "philosophical constellation" is the same one evoked in the final lines of the chapter "Bartleby" in *The Coming Community*. On this ontological level, Bartleby refuses to convert his riches of potentiality into the ready money of actuality. If in a "literary constellation" Bartleby is a despairing and disconsolate figure, in the "philosophical constellation" that interests Agamben a more heartening figure is seen. This constellation, though it includes such figures as Leibniz's pyramid of possible destinies and Nietzsche's eternal recurrence of the same,[14] has at its glowing center Aristotle's discussion of potentiality. Bartleby prefers to keep the wax tablet of his possibilities blank, and it is here that Agamben reads a special message for his community to come.

Bartleby in China

Agamben turns from this fictional figure to a real one—and one from the most recent history—for another example of inoperative resistance and political potentiality. As a rule, those who exercise their right and duty of civil disobedience do so in the name of specific causes and with a view to the righting of certain wrongs. In light of this fact, Blanchot found the motto of France's May 1968, "without project [*sans projet*]," of such interest. For him, it was the "unsettling and fortunate" rallying cry of what he called "an incomparable society" (Blanchot 1983, 52). "Unlike 'traditional revolutions,'" Blanchot continued, speaking of May 1968, the goal "was not to take the Bastille, the Winter Palace, the *Elysée* or the National Assembly—objectives without importance—and not even to overturn an old order, but to allow a possibility of *being-together* [être-ensemble] to demonstrate itself independent of any utilitarian interest" (52, italics in original). This same "being together" that we evoked earlier is what Blanchot finds most exemplary about the turn the events of May 1968 took.[15] Agamben too will prove interested in such a difficult-to-circumscribe "being together," but he will approach it by an unlikely route.

In the final chapter of *The Coming Community* Agamben turns to the student protests violently suppressed in Tiananmen Square roughly a year prior to his book's publication. *The Coming Community*'s first chapter had begun with the question, "What is a singularity?" This final chapter opens with the question, "What could be the politics of whatever [*qualunque*] singularity, that is, of a being whose community is mediated not by any condition of belonging (being red, being Italian, being Communist) nor by the simple absence of conditions (a negative community, such as that recently proposed in France by Maurice Blanchot), but by belonging itself [*dall'appartenenza stessa*]?" (CC, 85 [67]). The "negative community" that Blanchot invoked is, for Agamben, insufficient because it takes only the first step toward revising the idea of community; it knows what to reject but not what to put in its place. Regarding the question then posed— "What could be the politics of whatever singularity?"—Agamben claims that a "herald from Beijing carries the elements of a response" (CC, 85 [67]).

What Agamben found exemplary about the demonstrations in Beijing was not what they demanded but what they did *not* demand. "What was most striking about the demonstrations of the Chinese May,"[16] he wrote, "was the relative absence of determinate contents in their demands (democracy and freedom are notions too generic and broadly defined to constitute the real object of a conflict, and the only concrete demand, the rehabilitation of Hu Yaobang, was immediately granted)" (CC, 85 [67]). On the face of things, this fact makes the violence with which the Chinese government responded to these demonstrations all the more inexplicable.[17] Yet Agamben claims that "the disproportion is only apparent" and that "the Chinese leaders acted, from their point of view, with greater lucidity than the Western observers who were exclusively concerned with advancing increasingly less plausible arguments about the opposition between democracy and communism" (CC, 85 [67]). The "lucidity" of the Chinese leaders consists in their having seen quickly and clearly what was most dangerous for them and their interests. For Agamben—as for Foucault, Deleuze, Blanchot, and Nancy before him—a state will tolerate organized and articulate protest far more readily than undefined opposition. A society whose central strategy for control is observation and localized containment sees its greatest threat in that which it cannot identify. Such seemingly disorganized and unmotivated resistance is, from this point of view, the very last thing but anodyne. What is most threatening for the state powers that be is what deprives them of their most effective means of response, and it is in this light that Agamben speaks of a "lucidity" displayed by the Chinese leaders.[18]

In the light cast by this final chapter, it becomes clear that what Agamben saw in Bartleby was a one-man sit-in of the most radical sort. His civil disobedience shares with the Tiananmen protesters its relative absence of concrete demands. Because the nature of his discontent is not stated and because he cannot be precisely identified in his resistance, his presence, like that of the Chinese protestors, infuriates those in power. In Agamben's view, what truly provoked the Chinese authorities was the protestors' refusal to make more concrete demands that could then be granted or denied, revised, or ridiculed. The mute insistence of these protestors, their rejection of not just one incident or aspect of a corrupt system but that system as a whole, made their protest particularly threatening to the state—and explains, for Agamben, the violence with which it was met. For this reason, a seemingly incoherent insurrection may, in our times, be the most effective—and the most exemplary. Following Agamben's logic, the most threatening thing imaginable for a state—be it communist, democratic, or other—is a billion Bartlebys saying they would prefer not to continue to live in their society as it is. In the final words of the book's final chapter, Agamben notes, "Wherever these singularities peacefully demonstrate their being in common [*il loro essere commune*], there will be a Tiananmen, and sooner or later the tanks will appear" (CC, 87 [68]). Bartleby is thus a truly exemplary singularity in that he is the bearer of a lesson in potentiality, a lesson like that of the philosopher with his stylus suspended above a wax tablet on which nothing has yet been written, as well as a paradigm for *actual* resistance of the most singular—and, for Agamben, necessary—sort.

Spectacle and Shekinah

In the middle of a letter to Gershom Scholem from 1916, the young Walter Benjamin interrupts a catalogue of his recent readings to ask his friend, "What does *Shekinah* mean?" (Benjamin GB, 1.129). The question that Benjamin posed was at once simple and difficult to answer. *Shekinah* is a Hebrew term meaning the visible manifestation of the Divinity; it is strongly associated with *light*—"a glory or refulgent light symbolizing the Divine Presence," in the words of *The Oxford English Dictionary*—and etymologically associated with a sense of rest or dwelling (it derives from a term having both of these meanings). It is this sense of the word that one finds secularized in such metaphorical usages as George Eliot's "the golden sunlight beamed through the dripping boughs like a Shekinah," to which she immediately adds for clarification, "or visible divine presence" (Eliot 1858, 286). Theologians have frequently identified this visible glory with what was shown in fiery form on Mount Sinai, and Christian theologians have used it on occasion to refer to Jesus Christ. This is both a simple and complex answer to Benjamin's question. Giving a still more simple and more complex answer, however, is a task that Agamben assigns himself in *The Coming Community*.

The penultimate chapter of *The Coming Community* is entitled "Shekinah." Although Agamben had dwelt earlier in the book on Benjamin and on the theological concepts that Scholem communicated to him, this chapter begins neither with Benjamin's youthful question nor with Scholem's later answers—nor even with a definition of the term (thereby leaving many readers posing themselves the same question as had the young Benjamin). "Shekinah" begins with no mention of theology or divine presence whatsoever, but, instead, with Guy Debord.

In the introduction that Agamben wrote for the Italian translation of Debord's *Commentaries on the Society of the Spectacle* (1988) there is a section entitled "Tiananmen." Substantial parts of it are reproduced verbatim in the identically titled final chapter of *The Coming Community*, though the following passage is not: "Appearances notwithstanding, the spectacular-democratic world organization now emerging runs the risk of being the worst tyranny human history has ever seen and against which resistance and dissent will be ever more difficult—all the more so as, now more clearly than ever, this organization will have as [its] task to see to the *survival of humanity in an inhabitable world* [*un mondo abitabile*]" (MWE, 87 [71], italics in original, translation modified).[19] The terms that Agamben chooses here could hardly be more extreme, nor could the stakes be deemed higher. Debord was a thinker as incendiary and incisive as any of his generation, and though he was a serious one, he was not always considered as such. His early analyses of a mediatized global society's means of communication and control are without equal, and the predictions he made have proven uncannily accurate. Nevertheless, and in a darkly fitting irony, it is the mediatized, *spectacular* image of Debord that has prevailed: that of the playful Lettrist, the insurgent Situationist, the inventor of staged events, and the alcoholic anarchist. What has been stressed has been less the strategist or stylist than the filmmaker whose most famous film, *Cries in Favor of Sade,* consists of two alternating monochrome images and a lot of distressing noise, or the author who demanded that one of his books be published with sandpaper covers so that it would rub away the titles on either side of it.

For Agamben, however, Debord is a singularly serious and timely figure—one to whose memory he dedicated his eighth book, *Means Without End.*[20] Therein he writes that "Debord's books constitute the clearest and most severe analysis of the miseries and slavery of a society that by now has extended its dominion over the whole planet—that is to say, the society of the spectacle in which we live" (MWE, 73 [60]). In *The Coming Community* Agamben turns to Debord's own definition of this central term: "The spectacle is capital to such a degree of accumulation that it becomes an image" (cited in CC, 79 [63]). Agamben sees this spectacular nature of contemporary capitalist culture, with its increasing dependence on mediatized images, as having dire consequences for the constitution and construction of communities—consequences that have taken still clearer shape in the years since the publication of Debord's *The Society of the Spectacle* in 1967 (so clear that Agamben remarked in one of his most recent books that "contemporary democracies" as a whole might best be described as "the society of the spectacle" [RG, 10]). "When the real world is transformed into an image and images become real," writes

Agamben, "the practical power of humans is separated from itself and presented as a world unto itself" (CC, 79 [63]). What Agamben sees Debord expertly outlining is then nothing less than the dominant modern form of alienation seen in contemporary communities.

After crediting Debord for his remarkable foresight concerning the growing role of images in contemporary capitalist culture, Agamben turns to a more pressing question: "Today, in the era of the complete triumph of the spectacle, what can be reaped from the heritage of Debord?" (CC, 80 [64]). Agamben postpones answering this question, developing instead Debord's idea of the *spectacle*. In an article for an Italian newspaper published a year before *The Coming Community*, Agamben had written, "It is clear that the spectacle is language, the very communicativity [*la stessa comunicatività*] or linguistic being of mankind" (VS, 2). This bold equation represents a fundamental extension of Debord's definition and is one that Agamben will insist on, repeating it verbatim not only in his introduction to Debord's *Commentaries* but also in *The Coming Community* (see CC, 80 [64]). For Agamben, the term *spectacle* is concerned not only with *images,* as Debord had stressed, but also with *words*; not only with the flood of commercialized images that is the hallmark of our mediatized culture, but also with something involving all aspects of human communication.[21]

For Agamben, the consequence of his extension of Debord's *spectacle* from *image* to *word* is that "a fuller Marxian analysis should deal with the fact that capitalism (or any other name one wants to give the process that today dominates world history) was directed not only toward the expropriation of productive activity, but also and principally toward the alienation of language itself, of the very linguistic and communicative nature of humans, of that *logos* which one of Heraclitus's fragments identified as the Common" (CC, 80 [64]). Capitalist alienation is not only alienation from the material conditions of one's own production (work), but also alienation from the means by which one might share that which is common. Agamben argues that the *spectacle*—Debord's term for this extreme form of alienation—is so harmful for the world's communities because its alienating force stretches so far. The *spectacle* reaches not only into our homes through the ideological messages transmitted by our media, but also into our very "mediality"—our capacity to communicate what we have in common. The *spectacle*—in Agamben's widened use of the term—is at cross-purposes with the idea of community because it undermines human communicativity in both *image* and *word*. By vitiating the means of authentic communication, this modern form of social alienation undermines the means of constructing a community that might free itself from a logic of exclusion and violence.

The answer to Agamben's question as to what might be reaped from Debord's heritage is thus to be sought not only in image but also in word. It involves both realizing the dire states of the world's communities and understanding that the *spectacle*—the alienating means of communication characteristic of industrialized nations—concerns not only *images* but also our very communicative essence—our *language*. Yet there is still more to this heritage. "The extreme form of this expropriation of the Common is the spectacle, that is, the politics we live in," writes Agamben; "but this also means that in the spectacle our own linguistic being [*la nostra stessa natura linguistica*] comes back to us inverted" (CC, 80 [64]). Agamben's first book ended with these words: "According to the principle by which it is only in the burning house that the fundamental architectural problem becomes visible for the first time, art, at the furthest point of its destiny, makes visible its original project" (MWC, 115 [172]). For Agamben, as we saw in Chapter One, "where there is danger, also grows / that which saves," and it should then come as no surprise to find Agamben writing that "this is why (precisely because what is being expropriated is the very possibility of a common good) the violence of the spectacle is so destructive, *but for the same reason the spectacle retains something like a positive possibility that can be used against it*" (CC, 80 [64], italics added). What can be reaped from Debord's heritage, then, is not only clarity about the extremity of our situation, but also the means through which we might reverse it.

To say, however, that the extremity of our situation, the imminence of catastrophe, brings with it the possibility of reversal still tells us nothing about what this "positive possibility" *is*, or how we are to employ it. An answer to this question is not immediately given, but Agamben's argument does not end here. Without transition, he moves from his interpretation of the spectacle to a parable about the Shekinah. This diagnosis of the spectacle, he tells us, "is very similar to what the cabalists called 'the isolation of the Shekinah' and attributed to Aher, one of the four rabbis who, according to a celebrated Haggadah of the Talmud, entered into Pardes (that is, into supreme knowledge)" (CC, 81 [64]).[22] Agamben then offers his readers a concise version of the Haggadah in question:

Four rabbis, the story says, entered Paradise: Ben Azzai, Ben Zoma, Aher and Rabbi Akiba . . . Ben Azzai cast a glance and died . . . Ben Zoma looked and went mad . . . Aher cut off the branches . . . Rabbi Akiba left unharmed. [CC, 81 (64–65), ellipses in original]

Here we can at last begin to understand the reason this chapter bears the title "Shekinah" (rather than, for instance, "Spectacle"); but the connection to Debord's analyses of our mediatized age remains in the dark. To illustrate this unlikely parallel, Agamben then writes:

The Shekinah is the last of the ten Sefirot, or attributes of the divinity, the one that expresses the very presence of the divine, its manifestation or habitation on earth: its "word." Aher's "cutting off the branches" is identified by the cabalists with the sin of Adam, who instead of contemplating all of the Sefirot chose to contemplate the final one, isolating it from the others and in this way separating the tree of knowledge from the tree of life. [CC, 81 (65)]

Just as he did with Debord's *spectacle,* Agamben extends the Haggadic *Shekinah* to encompass not just "visible presence" but also "word." Once he has done this, his parallel becomes clear. In the parable, Ben Azzai and Ben Zoma, completely overwhelmed by the experience, are soon left out of account as one dies and the other goes mad. The remaining figures on whom Agamben fixes his attention are Aher (whose name means "Other") and Rabbi Akiba. Although Rabbi Akiba leaves unharmed, Aher does not. The harm done to him, however, is not easy to identify (like the madness and death befalling the other two figures). Aher "cuts the branches" and thereby, it seems, attempts to isolate and master a single aspect of the Divinity. By doing so, however, he severs the living connection to knowledge and is left with only the appearance of knowledge. In the terms used earlier in the chapter, he obtains the *spectacle* of knowledge, but not its reality.

"In this condition of exile," Agamben writes, "the Shekinah loses its positive power and becomes harmful (the cabalists said it 'sucked the milk of evil')" (CC, 82 [65]). What, however, does it mean for the Shekinah—for divine presence—to lose its positive power and become harmful? Clearly it means to isolate it—in precisely the same fashion as the spectacular organization of contemporary industrial societies has isolated the means of communication from anything truly *common* that they might communicate. The contemporary *spectacle,* like the cutting of the branches in the story from the Haggadah, "sucks the milk of evil" in that it isolates appearance from being, the means of communication from any common essence or nature to communicate.

Agamben is intrigued enough by this parable to retell it at no fewer than three other points in his work.[23] In the parable, Rabbi Akiba leaves the garden unharmed, but how and why is not made clear, and the question remains as to what Agamben sees as exemplary in Rabbi Akiba's case. The only means by which what Agamben calls "an authentic human community" could be constituted would be on the basis of what he describes as "the unpresupposable and unpresupposed principle . . . that, as such, constitutes authentic human community and communication" (P, 35 [20]). Here too we are confronted by a problem: How can a principle that is not only unpresupposed but unpresupposable be the basis for a community— or for that matter, for anything at all? And how would one even catch a glimpse of such an elusive principle? The answer to this second question is through the *experimentum linguae* examined earlier, through an experience of "a pure event of language before or beyond all possible meaning" (see P, 41–42 [28]). In the preface written for the French edition of *Infancy and History,* from the same period when Agamben was at work on *The Coming Community,* he writes that "the first outcome of the *experimentum linguae . . .* is a radical revision of the very idea of Community" (IH, 9 [xiv]). Agamben sees in this *experimentum linguae* the means for radically reconceiving the very idea of community. In other words, the reason such an experience and experiment are of such importance for Agamben is that a new conception of community is not to be had without a new conception of that which is most common: language. For this reason we can now better see why Agamben stressed that there was indeed a "powerful connection" between his reflections on language and those on politics to be found in the idea that "language is the common element that links all men and women" (IH, 9 [xiv]; UIGA, 33).

In the same parabolic chapter from *The Coming Community* with which we began our examination of the spectacle and the Shekinah, Agamben writes:

This is the sense in which the isolation of the Shekinah expresses the condition of our era. Whereas under the old regime the estrangement of the communicative essence of humans took the form of a presupposition that served as a common foundation, in the society of the spectacle it is this very communicativity, this generic essence itself (i.e., language), that is separated into an autonomous sphere. [CC, 82 (65)]

In our society of the spectacle, the branches of language have been cut from the living tree of experience—separating, in the language of the parable, the tree of life from the tree of knowledge. This is, for Agamben, a parable of nihilism, one that Debord's spectacle isolates. In the preceding chapter, we saw Agamben link the matter of language and the thinking of potentiality to what he calls an *experimentum linguae*. In his conceptions of spectacle and Shekinah, he extends this idea into the political sphere. "What is in question in political experience," he writes, "is not a higher end but rather being-in-language itself" (MWE, 117 [92]). For this reason, the "consequence of the *experimentum linguae* is that, above and beyond the concepts of appropriation and expropriation, that which demands reflection is the possibility and the modalities of a *free usage*" (MWE, 117 [93], translation modified, italics in original).[24] The *experimentum linguae* that Agamben describes is thus, for him, the "unique material experience possible of our generic essence" (MWE, 117 [92]).

Nihilism, or the Complete Consciousness of Language

In the essay "The Idea of Language," Agamben declares that "we are the first human beings who have become completely conscious [*coscienti*] of language," and claims further that "this is the Copernican revolution that the thought of our time inherits from nihilism" (P, 45 [33]). Before we can understand this singular consciousness of language we need to understand better the line of inheritance. In his essay on Bartleby and contingency, Agamben refers to "the ungrateful guest—nihilism—with whom we are all too familiar today" (P, 259).[25] Eleven years earlier, in *Language and Death*, Agamben had dedicated himself to exploring the forms and functions of negativity in Western philosophical thought and had evoked therein the "*nihilism* beyond which contemporary thought and praxis (its 'politics') have not yet ventured" (LD, xiii [5], italics in original, translation modified). Agamben's enterprise in that book was "conceiving of nihilism differently" than modern thought had hitherto done and involved understanding what he called mankind's "ungroundedness [*la sua in-fondatezza*] (or negative ground [*fondamento negativo*])"—a conception we first saw in relation to Agamben's idea of vocation (LD, xiii [6], translation modified). The idea of nihilism and how it is to be understood is evoked at numerous points in Agamben's writing from the period surrounding *Language and Death*. In an essay from 1985 he refers to "contemporary thought, in its somnambulant nihilism," and in another essay written the year before, he claims that whereas "nihilism . . . interprets the extreme revelation of language in the sense that there is nothing to reveal, the truth of language is that it unveils the Nothing of all things. The absence of a metalanguage thus appears as the negative form of the presupposition, and the Nothing as the final veil, the final name of language" (P, 115 [160], 46 [34]). It is important to note here that Agamben does not reject an experience of nihilism, he rejects interpreting it in the wrong fashion. The fact that "there is nothing to reveal" is taken itself as the subject of a revelation—and a catastrophic one spelling the loss of meaning, commonality, and any idea of community based on language. What Agamben enjoins his readers to do is to interpret this revelation differently: not as "the Nothing of all things"—the meaninglessness of existence—but as the absence of final revelation and the falseness of the idea that human history is unfolding with a progressive purpose in view.

This idea of a sacred truth to be revealed at the end of history is abetted by an idea of nihilism that Agamben endeavors to stand on its head. For this reason he claims that "the task of philosophy is . . . to be assumed exactly at the point at which contemporary thought seems to abandon it" (P, 46 [34]). The task of philosophy is thus to be found in awakening from this "somnambulant" state and confronting the "unwelcome guest" that is nihilism. It is for this reason that Agamben writes in the last lines of *Language and Death* that "the *ethos,* humanity's own, is not something unspeakable or *sacer* that must remain unsaid in all praxis and human speech. Neither is it a nothingness, whose nullity serves as the basis for the arbitrariness and violence of social action. Rather, it is social praxis itself, human speech itself, which have become transparent to themselves" (LD, 106 [133]). That *nihilism* presents a danger is visible in the very form of the word; but understanding Agamben's conception of it is far from simple. To understand this *nothing,* we must understand the *something* that it risks occluding. In this case, it involves the difficult task of determining what it would mean for "social praxis" and "human speech itself" to "become transparent to themselves." No clear answer to this question is offered in *Language and Death,* but one *is* offered in *The Coming Community* and in the "Copernican revolution that the thought of our time inherits from nihilism."

With this idea now in mind we can return to the nature of this revolution. In another essay from this period, Agamben goes so far as to define

philosophy itself as this experience: "Philosophy is the attempt . . . to become conscious of the meaning of the fact that human beings speak" (P,
67 [63]). This remarkable assertion is echoed in a host of essays and books
written in the years that follow, and this surprising historical diagnosis is
one that Agamben returns to in *The Coming Community.* Here he tells
his reader that "the era in which we live is also that in which for the first
time it is possible for humans to experience their own linguistic being—
not this or that content of language, but language *itself*" (CC, 83, italics
added). But what does Agamben mean by our becoming "completely conscious of language"? And how is it possible not only for an individual but
for an entire age to experience "language *itself*"?

In a similar vein, Agamben writes that "the age in which we live is
also the age in which, for the first time, it has become possible for mankind to experience its own linguistic essence—not this or that linguistic
content or true proposition, but the *fact itself of speaking*" (MWE, 115 [92],
italics in original, translation modified). This experiencing of language's
essence is conceived of in singular fashion: "The experience in question
here does not have any objective content and cannot be formulated as
a proposition referring to a state of things or to a historical situation. It
concerns not a *state* but rather an *event* of language" (MWE, 116 [92], italics in original). As had been the case for his *experimentum linguae*, what is
at issue here is the same matter of language that Agamben saw leading to
an experience of the potentiality of thought. "This experience," Agamben
stresses, "must be then constructed as an experiment concerning the very
matter—or the potentiality—of thought [*la materia stessa o la potenza del
pensiero*]" (MWE, 116 [92], translation modified). The reference here to
potentiality is a familiar one, but on this political terrain, what does it
mean to have such an experience of possibility and potentiality, and how
can it lead to a new idea of community?

Advancing Debord's insights concerning modern mediatized society, Agamben signals a chance offered to contemporary society by the very
alienation it is experiencing. For Agamben, the society of the spectacle
reflects man's alienated linguistic nature in inverted form, and he thus
refers to an "extreme [*estrema*][26] expropriation of language effected by the
spectacular state" (MWE, 115 [91], translation modified). In an essay published the same year (1990)[27] as *The Coming Community,* Agamben refers
to a "threshold of de-propriation [*de-propriazione*] and de-identification
of all modes and all qualities—a threshold in which those modes and

qualities first become purely communicable" (MWE, 100 [80], translation modified). Agamben's use of the terms *proper, expropriation,* and *depropriation* resemble their use in French philosophy (most notably in Derrida's writing) and are best understood through Heidegger's use of them. Heidegger's dialectic of the proper and the improper—of *Eigentlichkeit* and *Uneigentlichkeit*—has to do not with any greater or lesser correctness of conduct but with a dialectic of belonging and the ethical ramifications of such a dialectic. In Heidegger's philosophy there is no special or specific *essence* to either state; the proper is merely a form of the improper, and vice versa. For Agamben, this Heideggerian dialectic has the greatest relevance precisely in a realm where Heidegger was most reluctant to place it: the realm of language. For Agamben, language has no *proper* meaning and no *proper* content. It is a medium for communication, a medium made up of unmotivated signs that through the activity and ingenuity of man are used to communicate an astounding array of things. Developing this Heideggerian insight in the same direction as he does the linguistic insights of Saussure and Benveniste, Agamben arrives at a singular idea of language and at its corollary in a singular idea of community.

Agamben's expression "expropriation of language" thus can and should be understood in a simple sense: it is the rendering common of what one thought of as one's own—and only as one's own—province or property. Following the Hölderlinian principle that we saw in the first chapter of this book and that is such a fundamental element in Agamben's thought, this "expropriation of language," although devastating in its effects, is also the first step toward a truly "free usage" of that which is most common: our means of communication. This disastrous state of affairs, which Agamben calls "the extreme expropriation of language effected by the spectacular state," brings with it, however, a possibility for change. In this spectacular society, says Agamben, "we encounter our own linguistic nature inverted. For this reason (precisely because what is being expropriated here is the possibility itself of the Common), the spectacle's violence is so destructive; but for this same reason, the spectacle also contains something like a positive possibility that can be used against it" (MWE, 115 [91–92], translation modified). In Agamben's conception, "the spectacle's violence" is not the violence that the world's media report on—be it the documentary form of the violence of military conflicts or the fictional one of violent entertainment—but the violence they embody. The violence in question is that done to the means of communication by a system that pretends to communicate everything, to link all individuals and bring together all spheres, but instead effects increasing isolation and alienation. "In the sphere of the spectacle," Agamben remarked in a recent interview, "the media presents a language that has been drained of meaning. The problem then lies in how one might liberate the means [of communication] so that they do not again fall prey to this isolation and separation" (PWP, 21). The society of the spectacle has become so complete, the alienation so widespread, that we are offered a privileged glimpse of something that is normally obscured by the message: the medium itself. That the medium is the message is what, following Agamben, we can see with unprecedented clarity today; and this is what he means when he writes that, "We are the first human beings who have become completely conscious of language," just as it is for this reason that he will announce that "thought finds itself for the first time, today, confronted by its task without any illusion and without any possible alibi" (MWE, 111 [87]). René ten Bos (2005, 23–24) asks, "Can we . . . seriously ask people to forfeit the security of their imaginary integrity, identity, home, race, class, and so on?" Agamben's answer would seem to be that we already have; and to be, as he says, "without alibi" means to be without excuse for deferring the seizing of this opportunity.

The above would entail a reevaluation of our conception of the means and ends of history, and would require a reconception of the idea with which we began this study: the idea of vocation. It is for this reason that Agamben claims, "The fact that must constitute the point of departure for any discourse on ethics is that there is no essence, no historical or spiritual vocation, no biological destiny that humans must enact or realize" (CC, 43 [39]). Agamben stresses here something of which every serious modern observer is aware: the impoverishment of political discourse and the increasing reliance on spectacular situations, sound bites, and the seemingly endless resources of public relations. This situation is seen by Agamben as representing a crisis for communities of all sorts, but his answer is not a general strike or communist control. It is instead a call for a revaluation of the categories through which we view our political landscape. The most pressing political and ethical question for Agamben is how to encourage us to submit our thought and our language to a constant renovation, one that might counter the forces that seek to instrumentalize it and thereby undermine its commonality. For this reason Agamben writes in *The Coming Community*:

Even more than economic necessity and technological development, what drives the nations of the earth toward a single common destiny is the alienation from linguistic being, the uprooting of all peoples from their vital dwelling in language. . . . Contemporary politics is this devastating *experimentum linguae* that all over the planet unhinges and empties traditions and beliefs, ideologies and religions, identities and communities. Only those who succeed in carrying it to completion—without allowing what reveals to remain veiled in the nothingness that reveals, but bringing language itself to language—will be the first citizens of a community with neither presuppositions nor a state, where the nullifying and determining power of what is common will be pacified. [CC, 83 (66)][28]

This pacification of the nullifying power of the common and the liberation of its liberating potentiality is, as Agamben has not ceased to stress, no simple affair, and it is thus to more concretely political matters that he will turn in the essays and books following *The Coming Community*. In an essay from 2002 Agamben wrote that "only lucidity and imagination, freed at once from aging ideologies and a liberal-spectacular credo, can restore mankind to the space of their cities," and it is toward the employ of such imagination and the search for such lucidity that his efforts in the coming years will be directed (NSIV, 118).

Scholium I: Jacques Derrida and Aher, or
The Cutting of the Branches

The meaning and importance that Agamben ascribes to the Haggadic parable discussed in this chapter are easier to discern when we evoke, as does he, contemporary figures. In an essay published the same year as *The Coming Community*, Agamben retells this story—with an addition: the figure of Aher is identified with a contemporary thinker and a present danger. That thinker is Jacques Derrida and the danger is nihilism.

In *"Pardes:* The Writing of Potentiality," Agamben links the parable to the *experimentum linguae* of such importance to his ideas on language and potentiality (discussed in Chapter Four of this book). "The cutting of the branches," Agamben writes in *"Pardes,"* "is an *experimentum linguae,* an experience of language that consists in separating both speech from the voice and pronunciation from its reference. A pure word isolated in itself, with neither voice nor referent, with its semantic value indefinitely suspended: this is the dwelling of Aher, the 'Other,' in Paradise" (P, 207 [348]). For Agamben, Derrida resembles this Other, Aher. Unable to accept the final consequences of this *experimentum linguae,* he finds himself trapped in "the aporias of self-reference," thereby consigning deconstruction to "the exile of terminology" which Agamben also calls an "obstinate dwelling in the exile of the Shekinah" (P, 209 [350], 219 [363]). How are we to understand this parable and the severe judgment it passes on Derrida's thought?

Before answering this question we should note that Agamben's relation to Derrida and deconstruction is without parallel in his work. It is singularly, and at points intensely, polemical, yet chooses what seem the least polemical means for its expression—the indirect ones of parable, parallel, aside, and allusion. It should then come as little surprise that this relationship has been a source of much curiosity and confusion in the critical literature on Agamben. Most commentators agree that it is of fundamental importance. Simon Morgan Wortham writes that "one almost feels that the entire momentum of Agamben's critical re-elaborations of virtually the whole field of post-Enlightenment thought, not to mention his fascinating re-encounters with medieval texts and philosophy, builds ultimately towards a critique of deconstruction" (Wortham 2007, 90). But what is this critique? Adam Thurschwell finds that "Agamben's virtual charge . . . is the harshest that can be leveled: that Derrida, or rather deconstruction . . . is the false Messiah" (2005, 174). For her part, Eva Geulen claims that "while in his early texts Agamben cites Derrida as an unconditional authority [*unbedingte Autorität*] and lends some of [Derrida's] essays hagiographical traits [*hagiographische Züge*], with the *Homo Sacer* series, criticism of Derrida mounts" (2005, 127). Coming as it does in the first monograph dedicated to Agamben's thought, Geulen's assessment is remarkable for how much it misses. She traces this change in Agamben's attitude to a difference of philological opinion concerning Benjamin's essay "Towards a Critique of Violence." Although there was indeed such a disagreement, it was far from the first, and Geulen's characterization errs not only in neglecting decades of earlier opposition, but also in its description of Agamben's initial relation to Derrida.[29] The two philosophers enjoyed friendly relations (they were colleagues at the Parisian *Collège International de Philosophie* that Derrida helped found), and Agamben dedicated both the essay "The Thing Itself" and a chapter of *Idea of Prose* to Derrida. This does not mean, however, that there was a point in their respective developments when they were in complete agreement, and still less does it mean that Agamben moved from "hagiographical" adherence to apostate rejection, however appealing such a narrative might be.

A first step toward understanding this critique thus lies in uncovering its origins. While Mills and Geulen focus their attentions on *Homo Sacer*, Thurschwell offers a richer picture of this debate by directing his reader's attention to Agamben's critique of deconstruction in *Language and Death*, and thus to well over a decade earlier (Thurschwell 2005, 174; see also Mills 2004, 50–57). He does not, however, trace the matter back as far as he might have, for it is in *Stanzas,* from five years earlier, as both Kevin Attell (2006) and Wortham (2007, 89) have noted, that we first find a significant critique of Derrida and deconstruction. In the final chapter of *Stanzas,* Agamben distinguishes what he calls signification seen under the sign of Oedipus from signification seen under the sign of the Sphinx: "Every interpretation of signifying as the relation of manifestation of expression (or inversely, of encoding and concealing) between a signifier and a signified (and both the psychoanalytic theory of the symbol and the semiotic theory of language belong to this type) places itself necessarily under the sign of Oedipus" (S, 138 [165], translation modified). Agamben continues: "Under the sign of the Sphinx must be placed every theory of the symbol that, refusing the model of Oedipus, focuses its attention above all on the barrier between signifier and signified that constitutes the original problem of signification" (S, 138–39 [163]). In Agamben's view, Derrida focuses exemplary attention on this barrier but becomes transfixed by what he sees. "By restoring the originary character of the signifier," writes Agamben elsewhere in *Stanzas,* "the grammatological project effects a salutary critique of the metaphysical inheritance that has crystallized in the notion of sign, but this does not mean that it has really succeeded in accomplishing that 'step-backward-beyond' metaphysics" (S, 156 [187]). To this Agamben adds that "with greater prudence, the philosopher on whose thought that critique is based [Heidegger] hesitated to declare that step complete or even possible" (S, 156 [187], translation modified). More explicitly, Agamben states that "placing writing and the trace in an initial position puts the emphasis on this original experience, but certainly does not transcend it" (S, 156 [187], translation modified). One reproach made in *Stanzas* is that Derrida is crediting his thought with more originality in respect to Heidegger than it demonstrates, and in this vein Agamben also remarks that "like much of contemporary French thought, so too does Derrida's have its more or less openly declared foundation in that of Heidegger" (S, 158 [187]). As he also does later, Agamben expresses his criticism through an evocative figure (the Sphinx), followed by a restrained statement of disagreement. Part Four of *Stanzas* is, among other things, a response to Derrida's *On Grammatology* and questions Derrida's reading not only of Heidegger but also of Saussure—above all as concerns whether Saussure is really an advocate of semiological analysis of the sort that Derrida advocates. (In properly philological fashion, Agamben bases his argument on Saussure's notes published by Benveniste, which he finds that Derrida has neglected.[30]) Agamben reproaches Derrida for overvaluing his originality with respect to Heidegger and with missing the real import of Saussure's analyses. Beyond these local reproaches, however, looms a more general one—one concerned with language's communicative power and that he will return to for decades to come.

In an essay published three years after *Stanzas,* Agamben more explicitly traces "the limit of Derrida's thought, which identifies metaphysics with dependence on writing"—the same point he stresses in *Language and Death* (PS, 163).[31] In the latter publication, Agamben follows Aristotle's stress on the *grammata* through the manner in which this emphasis was treated by Aristotle's early interpreters (LD, 38 [52]). "This means," writes Agamben, "that, from the beginning the Western reflection on language located the *gramma* and not the voice in the originary place" (LD, 39 [53]). Although Agamben does not name Derrida here, the target of his critique is easily discernable. To remove all doubt, Agamben writes in the very next paragraph that "although we should certainly pay homage to Derrida as the thinker who has identified with the greatest rigor—developing Lévinas' concept of the trace and Heidegger's concept of difference—the original status of the *gramma* and of the signifier in our culture, it is also true that he believed he had opened the way to the surpassing of metaphysics, while in truth he merely brought the fundamental problem of metaphysics to light" (LD, 39 [53], translation modified).[32] As he had done in *Stanzas,* Agamben argues in *Language and Death* and in the essays leading up to it that not only are Derrida's insights less original than they present themselves to be—based as they are on those of Lévinas and Heidegger—they also make the more fundamental error of mistaking a beginning for an end.

In a talk first given in 1983, Agamben offered a more neutral account of deconstruction, speaking of "the theory of the supremacy of the letter or *gramma* (as the originary negative foundation of language), which, starting with Derrida, appears in innumerable forms in contemporary French thought"—although it is clear enough that this is a "theory" to which he himself does not adhere (P, 57 [49]). Two years later, Agamben refers to "an authoritative current of contemporary French thought" that "posits language in the beginning and yet conceives of this dwelling in the *arkhe* according to the negative structure of writing and the *gramma,*" and although Derrida is once again not directly named as its source, he is easily recognizable as its chief representative (P, 44 [32]). In another essay from that same year, Agamben turned to the rhetoric of entrapment that he would employ in the Haggadic parable, referring to "the structure of trace and originary writing in which our age has remained imprisoned" (P, 111 [156]). Although Derrida's name is once again avoided, the references to key terms in Derrida's thought such as *trace* and *originary writing* make the object of Agamben's criticism unmistakable.

What such a survey of Agamben's critique of Derrida and deconstruction shows is not only that it stretches back farther than critics have tended to note, but also that it displays a remarkable, if at times enigmatic, continuity. Although Geulen is indeed wrong to refer to a period of "hagiographical" adherence that comes to an end with *Homo Sacer,* and although it is false to trace the difference in views to an argument over how to interpret Benjamin's "For a Critique of Violence," it *is* the case that there is a rise in both the frequency and the intensity of Agamben's criticisms of Derrida during the period when *Homo Sacer* was written. In an essay from 1992 Agamben wrote that "the success of deconstruction in our time is founded . . . on its having conceived the whole text of tradition, the whole law . . . as a being in force without significance," and this charge is repeated almost verbatim in *Homo Sacer* (P, 170 [265]). After a discussion of the linguistic categories of meaning and denotation, Agamben remarks that what deconstruction does is "posit undecidables that are infinitely in excess of every possibility of signification" (HS, 25 [30]). In a later aside he notes that "the prestige of deconstruction in our time lies precisely in its having conceived of the entire text of tradition as being in force without significance, a being in force whose strength lies essentially in its undecidability and in having shown that such a being in force is, like the door of the Law in Kafka's parable, absolutely impassable" (HS, 54 [62–63]). During this period Agamben comes to characterize deconstruction as a "petrified or paralyzed messianism" and as existing in "a perpetual and interminable state of exception" (P, 171 [266]). It is presumably such remarks that led Thurschwell to the radical conclusion cited earlier, as well as to the more measured one of Mika Ojakangas that "only Derrida can be conceived as a truly messianic thinker, whereas Agamben's thinking represents post-messianism" (Ojakangas 2005b, 49).[33] In *Homo Sacer* we read that "it is precisely concerning the sense of this being in force (and of the state of exception that it inaugurates) that our position distinguishes itself from that of deconstruction. Our age does indeed stand in front of language just as the man from the country in the parable stands in front of the door of the Law. What threatens thinking here is the possibility that thinking might find itself condemned to infinite negotiations with the doorkeeper or, even worse, that it might end by itself assuming the role of the doorkeeper who, without really blocking the entry, shelters the Nothing onto which the door opens. As the evangelical warning cited by Origen concerning the interpretation of Scripture has it: 'Woe to you, men of the Law, for you have taken away the key to knowledge: you yourselves have not entered, and you have not let the others who approached enter either'" (HS, 54 [62–63]). Here the danger that Agamben sees in deconstruction is clearly stated. In threatening to lose itself in "infinite negotiations," deconstruction, for Agamben, is associated with the men of the law who, through love of the law, choose it over knowledge. It is this threat that Agamben chose to express in the parable of Aher and the cutting of the branches of signification. For Agamben, deconstruction has taken up residence in "the exile of terminology" and its position hinders a return.

As Agamben first remarked at the end of *Stanzas,* he finds Derrida to be transfixed by the barrier of linguistic presupposition, by the separation of signifier and signified. This line of criticism remains constant, although it is equally clear that Agamben is reluctant to focus a great deal of attention on it. His remarks are largely expressed through mythical and parabolic parallels—from Oedipus to Akiba—and frequently take place in asides. In a preface to a 1995 work by the Italian poet Antonio Delfini, Agamben discusses the idea of a divide between signifier and signified, between origin and trace, adding in a parenthetical aside that "it is here that the deconstructionist factory [*la fabbrica deconstruzionista*] establishes its residence" (EP, 77 [80]). Here as elsewhere, Agamben's criticisms of Derrida are far from completely transparent, but what is clear enough is the idea that there is something interminable and even mechanical in his deconstructions. Asked in an interview from 2001 to expand on what in deconstruction he found limiting, Agamben offered a characteristically oblique but nonetheless telling answer: "If I had to express it through a turn of phrase [*una battuta*], I would say that deconstruction was not able to maintain itself in pure destruction [*nella pura distruzione*] and, despite itself, ended up transforming itself into a *melacha*" (LSP, 45). Agamben is of course not obliged to express this assessment through a turn of phrase, and his decision to do so is characteristic of a polemic he made every effort to soften if not silence. At issue are types of destruction. What is forbidden on the Sabbath are *melachoth*—productive works that display a mastery over nature. Other activities, however, such as destruction in the sense of clearing away, are permitted. In this context, the distinction is a surprising one and at first sight seems obscure or even incoherent. That it has everything to do with Agamben's idea of community, however, is seen in his postface to *The Coming Community* where the distinction between *malacha* and *menucha* (rest) is presented alongside inoperativeness and de-creation as a conceptual paradigm for a community no longer waiting for a historical task to be accomplished or a set of conditions to be fulfilled. Agamben's *battuta* is focused on the idea of the "inoperative" that we saw earlier—an idea to which deconstruction is close but tries to instrumentalize and thereby reintroduces into the sphere of work and task. To summarize the import of these images, deconstruction, for Agamben, has set up shop in this place of exile and is content to remain there. This leads to relatively frequent and, though courteous, disappointed and dissenting references to deconstruction as choosing to dwell in aporias and harness their strength rather than seeking a way out of them.

As we saw earlier, "the *experimentum linguae*," for Agamben, "does not (as a common misunderstanding insists) authorize an interpretative practice directed toward the infinite deconstruction of a text, nor does it inaugurate a new formalism. Rather, it marks the decisive event of matter, and in doing so opens onto an ethics" (P, 219 [363]). Derrida's deconstruction falls prey to this "common misunderstanding" and consigns itself to an infinite process—"the infinite deconstruction of a text." This judgment has remained constant over more than thirty years and is found essentially unchanged in *Signatura rerum* where Derrida's "indefinite deferral of signification" is opposed to Foucault's archeological approach (see 79–81).[34] To what he sees as Derrida's infinite reading and interpretation, Agamben implicitly opposes the "genuinely Benjaminian hermeneutic principle" of the "now of legibility" (or "now of knowability"), which is "the absolute opposite of the current principle according to which each work may become the object of infinite interpretations at any given moment" (TTR, 145 [134]). "Our age does indeed stand in front of language just as the man from the country in the parable stands in front of the door of the Law," writes Agamben (HS, 54 [62–63]). Deconstruction either loses itself in "infinite negotiations" with the doorkeeper or takes the doorkeeper's place—"assuming the role of the doorkeeper who, without really blocking the entry, shelters the Nothing onto which the door opens" (the same metaphorical register that we saw Agamben borrow from Origen) (HS, 54 [62–63]). The door opens onto "Nothing," a "Nothing" that becomes dangerous for those around it only when it is closed off as sacred, presented and prized as something that is the province of the few. Derrida remains, for Agamben, in exile because he has found an aporia he considers supreme. Because he sees no way to clear the path, no way out of that exile, he misses what is for Agamben the most obvious, and necessary, response to our state of affairs.

As this discussion shows, Agamben's trenchant criticism of Derrida and deconstruction is the last thing but a recent development in his work and, on the contrary, displays a striking continuity from *Stanzas* (1977) to *Signatura rerum* (2008). As concerns the related question of *nihilism*, we might best close the question with another parable—this one not directed explicitly at Derrida—to express the problem that Agamben sees in deconstruction. The final "idea" in *Idea of Prose* is "The Idea of Awakening." It tells of the sage Nagarjuna, of his traveling and his teaching of the "doctrine of emptiness." Agamben writes of Nagarjuna:

What tormented him, however, were not the rebukes of the orthodox monks who called him a nihilist and accused him of destroying the four truths (his teaching—if truly understood—was nothing other than the meaning of these four truths). Nor did the ironic commentaries of the solitary ones—who, like rhinoceroses, cultivated illumination only for themselves—bother him (for had he not been and was he not still himself such a rhinoceros?). What distressed him were those logicians . . . who claimed to profess the same doctrine as himself. The difference between their teaching and his own was so subtle that at times he himself was unable to grasp it. Yet one could not imagine anything farther from his own position. For theirs was in fact the same doctrine of emptiness, but one constrained within the limits of representation. They employed the principle of reason and that of conditional production in order to show the emptiness of all things, but they did not reach the point at which these principles revealed their own emptiness. They upheld, in short, the principle of the absence of all principles! Hence they taught knowledge without awakening—they taught the truth without its invention [*la verità senza la sua invenzione*]. [IP, 131–32 (119–20), translation modified]

There is much that remains uncertain in the idea of a truth that is to be "invented," and much that remains open in the *euporias* that Agamben finds to resolve the *aporias* of language and history. The question of whether such criticism of deconstruction's "exile in terminology," of its "cutting the branches" of the tree of knowledge, is justified remains equally open. But what should not escape our attention, and what we can glean from even Agamben's most oblique criticisms of deconstruction, is that for him deconstruction represents a potent danger, one that is all the more potent for its proximity to what Agamben sees as the means of dynamic reversal—or in other words, the means to leave, as did Rabbi Akiba, the garden unharmed.

Scholium II: The Idea of Pornography

A reviewer of Vanessa Beecroft's 2005 performance art piece "VB55" at Berlin's Neue *Nationalgalerie* recounted that "one hundred women, aged eighteen to sixty-five—coached by a psychologist, fed vegetarian snacks, and wearing nothing more than skin-toned pantyhose and a sheer coat of almond oil—[were] standing around in Mies van der Rohe's spectacular glass box." Jennifer Allen added that next to her in line stood Beecroft's countryman Giorgio Agamben. "When we finally pressed our noses against Mies's grand vitrine," she wrote, "Agamben could hardly hide his disappointment: 'Pantyhose . . . *ma no!*'" "Speaking of the *vita nuda,*" she related, "the Italian philosopher asked me a question that has preoccupied him for decades. 'How do you imagine people in the perfect world: dressed or naked?'" (Allen 2005). This casual, if curious, question has more serious implications for Agamben than might appear, just as it has a more serious corollary in his writing: the paradigm of pornography.

Idea of Prose's "The Idea of Communism" begins and ends by discussing pornography. This is not the first time that Agamben has approached the subject. In one of his earliest essays he treated the image of pornography through the dramatic directions of Artaud and de Sade (SG, 69–70). Nearly forty years later his *Profanations* returns to the topic, offering a cursory history of pornographic photography and studying the gazes and gestures of the women depicted—from the coy averted glances of the first pornographic photos to the modern convention of the female porn star looking brazenly into the camera—which Agamben relates to forms of spectacular socialization characteristic of our time (PR, 102–6).[35] When Agamben turns to pornography in "The Idea of Communism," it is to do something unexpected. He does not invoke pornography to demystify communism as a manipulative ideology aimed at procuring maximum sexual freedom, or anything of the sort. What he finds so significant for his "idea of communism" in pornographic films is the role that clothing and class markers play in them. In such films there are indeed signs denoting that an individual belongs to this or that class or group, but they prove to be of little importance and they certainly do not serve to keep groups or individuals apart. In pornographic films the actors wear clothes that signify their place in society—whether they are rich or poor, Jew or Gentile, plumber or nurse—but these significations are suspended. That the clothes of the rich and the clothes of the poor, the clothes of the liberal and the clothes of the conservative, are let fall with the same abandon is what enchants Agamben in the idea of pornography and is the reason he sees a reflection of Marx's society without classes therein. These class markers persist in the same manner in which Paul claimed all vocations would persist in the time of the end. Of course, Paul says, Jews will remain Jews and Gentiles will remain Gentiles; the married will remain married and the single will remain single; the circumcised will remain circumcised and the uncircumcised will remain uncircumcised; the change is that these distinctions will cease to matter in the way they did before. "Circumcision is nothing," Paul proclaims, because it is no longer something that divides one people from another.

In the paradigm evoked in *Idea of Prose* and pursued in later works, in pornographic films the characters playing out their wooden drama still bear class markers but those markers no longer have any importance for their lives and no longer prevent individuals from taking pleasure in and from one another. They are rendered, in a term that will take on greater and greater importance for Agamben in the years following *Idea of Prose,* "inoperative." "In pornography," Agamben writes, "the utopia of a society without classes presents itself in the form of a caricatural exaggeration of traits that distinguish class, as well as in a transfiguration of those traits through the sexual act" (IP, 73 [55], translation modified). Pornography offers a glimpse of what Agamben had earlier called a *kairology*—an immediate potential for activity, fulfillment, and pleasure—and he finds therein the expression of an idea he sees as fundamental both to communism and the messianism that is its model: "the potential for happiness present in even the slightest and most everyday situation" (IP, 74 [56], translation modified).[36]

Agamben of course nowhere puts into question that pornography, as an industry, is largely composed of subjection and subjugation, but he also sees in it moments that reveal a far different figure. This is why in *The Coming Community*, as in a variety of other works, Agamben is so interested in the clothes taken off by figures in pornographic photos and films. Like the other paradigms in that book, pornography is evoked not as a global phenomenon to be praised or castigated, to be saved or censored, but for its paradigmatic power. This does not mean that free love need reign or that the rules of conjugal relation should be suspended in the profane order that Agamben calls "the coming community." But of necessity the ideas of property, propriety, and possession would be transformed in a community to come (and it is here that Heidegger's dialectic of belonging is brought into closest alignment with the Benjaminian idea of the profane order—a topic we will return to at the end of this book). The connection might seem capricious or even, in light of the sufferings and degradations of sex industry workers, simply callous. However, in *Idea of Prose, The Coming Community, Profanations,* and various essays touching on the matter, it is clear that what interests Agamben in pornography is the glimmer of equality that its banal scenarios strangely evoke. We saw earlier that for Benjamin "the elements of the final state are not to be found in formless progressive tendencies but are instead deeply embedded in every present as the most endangered, discredited, and mocked creations and thoughts" (Benjamin GS, 2.75). Agamben's search for paradigms takes him to just such discredited and mocked corners of our culture—what he called in *Infancy and History* "the folds and shadows of the Western cultural tradition."

Scholium III: Guy Debord, Strategy, and Political Ontology

In a recent lecture, Agamben recounted a conversation he once had with Guy Debord in which the latter interrupted him to point out, "I'm not a philosopher, I'm a strategist" (M). This is a remark that Agamben understood in all seriousness, and it is likely he had it in mind when he entitled the first section of his introduction to Debord's *Commentaries on the Society of the Spectacle* "Strategist." Just as Benjamin saw himself not only as analyzing the contemporary situation but also as developing strategies to combat opposing forces—a note clearly sounded in the first of his theses with its reference to historical materialism, its enemies, and the chessboard on which various strategies are explored—so too did Debord. The latter so clearly saw his work in strategic terms that he was at times reluctant to state his position openly, discretely noting in his published work that he might be forced to cloak or encode certain of his positions so they would not be appropriated by what he saw as the enemy.[37] This was much like what Benjamin noted in his essay on "The Work of Art in the Age of Mechanical Reproduction"—that the tools developed therein must be rendered unusable for the purposes of fascism. This pressingly political aspect of the works of both men clearly lends them, for Agamben, great appeal and great pertinence. For Agamben, the reason that the twentieth century knew so many political failures was that movements did not come to know their enemy well enough (see HS, 12 [16]). It is clearly this idea that led Agamben to such strategic observations as "One of the not-so-secret laws of the spectacular-democratic society in which we live is that wherever the powers that be are seriously in danger, the media establishment seemingly distances itself from the regime of which it is an integral part, so as to govern and direct the wave of protest so that it not turn into a revolution" (MWE, 125 [97], translation modified).

In light of these facts it should come as no surprise that Agamben came to understand Debord as a "strategist"; but what might surprise is the scope of Debord's strategic activity. Agamben writes that Debord is "a strategist whose field of action is not so much a battle under way in which to marshal troops as the pure potentiality [*potenza*] of the intellect" (MWE, 74 [61], translation modified).[38] Agamben's broadest criticism of a capitalistic society of the spectacle is that it strives to "depotentiate life [*depotenziare la vita*]" (MWE, 78 [64]). The strangeness of the expression stems from Agamben's strategy. For him, strategic choices concerning the present political landscape are to be made on a level that, although not merely abstract, is not narrowly political. For this reason he speaks in *Il Regno e la Gloria* of the "strategic function" of the concept of "secularization" in the hands of Carl Schmitt and Max Weber, just as in *State of Exception* he saw the exchange of views on violence between Benjamin and Schmitt as a "strategic" encounter. In his discussion of Aristotle's *Nicomachean Ethics* he repeatedly characterizes Aristotle's choice of terms as "strategic" (see especially PP, 366 [368]). The question of strategy is intimately linked to the questions of provocation and exaggeration that we looked at earlier. However, a still more fundamental element is involved. "If politics today seems to be going through a protracted eclipse and appears in a subaltern position with respect to religion, economics, and even the law," Agamben writes in *Means Without End*, "that is so because, to the extent to which it has been losing sight of its own ontological status, it has failed to confront the transformations that gradually have emptied out its categories and concepts" (MWE, i [9]). For Agamben, political thought and political strategy have to reconnect with a lost ontological element, have to acquire a meaning that is more than merely instrumental and a function that is more than merely superficial. They must become, for him, at once more comprehensive and more strategic.

Scholium IV: On Hope, Redemption, and
the Irreparable

One evening during a conversation with Kafka, Max Brod summarized his friend's position as being that there was, simply stated, no hope. Without hesitating, Kafka replied, "Oh no. There is indeed hope, hope enough, endless hope—only not for us" (Benjamin GS, 2.414). In the final words of Benjamin's study of Goethe's *Elective Affinities,* he reformulated Kafka's remark, stating that "only for the sake of the hopeless are we given hope" (Benjamin GS, 1.201). Given Kafka's and Benjamin's remarks on the matter, it should come as no surprise that this elusive hope was one with which Adorno would attempt to come to grips. He gave a dialectical interpretation of Benjamin's remark in his *Negative Dialectics,* proclaimed therein that "despair is the last ideology," and wrote, in a section entitled "Finale" at the end of *Minima Moralia,* that "the only philosophy that can be responsibly practiced in the face of despair is the attempt to contemplate all things as they would present themselves from the standpoint of redemption" (Adorno GS, 6.370–6.371; Adorno 1974, 247 [333–334]). To this end, "perspectives must be fashioned that displace and estrange the world, reveal it to be, with its rifts and crevices, as indigent and distorted as it will appear one day in the messianic light." In the haunting final words of the fragment and the work, Adorno wrote, "Beside the demand thus placed on thought, the question of the reality or unreality of redemption itself hardly matters" (Adorno 1974, 247 [333–34]). This imperative is felt so strongly by Adorno that the question of actual redemption appears of secondary importance. The thinker to whom *The Time That Remains* is dedicated, Jacob Taubes, excoriated this view—and this passage—as "the aesthete's variant" on the idea of the messianic (Taubes 2004, 75). In Adorno, says Taubes, "it hardly matters whether [redemption] is real. In Benjamin, it matters" (2004, 75). Whether Taubes's criticism is founded or not, it clearly formulates the question of how "actual redemption" is to be viewed—and awaited.

In *The Coming Community* this topic is approached through the curious term *irreparable.* Agamben says of the figures one finds in the fiction of Robert Walser—a favorite of both Kafka and Benjamin—that they are "irreparably astray" (CC, 6 [14]).[39] Both the tenth chapter and the appendix to Agamben's work bear this same term—*Irreparable*—as their title. The first of these—the chapter entitled "Irreparable"—evokes "the *post iudicium* world" (CC, 40 [38]). From this world, suggests Agamben, "both necessity and contingency, those two crosses of Western thought, have disappeared," with the result that "the world is now and forever necessarily contingent or contingently necessary" (CC, 40 [38]). The idea of making the necessary indistinguishable from the contingent is perfectly in line with Benjamin's idea of a "profane order." It is only on the basis of a transcendental and sacred realm beyond this world that such a dividing line could be drawn. A truly *profane* world—one that was conceived of as transient and thereby as "integral actuality"—would have no place for such a line. Agamben's *irreparable* is linked to a special form of *irreverence* singularly rendered in Walser's characters, who, having accepted the irreparable state of worldly affairs, lose their reverence for what are held up to them as sacred truths. In the appendix to *The Coming Community,* which also bears the title "Irreparable," Agamben writes that "how the world is—this is outside the world" (CC, 106 [88]). At the outset of this appendix Agamben informs his reader that it "can be read as a commentary on section 9 of Martin Heidegger's *Being and Time* and proposition 6.44 of Ludwig Wittgenstein's *Tractatus*," and adds that "both texts deal with the attempt to define an old problem of metaphysics: the relationship between essence and existence" (CC 89 [72]). As Agamben does not cite Wittgenstein's proposition, it bears noting here: "Not *how* the world is is the mystical, but *that* it is."[40] One thing Wittgenstein is saying is that the sheer fact that the world exists is so wonderful and strange that "mystical" is a fine word to describe it—and that what is far more "mystical" than any given inexplicable event in the world is the world itself. Saying "how the world is—this is outside the world" is Agamben's way of saying what Wittgenstein (and Heidegger) said before him. Because there is no transcendental perspective from which to see the world in its totality, and from that point to judge it, one cannot say "how the world," in its totality, *is*. And, ultimately, making a distinction between *existence* and *essence,* between the *necessary* and the *contingent,* would require precisely that. Recognizing that "how the world is" is something that could be said only from "outside the world" is a precondition for living in a world where *existence* and *essence, necessity* and *contingency,* are inseparable given that there is no transcendental instance or sacred exception that can draw the line between the two from within this life and this world. It is for this reason that in the chapter entitled "Irreparable" Agamben invokes a *post iudicium* world, not because the messiah has come and gone, and not because judgment has already been passed, but because we have every reason to cease waiting for such an impossible instance, and one way of conceiving this is as living in a world where judgment of this sort belongs only to the past.

Agamben's readers, as did Adorno's, often fail to distinguish between a harsh indictment and the relinquishing of hope. In the "Finale" to his *Minima Moralia* Adorno wrote of the idea of viewing the world from a philosophical remove as an "utterly impossible thing, because it presupposes a standpoint removed, even if by a hair's breadth, from the magic circle of existence, whereas we well know that any possible knowledge must not only be first wrested from what is, if it shall hold good, but is also marked, for this very reason, by the same distortion and indigence it seeks to escape" (Adorno 1974, 247 [333–334]). This "distortion and indigence" that so darkens Adorno's gaze is not something that Agamben wishes to turn away from. But the idea of this world as lacking something, as needing some addition from elsewhere, is an idea he rejects (and for which his study of "the original structure of negativity" in *Language and Death* laid the groundwork). For this reason, in his chapter entitled "Irreparable" Agamben is fundamentally concerned with what he calls the "salvation of the profanity of the world [*della profanità del mondo*]," which he concisely defines as "its being thus [*il suo esser-così*]" (CC, 89 [73]). The idea of the salvation of the profanity of the world is difficult to grasp—particularly because it is conceived of not as a sanctification of the profane but as a salvation that takes place simply through its being and remaining "thus"—or in the words with which Agamben began *The Coming Community,* "whatever." Agamben goes on to say that "the root of all pure joy and sadness is that the world is as it is," and it is here that we can best understand his idea of the irreparable and the importance of the idea of the profane—ideas that have guided his reflections to the present day (CC, 90 [74]).

To say that the world is "irreparable" is of course not to say that nothing is to be done, that nothing in the world is to be bettered and that no imperative like the one formulated by Adorno is called for. The term is not meant in the conventional sense of something that one would like to repair or remedy but cannot. Just as Agamben does not try to wish transience away, he also does not try to repair the *irreparable.* On the contrary, accepting that the world is *irreparable* in the sense that it is transient and profane is the necessary precondition for addressing the situations that are most in need of our attention and action.

CHAPTER SIX

The Potential of Paradigms:
Homo Sacer: Sovereign Power and Bare Life

Twenty years before *Homo Sacer* was to make him an intellectual celebrity, Agamben was leading a relatively quiet life of research and writing in Paris. He had left Italy for reasons that were in large part political and he met regularly with fellow expatriates Claudio Rugafiori and Italo Calvino. From 1974 to 1976 the three writers planned the publication of a journal that would address what they saw as the most pressing cultural problems of their day and treat its fundamental "categories" of thought and experience (see EP, xi [vii]; IH, 141–50; UIGA, 33; DTP, 5; and AA, xxxiv). The journal never materialized, but the work that went into it took many forms, the most singular of which was *Homo Sacer*.

Categories

The study of these *categories* was to proceed by conceptual pairs. Rugafiori set out to study "architecture and vagueness" while Calvino began with "speed and lightness" (it was with these conceptions that Calvino's career was to come to a premature end a decade later).[1] Agamben was to take up no fewer than three categorical pairings: tragedy and comedy, biography and fable, and the less conventional law [*diritto*] and creature [*creatura*] (see EP, xi [vii]). The results of his research on the first pair—tragedy and comedy—did not take long to find their way into print, with his essay on Dante's poetics appearing in 1978, two years after the project for the review was set aside.[2] The essay "Taking Leave of Tragedy" closed this circle of reflection in 1985, and the collection *The End of the Poem*— whose original Italian title, *Categorie italiane* ("Italian categories"), points to its origin in the planned journal—opens, appropriately enough, with the essay on comedy and ends with the one on tragedy. Agamben's second categorical pair—biography and fable—was also soon to play a central role in his work and found expression in a series of shorter and longer essays on poetic praxis written during the 1980s and early 1990s (many of which are also found in *The End of the Poem*). However, the third pair— law and creature—seemed for many years to vanish from the horizon of Agamben's interests—that is, until the publication of *Homo Sacer*.

It should perhaps come as no surprise that of the three pairs, law and creature was the last to be treated. *Tragedy* and *comedy* are not strange conceptual bedfellows, and although *biography* and *fable* form a less traditional pair, the questions they raise concerning the relation of life to work and of fact to fiction are not difficult to envision. Things stand quite differently, however, with the third categorical pair in which Agamben expressed such interest. Law and creature form a significantly less conventional pair. A *creature* indeed implies a creator, and *law* implies a legislator, but the parallel seems to stop there. In the way we customarily think of them, laws do not apply to all creatures but only to humans. (We do not, for instance, write laws in which dogs are held criminally responsible, even if we do write laws that are concerned with dogs.[3]) What, then, was this "creature" that Agamben proposed to study? And what was its relation to the law?

The beginning of an answer is that the unusual term *creature* is used here in a special sense. What Agamben means is something far from monstrous—as in the familiar euphemistic use of the term in fables and fictions in which the "creature" is an unidentifiable being somewhere between man and beast and thereby outside the law. In an essay examining the historical and theoretical underpinnings of conceptions of "human rights" written during the years when he was preparing *Homo Sacer,* Agamben employs the term *creature* in a fashion that helps clarify matters. Outlining the evolution of our conception of human rights, he invokes a "bare life [*la nuda vita*]" that the codification of inalienable human rights was meant to protect. Immediately thereafter he gives, in the space of a parenthesis, a gloss of what he means by this "bare life." The parenthetical

gloss is as revealing as it is brief: "bare life [*la nuda vita*] (the human creature [*la creatura umana*])" (MWE, 20 [24], translation modified).

The "creature" of Agamben's conceptual opposition is thus another
name for *life*—but not just any life. It is another name for *bare life*, so
it seems that we have merely replaced one enigmatic term with another.
Confronted by such a curious phrase—a bare life that is another name for
the human creature—Agamben's English translators reduced the strangeness of his formulation, rendering "the human creature" as "the human *being*" (MWE, 20 [24]). By designating *the human creature* as another name
for *bare life*, we rectify a mistranslation and enlarge the field of reference,
but we have yet to clarify the relationship that Agamben first glimpsed in
his categorical pairing of *law* and *creature*.[4] We have, however, reached the
central figure of *Homo Sacer* and the works to follow: *bare life*.

The Protagonist, or Law and Life

Early in *Homo Sacer* Agamben announces that "the protagonist of
this book is bare life" (HS, 8 [11]). But what is "bare life" and how has it
been bared? Is it a good thing, such as a purification; a bad thing, such as
a deprivation; or neither? Where do we glimpse this curious form of life,
and what relation does it bear to the categories of *creature* and *law*? "Bare
life" is the translation given in *Homo Sacer* for *la nuda vita*. The history
of this translation is, however, more complicated than might first appear.
In a brief discussion of the idea of the sacred at the end of *Language and
Death,* Agamben wrote that "even the sacralization of life derives from
sacrifice: from this point of view it simply abandons the naked natural life
[*la nuda vita*] to its own violence and its own unspeakableness" (LD, 106
[133]). This suggestive use of the term *nuda vita,* or "naked life," does not,
however, prepare us for the role it will play in Agamben's later thought. In
an essay from 1993 Agamben again invokes *la nuda vita,* and in a widely
read translation of that essay three years later the term is again rendered
as "naked life."[5] Daniel Heller-Roazen's translation of *Homo Sacer* (as well
as translations of other works in which the term occurs, such as *Potentialities* and *Remnants of Auschwitz*) chooses a different translation for *la nuda
vita*: "bare life." *Bare* and *naked* are indeed often synonymous, and this divergence might seem, at first sight, a negligible one reflecting a mere stylistic preference. It is, however, more than this, for *la nuda vita* is not a term

of Agamben's own invention. It too is a translation—a quotation without quotation marks from Benjamin.

In "Destiny and Character," Benjamin invokes *das bloße Leben,* "bare life," and employs it again in "The Critique of Violence" (see Benjamin GS, 2.175 and GS 2.199–200).[6] That Agamben conceived *la nuda vita* as a translation of Benjamin's "*das bloße Leben*" is not made clear to his reader in *Language and Death,* in the 1993 essay, or in any of the other essays leading up to *Homo Sacer.* Nor, for that matter, is it made clear in the opening sections of *Homo Sacer.* At the end of part one, however, Agamben turns to Benjamin's analyses of law and life and there underlines the relation of the one formulation to the other: "nuda vita (bloß Leben)." "*Nuda vita*"— naked or bare life—is thus, for Agamben, another way of saying *bloße Leben*—bare life—and this fact allows us to understand better not only Heller-Roazen's translation but also *Homo Sacer*'s protagonist. Benjamin's expression *das bloße Leben* designates a life shorn of all qualification and conceived of independent of its traditional attributes. Although Benjamin does not offer further directions for how it is to be understood, it is clear that *bare life* is not an initial state so much as what becomes visible through a stripping away of predicates and attributes, and in this respect Geulen offers an excellent paraphrase when she notes that "naked or bare (and bared) life is not a prior substance, but instead what remains after the withdrawal of all forms" (Geulen 2005, 82). Tracing and translating Agamben's enigmatic term, however, is only the first step in understanding what role he envisions for his protagonist and what he hopes to understand through him. The next step involves turning to the other member of the categorical pair on which he first began to reflect twenty years earlier.

To this end we would do well to return to the beginning of the work and examine what immediately follows the title *Homo Sacer.* The book's (untranslated) epigraph is from the German jurist Friedrich Karl von Savigny and reads *Das Recht hat kein Dasein für sich, sein Wesen vielmehr ist das Leben der Menschen selbst, von einer Seite angesehen* ("The law has no existence in itself; its essence is instead the lives of individuals—seen from a certain side"). As such a statement would incline its reader to expect, one of the objectives of the book is to examine the specific side from which law views life. Agamben's first formal studies were, as we saw, in law. His experiences with Heidegger in the south of France and the reading he undertook in their wake led him to revise his calling, and his idea of callings. "For a long time thereafter," Agamben once remarked, "I thought it was a mistake to have studied law. That is something, however, that I no longer think because without this familiarity I would probably never have been able to write *Homo Sacer*" (UL, 16). Signs of this renewed interest in law and the side from which it views life can be seen in an essay published three years before *Homo Sacer* in which Agamben makes a claim he finds important enough not only to place in italics but also to repeat at two other points: *"Philosophy is always already constitutively related to the law, and every philosophical work is always, quite literally, a decision on this relationship"* (P, 161 [252]; see also P, 163 [255], italics in original). Just as Agamben's first book examined an alienated conception of art and aesthetics, his second an alienated conception of scholarly study, his third alienated conceptions of history and experience, his fifth an alienated conception of representation, and his sixth alienated conceptions of language and community, his seventh, *Homo Sacer,* investigates an alienated conception of law.

Agamben turns, then, from the law of his epigraph to the life of the book's opening words. "The Greeks had no single term to express what we mean by the word *life,*" he begins (HS, 1 [3]). This seemingly innocuous observation proves full of consequences for what follows. In and of itself, the phenomenon in question need not be an occasion for surprise. There are many cases in which ancient languages employed more than one word for what modern languages have conflated or eliminated, and this general phenomenon, whether across historical or geographical distances, is perfectly familiar. In the most famous example, Franz Boas claimed in his *Handbook of American Indian Languages* (1911, 25–26) that the Inuit have four words for what we simply call *snow.* The number of words grew over time, Benjamin Whorf supported the claim, and one now easily finds references to Inuit cultures having hundreds of words for snow. Where one fixes this number lies in how one defines linguistic groups and lexical differences, but the reason the Inuit have more refined and specialized linguistic resources for discussing snow than, say, the Greeks is easy enough to understand. Our words are a reflection of our environment and experience (the point Boas wanted to illustrate in the case in question), but there is a fundamental difference between a word like *snow* and a word like *life,* just as for our political landscape there is a fundamental distinction between Greek and Inuit, as it is from the former that the majority of our political conceptions stem. Why then should *life,* that most common and shared of things, Agamben asks, have been separated by the Greeks into distinct words, and why should we not have retained this distinction?

Is it to be attributed to the Greeks having had a tiered conception of life that we have abandoned? Although to modern ears the Greek *zoē* conjures zoos and zoology and thereby the world of animals other than ourselves, the distinction between it and *bios* is not one between sentient life in the animal world and that special form of sentient life that is our own (a topic that Agamben takes up in connection with the term *creature* in *The Open*). The distinction is of a far different nature than a hierarchy of intensity or worth attached to living things.

As Agamben observes, for the Greeks the term *zoē* designated *life* in the sense of "the simple fact of living common to all living beings (animals, men, or gods)," and for this reason it tellingly admitted of no plural form (HS, 1 [3]). *Zoē* was then life in its most general sense, a sense every bit as general as *being*. The second term, *bios,* referred to the forms our lives take—to "the form or way of living proper to an individual or a group" (HS, 1 [3]). In addition to the undifferentiated fact of a thing being alive—*zoē*—there are specific ways of living—*bios*. This distinction corresponded to a fundamental division in the Greeks' political landscape. For them, "simple, natural life" (*zoē*) was not the affair of the city (*polis*), but instead of the home (*oikos*), while *bios* was the life that concerned the *polis*. There was thus in the very words the Greeks used to express the divisions of their culture a distinction between the life that was the business and concern of the (city-)state and the private life that lay beyond its province. As no less a work than *Antigone* graphically dramatizes, it was not always possible to separate these spheres, nor was it easy to decide which deserved one's allegiance when they came into conflict. Although we still have such conflicts of interest between family and country, we do not have separate terms to designate the life applicable to each. Why should we not have preserved such a fundamental distinction in the words we use to express our world? Agamben is intensely interested in the answer to this question, but he is interested in an idiosyncratic way. What interests him is not answering the question in merely historical or linguistic terms. His goal lies elsewhere: in seeing the conflation of terms as paradigmatic of our most pressing political concerns.

Homo Sacer

With these terms—*creature, law,* and *bare life*—brought into clearer focus, we are at last ready to turn to the enigmatic figure that gives its name to Agamben's book: the *homo sacer.* The first thing to note about this "sacred man" is that he was not sacred in any reverential sense—in fact, he was far closer to the opposite. *Homo sacer* is a juridical term from archaic Roman law designating an individual who, in response to a grave trespass, is cast out of the city. From the moment of his ritual pronouncement as a *homo sacer,* he can be killed with impunity by anyone but cannot be employed in sacrificial rituals that require the taking of a life. This "sacred man" is thereby removed from the continuum of social activity and communal legislation; the only law that still applies to him is the one that irrevocably casts him out of the communal sphere.

As Freud and Benveniste did before him, Agamben stresses that the word *sacred* exhibits a remarkable ambiguity in its semantic history, varying from that which is treasured as most pure and precious to that which is most contemptible and must be cast out of the community so as to preserve it from contamination. After analyzing the logic of sacralization, whereby an object is removed from the profane realm and raised to the level of the sacred, at the end of *Language and Death,* Agamben notes that "the sacred is necessarily an ambiguous and circular notion"—and as proof he evokes the figure of the *homo sacer* along with the juridical definition of his status (LD, 105 [131–32], translation modified). In the last chapter of *The Coming Community* he returns to this paradoxical status of the Roman conception of *sacer* (see CC, 86–87 [68–69]).[7] Thirteen years later this question has moved to the center of Agamben's interests—crystallized in the fragile figure of the *homo sacer.* Agamben told interviewers in 2001, "I was always fascinated by the Latin formula that describes the *homo sacer*" (UL, 17). Elaborating on this fascination he remarked, "I found this definition many, many years ago and for long years since always carried it around with me like a package, like a riddle, until I thought, now I must finally grasp [*begreifen*] it" (UL, 17).

What then is the relationship between this riddle that had long fascinated Agamben and the idea of bare life that he had first approached in *Language and Death?* After noting in *Homo Sacer* that "the protagonist of this book is bare life," Agamben offers a gloss of what he means by this: "that is, the life of *homo sacer* (sacred man), who *may be killed and yet not sacrificed,* and whose essential function in modern politics we intend to assert" (HS, 8 [11–12], italics in original). The figure of the *homo sacer* is indeed a mystifying and fascinating one, but wherein lies its relation to an "essential function" in modern politics? The *homo sacer* does not seem at first glance to be in such an inexplicable situation. One cannot, after all, sacrifice that which no longer has any worth, and in such a case of banishment the *homo sacer* cannot represent a sacrifice for the group for the simple reason that he is no longer a part of it. He cannot be used for ritual purposes because he has been declared unclean, his rights have been rendered forfeit, and his status as a member of the group has effectively been suspended. Wherein, then, lies the riddle? This was doubtless a terrible fate for an individual, but the psychological suffering and sociological implications of this practice in early Roman culture are not what Agamben is endeavoring to understand, and it is not toward this sort of psychological or anthropological explanation that he turns. Agamben finds a paradox in the *homo sacer*'s position with respect to the community that has cast him out—a paradox concerning law and its relation to the idea of the sacred. From the perspective of the social group that has cast him out, the *homo sacer* no longer has any of the customary forms or qualifications of specific lives (*bios*) in a community. Stripped of them, all that remains is a human creature, a bare life (*zoē*)—and it is this paradigmatic point that recalls Benjamin's "bare life" and that most interests Agamben in *Homo Sacer* and its sequels. For Agamben, this figure from the most remote past of Western legal history bears a message for today's readers—an ominous one.

Arendt and Foucault, or Biological Life as Such and Biopolitics

To assert the "essential function" of the *homo sacer* in modern politics and to solve the "riddle" it presented, Agamben turned with new intensity to two thinkers who had hitherto played comparatively minor roles in his published work: Michel Foucault and Hannah Arendt. Agamben first read Arendt during the tumult of 1968 and was surprised to discover that the Left in Italy considered her "a reactionary author one did not discuss" (UIGA, 33; see also UL, 17–18).[8] As noted in Chapter One, Agamben wrote to Arendt in 1970 to express his admiration, and although he had long read and admired her, it was not until the essays from the early 1990s preparatory to *Homo Sacer*—such as "Beyond Human Rights" and "What Is a People?"—that her influence figured prominently in his writing.

As concerns Foucault, he is the single most decisive influence on Agamben's later works, a fact on clear display not only in the *Homo Sacer* series but also in such works as *Signatura rerum*. Agamben has remarked, "I first began to understand the figure of the *homo sacer* after I read Foucault's texts on biopolitics" (UL, 17). Among the concepts that Agamben takes from Foucault and develops are what the latter called, in the first volume of *The History of Sexuality* (1976), "biopolitics," along with its corollaries "biopower" and "bioethics."[9]

In the essay "Form-of-Life" (1993), in which Agamben first takes up the questions treated in *Homo Sacer* and parts of which are reproduced verbatim therein, Agamben stresses that "what is left unquestioned in contemporary debates on bioethics and biopolitics . . . is precisely what before all else should be questioned—the very biological concept of life" (MWE, 7 [16], translation modified).[10] Agamben finds a rare treatment of this "biological concept of life" in Arendt's work and notes that some twenty years before the publication of Foucault's *The History of Sexuality* she "had already analyzed the process that brings *homo laborans*—and with it, biological life as such—gradually to occupy the very center of the political scene of modernity" (HS, 3 [6]). Agamben expresses surprise, however, that Arendt makes no connection between her research on "biological life as such" in *The Human Condition* and the analyses of totalitarian power she had conducted elsewhere and in which Agamben finds that "a biopolitical perspective is altogether lacking" (HS, 3–4 [6]).

To this first source of surprise Agamben adds another, observing not only that Foucault failed to note the precedent set for his investigations by Arendt's *The Human Condition,* but also that he never dwelt on what Agamben identifies as "the exemplary places [*luoghi*] of modern biopolitics: the concentration camp and the structure of the great totalitarian states of the twentieth century" (HS, 4 [6]). Foucault's failure to do this—which Agamben calls a "blind spot"—inspires Agamben to remedy this omission (HS, 6 [9]). In Foucault's neglecting to connect his own research with Arendt's, and in his not linking his novel conception of biopolitics to such extreme sites of its exercise as the concentration camp, Agamben sees a parallel to Arendt's own failure to connect the different areas of her research. He describes both of these as "blind spots," though he sees them not as stemming from carelessness on their parts, but instead as offering an "index of the difficulty" of studying "bare life" (HS, 3–4 [6], see also HS, 120 [132]).

These "blind spots" notwithstanding, it is only through the pioneering work done by Arendt and Foucault that Agamben sees the possibility for a better understanding of our political landscape. "Only within a biopolitical horizon," Agamben writes, "will it be possible to decide whether the categories whose opposition founded modern politics (right/left, private/public, absolutism/democracy, and so on)—and which have been steadily dissolving to the point of entering today into a real zone of indistinction—will have to be abandoned or will, instead, eventually regain the meaning they lost in that very horizon" (HS, 4 [7]).[11] Agamben first extends the field of Foucault's biopolitical inquiry to the origins of Western political experience in Greece and Rome. Doing so involves not only a longer historical lens (something examined in a scholium to this chapter) but also a shifting of disciplinary focus. Agamben moves from the fields Foucault studied to ones he tended to avoid: *law* and *theology*. "Foucault worked in many areas," Agamben notes, "but there are two he left out of account: law and theology. It seemed natural to me to direct my efforts in these directions" (DTP, 5).[12] Agamben is careful here and elsewhere to characterize Foucault's choice as a conscious, methodological one that makes perfect sense in light of Foucault's aims. Agamben stresses that for his own study, however, a treatment of legal structures could "complement" and "integrate themselves" into the line of speculation opened by Foucault, and that he tried to bring "Foucault's perspective together with that of the traditional juridical and political ones," adding that, "there is no reason to keep them apart" (LDV; UL, 18). In this light it should come as no surprise that the initial volumes of the *Homo Sacer* project—above all *Homo Sacer* and *State of Exception*—focused in large part on *law,* and that a more recent installment, *Homo Sacer II, 2: Il Regno e la Gloria* (2008), focuses on *theology*.

"I see my work as closer to no one than to Foucault," Agamben remarked in an interview from 2004, and the latter's contribution to the concerns of *Homo Sacer* is not limited to his reflections on biopolitics (DTP, 4). In regard to method, it is clearly reflected in Foucault's use of paradigms, as we will see later in this book, as well as in his concepts of *archeology* and *genealogy*.[13] This influence is also seen in Agamben's exploration of Foucault's idea of *sovereignty*. In such works as *Discipline and Punish,* Foucault shows how a *sovereign* model supremely interested in an elaborate display of power was replaced by a *disciplinary* one in which discrete control and concealed observation replaced the gory artifices of public punishment. Foucault was careful to stress, however, that the means for evading or abandoning the often insidious control exercised by the disciplinary model of political power that characterizes our modern age was not to be sought by somehow turning back the historical clock. As Foucault once remarked in a lecture, "it is not in returning to a sovereign model so as to oppose a disciplinarian one that one might limit the effectiveness of that disciplinary power" (Foucault 1997, 35). In his final books and lectures Foucault even suggested that historians abandon their focus on sovereignty, and in the first volume of his *History of Sexuality* he called for a "liberation from the theoretical privilege of sovereignty" (see HS, 5 [8]).

Agamben listens carefully to this advice—and does precisely the opposite. Instead of liberating his reflections from a theoretical privilege accorded to sovereignty, he radically intensifies them, joining them with Carl Schmitt's studies of sovereignty. The initial modification that Agamben effects to Foucault's historical schema is to show that the "bio-power" Foucault saw as most distinctive of the modern age—as the most distinctively modern thing about our political life and the specific forms that state power now takes—is actually as old as Western politics itself. It is therefore not an effect, as Foucault had claimed, of the shift from a sovereign to a disciplinary society. Agamben then stresses that Foucault's thesis must be "corrected," or at the very least "completed," given that "what characterizes modern politics is not so much the inclusion of *zoē* in the *polis*—which is, in itself, absolutely ancient—nor simply the fact that life as such becomes a principal object of the projections and calculations of state power," but rather the "state of exception" in which *bios* and *zoē* are no longer separable—nor are "right and fact"—but instead enter into a "zone of irreducible indistinction" (HS, 9 [12]).[14] This zone of indistinction characterized by a state of exception is one in whose shadows Agamben sees the fragile figure of the *homo sacer* play a fundamental role—and offer a surprising paradigm.

Borrowing Agamben's terms, Slavoj Žižek wrote in *Welcome to the Desert of the Real* (2002b, 100) that "ultimately, we are all homo sacer."[15] Benjamin Noys took up this same cry, writing, "If a well-known slogan of the 1960s was 'We are all German Jews!' then, for Agamben, the slogan of the new millennium should be 'We are all *homo sacer!*'" (Noys 2002, 56). Watching his small children play at a Swedish theme park, Richard Ek (2006, 379) wondered whether they were not "potential *homines sacri.*"[16] We should be careful not to exaggerate the scope that Agamben grants to his illustrative figure and see, for instance, all of the world's men and women as *homines sacri*, as figures indifferently cast out by a capitalist world order no longer interested in them. Yet the remarks of Žižek and Noys are not far from Agamben's. "If today," Agamben writes, "there is no longer any one clear figure of the sacred man, it is perhaps because we are all virtually [*virtualmente*] *homines sacri*" (HS, 115 [127]). This is a "virtually" that commentators such as Žižek and Noys do not include in their reformulations, but what we should focus on is that for Agamben the present historical situation indeed shows signs of this exceptional figure returning on a global scale. In short, Agamben's *homo sacer* is a figure from the remote past who brings into focus a disturbing element in our political present—and points toward a possible future.

The Concentration Camp

Homo Sacer is a work in three parts. The first part is entitled "The Logic of Sovereignty" and, revising Foucault's schema, traces the idea of sovereignty from modern instances and interpretations to its earliest appearances in ancient Greece and Rome. In his book on German tragic drama, Benjamin wrote that the sovereign "holds historical occurrence in his hand like a scepter" (Benjamin GS, 1.245). Although Agamben does not cite this remark, he clearly has it in mind, as well as what inspired it. In his *Political Theology: Four Chapters on the Concept of Sovereignty* (1922), Carl Schmitt gave a lapidary definition of the sovereign that led Benjamin to write to the future crown jurist of the Third Reich; and it is Schmitt's political theology that lies at the heart of Agamben's ongoing *Homo Sacer* project—both in *Homo Sacer* itself and in parts 2.1 and 2.2, *State of Exception* and *Il Regno e la Gloria*. The sovereign, Schmitt wrote, is "he who can decide on the state of exception [*Ausnahmezustand*]" and thereby suspend the rule of law. As such, the sovereign not only declares but also exemplifies this state of exception. The sovereign is within, and a functioning part of, a legal system based on the principle of sovereignty. But as its foundation, he or she is also in the unique position of standing beyond that same system, and for that reason can declare its suspension. As is evident, the "logic of sovereignty" that Agamben traces through Schmitt's work seems to contain a paradox in which its history is reflected.

Although the idea of sovereignty had interested Agamben throughout the preceding decade, from *Language in Death* to "Bataille et il paradosso della sovranità," the state of exception first comes to the fore in *Homo Sacer*. Its structure, however, is a familiar one. The logic of the state of exception is the same as that of the *example* seen in *The Coming Community* and involves the same seeming paradox of both belonging to a set of phenomena and being, as its representative, independent from it. Just as the example is at once a part and independent of that of which it is exemplary, so too is the sovereign a part and independent from the rule of law. Part One of *Homo Sacer* examines the historical, legal, logical, and ontological coordinates of this sovereign paradox and asks how a figure (the sovereign) can be at once within and set apart from a system that depends on it for its legal and logical coherence—a question that receives separate and ample consideration in *State of Exception*. The thesis of this first of the book's three parts is that "the original political relation is the ban (the state of exception as zone of indistinction between outside and inside, exclusion and inclusion)." This idea, Agamben tells us, "calls into question every theory of the contractual origin of state power and, along with it, every attempt to ground political communities in something like a 'belonging,' whether it be founded on popular, national, religious, or other identity" (HS, 181 [202]). Here we can recognize the subtle, if oblique, continuation of the concerns voiced in *The Coming Community*—and it is at this point that Agamben takes them in an unexpected direction: toward the figure of the concentration camp.

Homo Sacer's second part bears the same title as the book itself, and it is here that the titular figure is more closely studied. Through that figure, Agamben isolates nothing less than what he calls the "originary political element" in the West in "the production of bare life," revising thereby Foucault's analyses of sovereignty (HS, 181 [202]). It is the book's third and final part, however, that has polarized—and in many instances scandalized—readers. Agamben declares there that "in our age, the state of exception comes more and more to the foreground as the fundamental political structure and ultimately begins to become the rule. When our age tried to grant the unlocalizable a permanent and visible localization, the result was the concentration camp" (HS, 20 [24]). Whereas this formulation leaves some room for equivocation, Agamben's epigrammatic statement later in the book does not. "Today it is not the city," he writes, "but rather the camp that is the fundamental biopolitical paradigm of the West" (HS, 181 [202]). For Agamben, the camp is "the most absolute biopolitical space that has ever been realized"—a space in which "power has before it pure biological life [*la pura vita biologica*] without any mediation" (MWE, 41 [38], translation modified). For this reason it is the "paradigm of political space" in which we live, "the hidden matrix," and "the new biopolitical *nomos* of the planet" (MWE, 41 [38], 37 [35], 45 [41]).

It is not difficult to understand why this thesis sparked such controversy. The claim that the real, if concealed, character, the "hidden matrix," of our political landscape is the concentration camp is one that could hardly fail to divide opinion. This "paradigm" for our age might seem to outdo even the darkest predictions and the most hyperbolic commentators. Compared to the thesis that the concentration camp is the biopolitical paradigm for our age, Adorno's doubt about whether poetry might not be barbaric after Auschwitz might seem almost restrained (see Adorno GS, 10.30; see also Adorno GS, 6.355). In a less well-known remark from an essay composed in 1939 and 1940 as reports about the conditions in German concentration camps began to filter through to him in American exile, Adorno claimed that we were living in the "age of the concentration camp" (Adorno GS, 10.286).[17] It is one thing, however, to say in the midst of World War II that we live in "the age of the concentration camp" and quite another to say, as does Agamben fifty years later, that the concentration camp is our culture's political paradigm. For many, the concentration camp indeed served as an example, but of a different sort—an example of a horrendous *exception* to the civilized norm. Agamben presents it, however, not as the exception we are moving away from, but the rule toward which we are dangerously tending.

One critic has called Agamben's thesis an "outrageous provocation [*ungeheure Provokation*]" (Mayer 1997, 21). The term he employs—*ungeheur*—crystalizes a widespread response to the book. Many saw in Agamben's choice of paradigm both of the meanings the German word possesses: "outrageous" and "monstrous." What, then, is Agamben trying to express through this paradigm? Is it meant to shock readers to attention in a manner familiar from Adorno's extreme statements? Is it made to wake them from their mediatic stupor and political somnolence? Reflecting on precisely this question, Dominick LaCapra writes that in

Agamben's view "thought is to engage in unyielding, radical critique of the present in relation to the past. Hence the key role for aporia, paradox, and hyperbole as 'in-your-face' strategies of provocation" (LaCapra 2007, 161; see also Ternes 2007, 114). In other words, LaCapra answers these questions with a resounding *yes*. For him, Agamben's extreme claims are not only, in essence, provocative, they are also best understood as rhetorical devices, with "aporia, paradox, and hyperbole" the means employed to stir readers into realizing the dire state of affairs around them.

There can be no doubt that Agamben's statement surprised many readers and provoked many others, just as there can be little doubt that he knew it would. The question is whether Agamben advanced this claim only for its shock value or, instead, saw it as an essential part of a larger argument. LaCapra sees the matter in cynical terms, judging that "Agamben has recently risen to prominence in the field of critical theory, and there is a sense in which he seems constrained to raise the stakes or 'up the ante' (which is already astronomically high) in theoretically daring, jarringly disconcerting claims if he is to make a significant mark as a major theorist" (LaCapra 2007, 133).[18] LaCapra finds that what is jarring in Agamben's writing is the result less of genuine insight than of a theoretical arms race in which he is engaged. So as to profile himself against a dynamic cohort he must make extreme claims. A great deal rides on this question, and it is best tested by examining Agamben's single most provocative claim: that "the concentration camp is the biopolitical paradigm of the modern age." Understanding this claim, just like understanding *Homo Sacer* and the reactions it has elicited, entails grasping precisely what Agamben meant by calling the concentration camp a "paradigm" for our age. To this end, we must examine his idea, and use, of *paradigms*.

Foucault's Example

What does Agamben mean when he says that the concentration camps is the paradigm of our age? Is he suggesting that we will soon find our rights suspended and our persons given over to the arbitrary violence of a state like the Nazi one that created those camps? To answer these questions requires a careful understanding of Agamben's idea of the *paradigm*. *Homo Sacer* itself contains no definition of the term. The reason for this seems to be that Agamben assumed it would be clear to his reader. Although in a great many cases it has not been, we do not have to look far to find its essential coordinates.

The Coming Community's investigations of exemplarity offers an excellent introduction to this question, drawing on linguistics, set theory, ontology, and still other fields to articulate an idea of the paradigm. In the years immediately following the publication of that work, Agamben began to use what he with increasing frequency called *paradigms* to analyze political questions. He wrote, for instance, about the figure of the "refugee" as, for Arendt, "the paradigm of a new historical consciousness," and more generally of *Means Without End* as dedicated to seeking "genuinely political paradigms" (MWE, 15 [20]; and MWE, i–ii [9–10]). This search remained an essential part of much of Agamben's subsequent work, from the paradigms of *Remants of Auschwitz* to those of *Il Regno e la Gloria*. It did not escape Agamben's notice, however, that readers had difficulty understanding his use of paradigms, and in a series of interviews and lectures given in the wake of *Homo Sacer*'s publication, he sought to elucidate this point. In doing so, he again and again pointed to a precedent he thought was so obvious that he had not bothered to stress it in that work. "I have sought," he said, "to apply the same genealogical and paradigmatic method that Foucault employed" (DTP, 3).[19]

Because Agamben sees his paradigmatic method as having been pioneered by Foucault, to understand his use of paradigms we would do well to begin with this precedent. What, then, for Foucault, was a paradigm? Like Agamben, he offered no definition of the term in those works in which he first began to employ paradigms and so his meaning must be deduced from his method. In a certain sense, a *paradigm* was for him what it already was for Plato—an "example" (*paradigma* is Greek for example). However, it was not just any example, or rather it was an example used in not just any fashion. The most famous of Foucault's paradigms, which is also the one to which Agamben has most explicitly compared his own, is the *panopticon* presented in *Discipline and Punish* as an emblematic figure for a new age of disciplinary power and governmental control.[20] Its origin lay in Jeremy Bentham's design, first proposed in 1787, for a circular prison with cells arranged around a central well that would allow inmates to be observed at all times. "In a Panopticon prison," Bentham wrote, "there ought not anywhere be a single foot square, on which man or boy shall be able to plant himself . . . under any assurance of not being observed" (Bentham 1843, 86). Parliament accepted Bentham's design for a prison to be built at Millbank, London, in 1794, but when it was finally completed in 1816 the plan was no longer his. Thus, in the traditional terms of historical causality, Bentham's design exercised a very minor influence and Foucault's elevating it to the rank of "paradigm" might easily appear excessive. It was precisely this, however, that was so innovative about Foucault's use of paradigms. The influence that it is the traditional task of the historian to study was not what interested Foucault; he was not concerned with the panopticon as a design that had exercised a discernable historical influence, or even as a representative instance in its genre. For him, it stood in a different relation to its age—and to ours. For the unique historian that Foucault was, the paradigm of the panopticon exemplified far more than Bentham could have ever dreamed it would, and the representative or exemplary power that Foucault saw in it extended well beyond any direct historical influence it exerted. In the panopticon Foucault found what he deemed the concealed political coordinates of Bentham's age: deep historical structures underlying such surface phenomena as individual buildings. The spectacular display of state power whose emblem was to be found in gory acts of prolonged public torture, such as those inflicted on the French regicide Damiens, was ceding to a more subtle form of control. Instead of shocking and awing a population into subservience and thereby subjecting them to fear of the crown's sovereign will, the modern state, as Foucault argued, meticulously observed its subjects and let them know they were continually observed—thereby acquiring a new efficacy in their subjugation. Between the lines of Bentham's drawings Foucault saw a dream of institutional control that was being fully realized for the first time in the present day.

This manner of writing history through paradigmatic figures involved, however, viewing history in a way that was anything but orthodox, and it led many to question not only Foucault's historical claims, but his very right to call himself a historian. His use of paradigms entailed viewing history in terms other than those of traditional historical causality. In Foucault's hands, the panopticon became a paradigm for an entire governmental model, a manner of conceiving how best to regulate citizens, how best to discipline and punish those who have stepped out of the lines traced for them by the state. What is more, he presented his paradigm as a herald of what was to come: the panopticon was not only an example of something wide-ranging at a given moment in time; it was also an example of something wide-ranging *over* time. It was a representative instance of a larger phenomenon and a larger aspiration that was as much projected into the future as *goal* than placed in the present as *standard*.

Here we can see all that is remarkable as well as controversial about Foucault's use of the panopticon—and we can sense all the more clearly what is incendiary about Agamben's use of the paradigm of the concentration camp. Bentham's goal in designing a panopticon as a model for prison construction was not particularly sinister, although many modern sensibilities find this systematic suppression of the right to privacy to be just that. In retrospect, Bentham's panopticon seems to many a harbinger of dark things to come, a blueprint for a societal model that is every bit as relevant today as it was in 1787—and far more unsettling. To say, then, as Agamben does, that the paradigm of our age is the concentration camp is to say not only something about the recent past and the immediate present, but also something about a potentially dark future.

With this clearer understanding of Foucault's conception of what a paradigm is and how to use it, we can better understand Agamben's paradigmatic method and his particular claim that the concentration camp is the "biopolitical paradigm of the modern age." In such a statement two questions converge, one of which was largely absent from Foucault's use of paradigms. The first of these is concerned with intellectual coherence; the second with ethical propriety. Foucault was justifiably outraged by conditions in prisons, both ancient and modern, but there is a gulf between the design for a prison and the design for a concentration camp. With this difference comes the question of whether it is not an outrage to the memory of those who lived and died in those camps to employ—or in harsher terms, to instrumentalize—the site of their torture and murder as a paradigm for something else.

The Representative Power of the Concentration Camp, or Negri's Objection

It should come as no surprise that this second element, that of ethical propriety, was vehemently criticized in responses to *Homo Sacer*, and it is on precisely this point that Antonio Negri took Agamben to task. "Life and death in the camps," Negri wrote, "represents nothing more than life and death in the camps—an episode of the civil war of the twentieth century, a horrific spectacle of the destiny of capitalism and the ideologi-

cal unmasking of its will" (Negri 2001, 194). Negri's objection here is un-
equivocal: neither life nor death in the Nazi concentration camps should
serve to represent anything other than the horror that they were. This
clear and categorical criticism is, however, undermined by the fact that in
the very next clause Negri himself uses life and death in the camps to do
just what he charged Agamben with: representing something else—"the
destiny of capitalism." Although this weakens Negri's personal position,
it does nothing to weaken his general criticism; it remains perfectly legitimate and, indeed, imperative, to ask whether life and death in the camps
can be used to represent something else—be it our contemporary political
landscape, the destiny of capitalism, or anything at all.[21]

Negri was far from the only commentator to question this idea, and
in an interview a few years later Agamben was asked, "When you use the
camp in this fashion, do you not reduce or even annul the historical significance of the Holocaust?" Agamben's reply took the seemingly indirect
form of clarifying his use of the term *paradigm*: "When I say 'paradigm' I
mean something extremely specific—a methodological approach to problems, like Foucault's with the panopticon, where he took a concrete and
real object but treated it not only as such but also as a paradigm so as to
elucidate a larger historical context" (UL, 19). Elsewhere Agamben has
stated that "a paradigm is something like an example [*ein Beispiel*], an
exemplum [*ein Exempel*], a unique historical phenomenon" (LKA, 16).
Here, in the space of a single phrase, is crystallized all that is provocative
as well as mystifying in his use of paradigms. As early as *The Coming
Community* Agamben underlined the fundamental, if often overlooked,
fact that examples (and paradigms) are, per se, paradoxical things: "On
the one hand, every example is treated in effect as a real particular case;
but on the other, it remains understood that it cannot serve in its particularity" (CC, 10 [14]). As its etymology indicates and as Agamben underlines, the paradigm is neither clearly inside nor clearly outside the group or
set it exemplifies. In this it is like the sovereign: it is in a state of exception,
both within and lying beyond the set of phenomena it represents—and it
is no coincidence that Agamben chooses to pair these two investigations.
What, then, is the relation of the part to the whole, the particular example
to the whole of which it is an exemplary and representative part? In *The
Coming Community* Agamben goes on to discuss the example or paradigm in the terms of set theory, ontology, ethics, politics, and linguistic
theory (language being an exemplary case of exemplarity for the simple

reason that a given word—*tree*, for instance—serves at once to designate a specific tree as well as the class to which all trees belong). *The Coming Community* opens with the question "What is a singularity?" and tries both to isolate paradigms of singularity and to conceive of a community that would not negate its singularities in favor of universality. More recently, Agamben has written that "the paradigm implies the unconditional abandonment of the conceptual pair particular / general as model of logical inference" (SR, 23). The best way for Agamben to conceive of the relation of part to whole, singularity to generality, citizen to state proves to be through paradigms—through the "paradigmatic method" he adopted from Foucault. The coordinates of this paradigmatic method are different, however, when they are given greater historical and political specificity—and when Agamben employs as paradigm the most horrifying event in our recent past—and present. The fundamental question here, and the one on which the coherence of Agamben's method depends, is that of the relation of the *paradigm* as "real particular case," or singularity, to what it is set apart to exemplify.

Exemplary Places, or Critical Responses to Agamben's Paradigmatic Method

With this broader understanding of the problems and paradoxes of the paradigm, we can return to what precisely Agamben saw the paradigm of the camp exemplifying. Throughout *Homo Sacer* he refers to concentration camps as "exemplary places," and what he sees as exemplary is the legal no-man's-land in which its prisoners were placed—*not* the lives led and lost there to which Negri referred. In this respect, the cover of the American edition of *Homo Sacer* could be seen to reflect Agamben's intentions with particular clarity, showing as it does not an actual image of Auschwitz—a photograph or painting of individuals or of the place—but instead the camp's blueprint. This choice echoes not only Foucault's paradigmatic use of another blueprint (Bentham's), but also Agamben's use of the paradigm of the concentration camp in that work. It is precisely the concentration camp's *design*—spatial as well as juridical—that Agamben finds paradigmatic and wherein lies what he calls its "hidden matrix." What follows this image—the pages of the book itself—does not study the lives led and lost in the Nazi concentration camps (as will Agamben's next book, *Remnants of Auschwitz*), but instead examines possibilities for understanding our historical present and its concealed structures of discipline and control though its paradigm.

Negri's critique of *Homo Sacer* is indeed not the only one directed at Agamben's use of paradigms. In one fashion or another, most responses to the book have taken up this methodological question, although relatively few have couched it in terms that stress the idea of the paradigm. William Connolly's criticism of the excessive "formalism" of Agamben's approach seems to refer to this use of paradigm (although Connolly nowhere speaks directly of this paradigmatic method per se; see Connolly 2007, 27). The charges made by Ernesto Laclau also essentially concern Agamben's paradigmatic method. "Reading [Agamben's] texts," Laclau writes, "one often has the feeling that [he] jumps too quickly from having established the *genealogy* of a term, a concept, or an institution, to determine its actual working in a contemporary context" (Laclau 2007, 11, italics in original).

Such critiques are ultimately concerned with Agamben's aspiration to present paradigms as both real, concrete situations and representative instances. Because Laclau either does not see the nature or does not acknowledge the validity of Agamben's paradigmatic approach (or its heritage in Foucault), he dismisses part three of the book (concerning the paradigm of the concentration camp) as "a series of wild statements" (Laclau 2007, 22). He goes on to make the damning claim that "by unifying the whole process of modern political construction around the extreme and absurd paradigm of the concentration camp, Agamben does more than present a distorted history: he blocks any possible exploration of the emancipatory possibilities opened by our modern heritage" (Laclau 2007, 22). Laclau seeks to deal a double blow to Agamben's work, revealing it as both a false view of the past ("a distorted history") and a dangerous view of the present. If Agamben's paradigm of the concentration camp is to be understood as an example that *must* be followed, as a foregone historical conclusion, then Laclau would undoubtedly be right to characterize it as he does. But whatever objections one might raise against Agamben's paradigms, it is clear that they are not presented as predictions that nothing can be done to alter. On the contrary, they are the extreme means that Agamben employs to explore the same "emancipatory possibilities" that Laclau invokes. This is not to say that those extreme argumentative means are justified by such emancipatory ends, but to ignore those ends, or simply to characterize Agamben's analysis as deterministic,[22] is to miss both the thrust of the argument and the rationale behind it.

The difficulties that critics have experienced discussing Agamben's paradigmatic method are still more clearly displayed in the work of Andrew Norris. Unlike Laclau, Norris begins with a lucid statement that "Agamben's project [in *Homo Sacer*] hinges upon the paradigmatic status of the camp" (Norris 2005, 264). After acknowledging that for Agamben the camp is a "fundamental biopolitical paradigm," Norris asks, "But *on Agamben's own terms* what does this mean?" (2005, 273, italics in original). Norris's answer is that "the clear implication of Agamben's own explanation of what makes something exemplary or paradigmatic is that in claiming a paradigmatic status for the camps he is *and can only be* making an unregulated decision that cannot be justified to his readers in a nonauthoritarian manner" (2005, 273, italics in original). This is an exceptionally curious statement, and all the more so from the editor of one of the first volumes dedicated to the *Homo Sacer* project. Norris interprets "Agamben's own explanation of what makes something exemplary or paradigmatic" as "unregulated" and "authoritarian." To this judgment he adds a remarkable analogy, likening Agamben's paradigms to the decrees of a sovereign. In doing this, Norris is showing particular sensitivity to the analysis of sovereignty found elsewhere in *Homo Sacer*. His analogy presents a notable flaw, however. He goes on to claim that "on [Agamben's] own account, there is an isomorphism between the exception and the example or paradigm. Given his acceptance of Schmitt's analysis of the former as the product of the sovereign decision, this renders Agamben's evaluation of the camp as 'the fundamental biopolitical paradigm of the West' a sovereign decision beyond the regulation of rule or reason. As this casts his readers as either subject or enemy, it is hard to imagine how the politics it might produce will serve as a real alternative to what it contests" (Norris 2005, 264). For Schmitt, the sovereign is the figure who can declare a state of exception, suspending the rule of law. Norris claims that through his choice of paradigm Agamben is declaring a sort of conceptual state of exception where the rule of reason is suspended. The problem with this analogy is that the sovereign does not set out to persuade his or her subjects to accept a declaration of the state of exception; the sovereign simply declares. The real parallel for a sovereign decision would be not to write a work explaining in what sense the concentration camp can be understood as a paradigm for our historical past and political present, but to issue an authorial edict—and what is more, one that would somehow bind its readers to accept it.

In blurring the distinction between political power and intellectual persuasion, Norris characterizes Agamben's paradigmatic method as an arbitrary imposition because it is not the fruit of consensus. It is the product of an author, and in that sense Norris's description is perfectly accurate; but it would also apply equally well to *every* text that is the product of a single author—including, of course, Norris's own. Maintaining this analogy, Norris goes on to offer a summary judgment on *Homo Sacer*. "Unfortunately," Norris writes, "Agamben's acceptance of Schmitt's decisionism makes it impossible for his analyses to have any general validity. Perhaps worse, it puts him in the position of deciding upon the camp victims one more time, thereby repeating the gesture of the SS in precisely the way he says we must avoid" (Norris 2005, 278).[23] However flawed its reasoning, one thing this remark illustrates is the outrage that many readers have felt in finding Schmitt, crown jurist of the Third Reich, playing a shaping role in Agamben's analysis. Another thing it demonstrates is the ease with which Agamben's use of paradigms can be misunderstood.

Considering Agamben's paradigmatic method in this light, it should perhaps come as no surprise that it seems to have been best understood by those critics who have dismissed the concentration camp and replaced it with paradigms of their own. "I cannot conceal my perplexity at the central thesis: that the camp is the specific and typical figure of this inclusive exclusion," wrote Luciano Ferrari Bravo (1996, 169). In lieu of the concentration camp, he proposed Ellis Island as a more fitting paradigm (because of its role in the formation and preparation of masses of workers for the capitalist machine awaiting them in the New World). This paradigm serves Ferrari Bravo's philosophical purposes and is in line with his upbraiding of Agamben for insufficient materialism in his analysis; but it also shows a clear understanding of how Agamben uses the paradigm of the camp. In a similar vein, Robert Eaglestone has offered an alternative in suggesting that the *colony* would be a more suitable paradigm, as has Ojakangas in suggesting "the present-day welfare society" (Eaglestone 2002, 61, 64; Ojakangas 2005a, 27). Unlike the paradigm of Ferrari Bravo, those of Eaglestone and Ojakangas do not identify a concrete historical place or event and therefore represent a different sort of corrective. Whether Ellis Island, the colony, or a welfare society would be better paradigms are open questions, but what these suggestions share is a focus on the actual method Agamben employs.

What Is a Paradigm?

How then does Agamben balance an understanding of the historical specificity of a paradigm with its exemplary value? An initial way of approaching this question is by means of disciplinary distinctions. "I am not a historian," Agamben has stressed, "and I do not use paradigms as a historian" (LDV; see also LKA, 16). Elsewhere he has written that his paradigms' "goal is to render intelligible a series of phenomena whose relationship to one another has escaped, or might escape, the historian's gaze" (SR, 33). If he does not then use paradigms as a historian, we might well wonder as what, and to what end, he *does* use them. "I use a paradigm so as to circumscribe a larger group of phenomena," he has remarked, "and so as to understand a historical structure [*eine historische Struktur*]" (LKA, 16). Although he stresses that he is not a historian and is not using paradigms as a historian would, he makes clear that his undertaking nevertheless has a historical component; the horizon of understanding is "historical" and involves not only events but "structures." The reason Agamben stresses that although he employs historical materials and methods he does not do so as a historian is that his paradigms are aimed less at understanding the past than at understanding "the present situation" (LDV).

As the preceding makes clear, to be genuinely illuminating Agamben's paradigms must strike an exceptionally delicate balance between respect for the uniqueness of historical phenomena and the use to be made of those phenomena for understanding *other* situations. "For me," Agamben has remarked of the most controversial of his paradigms, "the camp is a concrete historical fact [*ein konkretes historisches Faktum*] that at the same time serves as a paradigm, making it possible to understand the present situation [*unsere heutige Situation*]" (UL, 19; see also LDV). Expanding on this point he has then noted, "The figures of the *homo sacer* and the camp serve as examples inasmuch as they are concrete historical phenomena. I do not reduce or cancel this historical aspect—on the contrary, I try first to contextualize them. And only then do I try to see them as paradigms through which to understand our present situation. This is simply another way of working historically, another methodological approach," to which he has added the radical claim that "every truly interesting book of history proceeds in this fashion" (UL, 19).[24] Agamben thus sees himself as "working historically," but not as a historian. Although this offers some development of the question, it does not offer an answer to the question of how his readers are to balance the two elements of his paradigms.

The first part of *Signatura rerum,* entitled "What Is a Paradigm?", aspires to answer exactly this question and thereby to correct those who "in more or less good faith believed that I intended to offer theses or reconstructions of a merely historiographical character" (SR, 11). As he has on earlier occasions, Agamben begins by addressing the dual nature of his paradigms: "In my work I have had occasion to analyze figures such as the *homo sacer,* the Muselmann, the state of exception, and the concentration camp that are, of course, discrete historical phenomena, but that I have also treated as paradigms whose function was to constitute and render intelligible a vast historico-problematic context" (SR, 11). Agamben's next move also proves to be a familiar one in that he stresses that there is ultimately nothing new in his paradigmatic method; that it is simply a continuation of Foucault's work. Because Foucault never defined the term *paradigm* in his work, Agamben seeks to elucidate his own idea of *paradigm* by first answering the question for Foucault. The definition of a Foucauldian paradigm at which Agamben arrives proves to be virtually identical to the one he gave of his own paradigm in the opening lines of the essay: "singular historical phenomena that . . . at once constitute and render intelligible a more ample problematic context" (SR, 19). Although this definition clarifies Agamben's relation to Foucault, it complicates his idea of the paradigm. For Agamben, the paradigms of Foucault's work and his own do not function merely as lenses through which to see things that are already there; they not only render intelligible a given context, they "*constitute*" it.

For this reason Agamben is careful to stress that the paradigm is not a "metaphor," that it follows not "the logic of the metaphorical transport of a signified, but instead the analogical one of an example" (SR, 19). In this respect the paradigm resembles more closely the "semantic structure" of allegory than that of metaphor (SR, 19–20). "To make of something an example is a complex act," he remarks, "one that supposes that the term that is to function as paradigm is disactivated from its normal usage not so as to be displaced into another area. . . . The paradigm is a singular case that is isolated from the context to which it belongs only to the extent that by exhibiting its singularity it renders a new group of phenomena intelligible whose homogeneity the paradigm itself constitutes" (SR, 20).

As these remarks make clear, the paradigmatic method, as Agamben understands it, involves the most fundamental—and creative—reflection. Far from finding, then, the original form of Foucault's—and by extension his own—paradigm in Thomas Kuhn's idea of the paradigm (expressed in *The Structure of Scientific Revolutions,* 1962), Agamben traces that form back to no less a figure than Aristotle, in whose philosophy he finds "the *locus classicus* of an epistemology of the example" (SR, 20). In Aristotle's *Prior Analytics* we read that "the example"—which Agamben translates as "paradigm"—"stands neither in the relation of part to whole, nor of whole to part, but rather of part to part" (Aristotle 1984, 110 [69a]; cited by Agamben in SR, 20). The relation that Aristotle outlines here is the one that governs Agamben's use of paradigms. Instead of a dialectical relationship between part and whole, he sees a "paradigmatic" relationship whose basis lies not in the inferential model of logic but in the more flexible one of analogy.[25]

Continuing his genealogy of the paradigm, which is also a search for examples that will help his reader better understand his method, Agamben turns from Aristotle to Kant and the latter's discussion of aesthetic judgment. A beautiful work of art offers Kant—and, in his wake, Agamben—an example for which there is no general rule: the work of art is beautiful, but that beauty is not deduced from laws, rules, or precepts. It is instead simply recognized as beautiful and thereby moves from part to part rather than from whole to part or part to whole (see SR, 22–23).[26] From Kant Agamben turns to Heidegger and his discussion of the hermeneutic circle. Heidegger famously stressed that it was never a question of avoiding the hermeneutic circle, only of entering it in the right fashion. Returning to the center of his first philosophical master's method, Agamben says of the hermeneutic circle that its "aporia can be resolved only if the hermeneutic circle is recognized as in reality a paradigmatic circle" (SR, 29). Heidegger's hermeneutic circle is condemned to remain a mystery as long as we fail to see that the relation in it of part to part and part to whole follows a paradigmatic line. Once we realize, however, that the hermeneutic circle was never anything else but a paradigmatic circle, its form and function are, for Agamben, suddenly clarified.

The conclusion that Agamben draws from these at once genealogical and conceptual excurses on the twin ideas of the example and the paradigm is that the model for paradigmatic reasoning, and for his own paradigmatic method, is neither inductive nor deductive but "analogical," and one in which "exemplarity and singularity are never fully separable" (SR, 32–33). He then ends his answer to the question "What is a paradigm?" on a poetic note. "I know of no better definition," he writes, "than the one contained in a poem by Wallace Stevens bearing the title 'Description Without Place': 'It is possible that to seem—it is to be, / As the sun is something seeming and it is. / The sun is an example. What it seems / It is and in such seeming all things are'" (SR, 34). In another poem Stevens offers the proposition, or makes the request, "Let be be the finale of seem" (Stevens 1997, 50). Agamben is focused not on a horizon where seeming and being would meet, whether in a joyous finale or otherwise, but instead on an idea of the paradigm as that which casts the light through which things first come to be known, but that does not, for as much, diminish the integrity of that source of light.

In sum, *Homo Sacer*'s strength is inseparable from its weakness: the radicalization of Foucault's paradigmatic method. Agamben sees the Nazi concentration camps as unique historical phenomena, and he treats them as representative ones. He uses paradigms heuristically—for how much they allow him to understand of the past, and for how starkly they throw the present situation into relief. The reader of *Homo Sacer* does not, of course, need to accept the legitimacy—whether logical or ethical—of ascribing such a double status to unique historical situations. It should be recognized, however, that this problem lies at the very center of his work.

Provocation and Progress, or the Intimate Solidarity Between Democracy and Totalitarianism

With this clearer sense of what, for Agamben, a paradigm *is,* let us return to his particular choice of paradigm. For Foucault, the panopticon was not the most absolute or cruel form of discipline or control in human history. It was instead far more innocuous than the things Foucault used it to exemplify. For this reason, although his method and its findings seemed provocative to many, the paradigm itself did not. Agamben's choice of paradigm, however, could hardly be more controversial. There can be little doubt that Agamben was aware of the risks entailed in his choice of paradigm. In the name of what, then, did he take this risk?

When Agamben says that the paradigm for our political age is not the *polis* but the concentration camp—the darkest, most terrifying phenomenon of modern times, the existence of which makes us doubt our humanity, fear our progress, and doubt our civilization—he is doing several things. One of these is provoking those who, in his view, naively cling to a belief in the idea of inevitable progress in history (a point we first saw in relation to *Infancy and History*). Agamben's skepticism about the dominant model of historical progress is expressed not only in his choice of paradigm but also in the comparisons he makes between democratic states and totalitarian ones. Despite all their very manifest differences, he sees nothing less than an "intimate solidarity" between them (HS, 10 [14]). In what does this solidarity consist? This is not a global conspiracy, and Agamben is careful to note real distinctions between the two forms. Nevertheless, for him the solidarity in question stems from a practice common to democratic and totalitarian forms of government: the appropriation of "bare life" by the mechanisms of the state.

Agamben's denunciation of this perceived solidarity is closely allied in his writing to the vision of the society of the spectacle announced and analyzed by Debord. In the years following the publication of *The Society of the Spectacle* Debord observed a growing similarity between what he called the "concentrated spectacle" of totalitarian regimes and the "diffuse spectacle" of Western democracies. One of the central ideas of his *Commentaries on the Society of the Spectacle,* for which Agamben wrote a preface, is precisely this. After noting that his goal of trying "to understand once and for all why democracy, at the very moment in which it seemed to have finally triumphed over its adversaries and reached its greatest height, proved itself incapable of saving *zoë,* to whose happiness it had dedicated all its efforts, from unprecedented ruin," Agamben writes that "modern democracy's decadence and gradual convergence with totalitarian states in post-democratic spectacular societies (which begins to become evident with Alexis de Tocqueville and finds its final sanction in the analyses of Guy Debord)" is "rooted" in precisely this "aporia" (HS, 10 [13]).

Although this explanation suggests a need for extreme means, it does not explain Agamben's use of Auschwitz as *leitmotif.* As we saw earlier, this choice was in large part motivated by the multiplying spaces in our societies where states of exception seem to have become the rule. On the other side of the analogy, and as his later work makes clear, Agamben sees a danger in according to the concentration camp the status of the unspeakable, in treating it as something to be honored through respectful silence. This does not mean that its figure can and should be instrumentalized, but it does mean that it is something from which we should not divert our historical gaze. In an essay published a year before *Homo Sacer* Agamben wrote that "the camp is the place in which the most absolute *conditio inhumana* ever to appear on Earth was realized." Elsewhere therein he states that "what happened in the camps exceeds the juridical concept of crime to such an extent that the specific political-juridical structure within which those events took place has often been left simply unexamined" (MWE, 37 [35]). This clear and compelling recognition of the immensity of the crime (so immense that it seems to exceed the concept) has, in Agamben's view, had as its natural result a failure to examine this "political-juridical structure" in as thorough a manner as it demands. For Agamben, failing to do so not only obscures our view of the past, it also endangers our societies in the present.

The "present situation" appears to Agamben extreme enough to call for extreme measures and extreme paradigms. What he wants to grasp is what he calls "the bare life [*la nuda vita*] of the citizen, the new biopolitical body of humanity" (HS, 9 [13]). Grasping this elusive bare life is no easy task, however, and it is for this reason that he develops conceptual paradigms that will cast it in a new and revealing light. And it is here that the idea of bare life relates to the other fundamental idea of *Homo Sacer,* the state of exception. Of what are the *homo sacer* and the concentration camp paradigms or examples? Agamben's answer is that they are examples of the state of exception. The only real rule of the camp was that the rule of law was suspended. This rule of misrule, or ruling outside of the norms governing social forms and human interaction, produces a gravely dangerous "state of exception"—one of the reasons that Schmitt's theories on that state are of such interest to Agamben both in this book and in its sequels.[27]

The Secret Connections Between Power and Potentiality

Although *Homo Sacer* is far and away the most amply commented on of Agamben's books, there remain two notable lacunae in the critical literature. The first is the one we looked at earlier: systematic discussions of Agamben's paradigmatic method. The second is more difficult to fill and concerns a chapter of the book that the majority of commentators have chosen either to avoid or to paraphrase without linking it to the principal concerns of the book. Entitled "Potentiality and Law," it presents us with something familiar—in an unfamiliar place.[28] It is a discussion of the idea of potentiality, here connected to questions of sacrality, sovereignty, and law.

We read here that

> only an entirely new conjunction of possibility and reality, contingency and necessity . . . will make it possible to cut the knot that binds sovereignty to constituting power. And only if it is possible to think the relation between potentiality and actuality differently—and even to think beyond this relation—will it be possible to think a constituting power wholly released from the sovereign ban. Until a new and coherent ontology of potentiality . . . has replaced the ontology founded on the primacy of actuality and its relation to potentiality, a political theory freed from the aporias of sovereignty remains unthinkable. [HS, 44 (51)]

Agamben clearly sets before his readers the aporia that forms the "knot" that his work will endeavor to loosen and that he gives the name *potentiality*. Were we to seek further confirmation that Agamben's conception of potentiality lies at the heart of the project, we might look to the next installment, where Agamben writes that "there is no human essence; the human being is a potential being [*che l'uomo è un essere di potenza*]" (RA, 134 [126]). For Agamben, a political theory freed from the dangerous aporias of sovereignty that *Homo Sacer* and its sequels graphically delineate will remain "unthinkable" until a "new and coherent ontology" that ceases to found itself on "the primacy of actuality" is developed. As noted, despite the capital importance that Agamben accords to this conception of *potentiality*, the majority of those who have thus far written on *Homo Sacer* have accorded little or no place to it in their analyses of the work; the majority of commentators have concerned themselves with the paradigm of the concentration camp.[29] However, as the preceding passage makes perfectly clear, to understand *Homo Sacer* and the questions that animate it, we must look to the idea of *potentiality* and its relation to political questions.

As Agamben noted in an essay from 1987, "We are used to thinking of the term potentiality [*potenza*] above all in terms of force, or power [*potere*]," and this is the habit that he endeavors to counter (BPS, 118). In an aside in *Idea of Prose* Agamben invoked "the secret connections that link power [*potere*] and potentiality [*potenza*]," and that peripheral question becomes a central one in *Homo Sacer* (IP, 51 [71], translation modified). It enters *Homo Sacer* through an analysis of the relation between the "constituting power" that founds a sovereign state and the "constituted power" that maintains it once it has been established—the same question that has occupied foundational thinkers of the modern nation state from Hobbes and Locke to Rousseau and, more recently, Schmitt. It is also the question that Benjamin, with characteristic boldness and concision, treats in his essay on violence and that he conceives through the figure of a "divine violence" that has proved so difficult for his interpreters to locate, just as it is the question that thinkers close to Agamben such as Negri and Paolo Virno have endeavored to reformulate in today's political context.[30]

For Agamben, the relationship of *constituting power* to *constituted power* forms "the secret connections that link power and potentiality." His examination of these powers in *Homo Sacer* involve his conceptions of *sovereignty* and *bare life* and their connection to an idea of potentiality. Let us first turn to the relation of *sovereignty* to *potentiality*. Agamben begins the chapter in question by focusing on power and the violence it can lawfully exercise. He first glimpses what he calls the "paradox of sovereignty" in the relationship between "constituting power"—the power that leads to a new (legal) order and that founds and grounds the constitution (in that order)—and the power that ensues from it, "constituted power," whose foundation and ground, in turn, is the new (legal) order's constitution. The practical and theoretical problem for thinkers from Hobbes to Schmitt arises from the fact that in the constitution and consolidation of every new state there is a transition from a revolutionary and anarchic force abundantly present in the "constituting power" that brings a new state into being and the conditioned and controlled form of "constituted power" that is its stabilized and, ideally, durable form. Although the difference is of course easy enough to understand, a problem arises as soon as we attempt to pinpoint the moment of transition and define how this transition from constituting to constituted power is to be justified and regulated.

As generations of political philosophers have stressed, one of the things that a constitution endeavors to effect is the defusing and domesticating of precisely this "constituting power," and the transformation of it into measures and guidelines for the exercise of a legitimate and properly legitimated "constituted power." "Here the basic problem," writes Agamben, "is not so much how to conceive a constituting power that does not exhaust itself in a constituted power (which is not easy, but still theoretically resolvable), as how clearly to differentiate constituting from constituted power" (HS, 41 [49]). The Trotskyist conception of a "permanent revolution" or the Maoist "uninterrupted revolution" are attempts in the one direction—that of retaining this constituting power in the constituted power. But as stated earlier, Agamben is asking his readers to focus on a different question, that of distinguishing constituting from constituted power.

In light of this argument, he criticizes Negri's *Constituting Power* [*Il potere costituente*] (1992) and its central claim that constituting power can be distinguished and isolated from sovereign power. "The strength of Negri's book," says Agamben, lies not here but "instead in the final perspective it opens insofar as it shows how constituting power, when conceived in all its radicality, ceases to be a strictly political concept and necessarily presents itself as a category of ontology" (HS, 43–44 [51]).[31] The political problem that Negri set out to understand and resolve is so fundamental that, following Agamben, it is best conceived of in ontological terms. As a result, Agamben likens the relation of *constituting power* and *constituted power* to *potentiality* and *act*. "The problem is therefore moved," claims Agamben, "from political philosophy to first philosophy (or if one likes, politics is returned to its ontological position)" (HS, 44 [51]). And it is via this path that Agamben arrives at the surprising and sweeping claim we saw earlier that "only an entirely new conjunction of possibility and reality, contingency and necessity . . . will make it possible to cut the knot that binds sovereignty to constituting power" (HS, 44 [51]).

Before cutting it, Agamben will pull this knot tighter in formulating the relation of constituting to constituted power in terms of *sovereignty*. "Every authentic understanding of the problem of sovereignty," Agamben argues, "depends on how one conceives of the existence and autonomy of potentiality" (HS, 44 [51–52]). Although the linking of the problems of constituting and constituted power to the problem of sovereignty, as well as the subsequent parallel linking of the problem of sovereignty to potentiality, is clear enough, what Agamben sees under the sign of "a new and coherent ontology of potentiality" remains exceedingly difficult for his readers to grasp—and for good reason. Agamben evokes here "the autonomy of potentiality." Yet what could he mean by such a formulation?

From what is potentiality rendered autonomous if not the actual realm in which questions of constituting and constituted power transpire?

On the one hand, this "autonomy" is clear enough. When Aristotle speaks of the architect's potential to design buildings even in moments when he is not designing, and of the kithara player's potential for playing even when he or she is not playing, this is a potentiality independent of (or autonomous from) its actualization that presents no problems of understanding. When we acknowledge an individual's potential for doing this or that thing, we do not ask that he or she do it without interruption. If what he or she does is not exercised for too long, we may consider its continued existence questionable or vitiated. If the kithara player ceases to play for many years, we may have reservations about whether he or she can still play with anything like his or her former skill. But the idea of such autonomy is easily grasped (we must decide only about the half-life of various acquired skills). Thus, this *potential* could be said to be autonomous because in these instances it is independent of its actualization. What Agamben is arguing is the same as concerns the sovereign exercise of political power: that the state or the sovereign retains this potential to suspend the rule of law even when not doing so, just as we might say that in the stabilized form of constituted power the state retains the potentiality for exercising its full power to suspend the rule of law. Yet is this truly to conceive of an "autonomy" of potentiality with respect to actuality? Do not these examples remain in "relation" to potentiality's actualization— both past and future?

Although this question about an "autonomous potentiality" is left open, the relation of Aristotle's conception of potentiality to sovereignty is not. Agamben tells his reader that "in thus describing the most authentic nature of potentiality, Aristotle actually bequeathed the paradigm of sovereignty to Western philosophy" (HS, 46 [54]). Agamben then states that "potentiality and actuality are simply the two faces of the sovereign self-grounding of Being" (HS, 47 [54]). For Agamben, the question of sovereignty, in both genealogical and ontological terms, is thus a question of *potentiality*. The relation of constitutive to constituted power that Negri explored is traced by Agamben back to a "logic of sovereignty," which is in turn related to the idea of potentiality first given clear expression in Aristotle's philosophy. Any attempt to resolve the aporias raised by the relation of constituting to constituted power that does not first confront the ontological problem posed by potentiality is condemned to remain, for Agamben, a partial one.

At this point in his reasoning Agamben states that for political theory to break the bonds of sovereignty and conceive of a new politics and a new idea of community—the task he has assigned himself—"one must think the existence of potentiality without any relation to Being in the form of actuality [*senz'alcuna relazione con l'essere in atto*]. . . . This, however, implies nothing less than thinking ontology and politics beyond every figure of relation [*al di là di ogni figura della relazione*], beyond even the limit relation that is the sovereign ban. Yet it is this very task that many today refuse to assume at any cost" (HS, 47 [55]). It is not difficult to see why this line of interrogation is the one least remarked on in critical treatments of *Homo Sacer*. Although lying at the conceptual center of the work, it is also the passage that is most difficult to integrate with the rest of the work. This difficulty is augmented by the fact that the question of how political theory and ontology might "think the existence of potentiality without any relation to Being in the form of actuality" finds little elaboration in the later sections of the book. Can we not, however, more closely approach what Agamben envisions here?

In this same passage Agamben observes that "in modern thought there are rare but significant attempts to conceive of being beyond the principle of sovereignty" (HS, 48 [55–56]). Among these attempts he numbers Schelling's *Philosophy of Revelation,* in which the latter endeavors to think "an absolute entity that presupposes no potentiality"; Nietzsche's doctrine of eternal recurrence of the same; and Heidegger's idea of *Ereignis* (HS, 48 [55–56]). To this list Agamben adds Bataille (in a sentence that was omitted from the English translation)—"who, although remaining a thinker of sovereignty, conceived in the ideas of negativity without employ and *désoeuvrement* a limited dimension in which the 'potentiality to not' [*potenza di non*] no longer seems subsumable within the structure of the sovereign ban" (HS, 56).[32] However, Agamben states that "the strongest objection against the principle of sovereignty" is not to be found in any of these thinkers but instead "is contained in Melville's Bartleby, the scrivener who, with his 'I would prefer not to,' resists every possibility of deciding between potentiality and the potentiality not to" (HS, 48 [56]). The problem of potentiality is not a problem among others in *Homo Sacer*; it is *the* problem that gives its logic, and its paradoxes, to all others. And as the reference to Bartleby makes clear, it involves thinking about potentiality in an unhabitual fashion. As Aristotle remarks in *On the Soul,* "He who possesses science [in potentiality] becomes someone who contemplates in actuality" (417b; cited by Agamben in P, 184 [286]). This is the horizon of Agamben's investigation. In a passage added to the Italian publication of a lecture on precisely this topic, Agamben stresses that "we still have to measure the consequences of this figure of potentiality," but it is already clear that it "obliges us not only to fundamentally reconceive the relation of potentiality to act, between the possible and the real, but also to consider in new fashion, in aesthetics, the status of the act of creation and of the work and, in politics, the problem of the conservation of constitutive power in constituted power" (PP, 286).

Politics and Ontology

There is much that is new to *Homo Sacer,* but there is also much that is familiar from his earlier works. One of the greatest difficulties that *Homo Sacer* presents is that of thinking on several levels at once, of linking ontological and linguistic categories with historical and political ones. Of capital importance to Agamben are what he calls "the analogies between politics and the epochal situation of metaphysics" (HS, 188 [210]). Early in *Homo Sacer* he remarks that "it is not by chance" that there is to be found in Aristotle's *Politics* a passage that "situates the proper place [*il luogo proprio*] of the *polis* in the transition from voice to language"—the same relation he has studied under a number of guises and that received particular attention in his analyses of *infancy* and of the relation of *voice* to *language* in *Language and Death* (HS, 7 [10–11]). For Agamben, "the question 'In what way does the living being [*il vivente*] have language?' corresponds exactly to the question 'In what way does bare life dwell in the *polis*?'" (HS, 8 [11]). Although he does not offer an immediate answer to these twinned questions, one is to be found therein. A few pages later he refers to "the link between *zoē* and *bios*, between voice and language" (HS, 11 [14]). Here, bare life, or *zoē*, is said to be like the voice of the individual living being whose relation to language is one of potential, although how that potential is actualized remains undetermined. Later in the book, however, Agamben writes that "today *bios* lies in *zoē* exactly as essence, in the Heideggerian definition of Dasein, lies (*liegt*) in existence" (HS, 188 [210]). The Heideggerian conception of facticity and the transcendental immanence, or immanent transcendence, that Agamben sees in Heidegger's ontology exhibits the same relation, and presents the same conceptual difficulty, as the relation of *bios* to *zoē*. They are mutually embedded in one another to the point that they have become indistinguishable. This has brought about a dire state of affairs, but it also, as is so often the case in Agamben's writing, points the way toward a possible reversal. In a biopolitical perspective, this state of affairs and its corresponding state of exception is the condition of possibility for the most abhorrent acts of state-sanctioned coercion. But this catastrophic state of affairs also reveals the means of ending this bloody reign and replacing the virtual state of exception that has become the rule with what Benjamin enigmatically called a "*real* state of exception" whose consequence would be a truly liberatory society (a question examined in a later installment in the *Homo Sacer* series, *State of Exception,* and to which I turn later in this book). The centrality of this idea is witnessed by Agamben's choice to liken this "*real* state of exception" to what Heidegger called a "factical life [*faktisches Leben*]," a life in which rule and exception, immanence and transcendence, existence and essence are indistinguishable from one another and come together in the being whose being at every moment is integrally and actually in question for itself. What is most difficult about Agamben's book is not what separates it from Foucault—that is, its conceiving of the history of sovereignty as having been from its outset a "biopolitics." Instead, it is seeing this biopolitical realm and its aporias as indissolubly linked to *linguistic* and *ontological* problems.

William Connolly has written, "Nowhere in *Homo Sacer . . .* is a way out of the logic actually disclosed." He goes on to note that "Agamben thus carries us through the conjunction of sovereignty, the sacred, and biopolitics to a historical impasse" (Connolly 2007, 27).[33] Agamben indeed sees us at a historical crossroads, and he describes a dire state of affairs, but it is not, in his view, an impassable one. *Homo Sacer* ends with a series of paradigmatic figures, from the ancient Roman priest Flamen Diale to the outlaw, from the Nazi *Führer* to the Muselmann of the concentration camp, from the Bosnian women at Omarska to the comatose body of Karen Ann Quinlan.[34] As Agamben makes clear, these are paradigms in the specific and special sense that he develops in this book. Like the *homo sacer,* they are heuristic figures chosen for their ability to help clarify "the present situation." "It is on the bases of these uncertain and nameless terrains, these difficult zones of indistinction," writes Agamben, "that the ways and the forms of a new politics must be thought" (HS, 187 [209]). This is the ultimate trajectory that *Homo Sacer* seeks to follow: a search for means, ways, forms, and lives through which "a new politics" can be arrived at, and it is this call that is heard, through one voice or another, on every page of his book.

The search for this "new politics" is, for Agamben, an unquestionably urgent one. The harsh conclusion he draws from a survey of our political landscape is that in our time, "thought thus finds itself, for the first time, facing its own task without any illusion and without any possible alibi" (MWE, 109 [87]). He sees the extremity of our present situation bringing with it a clarity as to the dangers at hand that no longer allows us to deny or defer them. As with all lucidity, this one brings with it a responsibility. "Contemporary politics," Agamben writes, is a "devastating experiment that disarticulates and empties institutions and beliefs, ideologies and religions, identities and communities"—only to re-offer them in "definitively nullified form" (MWE, 110 [88]). In *Language and Death* Agamben sought to explore the metaphysical trajectory of these nullified forms, and in *The Coming Community* he sought to study the effects of this "devastating experiment" on "identities and communities." Through this devastation he saw the glimmer of a new beginning—the one he continues to see in *Homo Sacer*, and continues to see endangered. For Agamben, we live at a watershed moment for political forms and democratic societies. In an essay written during this same period, he notes that the fall of the Soviet communist party and the subsequent rule of "the capitalist-democratic state on a planetary scale" have "cleared the field of the two main ideological obstacles hindering the resumption of a political philosophy worthy of our time—Stalinism on one side and progressivism and the constitutional state on the other"—and to make the measure of this transformation clear, he compares it to the first industrial revolution (MWE, 109 [87]). He writes elsewhere that it is "likely that if politics today seems to be passing through a lasting eclipse, this is because politics has failed to reckon with this foundational event of modernity" (HS, 4 [7]). Massive though this political transformation may be, it is not to be confined to the realm of politics. What Agamben calls the "politicization of bare life as such" constitutes for him "the decisive event of modernity and signals a radical transformation of the political-philosophical categories of classical thought" (HS, 4 [6–7]). At issue is thus very much a political transformation—a question of political economy and social control—but not only that. For Agamben, such a transformation of our political landscape requires a transformation of our philosophical landscape and of the categories through which we experience our world.

As in the ontological analyses of Heidegger, and as in the analyses in other realms that Agamben undertook starting as early as his first book, any hope of understanding—and changing—the present situation is predicated on an understanding of the origins of the problem. In our case, these are the origins of Western philosophical and political thought. That such archaeological work is necessary for understanding our present, and that failing to do this work carries with it dangerous consequences, is one of the most abiding principles in Agamben's work. In a later installment of the project published twelve years later, Agamben calculates "the price that must be paid every time theoreticians believe they can simply dispense with archaeological considerations," and reflects on how figures from the left such as Habermas reach positions about representative democracy and constitutional theory perilously close to those of conservative thinkers such as Schmitt and Erik Peterson because of their failure to trace the history of the concepts they employ (RG, 282). Of *Homo Sacer* Agamben wrote that it "was originally conceived as a response to the bloody mystification of a new planetary order" (HS, 12 [16]). This political project sent him back to remote reaches of our cultural tradition, and he noted that in his preparations for the work "it became clear that one cannot . . . accept as guaranteed any of the notions that the social sciences (from jurisprudence to anthropology) thought they had defined or presupposed as evident, and that many of these notions demanded—in the urgency of the catastrophe—to be revised without reserve" (HS, 12 [16], translation modified). In *Stanzas* Agamben saw himself working toward a "general science of the human." Thirteen years later he referred to "the project of a general science of the human, which reached its apex at the end of the 1960s" and which "dissolved with the political project of the same years" (P, 64 [60], translation modified; see also SR, 109–110). Continuing to look back at this aspiration in *Homo Sacer*, Agamben sees this project in another light, noting how many of the notions that would contribute to it need to be "revised without reserve" in light of "the urgency of the catastrophe" that is, for him, contemporary politics. At the end of *Homo Sacer* this call is redoubled. We must learn to reconceive, Agamben tells us, the disciplines of "politics and philosophy, medico-biological sciences and jurisprudence" (HS, 188 [211]). Our separate disciplines—be they political science or philology, jurisprudence or anthropology—have proven, in his view, inadequate to meet the dangers and demands of our day. Our failure to revise them radically, he warns at the book's close, presents the risk of "an unprecedented biopolitical catastrophe" (HS, 188 [211]).

A life stripped bare is what the state of exception that is rapidly becoming our rule effects, and what our every effort, following Agamben, should strive to counteract. The response he suggests, the counterfigure to this "bare life," is not *zoē* or *bios* but the two brought together in intimate, indistinguishable proximity, which he calls "form-of-life." In an essay important for the development of *Homo Sacer,* Agamben refers to a "form-of-life [*forma-di-vita*] in which it is never possible to isolate something like bare life" and whose corollary would be what he calls elsewhere, after Benjamin, "a *real* state of exception" (MWE, 9 [18], translation modified, italics in original). This dense claim is at first glance difficult to understand. Earlier in this programmatic essay Agamben offers a definition of such a "form-of-life." It is, he writes, "a life . . . in which the single ways, acts, and processes of living are never simply *facts* but always and above all *possibilities* of life, always and above all potentiality" (MWE, 4 [14], italics in original, translation modified). Here the more and less secret connections of power and potentiality, and their pertinence to the project at hand, become strikingly clear—as does the reason that Agamben has announced he will dedicate part four of *Homo Sacer* to this idea of a "form-of-life" (see RG, 11). Agamben's conception of "bare life" is a conception of life that is not the sum of its attributes, or the chronicle of its history, but a life whose essence exists only as *potential.*[35] To reduce life to any one of its attributes, or the attributes to which society assigns it, like assigning from on sacred and sovereign high an essential vocation to mankind, follows the same logic that has been the condition of possibility for the exclusion and violence that has marked our recent, and ancient, history. To think of "bare life" and its essence as potentiality is, for Agamben, not simply to remain petrified before some unthinkable limit, but instead to cut the knot that the logic of sovereignty has not ceased to tighten around our conception of life. What must be done is to develop a conception of life, and of "bare life," whose only necessary and universal attribute is its ability to make "free usage" of that potentiality.

Scholium I: Progress and Catastrophe, or
Clear and Present Dangers

In 2002, Agamben and other leading Italian intellectuals of the Left such as Dario Fo and Nanni Moretti were asked to contribute essays on the question of whether democracy under the current administration of Silvio Berlusconi was at risk. Agamben wrote of the "regressive" and "progressive" tendencies visible in contemporary politics that these were "categories in which, today, it is no longer possible to believe in good faith, poorly suited as they are to confront the problems with which mankind now finds itself faced" (NSIV, 118). This skepticism about the idea, and ideology, of progress recalls not only the analyses of *Infancy and History* but also the stated goal of *Homo Sacer*—"to bring the political out of its concealment and, at the same time, return thought to its practical calling" (HS, 4 [7]). In *Homo Sacer* this practical calling carries a note of particular urgency: "the urgency of catastrophe" (HS, 12 [16]).

This direct linking of the ideas of *catastrophe* and *progress* is rare but not unprecedented. The term *catastrophe* is one that Benjamin often employed to characterize the political situation in which he found himself during the final years of his life. In a passage from the *Arcades Project* dedicated to the "definition of fundamental historical terms" he defines *catastrophe* as "having missed the occasion," and *the critical instant* as "that the status quo threatens to remain" (Benjamin GS, 5.593). Elsewhere he writes, "that things 'continue so' *is* the catastrophe" (Benjamin GS, 5.592). *Catastrophe* is thus, for Benjamin, a "fundamental historical term," and as such it concerns time and its continuum. In the notes leading up to the *Theses,* Benjamin makes a still more categorical equation: "The catastrophe is progress; progress is the catastrophe" (Benjamin GS, 1.1244). In this same group of notes, Benjamin recommends an "empathetic understanding of the catastrophe [*Einfühlung in der Katastrophe*]" because, for him, "history does not only have the task of rendering accessible the tradition of the oppressed, but also of supporting it" (Benjamin GS, 1.1246). Benjamin's *Theses* identify a *catastrophe* that is present and ongoing: our current state of affairs and the model of progress that underlies it. To halt the *catastrophe* we have to interrupt not only this continuum but also the model of time on which it is based.

The reconceiving of models of time and history is clearly visible in such works as *Infancy and History,* but the linking of ideas of *progress* and *catastrophe* is best seen in Agamben's use, beginning in *Homo Sacer*, of a catastrophe without precedent as the paradigm for our age. Agamben's claim that the concentration camp forms the hidden matrix of our political landscape is, as the preceding chapter endeavors to illustrate, not a simple historical claim (it is, for instance, not verifiable, nor is it meant to be). That it is provocative is of the essence—and intention—of Agamben's project. Agamben's reader confronts a problem that, as we saw, is familiar from another of Benjamin's students—Adorno—who uses exaggeration as a stylistic and strategic tool to capture his reader's attention and to shake that reader from dogmatic slumber. The reader of *Minima Moralia, Negative Dialectics, The Jargon of Authenticity,* and a host of other works is asked to separate cunning exaggerations from those statements or diagnoses to which Adorno fully subscribes. Things stand similarly, but differently, with Agamben. Although he makes extreme claims calculated to provoke, he does not make any to which he does not literally adhere. We saw earlier, for example, how Agamben's idea of the paradigm is not merely provocative, and that there is a precise technical sense in which he employs it. Nevertheless, this provocative element remains, and in its light we might begin by asking who is being provoked? The first and clearest answer is that Agamben is provoking those harboring what he sees as a dangerously complacent view of history and its progressive development— the same progressive model of history that Benjamin castigated with such energy and that Agamben analyzed with such care in *Infancy and History.* One of the historiographical principles that Agamben inherited from Benjamin is a profound skepticism concerning the idea of progress in history. This skepticism should not be reduced, however, to a caricature. For both thinkers, progress can and does occur; societies and institutions can—and, in certain places and at certain times, do—become more just, fair, and equitable in the distribution of rights, goods, and power. But they do not do so on their own, or of necessity, simply because the arrow of history is pointing in that direction. No belief, in fact, is so dangerous, for Agamben, as the belief that whatever horrors have taken place are mere deviations from the real path of progress, and that the march of history is ineluctably moving toward generalized good.

Although there are differences in their conceptions of the dialectic and of time, in this skepticism is one that Adorno took from Benjamin, maintaining his vigilance in the face of contemporary events and denouncing what he called "that which is destructive in progress [*das Destruktive des Fortschritts*]" (Adorno GS, 3.13). In the preface Adorno wrote with Horkheimer for the 1969 edition of *The Dialectic of Enlightenment*, he clarified that "what we set out to learn was in fact nothing less than why mankind, instead of at last entering into a truly human state [*einen wahrhaft menschlichen Zustand*], is sinking into a new form of barbarity" (Adorno GS, 3.11). The danger in question remains clear and present. Adorno and Horkheimer also wrote of *The Dialectic of Enlightenment* that "the development recognized therein towards total integration is interrupted [*unterbrochen*], but not discontinued [*abgebrochen*], and threatens to stretch itself across dictatorships and wars" (Adorno, 3.10). Here we find an exemplary analogue for the argument that Agamben is making in *Homo Sacer* and in the essays leading up to it. Agamben's goal, in an updated version of the question that Adorno and Horkheimer posed, is "to try to understand once and for all why democracy, at the very moment in which it seemed to have finally triumphed over its adversaries and reached its greatest height, proved itself incapable of saving *zoē*, to whose happiness it had dedicated all its efforts, from unprecedented ruin" (HS, 10 [13]). As for Adorno and Horkheimer, for Agamben, the dangerous development in question is "interrupted, but not discontinued," and threatens at any moment to resume its course.

Although this is indeed the case, the question for Agamben is not only one of *old* forms of barbarism returning, but also of the development of *new* ones that threaten to be more bloody and more deadly than any that have preceded them. In view of what was transpiring in a Yugoslavia then breaking apart, Agamben wrote in *Homo Sacer,* "Political organization is not regressing toward outdated forms; rather, premonitory events are, like bloody masses, announcing the new *nomos* of the earth, which (if its grounding principle is not called into question) will soon extend itself over the entire planet" (HS, 38 [45]).[36] The period since World War II and its horrors seem to Agamben nothing so much as a stay of execution. For him there is no compelling reason to believe that the ravages of recent wars and genocides are truly behind us, just as there was no reason for such naive, if reassuring, faith after World War I—as Benjamin (whose calls went unheeded) vehemently repeated. This vision of contemporary politics is reflected everywhere in Agamben's writing—from his learned analyses of the foundations of Western law to his journalistic writings about political situations in Italy, America, Yugoslavia, Afghanistan, and Iraq. Agamben mistrusts the idea of historical progress and in this sense the thesis of the final section of *Homo Sacer* is indeed, as we saw it called, a "provocation." Yet it is the last thing but mere provocation. Its point is not only to arrest the reader's attention, but also to expose the hidden logic of the political paradigms that have governed our thinking for millennia.

Scholium II: Paradigm and Dialectical Image, or
The Shadow of the Present

The two most important paradigms that Agamben presents in *Homo Sacer*—the concentration camp and the figure of the *homo sacer*—are used in similar fashion but differ in fundamental respects. One of these differences is that although the concentration camp belongs to our historical present, the *homo sacer* dates from Western culture's most distant past. Given that Agamben employs both images as paradigmatic of the same idea—"bare life"—this historical distance raises a methodological question that has frequently troubled Agamben's readers. What some have valued as a depth and breadth of learning, lending Agamben's studies a weight that other considerations of related questions lack, others have characterized as simply *un*historical.[37]

More than any of Agamben's other works, *Homo Sacer* has given rise to this charge, beginning as it does with a Greek conception of life, followed by a Roman figure for its end before hurtling forward in time to comatose patients and concentration camp prisoners. In a radio interview Agamben denounced the pretension to scientific systematicity of today's historical disciplines, with their essentially "arbitrary" conventions for dividing the continuum of historical experience into such tidy units as centuries (LDV). To this manner of proceeding Agamben explicitly opposed the method pioneered by Foucault of employing paradigms, a method he calls both "more serious" and "more interesting" than any other (LDV). In another interview, Agamben's interlocutor questioned him about his use of figures and texts from the remote past to formulate what most interests and concerns him in the present, asking if this was a method he had adopted from Benjamin or Foucault. "From both," Agamben answered. "I believe that history—or better, what Foucault called the archaeology of one's own culture—is the only way to reach the present [*zur Gegenwart zu kommen*]. The historical object is never only in the past and never only in the present. It lies in a constellation formed by both: it is there where past and present meet" (PWP, 23). Agamben's reference to "the historical object" as "never only in the past and never only in the present" but found instead in "a constellation formed by both" is one that the reader of Benjamin's works will recognize as a citation without quotation marks. What Agamben is subtly evoking here is the most enigmatic figure in Benjamin's theory of knowledge: "the dialectical image."

Agamben dedicates significant attention to Benjamin's idea of a dialectical image, characterizing it at one point as "the fulcrum of [Benjamin's] theory of historical consciousness" (N, 58). It is this "fulcrum" that he wishes not only to understand in his work, but also to use. But before we can understand this usage, we must first understand Benjamin's term. Benjamin's "dialectical image" has proven so enigmatic for a simple reason: it seems to express an insoluble paradox in its very name. How, we might ask, can an image be dialectical? Is not an *image,* by definition, frozen, and a *dialectic,* by definition, in movement? It is clear from Benjamin's cryptic use of the term that he employs *image* [*Bild*] in a larger sense than we are accustomed to finding, and designates through it more than a simple visual image. Nevertheless, and even understood in a broader sense, the question remains as to how an image can be conceived of as "dialectical."

The answer to this question finds its corollary in the method that Benjamin, in equally enigmatic fashion, called "dialectics at a standstill." A dialectic is an exchange. By this token, dialectical images are those in which two parties enter into dialogue, in which two elements come into dynamic contact. What are these parties or elements? On this point Benjamin is clear: dialectical images represent the conjuncture of past and present. In his *Arcades Project* he writes, "It is not that what is past casts its light on the what is present, or what is present its light on what is past; rather, an image is that wherein what has been comes together in a flash with the now to form a constellation" (Benjamain 1999, 463; GS, 5.578). In the next lines Benjamin gives to this "image" the name "dialectical image," and observes that, "only dialectical images are genuinely historical" (Benjamin 1999, 463; GS, 5.578). A dialectical image is thus an image resulting from an element of the past and an element of the present entering into contact, or dialogue, with one another.

In the final cryptic notes on method that he left behind at the end of his life, Benjamin was intensely interested in developing a new theory of historical consciousness. We saw in connection with *Infancy and History* his vehement rejection of an ideology of progress and the model of time that corresponds to it. To this inert conception of historical experience Benjamin opposed a dynamic "time of the now" charged with an energy capable of "blowing elements out of the historical continuum" in which traditional historiography had imprisoned them. The "dialectical image" is an essential part of this methodological puzzle. Elsewhere in the *Arcades*

Project Benjamin writes that "a moment in time can be fully understood as a dialectical image only by means of another concept. This concept is the 'now of knowability'" (Benjamin GS, 5.1037). Only when it achieves a special legibility in what Benjamin calls the "now of knowability" can the "materialist historian" glimpse a "dialectical image," and it is only through this crucial concept that the method Agamben adopts from Benjamin can be fully understood.

At this point we can begin to see the similarity between what Benjamin mysteriously referred to as *dialectical images* and what Agamben calls *paradigms*. Agamben's paradigms are explicitly Foucauldian in the ways and for the reasons we saw earlier—but they are also of the order of what Benjamin called dialectical images. Like Agamben's paradigms, Benjamin's dialectical images represent a dynamic constellation of past and present where a moment in the past is not a simple element in a historical archive but a potentially dynamic means of understanding—and changing—the present situation, one that acquires its potentiality only at specific, and fortuitous, points. This process has a double character in that Agamben begins, as he notes, with the historical work of understanding given historical phenomena in their historical contexts. In this effort he works as a historian would, but he does not, as he has stressed on numerous occasions, use paradigms as a historian. Here we have the second stage of Agamben's "paradigmatic method," where, in the critical moment that Benjamin called "the now of knowability," he removes such texts and figures from their position in a continuum of historical experience and uses them to the dynamic end of elucidating the present. Such images are, for Benjamin and Agamben, "crystallizations" of historical experience—and not just any historical experience, but experience that at a given moment acquires unprecedented relevance. For Agamben, as for Benjamin, the past is not equally and everywhere accessible. This *potential* inhering in our past is, for both thinkers, truly dynamic. Much more is involved than simply removing a book from a shelf and turning to a page on which a given claim is made; for a document of our past to matter to us, a spark needs to be lit in our present.

When we consider Agamben's paradigms after the fashion of both Foucault's paradigms and Benjamin's dialectical images, the problem of historical method becomes clearer. Agamben is not troubled by the range of historical reference or by the charge that such broad range might be considered unsystematic and thus, ultimately, unhistorical. It should then come as little surprise that when asked whether his recourse to remote periods of our past was truly necessary and what he thought of charges that his manner of proceeding was ultimately "unhistorical," Agamben replied as he did. "Foucault once said something quite beautiful about just this," Agamben began. "He said that historical research was like a shadow cast by the present onto the past. For Foucault, this shadow stretched back to the seventeenth and eighteenth centuries. For me, the shadow is longer."[38] Elaborating on this metaphor, Agamben continued, "I tend to work in crepuscular regions, at sunset, where the shadows are very long. For me they reach into the deepest past. There is no great theoretical difference between my work and Foucault's; it is merely a question of the length of the historical shadow" (PWP, 23).[39]

CHAPTER SEVEN

The Unique and the Unsayable:
Remnants of Auschwitz: The Witness
and the Archive. Homo Sacer III

Niemand
zeugt für den
Zeugen.[1]

—PAUL CELAN, "ASCHENGLORIE"

"Initially it was the figure of the *homo sacer* that led me to see Auschwitz in a new light," Agamben remarked in 2001. "I tried to think through what sort of life had been led there," he continued, specifying that "the figure of the *homo sacer* was a means through which to see anew what happened in the camps" (UL, 19). *Remnants of Auschwitz* bears the subtitle *Homo Sacer III* (*State of Exception, Homo Sacer II.1,* did not appear for another five years, *Il Regno e la Gloria, Homo Sacer II.2* for another nine, and *Il sacramento del linguaggio, Homo Sacer II.3* for another ten years) and is a continuation of the concerns his readers first encountered in *Homo Sacer.* The paradigmatic figure from Roman antiquity that gave his project its direction and title is the same one through which he examines both the figure *of* the concentration camp and figures *in* the concentration camps. The most surprising thing, however, about *Remnants of Auschwitz* is the angle from which it approaches its question: that of *testimony.* This approach is not surprising in itself, as the question of testimony and testifying has been a central one in discussions of the Holocaust; but it *is* surprising as the next installment in the *Homo Sacer* project. Instead of taking up the provocative thesis of the final section of *Homo Sacer*—that the concentration camp is the "biopolitical paradigm" of our age—where he left off, he turns from the *paradigm* of the camp to *life* in the camps. In *Remnants of Auschwitz* the focus is not on how the *space* of the camp is a figure for the "biopolitical" spaces of modern society, as it was in *Homo Sacer,* but instead on bearing witness to the life led there.

    Remnants of Auschwitz is Agamben's most daring book. It promises a definitive response to those who would question the historical reality of the Holocaust, as well as an *"Ethica more Auschwitz demonstrata."* For this reason it is all the more regrettable that it is also his most flawed book. There are uncharacteristic gaps in the book's argument, and the fine line that the paradigmatic method of *Homo Sacer* requires he walk proves exceptionally difficult to follow. *Remnants of Auschwitz* has disappointed many readers, angered many others, and even cost Agamben some of his most enthusiastic supporters. The reasons for this, however, stem as much from the idea behind the book as from the flaws in its execution.

    Emil Fackenheim wrote in 1982 that "philosophers keep acting as if, philosophically, there is no difference between the six million and the one child dying of cancer," and that "so far as most philosophers and theologians are concerned, there simply is no Holocaust" (11). Whether or not this claim is true for philosophers as a group, it certainly does not apply to Agamben's individual case. In *Remnants of Auschwitz,* Agamben attempts to offer a philosophical response to the dilemmas posed by the Holocaust, and his manner of proceeding has sparked no little controversy. The *philosophical* method that Agamben employs in *Remnants of Auschwitz* is the same *paradigmatic* method we saw in *Homo Sacer* and must simultaneously treat Auschwitz as an absolutely unique event *and* as a paradigm for understanding other situations. The first question this philosophical method raises is whether such an approach is justifiable—whether using Auschwitz as a paradigm robs it of its historical singularity. Dominick LaCapra has called the book "a transhistorical *leçon de philosophie*" (2007, 162), and it is precisely this idea that has incensed so many readers. Esther Marion (2006) has written that "by appropriating Holocaust survivors and their testimonies . . . Agamben makes a lacuna of the horror of Auschwitz—of its empirical reality, victims and participants," and as a result he "turns genocide to pulp" and effects a "dehumanization of the Holocaust" (1022, 1018, 1021). Marion is not alone in offering such exceptionally harsh accusations. J. M. Bernstein (2004) has said of the book's philosophical approach that "at most, it is an aestheticization of [the *Muselmann's*] fate" (14). As we will see, however, the criticism leveled against *Remnants of Auschwitz* has focused more on the fact *that* Agamben dares to use such figures and events as Auschwitz and the *Muselmann* as paradigms than on *how* he does so and what his use of them reveals.

Survival in Auschwitz

Agamben makes no secret of the fact that the author whose life and testimony stands at the center of his tenth book is Primo Levi. Levi's most famous work, the one that chronicles his time in a concentration camp, *Se questo è un uomo*, was published in English as *Survival in Auschwitz*. When literally translated, Levi's title is less affirmative: "If this is a man." The rending conditional that Levi employs poses the simple and terrifying question of how men did what they did; how, if *this*—the concentration camp prisoner—is a man, he could be treated by other men in such fashion. This question concerning the project of dehumanization that lies at the heart of the Nazi concentration camps, and the ensuing doubt as to the solidity of our conceptions of humanity and its nature, is, from the book's first words, that to which Levi's work testifies.

In a later book, *The Drowned and the Saved*, Levi takes as his starting point the question of *testimony* and the singular problems raised by the sheer horror—and consequently the unbelievability—of what took place in the Nazi extermination camps. During and after World War II, as people both in Germany and abroad were told the truth of what took place in the Nazi extermination camps, the most common response was disbelief, that such things were not possible—something of which Nazi leaders were well aware.[2] Levi recounts a chilling remark made by an SS officer to Simon Wiesenthal that although the Nazis might lose the war against the Allies, the SS had already won their war against the prisoners. The war in question was a war of memory. They had prevailed, in the eyes of the SS officer, because they had done the unthinkable—and the unthinkable would not be believed. The SS officer told Wiesenthal that even if by some miracle he were to survive to tell his tale, it could be met only with incredulity, and he would suffer the indignity of being dismissed as a liar or madman. "The story of the *Lager* [camp]," claimed the SS officer, "*we* will tell" (Levi 1986, 3, italics in original).

The sign of testimony is the one under which Levi had written his two earlier books on life and death in and after the camps—*Survival in Auschwitz* [*Se questo è un uomo*] and *The Reawakening*—and under which he would also write *The Drowned and the Saved*. This was the sign of testifying to what he called "the worst crime in the history of mankind" (Levi 1986, 5). The problem of testifying begins, for Levi, with the simple and brutal fact that the victims who experienced the camp in all their horror did not live to tell their tales. He carefully stresses that the condition for survival in the camps was that they not be experienced in typical fashion, for the "normal" prisoner (Levi places the term in quotation marks) did not survive to tell his or her story. As a result, the task of testifying fell to those who had led *atypical* lives in the camps, who had benefitted from some exceptional privilege or aid without which they would never have survived. (In Levi's case, this came from his training as a chemist, which led to him working with civilians and, through them, receiving the extra rations and better treatment necessary for his survival.) The story of the camps, as Levi pointed out, is thus "virtually exclusively written by those—like myself—who did not touch bottom" (1986, 8). Those who did not touch bottom were called on to testify for those who did.[3]

The difficulty of testifying does not, of course, stop here. To this cruel fact were added others, such as the difficulties of gaining any sort of perspective on the nature and scale of what was taking place in the camps—or even, in the cases of the many prisoners who knew no German, the difficulty of even knowing where they were. To these impediments were added a sense of seemingly limitless injustice, inevitable feelings of desperation and guilt, and equally inevitable deformations of memory wrought by extreme suffering. As Levi all too clearly experienced, the mind, at least for a time, occludes that which is simply unbearable, and much of that to which he and others found themselves called to testify fell into this realm. Levi summarizes this question concerning *testimony* by suggesting that "the entire history of the brief 'Millenial Reich' could be reread as a war against memory" (1986, 20).

The German Army physician Peter Bamm remarked in *Die Unsichtbare Flagge* (1952) of the Sebastopol massacres that resistance would have been merely to sacrifice one's life but, in his words, "this is not to say that such a sacrifice would have been morally meaningless. It would only have been practically useless" (cited in Arendt 1963, 232–233). This consideration led Hannah Arendt to respond in *Eichmann in Jerusalem*:

It is true that totalitarian domination tried to establish . . . holes of oblivion into which all deeds, good and evil, would disappear, but just as the Nazis' feverish attempts, from June 1942 on, to erase all traces of the massacres—through cremation, through burning in open pits, through the use of explosives and flamethrowers and bone-crushing machinery—were doomed to failure, so all efforts to let their opponents 'disappear in silent anonymity' were in vain. The holes of oblivion do not exist. Nothing human is that perfect, and there are simply too many people in the world to make oblivion possible. One man will always be left alive to tell the story. Hence, nothing can ever be 'practically useless,' at least, not in the long run. . . . For the lesson of such stories is simple and within everybody's grasp. Politically speaking, it is that under conditions of terror most people will comply but *some people will not,* just as the lesson of the countries to which the Final Solution was proposed is that 'it could happen' in most places but *it did not happen everywhere.* Humanly speaking, no more is required, and no more can reasonably be asked, for this planet to remain a place fit for human habitation." [Arendt 1963, 233, italics in original]

The Nazis' attempts to "establish . . . holes of oblivion" did not, of course, work, although they came, in places, terrifyingly close. The response to such an attempt to create human "holes of oblivion," to wage what Levi calls "a war on memory," is simply *testimony.* And yet as Levi and so many others have born witness to, testifying is a harrowing experience—one that Levi invokes in the English epigraph to *The Drowned and the Saved:* "Since then, at an uncertain hour, / That agony returns: / And till my ghastly tale is told / This heart within me burns."[4]

The Aporia of Auschwitz, or On Historical Knowledge

In Levi's wake, Agamben begins *Remnants of Auschwitz* with an unexpected bit of testimony: that of a member of one of Auschwitz's *Sonderkommando.* The *Sonderkommando* (literally, special forces) were prisoners enlisted in the daily work of exterminating their fellow prisoners (principally in the gas chambers and crematoria) and who were themselves systematically executed and replaced by new prisoners. Several survivors of the *Sonderkammndo* claimed that they were like the other survivors, only more miserable.[5] They had chosen to live at all costs—whether in order to testify, to see their loved ones again, to avenge themselves, or simply to go on living—and the price they paid was that of killing their fellow prisoners—all day, every day. Levi says of the *Sonderkommando* that "conceiving and organizing the squads [the *Sonderkommando*] was National Socialism's most demonic crime" (1986, 38; cited by Agamben in RA 25 [23]). The testimony with which Agamben begins his book is a surprising remnant: a scrap of paper with a hastily scrawled note in Yiddish written by a member of a *Sonderkommando* and then buried under Auschwitz's third crematorium. Discovered seventeen years later, it says simply that it is "unimaginable that anyone could exactly recount how our experiences took place" (RA, 12 [8]). In response, Agamben quickly makes clear what sort of indescribability he faces and what sort of exactitude his study will aim for. His intention is not to detail daily life in the camps or to explain their organization; these tasks, he notes, have been admirably accomplished by other writers—by survivors such as Levi and Robert Antelme, and by historians such as Raul Hilberg in his *The Destruction of the European Jews* (1961). Agamben's *Remnants of Auschwitz* will instead be a reflection on the theory and practice of testimony itself—"a perpetual commentary on testimony" (RA, 13 [9]).

Agamben stresses that the problem he confronts is not the incommunicability of experience itself, as it was in *Infancy and History* (to which he does not refer here).[6] It is not "the difficulty we face whenever we try to communicate our most intimate experience to others" that interests him (RA, 12 [8]). Agamben's problem is stated systematically: "The aporia of Auschwitz is, indeed, the very aporia of historical knowledge: a non-coincidence between facts and truth, between verification and comprehension" (RA, 12 [8]). The immediate aporia—the aporia of an event and its recounting—is linked to an aporia of a more general order, one between *fact* and *truth*, between *knowing* ("verification") and *understanding* ("comprehension"). As was the case in *Homo Sacer,* the historical phenomenon in question is to be studied paradigmatically—both for itself *and* for the light it sheds on other problems. The specific "aporia of Auschwitz" concerns not only knowing what took place at Auschwitz, but also the broader question of our knowing *anything* about our past ("the aporia of historical knowledge"). *Testimony* is, for Agamben, the point at which specific questions about Auschwitz and general questions about historical knowledge converge. What is more, testimony also forms the point where knowledge and ethics meet. "As we shall see," writes Agamben, "almost none of the ethical principles our age believed it could recognize as valid have stood the decisive test, that of an *Ethica more Auschwitz demonstrata*," and it is precisely this test that he seeks to apply (RA, 13 [9]).

The Contamination of Law, or Ethics

Agamben has remarked that "the integral juridification [*la giuridicizzazione integrale*] of human relations that we witness today, the confusion between that which we might believe, hope, and love and that which we are held to do and not to do, to know and not to know, points not only to a crisis in religion, but also and above all to a crisis in law" (LSP, 44). This is a crisis that Agamben began to address in the first volume of the *Homo Sacer* series and that continues to occupy him in the next installment as *Remnants of Auschwitz* begins with a critique of the law. The confusion or, as Agamben polemically calls it, the "*contamination*" of ethical categories by legal ones is the book's starting point. In an essay published three years earlier, Agamben pointed to proof of "the irreparable collapse [*rovina*] of any ethical experience," seen in "the confusion between religio-ethical categories and juridical concepts that has today reached its paroxysm" (MWE, 130 [100–101], translation modified). This is a line of thinking he takes up in *Remnants of Auschwitz*. "One of the most common mistakes—which is not only made in discussions of the camp," writes Agamben, "is the tacit confusion of ethical categories and juridical categories (or worse, of juridical categories and theological categories, which gives rise to a new theodicy). Almost all the categories that we use in moral and religious judgments are in some way contaminated [*contaminate*] by law: guilt, responsibility, innocence, judgment, pardon . . . " (RA, 18 [16], ellipses in original). Elsewhere he writes that "the concept of responsibility is also irremediably contaminated [*contaminato*] by law" (RA, 20 [19]). In an interview following the publication of *Remnants of Auschwitz* Agamben stressed that "in our time moral and juridical categories have become irremediably confused" and that "Auschwitz is the place in which the insufficiency of the law is visible" (ATI, 39). Agamben's language could not be more extreme here as legal conceptions of "guilt, responsibility, innocence, judgment, pardon" not only prove insufficient for understanding the extreme instances offered by the camps but even hinder, or "contaminate," efforts to arrive at such an understanding. But what does Agamben find in the law that "contaminates" other realms of inquiry, and why does he feel the need to invoke the metaphorical register of infection and radioactivity?

This register complicates Agamben's point, implying as it does that there is something inherently harmful about the law. As we saw earlier, Agamben's first studies were in the law, and he later remarked of them that "for a long time thereafter I thought that it was a mistake to have studied law. That is something, however, that I no longer think, for without this familiarity I would probably never have been able to write *Homo Sacer*" (UL, 16). There is a strong antinomian element in Agamben's reflections that recalls another student of the law who came to criticize the law—the Paul to whom Agamben would dedicate his next book.[7] As he began to make clear in *Homo Sacer,* however, the target of Agamben's critique is not law in a conventionally understood sense but "the entire text of tradition in its regulative form, whether the Jewish Torah or the Islamic Shariah, Christian dogma or the profane *nomos*" (HS, 51 [59]; on this point see also Mills 2004, 57, n. 15). What is more, whatever "crises" law may be traversing and whatever problems inherent to legal discourse are at issue, the problem that Agamben attempts to isolate here concerns the *misuse* of legal conceptions—how legal conceptions of "guilt, responsibility, innocence, judgment, pardon" are used *as if* they were ethical conceptions. Agamben's contention is that law and ethics are separate areas and should be recognized as such. Ethics is "contaminated" by law in the sense that the project of developing truly ethical conceptions of "guilt, responsibility, innocence judgment, pardon" is abandoned in favor of an unthinking adoption of legal conceptions. As we saw in Chapter Six, the first words of the *Homo Sacer* project are Savigny's: "The law has no existence in and for itself; its essence is instead in the lives of men—viewed from a certain side." This viewpoint—that of law—is seen here as frankly dangerous for its tendency to obscure the *ethical* coordinates from which it must be distinguished.

Seeking to correct Agamben, LaCapra points out that "responsibility and guilt are concepts that are differentially shared by ethics and law," but such a corrective is unnecessary given that this is something Agamben himself stresses (LaCapra 2007, 155). Agamben is not claiming that ethics and law employ identical conceptions or that they are employed in an identical fashion. Instead, his claim is that in crucial instances ethics has borrowed its conceptions from law and that in doing so it has created significant problems for itself. LaCapra goes on to note that "Agamben does not provide any idea of a form of social life in which ethics would not involve these concepts," and in this he makes clear that he is arguing against a different idea than the one found in *Remnants of Auschwitz* (LaCapra 2007, 155). Agamben's goal is not, of course, "a form of social life" in which ethics has eliminated the categories of responsibility and guilt. It is instead a form of social life in which ethics no longer simply borrows its conceptions of such essential categories as responsibility and guilt from a different discourse (law), but instead develops its own truly ethical conceptions—ones that would allow us to better confront pressing questions concerning our past and present. In a certain sense, for Agamben it is not *law* that is the problem. It is, instead, our unthinking recourse to legal categories when we are confronted with problems that are not truly or purely legal but, rather, *ethical*. For Agamben, law can "contaminate" ethics not because law is *per se* noxious, but because the realm of law and the realm of ethics do not coincide. This leaves us with conceptions of, in the cardinal instance here, *responsibility* that Agamben judges inadequate for the ethical tasks imposed. Agamben's critique of the law becomes easier to understand when we understand it as a critique of *ethics*—of insufficiently developed ethical categories and of the fact that an "*Ethica more Auschwitz demonstrata*" needs to free itself from such "contamination."

The Game and the Grey Zone

From the question of *testimony* Agamben turns to that of *responsibility,* and it is along the lines of a new conception of *responsibility* that he continues his inquiry. He begins by noting the tendency to replace ethical problems with legal distinctions, and then embarks on a search for properly ethical conceptions. "The unprecedented discovery made by Levi at Auschwitz," he writes, "concerns an area that is independent of every establishment of responsibility, an area in which Levi succeeded in isolating something like a new ethical element [*un nuovo elemento etico*]. Levi calls it the 'grey zone'" (RA, 21 [19]). This "new ethical element" is what Agamben seeks—and he seeks it in the "grey zone" of responsibility, guilt, despair, and destitution that Levi endeavored to chart. This leads Agamben to claim that—alluding to Levi's prewar occupation, which allowed him to survive the camps (even after the war when asked if he saw himself as a writer or a chemist he routinely replied that he was a chemist)—one can glimpse here "a grey, incessant alchemy in which good and evil and, along with them, all the metals of traditional ethics reach their point of fusion" (RA, 21 [19]). Why does Agamben push Levi's formulations in this direction? An initial answer is to graphically demonstrate the shortcomings of ethical categories "contaminated" by legal ones. The question remains, however, of what are they to be replaced by.

In *The Drowned and the Saved*, Levi recounts a story told to him by a survivor of Auschwitz's final *Sonderkommando*. It is about a soccer match between the SS and the *Sonderkommando* that took place during an interruption in their "work" (of extermination). Levi writes: "Other men of the SS and the rest of the squad [the *Sonderkommando*] are present at the game; they take sides, bet, applaud, urge the players on as if, rather than at the gates of hell, the game were taking place on the village green" (cited RA, 25 [23]). The image of a moment of seeming normalcy around which the smoke of burnt bodies literally swirls is a haunting one. "This match might strike someone," Agamben suggests, "as a brief pause of humanity in the middle of an infinite horror" (RA, 26 [24]). For Agamben, however, the image is not one of hope. "To my eyes," he adds, "like those of the witnesses, this game, this moment of normalcy, is the true horror of the camp" (RA, 26 [24], translation modified). The illustrative import is clear enough: "For we can perhaps think that the massacres are over—even if here and there they are repeated, not so far away from us. But that match is never over; it continues as if uninterrupted" (RA, 26 [24]). This game expresses, for Agamben, "the true horror of the camp" not only because it is an all too brief respite, if one might call it that, from the "work" of extermination that both sides were to return to immediately thereafter, but also because it is a figure for our present historical situation. During the time of the game the horrors were not at an end, they were merely (and briefly) suspended; and it is here that Agamben sees a figure for our historical situation. As we saw, Adorno and Horkheimer wrote that the devastating developments they traced in their *Dialectic of Enlightenment* are "interrupted, but not discontinued, and threaten to stretch themselves across dictatorships and wars" (Adorno GS, 3.10). It is precisely this idea that Agamben sees reflected in the soccer game in question. The cruelty is not over, the barbarity has not been civilized and the evil not been eradicated. For him, at any moment the respite might end. For Agamben, the soccer game serves as a parable or emblem of the false sense of distance and security in which we live. Agamben's indirectly expressed message seems to be: You think that the evil is over and the time is now for play, relaxation, forgetting, but you are wrong; the game you play now is no different than the one played then. It is a brief respite, and at any moment the suffering and cruelty can come screaming back.

Agamben links this game to the "grey zone" that Levi names, claiming that it is "the perfect and eternal cipher of the 'grey zone,' which knows no time and is in every place" (RA, 26 [24]). Agamben then invokes the "anguish" and the "shame" of this unceasing spectacle: "our shame, the shame of those who did not know the camps and yet, without knowing how, are spectators of that match, which repeats itself in every match in our stadiums, in every television broadcast, in the normalcy of everyday life" (RA, 26 [24]). As in *Infancy and History,* the tone that Agamben adopts is one of outrage and impending danger. The closing words of this section of the book make clear the imperative of this work—and of the entire *Homo Sacer* project: "If we do not succeed in understanding that match, in stopping it, there will never be hope" (RA, 26 [24]). The horizon of the work is "hope"—but a hope that can be reached only by traversing the "grey zone" that Levi designates.

The Unique and the Unsayable

The "grey zone" in question—which is the space of *testimony*—is one whose language could not be more uncertain. This uncertainty also applies to the language of those who would learn from it. In *Remnants of Auschwitz* Agamben refers directly to a criticism like the one we saw earlier of the "outrageous provocation" of calling the concentration camp the paradigm of our age (Mayer 1997, 21). Before *Remnants of Auschwitz,* Agamben published an article in a French newspaper about the camps. A letter was sent to the paper's editor accusing Agamben, as he himself relates, of having "trampled upon the unique and unsayable [*unique et indicible*] character of Auschwitz" (see RA, 31 [29], translation modified). This letter clearly states the danger—or alternately, the potential for misunderstanding—involved in Agamben's use of paradigms. He endeavors to study the camp in all its historical specificity, but the horizon of his undertaking involves using the camp and the life led there as a paradigm through which to understand the dangers of the present. This approach requires the walking of a fine methodological line beneath which lies what might easily seem a lack of respect for the "unique and unsayable character of Auschwitz."

Agamben's response to this letter focuses on the second term of the accusation: the *unsayable*. As we saw in earlier chapters, he had often taken up Benjamin's project of "eliminating the unsayable" from language as part of a larger project of developing a profane conception of life and language—one in which the sacred and unsayable would cease to hold sovereign sway over our communities. Without referring to those earlier analyses, in *Remnants of Auschwitz* Agamben offers a short and erudite excursus on the semantic history of the term *euphemism* and its initial meaning of "adoring in silence." "To say that Auschwitz is 'unsayable' or 'incomprehensible' is equivalent," Agamben claims, to a *euphemism* in this original sense of the term: "to adoring in silence, as one does with a god" (RA, 32–33 [30]). The letter's charge gives Agamben the occasion to stress that this is precisely what he wishes to avoid. What is called for, in his view, is to dissipate any aura of sanctity and sacrality in favor of an effort to understand—with all that such an effort entails—what took place in, and what remains of, Auschwitz. This response leads to the claim that we should not remain silent about Auschwitz, that we should not make the mistake born of a laudable respect for the suffering of others of failing to perform the work of understanding necessary to prevent a renewal of such suffering. A question remains, however, as to how well Agamben has replied to the concerns voiced in the letter he himself singled out. The matter of the *unsayable* is one he convincingly argues against. But what of the *unique*?

The question of the *unsayable* character of Auschwitz remains specific to Auschwitz and is a question of how—and to what end—we should speak of what took place there. The question of the *unique* character of Auschwitz, however, touches directly on Agamben's paradigmatic method, and it is unfortunate that he does not reply to it. The letter writer may well have been aiming at the sheer pretense of Agamben discussing Auschwitz, preferring instead to shroud it in respectful silence. Yet this is not a common position, and Auschwitz is far more discussed than silenced (although of course its unrepresentability is frequently discussed). It is clear, however, that what the letter writer was objecting to was less the question of *testimony* that Agamben discusses in the first part of *Remnants of Auschwitz* than his use of the concentration camp as paradigm. In

Remnants of Auschwitz Agamben continues the paradigmatic practice developed in *Homo Sacer,* noting that "Auschwitz is precisely the place in which the state of exception coincides perfectly with the rule, and the extreme situation becomes the very *paradigm* of daily life" (RA, 49 [44], italics added). In light of the claims made in *Homo Sacer* and such occasional pieces as the French newspaper article, the accusation leveled by this letter writer can be seen in all its complexity, and Agamben's response in all its disappointing insufficiency.

To say that one should have been silent when one spoke is an accusation readily answered. The more pertinent part of the complaint is in the first part of the phrase—the part to which Agamben does not directly reply—"the *unique* . . . character of Auschwitz." For, in a certain sense, and by express design, Agamben does *not* treat Auschwitz as unique. His method—as he strove to make clear in later lectures, interviews, and essays and which I examined in the preceding chapter—requires that he understand and examine the paradigmatic case of Auschwitz in and for itself, embedded in its historical time and place, *as well as* a means for understanding other times and places—above all our own. Agamben never places the uniqueness of what transpired in Auschwitz in question. Nevertheless, his paradigmatic method uses the place of the concentration camp and the life led there to understand other situations, and it is precisely this approach that outraged many readers, such as the one who wrote to the French newspaper. As I showed in the preceding chapter, to understand Agamben's idea of paradigm, as well as his choice of paradigms, requires that we understand the danger he sees himself facing—a danger that has everything to do with the uniqueness of Auschwitz. Agamben makes no secret of the fact that for him there is a great risk involved in seeing Auschwitz as unique in the sense of an anomaly that could never happen again. He makes clear that he considers it possible for similar horrors to occur, and that the paradigm of *that* unique site of horror can help us understand—and avert—others.

The Incomprehensible Witness

The first chapter of *Remnants of Auschwitz,* "The Witness," ends on a doubtful note, and with a doubtful witness. Agamben relates Levi's reaction to the poetry of Paul Celan.[8] Although he was an outspoken opponent of what he called literary "obscurity," Levi found himself strangely moved by Celan's quintessentially obscure poetry. In what is difficult to see as anything other than a tenuous analogy, Agamben draws a parallel between Levi's description of Celan's poetry—full of incomprehensible sounds and words—and Levi's account of a certain child in Auschwitz. When Levi met him, the boy in question was roughly three years old, paralyzed from the waist down, with his small legs wasted and his eyes constantly wide with hunger and incomprehension. It seemed that no one had taught him to speak. The child was capable of uttering only a single word, which Levi transcribes as *matisklo* or *mass-klo,* and that despite the fact that the camp contained speakers of so many languages, no one recognized or understood. Of this child Agamben says that he "cannot bear witness, since he does not have language" (one might also note that it is because, as Levi tells his reader, he dies a few days after the liberation of the camp) (see RA, 39 [35]). Consistent with his avowed intention, Levi says he bears witness for those who were not able to, and that the boy in question "bears witness through these words of mine" (cited in RA, 39 [35]). At the chapter's close, Agamben says of Levi's act of testifying in the place of another, "but not even the survivor can bear witness completely. . . . This means that testimony is the disjunction between two impossibilities of bearing witness; it means that language, in order to bear witness, must give way to a non-language [*la lingua, per testimoniare, deve cedere il posto a una non-lingua*] in order to show the impossibility of bearing witness" (RA, 39 [36]).

What, then, are these "two impossibilities of bearing witness" that Agamben invokes? The first is the empirical one that Levi himself describes: that those whose stories most demand to be told did not live to tell them and it falls to the survivors to tell them in their name and memory. To this first "impossibility," however, Agamben links a second one that is not empirical but transcendental, insofar as it concerns not the actual possibilities and impossibilities of testifying for another but the structure of linguistic signification itself.

In light of the preceding discussion we might now return to the questions of unsayability and uniqueness raised by the French letter writer. Agamben begins with the empirical impossibility of testifying—that is, with the story of an individual boy in a place so horrible that its inhabitants have so little time or energy left that no one teaches him to speak. Levi's experience of an evocative but incomprehensible poetry—Celan's—is then compared by Agamben to Levi's experience of the haunting but incomprehensible sounds of this crippled child. Agamben brings together Levi's two experiences of incomprehensible language so as to establish what he calls an "impossibility of testifying" that extends far beyond the specific horror of a specific place to a postulate concerning the structure of all linguistic communication. "The language of testimony is a language that no longer signifies," writes Agamben, "and that, in not signifying, advances into what is without language, to the point of taking on a different insignificance [*insignificanza*]—that of the complete witness, that of he who by definition cannot bear witness" (RA, 39 [36]). Agamben's logic here is less than transparent—a weakness of this book not often found in his other works—but it is nevertheless possible to follow. What he is saying is that there where language does not make sense—in the obscure lyrics of Celan and the incomprehensible sounds of the child of Auschwitz—it becomes *like* the language of testimony in a new respect: its empirical inability to signify is akin to a transcendental inability to bear witness stemming from the structure of signification.

The child about whom Levi writes could not testify for two empirical reasons: he was incapable of speech and he did not survive the camp. The question, then, is what does the fate of the child, and Levi's haunting evocation of him, have to do with a signifying structure of bearing witness and a structural impossibility lodged therein? In what way is language to give way to "non-language," as Agamben says, and if so, to what end? The "complete witness" cannot bear witness; he who has seen the worst, who has "touched bottom" and experienced the camp in all its cruelty, does not survive to tell its tale. Only the exceptions to the camp's rule—like Levi—live to bear witness. Levi discusses this problem on an empirical level; Agamben extends it to cover a relation in human speech between language and what he calls "non-language." The "non-language" in question is a language of sound but no sense; a language whose semantic register seems empty and absent; a language that seems to be a "non-language" because, whether in the poetry of Celan or the utterances of the child, it means nothing to those who hear it. But to say that it "means nothing" is not completely accurate. On a semantic level, as the bearer of a determinate message, such language indeed means nothing insofar as Levi is unable to decipher the content of what either Celan or the child are trying to say. But on another and equally real level, both the poetry of Celan and the desperate utterance of the child mean something immeasurable to Levi. Agamben gives to this disjunction between intention and understanding, between sound and sense, the difficult name "non-language," thereby presenting a possibility for misunderstanding. The problem that Agamben raises at this point concerns the nature and structure of human language. Our language can never be the perfect and accurate reflection of some stable entity, because language by nature lies in an unstable relation to that which it expresses. No Adamic connection exists between the thing and the word (or sign) for the thing; language is a general system of signs ("unmotivated" in Saussure's terms) and its connections shift in time and space, from speaker to speaker and from instant to instant. Agamben cites a unique case of a literally unspeakable suffering to illustrate an impossibility present in all testimony because it is present in all language.

As we saw in an earlier scholium, this curious experience of a *factum loquendi* or *experimentium linguae* was an essential one for Agamben—and remains so. The sense behind the apparent paradox of an idea of experiencing language as a "nonlanguage" lies in conceiving of an experience that we all have and to which—for reasons easy to understand—we are rarely attentive. This is an experience of language independent of its signifying function—language seen as *sign* before it is seen as *sense* and that thereby highlights how our language is *articulated* (and is thus distinct from a natural but inarticulate *voice* possessed by other animals). For this reason Agamben evokes in a number of essays and works an experience of language as *voice* rather than as *meaning*, as *sound* rather than as *sense*—an experience that he expresses not only in formulae like *factum loquendi* and *experimentum linguae, infancy* and "speaking in tongues," but also through the sounds and songs of animals, from cricket to dolphin. To elucidate the idea of testimony requires, for Agamben, experiencing the respect in which our language is not completely natural—yet how far has this taken him from the incomprehensible suffering of the child in Auschwitz?

The *Muselmann*

Chapter Two of *Remnants of Auschwitz* identifies what "the witness" of Chapter One witnessed and in whose name he or she testifies: the *Muselmann*. In the language of the camps, the *Muselmann* was an individual who had crossed a fundamental line, who had reached a state of physical inanition and psychological desperation resembling autism and presaging death.[9] Various explanations of the origin of the term *Muselmann* have been offered, but the most common suggestion relates it to *muslim*— Arabic for he or she who has unconditionally submitted himself or herself to the will of God, and occasionally associated in European slang with unconditional submission. (Another account of the German term traces it to *mussel-man,* for the way that, like a mussel, such prisoners turned in on themselves). Whatever the origin of the term, the *Muselmann* was he or she who had ceased to react and interact, no longer responding even to hunger or physical pain.

The Nazi extermination camps were subject to periodic "selections," and it was the visibly weak and the sick who were "selected" for the gas chambers. Signs of sickness or weakness were routinely concealed for the simple reason that they could cost a prisoner his or her life. The *Muselmänner* were beyond such concealment and, as a result, effectively consigned to death in the next selection. They lived in a sort of stay of execution. As was widely noted by survivors from Levi to Bettelheim to Antelme, these figures were rarely treated with generosity or kindness by their fellow prisoners—in part because such kindness seemed pointless because met with no gratitude or even acknowledgement, and in part because these figures seemed eerie harbingers of their own imminent ends. One of the reasons that the *Muselmänner* were not immediately selected (killed) seems to have been their use value as living emblems of the fate awaiting all prisoners in the camps—the SS's manner of showing that becoming a *Muselmann* was not a matter of temperament or discipline, but of time.

If this then is what the *Muselmann* was, why does Agamben dedicate his second chapter to this figure, and what is revealing to him about it? The answer is precisely that which he glimpsed in the crippled child with whom he ended the previous chapter: because of his inability to testify. Levi talks of how those who lived to tell the tale of the camps had, by definition, not experienced the camps in all their horror. The *Muselmann,* on the other hand, was the exemplary prisoner insofar as he or she did experience the camp in its full horror; he or she, in Levi's phrase, "touched bottom," and for this reason either perished or survived unable to tell his or her tale.

Discussing Levi's testimony, Agamben then notes that "as suggested by the ironically rhetorical Italian title *Se questo è un uomo* . . . in Auschwitz ethics begins precisely at the point where the *Muselmann,* the 'complete witness,' makes it forever impossible to distinguish between man and non-man [*tra l'uomo e il non-uomo*]" (RA, 47 [42]). A figure of bare life, the *Muselmann* stands in a no-man's-land similar to that of the titular figure of the series, *homo sacer*. The testimony of survivors often echoes the sentiment that the *Muselmänner* were not considered like other men because they had sacrificed all dignity, because they had given up the hope that was necessary for survival, and because they had ceased to maintain a relation to the world beyond the camps. Agamben sees in them a seemingly endless "capacity" for suffering: "this almost infinite potentiality to suffer that is inhuman" (RA, 77 [72]). Reversing traditional attributes, to this figure of unlimited capacity he opposes a figure of *in*capacity—the executioner—and turns to the repeated claims of the SS that for their part they simply could not have done otherwise. Agamben notes the insistence with which the SS repeated after the war that they had no choice, that they were merely following orders. "In German, to act without being capable of acting is called *Befehlsnotstand,* having to obey an order," notes Agamben of the SS, "and they obeyed *kadavergehorsam,* like a corpse, as Eichmann said" (RA, 78 [74]).[10]

What remains to be asked and answered, however, is in what sense the *Muselmann* marks a limit "between man and non-man," and how that limit is to be understood. Agamben is careful not to situate the *Muselmann* beyond the human, and for this reason he says that the *Muselmann* "is not so much, as Bettelheim believes, the cipher of the point of no return and the threshold beyond which one ceases to be human" as something more difficult to formulate, and to which he then turns his attention (RA, 63 [57]). Rather than with Bettelheim's view, Agamben aligns himself with Levi's vision of the *Muselmann,* in which that figure does not mark a point of no return, a division between human and inhuman, between man and non-man, but instead is "the site of an experiment in which morality and humanity themselves are called into question" (RA, 63 [57]). What Agamben rejects in Bettelheim's conception of a point of no return is the idea of a human life without humanity—that it leaves a margin in life for a life without humanity. "Simply to deny the *Muselmann*'s humanity," Agamben argues, "would be to accept the verdict of the SS and to repeat their gesture. The *Muselmann* has, instead, moved into a zone of the human where not only help but also dignity and self-respect have become useless. But if there is a zone of the human in which these concepts make no sense, then they are not genuine ethical concepts, for no ethics can claim to exclude a part of humanity, no matter how unpleasant or difficult that humanity is to see" (RA, 63–64 [57–58]). The *Muselmann* represents an ethical paradox expressed in Levi's title: the paradox of treating a human being in inhuman fashion. But, for Agamben, the *Muselmann* represents a different ethical paradox because the categories of *dignity* and *responsibility* cease to apply; yet the *Muselmann* does not for as much cease to live. To consider such a figure already dead, or essentially dead, is, following Agamben, to conceive matters precisely as did the SS. Agamben's observation is a prescient one, but it should be made equally clear that there is a sense in which Bettelheim's claim is perfectly coherent. *Muselmänner were* essentially dead in that as soon as they showed these characteristic signs of radical withdrawal, their days were literally numbered. Nevertheless, and as Agamben argues, whatever stay of execution is granted to them cannot be anything but *human*.

The problem here is the same philosophical one with which Agamben began. The reason that such contradictory statements were made by those who witnessed the *Muselmänner* was that they lacked the ethical categories to describe such violently bared life. When they instinctively turned to their, and our, philosophical and political tradition for ethical terms with which to characterize this paradox, they found ones "contaminated" by juridical concepts. In an interview following the publication of *Remnants of Auschwitz,* Agamben said his intention was "not so much to explain Auschwitz as to understand the phenomenon of Auschwitz in its ethical and political aspects." Asked on what level this understanding was to take place, he responded, "on the ethical or the political—or more properly, the biopolitical level" (ATI, 38). In this case, the *biopolitical* level designates a life that is difficult to identify as human, and it is in this light that Agamben noted he was thinking of "the titles of the two books bearing the greatest intensity of testimony, *The Human Race* by Antelme, and *Se questo è un uomo* [*Survival in Auschwitz*] by Levi" (ATI, 38). The categories of *dignity* and *responsibility* seem to Agamben inapplicable because their heritage is juridical—making them ill-suited to their assigned task. What the position "between man and non-man" occupied by the *Muselmann* reveals is what Agamben said he would demonstrate over the course of the book: that "almost none of the ethical principles our age believed it could recognize as valid have stood the decisive test, that of an *Ethica more Auschwitz demonstrata*" (RA, 13 [9]).

It is at this point in *Remnants of Auschwitz* that the term first occurs that had played such a central role in *Homo Sacer* and in the articles both leading up to it and following it. For the initial sixty pages of the book, the idea of bare life is present everywhere but stated nowhere. In his discussion of the *Muselmann,* however, Agamben writes that "Auschwitz marks the end and the ruin of every ethics of dignity and conformity to a norm. The bare life to which human beings were reduced neither demands nor conforms to anything" (RA, 69 [63]). Dignity, Agamben argues, should no longer be the standard-bearer of the human. Undefined, non-normative life is bare life, but this area is far from explored, and this unpresupposable, undefinable place is, as he well recognizes, supremely difficult to chart. Agamben claims that "Levi, who bears witness to the drowned, speaking in their stead, is the cartographer of this new *terra ethica,* the implacable land-surveyor of *Muselmannland*" (RA, 69 [63]). Agamben's ironic reference to Kafka (Kafka is nowhere named in the passage—or thus far in the book—but the reference to a "land-surveyor" points clearly in the direction of *The Castle*) indicates several things. It indicates the importance of Levi's recognizing the terrain, the relation of this region to the sources of power and the rule of law (as in *The Castle*), as well as the uncertainty of the enterprise. In Kafka's book, the land-surveyor doesn't know what to survey; he has his tools and he has been summoned, but he does not know where or when to exercise his métier. Levi's uncertainty is equal to that of Kafka's land-surveyor—but to that uncertainty he opposes the urgency of his enterprise.

Bare Life and the Fabrication of Corpses

The next step Agamben takes is to turn his gaze from *bare life* to *death.* The corollary, for Agamben, of the fact that the *Muselmann* is he or she who experiences a life that no longer seems like life is that he or she experiences a death that is not like earlier ones. It is not surprising that Agamben evokes Heidegger at this point, referring to a passage in the latter's lecture on technology, "The Danger," where he employs the expression "fabrication of corpses" (a term whose genealogy Agamben traces through Rilke, Arendt, and the SS doctor Friedrich Entress). Of Heidegger's lecture Agamben remarks, "Not without reason, a few years later, the objection was raised that for an author implicated even marginally in Nazism, a cursory allusion to the extermination camps after years of silence was, at the very least, out of place" (RA, 74 [68]). Agamben's immediate interest is not the relation of Heidegger's person or philosophy to Nazism (a question he had already treated on numerous occasions)[11] but instead his sense that these deaths do not seem like deaths.[12] They were indeed the ends of lives but, akin to the modern mass-production deaths that Rilke discusses, Entress wishes for, and Arendt bemoans, they were deaths that were not experienced as such—"*ungestorbener Tode,*" in Heidegger's terms—and thus were not experienced in authentic fashion.

Agamben continues Heidegger's line of thought and its implicit reference to the central concept of "being-toward-death" from *Being and Time.* In the case of the camps to which Heidegger, while not directly naming them, is clearly referring, death experienced as "one's own" is impossible because of the very omnipresence of death. Death is not a "horizon" of experience because it never recedes. "The reason for which Auschwitz is excluded from the experience of death"—of the sort that Heidegger envisions—is that "it calls into question the very possibility of authentic decision and thus threatens the very ground of Heidegger's ethics. In the camp, every distinction between proper and improper, between possible and impossible, radically disappears" (RA, 75–76 [70]). This impossibility of experiencing an "authentic" death has nothing to do with being surprised by one's death or with deciding to accept or resist it. Agamben restates this dilemma as "in the camp, the most fundamental gesture [*il gesto più proprio*] of Heidegger's ethics—the appropriation of the improper [*l'appropriazione dell'improprio*], the making possible of existence—remains ineffectual" (RA, 77 [71], translation modified). In seeking new ethical coordinates, Agamben lingers with Heidegger's ethical conceptions before eventually dismissing them as inadequate for this extreme case. Here as elsewhere it is important to bear in mind the difficulty of translating Heidegger's special use of the term *proper* [*eigen*]. It has nothing of social or other *correctness* in its semantic register, and nothing of *authenticity* (another term used to render *eigen* and *Eigentlichkeit* in English translations of Heidegger's work) in the sense of an *authentic* article that one might oppose to a *fake*. The at once simple and complex meaning of *eigen* stems from the idea of that which is proper to a given person or thing—that which is literally "its own." The word's relevance for the discussion here is that the Heideggerian dialectic that Agamben sees put into question by death in Auschwitz is not about correctness—about what would be *proper* in the English sense of the term—but about what, if anything, is proper to the state of the *Muselmann*, this bare life stripped of all traditional ethical attributes (such as dignity and responsibility). Auschwitz does not render Heidegger's ethics invalid because of the shameful silence with which Heidegger reacted to it, nor because of his complicity in the regime that installed those camps. Agamben's point here is to put Heidegger's radical conceptions of ethics and of the source of values to the test of Auschwitz, to "the decisive test, that of an 'Ethica more Auschwitz demonstrata.'" Because of its focus on the appropriating of the experience of death, Heidegger's dialectic of the proper and improper is not, for Agamben, adequate to the task of understanding life in the extreme form taken by the *Muselmann*.

Only at the end of this chapter does Agamben approach the point from which so many of his readers doubtless expected him to begin his book: the "biopolitical machine" with which *Homo Sacer* ended. The real import for the *Homo Sacer* project of the tragic figure of the *Muselmann* reveals itself here: in the *Muselmann* "the final biopolitical substance [*ultima sostanza biopolitica*] in the biological continuum" is found and an "absolute biopolitical substance [*una sostanza biopolitica assoluta*]" is glimpsed (RA, 85 [79]). Only here is the camp then called a "biopolitical machine" (RA, 85 [79]) (a formulation that, incidentally, recalls Adorno's reference to Auschwitz as "the hellish machine that is history" [see Adorno GS, 4.268]). The camp is such a machine not merely because it produces cadavers but because it produces something truly *biopolitical*—something unlocalizable either in biological or in political terms and that marks the point at which the two domains—political life and biological life—dovetail.

The Resistance of the Muselmann, and the Critics

At the end of *Homo Sacer,* Agamben suggested that "the *Muselmann's* behavior . . . might be an unheard of [*inaudita*] form of resistance" (HS, 185 [207], translation modified). In light of the typological descriptions of Levi, Bettelheim, Antelme, and others, this might seem an absurd suggestion as in every case and for every observer the *Muselmann* seemed the very opposite: the ultimate figure of surrender. If the *Muselmann* is the prisoner who has completely succumbed to the barbaric forces brought to bear on him or her, wherein lies the resistance?

In *Homo Sacer,* Agamben saw this resistance in that the *Muselmann* did not "register any difference between an order and the cold" (HS, 185 [207]). Indeed, the *Muselmann* could be said to have offered resistance to the powers running the camp through his or her disobedience—a disobedience that was the result of having retreated so fully within him- or herself that he or she no longer had enough strength to attend to the outside world and the orders emanating from it. The *Muselmann* seems no longer to fear the blows of the SS, or even to distinguish those blows from other stimuli. Yet this response stems not from heroic opposition or courageous resistance but instead from the exhaustion, the trauma, the apathy, and the autism that characterize the *Muselmann*'s liminal state. Although Agamben does not return to this hypothesis in *Remnants of Auschwitz,* nothing in the book serves to contradict it or to indicate that Agamben has changed his mind on the matter. For him, the *Muselmann* is a figure—and a paradigm—of singular resistance. Like Bartleby, the *Muselmann* is an unlikely figure in that it seems to represent the opposite of resistance: a figure who has completely capitulated before the dehumanizing force bearing down on it. Bartleby, crushed by the weight of Wall Street and the law he serves there, or crushed by the weight of loss shown to him through his work at the office of "dead letters" in Washington, seems to succumb and to turn away from the world and die of self-imposed starvation. The war of attrition he led against either himself or his world is one he has lost—or so it seems. In the case of the *Muselmann,* the figure is still more charged—because more real. The *Muselmann* seems a figure of the success of the dehumanizing efforts of the SS; emotionally and physically exhausted, he or she no longer responds to the world, no longer distinguishes the blows of the SS from the stings of the cold. The *Muselmann* has lost the struggle for dignity and even individuality—reduced, finally, to bare biological life. Yet this is a figure Agamben finds exemplary? Although he does indeed, the exemplarity in question must be carefully understood. Agamben often stresses the simplicity of the term *paradigm,* pointing out that it comes from the Greek term for "example." Be that as it may, his manner of using paradigms is far from simple. The *Muselmann* cannot be exemplary in the classical sense of being an example of resistance to follow. Armed resistance, even suicidal revolt, seems more dynamizing, energizing, and thereby exemplary for a community confronting the most unjust treatment imaginable than a figure of final passivity like the one Agamben has singled out. The *Muselmann* is not exemplary or paradigmatic in the sense of being a figure to be emulated, in one paradoxical form or another; instead, as with all of Agamben's paradigms, it is a figure through which we might try to understand "a historical structure" full of relevance for our "present situation."

It should come as little surprise that this is a point that has frequently been misunderstood. As we saw earlier, Marion (2006) judges Agamben's book harshly ("by appropriating Holocaust survivors and their testimonies to articulate anonymous being and the unsayable in language, the inhuman, Agamben makes a lacuna of the horror of Auschwitz—of its empirical reality, victims and participants" [1022]). For her, "[Agamben's] use of the Holocaust in this paradigm disparages the real" (1019). Marion clearly formulates the question in terms of respect for and violation of the singularity or uniqueness of the "empirical reality" of Auschwitz. Albeit in less polemical terms, Robert Eaglestone (2002) also sees Agamben sacrificing historical reality for paradigmatic clarity; he writes that "Agamben's bare life is simply too bare: motivated by the clarity of a philosophical paradigm, it overlooks what is involved in living" (64–65). In their book on *Remnants of Auschwitz*, Philippe Mesnard and Claudine Kahan (2001) also raise a similar objection, judging that Agamben "conceives of politics *in abstracto*," and as a result "seeks to discover in history a central and unique paradigmatic function" (127).

Criticism of this aspect of Agamben's approach does not, however, end here. Levi and Rothberg (2003) focus on this same "empirical reality" invoked by Marion and others and ask of Agamben's book, "The *Muselmann* is meant to bear a certain truth about the nature of ethics 'after Auschwitz,' but is it not important when trying to articulate such an ethics to reflect on what Auschwitz was?" (30). The question posed here is of course rhetorical. The implicit charge that Agamben has failed to inform himself about Auschwitz, or to reflect on that information, is not the real one. What is actually at issue are the conclusions Agamben draws from his reflection. Levi and Rothberg continue: "Surely such an account [as Agamben's] should attend to the historical, legal and political conditions that led to the development of the camp system . . . such as a massive, morally indifferent bureaucratic apparatus that dehumanized its 'objects' and distanced its agents from a sense of responsibility for their actions. . . . If the *Muselmann* would not have existed without these factors, shouldn't an ethics focused on this figure also take account of them?" (30). Here too something unquestionable is asserted: that the "historical, legal and political conditions that led to the development of the camp system" should be attended to in any study of Auschwitz. And here too even a cursory glance at Agamben's writings shows that he indeed attends to these conditions. But it is also here where the real difficulty for Agamben's readers arises. He does not *only* attend to these conditions, and does not *only* examine the figure of the *Muselmann* in their light. He stresses at the outset of his book that others (such as Hilberg) have already done this admirably and extensively, but that there are still consequences—ethical and philosophical—to be drawn. On the larger *Homo Sacer* project, Benjamin Robinson (2003) reaches a conclusion similar to that of Levi and Rothberg, stating that "while [Agamben's] attention to the paradox of sovereignty is illuminating, his apocalyptic framework all but precludes historical analysis" (75, n. 26). More recently, Oliver Marchart (2007) has echoed this judgment, invoking Agamben's "apocalyptic vision" and arguing that "*because* [Agamben] refuses to delineate the historical genealogy of his paradigms the result is a radically pessimistic philosophy of history" (12–13, italics in original).[13] Here too the charge concerns history. At first sight it is surprising in that Agamben does include significant historical analysis in his work. But what becomes clear is that the paradigmatic purpose to which this analysis is put essentially nullifies it for such critics. In perhaps the most striking formulation of this critique—because it is made by the authors of the only book dedicated exclusively to *Remnants of Auschwitz*—Mesnard and Kahan write that "appealed to exclusively as limit situations, Auschwitz and the *Muselmann* . . . are not studied in their relation to the historical conditions that made them possible, but as paradigms of the normal and the everyday," and that "the real frames in which bearing witness appears seem to have no interest for [Agamben]" (2001, 124, 125).[14] As did Marion, Robinson, Levi, and Rothberg, Mesnard and Kahan claim that Agamben has not "studied" the "historical conditions" surrounding Auschwitz and the figure of the *Muselmann*.

Such criticism remains puzzling so long as one sees in it merely a question of historical information and analysis. What is really at stake is the *use* to which Agamben puts his historical analysis. Levi and Rothberg, like Mesnard and Kahan, are wrong to upbraid Agamben for not doing something that he in fact does (attend to the "historical, legal and political conditions that led to the development of the camp system"). Nevertheless, they, like the other critics noted above, are responding to something in Agamben's book that is genuinely unsettling and that we have already seen criticized by the unnamed French letter writer: his use of paradigms. Levi and Rothberg find that "for the Agamben of *Homo Sacer* a camp is a camp if anything is possible within it, . . . no matter whether or not it actually produces *Muselmänner* and corpses, while for the Agamben of *Remnants of Auschwitz* the important fact about the *Muselmann* is simply that such a figure happened, not where and how he became possible" (Levi and Rothberg 2003, 30). Here the contours of their criticism are clearly recognizable as criticism of Agamben's paradigmatic method. They charge Agamben with not attending to the historical reality of Auschwitz, but what they are really objecting to is the idea that his understanding of this historical reality can *also* be used to illustrate very different situations—in other words, can be used as a paradigm. In similar fashion, Mesnard and Kahan deduce from the fact that Agamben uses Auschwitz and the *Muselmann* as paradigms that he did not study the historical conditions behind them. Their explicit claim is that he is underinformed, but their far more powerful implicit one is that for him to use such figures as paradigms he *must* have been underinformed. Robinson says something similar in claiming that Agamben's use of such paradigms "all but precludes historical analysis" for the reason that, in his eyes, the first consequence of such historical analysis would be to rule out its use as a paradigm.

Traumatic Temporality, or the Eternal Continuation of Auschwitz

"The ethics of the twentieth century," Agamben writes, "opens with Nietzsche's overcoming of resentment" (RA, 99 [92]). Nietzsche's attempt to accept the pastness of the past—to transform the excruciating "it was" into "thus I wanted it to be," and whose motto is *amor fati*—meets, for Agamben, its limit at Auschwitz. Auschwitz, claims Agamben, "marks a decisive rupture" with this attempt at overcoming resentment (RA, 99 [92]). Reformulating Nietzsche's presentation of the idea of "the eternal recurrence of the same" in *The Gay Science*, Agamben proposes the thought experiment of "a demon that glides beside a survivor and asks: 'Do you want Auschwitz to return again and again . . . ?'" (RA, 99 [92]). Agamben claims that "this simple reformulation of Nietzsche's experiment suffices to refute it beyond all doubt, excluding the possibility of its even being proposed" (RA, 99 [92]). And yet this claim radically misrepresents

Nietzsche's idea. Here it is as if Agamben were responding to a vulgarized version of Nietzsche's doctrine—or to another idea altogether. Nietzsche's remarks were not meant as a *justification* of the past, not something of the nature of Hegel's epochal "what is is reasonable." The point of Nietzsche's arduous thought experiment was to place responsibility for human affairs, actions, and values in *this* world rather than in some transcendental other-world or afterlife. Its goal was precisely to confront the horrors of the past, not only the incidental oppositions to our whims and wills, not only disappointment, but injustice on the largest scale. To accept that the abominable has happened, that innocents have suffered and the guilty have gone unpunished, that the course of history has not been what Hegel claimed it was ("reasonable"), is what the experiment aimed to come to terms with. Nietzsche's question is whether we can accept this and carve out a limited justice in the shadow of a past rife with injustice and cruelty. And the reason he posed it was that he saw no other choice.

In Agamben's hands, the thought experiment is presented as if it were a callous suggestion. However unfair Agamben's "reformulation" of Nietzsche's thought experiment might be, the question remains of what Agamben is trying to do at this point in his argument. His "reformulation" seems at first sight to be the integration of Auschwitz into the series of things (history) to be willed an infinity of times. In this case, Agamben would be saying that no one who had lived through—or even learned about—something as horrible as Auschwitz could possibly will its return. We might understand this assessment from the side of history in the sense that hitherto nothing as horrible, nothing as monstruous as Auschwitz had happened, and in its wake such postulates as Nietzsche's needed to be reevaluated—and, perhaps, discarded. This assessment would correspond to the idea that history after Auschwitz should not be conceived of as was history before Auschwitz, and is in line with Agamben's attempt to put conceptions to "the decisive test" referred to earlier—that of an *Ethica more Auschwitz demonstrata.*

In this light it would seem that—though there has already been in the course of world history terrible pain and suffering—with Auschwitz the scales tipped, and the suffering, senselessness, and cruelty grew so great that an acceptance like the one for which Nietzsche strove was henceforth impossible. In short, one could no longer make peace with such a past. But this is not the position at which Agamben wants to arrive, as its only alternative is the very ethics of resentment Nietzsche set out to combat.

For this reason, Agamben claims that this "failure" that Nietzsche represents, this "failure of Zarathustra's lesson . . . does not depend on the fact that what happened at Auschwitz is too atrocious for anyone ever to will its repetition" (RA, 100 [92], translation modified). The English translation renders "will its repetition" as "wish for its repetition"—requiring the reader to imagine something quite different from that of which Nietzsche wrote, placing an unfathomably perverse "wish" in the place of a singular act of will. Agamben writes *"volerne la ripetizione"* and thereby reproduces Nietzsche's term *willing*. The point is not that one *like* the past, but that one *accept* it *as the past* and choose that irreparably past state of affairs over resisting and resenting that which no resistance or resentment could ever change.

Agamben is well aware that the alternative to accepting the past in the way that Nietzsche endeavors to do is to reject the past—a rejection that can lead only to resentment. Agamben finds just such an ethics based on resentment in the case of another survivor, Jean Améry, who, in his own words, refused to accept that "what happened, happened" (cited in RA, 100 [93]). Améry claims, "I believe to have recognized that a forgiving and forgetting induced by social pressure is immoral," and he feels that putting behind the past as past and laying aside one's resentments—and even one's fury—is to commit a *moral* trespass (cited in RA, 100 [93]). One could scarcely imagine a purer example of an ethics based on resentment. And yet while the staunch rejection of any form of reconciliation with the past is eminently understandable, it is also, for Agamben, ethically untenable.

As in many places in *Remnants of Auschwitz,* the path Agamben follows at this point is traced for him by Levi. The latter is as little disposed to "forgive" as Améry ("I am not inclined to forgive; I never forgave our enemies"; cited at RA, 101 [93]). Yet through the traumatic temporality that both Levi and Améry describe, Agamben finds a new formulation of his rejection of Nietzsche's attempt to make peace with the past, as well as, more broadly, a rejection of "twentieth-century ethics" (RA, 101 [93]). *"One cannot will* [volere][15] *Auschwitz to return for eternity,"* Agamben writes, *"since in truth it has never ceased to take place; it is always already repeating itself* [si sta già sempre riptendo]" (RA, 101 [93], italics in original, translation modified). In Levi's nightmares he finds himself back in Auschwitz—a terrifying if not uncommon phenomenon. This easily understandable psychological response is, however, raised by Agamben to the status of an ontological condition. Levi is not, as in Agamben's account of Nietzsche's experiment, engaged in the effort to "conquer the spirit of revenge in order to accept the past"; nor is he, as was Améry, endeavoring to "hold fast to the unacceptable through resentment" (RA, 102 [94], translation modified). The middle path that Agamben sees the traumatized Levi following is, however, unclear. What Agamben finds in Levi's poem "At an Uncertain Hour" is "a being beyond acceptance and refusal, beyond the eternal past and the eternal present—an event that returns eternally but that, precisely for this reason, is absolutely, eternally unassumable [*inassumibile*]" (RA, 102–3 [94–95]). Agamben then concludes that "beyond good and evil lies . . . a shame that is not only without guilt but without time," because the shame of which he speaks is not relegated to the past—and cannot be (RA, 103 [95]). This leads Agamben back to the path he had begun to follow earlier—that of the subject and of a shame without guilt. It is indeed laudable—it is even perhaps necessary—in the name of an "*Ethica more Auschwitz demonstrata*" not simply to accept the past (as Nietzsche asked) and also not simply to reject it (as did Améry). Beyond this opposition there lies, for Agamben, "a new, unprecedented ontological consistency of what has taken place," but it is a consistency that is extraordinarily difficult to grasp. Resentment is not overcome, as in Nietzsche, nor embraced as an ethical imperative, as in Améry, but suspended, as in Levi's case, like a *nightmare*.

Agamben here claims that one cannot accept the sheer horror of Auschwitz, of the remnants of Auschwitz with which we are confronted today, not because they are *per se* impossible to accept—whatever their horror and whatever suffering they represent. This emotional appeal that was Améry's—that of outraged refusal—is not the one that Agamben chooses, but he is no more prepared to have Auschwitz placed *ad acta* in the continuum of history. He is then left with a single possibility: have it remain in the present. The refutation of Nietzsche's "eternal recurrence of the same" that Agamben finds in Auschwitz is, in philosophical terms, a poor one: the past cannot recur because it is not the past. What is most important here is not the philosophical validity of Agamben's reading of Nietzsche (see the end of this chapter for a discussion of this question), but what Agamben is trying to express through it. If not on a philosophical then on a psychological level, Agamben's contention about the remnants of Auschwitz is consistent with the experience of survivors who lived to bear witness to Auschwitz and whose suffering did not end with their escape from it. As we have seen, Agamben focuses on the traumatic timelessness of Auschwitz for those who have survived it and who cannot relegate it to the past—and for this reason cannot even consider accepting or refusing it *as* past. This individual traumatic temporality (the fear that a dreadful past is not really past) is one that Agamben adopts as a paradigm—one that recalls his claim that the paradigmatic soccer game between the SS and the *Sonderkommando* is not horrible because it is so macabre, although it is indeed that, but because it is not over—that our present historical situation is not separate from that of World War II and the phenomenon of the camps.

The Subject of Shame

Chapter Three of *Remnants of Auschwitz* turns to the subject of shame—in both the subjective and genitive senses; it is an investigation both of the category of the *subject* and of the affect of *shame*. The *shame* with which Agamben begins is not, however, that of the Holocaust's more or less willing executioners, the shame of the *guilty*, but instead the shame of the *innocent* who lived to testify.[16] Agamben focuses his attention on the sense of shame experienced by the victims, on the shame that so many survivors have recounted plagued them for months, years, decades—or a whole life long—after their liberation. This shame came in many forms, but a particularly frequent one was, and is, the feeling that they lived, and live, in the place of others, that others died in their place. This shame could take concrete form in cases in which survivors feel, or felt, that they might have done more, helped more, been at a given moment braver, kinder, more generous, and that that might have made all the difference for one or more of their fellow sufferers. Given the conditions, the most pardonable lapses haunted, and still haunt, many survivors—something that Bettelheim, for instance, sees in a positive light, claiming that "only the ability to feel guilty makes us human, particularly if, objectively seen, one is not guilty" (cited in RA, 93 [86]). This sense of shame could just as easily take on the form of a sense of their relative merit or worth, that they were perhaps less worthy than those who perished, and even expand to metaphysical proportions as a sense that who or what governed who drowned and who was saved was simply incomprehensible. And finally, it can be a sense of shame of a secular but equally global nature—the shame named in Levi's haunting title ("If this is a man"), the shame over what Arendt and so many others expressed as something that simply should not have happened and that shames all who experience it, shames all who learn of it, shames us on the most general level possible: that of being human.[17] This sense of fundamental shame is, in this respect, easy to understand and to feel, and extraordinarily difficult to come to grips with.

At this point it is useful to recall that *Remnants of Auschwitz* is not Agamben's first encounter with the subject of shame. A chapter of *Idea of Prose* is dedicated to "The Idea of Shame" seen from the perspective of comedy and tragedy as well as in a historical evolution from the Greeks to the present day (see IP, 83–85 [67–69]). Agamben notes that the entry of shame into the affective discourse of the West seems to have occurred in the metaphysical speculation of the dialogue *Parmenides,* where Socrates shudders and feels something like a universal shame for the notion that ideas "of hair, filth, mud" and other "vile" and desultory things exist (IP, 83–84 [67–68]). In the case of our modern age and "modern man," "shame is the index of an unheard of and frightening proximity of man with himself [*l'uomo con se stesso*]" (IP, 84 [68]). To confront ourselves is, in this optic, to confront our transience—as well as to feel a sense of shame for not being able to take our mortal measure more fully, a shame at not truly understanding ourselves. In *The Coming Community* the question of shame arises in equally original form, in the question of the origin of the idea of original sin. For Agamben, a sense of shame is a fundamental part of our being because of our very uncertainty about our historical and personal *calling*—our uncertainty about our proper place and task both as individuals and as groups. "There is in effect," writes Agamben, "something that humans are and have to be, but this something is not an essence nor properly a thing: *it is the simple fact of one's own existence as possibility or potentiality*" (CC, 43 [39], italics in original). This experience brings with it not just something liberating and empowering, but also something harrowing, and leads to the sense that "insofar as humankind's most proper being—being potential—is in a certain sense lacking, insofar as it can not-be, it is therefore devoid of foundation, and humankind is not always already in possession of it," and for this reason, "humans have and feel a debt" (CC, 43 [39–40]). This sense of owing an uncertain "debt" leads Agamben to the idea that we "always already have a bad conscience without having to commit any blameworthy act"—which, in a characteristic turn, he says, "is all that is meant by the old theological doctrine of original sin" (CC, 44 [40]).[18] The sense of having a specific *vocation* that we fail to exercise, a specific *task* that we must accomplish, opens us, following Agamben's idea of shame, to the sense that we fail to fulfill it. The fundamental argument that Agamben makes in these works, however, is that we do not have, and should not have, any such determinate vocation. Turning to more directly political matters, in an essay on his self-imposed exile from Italy Agamben writes of *shame* from a variety of angles: a pervasive expression of shame in contemporary political debates in Italy, shame as Marx defined it—"a sort of anger turned upon itself"—and finally, the shame that will come center stage in *Remnants of Auschwitz:* "shame at being human" (MWE, 132 [102]). In all these discussions, what we should note is that Agamben examines shame as extending beyond the empirical coordinates of any specific acts or omissions.[19]

To return to *Remnants of Auschwitz,* this question of *shame* is at the heart of the book's reflections. Agamben begins the third and longest chapter, entitled "Shame, or On the Subject," by expressing surprise that the chapter in Levi's *The Drowned and the Saved* that follows his masterful account of the "grey zone" is entitled "Shame" and yet, in Agamben's eyes, proves to be such a disappointment. Agamben traces Levi's dismissal of collective guilt, and the "tragic" model of guilt that he finds in both Bettelheim and Des Pres, against whom Bettelheim inveighs, before beginning his own excursus on the topic by relating Antelme's account of a student from Bologna who, when arbitrarily called out from the ranks of prisoners marching from Buchenwald to Dachau at the end of the war, blushed a red that looked to Antelme like shame. Agamben says of Antelme's testimony, "Auschwitz also means this much: that man, dying, cannot find any other sense in his death than this flush, this shame" (RA, 104 [96]). "Why does this student from Bologna blush?" Agamben then asks, and answers that "it is as if the flush on his cheeks momentarily betrayed a limit that was reached, as if something like a new ethical material [*una nuova materia etica*] were touched upon in the living being" (RA, 104 [96]). In what might seem more like shock or fear than shame in the face of this Italian youth, Agamben identifies an ontological undercurrent. The surprising location of this "new ethical material" leads Agamben to Emmanuel Lévinas and from Lévinas to the latter's teacher, Heidegger. Agamben focuses his attention on Heidegger's lecture course dedicated to Parmenides in which the topic of shame receives ample treatment and in which, for Heidegger, the Greek term *aidos* touches on "fundamental . . . authentic Greekness," that shame is "more than a feel-ing" and, in Agamben's paraphrase, is "an emotive tonality that traverses and determines his whole Being. Shame is thus a kind of ontological senti-ment that has its characteristic place in the encounter between man and Being" (RA, 106 [98]). For Heidegger—and, in his wake, Agamben—shame is thus much more than an affect among others.

Heidegger finds this "ontological character of shame" most clearly in the experience of *disgust*. Agamben supplements Heidegger's scant reflec-tions on the *disgust* that leads to *shame* by turning to Benjamin. In the latter's *One-Way Street, disgust* is connected to what Benjamin calls an "obscure awareness" that there is something so "animal" in him that it can be "recognized" by the thing that disgusts him. This curious experience leads Agamben, in argumentation that is often difficult to follow because it is uncharacteristically schematic (or, alternately, hasty), to what he offers as a "provisional definition of shame": "[Shame] is nothing less than the fundamental sentiment of being *a subject,* in the two apparently opposed senses of this phrase: to be subjected and be sovereign" (RA, 107 [99]).[20] Here at last we can glimpse something of the sense behind Agamben's mystifying chapter title, "Shame, or On the Subject." In Agamben's ac-count, *shame* is more than an affect because the arc it describes is the same as that of "being a subject."

There is shame in being a subject because one is subjected to forces beyond one's control. Agamben thus employs the term *subject* in much the same way that Foucault did. For both thinkers, what is essential about the term *subject* is the conjuncture of passivity and activity. To be a subject is not merely to be a conscious and self-aware agent in a linguistic situa-tion, conceptual schema, or social forum; it is to be subjected by forces of subjectification, to be subjected to norms and constraints—what Foucault called "technologies of power." And it is this location, at the watershed between activity and passivity, that, in a certain sense, is also the source of shame.

The Subject of Testimony

At this point in his argument, Agamben turns from *shame* to the *subject,* from what he describes as the ontological character of shame to the linguistic phenomenon of "desubjectification," to forms of reflexivity or self-reflexivity visible in Spinoza's observations on Hebrew grammar and in Keats's letters on poetic creation. "In the Western literary tradition," writes Agamben, "the act of poetic creation and, indeed, every act of speech implies something like a desubjectification" (RA, 113 [105]). Poets have often experienced this phenomenon as a visitation from the Muse, but whatever its character, a constant has been the poet becoming, if only for a moment, other (as in Rimbaud's epochal self-description *je est un autre*). Agamben does not leave this experience in the province of the poets but extends it to all acts of speech. What is writ large in poetry is, for Agamben, writ small in every act of speech: *desubjectification*.

What does this have to do with Auschwitz, with those who survived it, those who testified to it and to its "remnants"? The connection is not an easy one to make, and Agamben first leads his readers through an excursus on poetic subjectivity, discussing Keats,[21] Dante, Pessoa, and others, without a clear end in sight. Agamben continues to relate these poetic experiences of "desubjectification" to grammatical or linguistic coordinates present in every speech act, and along the way invokes a cardinal point of reference from his earlier work: Benveniste's researches into the impersonal function of pronouns (this same aspect of Benveniste's research plays a decisive role in the final section of Agamben's essay "Infancy and History," from the work of the same name). To this constellation of linguistic experiences and experiments is added the Apostle Paul's account of *glossolalia* (his reminders to the people of Corinth that speaking in tongues should always be accompanied by interpretation and should not run afoul of sensible speech), which Agamben also sees as paradigmatic of desubjectification (see RA, 114 [106]).[22] It is at this point, then, that it becomes for Agamben "possible to clarify the sense in which shame is truly something like the hidden structure of all subjectivity and consciousness. Insofar as it consists solely in the event of enunciation, consciousness constitutively has the form of being consigned to something that cannot be assumed" (RA, 128 [119–120]).

This excursus on poetic speech and the shifting spaces of the self in poetic creation at last leads Agamben back to Auschwitz, and he proposes to "reread the phenomenology of testimony" in its light (RA, 120 [111]). Both the linguistic and the poetic offer new perspectives on the question of testimony; language's structure (linguistics) and its most exploratory instances (poetry) cast light, for Agamben, on the matter at hand. With this broadened perspective, he returns to the two sides of the equation of testimony examined in the first chapter: the relation between those who "touched bottom"—or in Levi's other evocative phrase, "saw the Gorgon"—who lived the camps in all their integral cruelty, and those who, like Levi, did not and as a result lived to bear witness. In response to this perspective on subjectivity and shame, Agamben's newly weighted question becomes "*Who is the subject of testimony?*" (RA, 120 [111], italics in original).

The fine line that Agamben walks throughout this section of the book—in particular as concerns the question of the paradigm Auschwitz offers—can be seen with special clarity in the rebuke that J. M. Bernstein lodges against it and that resembles many of the criticisms noted earlier:

It is surely right to say that the extremity of human suffering involves a systematic undoing of a subject's linguistically realized intentional relation to the world. Our own experiences of extreme pain could have informed us of as much. And thus it must be equally right to say that, even as speaking animals, we belong to a world whose emphatic presence would vitiate our relation to it. From this, it equally follows that the biopolitical world of the camps operates through the disarticulation of subjectification (our speaking being) from desubjectification (the contingency of life). But none of this directly or meaningfully seems to be an *ethical* response to the fate of the *Muselmann*. [Bernstein 2004, 14, italics in original]

From this charge of irrelevance Bernstein rapidly moves to the harshest of judgments: that what Agamben effects is "at most, an aestheticization of [the *Muselmann*'s] fate for the sake of a metaphysics of language" (14). Mesnard and Kahan also speculate that Agamben's "failure to understand historiographical debates on the Holocaust" stems from "an aesthetic position" (Mesnard and Kahan 2001, 126).[23] A more scathing criticism of Agamben's enterprise would be difficult to formulate, characterizing as it does his investigation of the figure of the *Muselmann* as an "aestheticization" of that figure's awful fate for the purposes of advancing a metaphysical theory of language. Bernstein is doubtless right that Agamben's study of modes of desubjectification is not "directly . . . an *ethical* response to the fate of the *Muselmann*," but this is also not what Agamben is claiming to offer. Whether Bernstein's criticism is justified hinges on the actual claim that Agamben is making: not that such study is a "direct . . . ethical response to the fate of the *Muselmann*," but that it is a useful link in the chain of understanding the subject of shame that Agamben has set out to follow.[24]

Although Agamben's readers might easily be forgiven for not finding and following such a chain, it is at this point that the motivation behind Agamben's excursus on traumatic temporality and ways of approaching a terribly present past, along with his reason for immediately following it with a study of the modes of speech and desubjectification, becomes clear. One of the most fundamental components of what Agamben calls "the phenomenology of testimony" is an experience of the time in which such shame transpires: "a shame that is not only without guilt but even without time" (RA, 103 [95]). With Heidegger's phenomenology clearly in mind, Agamben advances the claim that "Auschwitz marks the irrecoverable crisis of authentic temporality [*temporalità propria*], of the very possibility of 'deciding' on the disjunction. The camp, the absolute situation, is the end of every possibility of an originary temporality, that is, of the temporal foundation of a singular positioning space, of a *Da*. In the camp, the irreparability of the past takes the form of an absolute imminence" (RA, 128 [119]). Just as Agamben saw in Auschwitz the "refutation" of Nietzsche's thought experiment on the "eternal recurrence of the same," he also sees in it the "irrecoverable crisis" of Heidegger's experiment in reconceputalizing "authentic temporality." This "absolute imminence" recalls "kairological" and "messianic" conceptions of time from *The Man Without Content* to *Infancy and History* to *The Coming Community*. Like those conceptions, this temporality is based not on sequentiality and chronology but rather on a more complex and dynamic interweaving of past and present. What is imminent in the camp is "a time of the now," characterized above all by the suffering and shame of a past that one cannot relegate to the past, and what remains of the camp for so many of its survivors is a past that is not past.

This paradox of traumatic temporality leads Agamben to Derrida. Proceeding along precisely the same polemical lines as we saw earlier, he takes Derrida to task for conceiving of time as infinite deferral. Agamben writes, "It is hardly astonishing that it was precisely from an analysis of the pronoun I in Husserl that Derrida was able to draw his idea of an infinite deferral, an originary disjunction—writing—inscribed in the pure self-presence of consciousness" (RA, 123 [114]). Here as elsewhere, Agamben agrees with much of Derrida's analysis, but diverges at the point where he sees Derrida remain in an aporia or "infinite deferral," rather than seeking to transform that aporia into a "euporia." Of the disjunction between world and text that Derrida highlights—the disjunction between "living being and language"—Agamben surprisingly claims that "far from authorizing the infinite deferral of signification—[it] is what allows for testimony" (RA, 130 [120]). Returning (though not referring) to his earlier analyses of the difference between the inarticulate voice of the natural world and the articulate voice of man that Agamben analyzes in essays such as "Vocation and Voice" and books such as *Language and Death,* Agamben programmatically claims that, "*testimony takes place in the non-place of articulation. In the non-place of the Voice stands not writing, but the witness*" (RA, 130 [121], italics in original). He continues: "And it is precisely because the relation (or rather, non-relation) between the living being and the speaking being has the form of shame, of being reciprocally consigned to something that cannot be assumed by a subject, that the *ethos* of this disjunction can only be testimony—that is, something that cannot be assigned to a subject but that nevertheless constitutes the subject's only dwelling place, its only possible consistency [*consistenza*]" (RA, 130 [121]).

The link that Agamben asks his reader to make here is a difficult one and involves several connections. Agamben presents the witness as being in an important respect like the poet, and like any speaker seriously reflecting on the significance of his or her speech, in recognizing a disjunction between a *natural* voice (like the one that other animals possess) and a *cultural* voice (which sets us apart from other animals). This is a disjunction—the disjunction of an unmotivated sign-system—that we are eager to forget and that, when we remember, produces an uncertainty, anxiety, and even something like *shame.* This disjunction means that, in Agamben's words, "we are consigned to something that cannot be assumed by a subject"—and that is, precisely, being a *subject.* Agamben then links this *linguistic* state of affairs—common to all who speak, whether they must testify to the evil that man does or to something completely quotidian and desultory—to Heidegger's phenomenological analyses of *shame.* In this tightly circling constellation of ideas, Agamben brings together the figure of the witness ashamed of him- or herself with a sense of shame that is constitutive of human subjectivity. What is revealed in the spotlight of Auschwitz is a shame that is ours at every moment and every step—whatever our individual share of guilt and whether we are aware of it or not.

With this in mind, Agamben turns from a theory of testimony and the shame it incites back to Auschwitz and Levi's question concerning the human and its limits. Agamben writes, "Let us then formulate the thesis that summarizes the lesson of Auschwitz: *The human being is the one who*

can survive the human being [l'uomo è colui che può sopravvivere all'uomo]"
(RA, 132 [124], italics in original). As Levi remarked, the *Muselmänner*
were the "complete" or "integral witnesses [*i testimoni integrali*]," and what
they bore witness to, in Agamben's words, is that "*the human being is the
inhuman; the one whose humanity is completely destroyed is the one who is
truly human*"(RA, 133 [125], italics in original). This seeming oxymoron is
not as counterintuitive as it might first appear when we recall how we actually use the word *inhuman*. As noted earlier, the *inhuman* is something
that is in fact all too human. We use the word inhuman not to denote
higher or lower orders (such as gods or animals) but instead to refer to
human behavior that is, for us, below the bar of civilization, unworthy of
how we would like humans to be. What Agamben sees in this paradoxical
"lesson of Auschwitz" is that the human and the inhuman are not equal
and inverse images. This idea about the human as inhuman at last leads
Agamben to the title of his work: "The paradox here is that if the only
one bearing witness to the human is the one whose humanity has been
wholly destroyed"—Agamben is here referring to the reduced state of the
Muselmänner—"this means that the identity between human and inhuman is never perfect and that it is not truly possible to destroy the human,
that something always *remains* [*che* resta *sempre qualcosa*]. *The witness is
this remnant* [il testimone è quel resto]" (RA, 133–134 [125], italics in original). The literal translation of Agamben's Italian title is "What Remains of
Auschwitz," and here he tells us that what remains is the *witness*.

Agamben next links this paradox—"*the human being is the inhuman; the one whose humanity is completely destroyed is the one who is truly
human*"—to another. After reading Antelme's *The Human Race*, Blanchot
concluded that "man is the indestructible that can be infinitely destroyed"
(cited at RA, 134 [125]).[25] Agamben interprets these two paradoxes in light
of one of his most fundamentally held ideas—one about human nature
and its essence: "There is no human essence; the human being is a potential being [*un essere di potenza*]" (RA, 134 [126]). By claiming that "the
human being is a potential being" Agamben is drawing what he sees as
the necessary consequence of the absence of a human essence. For him,
it is not some already attained state or already developed faculty (such as
speech or reason) that defines human being, just as it is not some specific
historical task or vocation. For this reason, human essence and human
existence are not to be separated. *Human being* is, for Agamben, *potential
being* in the sense that the only coherent definition of a being without

fixed essence is *potentiality.* Alongside the unmitigated horror of what humans are capable of doing to one another—for which there seem to be no limits—what the *witness* of Agamben's title bears witness *to* is precisely this potentiality in all its ethical complexity.[26]

For Agamben, Auschwitz is the most harrowing proof conceivable of the contingent, profane, and potential nature of human being. The catastrophic situation it represents provides the elements for a clearer conception of what it means to be human and what it means to be a speaking subject. In other words, there is for Agamben a lesson to be learned from the remnants of Auschwitz about what it means to be human. The hardest aspect of this lesson lies in the idea that the same freedom—the same potentiality that is man's essence—that made such horrors possible is also the only one that can help us understand and combat those horrors. For this reason, in the catastrophe to which Agamben is directing his reader's attention there is contained a fragile truth about the nature of being human that, in his view, could all too easily slip through history's hands.

The Archive

To understand what "remains" of Auschwitz, of the "archive" and of "testimony," we must turn to the fourth and final section of the book. Ewa Ziarek (2003) has written that "Agamben's reflection . . . leads not only to a redefinition of testimony but also to a new theory of enunciation and subjectivity" (202). In this estimation, however, she has stood relatively alone. Düttmann, who offered glowing praise for such works as *Idea of Prose* and *The Coming Community,* felt impelled to note that "the last chapter of *The Remnants of Auschwitz* is hardly more than a sketch, a first draft which announces the unfolding of the argument," though without explaining why Agamben chose to publish such premature findings (Düttmann 2001, 5). This last chapter of *Remnants of Auschwitz* shares the book's subtitle: "The Archive and Testimony." Whereas the question of testimony has been present since the book's first lines, the question of the *archive* is first introduced here. The chapter begins with an anecdote that at first sight has nothing to do with Auschwitz or an archive: how one of the most brilliant theoreticians of speech lost the ability to speak. As Agamben relates, one evening in 1969 Émile Benveniste suffered a stroke in a Parisian street. The world-renowned linguist and member of the *Collège de France* awoke to find himself unable to speak—a state in which he would remain for the final three years of his life.[27]

Although it remains implicit in Agamben's account, Benveniste's fate offers an emblematic beginning to this final section of the book in its posing anew the problem of bearing witness. Perhaps more than any other thinker of his generation, Benveniste focused his attention on the structure of the situations in which statements were made, on how such statements were socially circumscribed, and how they were conditioned by a process of subjectification in which language played the leading role. That this thinker who saw more clearly than any other into this dizzyingly complex field of subjectivity and speech suffered the cruel irony of being himself struck silent and thereby prevented from finally developing his project of a "metasemantics constructed on the basis of a semantics of enunciation" is, it appears, the reason he is placed at the chapter's outset.[28] With this final and unfinished project in mind, Agamben asks, "What did Benveniste glimpse before falling into aphasia?" (RA, 138 [128]). For Agamben, an indication is to be found in the thinker who developed this theory of enunciation into the same realm of a general metasemantics of enunciation that Benveniste had planned: Foucault. (It was this same concept of *enunciation* that proved so important for Foucault in a work that appeared the same year in which Benveniste fell tragically silent: *The Archaeology of Knowledge*.)[29] Despite the clarity and insight of Foucault's explorations in this domain, Agamben sees Foucault as having omitted a key aspect of Benveniste's theory: "In his understandable concern to define archeology's terrain with respect to other knowledges and domains, Foucault appears to have neglected—at least to a certain point—to consider the ethical implications of his theory of statements" (RA, 141 [131]). What Agamben claims that Foucault neglected is thus no peripheral matter, but instead the very "ethical implications" without which any such theory remains incomplete. To remedy this shortcoming, Agamben turns to a different work of Foucault's—his late essay "The Life of Infamous Men," originally written as a preface to an anthology of archival *lettres de cachet*. In Agamben's words, "a name lives solely in the disgrace that covered it"—a "disgrace" that for Agamben "bears witness to life beyond all biography" (RA, 143 [133]).[30] What Agamben sees here is "not the subject's face, but rather the disjunction between the living being and the speaking being that marks its empty place" (RA, 143 [133]). Before offering his own version of this ethical element that Foucault neglected in his metasemantics of enunciation, and before elucidating this "life beyond all biography" that he saw in another of Foucault's texts, Agamben turns to the *archive* named in the book's subtitle.

To what sort of archive is Agamben referring? Is he interested in an idea of the archive after the fashion of Derrida's *Archive Fever* (1995), in the feverish unease that an archive can produce, and in the difficulty of archiving, of fixing and locating, the remnants of the past in a way that is true to that past and that can be true for the present—and for the future? For Agamben, as for Derrida, the *archive* poses a problem of historical knowledge and of the codification of culture. It is concerned with both conservation and renovation, and it reflects their tensions. It would also seem from Agamben's title that the remnants of Auschwitz are real and concrete—the witnesses and the archive formed from their testimony, from the documents of those who perished and those who planned (as in the case of the documents on the Final Solution that survived the SS's attempt to destroy their extensive archives). To these archives would presumably be added the archive represented by the remnants of Auschwitz—the physical place—itself. Converted into a place of mourning and memory for the past and the future, it is also a site of contention (amply reflected in recent years by the attempt on behalf of the area's Catholic community to erect a cross there, as well as in the visit of a German pope, Benedict XVI, in 2006). All of these things remain of Auschwitz, and one might with justice call these remnants an *archive*. Yet none of these things corresponds to the *archive* that Agamben has in mind in his book's final chapter.

The term so long awaited—named as it is in the subtitle but not appearing until this late in the work—is thus introduced not in any of its conventional senses but instead, as a technical term. "Foucault gives the name 'archive,'" Agamben reminds his readers, "to the positive dimension that corresponds to the plane of enunciation [*enunciazione*], 'the general system of the formation and transformation of statements [*enunciati*]'" (RA, 143 [153]). Agamben's citation here is from *The Archaeology of Knowledge*, wherein *archive* is understood in a special, metaphorical sense; it is not a collection of objects and documents, a catalogue or collection preserved from the past for the future, but rather a systematic matrix or "general system" for the making of statements at a given time and in a given place. (Agamben paraphrases Foucault's idea of the archive as precisely "the set of rules which define the events of discourse" [RA, 143 (133)].)

Agamben's special use of the term *archive* is initially close to the one Foucault developed from Benveniste, and Agamben will thus define "the archive" as "the mass of the non-semantic [*non-semantico*] inscribed in every meaningful discourse as a function of its enunciation; it is the dark margin encircling and limiting every concrete act of speech" (RA, 144 [134]). In Agamben's hands, *archive* thus means the opposite of what is often meant by the term, the opposite of existing collections containing the remnants of the past. *Archive* signifies here not an aggregate body of actual documents or statements but "the dark margin encircling and limiting every concrete act of speech." In the counterintuitive sense Agamben is employing here, the archive is not the storehouse of the said but the shadowy domain of all that went unsaid. In other words, the *archive*, in Agamben's modified sense, is precisely that which does not appear in any archive; it is what does *not* appear in statements; it is their "dark margin," illegible but shaping.[31]

   After recasting the idea of the *archive* in the wake of Benveniste and Foucault, Agamben is at last ready to clarify the full sense of his subtitle: "In opposition to the *archive*, which designates the system of relations between the unsaid and the said, we give the name *testimony* to the system of relations between the inside and the outside of *langue*, between the sayable and the unsayable in every language—that is, between a potentiality of speech and its existence, between a possibility and an impossibility of speech" (RA, 145 [144], italics in original). Chapter and subtitle do not thus name two terms that are simply opposed. Instead, they name different modalities, different perspectives on the potentialities of speech. *Archive* is concerned with "the relations between the unsaid and the said" and thus points toward the past, the "unsaid" in the margins of the "said." *Testimony* is concerned with the same *thing*—the act of speech—but it considers it in another light. For Agamben, *testimony* is "the system of relations between . . . the sayable and the unsayable," and thus the potentiality of the present. Although the parallel is not offered with as much clarity as one is accustomed to finding in Agamben's writing, it is clear that what the archive is on the level of the *said*, testimony is on the level of *the sayable*. By this same token, what the archive is on the level of *actuality* (the said), testimony is on the level of *potentiality* (the sayable). For this reason Agamben can go on to say, summoning the terms familiar from his analyses of Aristotle, that "because testimony is the relation between a possibility of speech and its taking place, it can exist only through a relation to an impossibility of speech—that is, only as *contingency*, as a capacity not to be [*un poter non essere*]" (RA, 145 [135], italics in original). These two terms that form the subtitle and explain the title of Agamben's tenth book are thus an integral part of his project of conceiving the question of potentiality in immediate conjunction with the question of language and its speaking subject. "The human being is the speaking being [*L'uomo è il parlante*]," says Agamben, returning to a decisive term from an earlier phase of his work, "because it is capable of its own in-fancy [*in-fanzia*]" (RA, 146 [135–136]). It is here that Agamben renders explicit his choice of terms and makes clear the relationship of his idea of *contingency* to *potentiality*: "contingency is not one modality among others, alongside possibility, impossibility, and necessity: it is the actual giving of a possibility, the way in which a potentiality exists as such. . . . Contingency is possibility put to the test of a subject" (RA, 146 [136]).

The introduction here of the term *contingency* leads Agamben back to the subject with which he started. *Subjectivity* is, in his words, "that which, in its very possibility of speech, bears witness to an impossibility of speech" (RA, 146 [136]). If speech is contingent, the possibility that speech might *not* be possible must be taken in all its seriousness. This seriousness is to be viewed not only on an empirical level (as in the case of someone— be it Benveniste or the *Muselmann*—deprived of speech), but also on a *modal* one. For Agamben, "testimony is a potentiality that becomes actual through an impotentiality of speech" (RA, 146 [136]). This formula too risks being misunderstood if we do not recall Agamben's point of departure: the structural impossibilities of testifying to the remnants of Auschwitz that Levi details. In Levi's vision, those who truly witnessed the camps in all their horror—those he calls "integral witnesses"—were forever rendered speechless, and it was thus (empirically) impossible for them to testify to what they had witnessed. Following Agamben, this "impossibility" provides the foundation for the vocation of the survivor (such as Levi) who is bearing witness. To adopt the terms of another one of Levi's titles, it is the testimony of those who were drowned by those who were saved. The axiom that Agamben draws from Levi's experience is that "testimony is a potentiality that becomes actual through an impotentiality of speech." What was in Levi's account merely an empirical "impotentiality of speech" is extended by Agamben to encompass the contingent nature of all speech acts. This does not mean that those speech acts were meaningless, only that they carry with them an "impotentiality" in the sense that—given that our world is a contingent one—no absolute necessity guided them, and it might just as well have come to pass that they were not spoken.

At this point Agamben turns to something that was not explicit in *Homo Sacer* and that has led so many readers to pass over in silence the section of that work where the question of potentiality is raised. What is rendered explicit in *Remnants of Auschwitz* is the relation of those categories to the biopolitical struggle that Agamben dedicated himself to analyzing. As early as 1990—five years before *Homo Sacer*—he had stressed the philosophical stakes of a reconceptualization of the modalities of potentiality, actuality, necessity, and contingency, claiming that "the task of the coming philosophy" would be "to redefine the entire domain of categories and modality" (P, 76 [75]). In the years that followed he would emphasize that this was also the task of a *political* philosophy.

The sense in which this reconceptualization is a pressing concern not only for an ontology but also for a political philosophy worthy of our times is made clear in *Remnants of Auschwitz* where Agamben states that "it is time to attempt to redefine the categories of modality from the perspective that interests us. The modal categories—possibility, impossibility, contingency, necessity—are not innocuous logical or epistemological categories that concern the structure of propositions or the relation of something to our faculty of knowledge. They are ontological operators [*operatori ontologici*]—that is, the devastating weapons used in the biopolitical struggle for Being [*la gigantomachia biopolitica per l'essere*], in which a decision is made each time on the human and the inhuman. . . . The field of this battle is subjectivity" (RA, 146–47 [136–37]). Not only does this declaration bring together what in *Homo Sacer* remained only indirectly linked, which the reader needed to read between the lines of that work—the relation of *potentiality* to *biopolitics*—it also closes a larger arc of Agamben's efforts over the preceding twenty years. This is what binds *The Coming Community* with *Homo Sacer:* the former is a work focused on modal thinking and its relation to collective identities, whereas the latter turns to political paradigms for such potentialities. In books and essays throughout this period, Agamben approaches modal categories from a striking variety of perspectives. His aim, however, remains constant: the development of a philosophy of potentiality and an authentic idea of individual and collective vocation. In *Remnants of Auschwitz*, Agamben is thus voicing one of his innermost convictions: the inseparability of metaphysical from political concepts. For Agamben, exploring logical and ontological categories is necessary for effecting real political change, and for this reason he speaks of ontological *operators*. For him, ontological operators—the modal categories of possibility, impossibility, contingency, and necessity—are *operative* elements shaping our political landscape.

What then remains for Agamben is how to reconceive these modal categories. He stresses that it is crucial that we *not* approach them as the consequences of a modern conception of the *subject*. (The reader should recall that Agamben traced a genealogy of the modern conception of *subjectivity* twenty years earlier in *Infancy and History*.) "The categories of modality are not founded on the subject, as Kant maintains, nor are they derived from it," writes Agamben, "rather, the subject is what is at stake in the processes in which they interact. They divide and separate, in the subject, what is possible and what is impossible, the living being and the speaking being, the *Muselmann* and the witness—and in this way they decide on the subject" (RA, 147 [137]). For Agamben, it is not the subject that *decides* on its modalities of being; instead it is these modalities that shape the forms subjectivity takes. In other words, the "subject," for Agamben, is not a self-certain actant that chooses this or that mode, but rather the point on which the ontological operators of a given place and time are turned. Agamben stresses that "modal categories, as operators of Being [*operatori dell'essere*], never stand before the subject as something he can choose or reject; and they do not confront him as a task that he can decide to assume or not to assume in a privileged moment. The subject, rather, is a field of forces always already traversed by the incandescent and historically determined currents of potentiality and impotentiality" (RA, 147–148 [137]). Agamben is here criticizing not only the Kantian conception of the subject, as he explicitly states, but also the radical decisionism of Heidegger's idea of subjectivity. Whereas Heidegger's *Dasein* can choose to accept its contingent nature, can recognize or reject modal categories, we find in *Remnants* a vision of subjectivity closer to that of Foucault. This is a subject that is above all *subjected*—that is, subject to forces, as much as it is a self-affirming source of action. "From this perspective," Agamben then writes, "Auschwitz represents the historical point in which these processes collapse, the devastating experience in which the impossible is forced into the real [*nel reale*]" (RA, 148 [137–38]). What Agamben is voicing here is not a moral imperative such as that Auschwitz represents something "impossibly" bad brought into the world ("forced into the real"). Instead, the "impossible" in question is the literal passivity of subjectivity and it directs Agamben's reader to the point where a subject is subjected to so much, is forced to integrally experience its own impotence, its own powerlessness, its own inherently subjected state so mercilessly, that that very subjectivity seems to contract to a flickering point.

Agamben's discussion of Foucault had at an earlier point touched on the latter's reconceptualization of the author and what Foucault called the "author function." Returning to the idea of the author, Agamben offers a concise history of the term, stressing that its modern meaning appears relatively late. "In Latin," Agamben notes, "*auctor* originally designates the person who intervenes in the case of a minor (or the person who, for whatever reason, does not have the capacity to posit a legally valid act) in order to grant him the valid title he requires," but he also points out that older meanings of the term include "vendor," "he who advises or persuades," and "witness" (RA, 148 [138]). "In what way can a term that expressed the idea of the completion of an imperfect act [*un atto imperfetto*] also signify seller, adviser, and witness? What is the common character that lies at the root of these apparently heterogeneous meanings?" (RA, 148 [138]). The last of these is the one that most interests Agamben, bringing together as it does *witness* and *author*, and thereby evoking the authorial witnesses with which he began his investigation.

To clarify this conception of *authority*, as well as its attendant conception of *subjectivity*, involves, for Agamben, distinguishing the various Latin terms for *witness*. "If *testis* designates the witness insofar as he intervenes as a third [party] in a suit between two subjects," Agamben writes, "and if *superstes* indicates the one who has fully lived through an experience and can therefore relate it to others, *auctor* signifies the witness insofar as his testimony always presupposes something—a fact, a thing, or a word—that preexists him and whose reality and force must be validated or certified" (RA, 149–50 [139–40]).[32] Agamben continues: "It is thus possible to explain the sense of the term *auctor* in the poets as 'founder of a race or city,' as well as the general meaning of 'setting into being' identified by Benveniste as the original meaning of *augere*. As is well known, the classical world is not acquainted with creation *ex nihilo*; for the ancients every act of creation always implies something else, either unformed matter or incomplete Being, which is to be completed or 'made to grow.' Every creator is always a co-creator, every author a co-author. The act of the *auctor* completes the act of an incapable person, giving strength of proof to what in itself lacks it and granting life to what could not live alone. It can conversely be said that the imperfect act or incapacity precedes the *auctor*'s act, and that the imperfect act completes and gives meaning to the word of the *auctor*-witness. An author's act that claims to be valid on its own is nonsense, just as the survivor's testimony has truth and a reason for being only if it is completed by the one who cannot bear witness. The survivor and the *Muselmann,* like the tutor and the incapable person and the creator and his material, are inseparable; their unity-difference alone constitutes testimony" (RA, 150 [140]).

The semantic histories of these Latin terms for *witness* that are necessary for a revision of our modal categories also serve to explain the situation in which those like Levi found themselves. In a certain respect, this situation, following Agamben, was that of every *author*—understood in the original sense of the term—no matter if of poetry or of prose, of fiction or of nonfiction, no matter if their creation is a city or a poem. The *author-structure*—which Agamben links via the semantic history of the Latin term to a *creation-structure* understood as the shaping of preexisting material—serves to explain the sense of unease of an author such as Levi. This might seem a strange task, for on an empirical level it is hardly difficult to imagine why Levi should have felt such unease in his particular author-function. He felt the confusion and sorrow of having survived where others perished, of owing his survival to a seemingly random contingency—that he was a chemist in a place and at a time where that fact could save his life—as well as the despair of belonging to the same "human race" that acted with such unrelenting and seemingly inhuman cruelty. Agamben's task, however, is not simply to understand Levi's authorial unease, but to understand an unease far more vast, which Agamben sees as inhabiting all attempts to bear witness.

Levi's Paradox

Although Levi is not discussed in this section on author and *auctor,* his situation is not difficult to read between its lines, and it is thus hardly surprising that in the following section Agamben returns to what he names "Levi's paradox," laconically formulated as: "the *Muselmann* is the complete witness [*il testimone integrale*]" (RA, 150 [140]). This integral or complete witness, which one might have taken lightly as a figure of difficult speech, is one that Agamben takes literally, developing it into an axiom of *testimony* and the *authority* that grounds the act of testifying. As we have seen, the "integral witness" (the *Muselmann*) is one who could never bear witness. Therefore, the true or integral witness is he or she who cannot bear witness (this is "Levi's paradox"). What Agamben sees expressed in this paradox is "nothing other than the intimate dual structure of testimony as an act of an *auctor,* as the difference and completion of an impossibility and possibility of speaking, of the inhuman and the human, a living being [*un vivente*] and a speaking being [*un parlante*]" (RA, 151 [141]).[33]

With the clarification of this authorial structure and the modal categories that determine it, Agamben can return to the question of the unique and the unsayable. Of those who wish to qualify Auschwitz as precisely that, Agamben says, "If they mean to say that Auschwitz was a unique event in the face of which the witness must in some way submit his every word to the test of an impossibility of speaking, they are right. But if, joining uniqueness to unsayability, they transform Auschwitz into a reality absolutely separated from language, if they break the tie between an impossibility and a possibility of speaking that, in the *Muselmann,* constitutes testimony, then they unconsciously repeat the Nazi's gesture [of silencing]" (RA 157 [146]). Just as in *Language and Death*—as well as, in less direct fashion, in virtually all of Agamben's works from *Infancy and History* to *The Coming Community*—the Benjaminian project of "eliminating the unsayable" is continued. In those earlier instances the concern was a general one: "eliminating" the idea that language carried a concealed secret, a transcendent formula, a sacred kernel that it was humanity's task to uncover. In *Remnants of Auschwitz* what is at issue is the elimination of something more concretely unsayable. For Benjamin, as for Agamben, the "unsayable" is an illusion fostered by an idea of the sacred. Here, in the context of the specific historical event that was Auschwitz, the contours of Agamben's question can be seen with unprecedented precision. To relegate something to the realm of the unsayable is to give it a sacred aura that does it a disservice. For Agamben, to leave Auschwitz in silence, to raise or lower it to the status of the "unsayable," not only repeats the gesture of the Nazis endeavoring to consign those who perished there to oblivion, but also plays into the hands of those today who would strive to negate the Holocaust. In other words, trying to appropriate the prerogative of the unsayable is, for Agamben, supremely ill advised.

We would do well to recall at this point that *Holocaust* is not a term that Agamben himself employs; it is a term that he in fact objects to, offering compelling arguments against the use of both it and *Shoah*. He does so for the same reason that he combats the idea of an "unsayable" encircled by a sacred aura. As early as *Homo Sacer* he denounced the term *Holocaust* for its sacred and sacrificial tones, writing that "the wish to lend a sacrificial aura to the extermination of the Jews by means of the term 'Holocaust' was . . . an irresponsible historiographical blindness" (HS, 114 [126]). Elaborating on this same point in *Remnants of Auschwitz,* he notes that *holocaust,* deriving from the Greek for "completely burned," was a patristic term used by the Church Fathers in more or less anti-Semitic fashion to ridicule the offering of bloody or burnt sacrifices. Agamben says that "insofar as it implies the substitution of a literal expression with an attenuated or altered expression for something that one does not actually want to hear mentioned, the formation of a euphemism always involves ambiguities. In this case, however, the ambiguity is intolerable" (RA, 31 [29]). This ambiguity is found almost as intolerable as the other euphemism in question— *Shoah* (a Hebrew term meaning catastrophe)—which is used in the Old Testament in the context of divine retribution and thereby implies that the Jews were being punished for their waywardness.

To return to the charge of the unsayable and the ways in which such an attitude not only corresponds to the intentions of the Nazis but also plays into the hands of Holocaust deniers, Agamben writes that "Levi's paradox contains the only possible refutation of every denial of the existence of the extermination camps [*ogni argomento negazionista*]" (RA, 164 [153]). As we saw earlier, "Levi's paradox" is defined as "the *Muselmann* is the complete witness." That this is a paradox and that it should bear Levi's name is easy enough to understand, but how it constitutes the refutation of *every* negationist argument is another matter. Agamben claims that if Auschwitz is "that to which it is not possible to bear witness" and the *Muselmann* is "the absolute impossibility of bearing witness," then if the *Muselmann* bearing witness through another is effected, so too can Auschwitz be attested to as a whole. If the *Muselmann* is he who cannot bear witness and yet the survivor bears witness for him or her, an (empirical) impossibility is made possible. Agamben's argument holds that this applies to the camps as a whole. He writes, "If the witness bears witness for the *Muselmann*, if he succeeds in bringing to speech an impossibility of speech—if the *Muselmann* is thus constituted as the whole witness [*il testimone integrale*]—then the denial of Auschwitz is refuted in its very foundation" (RA, 164 [153]). This analogy is one that, for Agamben, must hold in order for his position to hold, yet it requires that one see a seeming impossibility overcome in one domain as tantamount to it being overcome in another.

"If the survivor bears witness not to the gas chambers or to Auschwitz but to the *Muselmann,* if he speaks only on the basis of an impossibility of speaking," Agamben claims, "then his testimony cannot be denied" (RA, 164 [153]). Yet we might easily ask why this should be so. If the basis of negationist arguments is a question about the reliability of testimony, then it seems that the specter of relativism cannot be banished with an argument such as Agamben makes here. In consequence, the next sentence in Agamben's book is almost disquieting in its peremptory certainty: "Auschwitz—that to which it is not possible to bear witness—is absolutely and irrefutably proven" (RA, 164 [153]). On the one hand, it is not only reasonable but necessary to concede the structural impossibility of integrally testifying to what took place in the camps (because those who experienced it in full paid with their lives). Levi's decision to begin *The Drowned and the Saved* with this point gives what follows all the more persuasive power. Agamben's extension of this observation leads to an argument that can function only by displacing the question of the reliability of witnesses with the question of the structure of witnessing itself. His reasons for claiming that such speculation is preferable to a sanctifying silence are compelling, but what is less so is that such an analysis provides an "absolute and irrefutable proof" against negationist arguments. Showing that those arguments are evidence of the most historically blind and morally base prejudice is one thing, but the effecting of a complete *theoretical* victory over them is something of another order. That Agamben achieves this on a theoretical or structural level is much to be doubted—just as it is to be doubted that he needed to achieve this.

This last short section of Agamben's text introduces its afterword—which seems at first glance like the book's refutation. The last word is left to the integral witnesses: the *Muselmänner* themselves. In 1987, one year after Levi's death, the first study dedicated to the *Muselmann* was published and included brief testimonies from those who survived their condition as *Muselmänner* to tell their tale. The name given to this section of this study is "I Was a *Muselmann,*" and with it Agamben ends his book. For him, it does not bring into question his long elucidation of the impossibility of the *Muselmann* bearing witness—instead it "not only does not contradict Levi's paradox but, rather, fully verifies it" (RA, 165 [154]).

Even more than *Homo Sacer, Remnants of Auschwitz* has polarized readers—and with good reason. It is the only one of Agamben's works where steps in reasoning seem to have been silenced or skipped, and it is the only one that shows signs of haste. Its aim seems to shift and its final claim—a refutation of any and all negationist arguments—appears doubly dubious in that such a theoretical refutation is not compellingly presented as something in which readers are in need, and because the theoretical argument offered rests on a strained analogy. Geulen claims that in this work "the possibilities of Agamben's technique seem to be overextended" and that "the contrasting opposition of the testimony of witnesses with countless theoreticians (Benveniste, Foucault, and Lévinas, among many others) shows a lack of discipline" (2005, 113).[34] Along similar lines, Mesnard and Kahan note a "tendency to move carelessly from the registers of affect, subjectivity and lived experience to theoretical registers" (2001, 125). Whether the problem lies in the technique or in its execution, there can be little question that a problem exists. In both earlier and later works, Agamben demonstrated a remarkable ability to move precisely and insightfully from theoretical reflection to the study of individual cases, but there can be little doubt that this ability seems to fail him at moments in this book, and that the argument is strained at points. In a review from 2003, Lorenz Jäger called the book "a work that must be counted as one of the greatest philosophical experiments of our time" (37). Jäger's terms are well chosen: the work is very much an experiment, and its implications are as much philosophical as historiographical or political. Its success, however, is another question.

Scholium I: What Is a Remnant?

Both Agamben's tenth and eleventh books—*The Remnants of Auschwitz* and *The Time That Remains*, published two years later—employ a singular concept that figures in their titles: *the remnant*. What then is this *remnant* and why is it of such importance to Agamben? To begin with the first of these works, *the remnants of Auschwitz* that gave his tenth book its name would seem, at first, to refer to those who survived Auschwitz. The book's epigraphs, among which figures *Isaiah* 10:22— "For although thy people be as the sand of the sea, yet a remnant of them shall be saved"—seem to confirm this. However, there is more to this *remnant* for Agamben than those who have testified and the archive their testimony forms. Agamben is careful to point out that "the remnant [*Resto*] is a theologico-messianic concept" (RA, 162 [151]). Unsurprisingly, this "theologico-messianic concept" is concerned with salvation—and a salvation that is to all appearances *limited*. The Apostle Paul writes that "for they are not all Israel, which are of Israel," as well as "Even so then at this present time also there is a remnant according to the election of grace" (*Romans* 9:6; *Romans* 11:5). As the book's epigraphs from the prophetic books of the Old Testament, as well as those from Paul's Letter to the Romans, underline, not all of Israel will be saved, but only a "remnant." One question, then, is why only a remnant will be saved. Is it because a purifying sacrifice is called for? Is it because only a part of Israel is worthy of salvation?

Agamben rejects not only these particular notions but also the fundamental ideas that underlie them. "What is decisive," he writes, "is that . . . 'remnant' [*il resto*] does not seem simply to refer to a numerical portion of Israel" (RA, 163 [152]). *Remnant* must then be meant in another sense than the conventional one of a *remainder* left over from some larger *whole*. This is a matter that Agamben addresses in *The Time That Remains,* where he asks, "How should we conceive of this 'remnant of Israel?'" and answers, "The problem is misunderstood from the very start if the remnant is seen as a numeric portion, as it has been by some theologians who understand it as that portion of the Jews who survived the eschatological catastrophe, or as a kind of bridge between ruin and salvation" (TTR, 54–55 [56], translation modified). This does not, however, resolve the problem, and Agamben is careful to stress that "it is even more misleading to interpret the remnant as outright identical to Israel" (TTR, 55 [56]).

"A closer reading of the prophetic texts," he continues, "shows that the remnant is closer to being a consistency [*consistenza*] or figure that Israel assumes in relation to election or to the messianic event. It is therefore neither the whole, nor a part of the whole, but the impossibility for the part and the whole to coincide with themselves or with each other" (TTR, 55 [57], translation modified). Agamben thus sees the "theologico-messianic concept" of the remnant as articulating a relation of *part* to *whole*[35] that does not fall within the traditional lines drawn by dialectical thought, and that has affinities with Adorno's "negative dialectics," Derrida's *différence,* and the Spinozist ideas of "immanence" and "multitude" that were important for Deleuze and Guattari and for Negri and Hardt. Like those ideas, the *remnant* is located in a singular conceptual and strategic space, with the result that "the remnant is precisely what prevents divisions from being exhaustive" (TTR, 56 [58]).

Concerning divisions as it does, this "theologico-messiainic concept" offers Agamben an important paradigm for his idea of a coming community. "If I had to point to a political legacy in Paul's letters that was immediately traceable," he writes in *The Time That Remains,* "I believe that the concept of the remnant would have to play a part" (TTR, 57 [58]). The reason he gives is that "it allows for a new perspective that dislodges our antiquated notions of a people and a democracy, however impossible it may be to completely renounce them. The people is neither the whole nor the part, neither the majority nor the minority. Instead, it is that which can never coincide with itself, as whole or as part, that which infinitely remains or resists each division, and with all due respect to those who govern us, never allows us to be reduced to a majority or a minority. This remnant is the figure, or the consistency [*la consistenza*], assumed by the people in the decisive moment—and as such, is the only real political subject [*l'unico soggeto politico reale*]" (TTR, 57 [58–59], translation modified). Elsewhere Agamben uses these same terms, stressing that "the real political subject is always a 'remnant'" (UL, 20).

In Agamben's hands, the *remnant* is a concept through which we can view how a totality conceives of itself and of its component parts. At first sight, the claim that "the only real political subject," "the true political subject," is a "remnant" may seem gnomic, or paradoxical, but its sense lies in the idea that a true political subject is not merely a part of a totalizing whole. This singular and separate identity or subjectivity is one that Agamben chooses to call by the theologico-messianic term *remnant.*

What is at issue is thus what Agamben calls "the decisive point" of "opening up a highly interesting way to solve the problem of identities—ethnic or other. Such a thing as an ethnic identity will never truly exist because there will always remain a remnant" (UL, 20).

Of the genesis of his singular term for political subjectivity Agamben remarked in 2001, "I began to think about how a people could be thought of as a remnant. Not as something substantive, and also not after the fashion of our contemporary democratic tradition—that is, having to do with majorities and minorities—but as something that is always left over. . . . I think of the people as something to which a position can never be ascribed; it is neither majority nor minority. The people as a whole can never coincide with itself, and every attempt to effect such has resulted in catastrophe" (UL, 20). It is precisely this idea for which Agamben argues in his essay "What Is a People?" from *Means Without End,* and to which he returns in *The Time That Remains,* where he traces the theological and linguistic history of the idea of a *people* (see TTR, 47ff. [50ff.]). This divided people becomes a paradigm for the notion that the idea of a people cannot and should not be thought of as pure, whole, or without remainder. Following the philological and theological paths that the term *people* has taken, Agamben notes how the Septuagint translates *am* with *laos* and *goyim* with *ethne,* and that "a fundamental chapter in the semantic history of the term *people* thus begins here and should be traced up to the contemporary usage of the adjective *ethnic* in the syntagma *ethnic conflict*" (TTR, 47 [50], italics in original). It is this "originary theological-political fault line" that interests Agamben (TTR, 47 [50], translation modified). In his reading, for both Jews and *goyim* "it is impossible to coincide with themselves [*coinicidere con se stessi*]" and there is thus "something like a remnant between every people and itself, between every identity and itself" (TTR, 52 [54]). A *remnant* is what results from every dialectical attempt at exhaustive identification and classification, every attempt to create a community that would completely subsume the singularity of its members. For this reason, the *remnant* is a concept that can apply not only to an entire people, but also to its individual members, and for this reason Agamben can claim that "the subject is a sort of remnant. . . . It is something that is left over—it represents a difference. It is the impossibility for a subject to completely coincide with itself [*mit sich selbst übereinzustimmen*]; there always remains a remnant" (UL, 20). Here we can understand why Agamben was so emphatic in rejecting the idea that his idea of the *remnant* was numerical, for it refers here to an entire people *as well as* to its individual members. What it represents is a novel way of conceiving of parts and wholes, singularities and communities, that does not focus its attentions on minority and majority positions to be dialectically merged. The remnant is a response to the totalizing nature of dialectical thinking and, at least in some readings, its gradual elimination of differences. It is thus a *paradigm* for a conception of both part *and* whole. For Agamben, the theologico-messianic concept of *remnant* is interesting and illustrative in its own right—as a figure in a theologico-messianic context—as well as a paradigm for parts and wholes in a community to come. Here we can see another of the secret connections that link Agamben's so seemingly disparate books, for in this light the *remnant* can be seen as a means of continuing the lines of thinking, and the search for paradigms, of *The Coming Community.*

In *Remnants of Auschwitz,* Agamben writes that *"remnant designates the consistency* [la consistenza] *assumed by Israel when placed in relation with an* eskhaton, *with election or the messianic event"* (RA, 163 [152], italics in original). In this light, the *remnant* in no way designates something less than a whole, but instead designates the whole (people, individual, language) seen in a new light and having taken on a different and new "consistency." As in so many of Agamben's works, this displacement is predicated on a different conception of *time.* Agamben writes, "We must cease to look toward . . . historical processes as if they had an apocalyptic or profane telos in which the living being and the speaking being, the inhuman and the human—or any terms of a historical process—are joined in an established, completed humanity and reconciled in a realized identity. This does not mean that, in lacking an end [*un fine*], they are condemned to meaninglessness or the vanity of an infinite, disenchanted drifting. They have not an *end* [*un* fine] but a *remnant*" (RA, 159 [148], italics in original). In light of this final sentence we can better understand why his book bears the title *The Time That Remains,* as what is at issue is a model of time based on "the decisive moment" we first saw in *Infancy and History.* To a nondialectical conception of the relation of singularity to community Agamben joins a nondialectical conception of time—stressing that, for him, the *remnant* corresponds precisely to what Paul calls "the time of the now" and Benjamin calls "now-time" (TTR, 57 [58]). Whether this wholly removes the concept of *remnant* from its theologico-messianic context or returns it to its original vocation is a question of perspective.

"The messianic Kingdom," Agamben writes, "is neither the future (the millennium) nor the past (the golden age): it is, instead, a *remaining time* [un tempo restante]" (RA, 159 [148], italics in original). As he has shown in books from *Infancy and History* to this one, for Agamben this remaining time is *now*—a time that is *messianic* not in the sense that it is waiting for the machine of history to move the proper pieces into place so that the lever of revolution at last falls, but, instead, in the sense that we ought to conceive of every moment as what Benjamin called "the narrow gateway through which the Messiah might enter," every moment as the time of the now in which we must act.

Scholium II: On Genius, or Heidegger's
Poison and Benjamin's Antidote

As we saw earlier, Agamben claimed that "the real interest of en-counters—in life as in thought," is that "they serve to make life possible (or at times impossible)" (AC, ii–iii). Of his own most decisive encounters he then said, "That is what happened with my meeting Heidegger—and at nearly the same time, with my coming into contact with Benjamin's thought. Every great work contains an element of darkness and poison— for which it does not always offer an antidote. Benjamin was the antidote that allowed me to survive Heidegger" (AC, ii–iii). With the preceding in mind, we might attempt to answer the question raised earlier as to what in Heidegger's work Agamben found poisonous and what in Benjamin's allowed him to survive it.

As a first step toward answering this question, we would do well to turn to Benjamin's own views on the relation of his work to Heidegger's. In 1916, the twenty-four-year-old Benjamin wrote to Gershom Scholem to report on his recent reading. In his letter he mentions an essay called "The Problem of Historical Time" that he had read "in the last or second to last" issue of the journal *Zeitschrift für Philosophie und philosophischen Kritik*. He either does not recall or does not bother to note the author of the essay in question, singling out the "frightful work," as he calls it, for how it "shows exactly how one should *not* go about approaching such a question" (Benjamin 1966, 129, italics in original). The study in mediocrity that Benjamin refers to here was one of the first publications of Martin Heidegger.

Fourteen years later, during which time Heidegger's philosophical star had not ceased to rise, Benjamin again wrote to Scholem of his read-ings and projects, and again invoked Heidegger. He told Scholem that he had come to see that the *Arcades Project*, like his earlier *The Origin of German Tragic Drama*, would need an introduction offering nothing less than a "theory of knowledge [*théorie de la connaissance*]" (Benjamin 1966, 506).[36] He wrote that the novelty of his new work was such that it required not a "theory of knowledge" like the one he had written for his earlier work, but a "theory of historical knowledge" (Benjamin 1966, 506). "It is here," continues Benjamin, "that I shall find Heidegger on my path, and I expect sparks to fly from the impact of our very different ways of viewing history." Following in this combative vein, Benjamin wrote to Scholem later that year of his plan to form a "reading group" to be led by Brecht and himself with the goal of "demolishing Heidegger" (Benjamin 1966, 514). Brecht, however, fell ill and the destructive summer reading group came to naught.

Years later, in 1938, Benjamin was dismayed to read an article in a German language Soviet journal that he felt portrayed him as, in his own words, "a follower of Heidegger."[37] In a certain respect, this is the end of the story. Neither with the help of the powerful Brecht nor alone did Benjamin ever set about demolishing Heidegger, and it seems never to have occurred to Heidegger to try to demolish, or do anything with, Benjamin. If Heidegger ever read any of Benjamin's works, the experience left no discernable traces (no great mystery given that it was only toward the very end of Heidegger's life that Benjamin's works began to receive anything approaching the attention they enjoy today). For a real attempt at "demolishing," the public had to wait for Adorno's vitriolic attack on Heidegger in *The Jargon of Authenticity*, focused on what the former described as Heidegger's unbearably clichéd playing of the "*Wurlitzerorgel des Geistes.*" For all that work's polemical intensity, whether conceptual sparks of the kind Benjamin envisioned flew is open to question. (Many have seen Adorno as so emphatically put off by his object of study that it seems to dull his otherwise so sharp analytical faculties.)

In the years after Benjamin's untimely death, Adorno asserted that the former's book on tragic drama contained an implicit critique of Heidegger's concept of historicity. Beyond this point, however, Adorno acknowledged little or no common ground and next to nothing of a common cause between the two thinkers. In her insightful and influential introduction to a collection of Benjamin's works, Hannah Arendt, however, saw the contrary. For her there was a "close affinity" between Benjamin's figure of the collector and Heidegger's reconceptualization of tradition (Arendt 1968, 46). In ways that will already have become clear, Agamben is clearly far more of Arendt's mind on the matter—and saw a close affinity not only between the figure of the collector and an idea of tradition, but also between a whole constellation of terms and ideas concerning everything from first philosophy to contemporary politics. The two final chapters of *The Man Without Content* are devoted, respectively, to Heidegger and Benjamin. The first paragraph of Agamben's *Stanzas* calls on Benjamin as a model, and this preface is followed by the dedication *"Martin Heidegger in memoriam."* As he does in many later essays and books, Agamben brings Benjamin and Heidegger into close connection and makes every effort to see whether sparks can be made to fly from their very different ways of approaching the most varied questions. This gives us something of a sense for the singularity of Agamben's claims, but it still tells us nothing specific about the poison contained in Heidegger's work or about the antidote to be found in Benjamin's.

As virtually all who came in contact with Heidegger stressed, his intentions were not easy to fathom. During his inauguration speech as Rector of Freiburg University in 1933 he announced that "the *Führer* is himself and alone the present and future German reality and its law [*Der Führer selbst und allein ist die heutige und künftige deutsche Wirklichkeit und ihr Gesetz*]." This was at once shocking and confusing for many present. One of Heidegger's students, Karl Löwith, remarked that those in attendance were unsure as to whether they should go home and study the pre-Socratics or join the SA (cited by Safranski 1998, 264 [282]). After the war, most of those who had known Heidegger, like those who came to know him later, were unsure how to understand his political engagement. Was he to be compared to Plato in Syracuse—taken in by a dictator and held hostage—as some of his followers argued? Was his naïveté still greater, and was he, like Thales, staring so intently up at the philosophical sky that he fell into a political well? Or was his choice a cunning one—and, still worse, one perfectly in line with his philosophy?

An important perspective on these questions is offered by returning to Hannah Arendt. She was uniquely close, personally and philosophically, to both Heidegger and Benjamin, and was among the first to see the storm of progress caught in the wings of Benjamin's angel of history, as well as another storm—"the storm that blows through Heidegger's thought," which she said is "like the one which blows across centuries against it from Plato's works" (Arendt 1988, 232). Gilbert Ryle's laconic judgment about Heidegger—"Bad man. Can't be a good philosopher" (cited in Thrower 1989, 12; and M. A. Bernstein 2000, 63)[38]—was shared by many, but Arendt did not accept either of these assertions in such simple fashion. Karl Jaspers, a harsher critic of his former friend, wrote to Arendt in 1949 denouncing the "impurity [*Unreinheit*]," as he chose to call it, of Heidegger's "soul." She saw her former teacher's shortcomings all too clearly, but she also saw them in a more nuanced fashion and replied to Jaspers, "What you call impurity I would call lack of character [*Charakterlosigkeit*]—but in the sense that he literally has none—definitely not an especially bad one. But all the while he lives at a depth and with a passion that one cannot easily forget" (Arendt and Jaspers 1985, 178).

Arendt clearly never forgot this depth or intensity and continued to try to better understand its singular nature and character. Four years after writing this letter she composed a fable about the love of her youth that would not appear in print until after her death (it was first published in English translation in the posthumous collection *Essays in Understanding* from 1994). She consigned it to her diary and gave it the title "Heidegger the Fox." It reads as follows:

Heidegger says proudly: "People say Heidegger is a fox." This is the true story of Heidegger the fox.

There was once a fox who was so utterly without cunning that he not only constantly fell into traps but could not even distinguish a trap from a non-trap. . . . After this fox had spent his entire youth in other people's traps . . . he decided to completely withdraw from the fox world, and began to build a den. . . . He built himself a trap as a den, sat down in it, pretended it was a normal den (not out of cunning, but because he had always taken the traps of others for their dens). . . . This trap was only big enough for him. . . . Nobody could fall into his trap, because he was sitting in it himself. . . . If one wanted to visit him in the den where he was at home, one had to go into his trap. Of course everybody could walk right out of it, except him. . . . The fox living in the trap said proudly: so many fall into my trap; I have become the best of all foxes. And there was even something true in that: nobody knows the trap business better than he who has been sitting in a trap all his life. (Arendt 2002, 403–4)

The points of reference in this private parable seem clear enough. Arendt begins by referring to Heidegger's pride at being thought cunning ("a fox"). Machiavelli had noted in *The Prince* that "it is necessary to be a fox so as to recognize traps." She then turns the metaphor into a fable and Heidegger's pride against him.[39] She evokes the vanity and blindness of a man she once adored, the instinctive mistakes he made in political and personal life, the traps of thought and deed he fell into and was unable to recognize as traps. The fable she composes is ironic in ways that are difficult to grasp— from the fact that she compares Heidegger to an animal—never a flattering analogy, but all the less for a philosopher who singled himself out for his claim that animals were "without world"—to more personal matters. In Heidegger's philosophy the term *dwelling* and references to a capacious "house of being" are frequent, and there is an added irony in her choosing the most cramped of dwellings for the cunning philosopher.[40]

However we are to understand its allusions, the general outline of

Arendt's indictment is clear enough. The fable depicts Heidegger's problem as that of a weakness turned into a strength and of that strength turned against itself. His ability to discern logical inconsistencies and metaphysical mystifications, his suspicion concerning the freezing of the constant and manifold flow of life, thought, works, and Being into the fixed forms of concepts and systems left him, for a time, without a home under the stormy skies of ceaseless change. Having isolated and denounced so many homes as traps, as limitations to thought, so many constructions of habit as limiting the productive anxiety of authentic reflection, he found himself in a difficult position when it came time to seek a refuge for himself. Following the logic of Arendt's parable, his acuity poisoned his thinking and blinded him to a fundamental fact about homes, so when he set about to build himself one, he built himself a trap. In other words, his understanding of the ineluctability of traps led him no less ineluctably into a trap.

This much Arendt makes clear—but how should we view this trap? Is what is at issue as simple and self-evident as his political engagement? Did the trap that was the Nazi Party seem for a brief period like a home because it promised the end of traps? (There can be little doubt that despite Heidegger's cynical manipulations within the Nazi party, he at least for a time saw it as a genuinely revolutionary movement.) And more to the point for our purposes here, is the poison to which Agamben enigmatically refers of the same nature?

As we saw earlier, in *Remnants of Auschwitz* Agamben takes issue with Heidegger's startlingly callous reference to the concentration camps organized and run by the leader and party he had actively supported. On a more personal level, Agamben was well aware of the differences—or at least what seemed like differences—between the man he had known years after the war and the one of earlier times. Agamben has recounted on several occasions a conversation he had with Emmanuel Lévinas about the teacher they had known at different periods. The image of an "extraordinarily hard" man that Lévinas had retained of Heidegger in 1928 and 1929 was offset by Agamben's recollection of a man who, nearly forty years later, singled himself out for what Agamben called the "gentleness" of his demeanor (LDV). The man Agamben knew seemed a peaceful one with little resemblance to the glintingly hard and willful thinker Lévinas had known. Yet all such differences and details risk missing the point of Agamben's remark. Heidegger famously began his lecture course on

Aristotle with all the biographical information he thought relevant for his undertaking: "Aristotle was born, he worked, he died."⁴¹ For his own philosophy he would have doubtless asked for the same focus. When Agamben evokes a shadow and a poison in Heidegger that Benjamin helped him "survive," he is careful to make clear the terms of the operation: not that of the "man" but of his "work." What then of that work?

Agamben indeed saw shortcomings in the work of his first philosophical master—including the central concept of his late philosophy. In an essay from 1992 Agamben characterized Heidegger's concept of *Ereignis* as an effort to think "the end of the state and the end of history *together*," which was "insufficient"; and in *Il Regno e la Gloria* he wrote that "Heidegger was unable to master the problem of technology because he failed to return it to its political *locus*" (MWE, 111 [88–89], italics in original, translation modified; RG, 276). For Agamben, this diagnosis was important enough to repeat in *Homo Sacer* (se HS, 60–61 [70]). But a philosophical shortcoming need not imply something poisonous. Daniel Binswanger (2005) has accused Agamben of clearing Heidegger of his Nazism, writing that "via a detour through Verona and Paris [where Agamben held teaching posts] the Master from Germany has been definitively denazified [*endgültig entnazifiziert worden*]" (6). The "Master from Germany" is none other than Heidegger (the epithet is from Paul Celan's poem "Death Fugue," in which "the Master from Germany" is "death"). Although Agamben by no means attempts to absolve Heidegger of his dark past, he does ask about the relation of Heidegger's politics to his philosophy. In an essay entitled "Heidegger and Nazism," Agamben takes as his point of departure Lévinas' texts on what the latter saw as a dangerous element in Heidegger's work. In an essay from 1934 whose point is sharpened by a note he added to its republication in 1991, Lévinas locates the seeds of Nazism in Western philosophy—and most intensely in Heideggerian ontology (see PP, 322–25). "The true point of [Lévinas'] essay from 1934," writes Agamben, "is in the radicality of this diagnosis which it would be vain to seek to exorcise through condemnations or apologies" (PP, 325). The true point in question is the idea that "if Nazism was able to coincide—at least at its point of departure—with the great philosophy of the twentieth century, it would be foolish to believe it possible to extricate oneself from this uneasy proximity [*scomodo vicinato*] by condemning one philosopher and absolving another. Sixty years later the question that

[Lévinas'] essay poses continues to demand a response." Agamben then asks, "What is the meaning of his proximity?" (PP, 325).

In *Homo Sacer* Agamben offers a direct answer to this question, judging Heidegger's philosophy and Nazism as "radically divergent." The "immediate unity of politics and life" that Agamben diagnoses in the biopolitics of our day—and for which the concentration camps are, for him, a privileged example—"shed light on the scandal of twentieth-century philosophy: the relation between Martin Heidegger and Nazism" (HS, 150 [167]). Expressed differently, the biopolitics of the sort he is studying in that work presents a lens through which to understand the mystifying relation between Heidegger's philosophy and Nazism. Agamben notes that "only when situated in the perspective of modern biopolitics does this relation acquire its proper significance (and this is the very thing that both Heidegger's accusers and his defenders fail to do)" (HS, 150 [167]). What the accusers and defenders in question have failed to do becomes Agamben's aim. This relation is best seen, for Agamben, in Heidegger's idea of "facticity" or "factical life" (which he had analyzed in an essay entitled "The Passion of Facticity"). In *Homo Sacer* Agamben tries to understand what Heidegger described in his 1935 course *Introduction to Metaphysics* as "the inner truth and greatness" of the National Socialist movement, which "the works that are being peddled about nowadays as the philosophy of National Socialism have nothing whatever to do with" (see HS, 152 [169]). Agamben writes, "From Heidegger's perspective, National Socialism's error and betrayal of its 'inner truth' consists in its having transformed the experience of factical life into a biological 'value'" (HS, 152 [169]). When understood correctly, however, "the experience of facticity is equivalent to a radicalization without precedent of the state of exception (with its indistinction of nature and politics, outside and inside, exclusion and inclusion) in a dimension in which the state of exception tends to become the rule" (HS, 153 [170]). A facticity of this sort would represent a *real* state of exception like the one for which Benjamin argued because it would break down the distinction between existence and essence, sacred and profane, and would thereby form a political order freed from the violent dictates of sacred privileges and sovereign proclamations. Heidegger had hoped of Nazism that it would bring about precisely such a political order, but, in Agamben's reading, found himself deceived, for Nazism presented something very different, basing its classifications on a "biological 'value'" foreign to Heidegger's thinking. It is at this point that, for Agamben,

"Nazism and Heidegger's thought radically diverge," as "Nazism determines the bare life of *homo sacer* in a biological and eugenic key, making it into the site of an incessant decision on value and nonvalue in which biopolitics continually turns into thanatopolitics and in which the camp, consequently, becomes the absolute political space. In Heidegger, on the other hand, *homo sacer*—whose very own life is always at issue in its every act—instead becomes Dasein, the inseparable unity of Being and the ways of Being, of subject and qualities, life and world, 'whose own Being is at issue in its very Being'" (HS, 153 [170]). This extensive discussion leaves us, however, with a stubborn question: if the poison and shadow to which Agamben refers is not to be sought in the man but in the *work,* and if this work, following Agamben, is "radically divergent" from the Nazism in which Heidegger placed his faith, where are we to locate this poison and shadow?

In one of his first essays Agamben describes a response to the idea of original sin in Kafka's works as "a curious antidote that, like all real antidotes [*contravveleni*], partakes of the nature of the poison it wishes to counteract" (PB, 49). Many years later Agamben again employed this metaphor of poison and antidote, writing of how Simone Weil "evoke[s] the figure of the scapegoat, in whom sacrificial innocence and guilt, sanctity and abjection, victim and executioner are unified for the sake of catharsis. It is necessary to recognize this temptation in both Morante and Weil for what it is, and to search in their own work for the antidotes [*i contravveleni*] contained therein" (EP, 106 [110], translation modified). To characterize *intellectual* relations as if they were *bodily* ones in which the very life of the individual was at stake is to depict a passionate state of intellectual affairs. It implies that all truly vital ideas and decisive encounters contain an element of radical uncertainty—and, thereby, danger.

These remarks are, however, not the only ones Agamben made in which this special metaphorical register is invoked. Two years after recounting how Benjamin offered an antidote to Heidegger's poison, he remarked that "in a certain respect Benjamin is as important for me as Heidegger—or even more important. The relation between the two is that of poison and antidote [*Gift und Gegengift*]" (UL, 17). In 2004, Agamben returned to the metaphor and said that *all* great thinkers have their poison and antidote, and that in the case of Heidegger and Benjamin he used "one as the antidote to the other." When one of his interviewers then asked him how Heidegger could be used as an antidote to Benjamin, Agamben laughed and said that it would be "easier to show the inverse" (LDV). Pushed farther, Agamben remarked, "I'm not sure that the dangerous element in question concerns only Heidegger. Is there not an implicit risk in every vocation (or revocation) as in every truly decisive reading?"[42] In a still more recent interview, Agamben retained the metaphor while giving it a counterbalance, noting that "perhaps Benjamin was the antidote that saved me from Heidegger, and Heidegger, in some sense, what prevented me from losing myself in Benjamin" (DTP, 4). The poison that Agamben thus evokes is not limited to the philosophy of Heidegger. It is instead something intimately bound up with philosophy and its vocation.

What then of the "shadow" that Agamben links with this "poison" in Heidegger's work? In an essay entitled "On Potentiality," Agamben examines Aristotle's remarks on vision in *On the Soul* (418b-419e) and offers the following paraphrase: "The object of sight . . . is color; in addition, it is something for which we have no word but which is usually translated as 'transparency,' *diaphanes. Diaphanes* refers not to transparent bodies (such as air and water) but to a 'nature,' as Aristotle writes, which is in every body and is what is truly visible in every body. Aristotle does not tell us what his 'nature' is; he says only 'there is *diaphanes,' esti ti diaphanes.* But he does tell us that the actuality (*energeia*) of this nature is light, and that darkness (*skotos*) is its potentiality. Light, [Aristotle] adds, is so to speak the color of *diaphanes* in act; darkness, we may therefore say, is in some way the color of potentiality" (P, 180 [278]). In another essay from the same years, Agamben again speaks of potentiality as shadow or darkness. The darkness that Agamben associates with potentiality here and elsewhere is thus something perilous, something that must be confronted, traversed, and survived but is of itself nothing other than "the experience of potentiality." For this reason, Agamben could refer to this experience elsewhere as "the hardest and bitterest experience possible" (P, 178). A potentiality is by nature shadowy, and it is the task of the philosopher to identify and utilize what in that shadow can be illuminated and employed.

Agamben has written that were we to attempt to identify "something like the characteristic *Stimmung* of every thinker, perhaps it is precisely a being delivered over to something that refuses itself that defines the specific emotional tonality of Heidegger's thought" (O 65 [68], translation modified). That *Stimmung* is to be understood in the broadest and most fundamental sense is made perfectly clear in an essay from 1980 in which Agamben offers a philological analysis of this quintessentially untranslatable term (see PP, 77ff.). In Heidegger's case, this *Stimmung*, this emotional tonality, is a curious one of gift and refusal. In *Language and Death* Agamben relates an anecdote important enough to him that he recounts it again in his next book, *Idea of Prose*: "One day, when the seminar was nearing its end and the students surrounding him were no longer able to contain their questions, Heidegger remarked, 'You can see my limit, but I cannot'" (IP, 59 [39], translation modified; see also LD, xi [3]).[43] In an afterword written for the second French edition of *Stanzas*—a book, we should recall, dedicated to Heidegger—Agamben takes this principle as his own, remarking that "someone else will always be able to better judge whether . . . the present work was truly written in response to the . . . possibilities here opened" (PO, 271). The questions of personal limit and the relation of one work to another converge here. Benjamin wrote that "in every true work of art there is a passage from which blows a breeze cool like the coming dawn" (Benjamin GS, 5.593). This "passage" can never be a point in a work but is instead a part of every work. For readers to come it is this part that matters most.

One of Agamben's most recent books contains a chapter entitled "Genius." Therein he treats ancient conceptions of genius, of how the Romans spoke of both a good and a bad genius—a "white Genius" and a "black Genius"—the first counseling us to do good, the second its opposite. "Horace was probably right," Agamben concludes, however, "in suggesting that in reality there is but a single Genius, which is, however, mutable—at times clear and at others shadowy, at times sage and at others corrupting. If carefully reflected upon, this means that what changes is not Genius but our relation to it, which moves from clear and luminous to shadowy and opaque" (PR, 15). Agamben suggests here that the more and less genial works that influence our thought and lives are like *genius* in this antique sense. They each contain something clear and something shadowy, something that can inspire us as well as something that can overwhelm us. In other words, they are mutable. But in light of Agamben's remark it is perhaps more accurate to say that it is we who are mutable, and that what we experience in an author's work as clear or shadowy, poisonous or redemptive, has every bit as much to do with ourselves as with the idea of the work.

In the closing lines of *The Time That Remains* Agamben at last names the principle that has guided that work—and all his work. He does so, in characteristic fashion, by quoting the passage from Benjamin in which the latter announces the most fundamental idea behind his idea of history and his idea of prose: that "each now is the now of a particular knowability" and that "the image that is read—which is to say, the image in the now of its recognizability—bears to the highest degree the imprint of the perilous critical moment on which all reading is founded" (Benjamin GS, 5.578; cited in TTR, 145 [135]). If there is an antidote to be sought in Benjamin's work it is in this idea: that reading is based on a critical act—an act touching on the limits of our lives and thought—and for this reason it will always bring with it both an element of peril and an element for which we possess no better word than potentiality.

Scholium III: Eternal Recurrence of the Same, or
Nietzsche and the Potentiality of the Past

Agamben's first book begins with a long citation from Nietzsche's
The Genealogy of Morals. Given *The Man Without Content*'s project of a
"destruction of aesthetics," Agamben's decision to open the book with a
remark from the most vehement opponent of the Kantian conception of a
disinterested view of art is fitting, and one way of reading *The Man Without Content* is as a long and artful gloss of Nietzsche's position as stated
at its outset. Although Nietzsche is seldom mentioned in Agamben's next
book, *Stanzas,* his presence can be felt throughout it. As much as any other modern thinker, Nietzsche theorized and practiced just what Agamben
calls for in *Stanzas:* a poetizing philosophy and a philosophizing poetry
that would break down the barriers between the two. In essays both early
and late Agamben has offered lucid and insightful readings of the most
central ideas in Nietzsche's philosophy, from a "gay science"—which Agamben traces to a "gay saber" found in the poetry of the troubadors and to
Las Leys d'Amors (see PS, 155–156)—to "stellar friendship" (see F), to "the
lucid threshold of madness" that Nietzsche crossed (see PR, 45). Yet more
than the idea of the arid products of modern aesthetics, more than the
merging of poetry and philosophy, more than a science rendered gay or a
friendship rendered stellar, the idea of Nietzsche's that most intrigues Agamben is without question "the eternal recurrence of the same."

Just as Spinoza's idea of a circle is not round, Nietzsche's idea of
"the eternal recurrence of the same" is neither eternal nor identical.
Although it is indeed recurrent—not only in the variety of forms it takes
in Nietzsche's published and unpublished writings, but also in the reception of his work—it is the last thing but a unified doctrine. Nietzsche's
French translator, Pierre Klossowski, had good reason for stressing that it
was in fact not a doctrine at all but something more like "a simulacrum of
a doctrine."[44] For Nietzsche himself, the idea of the eternal recurrence of
the same began indeed not as a doctrine but as an *experience.* It was not a
conclusion he reached through careful and consecutive meditation, but,
instead, an idea or "vision" that came to him one August day in 1881 as he
walked on the Alpine Surlej-Felsen of Sils Maria, Switzerland. He wept
for joy.

An evocation of this experience and an expression of this idea first
appeared some time later in Nietzsche's writing. At the end of the first

version of *The Gay Science* it is presented as a thought experiment: "What if some day or night a tempter were to steal after you into your loneliest loneliness and say to you: 'This life as you now live it and have lived it, you will have to live once more and innumerable times more; and there will be nothing new in it, but every pain and every joy and every thought and sigh and everything unutterably small or great in your life will have to return to you, all in the same succession and sequence—even this spider and this moonlight between the trees, and even this moment and I myself. The eternal hourglass of existence is turned upside down again and again, and you with it, speck of dust!' Would you not throw yourself down and gnash your teeth and curse the tempter who spoke thus? Or have you once experienced a tremendous moment when you would have answered him: 'You are a god and never have I heard anything more divine.' If this thought gained possession of you, it would change you as you are or perhaps crush you" (Nietzsche 2001, 194–95). Nietzsche poses a question to his reader: Can you conceive of your existence as without an essence lent to it by some other place or force? Can you accept the world's transience, and do you see that the most apt figure for conceiving of that transience is the circle? That there will be no *other* life, no *other* world than this one, that all dreams of transcendence are nothing more than that—dreams— is the idea that Nietzsche's thought experiment sought to express. What we know of the world is of this world, said Nietzsche, so what if we were to live in function of this knowledge instead of divine, transcendental hypotheses? If God is dead, if the center of all your values has disappeared from your intellectual and moral firmament, you need a new means of ascribing value to the world and your actions in it. Nietzsche's thought experiment is aimed at effecting a revaluation of all values without recourse to a transcendental space or order of pure value. "Eternal recurrence of the same" is a continuation of the statement "God is dead." If there is no god, our world must be conceived of in purely profane terms. What Nietzsche's thought experiment sought to pose to his readers with new clarity was the question as to whether they could bear this "greatest weight," whether they had the strength to find the source of all value in *this* world and *this* life.

A few years after *The Gay Science,* Nietzsche returned to his vision, dramatizing it in *Thus Spoke Zarathustra.* Therein the animals that speak Zarathustra's doctrine say, "I come again, with this sun, with this earth, with this eagle, with this serpent—*not* to a new life or a better life or a similar life: I come back eternally to this same, self-same life, in what is greatest as in what is smallest, to teach again the eternal recurrence of the same" (1966, 221). What Nietzsche says is that what has come and what is and what will come will not come again as anything other than what it was and is; it will not come again transcended, purified, or spiritualized; there will be no sea changes, nothing rich or strange will it suffer. It will come back again as it was and is. Does this mean a literal recurrence of everything that happens in this life? Or is this merely a manner of eliminating the transcendental from the equation? Everything points here to an idea of *absolute transience* as *absolute permanence.* This intuition is clearly expressed by Nietzsche's initial title for the work that became *Thus Spoke Zarathustra:* "Noon and Eternity." The difficulty here is that of formulating an idea of absolute transience, of locating value and reality only in this world. Paul Celan was to confront this same difficulty in "Counter-light," where he asks, "'All passes': does this thought too not bring all to a halt?" (1983, 3.165). Celan's remark succinctly expresses the essence and the paradox lying at the heart of Nietzsche's doctrine. The transience expressed is transience frozen in the form of a circle.

As concerns this singular idea, many of Nietzsche's first readers and most of his first commentators did what one often does with the unheard of: they avoided it. Some excused it as a poetic flight of fancy, as the product of a rhapsodic cast of Nietzsche's adventurous mind. Others saw it as a perverse thought experiment, and still others as some sort of intellectual trap (encouraged in this by Nietzsche himself, who on occasion called it a "Medusa's head" and a "hammer"). Still others viewed it as a mystical revelation facilitated by the high alpine altitudes in which Nietzsche was wandering and treated it with the discretion accorded to religious experiences. A few interpreted it as a scientific hypothesis. (In posthumously published notes collected in *The Will to Power,* Nietzsche did indeed toy with theories that deduced from the hypotheses of infinite time and finite matter that all states would eventually recur, but these did not lie at the heart of his idea.) But the majority of these first readers saw this idea as a harbinger of Nietzsche's impending madness.

It was with Heidegger and other interpreters of his generation that the idea first came to be taken seriously as a fundamental part of Nietzsche's philosophy—and thereby as an idea that could not simply be occluded or removed, leaving the rest of Nietzsche's thought intact. Shortly after citing the passage from *The Gay Science,* Agamben states precisely what

Heidegger had before him: "Will to power and eternal recurrence are not two ideas that Nietzsche casually places next to each other; they belong to the same origin and metaphysically mean the same thing" (MWC, 91 [137]).[45] More laconically, in a later essay Agamben simply refers to eternal recurrence as the *experimentum crucis* of Nietzsche's thought (MWE, 79 [64]). In short, Agamben sees eternal recurrence as "meaning the same thing" as Nietzsche's most celebrated thought (will to power) and as the crucial experiment with which Nietzsche's thought stands or falls.

In "Clearings," Agamben evoked being "in the obscure / circle of existence" (R, 54). This circle is one that much interested him in the years that followed. As noted earlier, in *The Man Without Content* Agamben explores Nietzsche's eternal recurrence first in his discussion of the role of will in artistic creation and then, a few pages later, in the context of an overcoming of nihilism (see MWC 78 [118], 85–93 [127–140]). In his ample treatment of the notion in that book, he writes, "In the idea of the eternal recurrence, nihilism attains its most extreme form, but precisely for this reason it enters a zone in which surpassing it becomes possible" (MWC, 89–90 [134]). For Agamben, the very extremity of Nietzsche's position brings with it the possibility for a radical change in viewpoint. Eternal recurrence offers a way out of nihilism and a way to action, as it did for Heidegger, who wrote, "While at first blush the doctrine of return introduces an immense, paralyzing indifference into all beings and into human behavior, in truth the thought of thoughts grants supreme lucidity and decisiveness to beings at every moment." As concerns the subject of that crucial chapter from Agamben's first book—which ends with a quotation from Nietzsche on "the world as work of art"—eternal recurrence and its capacity for traversing and surpassing nihilism offers a way of conceiving of artistic activity unmoored from the aesthetic frameworks that Agamben is endeavoring to overcome (see MWC, 93 [140]).

Agamben returns to the idea in his fifth book, *Idea of Prose*—but this time he is no longer concerned with the history of aesthetics. In a chapter entitled "The Idea of Truth," he calls on eternal recurrence to express the fundamental idea behind his *Idea of Prose*—"the absence of any final object of knowledge" (IP, 56 [36]. "The eternal return is, in fact, a final thing, but at the same time the impossibility, also, of a final thing" (IP, 56 [36]; translation modified). Here, Nietzsche's special conception of repetition is a means of breaking free from the spell of transcendence and its unfulfillable promise of a final truth. It is what it was in *The Man*

Without Content: an idea that helps Agamben express his most profound intention.

The following year Agamben speaks of eternal recurrence in a related light. As we saw, Nietzsche announced his idea as that of the "greatest weight." Of his last conversation with Calvino Agamben recounts that they spoke not of the greatest weight but of the greatest lightness—of the "lightness" that was to be one of the topics his friend was scheduled to treat in the Harvard lectures that his untimely death prevented him from giving (QGK, 40). Reflecting on this discussion Agamben wrote that eternal recurrence was an exemplary manner of thinking about the idea of reversibility (QGK, 32). That same year (1986) Agamben dedicated an entire essay to Nietzsche's thought experiment in which we read that "the idea of eternal return is primarily an idea of the like [Agamben had been exploring and explicating the etymology of *Gleich* (German for *like*) in Nietzsche's phrase *ewige Wiederkehr des* Gleich*en*], something in the order of a total image, or to use Benjamin's words, a dialectical image" (ER, 10). Agamben's reading here is a radical one. Eternal recurrence of the same is explicitly interpreted as eternal recurrence not of the same but of the "*like*," of the similar. As in Gilles Deleuze's brilliant and idiosyncratic interpretation of eternal recurrence in his *Nietzsche and Philosophy* (1962), eternal recurrence is liberated from that which is most binding in it: its sameness. With good philological and philosophical reason, Agamben chooses to interpret Nietzsche's idea here not as a cosmic hypothesis but as a philosophical thought experiment, an experiment in finding value in and through *this* world (as well as likening it, in something of a conceptual encomium, to Benjamin's dialectical image).

Agamben was to find still other ideas that Nietzsche's remarkable thought experiment was capable of illuminating. In an introduction to Guy Debord's *Commentaries on the Society of the Spectacle* from 1990, he endeavors to explicate for his readers what a "situation" is in the Situationist sense of the term. Although Debord himself makes no recourse to eternal recurrence, or to Nietzsche, in his own explanations, Agamben writes that "nothing could give a better idea of a constructed situation . . . than the bare scenography in which Nietzsche, in *The Gay Science,* develops his thought's *experimentum crucis.* A constructed situation is the room with the spider and the moonlight between the branches exactly in the moment when—in answer to the demon's question, 'Do you desire this once and innumerable times more?'—is said 'Yes, I do'" (MWE, 79 [64–65]).

Eternal recurrence is presented here as a manner of ascribing supreme and exclusive importance to the here and now. It is a question posed to the reader: Is this world enough for you? Can you live without the consoling idea of transcendence? Agamben continues: "What is decisive here is the messianic displacement that *integrally* changes the world, leaving it at the same time *almost* intact. Everything has remained the same and yet has lost its identity"—the world remains as it was, but our manner of seeing it effects a change so radical that Agamben calls it "messianic" (MWE, 79 [64–65], italics in original, translation modified). What is constant throughout these readings is that Agamben does not take the idea of "eternal recurrence of the same" as necessitating a literal recurrence of some same state of affairs—an interpretation compatible with Nietzsche's remarks on the matter (and bolstered by the interpretative efforts not only of Heidegger, but also of Klossowski and Deleuze). In an essay on gesture written two years later, Agamben again speaks of the idea in the most positive terms, as an elucidation and exploration of the idea of *potentiality:* "The thought of the eternal return is only intelligible as a gesture in which potentiality and act, natural and mannered, contingency and necessity become indistinguishable" (MWE, 53 [48], translation modified). In every one of these instances, Agamben presents eternal recurrence as a radical thought experiment aimed at ascribing value only to and through *this* world and *this* life. As such, it is an experiment in which the moment is filled to bursting with potentiality and a paradigm of profane life.

This is not, however, Agamben's last word on the matter. Elsewhere during these years there are both silent and vocal departures from this view of Nietzsche's "simulacrum of a doctrine." A silent departure is found in *Infancy and History,* where Nietzsche's eternal recurrence is absent from the list of thought experiments exploring radically present-centered or now-centered *kairotic* conceptions of time that might help formulate a "critique of the instant and the continuum." This is at most a minor matter, but just one year after the essay on gesture cited earlier, Agamben offers an emphatic departure from his earlier readings. Although in "The Eternal Return and the Paradox of Passion" (1986) he refers to Nietzsche's doctrine as "this paradox of passion, this giving of self to self . . . which marks the dawning of all consciousness and all subjectivity" (ER, 16), such a view is replaced in "Bartleby, or On Contingency" (1993) by a devastating aridity. The dynamic oscillation that Agamben found in his earlier explorations of the idea comes to a grinding halt. In the later essay Agamben observes that "potentiality can be turned back toward the past in two ways. The first one Nietzsche assigns to the eternal return" (P, 267). Referring to Nietzsche's own description of the genesis of the doctrine of eternal recurrence through the painful experience of the individual confronted with the fact that "the will cannot will backward" (what Nietzsche calls "the will's loneliest melancholy"), Agamben examines the role of the *possible* therein. Summing up the doctrine and offering a new reading of it, Agamben states, "Solely concerned with repressing the spirit of revenge, Nietzsche completely forgets the laments of what was not or could have been otherwise" (P, 267). Whereas earlier Agamben had written that "what Nietzsche tried to do in the concept of eternal return is precisely to conceive the final identity of the two *potentiae* [*potentia activa* and *potentia passiva*], the will to power as a pure passion affecting itself," in the later essay Nietzsche's eternal recurrence is branded as having, in the interest of suppressing "the spirit of revenge," taken the extreme measure of evacuating the past of its potentiality to have been otherwise (and thereby of its contingency) (ER, 17). Rather than being the shimmering point of identity between two modalities, eternal recurrence is, in Agamben's radically revised view, that which evacuates the past of its potential. That this is a crucial issue is stressed by Agamben's employing the harshest terms, as Nietzsche is said to turn a deaf ear to the "laments" of those things that might have been and were not. Nietzsche's idea of eternal recurrence of the same goes from a unique expression of potentiality to its very opposite.

In *Homo Sacer,* published two years after the essay on Bartleby, Agamben returns to eternal recurrence. Here we read that "in the late Nietzsche, the eternal return of the same gives form to the impossibility of distinguishing between potentiality and actuality, even as the *Amor fati* gives shape to the impossibility of distinguishing between contingency and necessity" (HS, 48 [56]). Whereas "Bartleby, or On Contingency" had seen the foreclosing of contingency in Nietzsche's rigid repetition, here Agamben returns to an idea of indistinguishability—between transience and permanence, light and weight, potentiality and actuality, contingency and necessity—that we saw in his earlier treatments of the idea. Yet this view too will be soon changed in favor of the most limiting and peculiar of Agamben's references to Nietzsche's idea. In *Remnants of Auschwitz,* the polemical thrust of Agamben's reading of Nietzsche surpasses anything seen in "Bartleby, or On Contingency." Turning his attention away from the question of potentiality to ideas of transience and contingency, he offers a diametrically opposed interpretation of eternal recurrence. All talk of a "displacement," of thinking of a "like" instead of a "same," all talk of giving potentiality to past and present is abandoned as Nietzsche's thought experiment is described as a means for handing down a judgment on human history. Agamben categorically opposes himself to Nietzsche's idea of eternal recurrence on the grounds that the event of Auschwitz shatters its foundation, that it "refutes it beyond all doubt, excluding the possibility of its even being proposed" (RA, 99 [92]). The intricacies of this singular argument were explored earlier and are further examined in the following few pages. But, for the moment, we might first ask what brought about this radical change in Agamben's position.

Agamben was asked in an interview in 2004 why Nietzsche had not played a more fundamental role in his writings, considering what a consistent point of reference Nietzsche was for those interested in developing or inventing a "non-exclusive conception of the political." (The interviewer seems to be alluding to figures such as Nancy, Badiou, Deleuze, Foucault, Derrida, Negri, and Virno.) Agamben's answer to the question is characteristically indirect. The interviewer's interest is clearly focused on political philosophy, yet Agamben's answer departs in a completely different direction. "Nietzsche was important for me," he begins, "but a bit like Benjamin I see eternal recurrence as like having to stay after school, when you have to write the same sentence a thousand times" (LKA, 16).[46] Despite the fact that his interviewer had not mentioned eternal recurrence, and despite the fact that those thinkers to whom he was alluding, who turn to Nietzsche for political coordinates, do not accord great place to eternal recurrence in their *political* analyses (they are more focused on the ideas of *will, truth, power,* and *genealogy*), it is precisely to this point that Agamben returns, and he does so not "a bit like Benjamin," but exactly like him.

Benjamin found the idea of eternal recurrence of singular interest, but what he saw in it was, above all, something *mechanical* and mindlessly repetitive. Most famously, Benjamin raises a question of precedence, noting, as Agamben would after him, that the nineteenth-century French revolutionary and autodidact Louis-Auguste Blanqui wrote of an idea that, in its essential outlines, anticipated Nietzsche's doctrine of eternal recurrence by ten years. After noting this, Benjamin makes the radical claim that "the belief in progress, in an endless perfectibility—an endless moral task—and the representation of eternal recurrence are complementary" (Benjamin AP, 119; GS, 5.178, translation modified). Whether the improvements that Nietzsche imagined in the state of the world to come were "complementary" with the ideology of progress that Benjamin set out to combat is debatable, but Benjamin goes still farther in drawing conclusions from this complementarity. He finds that Nietzsche's teaching is complicit with imperialism ("Nietzsche had an inkling of his doctrine's complicity with imperialism" [Benjamin AP; GS, 5.175]) and that eternal recurrence is in opposition to the concept of messianic time, "now-time," as explosive, nonhomogenous time, bursting with revolutionary promise. For Benjamin, eternal recurrence offers a vision of time as blandly and blankly "progressive."[47] As is often the case, Benjamin concentrates his criticism in the form of a particularly striking image—that of having to stay after school and copy out the same sentence ad nauseum (Benjamin GS, 1.1152). For Benjamin, eternal recurrence of the same was an idea of mechanical repetition, and for this reason he likened it to the ideology of progress, and to a punishment. Instead of allowing the childlike exercise of newfound potentiality so as to write all manner of creative things, eternal recurrence offered the numbingly adult task of mindless repetition.

While Heidegger saw traces of the mechanical in the idea, he never came close to reducing it to that element. For him, eternal recurrence had all the earmarks of what he called "authentic temporality" and what Benjamin called "now-time" (a conception of time whose central focus is on the dynamic possibilities of the present). In a lecture course Heidegger stated that what is expressed in Nietzsche's concept of eternal recurrence is "eternity not as an arrested now, but as a now that resounds back upon itself [*in sich selbst zurückschlagende Jetzt*]" (Heidegger GA, 6.17). Benjamin sees it, however, as something diametrically opposed to this. For him, it is a conception of time and of its moment evacuated of dynamic potentiality. His most striking image for this progress-oriented doctrine complicit with the forces of imperialism is the child made to stay after school to copy out morally sententious sentences aimed at making him a better, or more docile, adult. Appropriating the story of an adult copyist (Bartleby, the scrivener), Agamben moves farther away from a Heideggerian reading of Nietzsche and closer to Benjamin's idea of punishment. Initially, for Agamben, a figure of absolute indistinction or indetermination, eternal recurrence was *rich* in potentiality. Here, in Benjamin's wake, it could not be poorer in it.

What we have here is perhaps nothing mysterious. Over the course of several decades of continued rereading and reflection Agamben appears to have changed his mind as to the ultimate import of a complex and notoriously enigmatic philosophical idea. This move in his thinking corresponded to a move away from the line drawn by one treasured thinker in the direction of a line drawn by another. But what is of greatest interest here is a correlate of this change in position. The reason for the singular uncertainty expressed by Agamben concerning Nietzsche's idea lies in that which he is trying to think through it: "pure potentiality." For Agamben, to think "pure potentiality" is also to think the dynamic potentiality of the past. Agamben is right to see that Nietzsche wished to eliminate from the past its potentiality (if not, as Agamben argues, its contingency). Nietzsche endeavored to conceive of the past not as *necessary* but only as—to choose a term that will play a programmatic role in Agamben's *The Coming Community*—irreparable. Nietzsche wished to freeze the past so as to confront the most painful aspect of human experience: that we cannot turn back time, undo wrongs, and eliminate the monstrous suffering of the past. Eternal recurrence was a thought experiment aimed at freeing individuals of the longing for the past to have been other than it was. The bottom line in Nietzsche's doctrine of eternal recurrence, as we saw, is that the teeth-gnashing will cannot change the past. If read in a liberal light, Nietzsche's goal was to direct humanity's gaze more fixedly on what was to be done to bring about a new order that might avoid such things repeating themselves in the future. Awakening the potentiality of the past as Agamben conceives it cannot simply be an act of *will* that accepts the past in all its irrevocability, that appropriates the past's contingency as the will's necessity (what Nietzsche called *amor fati*). Whether Agamben's initial or his subsequent reading of Nietzsche's eternal recurrence has better philosophical justification is not the most important question to ask here. Instead, the question is best posed in terms of how Agamben adopts and develops the idea, and his singular ambivalence exemplifies the difficulty for him—both in *Remnants of Auschwitz* and elsewhere—of developing a philosophy of potentiality able to come to terms with the past.

CHAPTER EIGHT

The Suspended Substantive:
The Open: Man and Animal

With a title as enigmatic as *The Open,* the book's reader might well wonder, the open *what?* Is the title's adjective to stand alone? Does it need no substantive to support it? This unusual title is not what one might first suspect—it is not an awkward translation of the work's original title. No substantive follows in the original, and none is meant to. The idea that gives Agamben's book its title is that of an openness that is unconditioned—and perhaps unconditional, unspecified—and perhaps unspecifiable.

If the question "the open *what?*" can be answered with no substantive, we might ask *in* what this opening occurs. *Between* what more substantive things has an indefinable space opened? The first answer to the question can be found in the work's subtitle: *Man and Animal.* The open space in question is that which separates and distinguishes man from animal. Philosophers, anthropologists, social scientists, zoologists, chemists, taxonomists—and many others—have had no small difficulty in agreeing on the matter. Philosophers have traditionally held a low opinion of animals.[1] Descartes had especially little respect for their minds and influentially classified them as *automata mechanica.* As Agamben notes, the great naturalist and taxonomist Linnaeus responded to this assertion with the laconic rejoinder, "Descartes obviously never saw an ape" (see O, 23 [30], translation modified).[2] Philosophers have been more eager than taxonomists to put distance between themselves and animals—and for this reason have been particularly interested in studying what separates man from animal. The last great attempt in this regard was Heidegger's. Despite his preference for the primordial and his openness to the woods and the wilderness, his opinion of animals' faculties was not much higher than that of Descartes. In his view, animals live in an environment in which they are receptive to various stimuli but where they have nothing approximating what we call a "world." Animals are, as he claims, "poor in world [*weltarm*]"—or even "without world [*weltlos*]." They live in such intense and incessant proximity to their environment and its stimuli that they do not see the existential forest for the environmental trees. They can never take a step away from the immediacy of their perception and for this reason cannot be said to possess a "world" in the sense that man, in Heidegger's view, does.

In its opening lines, *Language and Death* cites Heidegger's remark that "Mortals are they who can experience death as death. Animals cannot do this. But neither can they speak" (cited in LD, xi [3], translation modified). Heidegger saw a connection between these two privations, and it was this link that Agamben followed in his fourth book. Animals cannot speak in the sense that they can take no distance from their means of expression and communication. Just as they cannot take a step away from their world to reflect on it (and for this reason, Heidegger claims, they have no *world* in his special sense of the term), neither can they take a step away from their voice to reflect on it (and thus have no *language*). Long before Heidegger, Aristotle had noted in his *Politics* that "among living beings, only man has language." Like animals, we make sounds of pleasure and pain with our voices, but we are unique in possessing a language—and as Aristotle says, "language is for manifesting the expedient and the inexpedient, the just and the unjust" (Aristotle 1253a; 1984, 10–18). This difference is the source of our ethical responsibility and the loss of our animal innocence. (For this reason, in *Idea of Prose* Agamben describes an experience of language independent of signification as "the innocence of language.")

Aristotle and Heidegger present this inability as something on the order of a privation (" . . . cannot . . . neither can they . . . "). Agamben, however, stresses in numerous places that our human state might with equal justice be viewed as a privation. As we saw earlier, Agamben has often evoked the immediacy of what Mallarmé called "*la voix sacrée de la terre ingénue"*—the chorus of natural and animal life that can sound so joyous to human ears. In a short, largely narrative text from 1982 entitled *The End of Thought,* Agamben writes of walking in the forest and being surprised by "the variety of animal voices": "Ultimately, the double note of the cuckoo mocks our silence and reveals our being, unique and without voice in the infinite chorus of animal voices [*nel coro infinito delle voci animali*]" (FP, 1). As Western philosophy has not tired of stressing, the voices of animals have no capacity for reflection because they take no distance from their experience—but as Agamben points out, this also means they have an immediacy that we lack. This is what forms the kernel of Agamben's many interrogations of the double-edged idea of *voice* and of what separates our voices from those of animals. In essays such as "Voice and Vocation," this idea lies at the center of his interests and is even found in the title of one of Agamben's books, as Benjamin's "idea of prose" is a "celebration" of language that "is the idea of prose itself, and which is understood by all humans just as the language of birds is understood by those born on Sunday" (Benjamin GS, 1.1239).[3] For Agamben, the birth of thought is located in our reflection on the animal voices surrounding us. In *The End of Thought* he stresses that when we are in the midst of nature and its many voices, "it is then that we try to speak and to think" (FP, 1). This initial reflective moment is not one of exuberance or joy, and Agamben notes that the word *thought* [*pensiero*] originally meant "anguish" and "torment" (FP, 1). "Thinking in language is something we can do," Agamben writes, "because language at once is, and is not, our voice" (FP, 3). This passage from innocence and immediacy to experience and reflection is also the passage traced between *infancy*—an important concept for Agamben during the years when he was developing his ideas of *voice* and *language*—and *speech.* We should as little simply bemoan our loss of infancy as vaunt our possession of an articulate language; the interest of the experience lies, for Agamben, elsewhere. In an essay from 1980, he refers to a nineteenth-century children's book that doubled as an illustrated grammar (*La Grammatica della signorina Mimi*) in which Mimi learns that to speak is not simply to make certain noises, as animals do, but to learn language's rules, of which Agamben writes, "in the illustration to this passage we see the young girl between a dog and a cat, symbol of the human word in danger of losing itself in the animal voice" (PS, 157–158). Our experience—and our reflective capacities—come into being in response to this "animal voice." In *Infancy and History, Language and Death, The End of Thought,* and essays such as "The Celebration of the Hidden Treasure," the voices of animals are of the greatest importance for Agamben, and it is this reflection on the relation of voice to language that lies at the center of his interest in *The Open.*

As mentioned earlier, the title *The Open* is, for all its strangeness, not the result of an awkward translation from Agamben's Italian. Nevertheless, its strangeness does stem in large part from a translation—or to be more precise, from two translations. The first of these is from the German. The German in question is a special one: the profoundly idiosyncratic technical vocabulary that Heidegger fashioned for his philosophical purposes. For Heidegger, the "open" is something literally fundamental and it lies at the heart of his thought. This "open" is the space revealed to us in the moment when the world we live in, which because of our many tasks and travails we tend to take no distance from (like animals from their stimuli), opens out onto something larger. This moment of distancing ourselves from our everyday concern with means and ends, with stimuli and response, is what gives us not just an environment but, in his words, a "world." The "open" is what we then find ourselves in when the bustle and haste of our environment recedes and we see that environment in all its strangeness and immensity, as a "world"—one that is greater and less graspable than our representations of it. This experience of "the open" is, for Heidegger, what makes us human, and what separates us from the animals. This open moment is the one that lies at the origin of philosophy: the humbling—and potentially frightening—moment of wonder that first spurred human speculation into the finer and deeper reasons for things. As was his wont, Heidegger came up with a special phrase to describe this experience of acceding to the open—"the world worlds [*die Welt weltet*]"—and in the very next sentence of the text where he introduces this formulation states that "the rock has no world. Plants and animals also have no world" (Heidegger 1950, 31).[4] When the world, strangely enough, "worlds," we find that world open before us; we are standing, to adopt Heidegger's terms, in a "clearing," a step away from both trees and forest. The world is no longer too much with us and we suddenly see trees, forest, and ourselves in an uneasy and changing relation to one another.

The open is one term among many in Heidegger's technical vocabulary—and it was ultimately one that found little place in his later philosophy. It played, nevertheless, a crucial role in the development of that philosophy. This is most clearly visible, as Agamben points out, in Heidegger's lectures in Freiburg in the fall semester of 1942–43. In the midst of the most unsparing combat, Heidegger was lecturing on Parmenides. The course was dedicated in large part to the translation of a single word—*aletheia,* Greek for "truth." Heidegger suggested a number of ways of translating the term, but his fourth and final suggestion was, "*das Offene und das Freie der Lichtung des Seins*"—literally, "the open and the free in the clearing of being"—or more simply, "the open" (Heidegger GA, 54.195). In his woodland terminology, *Lichtung,* a clearing (as in a forest), is etymologically a "light-ing," an opening and an illumination. Given the pride of philosophical and poetic place that Heidegger accorded to his own "clearings [*Lichtungen*]" as openings onto a place that is of primary and primordial meaning and being, it should come as little surprise that the twenty-five-year-old Agamben entitled an early poem "Clearings." In Heidegger's ontological register, the "open" corresponds to originary truth: it is the open space in which truth in its original (Greek) meaning took place. It stands thus, for Heidegger, at the heart of philosophy: at the heart of its history and its essence.[5]

In these lectures first published in 1993, it seems that Heidegger arrived at his translation not only by sounding the concealed depths of ancient Greek, but also by sounding the concealed depths of modern German.[6] This modern German was a poetic one—that of Rilke. As he introduces his translation of Parmenides' term for truth, Heidegger is well aware that the unusual expression "the open" will lead his listeners to think of Rilke's *Duino Elegies* (1923), and in particular of Rilke's repeated use of the curious term in the eighth elegy. (Although neither Heidegger nor Agamben notes this, the term had a longer poetic history and in fact had been used by Hölderlin in one of his most famous poems, "Bread and Wine": "*So komm! dass wir das Offene schauen . . .*") Rilke's elegy begins, "With all its eyes the creature sees / the open [*das Offene*]" (Rilke 1996, 2.224). In his poem, we (humankind) are excluded from this glimpse of the open granted to all other creatures. Years earlier, on a visit to Paris's *Jardin des Plantes,* Rilke's sensitive eye had been captured by a panther. For Rilke's panther, captivity was the central fact of his existence. "It seems to him," wrote Rilke of the great cat, that, "there are / a thousand bars; and behind the bars, no world" (Rilke 1996, 1.469). What interested Rilke was how impenetrable, how full of incommunicable will, strength, and silence, the animal was; what awakened his poetic sensibilities was how closed-off that animal's world was. The worldlessness of the animal proves in the later poem to be the fruit not of its nature but of its confinement. In the eighth elegy, the unnamed animal (*die Kreatur*) is accorded a different glimpse of the world: it sees the world in all its openness. It sees what fear of death and fear of life prevent us, the smartest and saddest of creatures, from seeing: the world in all its intense and interconnected immediacy.

Heidegger is quick to distance himself from this immediacy. Although, as he notes, he and Rilke are employing the same term, the same "wording" (Heidegger repeatedly uses the term *Wortlaut* instead of the simpler *Wort*), "what is being named," says Heidegger of his use of the term "the open," "is so different that no opposition could hope to convey it," because "oppositions—even the most extreme—demand that those things which are to be opposed to one another can be placed in the same realm" (Heidegger GA, 54.226). "The open" that Rilke praises and that he sees reflected in the eyes of animals is, for Heidegger, mere blindness. This blindness is of a particular sort: historical blindness. Rilke's problem, his misapprehension of the deep meaning of the term "the open" and, according to Heidegger, his inconsequent use of it stems from his unthinking adoption of a traditional view of the relation of man to animal that is typical of a fundamentally unreflective modernity (see Heidegger GA, 54.231, 54.235). The "open" with which Heidegger translated the Greek *truth* is another one than that which Rilke famously invoked. For Heidegger, it is not the animals that see "the open"; they are open to nothing but stimuli. According to him, the experience is reserved for us alone.

This is the point at which Agamben takes his title and enters the discussion. The difficulty of acceding to this "open" place is one that he had referred to as early as the end of his second book, *Stanzas*: "Even if it were possible to reveal the metaphysical inheritance of modern semiology, it would still be impossible for us to conceive of a presence that, finally freed from difference, was only a pure and undivided station in the open [*una pura e indivisa stazione nell'aperto*]" (S, 156 [188]). Three years later, Agamben's interest in this terminological connection is attested to in an essay in which Agamben not only points out Rilke's use of the term "the open" but claims of the *Duino Elegies* that "Heidegger had them constantly in mind while writing *Being and Time*" (PP, 81). Agamben's essay

"The Face," from 1990 (the English translation incorrectly dates it as from 1995), begins, "All living beings are in the open" (MWE, 91 [74]). In that essay Agamben notes that "animals are always already in the open," and humans are singled out in that they "transform the open into a world" (MWE, 93 [75]). In *Remnants of Auschwitz,* Agamben refers in passing to "the pristine adhesion to the Open that Rilke discerned in the gaze of the animal" (RA, 122–123 [114]).

In *The Open* Agamben neither laments Rilke's historico-ontological naïveté nor accuses Heidegger of insensitivity toward poetry or animals. His interest is fixed on another point: the open place where he feels that the two irreconcilable positions meet—the point at which the animal's unhindered openness, or receptivity, to stimuli in its environment and man's openness to the world in all its ungraspable immensity converge. One might ask whether these two types of openness, these two types of receptivity, have anything in common, whether they bear the weight of comparison. For Heidegger, they clearly did not. Agamben assumes that they do, and this assumption leads him to posit another type of openness than either Rilke or Heidegger had conceived of, an openness of inactivity, of *dis*engagement from one's environment, and perhaps from one's world.[7]

This openness that interests Agamben is not one of immersion in immediate stimuli and short-term tasks, nor is it an exalting in the immensity and strangeness of the world; rather, it is a special sort of inactivity that he denotes using another strange substantive—the French term *désoeuvrement* ("inoperativeness," *inoperosità*). Agamben dedicates a significant amount of *The Open* to the exegesis of this term (which I examined in an earlier scholium), both at the beginning of the book in his discussion of the debate concerning it between Georges Bataille and Alexandre Kojève, and at the book's end, where the penultimate chapter bears the title *Désoeuvrement*.[8] As we saw, this is far from the first time that Agamben confronted the idea. As early as *Language and Death* he examined—and quoted long passages from—the correspondence between the two men in the context of his investigation of the role of negativity in Hegel's dialectic (see LD, 50–53 [65–67]). *Désoeuvrement* is an idea that excited the intense interest of two other writers to whom Agamben feels close—Blanchot and Nancy, who both, as we also saw earlier, wrote works centered around this term's use in Bataille's work and its applications beyond it. In *The Coming Community* Agamben indirectly responded to Blanchot's and Nancy's speculations on *désoeuvrement*, community, communism, and identity. In his next work, *Homo Sacer*, he traced the term's genealogy and offered his own singular interpretation of it. Therein he writes that "the only coherent way to understand inoperativeness is to think of it as a generic mode of potentiality that is not exhausted (like individual action or collective action understood as the sum of individual actions) in a *transitus de potentia ad actum*" (HS, 62 [71]). For Bataille, the term meant a radical refutation of the utilitarian aims of modern society and modern philosophy (represented for him by Hegel's dialectic), a commitment to inactivity and excess, and a refusal to contribute to the great work (the *oeuvre* of *dés-oeuvre-ment*) of history. For Agamben, it is this and more. As we saw earlier, *désoeuvrement* is not about exhaustion or even excess, but, instead, what Agamben calls *potentiality*. It represents an energy that has not been exhausted and that *cannot* be exhausted in the passing of the potential to the actual (*transitus de potentia ad actum*). In the postface to a new Italian edition of *The Coming Community*, Agamben recenters his speculations in that work around the idea of inoperativeness and suggests that the term might form a "paradigm for politics": "Inoperativeness does not signify inertia, but rather *katargesis*—that is to say, an operation in which the *as if* integrally replaces the *that*, in which formless life and lifeless form coincide in a form of life [*una forma di vita*]"; "not work, but inoperativeness [is] the paradigm of the coming politics" (CCV, 93). Inoperativeness is not laziness or inactivity; it is the open space where formless life and lifeless form meet in a distinct life-form and form of living that are rich with their own singular potentiality. This is the "open" that Agamben's title strives to name.

From *The Man Without Content* onward we have seen something of a recurrent pattern: a sort of *Benjamin ex machina* where at the end of an essay or work the contradictions uncovered or problems posed are, if not resolved, placed in a new—and more hopeful—light thanks to insights culled from Benjamin's thought. *The Open* is no exception in this regard. After six chapters of Heideggerian exegesis (Chapters Twelve through Seventeen), Agamben turns abruptly to Benjamin. Just as the knot of Heideggerian reasoning has begun to tighten around man and animal, Agamben appeals to a conception of the open taken from Benjamin's reference in a letter from 1923 to "the saved night." The chapter's title is

"Between [*Tra*]" and suggests a different form of the open glimpsed in this strangely redeemed night. This openness is what Benjamin elsewhere called "dialectics at a standstill," the "between" or "interval" between two terms or two coordinates—an unresolved opposition, a *désoeuvrement* at the heart of a dialectic that had hitherto known no pause (O, 83 [85]).

In a number of his essays Agamben speaks of an author's having a single most personal and intimate "gesture." If we were to apply this principle to Agamben's own writing, we might find such a defining gesture in the curious idea of a "division of division." This gesture is best seen in a philological emendation that Agamben makes in *The Time That Remains* and that I examined earlier (concerning Benjamin's "line divided by Apelles' incision"). Agamben takes Benjamin's hitherto misunderstood figure as a metaphor for the Paulinian division and suspension of earlier divisions (Jew / Gentile, circumcised / uncircumcised, married / single, and so on). "Wherein lies the interest of this 'division of a division'?" asks Agamben. His reply is, "Above all in that it obliges us to think the question of the relation of universal to particular in a completely new fashion, not only in the realm of logic, but in that of ontology and of politics" (TTR, 51 [53–54]). What was at issue in Agamben's idea of community was precisely this: finding figures "to think the question of the relation of universal to particular in a completely new fashion." Further glossing this division of a division, Agamben says that it is "an operation that divides these divisions of the law themselves and renders them inoperative, without forasmuch leading them to an ultimate stage [*un suolo ultimo*]" (TTR, 54–55). Here we can follow the line of reflection linking Agamben's reflections on the idea of the "inoperative" from *Language and Death* to *The Coming Community, Homo Sacer,* and *The Open.* What is more, we can trace his interest in the figure still farther back, both to his remarks on *vocation* as that which renders inoperative an earlier vocation rather than simply replacing it with a new goal, and to his first book, where writing about the divisive nature of modern aesthetic experience he claims that the spectator "has no other way of finding himself . . . than wholly to assume his contradiction"—which means to "split asunder his own split [*lacerare la propria lacerazione*], negate his own negation [*negare la propria negazione*]" (MWC, 48 [72]). This division of division that Agamben finds and focuses on in Benjamin and Paul, this characteristic gesture, is not one that pretends simply to efface the divisions that isolate and alienate communities, but rather one that, without effacing them, renders them, as instruments of political division, "inoperative."

Whatever gesture might be most characteristic of Agamben's thought, the question remains as to why he turned to the issues he did in *The Open.* We might then ask ourselves why he should be interested in the relation of man to animal. It is indeed a classical philosophical *topos,* one treated by Aristotle, Descartes, Kant, Heidegger, and more recently such figures as Deleuze and Derrida.[9] But why should Agamben turn to it at *this* point in his itinerary? The best place to seek an answer is in the idea of "bare life" that has guided much of Agamben's thought since *Homo Sacer.* Although *The Open* is not a numbered part of the series, it shares with it an effort to explore the conceptual confines of the concept of "bare life." In the opening lines of *Homo Sacer* Agamben distinguishes specific forms of life, named in Greek *bios,* from *zoē,* a term that "expressed the simple fact of living common to all living beings (animals, men, or gods)" (HS, 1 [3]). This point is worth stressing not only to give a sense of the continuity of Agamben's concerns, but also to understand the form they take in *The Open.* In this light, to read Agamben in the context of debates about animal rights is, though illuminating for those debates, somewhat misleading as a frame through which to understand *The Open.*[10] For Agamben, the point is not to locate a continuity or an interruption in the line of evolution, not to align himself with those advocates of continuity like Aristotle or those who see a fundamental break between man and animal like Descartes and Heidegger, and not to bring about more just treatment of animals, but instead to glimpse a new and different paradigm for human life.

This division of a division that Agamben sees through the lens of Benjamin's work, and that he traces in part to the influence of Paul, would bring about a standstill of the dialectic of ontological unity and historical progress that has led to so many of our present travesties. This dividing of a division, or bringing to a standstill of the dialectic, would also, for Agamben, be the freezing of the "anthropological machine" that he sees as menacing today's societies (O, 83 [85]). In the wake of Foucault's analyses of the powers and dangers of "biopolitics"—the new forms of discipline, control, and domination that modernity has brought with it—Agamben identifies what he calls an "anthropological machine" that threatens to close that which is productively and promisingly open in contemporary politics.[11] The openness in question is the open vocation of man, the free-dom to refuse to accept the demands of institutionalized forms of power that Agamben sees as seeking to identify, to isolate, and to control. This "open" is then an openness of historical task, an openness of how we choose to see our historical task—or the lack thereof. The "biopolitical machine" serves to define the human in its distance from the animal, and to seize hold of something Agamben calls bare life. It is this menace, which the work of Foucault helped to move to the center of Agamben's interests, that leads Agamben to undertake an investigation of the reigning conceptions of *life*—and of the way human life is distinguished from animal life, the way qualified, categorized life is distinguished from a merely animalic life, a "bare" and "unprotected" life. "To render inoperative the machine that governs our conception of man," writes Agamben, "would not mean to search for new—more effective or more authentic—articulations of this conception, but rather to display the central void, the hiatus which—within the human—separates the human from the animal" (O, 92 [94], translation modified). This would mean, following Agamben, "to take the risk upon ourselves involved in such a void, in such a suspension of suspension, a *Shabbat* both of animal and man" (O, 92 [94], translation modified). It is this open-ended risk for which Agamben's work wishes to make a plea—neither strictly human nor strictly animal, but from the open space between the two.

CHAPTER NINE

The Exceptional Life of the State:
State of Exception. Homo Sacer II.1

The exception is more interesting than the regular case. The latter proves nothing, the exception proves everything.

—CARL SCHMITT, *Political Theology*

Philosophers have often written of the nature of the state and of the state of nature. They have often written of the state of culture and the culture of the state. Rarely, however, have they written of a state of exception in which the state's habitual nature and culture are suspended. It is to just such a state of exception—and to the possibility that such states of exception lie at the heart of the functioning of modern states—that Agamben dedicated the next installment of his *Homo Sacer* series, *State of Exception.*

Like the larger project of which it is a part, *State of Exception* is a book about *life.* It is not about life in any banal or belletristic sense. It is an earnest and erudite analysis of the ethical, juridical, and ontological coordinates through which Western culture has developed and defined a concept of *life*—of its essence and its limits. The book's subtitle (which the English translation fails to render), *Homo sacer, II.1,* refers the reader to the project that Agamben inaugurated in 1995. This investigation of the life of power was continued in *Homo sacer III, Remnants of Auschwitz.* That work pursued its analysis of life and its limits into the Nazi concentration camps, and the prodigious difficulties of those who lived to bear witness to them. *State of Exception: Homo sacer II.1* focuses its attention on the suspension of the rule of law that was the condition of possibility for the establishment of those camps—and for much more.

The work of Agamben's that directly preceded *State of Exception* did not belong to the *Homo sacer* series. As we saw, *The Open* followed the conceptual history of the term *life* in light of what separated the life of man from the life of animals. As we also saw, *The Open* took its title from a singular term to which both Rilke and Heidegger had accorded special importance. *State of Exception*'s title is also a translation, and also a translation from the German. It refers to the laconic definition of sovereignty given by a figure familiar to Agamben's readers from the beginning of the *Homo Sacer* project: the German jurist and scholar Carl Schmitt. As we saw earlier, Schmitt began his *Political Theology* (1922) by defining the sovereign as "he who can decide on the state of exception [*Ausnahmezustand*]" in which the rule of law is suspended—and it is this suspension that gives its name to Agamben's work.[1]

What does Agamben isolate in this phenomenon that Schmitt expertly identified and for which he personally militated? Does it interest him only as a fact of legal history—one that paved the way for the denationalization and subsequent genocide of European Jewry? Agamben does indeed closely examine the regime that first called on Schmitt's teachings and person—but his analysis of the phenomenon of a state of exception where a sovereign leader suspends the rule of law does not restrict itself to this instance. One of the first points that Agamben wants, in fact, to make clear is that in the life of the state such exceptional instances are not so exceptional. To this end, he sketches a genealogy of states of exception from their origins in Roman law to more modern cases such as the states of exception declared by France's revolutionary governments, Abraham Lincoln's authorization in 1862 of the summary arrest and detention of persons suspected of "disloyal and treasonable practices," and the "unlimited" national emergency declared following the bombing of Pearl Harbor that led to the expulsion of seventy thousand American citizens of Japanese origin (along with forty thousand Japanese citizens) (see SE, 20ff. [30ff.]). This historical background is in no way offered as a relativization of the long and deadly state of exception put into effect by Hitler's decrees. It is meant instead to alert the reader that the conditions that allowed for such a state of deadly exception had existed in the West for some time—and have not disappeared from it.

As we have seen, in Benjamin's final works he repeatedly attacked the reigning ideology of progress and the concomitant idea that with time states and societies grow more just and more wise. He wrote in 1940, in regard to the barbarities then under way, that "the wonder occasioned by the fact that the things we are at present experiencing are 'still' possible in the twentieth century is no philosophical wonder" (Benjamin GS, 1.697). As he makes clear, Agamben could not more fully subscribe to this view. He consequently isolates not only historic states of exception but also contemporary ones. The most notorious of these is George W. Bush's declaration in November 2001 providing for the "indefinite detention" of noncitizens suspected of terrorist activities. In a provocative analogy, Agamben claims that "the only available comparison" to this legal no-man's-land into which the detainees in Guantánamo have been thrown, and in which so many still dwell, is "the legal situation of Jews in the Nazi *Lager* [concentration camps]" (SE, 4 [12]). It is important to pay careful attention to the terms Agamben employs here: the analogy between detainees in Guantanamo and imprisoned Jews in Nazi concentration camps concerns their "juridical situation"—the rights and recourses they have—not the political intentions of the regimes in question, or the physical treatment of those indefinitely imprisoned.

For Agamben, the violence of states of exception is a problem more present and pressing now than ever before. In a newspaper article from 1997 he points to the "special laws" passed during Italy's *anni di piombo,* which are still in force and "cast a sinister shadow on the life of our democratic institutions" (CM, 5). This observation leads Agamben to judge that "in Italy the exception has become the rule" and to offer an incendiary parallel between those laws and the *Verordnung zum Schutz von Volk und Staat* through which the Nazi government suspended the articles of the constitution concerning personal and civil liberties, the right to free assembly, the inviolability of the home, and the privacy of epistolary and telephonic communication (CM, 5).[2] In *State of Exception* Agamben isolates the case of the United States, judging that its government has declared nothing less than a "global state of exception" that is "mobile" and thus can apply itself wherever it likes through the occasion presented by the "war on terrorism." "When the state of exception . . . becomes the rule," he continues, "then the juridico-political system becomes a machine which may at any moment turn lethal" (SE, 86 [110]). It is this lethal machine whose biopolitical motor is the state of exception that is, in Agamben's analysis, "leading the West toward a global civil war" (SE, 87 [III]).

The Original Structure of the State of Exception

Agamben examines this biopolitical machine not only as a historical, juridical, and political phenomenon, but also as something more. The state of exception is what he calls an "original structure [*struttura originale*]" (SE, 3 [II]). In this original structure, "the law includes . . . the living [*il vivente*] through its own suspension" (SE, 3 [II]). This dense formulation refers to the central paradox of such states of exception: the state of exception is the point at which the law provides for its own suspension; it is the legal suspension of the distinction between legality and illegality. Agamben is profoundly interested in Schmitt's "state of exception," not merely as a key juridical term among others but as a concept marking the very limits of the law. For this reason, Agamben speaks, in regard to the state of exception, of a "no-man's-land" he sees lying between "civil law and political fact," between "juridical order and life" (SE, 10). The state of exception is the political point at which the juridical stops and a sovereign unaccountability begins; it is where the dam of individual liberties breaks and a society is flooded with the sovereign power of the state—what Judith Butler calls "a paralegal universe that goes by the name of law" (Butler 2004, 61).[3]

Isolating this "original structure" is no easy task, however, lying as it does in an "anomic space" (a literally "lawless" space). Agamben endeavors to delineate this space by directing his readers to Derrida's analysis of "the force of law." The general problem here is one that generations of jurists and political philosophers have struggled with: the force the law is justified in employing. Seen from a different angle, the question is one of violence—the distinction between legitimate and illegitimate violence. From the perspective of the state, what is at issue is drawing the line that separates the one from the other. Plotting the points this line should follow usually sends theoreticians back to the origins—the founding of a state—and to the shadowy but necessary distinction, so vividly present in revolutions, between *constitutive* violence—the violence that founds a state (and was used to overthrow what came before it) and *constituted* violence—the violence that is then part and parcel of the state's functioning (the extreme means it holds in reserve to handle special cases of external threat or internal unrest). As we saw in *Homo Sacer* and in the response to Negri that Agamben offers therein, constitutive violence *establishes* law, and constituted violence *maintains* that law. In theory, the distinction is already difficult to make; in practice, it is often next to impossible.

When left to speak for themselves, states have little trouble distinguishing between legitimate and illegitimate uses of force, and they employ a simple and circular reasoning: the use of force is legitimate because it is legitimated (by the state). Constitutive violence with its unavoidable excesses and anarchic appearance is to be distinguished, following the standard explanation that states offer, from constituted violence in being channeled and codified—even if this codification includes an extralegal realm that is not, however, explicitly illegal; it is a state of exception in which certain constitutionally guaranteed rights and protections are suspended so as to confront a clear and present danger to the state. A telling icon for this exceptional state that states impose is found in an essay by Agamben from 1992 in which he recalls Montesquieu's observation that a veil was placed on the Statue of Justice at the moment of the declaration of a state of exception (see MWE, 113 [90]).

With this as his background, Agamben traces the history of the French phrase that captivates Derrida, *force de loi* ("force of law"), and reformulates it in light of the state of exception he is illustrating. In the state of exception, the force of law is changed. *Force* and *law* then no longer stand in a relationship of means to ends (with *force* as the recourse that *law* may employ to achieve certain ends) but are, so to speak, contracted into a single point or line. Agamben expresses this relationship through the typographical recourse "force-of-law [*forza-di-legge*]" (SE, 39 [52]). Yet for this to be possible, *law*, as a separate entity limiting and controlling the *force* used in its exercise, is suspended, or even cancelled—which Agamben expresses through the alteration "force-of-~~law~~ [*forza-di-~~legge~~*]" (SE, 39 [52]). Such typographical measures, employed by Agamben's teacher Heidegger—and also often by Derrida—amply reflect the difficulty of finding an adequate expression for such an original structure and the "anomic space" it outlines.

The conclusion that Agamben draws from this contraction and suspension of force and law is not limited to the exceptionality of state structures. Such a juridical form reveals a philosophical relation—one in which "potentiality and act" are "radically separated" (SE, 39 [52]). A reader unfamiliar with Agamben's other works may be surprised to find such terms as *potentiality* and *act* in such a context. He or she might be equally surprised by the suggestion of an *act* or *actuality* separated from the *potentiality* that would precede it. If everything that is actual must have been first possible—for if it had not been possible, then it never could have become actual—how are the two to be separated? How can act be divorced from potentiality? And what does this have to do with the dire political situation that Agamben diagnoses—with the "planetary civil war" toward which he sees us heading?

This reflection on the categories of potentiality and actuality is no new element in Agamben's speculations. Not only has the idea of potentiality (and its avatars, "latency" and "infancy") been at the center of his earlier investigations, but it has also played a central, if at times enigmatic, role in the *Homo sacer* project. As we saw earlier, in a passage from *Homo Sacer* that caused its readers the greatest confusion, Agamben declared that

only an entirely new conjunction of possibility and reality, contingency and necessity . . . will make it possible to cut the knot that binds sovereignty to constituting power. And only if it is possible to think the relation between potentiality and actuality differently—and even to think beyond this relation—will it be possible to think a constituting power wholly released from the sovereign ban. Until a new and coherent ontology of potentiality . . . has replaced the ontology founded on the primacy of actuality and its relation to potentiality, a political theory freed from the aporias of sovereignty remains unthinkable. [HS, 44 (51)]

Although that work does not expand on this point, or offer insight into the form that a thinking that no longer relates potentiality to actuality might take, the question remained at the heart of Agamben's project in the works and years to follow. In the state of exception that Agamben isolates, potentiality and act are "radically separated." Is this not, then, in light of what the first volume of the series longs for (a "new and coherent ontology" that ceases to found itself on "the primacy of actuality"), to be desired? And is this not what is ushering in the "planetary civil war" about which Agamben warns us?

The Real State of Exception

Benjamin's eighth thesis on the philosophy of history reads as follows: "The tradition of the oppressed teaches us that the 'state of exception' [*Ausnahmezustand*] in which we live is the rule. We must arrive at a conception of history that corresponds to this fact. Then we would have before our eyes as our task the bringing about of a *real* state of exception [*wirklichen Ausnahmezustands*] which would better our position in the struggle against fascism" (Benjamin GS, 1.697, italics added). Agamben wrote of this thesis in an essay from 1992 that "fifty years later, Benjamin's diagnosis has . . . lost none of its currency. Since then, the state of emergency[4] has become the rule in every part of our cultural tradition, from politics to philosophy and from ecology to literature" (P, 170 [265]). In a seminal essay from the following year Agamben cites Benjamin's eighth thesis, observing again that "fifty years later" it has lost none of its "relevance" (MWE, 6 [15]). In a citation without quotation from an essay on contemporary politics from 1992, Agamben declares that "*the state of exception is the rule,*" and in these same years he refers to "the new planetary political space in which the exception has become the rule" (MWE, 113 [90], italics in original; MWE, 139 [107], translation modified). "The state of exception," he writes in the book of that name, "has now reached its maximal planetary expansion," and in an essay published that same year he invokes the threat of "a permanent state of exception" (SE, 111; EDL, 44). Connecting this idea to the most controversial paradigm in his writing, Agamben remarked elsewhere that "*the camp is the space which opens when the state of exception starts to become the rule,*" and thereby inscribes his studies of the concentration camps both in these essays and in *Remnants of Auschwtiz* as part of a larger reflection on the idea of a state of exception (MWE, 39 [36], italics in original, translation modified).

To show that this formulation and the "diagnosis" it contains are crucial for Agamben is not, however, to understand them. The "tradition of the oppressed" has an important lesson to teach us, Benjamin writes, but what is this lesson? What is more, how are we to understand the titular "state of exception," and what is to separate it from what Benjamin called a "real state of exception"? The word that Benjamin first introduces in quotation marks—*Ausnahmezustand*—and then adopts as his own is one that he himself has borrowed—from what many have found to be a surprising source: Carl Schmitt. This subtle reference to Schmitt is not the only one of its kind in his work. Benjamin respectfully referred to Schmitt as early as *The Origin of German Tragic Drama,* and two years later, in 1930, he wrote a complimentary letter to Schmitt (see Benjamin GS, 1.245ff.). Benjamin's admiration for the Third Reich's most prominent jurist has often appeared to his commentators as puzzling, and even scandalous. What is more, although the origin of the key term used in this thesis— *Ausnahmezustand*—has been identified as from Schmitt, Benjamin's use of it has remained something of a mystery. No theorist of the twentieth century has been so exhaustively commented on and analyzed in recent years as Benjamin. Yet this attention has been unable to give a coherent account of this enigmatic passage. One of the goals of *State of Exception* is to remedy this lack.

The subtext of the state of exception—and of *State of Exception*—is a covert engagement between Schmitt and Benjamin (which Agamben had begun to reconstruct in an aside in *Homo Sacer*; see HS, 27–28 [33–34]). To this end, Agamben examines not only the "exoteric dossier" on the known—scanty—relations between the two thinkers, which consists of the reference to Schmitt in Benjamin's work on Baroque drama, Benjamin's letter to Schmitt, and a reference by Schmitt to Benjamin in the former's *Hamlet or Hecuba* (1956), written many years after Benjamin's death.[5] Beyond these few established connections, Agamben also examines what he calls the "esoteric dossier" of the case (see SE, 52 [68]). In doing so, he begins by turning the clock of the encounter back several years to Benjamin's "For a Critique of Violence," published in 1921 in a journal that Agamben shows Schmitt regularly read and for which he even wrote. In this early essay Benjamin evokes something he enigmatically calls "pure violence [*reine Gewalt*]," which is described as having no connection to law (see Benjamin GS, 2.183). This violence becomes, for Agamben, the real point of departure for his intellectual exchange with Schmitt, which would reach its highest pitch in the eighth thesis on the philosophy of history. Reversing the customary conception of this relationship as beginning with a work of Schmitt's (*Political Theology*), Agamben traces it first to Benjamin. He then sees Schmitt's celebrated remarks in his *Political Theology* not as the beginning of the exchange but as a response to Benjamin's earlier essay. "Schmitt's doctrine of sovereignty pursued in his *Political Theology*," argues Agamben, "can be read as a punctual response to Benjamin's essay" (SE, 54 [70], translation modified).

"The state of exception," he continues, is then the concept through which "Schmitt responds to Benjamin's assertion of an integrally anomic human action" (SE, 54 [71], translation modified).

In this "esoteric" light, Benjamin's relation to Schmitt is suddenly less scandalous, and more comprehensible. If Agamben's claim is correct, then it was not Schmitt who was controlling the game and its rules of engagement, as had hitherto been thought, but Benjamin. The decisive move in the esoteric conflict between the two theorists—and it is clear that Agamben sees the two as playing a strategic game, or locked in a struggle, with one another—is the enigmatic eighth thesis that Agamben had, as early as 1992, sought to gloss (in "The Messiah and the Sovereign: The Problem of Law in Walter Benjamin").[6] The question that Agamben then endeavors to answer is the question that every one of the theses' interpreters has endeavored to answer: What did Benjamin mean by calling for a "*real* state of exception" (in an earlier version of the theses Benjamin himself underlined the word *real* [*wirklichen*]")? It is difficult to imagine that Benjamin is welcoming here a state of legal exception or emergency like the one that, at the time of his writing, had already reigned in the country of his birth for seven years. His use of the simple adjective *real* implies, however, that a clear distinction is to be made, and that the state of exception in place—which threatened to become the rule—was in one manner or another a *fictive* one. It was of course not fictive in the sense of imaginary—the state of exception was real enough—but its recourse to law and justice, its all-encompassing suspension of individual rights and incorporation of the personal sphere of the state's citizens, seemed to be based on a juridical *fiction* that was at the same time a fiction of justice. Benjamin's intention then appears to have been to stress the falseness of that fiction through the idea of a "real" state of exception that would give the lie to the one that, for him, had become the rule. This idea is perfectly consistent with Agamben's remark in *Homo Sacer* that "the violence that Benjamin defines as divine is situated in a zone in which it is no longer possible to distinguish between exception and rule. It stands in the same relation to sovereign violence as the state of actual exception, in the eighth thesis, does to the state of virtual exception" (HS, 65 [75]). For Agamben, Benjamin's intention, early and late, is a strategic one, and this eighth thesis is explicitly aimed at what Benjamin called elsewhere "bettering our fight against fascism" (Benjamin GS, 1.697). How precisely this "*real* state of exception" is to be distinguished from a "state of exception" increasingly in effect is a dilemma that no commentator has yet succeeded in solving—and it is doubtless such passages in the theses that, as we saw, led Brecht, on first reading them, to think with dismay of how readers were in a position even to *mis*understand them.

It should come as little surprise that Agamben's own position in exploring this difficult distinction in Benjamin's thought has often left his readers uncertain. Kalyvas (2005) observes that "Agamben's assertion that the new politics will be a 'nonstatal and nonjuridical politics' . . . comes dangerously close to the one of an extralegal, permanent (though sovereignless) exception," and in doing so it echoes the reservations to Benjamin's conclusions voiced by readers from Scholem to Habermas (116). De Boever (2006), for his part, has written, "The confusing thing . . . is that the state of exception . . . also emerges in Agamben's work in another light, as a state that should not be avoided but that is, in fact, almost desirable" (153). The current state of exception is indeed not desirable—it is in fact the last thing but desirable. Nevertheless, something that often seems or sounds remarkably similar to it—what Benjamin called "a *real* state of exception"—is for Agamben absolutely desirable.

Agamben's attempt at outlining this deceptive distinction and at glossing this passage is motivated by his sense that in this eighth thesis Benjamin expresses an "undecidability between norm and exception" that he sees as "putting Schmitt's theory into check" (SE, 58 [76]).[7] This decisive move is preceded, however, by several delicate ones. The first of these is Benjamin's positing of a sphere of "anomic human action"—a sphere of action outside the sphere of the law for which he chooses the simple and striking term *violence* [*Gewalt*]. Agamben reads Benjamin's references to "violence" and "pure violence" as denunciatory, strategic—and essentially esoteric. For Agamben, Benjamin is not referring to actual acts of physical violence that he wishes to isolate, glorify, or purify but is instead playing a conceptual game with theorists of the state who instrumentalize the use of violence. His surprising recourse to the term is, for Agamben, a subtle and unexpected move that allows him to surprise—and to checkmate—his conservative opponents.

The real state of exception that Benjamin envisioned has, for Agamben, not only a strategic function but also a positive content. Following Agamben's reading of the eighth thesis, this *real* state of exception is a revolutionary state in which a totally different—and difficult to define—relationship of law to life would prevail. In *Homo Sacer*, Agamben wrote of Kafka's curious conception of law and of the debate Benjamin had on the question with Scholem, adding in his own cryptic gloss, "Law that becomes indistinguishable from life in a real state of exception is confronted by life that, in a symmetrical but inverse gesture, is entirely transformed into law" (HS, 55 [64]). Life entirely transformed into law is a place of nightmarish control. Its mysterious inverse figure, however, seems to offer the greatest promise, and it is this figure that Agamben sees in a "*real* state of exception." Schmitt wanted to retain for the sovereign and the state the instrumental use of violence within a traditional legal context deriving from the distinction between constitutive violence and constituted violence. For Agamben, by showing the impossibility of such, Benjamin suggests a fully different conception of law—one with revolutionary (and messianic) traits in which what is combated and overturned is an entire logic of discipline and control, as well as attribution and possession. The relations of state to law, of law to violence, of individual to collective, and of potentiality to actuality are all to be seen anew in this revolutionary light and messianic life.

Utopianism, Nihilism, and Agamben's Critics

The state of exception represents, for Agamben, a "catastrophic" development. Asked in an interview precisely what he saw as signaling such a catastrophe, he replied, "There is a point—one already noted by Benjamin when he said that the state of exception in which we live has become the rule. I have simply extended this observation to its extreme point. This need not appear as a catastrophe, and can, on the contrary, present itself as something natural. You can find this area of indistinction in everyday life, in that the distinctions between private and public, political and biological, disappear. We no longer have clear criteria to distinguish between these spheres" (UL, 18). Given this radical state of affairs, a radical solution must be sought; and as in Agamben's earlier efforts, it should be sought not in distant models and utopian schemes but instead in the catastrophic process itself. Thirty-three years before *State of Exception* Agamben wrote, "According to the principle by which it is only in the burning house that the fundamental architectural problem becomes visible for the first time, art, at the furthest point of its destiny, makes visible its original project." The political house in flames of today's "planetary state of exception" is one in which Agamben believes its "original project" (or "original structure") can be glimpsed, and it is in this burning house that the perennial problems of Western politics appear to him most clearly. If we can no longer distinguish between these spheres, we must accept—and utilize—this irrevocable fact, to see and understand better not only our point of departure, but also our points of potential arrival.

In the *Homo Sacer* books, the exception becomes the fundamental paradigm for the very functioning of the law because, for Agamben, "the exception is the originary form of law [*la forma originaria del diritto*]" (HS, 26 [32]). Yet, if the exception is the originary form of the law, and this fact is often occulted in legal debates, how is one to bring about its revelation—and what would this revelation effect? Part III of the *Homo Sacer* series, *Remnants of Auschwitz,* laid particular stress on the danger of replacing ethical concepts with juridical ones. If our ethical concepts must be extricated from the paradoxes of sovereignty and the legal systems based on them, what is to be made of the law? Asked whether the aspiration behind the *Homo Sacer* project was somehow "to do away with the law [*das Recht abzuschaffen*]," Agamben replied: "I've often asked myself how one should deal with the law [*wie man mit dem Recht umgehen muss*]. I am, however, very skeptical as concerns the simple demand to do away with the law that we find in some revolutionary movements, and even in some religious ones. Would not the best strategy be to confront the means and methods of law—and to try to invent a potentially new use of the law [*Gebrauch des Rechts*]? In other words, could we play with the law? [*Können wir mit dem Recht spielen?*]" (PWP, 24). This final suggestion, that we might try to "play with the law," is so difficult to envision that we might wonder whether it is a misunderstanding of the sort often found in interviews. If we look, however, to Agamben's work—both early and late—we find that this comment corresponds to his manner of conceiving the problem of sacred privileges and is far less flippant than it risks sounding. Agamben is indeed intent on irreverently toying with law—it is, in fact, one of his most fundamental intentions. In an arc of speculation that stretches from *Infancy and History* to *Profanations,* he offers paradigms for playing with sacred objects protected by the law. But how does this encounter with the idea of the law relate to the idea of the state of exception?

Unsurprisingly, answering this question has led to no small uncertainty among readers and critics. A frequent reaction to *State of Exception*, and to the *Homo Sacer* project more generally, is clarity concerning the diagnosis and uncertainty concerning the remedy. Jenny Edkins (2007) voices a common sense of uncertainty when she asks what is being advocated and observes that "whether Agamben's work calls for an overarching eschatological move of redemption, or a patient politics that moves step by step within the constraints of existing power, is . . . debatable" (73). As concerns the specific question of play, even Agamben's most favorably disposed critics have stressed that "it is difficult to imagine how we might actually take this 'truly political' action, which Agamben calls 'play'" (Morgan 2007, 47). This idea of a disactivated law that is to be played with has seemed cavalier and even incoherent to some readers—particularly those whose background is in law. Legal scholars such as Stephen Humphreys (2006), who finds that "together with *Homo Sacer . . . State of Exception* permits a reinvigoration of the relationship between philosophy and law—to the latter's enrichment" (687), and David Fraser (1999), who writes that "there are possibilities and complexities inherent in Agamben's approach which might allow us to come to a more complete understanding of law and ethics before and after Auschwitz" (406), are far less common than those who argue the contrary to be the case. Fleur Johns (2005), for instance, not only locates what she feels to be a deterministic strain in Agamben's thinking about epochal shifts in legal culture (akin to the one that both Laclau and Norris identify), but also argues that for those working toward judicial reform of states of exception like the one reigning at Guantánamo Bay, "the effect of such commentary [as Agamben's] is to *compound* efforts to curtail the experience of deciding on / in the exception" (634, italics in original). More generally, Fitzpatrick and Joyce (2007) find that "not without a touch of the tendentious . . . we find . . . Agamben instancing persistent irresolutions in jurisprudence and in the field of law and society" (69).

This uncertainty has led to such categorical critiques as that of Paolo Virno (2002), who, as we saw earlier, judged that Agamben was "a thinker with no political vocation" (54).[8] A number of other prominent critics have responded to this uncertainty by characterizing Agamben's political reflections as "utopian." In 2002 Negri remarked of Agamben's guiding concept of "bare life" that it "sounds like a utopian escape" (10). Following the publication of *State of Exception* a year later, Negri found in that work "a feverish utopian anxiety" with the same evasive traits as *Homo Sacer* (2003, 21).[9] LaCapra (2007) also employs this term to articulate his reservations. Of the idea of divorcing legal from ethical concepts, he writes, "The unstated horizon of this view would seem to be an ecstatic, anarchistic Utopia that remains terra incognita and whose relevance to present problems or commitments is left utterly blank" (155). LaCapra thus reaches a similar conclusion as Virno—that Agamben is a thinker with no political vocation, or in his words, "relevance." Elsewhere, LaCapra uses this same term, lamenting "a blank, Utopian, messianic (post)apocalypticism" in Agamben's thought (LaCapra 2007, 161). The recurrent term *blank* expresses all that LaCapra finds lacking in Agamben's political reflections. Carlo Formenti's criticism of the *Homo Sacer* project is also in this vein, as for him it is "more than a refoundation *of* the political, an escape *from* it" (Formenti 1996, 23, italics in original). The question posed here is whether the "*real* state of exception" that Agamben evokes is merely a vague expression and hollow paradigm or, on the contrary, a real *political* response to a dire state of affairs.

Other commentators have seen Agamben, instead of fleeing from the political into utopian speculation, doing something more dangerous: misaligning himself in the political arena. Johann Frederik Hartle (2004) offers a particularly harsh judgment of Agamben's attempt to isolate a "pure violence" in Benjamin's thought, saying of this passage in *State of Exception* that "it sounds nice, but does not mean much, and means especially little when one reads it in relation with what Agamben sees under the sign of a machine made of law and violence." Far from depriving fascism of the means of functioning, Hartle sees Agamben playing into the hands of such forces. "Because this 'off' button of 'mystic' violence seems to lie beyond all real political conflicts," he writes, Agamben's thought is "only poorly protected from right-wing conservative (mis)-interpretations and authoritarian appropriations in the name of a supposedly messianic political subjectivity." In essence, Hartle accuses Agamben of something highly dangerous. Agamben has repeatedly recounted an anecdote about Benjamin told to him by Pierre Klossowski. When confronted with the endeavors of the secret society *Acéphale* (of which Bataille was a member), Benjamin exclaimed, "You are working for fascism!" (see HS, 113 [125]; and BPS, 115). Benjamin was of course not accusing Bataille of knowingly fighting for the enemy but, instead, of unwittingly supplying them with conceptual arms.[10]

For those who are more favorably inclined toward Agamben's political vocation, the question of how to understand the idea of a state of exception remains profoundly uncertain. Giuseppe Goisis (2007), for instance, asks if the harrowing paradigm of the state of exception that threatens to become the rule is meant to "reawaken . . . the intellectual energies and the moral resources" of democracies, or instead is to be understood as "an absolutely realistic paradigm" pointing to the fact that "certain profound dynamics cannot be modified" (283).[11] Goisis leaves the matter undecided, noting simply how much he would like to know "Agamben's genuine point of view on the question" (283–84). When he asks himself this same question of whether Agamben is diagnosing an inoperable disease or merely alerting us to a dangerous state of affairs, Ernesto Laclau (2007) emphatically responds that "political nihilism is [Agamben's] ultimate message" (22). For Laclau, Agamben "draws a picture by which the becoming rule of the exception represents the unavoidable advance towards a totalitarian society" (17). (For his part, Laclau claims to counter such analyses: "I try to determine with the generalization of the 'exceptional,' also countertendencies that make it possible to think about the future in more optimistic terms" [17].)

As we saw earlier, Agamben was fond of remarking, in a paraphrase of Marx, that "the absolutely desperate state of affairs in the society in which I live fills me with hope," and this mixture of denunciation and hope is one that many critics have understandably found difficult to gauge. Concerning Goisis's question, however, it seems that Agamben's "genuine point of view" is that the state of exception is both of these things. Agamben's use of the paradigm is clearly not meant to be paralyzing. On the contrary, his extreme positions on political states of affairs are clearly made with the intent of both shaking readers from dogmatic slumber and instilling the belief that something can still be done to avert impending catastrophe. But these are not mere rhetorical devices employed to attract the reader's attention. They are also paradigms for more precisely understanding our present situation. The question, then, is whether they should be called, as Goisis asks, "absolutely realistic." Following Agamben, a paradigm is at once embedded in a given historical situation and a tool for better understanding "the present situation." These paradigms must then walk a fine line between past and present, and for this reason they require the most careful understanding—at once historical and hermeneutic—if they are to achieve their end.

One of the central issues in such criticisms is a characteristic of Agamben's thought present from the outset, and which we noted in relation to his first book—the proximity of danger to salvation, of poison to remedy, which is as visible in his paradigms for political change as in his initial examination of the arts. Focusing on precisely this point, Thomas Khurana (2007) writes of a "disturbing proximity that makes Agamben's thought at once so fascinating and so precarious" and that, Khurana notes, "appears in a series of exceptionally delicate distinctions," such as the difference between the state of exception that spells disaster and the real state of exception that would be our liberation from it (30). With this point in mind, Khurana judges that "Agamben's project can neither be understood as utopian nor as restorative," and he perceptively shifts the question to "how convincing a political analysis can be in which the promising paradigms of a coming community are so intimately interlaced with the structural characteristics of the status quo under attack" (43). To answer this question we need to look more closely at the precarious proximity of the disastrous state of exception that characterizes our age and at the "*real* state of exception" that would represent our liberation from it.

"The thought of our time finds itself confronted with the structure of the exception in every area," Agamben remarks (HS, 25 [30]).[12] Given this sweeping status, it should come as little surprise that Jan Assmann (2006, 54) has called the state of exception Agamben's *Lebensthema*. If it is the case that, as Agamben stresses, "the thought of our time" is "confronted with the structure of the exception in every area," how then are we to grasp this omnipresent "structure"—and to what end? Elsewhere, Khurana (2002) has written that Agamben's project more closely resembles "a Heideggerian history of being than a Foucaldian archaeology," and that what is at issue is "a conception of political being present in and traversing our past . . . which in the modern era reveals itself as what it always was: biopolitics" (124). He notes that the state of exception that Agamben finds in so many times and places and that he characterizes as "the originary form of the law" is not traced and not traceable as a historical phenomena among others. It has a special status—a structural one—and beneath the changing historical manifestations, from *homo sacer* to *Muselmann* to Guantánamo detainee, lies a latent and identical structure: the state of exception. Khurana notes in this connection that "what is problematic in Agamben's theory of exception is that it is at points close to locating not only the origin of politics in a state of exception, but also in locating the true vocation of all politics in its becoming its own state of exception" (2002, 123). Khurana is singularly sharp-sighted in isolating this issue as the watershed problem raised by the book—the distinction between a state of exception ravaging our political landscape and "a *real* state of exception" that would spell its end. If politics as a separate sphere of human activity arose as a result of a state of exception, and if this exceptional structure has taken on ever more sinister traits in recent history, the answer cannot be sought by somehow magically starting over—and it is this suspicion that led such incisive critics as Virno, Negri, LaCapra, Formenti, and Laclau to isolate something like a utopian element in Agamben's analyses.[13]

The Idea of the Profane

For Agamben, the destructive powers of the state of exception can be neutralized only through what he calls a "real state of exception." However, the state of exception that Agamben sees in the founding of the state is not the same as the "*real* state of exception" he sees as its desired destination. This distinction is one that we can best understand through one of the central ideas of Agamben's recent writing: the idea of the profane.

In the *Homo Sacer* project, the idea of the profane has followed Agamben's studies of the sacred like a shadow. In one of his first published essays he refers to our modern world as one where "a total abolition [*abolizione totale*] of the sacred" has come about (FF, 21). As readers of *Homo Sacer* and its sequels can easily attest, this is a position that he has radically altered. Appearances notwithstanding, a total abolition of the sacred has, in Agamben's view, by no means taken place. Although the sacred has, in our secularized age, receded from view, this retreat has led not to its abolishment but only to its adopting ever more subtle guises. What Agamben sees in the ambiguous figure of *homo sacer* that gave his project its impetus and title—and that he glimpsed in the interstice between the two Greek terms for life, *zoē* and *bios*—was "a figure of the sacred that, before or beyond the religious, constitutes the first paradigm of the political ream of the west" (HS, 9 [12]). This paradigm reveals that, far from being abolished, the idea of the sacred is as present as ever in the divisions and distinctions of contemporary society.

In an essay from 1992, Agamben refers to the task of "the thought to come" as the conceiving of "an absolutely profane life which has attained the perfection of its own potential and of its own communicability and over which sovereignty and law no longer have any hold" (MWE, 114–15 [91]). As we saw in the context of *The Coming Community*, much rides on properly understanding what Agamben sees under the sign of the *profane* and what he calls here "an absolutely profane life." Although a "total abolition of the sacred" has by no means come to pass, we must unconditionally strive for it if an "unprecedented biopolitical catastrophe" is to be averted.

Where are we then to seek such an absolutely profane life—or alternatively, a total abolition of the sacred? In the closing pages of *Homo Sacer*, Agamben, expressing skepticism about the Foucauldian project of discovering a "different economy of bodies and pleasures," states, "Just as the biopolitical body of the West cannot be simply given back to its natural life in the *oikos,* so it cannot be overcome in a passage to a new body—a technical body or a wholly political or glorious body—in which a different economy of pleasures and vital functions would once and for all resolve the interlacement of *zoē* and *bios* that seems to define the political destiny of the West. This biopolitical body that is bare life must itself instead be transformed into the site for the constitution and installation of a form of life that is wholly exhausted in bare life and a *bios* that is only its own *zoē*" (HS, 188 [210]). A "form of life" that could not be placed in a state of sacred exception is a profane life, one where *bios* would coincide with *zoē*. It is thus not the "passage to a new body," but, instead, a reconception of the idea of life. Agamben's intention is not to theorize a new body that would escape the powers of capture and recuperation of a state system—as was the desire of Foucault and, following him, Deleuze—but instead the "free usage" of "bare life" that is, for him, best understood as "profane."

At the end of *Language and Death* it is this empty aspect of the *sacred* that Agamben approaches. He writes of *sacrifice* and the *sacred* in a passage he found important enough to repeat verbatim in another essay that same year:

> However one interprets the sacrificial function, the essential thing is that in every case, the action of the human community is grounded in another action. . . . At the center of the sacrifice is simply a determinate *action* that, as such, is separated and marked by exclusion; in this way it becomes *sacer* and is invested with a series of prohibitions and ritual precepts. Forbidden action, marked by sacredness, is not, however, simply excluded; rather it is now only accessible for certain people and according to determinate rules. In this way, it furnishes society and its ungrounded legislation with the fiction of a beginning: that which is excluded from the community is, in reality, that on which the entire life of the community is founded. [LD, 105 (131), italics in original, translation modified; see also P, 135–136 (188)]

It is precisely against this sacred exclusion as the foundation of the community that Agamben's coming community and his practice of profanation are directed, and it is precisely this "ungrounded legislation" that becomes the central target of a book written nearly twenty-five years after *Language and Death—Profanations.*

In the central chapter of *Profanations,* programmatically entitled "In Praise of Profanation," Agamben chooses a point of departure that, as in *Homo Sacer,* is both juridical and historical. "Roman jurists knew perfectly well what it meant 'to profane,'" Agamben writes, but although they may have been clear as to what it meant, we today lack this clarity and are thereby open to real and terrible dangers (PR, 83). As early as *Language and Death,* Agamben stressed that "the sacred is necessarily an ambiguous and circular notion," and in the works that followed he graphically illustrated this fact (LD, 105 [131–32]). Unsurprisingly, the *profane* also contains ambiguities and circularities in need of clarification.

"Sacred or religious," writes Agamben in *Profanations,* "are those things that belonged in one fashion or another to the gods." For this reason, "they were removed from the free usage [*al libero uso*] and commerce of men, and could not be sold, given as deposit, or ceded in usufruct" (PR, 83). The idea of "sacrilege" stemmed from this sacred exception and its corresponding rules, but for Agamben profanation is best understood in relation to another term: *consecration.* "If consecration was the term that denoted the leaving of the sphere of human law, profanation signified the return to the free usage [*al libero uso*] of mankind" (PR, 83). To know how to profane is to know how to return things that have become subject to a state of sacred exception—things that have been consecrated—to their original—profane—context. "To profane," Agamben thus writes, "does not simply mean to abolish or cancel separations, but to learn to make new uses of them" (PR, 100). The goal of *profanation* is therefore at once to repeal this ungrounded legislation referred to earlier and to find new uses for what remains. "The creation of a new use," Agamben writes, "is only possible through disactivating an old use—rendering it inoperative" (PR, 99). It is for this reason also "a pure means [*un mezzo puro*]"—that is to say, "a means without end [*un mezzo senza fine*]" (PR, 99). The idea of *profanation* is in this respect closely linked to the ideas of *vocation* and the *inoperative*, to *potentiality* and a conception of *means without ends*. At the end of *Language and Death* Agamben writes that "philosophy is precisely the foundation of man [*la fondazione dell'uomo*] as human . . . and the attempt to absolve [*assolvere*] man of his ungroundedness and the unsayability of the sacrificial mystery" (LD, 106 [133], translation modified). It is this sacrificial mystery that will be explored in the ongoing *Homo Sacer* series, as well as in the new perspective offered by *Profanations*. "Pure, profane, and liberated from sacred names," Agamben writes, "is the thing returned to the common use of mankind" (PR, 83).

In "The Critique of Violence"—written in 1919 and 1920—Benjamin made a passing suggestion that lay dormant until Agamben undertook *Homo Sacer*. "It might be worth while," he speculated, "to investigate the origin of the dogma of the sacredness of life" (Benjamin GS, 2.155; cited in HS, 66 [75]). From its title page to its final lines, *Homo Sacer* concerns itself with precisely this—as had, in less direct fasion, earlier works such as *Language and Death* and later ones such as *The Time That Remains, State of Exception, Profanations,* and *Il Regno e la Gloria*. It is this "dogma of the sacredness of life" that Agamben traces to the most remote corners of Western intellectual history. And although his investigation of the idea of "the sacredness of life" is not singular, what he pairs with it—an investigation of the idea of the profaneness of life—is.

Agamben has shown that investigating the origin of the dogma of the sacredness of life has as its corollary demonstrating that this dogma is essentially that—dogma—and that for communities to come it should be replaced by a focus on the "integrally profane" nature of human existence. As he made clear as early as *Language and Death*, the sacred is set apart by nothing so much as the rituals that separate it from the continuum of everyday life, thus creating and cordoning off a sacred space and sacred powers to be wielded over the many by the few. In *Homo Sacer,* Agamben restates this point, stressing that for societies like classical Greece, "life became sacred only through a series of rituals whose aim was precisely to separate life from its profane context" (HS, 66 [76]). Agamben's intention—on particularly clear display in *Profanations*—is to reverse this process and return life to its profane context. Consequently, to profane something—in the special use he ascribes to that activity—is not to defile it but instead to liberate it, to remove it from the sphere of the sacred and free ourselves from the idea that there are some things that are sacred and some that are profane and that they should be held separate lest the hidden balance of the world be lost. In simpler terms, Agamben's conception of the relation of sacred and profane is a *desacralized* one. By his account, there is nothing inherently sacred in sacred things and nothing inherently profane in profane ones. They are categories like others, buttressed by those in whose interest it was to have and hold fast to such distinctions. For Agamben, to profane something is thus in no sense to debase its nature or reduce its value. To profane is, for him, first and foremost a positive act serving to liberate things and practices for communal usage. For this reason, Agamben writes that "pure, profane, and liberated from sacred names is the thing returned to the common use of mankind" (HS, 66 [76]). This chain of adjectives—*pure, profane, free*—shows both the intent of profanation as well as the reason Agamben wishes to praise it. The goal of profanation is to purify and free things of the "sacred names" that cordon them off as the province of the few; it is to return the things of the world to their natural context: "common usage."

Given this view, the return of the things of the world to their original context where they would be subject to free usage seems like a natural movement, but how one is to envision this transition to a purely human context is another matter. One answer to the question of to what one is to return these profaned things is, simply, to the sphere of free usage. In *Means Without End* Agamben had already declared, "that which demands reflection is the possibility and the modalities of a *free usage*" (MWE, 117 [93], translation modified, italics in original). In an interview with the French journal *Vacarme,* he offered an illustration of what he saw as such free usage in the debate that sprang up between the Catholic Church and the Franciscan order over a free usage of the things of the world. Not only did the Franciscans reject the idea that they possessed personal property, but they also refused to accept communal property (in the name of the order). The Church suggested that they classify their manner of living as *droit d'usage* (*usufructus*, as distinguished from the right of ownership). Agamben relates that the Franciscan order retorted (in his own paraphrase), "*Non, ce n'est pas un droit d'usage, c'est de l'usage sans droit* [No, this is not a lawful usage, it is lawless usage]" (BM, 7). This example makes clear that the free usage in question is not simply a usage with a more ample or liberal legal definition, but a usage that categorically rejects the idea of legitimate possession. This "lawless usage" is not a purely anarchic one, but it does reject the paradigms offered by the juridical culture of its day—with the truly revolutionary implication that "lawful usage" as then understood by church and state was far from just. It should then come as no surprise that Agamben returns in *Profanations* to the idea of free usage advocated by the Franciscans and that Pope John XXII responded to with such vehemence (see PR, 94–96).[14] The idea of a lawless usage corresponds to a free usage in which the things of the world—and above all those things and practices that have been consecrated by a sacred few—would be "returned" to their original context.

If one agrees with the necessity of such a revaluation of value, with the need for such a change in our conceptions, how then does one go about profaning? "To profane," we read, "means to open the possibility of a special form of negligence [*negligenza*] that ignores the separation—or rather, makes a particular usage of it" (PR, 85). The first form of this negligence that Agamben offers as paradigmatic easily risks seeming light-hearted, as simply anarchic or unserious—and returns us to a topic raised in relation to the law: play. This too is far from a new concern for Agamben, and the movement from rite to game and the profanizing of sacred practices is something that Agamben first studied in the essay "In Playland: Reflections on History and Play," a largely structuralist attempt (the essay is dedicated to Levi-Strauss) to understand the "systems" and "mechanisms" whereby rites become profaned—which is to say, become games—and vice versa. "The majority of our games," Agamben observes in *Profanations*, building on these earlier reflections, "derive from ancient and sacred ceremonies, from rituals and divinatory practices that belonged for a time to the religious sphere" (PR, 85–86). He then cites a series of such games—ball games "that reproduce the gods' struggles to possess the sun," and such objects as the spinning top and the chessboard that were initially divinatory instruments. The conclusion that Agamben draws is that "this signifies that the game liberates and diverts humanity from the sphere of the sacred, but without simply abolishing it" (PR, 86). Abolition would invite a restoration—a dialectical reversal that would reinstate the sacred. The change that Agamben wishes to effect would be more radical and more durable.

However, and as Agamben points out, recourse to games and play is not a simple activity in our day and age—above all because "the game as means of profanation has fallen into disuse" (PR, 87). This does not mean that games as such have disappeared from our culture—on the contrary, they are more present than ever. But they do not play the profanizing role that Agamben identified in earlier cultures. "That modern man no longer knows how to play," he writes, "is to be seen precisely in the vertiginous multiplication of old and new games" (PR, 87). What one finds in these new games is not a profanizing instrument or force, but a "desperate and obstinate" search to "return to the lost festival [*alla festa perduta*], a return to the sacred and its rites" (PR, 87). "In this sense, the televised games for the masses are part of a new liturgy, secularizing an unconsciously religious intention" (PR, 87–88). For this reason, "To return the game to its purely profane vocation [*alla sua vocazione puramente profana*] is a political task" (PR, 88).

Agamben seeks in the profane a response to the sovereign state of exception and the logic of sacrality on which it depends. In light of Agamben's idea of the profane, the dissimilar books *Homo Sacer, Remnants of Auschwitz, The Time That Remains, State of Exception, Profanations,* and *Il Regno e la Gloria* are ultimately responses to the same problem, and all envision special and paradigmatic forms for playing with sacred objects so as to effect their desacralization. A state of exception extended without limit would be a *real* state of exception with, as corollaries, a truly exceptional state and a truly exceptional existence in which the violent divisions of sovereignty and sacrality, with their instrumentalization of partial states of exception, would be rendered inoperative. Such a *"real* state of exception" would correspond to a world that is "integrally profane"—a world that had employed the devices of profanation so as to disarm the sovereign order and suspend the divisions between the sacred and the profane.

When seen in this light, a long arc of Agamben's work becomes visible. The concern with sacrality raised at the end of *Language and Death* is taken up with greater focus and intensity more than ten years later, and it is this idea that links such dissimilar books as the scholarly *Homo Sacer* and the more personal *Profanations*. These books approach the same idea from radically different sides—*Homo Sacer* from the side of law, *The Time That Remains* and *Il Regno e la Gloria* from the side of theology, *Profanations* from the side of personal experiences—with the goal of defining a *real* state of exception that would also form a truly profane order.

The fictive state of exception that maintains a distinction between sacred and profane, immanence and transcendence, that which is within the juridical order and that which is beyond it must, for Agamben, be replaced if we are to avoid a "planetary civil war"—and the remedy lies periously close to the poison. In 1993, Agamben had already written, "before extermination camps are reopened in Europe (something that is already starting to happen), it is necessary that the nation-states find the courage to question the very principle of the inscription of nativity as well as the trinity of state-nation-territory that is founded on that principle" (MWE, 24 [27]). For Agamben, if we want to abandon as our "biopolitical paradigm" the concentration camp, we must bring about a *real* state of exception, an integrally actual and integrally profane order in which the destructive distinctions between sacred and profane, the exception and the norm, the singular and the universal are neutralized—and put behind us. They are not to be somehow magically destroyed, not to be annihilated from the memory of man, but instead are to be seen in a new light—the same light that Agamben elsewhere calls messianic and that we will turn to shortly. In such a profane order, distinctions would continue to exist; all persons and all objects would not float freely in a space without meaning, but they would cease to have the divisive force they carry today; they would cease to be instruments in the hands of those in power. At such a moment we could literally "toy" with them, because they would have become relics, and they would be open to whatever new usages lie at hand. Although this subtle coherence of Agamben's interests is often missed in analyses of his thought, it does not, however, offer a concrete answer, or a definite paradigm, for how we would "invent a new use of the law," and for the moment this remains the most pressing question to be posed to Agamben's political philosophy—a question that the essays and books to come will, his readers can only hope, seek to answer.

In a crucial passage from *Remnants of Auschwitz,* Agamben speaks of a singularly dangerous process, alluded to earlier—what he calls the contamination of ethical concepts by legal ones. "As jurists well know," he remarks, "law is not directed toward the establishment of justice. Nor is it directed toward the verification of truth. Law is solely directed toward judgment, independent of truth and justice" (RA, 18 [16]). At the end of *State of Exception,* Agamben states that "politics has suffered a lasting eclipse because it has become so contaminated by law" (SE, 88 [112]). For this reason, "to show law in its nonrelation to life and, consequently, life in its non-relation to law, means to open between the two terms a space for human action" (SE, 88 [112], translation modified). What Agamben is then striving for is the realization of another—a *real*—state of exception open enough for the potentiality to think, to act, and to live to be given free reign.

Scholium I: Adorno, Profanity, and the Secular Order

There are few thinkers whose concerns coincide with Agamben's so often as Adorno's. Given this fact, it is surprising how rarely Agamben refers to Adorno. Asked about this, Agamben remarked, "My relation to Adorno has taken place from the beginning under the sign of Benjamin."[15] After the essay in *Infancy and History* centered around an exchange of letters between Benjamin and Adorno, the latter is only rarely referred to or cited in Agamben's work—even when Agamben's reader might most expect it. In *Homo Sacer* Agamben claims that "today it is not the city but rather the camp that is the fundamental biopolitical paradigm of the West" (HS, 181 [202]). Although Agamben does not mention the precedent, he was not the first student of Benjamin's to see such a dark figure at the heart of our era. Before he questioned the status of poetry after Auschwitz, Adorno wrote, in an essay composed in 1939 and 1940 as reports about the conditions in German concentration camps began to filter through to him in American exile, that our age was the "age of the concentration camp" (Adorno GS, 10.286). Considering the fame of Adorno's categorical imperative concerning Auschwitz ("that Auschwitz not happen again . . . that it not repeat itself"; see Adorno GS, 10.674) and his remarks on art after Auschwitz ("after Auschwitz, writing a poem is barbaric"; Adorno GS, 10.30; see also Adorno GS, 6.355), it is indeed surprising that they are not even mentioned in the sections on categorical imperatives and art in *Remnants of Auschwitz*. In addition, Adorno's denunciation of "the nothingness that the concentration camp demonstrated to its subjects"; of the "drastic guilt of the one who was spared" in Auschwitz and who, "in revenge for being spared will be visited by dreams, such as that he did not survive"; of the invocation of a "bare life [*bloßem Leben*]"; as well as of the idea that the failure of culture that Auschwitz emblematizes "irrefutably proved" the invalidity of Kant and Hegel's faith in freedom are ideas that one might have expected Agamben to invoke here and that he does not (Adorno GS, 4.14, 6.356, 6.368, 6.359).[16] In *Remnants of Auschwitz* Agamben refers to Adorno in passing, and rather dismissively, at the conclusion of his discussion of Heidegger's dialectic of death, stating there that "the ambiguity of our culture's relation to death reaches its paroxysm after Auschwitz. This is particularly evident in Adorno, who wanted to make

Auschwitz into a kind of historical watershed" (RA, 80 [75]).[17] Considering the similarity—or at least the proximity—of their reflections, one of the surprises that *Remnants of Auschwitz* offers is that Adorno and his strident proclamations do not play any significant role therein.

Another point of equally close proximity and subtle, and silent, divergence is found in the idea that lends Agamben's *Profanations* its title. Adorno wrote to Benjamin that he planned to make himself "the advocate of theological motifs in your—and, perhaps I might say, my own—philosophy." He went on to write of "saving" theology through what he saw as Benjamin's "alterations" of theology (Adorno and Benjamin 1994, 324 [323]). Adorno also noted wherein he saw these alterations lying—in what he called theology's "immigration into profanity [*Einwanderung in der Profanität*]" (324 [323]). In the same letter he also wrote of "making the power of theological experience anonymously available in profanity [*die Kraft der theologischen Erfahrung anonym in der Profanität mobil zu machen*]" (324 [323]).

This much of Adorno's declared intention appears identical to Agamben's efforts in *Profanations* and the studies leading up to it. Years later, however, Adorno would return to the idea of the profane and to the movement of theological experience into its realm, writing that "nothing of theological content will remain unchanged; everything must be put to the test of immigrating into the secular, the profane" (Adorno GS, 10.608). Here Adorno returns to the idea of an "immigration into profanity" while appending to it a second term—the *secular*. And it is here that we find a crucial divergence between Adorno's and Agamben's praise of profanation. Whereas for Adorno the profane and the secular could be named in a single breath and as a single destination, for Agamben it is imperative that they be clearly distinguished from one another.

"Profanation is something completely different from secularization," Agamben remarked in a recent interview. "Secularization takes something from the sacred sphere and *seems* to return it to the worldly sphere. But in this case power's mechanisms are not neutralized. When theological power is transformed into secular power, this provides a foundation for secular power. But secularization never truly does away with the sacred. And it is for this reason not a good solution to our problem—on the contrary. We must neutralize this relation to the sacred—that is what profanation first makes possible" (PWP, 22, italics in original).[18] This is the last thing but an isolated line of reflection, and it is to this point that Agamben returns in *Profanations,* where he writes that "secularization is a type of removal which leaves forces intact, which limits itself to moving them from one place to another" (PR, 88). For this reason he claims that the political secularization of theological concepts "only displaces the celestial monarchy into a terrestrial one" (PR, 88). In light of the "political task" currently facing us, we must, he argues, "distinguish between secularization and profanation" (PR, 88).[19]

Agamben's adoption of Benjamin's idea of the profane differs from Adorno's interest in that same concept through its separation of secularization and profanation. Although Adorno sets the two terms alongside one another, Agamben opposes them, and in so doing he clarifies what he sees as the function and goal of profanation. For Agamben, the change that secularization brings about is a superficial one: it *seems* to return something from the otherworldly to the worldly sphere, but this is often deceptive. Secularization may appear to liberate ideas and things from the sacred sphere in which they had dwelt, but, actually, that process only changes the location of the closed-off area. For Agamben, secularization "conserves" the divisions inhering in theological concepts, merely displacing their center of power while retaining their structure and their illegitimate privileges. What he envisions under the sign of profanation is more radical. In his words, secularization does not "do away with the sacred"— and that is precisely the goal of his profanations.

Scholium II: Carl Schmitt, or Politics and Strategy

The prominence of Carl Schmitt in Agamben's political writings of the last twenty years has surprised and troubled many readers. Schmitt not only theorized a state of exception, he also helped bring about an effective declaration of such a state. In 1934 he prominently supported Hitler's mounting sovereignty and, in 1936, wrote of the need to purify German legal culture of the "Jewish mentality [*jüdischem Geist*]" he saw corrupting it. A year later he began to recede from the important role he had hitherto played in the Nazi party and their violent state of exception, later claiming that he underwent an "inner emigration." In 1945, Schmitt was arrested and imprisoned by the Allied authority. Upon his release in 1950 he was forbidden from playing any role in the legal or academic institutions or debates of the day, and he lived out the rest of his long life (he died in 1985 at the age of 96) guarding a defiant silence on the question of his personal responsibility. This silence appears to have been broken only in discussions he had late in his life with the Jewish philosopher Jacob Taubes, who felt their talks were subject to the same rules of secrecy as religious confession.

In an essay on Agamben, Daniel Binswanger (2005) spoke for many when he observed how "remarkable is the renaissance of the political philosophy of Carl Schmitt"—in particular, what Binswanger characterized as "the fascination on the Left for the conservative revolutionary and later 'crown jurist' of the Third Reich" (6). The confusions in which Agamben's studies of Schmitt have resulted are nowhere on more striking display than in an essay by the editor of the first English-language work on *Homo Sacer,* Andrew Norris, whose dismissal of Agamben's paradigmatic method is linked to the role Schmitt played in Agamben's thought. "Unfortunately," Norris declares, "Agamben's acceptance of Schmitt's decisionism makes it impossible for his analyses to have any general validity."[20] "Perhaps worse," Norris continues, "it puts [Agamben] in the position of deciding on the camp victims one more time, thereby repeating the gesture of the SS in precisely the way he says we must avoid" (Norris 2005, 278). The flaws in Norris's analogy between philosophical argumentation and legal declaration are noted in an earlier chapter, but what we should attend to here is the extent to which Agamben is seen by such an informed reader as uncritically accepting Schmitt's ideas and, what is more, dangerously close to complicit with past crimes.

This note sounded by Binswanger and Norris is indeed not the only one heard in the critical literature on Agamben. Anselm Haverkamp (2004, 321) has written that "*Homo Sacer* confronts and refutes Schmitt's mythic superstructure of the exception with its proto-typical application in Roman law"; and Sarah Pourciau (2005, 1089) has aptly characterized that book as "an attempt to think the Schmittian political from the inside out." Deeming Agamben's use of Schmitt's ideas as a reflection on those ideas from the inside out is a provocative suggestion, and one where Agamben is seen as not merely following Schmitt's dark lead; but the question remains as to how we might better understand this relationship. Four elements seem worth noting here. The first concerns a general mystery; the second, Benjamin; the third, the law; and the fourth, strategy.

The enigma of a man of Schmitt's formidable acumen and erudition making the political decisions he did is every bit as remarkable, and every bit as disconcerting, as Heidegger's very different case. In many respects it is still more disconcerting given the far more profound influence that Schmitt had on the course of events. This individual mystery, which motivated such visitors as Taubes and Alexandre Kojève to seek Schmitt out, bears noting, but this is not something that Agamben focuses on or that plays any explicit role in his reflections. Turning to the second element, just as many of Agamben's readers find Schmitt's presence in his works surprising, and even scandalous, so too do readers of Benjamin (as we saw earlier). Although this parallel answers no questions concerning Agamben's interest in Schmitt's ideas, it does point to one of the paths that led Agamben there. As is on particularly clear display in *State of Exception,* Agamben endeavors to understand the riddling relationship between Benjamin and Schmitt—and to see it in a new light. The third element contributing to Agamben's interest in Schmitt also dates from the beginning of Agamben's career—his legal studies. Agamben's criticism of legal conceptions—such as sovereignty—as well as his more general critique of the manner in which legal conceptions have served as stand-in's for ethical ones, is informed by Schmitt's example. The critique of the law, and the need to distinguish ethical conceptions from legal ones, finds, for Agamben, a test case in Schmitt. The fourth, final, and most important element is strategic.

As is particularly clear in *Means Without End* and *Homo Sacer,* Agamben's idea of political philosophy is intimately linked to his conception of political strategy, and as is equally clear in *State of Exception* and *Il Regno e la Gloria* Agamben finds Schmitt a formidable strategist. What is at issue in the latter's reflections are nothing less than our most fundamental political conceptions. As he stressed in his discussions of Debord, Agamben is profoundly interested in the strategic possibilities present in political conceptions. That he began to write about Schmitt during the period in which he was exploring "the paradox of sovereignty" should then come as no surprise.[21] Far from uncritically accepting Schmitt's ideas on political theology, however, Agamben clearly aspires to oppose Schmitt's strategic shaping of such conceptions as sovereignty and its defining state of exception. If Agamben is to illustrate successfully the illegitimacy of certain systematic uses of state power, and to retrace the theological origins of our political conceptions, then he has every reason to engage with one of its most subtle and resourceful defenders.[22]

CHAPTER TEN

The Messiah, or On the Sacred
and the Profane

No idea is so central to Agamben's philosophy of potentiality, and none plays so enigmatic a role therein, as the "messianic." Agamben frequently invokes "messianism," "the Messiah," "messianic time," "the messianic event," "the messianic Kingdom," "petrified messianism," "messianic displacement," "messianic concepts," and "the concept of the messianic." Yet what precisely he envisions under the sign of the messianic is far from self-evident. If we turn to the critical literature for clarification, we find the term used with equal frequency by Agamben's interpreters, but the simple if difficult question of what is meant by it is rarely raised, with both defenders and detractors seeming to take its meaning for granted. LaCapra (2007, 161), for instance, denounces a "a blank, utopian, messianic (post) apocalypticism" in Agamben's thought, and although we can easily gather that he is lamenting this state of conceptual affairs, the role of messianism therein is not immediately clear. At the other end of the critical spectrum, Heller-Roazen (1999) notes that "whether the subject is Aristotle or Spinoza, Heidegger or Benjamin, what is at issue [in Agamben's writing] is always a messianic moment of thinking in which the practice of the 'historian' and the practice of the 'philologist,' the experience of tradition and the experience of language, cannot be told apart" (1). Here the messianism in question is clearly a virtue, but its precise nature is, again, left for the reader to formulate. Does Agamben's idea of the *messianic* refer to something to come, something that is here, or something already come and gone—to something in this world, something in another, or something in both? Is the "Messiah" merely a metaphor, or is it something more? If it is the former, what is the figural meaning it is meant to convey? And if it is the latter, what is that something and how should we understand it? Whatever else they are, *Messiah, messianic,* and *messianism* are quintessentially theological terms. To answer these questions, we might then begin by clarifying Agamben's idea of theology.

Agamben's Idea of Theology, or
The Blotting-Paper and the Ink

Few aspects of Agamben's thought are so difficult to grasp as the role of theology. To begin with an exemplary work from the middle of Agamben's career, *The Coming Community* presents characteristic challenges in this regard. Published in the immediate aftermath of the fall of communism, the book seems to be first and foremost—to borrow a chapter title from the work that preceded it—a reflection on "the idea of communism," offering as it does a series of provocative paradigms through which the ideas of community and communism might be newly conceived. References to debates about the status of identity and difference and about the relation of part to whole in communist theory and praxis abound therein and chapters such as "Without Classes" and "Tiananmen" clearly invoke both a laudable communist idea (a society without classes) and the deplorable results of certain attempts to bring it about. In short, much points to our understanding Agamben's coming community as an essentially communist one. Yet no sooner is this noted than a glaring contradiction seems to arise. The coming community that Agamben evokes is clearly not *only* a political one. References in the book to Aquinas and Augustine; to halos, limbo, and purgatory; to the Kabbalah, Halacha, Haggadah, Skekinah, and Tikkun all clearly direct the reader's attention toward religious paradigms for life in such a community. Yet are these two fields of reference not mutually exclusive? Does not the novelty of communism lie in its dismissal of conceptions of inclusion or exclusion based on religious belief, and is not its founding gesture a dismissal of religion as the organizing principle of community? How do we then reconcile these communist elements with the theological ones, and what might they have to do with the central figure of these discussions—the Messiah?

To answer these questions we should begin by observing that

religious and communist paradigms are by no means opposed to one another in *The Coming Community.* They are, on the contrary, intimately linked. Aquinas and Augustine, limbo, halos, and even the Shekinah are all evoked in *The Coming Community* as paradigms for conceiving of a community no longer based on exclusive conditions of belonging. This is equally true for the more central terms *Messiah* and *messianic*, which, in Agamben's hands, prove so difficult to grasp. At first sight, the idea of the messianic seems simply and irreducibly religious, and any attempt to understand it as anything else incoherent. We might then well ask, if the Messiah is not a religious figure, who or what is? Yet given Agamben's vehement rejection of all models of history based on the idea of a culminatory event, the idea of the messianic—of a Messiah to come (or to return)—seems to run counter to the vision of history he has espoused since the beginning of his career. In the place of such models of history, Agamben appeals to what Benjamin called a "now-time" and what he himself calls a "kairology." Everything about Agamben's approach seems to exclude such millennial expectations and mystical interventions as are so often expressed in the idea of a coming, or returning, Messiah.

For Agamben, the proximity of messianic and Marxist ideas has an important precedent, first discussed in Chapter Three in relation to *Infancy and History.* Throughout Benjamin's career—but particularly in the notes leading up to and including his *Theses on the Philosophy of History*—he linked Marx's communist conceptions with messianic ones. Benjamin appears to have been prompted to write these theses by the shock he experienced on learning of the Hitler-Stalin pact in August 1939. Shortly after their completion, he read them aloud to his friend Soma Morgenstern. In a letter written years later to Scholem, Morgenstern recounts this event, noting his surprise at the amount of faith Benjamin had placed in the Soviet project,[1] and telling of his having asked Benjamin at this time whether he had noticed that his faith in Marxism-Leninism "was related to the Jewish belief in the redemption of the world through a Messiah" (Benjamin GS, 7.772). Morgenstern reports that Benjamin replied—"not without irony"—"you might go farther and say that Karl Marx and all of nineteenth-century socialism is but a different form of messianic faith" (Benjamin GS, 7.772–7.773). This remark made of Marx and his socialist fellow-travelers secularizing thinkers of the messianic—whether they were aware of it or not. That this was for Benjamin more than a merely occasional, or ironic, idea can be seen in the *Handexemplar* of his *Theses* that was lost after his flight from Paris and that Agamben rediscovered in the *Bibliothèque Nationale.* It contains an additional thesis in which Benjamin writes that "in his conception of the classless society, Marx secularized the conception of messianic time" (Benjamin GS, 1.1231). To this observation Benjamin appended an appraisal: "And he did well to" (Benjamin GS, 1.1231). It was precisely this bringing together of such strange bedfellows that, as we saw in connection with *Infancy and History,* mystified so many readers of Benjamin's *Theses,* including such friends as Scholem, Adorno, and Brecht. Where these diverse thinkers saw a glaring inconsistency concerning religion and communism, messianism, and Marxism, Benjamin saw a subtle parallel—as does Agamben.[2]

Asked in an interview why he so frequently returns to religious or theological motifs in his work, Agamben answered, "I think that it is only through metaphysical, religious, and theological paradigms that one can truly approach the contemporary—and political—situation" (PWP, 22). Agamben's interviewer then asked, "And how close does one thereby come to the doctrine of a Divinity?" to which Agamben replied:

My books . . . are confrontations with theology. Walter Benjamin once wrote: my relation to theology is like that of blotting paper to ink. The paper absorbs the ink, but if it were up to the blotting paper, not a single drop would remain. This is exactly how things stand with theology. I am completely steeped in theology, and so then there is no more; all the ink is gone. [PWP, 22]

In characteristic fashion, Agamben presents the role of theology in his thought through an enigmatic figure borrowed from Benjamin. This is not the first time he has employed this image; he cited it both in an essay on Benjamin in 1982 and in an introduction to Caproni's *Res amissa* in 1991.[3] These repeated references make clear how apt an image he finds it, but we might well ask what precisely Benjamin—and through him, Agamben—is trying to express through it.

The remark to which Agamben is alluding is from Benjamin's *Arcades Project* and reads as follows: "My thinking is to theology what the blotting paper is to ink. The latter is completely steeped in the former. Were it up to the blotting paper, nothing that was written would remain [*Mein Denken verhält sich zur Theologie wie das Löschblatt zur Tinte. Es ist ganz von ihr vollgesogen. Ginge es aber nach dem Löschblatt, so würde nichts was geschrieben ist, übrig bleiben*]" (Benjamin AP, 471; GS, 5.588, translation modified). In this singular analogy, Benjamin equates the blotting paper to his thinking and theology to ink. If it were up to his thinking (to the blotting paper), there would be no theology (ink) left. Following the logic of the metaphor, his thinking would fully absorb theology and nothing of it would remain visible on the page. Yet this leaves us with an important question: What are we to make of what *does* remain on the page?

To answer this question demands of the reader something difficult: to grasp Benjamin's conception of theology. From his first writings to his last, Benjamin employed the most varied theological motifs—from his iconic angel of history to the figure of the Messiah, from "catastrophe" to "redemption." What is more, he did so in *esoteric* fashion. In a statement of philosophical purpose, Benjamin wrote in a letter from 1931, "I have never been able to study or to think in other than—if I might say so—a theological manner—and namely one that follows the Talmudic doctrine of the forty-nine levels of meaning contained in every passage of the Torah" (Benjamin 1966, 2.524). Although he stridently opposed what he found to be the hollow and schematizing theological interpretations of Kafka produced by "the school of Prague" (principally by Max Brod), he nevertheless read Kafka in the light cast for him by theology—even if it was, as he once called it, "theology on the run" (see Benjamin GS, III.277).[5] In the preface to *The Origin of German Tragic Drama*, Benjamin notes that his use of the scholastic term *tractatus* therein is a "subtle allusion to theological matters" and that without such devices "it is impossible to think of truth" (Benjamin GS, 1.208). In a letter to Max Rychner endeavoring to clarify the esoteric elements in that same preface, Benjamin was still more explicit, claiming that "one can only understand [it] if one knows the Kabbalah" (Benjamin GS, 1.885).[6]

In a passage to which Agamben pays special attention at the close of *The Time That Remains*, Benjamin compares "theology" to a "small and ugly figure that by no means is to be seen," but whose concealed presence can ensure the victory of historical materialism over its enemies (Benjamin GS, 1.693). This tiny parable is from the first of Benjamin's *Theses*. Upon first hearing them, Morgenstern deduced that "all following theses are a development of this first one" (GS, 7.772). Later in the *Theses* Benjamin employs further theological figures such as "messianic force," "messianic time," and "a messianic freezing of events" that he describes as "a revolutionary opportunity in the fight for the oppressed past" (Benjamin GS, 1.694, 1.703). In a crucial fragment from his *Arcades Project*, Benjamin says of our "experience" of the special form of remembrance he calls *Eingedenken* that it "as little allows us to conceive of history as a-theological as it allows us to write history in unmediated theological terms" (Benjamin GS, 5.589).[7] Benjamin's method then became to think and to write through theological figures—but never to do so in "unmediated terms," thus keeping the figure of theology concealed beneath the strategic surface of his works.

With this in mind we can return to the evocative image of theology and writing that Agamben adopts and venture an interpretation of it. If thought absorbs theology so fully that one does not see it on the page, this does not mean that theology is absent. On the contrary, it is present in every word of every line. At the end of *Il Regno e la Gloria* Agamben praises a passage from Bossuet in which the latter envisions God having created the world as if there were no God (RG, 314). In a similar vein, one of the final fragments in *The Coming Community* reads, "The world—insofar as it is absolutely, irreparably profane—is God" (CC, 89 [74]). To experience the world as "irreparable"—transient in its passing and unchangeable in its past—and "profane" by no means requires that one deny the existence of God. One might just as well equate every atom and instant of the world with such a Divinity.

The Messiah

Although the preceding discussion addresses both the relation of messianism to Marxism and the invisible, or barely visible, presence of theological concepts in Agamben's writing, it does not account for all of the places where Agamben directly employs theological figures, or for that matter, what, precisely, he understands under the crucial heading "the messianic." Agamben is indeed often drawn to theological figures and, fittingly enough, to none so intensely as the Messiah. As we glimpsed earlier in this book, Agamben's references to the Messiah, messianic time, and the messianic are frequent and play an essential role in his reflections. Yet, as has also been noted, no idea has so thoroughly perplexed, and even frustrated, his readers. Messianic time is an idea we encountered and elucidated earlier in this book. What then of the messianic and the Messiah?

In *Means Without End* Agamben writes that "the Messiah is the figure in which religion confronts the problem of the law," and in *Homo Sacer* he writes that "the Messiah is the figure in which the great monotheistic religions sought to master the problem of law" (MWE, 135 [104], translation modified; HS, 56 [65]). The Messiah is thus a "figure" that allows us to see better a historically decisive confrontation between the claims of religion and those of law. Agamben writes that "in Judaism, as in Christianity or Shiite Islam, the Messiah's arrival signifies the fulfillment and the complete consummation of the Law" (HS, 56 [65]). The consequence he draws from this is that "in monotheism, messianism thus constitutes not simply one category of religious experience among others but rather the limit concept of religious experience in general" (HS, 56 [65]).

Although this is a great deal to see under the heading of the messianic, Agamben sees still more. Just as for him the state of exception is not a category of political experience among others but instead marks the limit of *political* experience, messianism marks the limit of *religious* experience and the point where it confronts questions of law. This limit, however, does not link religion only with law. Elsewhere Agamben writes that "messianism represents the point of greatest proximity between religion and philosophy," and he echoes this position in an interview in which he notes that "because philosophy is constitutively bound up in a confrontation with the law [*un confronto con la legge*], the messianic represents the point of greatest proximity between religion and philosophy" (P, 163 [255]; LSP, 44). The figure of the Messiah is thus a figure standing at the crossroads of *law, religion,* and *philosophy.* But locating *where* this figure stands is but one element in understanding its role in Agamben's thought.

Because so many of Agamben's references to the Messiah, messianic time, and the messianic are made in the context of discussions of Benjamin's work, here too the best way to approach the question is through that which so mystified readers such as Adorno, Scholem, and Brecht and so clearly entrances Agamben: *Benjamin's* idea of the messianic. The most famous and most enigmatic of Benjamin's fragments, his early "Theologico-Political Fragment," begins with the Messiah.[8] "Only the Messiah himself," he writes, "completes all historical occurrence, in the sense that He alone redeems, completes, creates [*erlöst, vollendet, schafft*] its relation to the messianic" (Benjamin SW, 3.305; GS, 2.203). In the tradition in which Benjamin is writing, these opening lines present no great interpretative difficulties. The Messiah will come, and when He does, that coming will "complete" human history. For Christians, the Messiah has already come—and until His Second Coming He offers redemption by visiting the individual hearts of mankind. In this sense, redemption through Christ occurs in the private world of each individual touched by grace. In the Jewish tradition in which Benjamin is writing, however, redemption through the Messiah is nothing of this sort. Not only has the Messiah not yet come, but what is awaited when He does arrive is not an individual experience but instead a communitarian—a public and political—event that will take place, to borrow Scholem's canonic definition, "on the stage of history and within the [Jewish] community" (Scholem 1972, 1).

Whereas the first clause in Benjamin's fragment is perfectly uncontroversial, the second clause asserts something that has long divided messianic thought. Therein Benjamin writes of the Messiah that "He alone redeems, completes, creates its relation to the messianic." Benjamin seems to say here that we can do nothing to influence the relation of human history to the Messiah, nothing to hasten or slow His arrival. It is the Messiah who not only "redeems" and "completes," but also "alone . . . *creates*" a relation to human affairs and human history. Although this is a point of some controversy, it is nevertheless clearly part of the messianic tradition. The question that the fragment raises, however, is how Benjamin moves from this more or less orthodox conception of the Messiah and His coming to, at the end of the fragment, a "method" called "nihilism" that, so he claims, is nothing less than "the task of world politics [*die Aufgabe der Weltpolitik, deren Methode Nihilismus zu heißen hat*]"; (Benjamin GS, 2.204).

To understand this singular constellation of ideas, we must note that for Benjamin *nihilism* has none of its customary negative connotations. For a thinker like Nietzsche, nihilism is an all-too-human consequence of "the death of God" and of the "devaluation of all values" that follows in its wake. Such "nihilism," however, is far from what one could call a "method" having something decisive to offer "world politics" (although it could of course be a precursor to such). The nihilism that Benjamin has in mind, however, is closer to the anarchism of the Russian "nihilists" (such as Nikolai Chernyshevsky and Dmitri Pisarev). We will return to what Benjamin might mean by his nihilistic method, but for the moment it is essential to note that Benjamin's conception of nihilism is difficult to grasp, above all because of its unconventional valorization. The link, however, between this most positive of presences, the Messiah, and the "method" that Benjamin calls "nihilism" is fully comprehensible only through two other terms that play decisive roles in Benjamin's fragment: *transience* and the *profane*.

Benjamin continues his reasoning in this fragment by noting that "the rhythm of this eternally transient worldly existence, transient in its totality, in its spatial but also in its temporal totality, the rhythm of messianic nature, is happiness [*der Rhythmus, dieses ewig vergehenden, in seiner Totalität vergehenden, in seiner räumlichen, aber auch zeitlichen Totalität vergehenden Weltlichen, der Rhythmus der messianischen Natur, ist Glück*]" (Benjamin SW, 3.306; GS 2.204). Two things are asserted here and both of them are surprising. Benjamin looks at the world and sees "transience"— complete and total "transience." This emphasis is far from self-evident. *Transience* is of course an essential part of our experience of the world and makes for much of the beauty we find in it. We are moved by its fragility, by the unimaginable touch of time that will soon take it from us. For this reason, transience is at the heart of poetry, but it is also, less evidently, at the heart of philosophy. It is, on the contrary, far easier to claim that transience is opposed to philosophy, for if philosophy is about things that are not just temporarily and contingently true but that also pretend to universal validity, they cannot be founded only on the basis of things that are ceaselessly passing away. Plato's project of "saving appearances" was to show that this *transience*, this continual passing away of the things of the world, was not the ultimate reality of human existence but, instead, merely its imperfect reflection. Things do not *really* pass away, for as Plato said in the *Timaeus*, "the creator of the world constructed a moving image of eternity, and in ordering the heavens he made this image eternal but moving according to the laws of number, while eternity itself rests in unity, and this image we call time" (Plato, *Timaeus*, 37d; 1167). The seeming transience of this world is redeemed by the real eternity of another.

In the Christian redemption of the transitory, this eternity is given a single divine face and it is the loving and watchful eye of God whose grace transforms the transient into the lasting, and the desultory into the meaningful. In the Gospels of both Matthew and Luke, we hear this vigilance extended even to the most insignificant elements of our worldly existence and mortal person, and we are told that even "the very hairs of your head are all numbered" (*Matthew* 10:30; *Luke* 12:7). In a world in which everything seems to pass away, in which everything is consigned to ruin and loss, there is a principle that preserves everything. In both classical and Christian conceptions, there is another world or place—a timeless one—that transcends this time and this place. By asserting that the world is "eternally transient," Benjamin is rejecting this millennial heritage.

Benjamin draws two conclusions from the "eternal transience" he sees: that this transience corresponds to "messianic nature" and that it is "happiness." Benjamin is not ignoring the fact that nothing in life is so difficult to accept as that it will end. On the contrary, he acknowledges that it is supremely difficult to accept that not only we ourselves but all that we experience—all that we love and lose—is destined to pass and fade into nothingness ("nihilism," in the singular turn Benjamin gives to the term). Our mortal sense of justice demands that the world *not* be a nihilistic one—that there be a positive principle of judgment and retribution for all the cruelty and suffering we see around us. We ask that the just be rewarded and the unjust punished. Our mortal sense of beauty demands that these passing things have some durable reality. It is not singular or strange to look at the world and see, as Benjamin did, transience; and it is not singular or strange to claim that this is all there is to the world. But for all the reasons noted above, it *is* singular and strange to find in this fact the source and idea of "happiness." On the contrary, would we not expect to find melancholy and despair in its stead?

It is for this reason that, in the compressed logic of Benjamin's fragment, he refers to a "messianic intensity of the heart" that consigns it to "unhappiness [*Unglück*] in the sense of suffering" (Benjamin SW, 3.305; GS, 2.204, translation modified).[9] The extraordinary nature of Benjamin's conception lies in his effort to locate happiness not in a transcendent realm lying elsewhere, but instead here and now in this, and only this, world; in this, and only this, life. What Benjamin is asking his readers to envision is perfectly analogous in its conceptual coordinates to Nietzsche's thought experiment on the eternal recurrence of the same that Benjamin so peremptorily dismissed.[10] In both Nietzsche's eternal recurrence and Benjamin's "rhythm" of "messianic nature," the goal is the acceptance of this transience and the consequent rejection of the idea of an unknowable transcendental realm lying beyond it.

That Agamben is perfectly aware of this element in Benjamin's thought, and that it is a crucial one for him, is seen in *The Time That Remains* where he contrasts Benjamin's vision of transience with the

Apostle Paul's: "While, for Paul, creation is unwillingly subjected to transience [*caducità*] and destruction and for this reason groans and suffers while awaiting redemption, for Benjamin, who reverses this in an ingenious way, nature is messianic precisely because of its eternal and complete transience, and the rhythm of this messianic transience is happiness itself" (TTR, 141 [131], translation modified). *Nihilism* for Benjamin is thus not meaninglessness but instead an acceptance of the *transience* of this world and a rejection of the idea that our happiness should be shaped and our acts guided by a transcendental realm seen only in sacred glimpses by privileged individuals. In the face of worldly transience, the best "method," the best path to follow, is not one that follows an endless route toward some transcendental plane or place, but one focused fully on *this* time and *this* place.

It is at this point that we can more fully integrate Benjamin's—and Agamben's—idea of "messianic time" with his idea of the Messiah and the messianic. For Benjamin, to conceive of transience and the messianic together is to grasp "the present as the 'now-time' . . . loaded with splinters of the messianic [*Splitter der messianischen*]" (Benjamin GS 1.704). By this token, when Benjamin wrote of "messianic time," he meant not the time while one waited for the coming of a Messiah but instead a manner of experiencing and acting on what is already here in the present. In other words, what is messianic in Benjamin's conception of messianic time is not what is to come but what is already here. "Messianic time" (the term that came to replace the "kairology" we first saw in *Infancy and History*) rejects a historical dialectic of progress and its logic of deferral; it rejects the positing of the completion of a historical task in an indeterminate future. To many, "messianic time" suggests indeterminate waiting for the Messiah to come, redeem mankind, and complete human history. For Agamben, however, "messianic time" means, as it did for Benjamin, the very opposite.[11] This messianic time is not one of apocalypse, but of immediacy. About this point Agamben is perfectly explicit, noting that "the sole possibility we have to truly grasp the present is to conceive of it as the end [*das Ende*]. That was Benjamin's idea, and his messianism is to be understood above all after this fashion" (UL, 18). For Agamben, Benjamin's messianism, like his own, is an attempt to grasp the potentialities of our present situation. For this reason, "the paradigm for the understanding of the present is messianic time" (UL, 18). In *Infancy and History* Agamben writes that the "kairology" he envisioned is one that should be sought not at the millennium but "*now,*" and it is this dynamic possibility inherent in every historical moment that he hears, like Benjamin's surrealist alarm clock, ringing "sixty seconds every minute."

The Profane Order

Although we have localized the message and meaning of *transience* in Benjamin's fragment, there remains a still more central term—for both Benjamin and Agamben—that is necessary for understanding how the two thinkers conceive of the Messiah and the messianic. That term is the *profane.* After acknowledging the transience of "worldy existence," Benjamin introduces this decisive term into his discussion. The English translation makes this passage extremely difficult to understand. It reads: "The secular order should be erected on the idea of happiness" (Benjamin SW, 3.305). This is not *per se* a difficult idea to envision, but it is difficult to align with Benjamin's other claims in that fragment. There is a good reason for this: it is not what Benjamin wrote. What he did write is both more radical and more coherent: "The profane order [*Die Ordnung des Profanen*] is to be erected on the idea of happiness" (Benjamin GS, 2.203). The choice made by Benjamin's translator is at once understandable and unfortunate. On the one hand, as we saw earlier, Benjamin frequently discusses the idea of "secularization"—from the secularization of the idea of the messianic in Marx to the more general secularization of the theological in politics to the secularization of a religious "aura" in aesthetic experience. The term that Benjamin employs here, however, is a different one— one that should have presented no problems of translation. Although such a choice initially appears to ease the reader's task by offering a familiar concept (the *secular*) in familiar fashion, it ultimately hinders any full understanding of what is being discussed.[12]

As we saw, Benjamin often employed the term *secular* and had a clear and systematic use for the term, but he chose to evoke here not a "secular order" but a "profane order." What then is this profane order? A secular order would be, after all, easy enough to identify: a worldly as opposed to a religious order, with the operative distinction between the *religious* and the *secular*. The profane, however, is part of a still more ancient pairing—older than Christianity, which forged the term *secular* in its modern sense—and is in fact one of the oldest and most deeply ingrained of cultural distinctions. It is paired with and opposed to the *sacred* and once distinguished those who were allowed inside the temple (the sacred) and those who were kept from it (the profane). The "profane order," we can then assume, is opposed to a "sacred order"—and indeed Benjamin's vehement rejection of "theocracy" in the fragment points precisely in this direction.

To dismiss "theocracy" as Benjamin does is to dismiss a sacred order outside this world, choosing instead to dwell more fully in a transient world where things pass and fade, a world without absolute distinctions or privileges. Transience can be a source of sadness and despair and can push individuals to the brink of their endurance, just as it can be a source of liberation. The idea of happiness that Benjamin expresses is profane in precisely the same sense as Agamben's idea of a coming community— in its all-inclusiveness—in that it does not base its rights or practices on a connection with a sacred or transcendental realm. *Profane* here means being integrally focused on *this* world and *this* life. Opposed to this happiness is then not only the pain we feel at the passing away of things, but also the privileges of a sacred order that introduces divisions of power and prestige, property and permission, and so often employs the most violent means to retain them. Benjamin's "profane order" (like the "profane illumination" he was to see years later) is a consequence of an "eternally transient" world and implies the rejection of a distinction between the sacred and the profane. If the world is truly to be conceived of as transient, such distinctions as those between the sacred and the profane are arbitrary ones—human distinctions masked as divine ordinance.

It is in relation to this idea that Agamben claims that it is through the figure of the messianic that we can best see the relation of religion to law and religion to philosophy. In his reading, the great monotheistic religions sought "to control and reduce the essential messianic properties of religion and philosophy" (P, 163 [255]). They could never fully succeed, however, because "the messianic is precisely that element which, in religion, goes beyond it, exceeds and completes it at every point [*la eccede e compie in ogni punto*]" (LSP, 44). Nevertheless, this has led not only to the consistent repression of messianic movements within the great monotheistic religions, but also to a singular use of messianism's central feature: the *real* state of exception it calls into being. That for Agamben the idea of the profane is intimately linked with the idea of the real state of exception can be seen where he writes that "messianic time has the form of a state of exception" (P, 160 [252]). Elsewhere he notes that "from the juridico-political perspective, messianism is . . . a theory of the state of exception—except for the fact that in messianism there is no authority to proclaim the state of exception; instead, there is the Messiah to subvert its power" (HS, 57–58 [67]). The messianic state of exception that Agamben evokes here would correspond to what Benjamin enigmatically called "a *real* state of exception" where the state of exception that has become the rule is stripped of its divisive power. It is for this reason that Agamben speaks of "the task that messianism has assigned to modern politics," and which he defines as "to conceive of a human community that would have not (only) the figure of the law" (MWE, 135–136 [105], translation modified).

The *post iudicium* kingdom that Agamben conceives of is thus not one where the temples are destroyed or where all are crammed into them but where the distinctions that separate sacred and profane are rendered, to choose one of Agamben's central terms, *inoperative*. The "profane order" is given that name because it is an order from which the sacred—the source of exclusion and exception—is removed. The messianic kingdom serves as a paradigm for the coming community because it has neither an *in*clusive nor an *ex*clusive identity. The divisions that separate groups and individuals cannot be simply and instantly made to disappear, and indeed they do not need to be annihilated or forgotten; but for Agamben they do need to be neutralized, to be rendered *inoperative* and thereby deprived of their destructive power. The figures that *The Coming Community* presents are paradigms for such a profane order. Within the context of Benjamin's fragment, this explains the relation of *transience* to the *profane,* as well as Benjamin's later reference to an "integral actuality" reflected in a singular idea of prose. And it is this idea of the messianic—which is at once an idea of the profane—that leads Agamben to speak of a "messianic moment in which art stays miraculously still, almost astounded—fallen and risen in every instant." Agamben writes "fallen *and* risen" in every instant because in the light cast by a profane world there is no operative distinction between the two. Every creature and every gesture in such an integrally profane and integrally actual world is equally and at every moment "fallen and risen."

How to Bring About the Coming of the Messiah

Although this discussion might clarify the relation of the profane to the sacred, and the meaning of a profane order as it relates to the ideas of nihilism and transience, we are nevertheless left with the figure that Benjamin placed at the outset of his reflection and to which Agamben so often returns: the Messiah. What place, if any, does the Messiah have in such a profane order?

There is a passage in Benjamin's writing where he tells of the most difficult thing in the world: bringing about the coming of the Messiah. With this in mind, Agamben notes in *The Coming Community* that "there is a well-known parable about the Messianic Kingdom that Walter Benjamin (who heard it from Gershom Scholem) recounted one evening to Ernst Bloch, who in turn transcribed it in *Spuren*" (CC, 53 [45]). Bloch writes: "A rabbi, a real cabalist, once said that in order to establish the reign of peace it is not necessary to destroy everything nor to begin a completely new world. It is sufficient to displace this cup or this brush or this stone just a little, and thereby everything. But this small displacement is so difficult to achieve and its measure is so difficult to find that, with regard to the world, humans are incapable of it and it is necessary that the Messiah come" (quoted at CC, 53 [45], translation modified). The parable that passed through the hands of Scholem and Benjamin, and that Bloch here recounts, concerns the most divisive question in Jewish messianic thought: What, if anything, can we do to hasten the arrival of the Messiah? Many thinkers have held that the Messiah is waiting for certain worldly criteria to be fulfilled. Once this criterion, or these criteria, are fulfilled, the Messiah will come, "complete" human efforts, and close human history. *What* exactly this is—the coming of a truly just man, the forming of a truly just community, the reaching of a certain global state of affairs such as peace on earth or a return to the Holy Land—is a matter of the greatest uncertainty and contention.

This basic premise, however, has not been adopted by all thinkers in the messianic tradition. Another school of thought has seen the coming of the Messiah as determined in advance, independent from human actions and thus from the fulfilling of any worldly criteria. The Messiah will come when He is destined to come, and there is nothing we can or could do to hasten or slow His arrival. Whatever the current state of the world, whatever its measure of justice or injustice, He will come. In the former case, everything depends on finding out how to fulfill seemingly unknowable criteria. In the latter case, nothing can be done to slow or hasten His arrival, and one has only to wait.

In relation to these two currents of messianic thought, Bloch's recounting of the parable represents something radical. Although there is indeed something we must do in order for the Messiah to come, this is nothing monumental—nothing to do with social justice (a just community) or political hegemony (a return to the Holy Land), but instead something so subtle and so small—if perhaps ineffably genuine—as to seem perfectly insignificant. Here, however, is where the contours of the parable begin to blur. How can we discern which stone or which cup to displace—and how far? Because this "small displacement" is so tiny, we will never find it (we are "incapable of it," says Bloch) and for this reason we need the Messiah to come—of His own calling. With this idea of the "small displacement," Bloch brings the two schools of messianic thought into the greatest possible proximity.

As Agamben reminds his reader in *The Coming Community*, Bloch was told the parable—or something like it—by Benjamin, and he is not the only writer to have committed a version of it to paper. As Benjamin chose to recount the parable heard from Scholem, things stand a tiny but decisive bit differently. He wrote, "The *Hassidim* tell a story about the world to come that says everything there will be just as it is here. Just as our room is now, so it will be in the world to come; where our baby sleeps now, there too will it sleep in the other world. And the clothes we wear in this world, those too we will wear there. Everything will be as it is now, just a little different" (Benjamin GS, 2.432).[13] It seems that Benjamin's vision of the messianic kingdom is more radical—and more perplexing—than what Bloch understood, or chose to understand, of it. In Bloch's telling, the messianic kingdom and this world are astonishingly close, but nonetheless separate. The tiny displacement in Benjamin's telling focuses instead on something absolutely different. The emphasis is no longer on what we must do to bring about the coming of the Messiah, but on what the world will be like *after* He has come. And, surprisingly enough, the coming of the Messiah seems almost superfluous. The messianic world is not this world, yet *nothing* will be changed in it. *"Everything,"* says Benjamin "will be as it is now"—all things will remain in their places and the various vocations of men and women will remain the same—or almost. "Everything will be as it is now," says Benjamin, "just a little different." Everything then lies in understanding this difference.

The Messiah is the anointed one come to transform the world and to mark a fundamental change in all its distinctions. Paul seems to say something akin to this in the First Letter to the Corinthians, where he notes that in the time of the end we will remain in our places—men will remain men and women will remain women, rich and poor will remain rich and poor; it is only that these distinctions will cease to divide them as they had in the past; they will not change their callings, but their relation to the categories, qualities, possessions, and properties that had hitherto defined them will change.[14] The circumcised will remain circumcised, the uncircumcised will remain uncircumcised, but circumcision will become, in Paul's words, "nothing" (1 *Corinthians* 7:19)—that is, nothing that need divide us. But how are we to envision such a world where everything remains the same—except for a small difference? Are we to wait for His coming to actualize such an integral vision of a transient world? Clearly not. For Benjamin, it is a false messianism that sees "the Divine Kingdom . . . as the telos of a historical dynamic" (Benjamin GS, 2.203–2.204). Such a kingdom is, for him, "not the goal [*Ziel*], but instead the end [*Ende*]" of history (GS, 2.203–2.204). *Nihilism* is the "task" of world politics because it represents the effort to see the world as nothing more than it is—to construct world politics not on the basis of a sacred order to come, but instead on a profane order that is already right before our eyes and that is the only world we have ever known. In no way does he exclude the idea of a divine order beyond this world or a Messiah to come. What he does wish to isolate are the dangers inherent in the idea of a sacred order. And it is for this reason that he begins by evoking the decisive figure in that order: the Messiah. A connection to the Messiah, Benjamin claims, is not to be created from *this* side, from the transient and profane world that is our own—whether it takes up the mantle of the sacred or not. If there is a Messiah and if he is coming is something we cannot know. It is a "relation" that, for both Benjamin and Agamben, can be made only from the other side. In the meantime, we have only this world and this life. And we have no time to waste.

Conclusion: The Idea of the Work

In a preface to one of his works, Agamben remarked that "every written work can be regarded as the preface (or rather, the broken cast) of a work never written, and that of necessity remains so because in relation to it later works (in turn prefaces or moulds for other absent works) represent but sketches or death masks" (IH, 3 [vii]).[1] Elsewhere he has noted that "in a certain sense my books are in reality but a single book which is, in turn, nothing but a sort of preface to a work never written, and impossible to write" (UIGA, 33). At first sight these characterizations of every completed work as but a preface to an unwritten one might seem to express a sense of the unattainability of aspirations. As becomes clear to Agamben's reader, however, he has a very different idea in mind.

The Idea of Incompletion

Agamben's remarks on the secret life of prefaces and books reflect an important idea for him—the idea of incompletion. At issue here are not merely the obstacles that stand in the way of individual creations, and Agamben does not mean that authors always undershoot their mark or overestimate their capacities, nor is he referring to the external factors that prevent a work from attaining the fullness it might have achieved had not greedy wine merchants, harrying tailors, and eloquent panderers distracted the great minds from their tasks. What he is trying to elucidate through his remarks on incompletion is something stranger and more elusive: his idea of the work.

Although he nowhere indicates this, in his earlier remark Agamben is practicing an art he has long mastered—Benjamin's "art of citing without quotation marks." In a letter to Florens Christian Rang from January 10, 1924, the young Benjamin wrote that "a consideration of the relation between the work and its first inspiration . . . leads me to the conclusion that every completed work is the death-mask of its intuition" (Benjamin GB, 2.406). Four years later Benjamin returned to this singular image in a section of his *One-Way Street* entitled "The Writer's Technique in Thirteen Theses." The thirteenth and final thesis therein reads: "The work is the death-mask of conception" (Benjamin GS, 4.107). In Benjamin's image, the work appears as a rigid and lifeless form—not life, but its imprint. Given Agamben's impassioned familiarity with Benjamin's work, there can be little doubt that he had this image in mind when he wrote the passages cited above, just as there can be no doubt that the image carries a special significance for him. The question remains, however, as to why the idea of the completed work should conjure such dark associations for the two writers.

Benjamin's image associates completion with death, and what is alive, by contrast, is the conceiving and creating of a work. For Benjamin there is a melancholic note to be heard at the end of any work, as at the end of any enlivening experience. But the figure here is not only that of a creator taking leave of a cherished creation; it also involves leaving the limitless realm of potentiality for the confines of actuality. Benjamin's image consigns every completed work to *in*completion, but as we saw, the manner in which he understands such incompletion is idiosyncratic. In his final, and unfinished, work he claimed that, "remembrance can make the incomplete (happiness) complete, and the complete (pain) incomplete" (Benjamin GS, 5.589).[2] In this surprising reversal of categories, it is the complete—frozen in place—that Benjamin equates with pain, whereas happiness is found under the more mobile sign of the *in*complete.

This reversal lends Benjamin's idea of prose its singular form. In a fragment that gave Agamben's fifth book its title, Benjamin states that "the messianic world is the world of complete and integral actuality." In such a world, Benjamin writes, "history is not written: it is celebrated as a festival. As a purified festival, however, it does not have the character of a ceremony and knows no hymns. Its language is a freed prose, a prose that has broken the chains of writing" (Benjamin GS, 1.1235). This festive life is one where the division between sacred and profane no longer has any meaning and is without rite because there is no longer anything to separate the two spheres; it is the festivity of a life where all illuminations are profane. Such a world no longer waits for any transcendental consecration or culmination and what it celebrates it celebrates simply, every moment of every day. The language it employs is, from our perspective, an inconceivable one: a "freed prose" that has "broken the chains of writing." To break the chains of writing can only mean to free the written work from its frozen form—or in other words, to experience it in all its potentiality. In an essay that gave its title to a collection of Agamben's essays, "The Potentiality of Thought," he reminds his reader of "the most demanding and inescapable experience possible: the experience of potentiality"[3]; and it is precisely this experience that the completion of a work offers (P, 178 [274], translation modified).

As we saw earlier, Agamben took Benjamin's ideas about incompletion and happiness with the utmost seriousness. Showing perceptible admiration, Agamben cited Vasari's remark about Leonardo da Vinci that, "thanks to his intelligence in the arts, he started many projects, and finished none" (LDV). Yet the idea of incompletion that so occupies Agamben clearly extends beyond questions of the actual completion of individual works. In the poem "Clearings," Agamben evokes how "all in us / remains incomplete," and in the opening words of an essay published a year earlier—in 1966—he remarked that "it is to be doubted whether the concept of the work is even conceivable in unambiguous fashion" (R, 53; PB, 42).[4] This is a doubt that from that day to the present Agamben has retained, stressing in many subsequent works all that is ambiguous about the idea of the work. The second part of Agamben's second book dedicates a section to the idea of "The Un-finished [*Il non-finito*]" and another to what he calls the "Eclipse of the Work" (see S, 34 [43], translation modified; and S, 54–55 [63]). Indeed, in each of Agamben's books the idea of the incomplete as it relates to the idea of the work has been formulated in one manner or another. Christopher Budd (1999) has written that "[Agamben's] work is one that sparks great new trains of thought in the reader, but does not bring any to closure itself" (55). Although Agamben might not agree with Budd's analysis, there is every reason that he would agree with the conclusion. This is likely the reason that Agamben repeatedly spoke of the properly philosophical element in a work as its "capacity for development." At the heart of every finished work Agamben finds not only something that is not finished, but something that cannot be finished, and this is likely the reason he has noted that he "always found himself more interested in the before and the after of the work than in the work itself" (LDV).⁵ Rather than impatience with the act of writing or eagerness to move on from one project to the next, this idea reflects first and foremost Agamben's interest in all that the completed form of a work cannot bring into its closed confines. In short, for Agamben, the idea of incompletion is inseparable from the idea of the work.

The incompletion of inspiration and the completion of the finished work meet, for Agamben, in the idea of study. In a chapter from *Idea of Prose* entitled "The Idea of Study," which Agamben found important enough to repeat verbatim in another essay, he notes that "the end of study may never come—and in this case the work forever remains a fragment or a sketch—or coincides with the moment of death, when what had seemed a completed work reveals itself simply as study" (IP, 65 [45]; see also QGK, 44). As with Benjamin's figure of a death-mask, Agamben's end of the work has a finality to it like the finality of life. The completion of a life like the completion of a work is a question of perspective and is brought about, simply enough, by its end. In an afterword written for the French edition of *Stanzas,* Agamben employs Leibniz's figure of a "palace of destinies" to imagine a library, "on the infinite shelves of which are conserved the possible variants of each work, the books we might have written had something not intervened at a given moment, leading us to write and publish the book we did" (PO, 270). In the company of these possible works never made actual, the actual work appears to him, and to many of his readers, in a new light.

The End of Days

In *Profanations* Agamben asks a question he first raised in all its complexity in *The Coming Community*: "Is a society without separations possible?" (PR, 100). The answer he offers is that the question as such is poorly formulated. "The society without classes is not a society which has abolished and lost all memory of the difference of class," he writes, "but rather a society that has learned to disactivate its protocols so as to render a new usage possible" (PR, 100). In an essay published the same year as *The Coming Community* (1990), Agamben refers to a "threshold of de-propriation [*de-propriazione*] and de-identification of all modes and all quali-ties" (MWE, 100 [80]).[6] This is the Pauline message that Agamben sees everywhere in *The Coming Community*—from Heideggerian ontology to the preferences of Bartleby to pornographic films where the signs of class are retained but no longer carry any meaning that separates individuals from one another. What these varied paradigms outline are the contours of what Agamben called in a different work "a *political* community orient-ed exclusively toward the full enjoyment of worldly life" (MWE, 114 [90], italics in original, translation modified). In such a community, the exclu-sionary logic of belonging that dictates that one can enjoy a community's protection only if certain sanctified criteria are fulfilled—only if one is Muslim, Italian, communist, or whatever else—is replaced by a different conception of community, conceived of through such theological figures as *the messianic kingdom* and the *remnant*. What sort of political task is born of such a messianic vision? In an essay on Benjamin first published in 1983 and to which, in a recent Italian republication, Agamben added a final page, he writes, "To conceive of a human community and a human language which would no longer refer itself to an unsayable foundation and would no longer destine itself to an infinite transmission [is] certain-ly an arduous task" (PP, 54).[7] Yet to employ the terms that Agamben uses elsewhere—the understanding and the forming of "this empty and unpre-supposable community [*questa comunità vuota e impresupponibile*]"—is for him the "task of generations to come" (IH, 10 [xv]). In such a concep-tion, we have a task—but one that is completely undefined—and it is for this reason that it is so arduous.

A communal task or vocation of this order recalls the individual vocation seen in the introduction to this book. As we saw there, Agamben believes that "the fact that must constitute the point of departure for any discourse on ethics is that there is no essence, no historical or spiritual vocation, no biological destiny that humans must enact or realize." He adds that "this is the only reason why something like an ethics can exist, because it is clear that if humans were or had to be this or that substance, this or that destiny, no ethical experience would be possible—there would be only tasks to be done" (CC, 43 [39]). The "*post iudicium* world" that Agamben envisions is not a coming community in which some set state of affairs must first come about or to which a judgment must be handed down from a sacred source. It is not even one in which an end- or tipping-point of dialectical progress has to be reached. In a postface to *The Coming*

Community that Agamben wrote eleven years after completing that book, he rendered explicit what was implied therein: "*coming* does not mean *future*" (CCV, 92, italics in original). At first sight this is a confusing gloss of that work's title. As in the conceptions of messianic time that he studied in Benjamin and Paul, Agamben's own "time of the now" is one no longer waiting for a final form. For him, mankind has no set "destiny" it must follow, just as it has no determinate work, essence, task, or vocation. It can hardly be overstressed that this is not quietism; that there is no specific "task" to fulfill or "vocation" to exercise does not mean that there is nothing to be done. Agamben's rejection of the idea of a singular human "essence" or "destiny" is made in the name of a time that is now and an action that is pressingly and unavoidably our own. In his view, what truly leads to apathy and quietism is a naive belief in historical progress like the one he attacked in *Infancy and History*. It is this same idea that leads him to claim in *Idea of Prose* that "the one incomparable claim to nobility our own era might legitimately make in regard to the past" is "*that of no longer wanting to be a historical epoch*" (IP, 87 [71], italics in original).

This idea of "the end of history" is easily misunderstood, and for good reason. It is not truly the end of history but is instead merely the end of a certain conception of history. Its modern origins are found in Hegel's dialectic and its ancient ones in early Christianity's Judgment Day. Humanity will have a final day, whether in a dozen, a hundred, a million, or a hundred million years. But what if, in the meantime, we were to do away with the idea of a Last Judgment? The curious messianism that Agamben inherited from Benjamin does not dictate that it is impossible for there to be an End of Days, a Day of Reckoning, or even a Messiah; it only indicates that we should direct our efforts to this world and to our time rather than await a religious rapture or a secular culmination. "The end of history" is thus best understood as the end of a certain type of history, one that views human history as on a set dialectical course. For Agamben, there is an absolutely crucial distinction to be made between the end of days and the days of the end, the end of time and the time of the end. The one is apocalyptic, the other messianic. What is so difficult about Agamben's use of the term *messianic* is precisely this difference.

In this light we can at last fully understand Agamben's repeated claims that mankind has no historical task, calling, work, or vocation—whether individual or collective. When Agamben writes that mankind is "inoperative" he is not saying that it is dysfunctional or that its natural state is rest. He is saying, instead, that "man is a being of pure potentiality, and which no identity and no vocation can exhaust" (PP, 330). By this token, human history and human life are contingent. To say that human history and human life are contingent is also to say and to see that they are free—free to continue as they are going, free to commit and undergo unimaginable atrocities, just as they are free to change the course of events and bring about a more just and egalitarian order.

In the same postface to *The Coming Community* Agamben stresses that "the idea itself of a calling . . . or of a historical task . . . needs to be integrally rethought" (CCV, 91). What is called for here is a breaking with the millennial idea of a task to be completed and the need to form an elect corps to accomplish it. This is precisely the sense in which Agamben means—in what may seem at first sight an enigmatic formulation—that ours is the first era that might not be a historical one. This does not mean that human history will end with our generation, but it does mean that a hitherto dominant mode of conceiving that history might end. "There is in effect," writes Agamben, "something that humans are and have to be, but this something is not an essence nor properly a thing: *it is the simple fact of one's own existence as possibility or potentiality*" (CC, 43 [39], italics in original). An ethics worthy of the name could never simply be a list of historical tasks to accomplish or spiritual exercises to perform. It must remain, for Agamben, precariously open. Benjamin wrote that "nihilism" is the "task" of "world politics." Agamben's version of this remark is that world politics has no set "task" at all.

In *Men in Dark Times* Hannah Arendt writes, "What begins now, after the end of world history, is the history of mankind" (Arendt 1955, 90). With a similar idea in mind, Agamben writes that "the life that begins on earth after the last day is simply human life" (CC, 7 [12]). The name that Agamben gives to the profane order, to the life that begins after the last day—*irreparable*—is, as we have seen, to be understood not in the sense of "not being capable of being bettered," but instead as meaning that no magic wand or sacred scepter will end our woes. Such a life no longer waits for a culminatory event that will crystallize, dissolve, transform, or transubstantiate it—whether after the fashion of a dialectic of progress or an End of Days. For this reason all our efforts—individual and collective—should be directed toward what Agamben calls in a recent work "the end of days that is every day" (PR, 30).

Notes

ABBREVIATIONS OF AGAMBEN'S WORKS

1. In Agamben and Deleuze, 1993.

2. Three unofficial but extensive electronic bibliographies of Agamben's works and one print bibliography are currently available. The electronic ones are Eddie Yeghiayan's "Giorgio Agamben. A Selected Bibliography" at http://sun3.lib.uci.edu/eyeghiay/Philosophy/Colloquia/agamben.html; the bibliography compiled by the European Graduate School, http://www.egs.edu/faculty/giorgioagamben.html; and the bibliography of the unofficial Agamben website Agambeniana, http://agambeniana.at.infoseek.co.jp/index.html. Most recently, a selected bibliography of Agamben's works has appeared in print as an addendum to Calarco and DeCaroli's *Giorgio Agamben: Sovereignty and Life* (2007). The latter is a valuable resource but its compilers give misleading dates and sources for a number of key works. For example, Agamben's 1975 essay "Aby Warburg e la scienza senza nome" is dated not 1975 but 1984 (when it was republished with a postscript). The same dating and republication problems are found with the new and expanded editions of Agamben's books, which are either not indicated as such or simply absent (as is the case, for instance, for the revised editions of both *La comunità che viene* and *Idea della prosa*). Although this bibliography goes through the year 2005, it fails to note either of the books that Agamben published that year (*La potenza del pensiero* and *Profanazioni*). All of these bibliographical resources are of genuine assistance, but it is recommended that the reader use them in conjunction with one another and bear in mind that even then the list they form will be incomplete.

PREFACE

1. On this library, see Ernst Gombrich's *Aby Warburg: An Intellectual Biography,* especially Fritz Saxl's memoir on its history, published as an appendix to that work (Saxl 1970). Agamben himself writes of this library in an essay from 1975, "Aby Warburg and the Nameless Science" (P, 89–103) and refers to this "law of

the good neighbor" in his *The Idea of Prose* (IP, 64 [44]). For more on Agamben's relationship to Warburg, see Chapter Two of this book.

2. Reported by Saxl 1970, 331.

INTRODUCTION

1. Char led a Resistance cell in his native Provence. His experiences of this time are poetically chronicled in his *Feuillets d'Hypnos* [Leaves of Hypnos] (1946). This work so impressed Arendt that it formed the starting point for her *Between Past and Future* (1961).

2. Agamben was present at the seminars held in 1966 and 1968 (on Heraclitus and Hegel, respectively). Protocols from the seminars can be found in the complete edition of Heidegger's works. These protocols do not explain the genesis of the seminar, or its makeup, beyond the remark, "Vezin, Fédier und Beaufret were joined by two Italian friends, Ginevra Bompiani and Giorgio Agamben" (Heidegger GA, 15.267). Agamben is seen alongside Heidegger in several of the photos published by another member of the seminar, François Fédier, in his *Soixante-deux photographies de Martin Heidegger* (1972). Not noted in any published account of the seminars is how Agamben came to be among such a select few. In 1966, the year of the first seminar, Agamben was in Provence with Char's student, French poet Dominique Fourcade. Agamben's proximity led to his being invited to that seminar, which consisted of five students who were fed and lodged in the small *Hôtel du Chasselas*.

3. The term that Agamben leaves in German is the central one in Heidegger's *Being and Time*. It posed such a problem of translation that the first English edition of that book (by John Macquarrie and Edward Robinson, 1962) simply left it in German. Although there were good philosophical reasons for doing this, it created the impression that the term was so arcane, so philosopohically specialized, that no corresponding word existed. Although it is true that it is phenomnally difficult to find an equivalent term, this is not because the word is so rare or obscure. Its elements are *da*—"there"—and *sein*—"being"—and it is far from technical in its resonance. Unsurprisingly, one translation has been "being there," but this has often been rejected because the *being* that is *there* about which Heidegger speaks is our own, and ourselves—which is the reason the first French translation chose to render it as "human reality [*la réalité humaine*]." Here as elsewhere Agamben leaves the term untranslated.

4. Agamben expresses this same idea in a work that has *vocation* as one of its principal topics—*The Time That Remains: A Commentary on the Letter to the Romans* (2000). Therein Agamben claims that, for Paul, "messianic vocation is the revocation of every vocation" and goes on to note that "in this way, it defines what to me seems the only acceptable vocation. What is a vocation but the revocation of each and every concrete factical vocation [*di ogni concreta vocazione*

fattizia]?" (TTR, 23–24; 29; translation modified). A chapter entitled "The Idea of Vocation" in Agamben's fifth book stresses the difficulty of "thematizing" the subject of a vocation (IP, 45–46; 27–28). For an analysis of the term *vocation* from a different perspective, see also Agamben's essay "Vocation and Voice" (in PP, 77–89).

5. See Daniel Heller-Roazen's remark in the introduction to the collection of Agamben's essays he edited that "a single matter animates the works gathered together here"—a matter expressed in the title he chose for that volume: *Potentialities* (Heller-Roazen, 1999, 1).

6. The Greek term *argos* is a privative form of *ergon*, activity or work.

7. It might be objected that this is forcing the terms of the debate—at least as they are raised in Aristotle's *Ethics*—by tying accomplishment to function. Mankind might have as an—or the—activity proper to it to live well, or to reason, without this implying a *productive* function it must fulfill.

8. His reasons for this resignation are given in an article published in *La Repubblica* ("Se lo stato sequestra il tuo corpo," January 8, 2004, 42–43) and syndicated in the *New York Times* and a host of other leading national newspapers. For another example of Agamben's journalistic interventions, see his vehement response to a proposal that would legalize torture under certain circumstances (connected to combating terrorism), "Violenza di diritto," in *L'Umanità*, May 12, 2004.

9. This definition is one to which he had often turned in the past (see LSP, 45; LDV; and DTP, 4).

10. This conception of the unsaid has a precedent, or finds a kindred echo, in Wittgenstein's remark that "my [*Tractatus*] consists of two parts: of the one which is here, and of everything which I have *not* written. And precisely this second part is the important one" (undated letter to Ludwig von Ficker from late 1919; cited by Monk, 178; italics in original).

11. *Homo Sacer* began as a book and became a series. To date, five volumes have appeared and at least one more is forthcoming. The next—nonsequential—volume to appear after *Homo Sacer* was *Remnants of Auschwitz, Homo Sacer III*, in 1998, followed by *State of Exception, Homo Sacer II, I*, in 2003; *Il Regno e la Gloria, Homo Sacer II, 2*, in 2007; and *Il sacramento del linguaggio. Homo Sacer II, 3*, in 2008. The fourth and final part of the project will treat the concepts of "forms of life" and "styles of life." Although *Means Without End*, published in 1996, is not a numbered part of the series, Agamben notes that it belongs to the same "set of investigations" as *Homo Sacer* (MWE, ii [10]). It bears noting that *Homo Sacer* is so difficult and so controversial a book in part because it is a model in miniature for a larger project. Its three parts—and even the individual sections composing those parts—present certain discontinuities that have proven baffling to even the best disposed readers. (A prominent example of such is the chapter "Po-

tentiality and Law.") In the successive volumes in that series the different strands that are so tightly interwound in *Homo Sacer* have tended to become detached from one another, thus making *Homo Sacer* an easier book to read in the backward light they cast.

12. Franchi goes on to stress the continuity of interest in *aesthetic* issues in Agamben's work. He sees the "common ground" of the political and aesthetic sides of Agamben's production in the theme of "passivity." Franchi links the politics of passivity that he finds in Agamben with Paolo Virno's concept of "exodus" (see Franchi 2004, 38).

13. Although these are the first two books in English to be exclusively dedicated to Agamben's work, the first book in English to treat Agamben is Thomas Carl Wall's *Radical Passivity: Lévinas, Blanchot, and Agamben* (1999). Wall's analysis is focused on Agamben's *The Coming Community*.

14. For representative examples, see Kalyvas, Rancière, and Passavant. Kalyvas (2005) writes that "by assimilating political relations to a single master concept, that of sovereignty, Agamben can no longer localize the contingency of political and social struggles" (115). Rancière (2004) finds that "Agamben's argument is in line with the classical opposition between the illusion of sovereignty and its real content. As a result, he misses the logic of political subjectivization" (305). Passavant (2007) argues that Agamben employs "two contradictory theories of the state" (one that is, in Debord's sense of the term, *spectacular* and another that is modeled on judicial sovereignty and its defining state of exception) (147). A host of other correctives to individual political concepts are discussed in Chapters Six, Seven, and Nine.

15. In another interview, he offers a more lighthearted version of this remark: "Well, the situation is grave, but not desperate—or it is desperate, but not grave" (PWP, 24).

16. Michael Hardt (1996, 2) writes of this slogan that "it did not mean a refusal of creative or productive activity but rather a refusal of work within the established capitalist relations of production." On these workers' movements, see also Tronti 1980, 28–34.

17. For Agamben's discussion of this formula, see LD, 49ff [65ff].

18. The English translators chose "power" to translate *potenza* here, although later in the same paragraph they translated the same word as "potentiality." The choice is by no means wrong, but it obscures the terms at issue here, and the wedded sense of actual and potential power expressed by the Italian *potenza*. This is a recurrent problem in translations of Agamben's work. Speaking of his collection *La potenza del pensiero* (The Potentiality of Thought), Agamben remarked, "in my book *potenza* does not mean so much 'power' [*potere*] as 'possibility,' 'potentiality' [*possibilità, potenzialità*]" (DTP, 5).

19. *The Gospel of Saint Matthew* uses many nonprofessional actors—including Pasolini's own mother (as Mary). The then twenty-two-year-old Agamben plays the Apostle Philip. Agamben speaks briefly of the experience in an interview from 1985, noting among other things that he did not particularly enjoy it (see UIGA, 33).

20. Weil was an important thinker for Elsa Morante, with whom Agamben was intellectually and personally close. One of the few places in Agamben's published work where Weil is mentioned is in an essay on Morante, where he notes in passing the importance of Weil to Morante's thought (see EP, 102 [105]).

21. See Weil [1948] 1997. Although Weil does not note this, the word is derived from a fourteenth-century French term. It too is absent, however, from even the most exhaustive modern dictionaries and does not appear in *Le Grand Robert,* in *Littré,* or in the *Trésor de la langue française.* The term is found, however, in Frédéric Godefroy's *Dictionnaire de l'ancienne langue française, et de tous ses dialectes du IXe au XVe siècle,* where it is defined as "diminution." It was through Weil's use of the term that poet Anne Carson was led to it. Carson uses poetry, essay, and even opera to explore the term in her *Decreation* (2005). See also Stevens 1997, 750.

22. Asked about his intellectual masters in an interview from 1985, Agamben spoke of both Heidegger and José Bergamin, noting that during their lifetimes he thought of them as "examples and as friends" and that "only after their deaths did I come to think of them as masters [*maestri*]" (UIGA, 32).

23. In a similar vein, Heidegger had announced in a lecture a year earlier (1925), "If I am forced to employ here cumbersome and unattractive expressions, this is no mere whim on my part and stems from no special fondness for having my own terminology. Instead, it responds to the constraint placed upon language by the phenomena themselves" (Heidegger GA 20.205). Not everyone, of course, was convinced of the phenomenological necessity of such a singular language. In a recently discovered letter sent to Paul Tillich on April 13, 1944, Thomas Mann wrote, "Heidegger—I could never stand this Nazi *par existence.* The challenge of reading his philosophical jargon of terror made it difficult to keep hold of the book. *One's-own-ness!* Should not such writing be subject to punishment?" (first published in the *Feuilleton* of the *Frankfurter Allgemeine Zeitung,* June 20, 2002, 45). Mann's friend Theodor Adorno was to take Heidegger aggressively to task for what Mann called Heidegger's *Schreckensjargon* in *The Jargon of Authenticity* (1964; see Adorno GS 6.413–523).

24. This element in Heidegger's philosophy was early and often criticized—and by no one so vehemently as Adorno, who from his first attacks on Heidegger and the new ontology of the 1930s to his more strident *Jargon of Authenticity* castigated the idealism he saw in Heidegger's conception of potentiality. On these earlier attacks, in which Adorno does not mention Heidegger by name, see

Beatrice Hanssen's discussion of Adorno's essay "The Idea of Natural History" (1998, 13ff.).

CHAPTER I

1. The English translation of *The Man Without Content* (1999) has on its title page the following note: "Originally published in Italian in 1994 under the title *L'uomo senza contenuto* © 1994 by Quodlibet." The book was in fact published twenty-four years earlier; the edition referred to here is the second one. It is important to bear this in mind not only so as not to rob the book of its right of primogeniture, but also so as to allow the reader to better situate its claims in debates of the day. In Eva Geulen's book-length introduction to Agamben's work, *Giorgio Agamben zur Einführung* (2005), although she announces that she will be employing "scarcely known earlier texts" in her investigations, her chronology for even Agamben's best known texts is inaccurate. Early in her study she refers to Agamben's "first book, *Infancy and History*" (Geulen 2005, 15). *Infancy and History,* from 1978, was published eight years after Agamben's first book, *The Man Without Content,* and is his *third* book. In a later chapter, Geulen refers to *The Man Without Content* (by its Italian title) and gives as its date of publication 1994—which shows that she was consulting neither of the two Italian editions of the work but instead the English translation from which this error stems (see Geulen 2005, 34). To complete this chronological confusion, Geulen refers at still another point to Agamben's "first book, *Stanzas*"—which she also goes on to designate as "Agamben's first publication" (see Geulen 2005, 37, 38). Published in 1977, *Stanzas* is Agamben's second book, and not only does another book precede it but so too do more than a decade of other publications. These errors are in no way characteristic of the reception of Agamben's work in Germany and are counterbalanced by many fine insights in Geulen's own work.

2. The initial English translation of *Being and Time* by John Macquarrie and Edward Robinson from 1962 translates *Destruktion* simply as "destruction." Trying to capture its unconventional usage, J. Glenn Gray, David Farrell Krell, and Joan Stambaugh translate *Destruktion* as "destructuration" (see Heidegger 1993, 1996).

3. Heidegger often turns to Hegel's epochal claim. An important instance of this is found in the afterword to his "The Origin of the Work of Art" and is echoed in his lectures from the period. For a further example, see Heidegger's seminar from 1936–37 on Schiller's *Letters on Aesthetic Education* (Heidegger 2005, 13ff.). The reason Hegel's statement was of such enduring interest to Heidegger was that the role of art was a central topic for Heidegger. In an interview given the year that Agamben met Heidegger (1966) he remarks, "That is the great question: Where does art stand? What is its place?" (GA 16.682). In this same in-

terview he refers to "contemporary literature" as "primarily destructive [*weitge-hend destruktiv*]" (Heidegger GA 16.670).

4. The clearest expression of this is to be found in the *Republic*. See *Republic* 398a: "If a man, then, it seems, who was capable by his cunning of assuming every kind of shape and imitating all things should arrive in our city, bringing with himself the poems which he wished to exhibit, we should fall down and worship him as a holy and wondrous and delightful creature, but should say to him that there is no man of that kind among us in our city, nor is it lawful for such a man to arise among us, and we should send him away to another city, after pouring myrrh down over his head and crowning him with fillets of wool, but we ourselves, for our souls' good, should continue to employ the more austere and less delightful poet and tale-teller, who would imitate the diction of the good man and would tell his tale in the patterns which we prescribed in the beginning, when we set out to educate our soldiers" (Plato 1984, 643). See also *Republic* 605c: "And so we may at last say that we should be justified in not admitting him into a well-ordered state, because he stimulates and fosters this element in the soul, and by strengthening it tends to destroy the rational part, just as when in a state one puts bad men in power and turns the city over to them and ruins the better sort. Precisely in the same manner we shall say that the mimetic poet sets up in each individual soul a vicious constitution by fashioning phantoms far removed from reality, and by currying favor with the senseless element that cannot distinguish the greater from the less, but calls the same thing now one, now the other" (Plato 1984, 830).

5. This element of Agamben's argument bears a clear debt to Edgar Wind's *Art and Anarchy* (1963). Wind's work takes as its point of departure the same idea, that the divine madness Plato both revered and feared has disappeared from our experience of the work of art. Like Agamben, Wind follows the historical stations of this loss. "The sacred fear is no longer with us," Wind writes, and "art is so well received because it has lost its sting" (1963, 9). Wind stresses that "the outward circumstances under which great art is produced are often far from reassuring" and that "art is—let us face up to it—an uncomfortable business, and particularly uncomfortable for the artist himself" (1963, 1, 2). This is a point that will prove central to Agamben's argument, although Agamben will shift the debate from a cultural to an ontological level that Wind does not discuss. The ideas that Wind follows in *Art and Anarchy* can be found first in his inaugural lecture as *Privatdozent* for philosophy in Hamburg in 1930 (see "On Plato's Philosophy of Art" in Wind 1983, 1–20). Wind remains a point of reference for Agamben in his next work and is named in one of Agamben's most recent books (see S, 64 [55]; SR, 70).

6. "The man without content" evokes one of his relatives, Robert Musil's *The Man Without Qualities* (*Der Mann ohne Eigenschaften*, which translated into Ital-

ian is *L'uomo senza qualità*, making the symmetry of the titles as clear in Italian as in English). It bears noting that by the point in Agamben's book when he has at last revealed to his reader the meaning of the title, he has already twice referred to Musil's novel. In Musil's German, what his man lacks are *Eigenschaften,* which are indeed "qualities" in a certain sense, but qualities that, as the German word's etymology reflects, are of one's "own crafting" or "creation" (the respective elements of the composite noun *Eigenschaften* are "own," *eigen,* and "create," *schaffen*). Like Musil's protagonist, Agamben's artistic man without content has nothing that is his "own" and thus struggles greatly in the act of "creating." Concerning Agamben's continued interest in Musil, see S, xix [xvi] and 26 [33]; and AE.

7. In an essay written almost forty years later, Agamben places Artaud in an Averroist legacy alongside Dante, Spinoza, and Heidegger (TDI, xi).

8. References to Pasolini's influence on Agamben's conceptions of art and life are rare. An exception is found in Daniel Morris's "Life, or Something Like It" (2004, 1). A second exception is found in Fabio Vighi (2003), who sees Agamben's interest in the figure of the refugee as "reminiscent of Pasolini's uncompromising radicalism" and, more generally, his linking of the "wretched" and the "sacred" in the figure of the *homo sacer* as reminiscent of Pasolini's aesthetic vision. (2003, 105). In a recent work Agamben refers to Pasolini in the context of the idea of "serious parody [*parodia seria*]" that he saw Pasolini sharing with Elsa Morante (see PR, 51). For a polemical treatment of the role of the author in an age in which literature seems to decline ever more in cultural influence and importance, and that makes its arguments via two artists who were personally close to Agamben, see Carla Benedetti's *Pasolini contra Calvino* (1998). Therein, the virulently engaged Pasolini is placed against the distanced formalist Calvino to expose the contradictions of our artistic age.

9. Continuing in this vein, Agamben states that for the view of art that aesthetics has outlined, "the supreme truth of the work of art is now the pure creative-formal principle that fulfills its potentiality [*potenza*] in it, independently of any content" (MWC, 47 [71]).

10. With his customary wit, Wind (1963, 11) remarks: "It is worth listening to Hegel on this point. Whatever the weakness of his metaphysics, as an observer of the world of men he was as sharp-sighted as Montaigne."

11. In a number of his works Heidegger employs crossed-out terms to indicate that they are "under erasure"—a practice that Agamben also employs in later works such as *Homo Sacer* and *State of Exception* (and that he shares with, among others, Derrida).

12. See also: "While in the 'ready-made' the spectator was faced with a technologically fabricated object which inexplicably presented itself charged with a degree of aesthetic authenticity, in pop art the spectator was faced with a work

of art which appeared to strip itself of its aesthetic potential to assume paradoxically the status of an industrial project" (MWC, 62 [93], 63 [95], translation modified).

13. An added illustration of this idea might be found in a work such as Robert Morris's "Document" (1963), housed in the New York Museum of Modern Art. "Document" accompanies Morris's "Litanies" and takes the form of a notarized statement in which the artist declares, "I hereby withdraw . . . all esthetic quality and content" from the work in question.

14. In a recent work, Agamben calls this trend, "the museification of the world [*la museificazione del mondo*]" (PR, 96). Clarifying his curious choice of words, he notes, "*museum* does not designate here a place or a physically circumscribed space"; rather, it is "the isolated dimension into which is transferred all that once was, but no longer is, felt as true and decisive" (PR, 96). Agamben specifies here that a museum in this sense might coincide with an entire city, with a region, or even with a group of individuals.

15. Agamben's interest in Heidegger's "The Origin of the Work of Art" is seen not only in *The Man Without Content* but also in an essay published four years earlier, *"Il pozzo di Babele"* (see especially PB, 42).

16. Such evocations of ontological origin have indeed sounded vague, incantatory, or worse to some ears—such as those of Adorno, who vigorously attacked "that prestige-word *origin*" (see Adorno GS, 7.481).

17. The term *structuralism* is of course the coinage of neither Barthes nor Todorov (it stems from Roman Jakobson and dates from 1929). It was, however, in the years when *The Man Without Content* was written and published that it came to hold sway not only in the linguistic circles from which it emerged (primarily through Jakobson, Saussure, and Benveniste), but also in virtually all realms of the social sciences and the humanities. For an overview of this historical and conceptual process, see Culler 1975.

18. The crucial role assigned here to the concept of *rhythm* with its central points of reference in Hölderlin and Greek antiquity is echoed by a short essay of Heidegger's in which he turns from Rimbaud to the Greek poet Archilochus and attempts to answer the question, "What does the Greek word *rhythm* here mean?" (Heidegger GA 13.226). Another unnamed source for Agamben's stress on *rhythm* can be found in Benjamin's *The Origin of German Tragic Drama* (1928). In that work's preface Benjamin writes of the rhythm that marks the idea of origin: "Origin [*Ursprung*], although an entirely historical category, has, nevertheless, nothing to do with genesis [*Entstehung*]" (Benjamin 1977a, 45–46 [GS I.226]). Origin is thus not confined to a single moment at the beginning of the creation of a work of art. It is something, in Benjamin's conception, more abiding. This surprising claim is offered some (poetic) clarification: "Origin is an eddy in the stream of becoming and in the rhythm set by its current [*in seine Rhythmik*] it swallows

up the material of its genesis." "That which is original," Benjamin continues, "is never revealed in the naked and manifest existence of the factual; its rhythm [*Rhythmik*] is apparent only to a dual insight" that includes something restorative and reestablishing alongside of something unfinished and incomplete (Benjamin 1977a, 46 [I.226]). Hölderlin's ecstatic claim that "everything is rhythm, the entire destiny of man is one heavenly rhythm, just as every work of art is one rhythm" is followed by Agamben to the heart of the idea of a special structure to the work of art. This rhythm that is in "everything" and that makes of every work of art "one rhythm" may ring of pantheistic outpouring, but it also anticipates the singular idea of *origin* that Benjamin develops and that will be a lasting influence on Agamben's conception of history.

19. "Politics in a literary work is like a pistol fired in the midst of a concert [*La politique dans un oeuvre littéraire, c'est un coup de pistolet au milieu d'un concert*]" (Stendhal 1959, 236).

20. This letter (written in English) is dated Feburary 21, 1970, and is to be found in the Hannah Arendt papers housed in the Library of Congress (item 004722). Agamben noted that he first read Arendt in the summer of 1968 (see UL, 17–18).

21. For Emerson's remark, see Emerson, 1.56. Nietzsche's reflections are found in his essay "On the Use and Misuse of History for Life" in *Untimely Meditations*).

22. For a broad range of approaches to the role of this central term in Benjamin's thought, see Benjamin and Osborne 1994.

23. A passable analogy in the realm of English letters would be the revival of interest in the poetry of John Donne that took place during roughly these same years.

24. Agamben's continued interest in the figure of the collector is returned to in the context of an analysis of fetishism in *Stanzas* (see S, 35 [43]). Benjamin's—and Agamben's—ideas about citation are treated in a Scholium to Chapter Four.

25. In a later work Agamben entrusts this task to (a broadly conceived) philology: "The abolition of the distance between the thing to be transmitted and the act of transmission, between writing and authority, has in fact been philology's role since its beginning" (IH, 146 [146], translation modified).

26. In an essay published four years earlier, Agamben evoked Kafka in other terms—as the writer who most deeply felt and authentically responded to the paradox of the work of art as that which would exhaustively express what can never be exhaustively expressed: life. Therein he writes that "Kafka is the writer who has felt in all its depths this predestined failure [*naufragio*] of the work . . . " (PB, 45). Kafka will remain a central figure not only for Agamben's conception of the work of art but also for a host of other central ideas. For one instance among

many, Agamben refers in a recent essay to Kafka as "the greatest theologian of the twentieth century" (BH, 13).

27. The story of Benjamin's intimate relation to this painting is well documented enough to omit here. It bears noting, however, that in a recent essay Agamben returns to the image not in relation to the philosophy of history but through a genealogy of angels. Therein he makes the surprising claim that "in our culture angelology and the philosophy of history are so intertwined that only whoever is able to grasp their relation to one another is in a position to interrupt and dissolve it—not so as to reach a suprahistorical beyond, but instead to grasp the very heart of the present moment" (BH, 27–28).

28. Rimbaud's enigmatic remark is from a letter dated May 15, 1871. In Char's 1957 introduction to a selection of Rimbaud's verse, he singles it out as essential to understanding Rimbaud's conception of the role of the poet. In a text from 1972 (published in 1976) entitled *"Rimbaud vivant,"* Heidegger analyzes this same remark, asking whether the *"en avant"*—which he translates as *"im Voraus sein"*—is meant temporally, as a privileging (*"Vorrang"*), or as something more mysterious (Heidegger GA, 13.225–13.227). Asked in an interview from 1966 whether an individual or philosophy can influence the course of events, Heidegger answered, "Philosophy will not be able to effect any immediate and unmediated [*unmittelbare*] change in the state of contemporary world affairs" (GA 16.671). He then added, "This applies not only to philosophy but to all merely human reflection," before offering the Delphic utterance, "Only a god can now save us [*Nur noch ein Gott kann uns retten*]" (GA 16. 671). What philosophy and poetry, *Denken und Dichten*, can effect, following Heidegger, is to prepare the way for the coming of such a god (GA 16. 671). For an understanding of the poetic relationship between Heidegger and Char, see also Heidegger's collection of short poems, *"Gedachtes,"* which bears the dedication *"Für René Char in freundschaftlichem Gedanken,"* published in German and French in 1971 in a special issue of *L'Herne* dedicated to Char (Heidegger GA, 13.221–13.224). See also UIGA, 32.

29. The possibility of a dynamic reversibility is evoked in a number of Agamben's later works—including most recently his *Il sacramento del linguaggio,* which closes with a similar injunction (see SL, 98). In "Program for a Review," written in the years directly following *The Man Without Content*, Agamben found a name for his singularly destructive enterprise. Of the objective he wished to assign to this review (which never materialized) he writes, "The task imposed upon this review by its situation cannot therefore simply be defined as a 'destruction,' albeit a necessary one, of tradition, but rather a 'destruction of destruction,' in which the destruction of the mode of transmission, which marks our culture fundamentally, is dialectically brought to light" (IH, 145 [145]). It was this "dialectical bringing to consciousness" of the "destruction of the transmissibility of cul-

ture" that was to be the goal of the review. That his "destruction of aesthetics" was to be seen as of a pair with the "destruction of destruction" from this proposed project for a review is made clear by the image that directly follows Agamben's evocation of a "destruction of destruction": "It is only in a 'destruction' of this kind that the categorical structures of Italian culture can become visible, like the fundamental architectural project [*il progetto architettonico fondamentale*] of a house in flames" (IH, 145 [145], translation modified).

30. This question is discussed in Hugo Ott's *Martin Heidegger: A Political Life* ([1983] 1993). The most balanced account of Heidegger's political affiliations and their relation to his philosophy is found in Rüdiger Safranski's unforgivingly titled *Ein Meister aus Deutschland: Heidegger und seine Zeit* [*Martin Heidegger: Between Good and Evil*] ([1994] 1998).

CHAPTER 2

1. Errors in the critical literature concerning the publication dates and chronological order of Agamben's first books are found here as well (see Chapter One, note 1). Both Geulen (2005) and Mesnard and Kahan (2001, 99) refer to *Stanzas* as Agamben's first book.

2. Derrida's fluid terminology gave many names to this phenomenon, such as *phonocentrism, grammatology, différence, dissemination,* and *deconstruction,* as well as other, closer and more distant cognates. As Derrida often stressed, that this phenomenon cannot be circumscribed by a single fixed term was an essential part of his philosophy.

3. Letter to the author, April 26, 2005. The latter remark ("*Dichtung kann man nur philosophieren*") is a paraphrase of a statement made by Wittgenstein that Agamben cites at the close of "The End of the Poem": "Philosophy should really only be poeticized [*Philosophie dürfte man eigentlich nur dichten*]" (EP, 115, 119). The remark in question is found in Wittgenstein's *Culture and Value* (1984, 24). In an analogous fashion, Furio Jesi, an author to whom Agamben felt close and whose work he helped support, wrote of the "scientific *and* artistic" aspirations of his own philological work, saying, "To the question, 'Do you never think of writing a novel?' I can only reply: I have never done anything else" (Jesi 2001, 356, italics in original).

4. Earlier (and shorter) versions of Parts I and II of *Stanzas* were published in 1974 and 1972, respectively.

5. The fact that the essays in the collection are called parts (implying a unified whole of which they are parts) underlies this continuity. It was perhaps this that led the translator of the English edition to lend a still greater continuity to the four parts of the book by continuously enumerating their individual chapters (that is, the final chapter in the volume is not, as in the original, Chapter Three of Part Four but Chapter Nineteen).

6. Fénéon (1861–1944) is best remembered for his remarkable critical insight (he was an early champion of Rimbaud, Apollinaire, and the Impressionist painters), as well as for the extreme laconism of his literary production.

7. The English translation falsely renders the Italian *scadimento* as "extinction." *Scadimento* belongs to the same linguistic family as the English word *decadence* (the act of falling off, -*cadere*) and means "decadence" or "decline."

8. *Melancholy* will remain an abiding interest for Agamben. See, for an important instance, RA, 125ff. [117ff].

9. Agamben takes issue with their findings in both of his first two works, as well as in an essay from 1975—see P, 285, n. 19.

10. The translator uses the term *phantasy* instead of *fantasy* to translate the Italian *fantasia*. The rationale for this choice seems to be reflected in the *Oxford English Dictionary*'s description: "In modern use *fantasy* and *phantasy*, in spite of their identity in sound and in ultimate etymology, tend to be apprehended as separate words, the predominant sense of the former being 'caprice, whim, fanciful invention,' while that of the latter is 'imagination, visionary notion.'"

11. As in Agamben's Italian original, the English translation leaves this motto in German but unaccountably changes it from "*Der* liebe *Gott steckt im Detail*" to "*Der* gute *Gott steckt im Detail*." Agamben also discusses this motto in the context of the idea of divine and natural signatures in *Signatura rerum* (see SR 72).

12. Warburg, however, never employed it in his writing. It first appeared in print under the pen of Warburg's friend and colleague E. R. Curtius in the published text of the eulogy he gave at Warburg's funeral in 1929. It first gained wide currency nearly twenty years later through the two references Curtius makes to it in his *European Literature and the Latin Middle Ages* (45; 386). Its actual origin, however, remains uncertain. In his *Aby Warburg: An Intellectual Biography*, Ernst Gombrich, then head of the Warburg Institute, claimed that it was a translation of a phrase of Flaubert's, "Le bon Dieu est dans le detail," although he does not indicate where Flaubert allegedly employed this formula (see Gombrich 1970, 13). Although another figure close to the Warburg Institute, Erwin Panofsky, expressed skepticism about this derivation as early as 1949 (the bulk of Gombrich's book on Warburg was composed during these years), and despite Gombrich's subsequent inability to find the source despite its supposedly stemming from one of the best known and most studied corpuses in French literature, this dubious derivation is still cited to this day. (For a sign of the spread of Gombrich's apocryphal derivation, see a telling instance in Italo Calvino's *Lezioni americane* where he cites "Flaubert's affirmation" that "Le bon Dieu est dans le detail" [77], although without reference to Warburg or Gombrich). Another former director of the Warburg Institute, Edgar Wind, was more outspoken than Panofsky, remarking that the attribution was made "without any reference to an authentic sentence in Flaubert, whose writings are not inaccessible" (from a review of

Gombrich's *Aby Warburg* in the *Times Literary Supplement,* June 25, 1971, 735–36; reprinted in Wind's *The Eloquence of Symbols,* 112). In the editorial afterword to Warburg's *Ausgewählte Schriften und Würdigungen,* Dieter Wuttke restates what Wind had noted concerning the motto's provenance (see Warburg 1979, 623–25).

13. Agamben brings together the two writers at a number of points in his writing, most notably in "Nymphae." For more on Benjamin's interest in Warburg's work, see Galitz and Reimers 1995, 10ff.

14. The latter essay, from 1996, is entitled "Absolute Immanence" (see P, 220–39). The conception of immanence that Agamben finds in Deleuze (and in Foucault) is explicitly related therein to a concept of "life" that Agamben sees as "the subject of the coming philosophy" and that will necessitate "a genealogical inquiry into the term *life*—precisely the project that the *Homo Sacer* series takes upon itself" (P, 238 [239]). For a more recent reference to Deleuze, see the beginning of Agamben's essay "Friendship."

15. Concerning the question of how art historians have considered Warburg and his place in their discipline, compare Ulrich Raulff's remark in a recent book on Warburg: "Twenty years ago one would have received as answer to the question as to what discipline Warburg belonged that he was an art historian. Today . . . art historians see Warburg not as an art historian but as a 'scholar of images' [*Bildwissenschaftler*] who liberated their discipline from a narrow study of works of high art" (Raulff 2003, 7).

16. See Warburg's "Italienische Kunst und internationale Astrologie im Palazzo Schifanoja zu Ferrara" in Warburg 1988, II, 459ff.

17. This final term is found in art-historical treatises as far back as the seventeenth century but was rarely employed before Warburg revived its use and recoined it in polemical distinction to the established subdiscipline of *iconography* (generally seen as that part of art historical study involving the deciphering of the *content* of a work in relative independence of the stylistic means used to render it). With time, however, *iconology,* like its terminological predecessors, proved too narrow for Warburg's needs, and it was left to one of his students—Erwin Panofsky—to make *iconology*'s fame and fortune. It is a matter of general consensus that *iconology* as developed by Panofsky does not correspond to the larger interdisciplinary aspirations of Warburg's study. Modern interpreters have been careful to point out that Panofsky's psychological reductiveness was not in the spirit of Warburg's inquiries. This is noted by Agamben as well as, in less pointed form, by Carlo Ginzburg, and in more pointed form by Georges Didi-Huberman. Raulff falsely credits Didi-Huberman with first drawing attention to the distance that separates Panofsky's approach from Warburg's (Agamben precedes him in this respect by many years; see Raulff 2007, 15).

18. Agamben writes of his essay on Warburg from 1975 that it was conceived "as the first of a series of portraits dedicated to exemplary personalities, each of

which was to represent a human science," and he notes that this series of portraits was to be made in the interest of "the project of a general science of the human" (P, 101 [144]; the only other portrait on which Agamben began work—dedicated to the linguist Émile Benveniste—remains uncompleted). Benveniste suggested that "the fundamental character of our language—to be composed of signs—might prove common to the totality of social phenomena which constitute *culture* [*l'ensemble des phénomènes sociaux qui constituent la* culture]," and it is doubtless this aspiration that led Agamben to place him alongside Warburg (Benveniste 1966–1974, 1.44; italics in original). In *Stanzas* Agamben says of Benveniste that he is "a linguist who has, in our opinion, effected a new 'situation' of the science of language" and that to him "we owe the most lucid perception of the inadequacy of the semiotic perspective (understood in the narrow sense) for an understanding of the linguistic phenomenon in its totality" (S, 158 [186]). As we will see in Chapter Seven, Agamben returns to Benveniste in the context of the idea of the archive in the final section of his *Remnants of Auschwitz*. Benveniste also plays a central role in Agamben's analyses of vows and oaths in *Il sacramento del linguaggio* (see especially SL, 7ff.)

19. Agamben refers in Part 4 of *Stanzas* to "a *Nachleben* of the emblematic form" in such authors as E.T.A. Hoffmann, Edgar Allan Poe, and Kafka, and in the caricatures of J. J. Grandville and Sir John Tenniel, as well as to a *Nachleben* of images from our culture's mythic past in an essay from *Infancy and History* (see S, 144 [171]; and IH, 85 [91]).

20. Agamben defines and praises Warburg's celebrated neologism *Pathosformel* elsewhere in saying that it "designates an indissoluble intertwining of an emotional charge and an iconographic formula in which it is impossible to distinguish between form and content," and that it "suffices to demonstrate that Warburg's thought cannot in any sense be interpreted in terms of such inauthentic oppositions as those between form and content and between the history of styles and the history of culture" (P, 90 [124]). In a more recent essay, Agamben says of *Pathosformel* that it is a "hybrid of matter and form, creation and performance, first-time-ness [*primavoltità*] and repetition"—and he employs the same terms in *Signatura rerum* (N, 56; SR, 31; see also SR, 58).

21. Lévi-Strauss also plays a decisive role in Agamben's early thought and in his project for a broadened multidisciplinary study. The influence of Lévi-Strauss is most strongly felt in Agamben's next book, *Infancy and History*, most particularly the chapter dedicated to him: "In Playland: Reflections on History and Play" (see IH, 65ff. [67ff.]). Although references to Lévi-Strauss are more rare in the works that follow this one, he remains an important figure for Agamben. For a treatment of Lévi-Strauss's thought as it pertains to the logic of *example* and *exception*, see Agamben's *Homo Sacer* (25 [30]).

22. Agamben returns to Warburg's "nameless science" in SR, 59.

23. The translator curiously renders "approach" here as "history": "a global *history* of culture. . . . "

24. Agamben's later collection of essays *The End of the Poem* testifies to his abiding interest in the beginnings of vernacular poetry and in the troubador, stilnovist, and Dantean poetic projects.

25. It bears recalling that Corbin's own interdisciplinary interests led him far from his principal field of study—Islamic culture—to not only poetics but also philosophy. (He was the first French translator of Heidegger with his translation of "What Is Metaphysics?" from 1937.) More recently Agamben discusses Corbin's studies of the theological figure of the angel in BH, 25–26.

26. The English translation falsely renders the term *ritrovare* not as "recover" but as "discover."

27. In the first book in English to analyze Agamben's work extensively, Thomas Carl Wall (1999) discusses what he calls a "sense of almost comical erudition" in Agamben's writing (122).

CHAPTER 3

1. The original as well as the revised Italian editions of the work contain six chapters. The English translation contains a seventh chapter entitled "Notes on Gesture." This addition is nowhere acknowledged as such in the edition and is neither explained nor even noted (thus creating the false impression that the essay from 1992 was an original element of the work from 1978). Agamben himself included "Notes on Gesture" in his 1996 collection of essays *Means Without End*. The English translation of *Means Without End* (from 2000) also includes this essay (in a new translation and nowhere noting the earlier existence of a published English translation).

2. Agamben offers no reference for his citation—a practice that in Italy's academic culture is not exceptional. Somewhat more exceptional is that he does not directly name the essay from which it is drawn, merely stating that it is "from 1933" and that it discusses a "poverty of experience" (an expression that Agamben leaves in quotation marks, assuming that this indication would suffice for the curious reader to locate the essay in question). Instead of simply reproducing Agamben's remarks, the English translation gives a full bibliographical reference—but to the wrong essay (see IH, 62, n. 1). The information given is for Benjamin's "The Storyteller." That this is not the essay in question can easily be seen not only in the allusion to the work's title but also in the fact that "The Storyteller" is not from 1933 but from 1936. It should be noted, however, that "The Storyteller" deals with themes very similar to those in Benjamin's earlier essay and even includes passages reproduced verbatim from it.

3. It should be noted that Benjamin's interest in the term and category of *experience* has not only sociological but also philosophical sources. The latter are found in his responses to Kant undertaken in the late teens and in his rejection of the neo-Kantian philosophical school so influential in the German universities of the day (whose views were crystallized in Herman Cohen's *Kant's Theory of Experience*, published in 1871). As late as 1917, Benjamin still planned to write a dissertation on Kant focusing on the category of experience. Remnants of that project are to be found in essays such as "On the Program of the Coming Philosophy" (1918), with its calls for a correction of the dominant reading of Kant and for "a deeper, more metaphysically fulfilled experience" as opposed to the "mathematical" and "mechanical" one found in Kant, alongside a call "to create on the basis of the Kantian system a concept of knowledge to which a concept of experience [*Erfahrung*] corresponds" (Benjamin GS, 2.160). Of the "actual value" of Kant's conception of "experience" Benjamin claimed it was "virtually nill" (Benjamin GS, 2.159).

4. It is useful to bear in mind that Benjamin's position on experience was once very different. In one of his first publications, the short essay "'Experience [*Erfahrung*]'" (Benjamin himself places the titular "Experience" in quotation marks) from 1913, the twenty-one-year-old Benjamin attacks "experience" as the means of repression employed by older generations—above all the "philistines" among them—against the young. "Because he has never gazed upward toward the great and the meaningful, the Philistine makes of experience [*Erfahrung*] his gospel," writes Benjamin (GS, 2.55). This early and passionately idealistic essay levels an attack on the restricted imagination of the "Philistine," who is ignorant and boastful of everything "experience" has given him. Parents and Philistines (in secret collaboration) use the word *experience* as a magic wand to convert their own arbitrary opinions into facts that the young are expected to accept blindly. The "experience" excoriated in this essay is an experience unworthy of the name (thus the scare quotes in which he keeps it), and rather than being that which he will later lament his generation having lost, it is an early sign of that loss already under way. Nevertheless, the paradox implied in his later championing of the term *experience* did not escape Benjamin, and in a note written years later (undated but in all likelihood from 1929), he writes of his work from 1913: "In this early essay I mobilized all the rebellious energies of youth against the word 'experience [*Erfahrung*].' Now this word is a fundamental element in many of my writings. Despite this I have remained true to myself. My attack pierced the word without annihilating it. It maneuvered itself into the heart of the matter" (Benjamin GS, 2.902). In the notes for his *Arcades Project* he lists a solid recourse to "experience [*Erfahrung*]" as part of the "elementary doctrine of historical materialism" that guided his investigation (see Benjamin GS, 5.595).

5. The English translation omits the term *structure* [*la struttura*] from this passage.

6. Agamben's remarks here are substantially reproduced in an essay published two years later (see PS, 157–158).

7. Although this preface was adopted in the English translation of *Infancy and History*, its special provenance (the French translation) and later date of composition (1989) is nowhere noted therein.

8. Agamben returns to this idea in his most recent book (see SL, 97).

9. One of the dedicatees of this chapter of *Infancy and History* is French scholar and Gnosticism specialist Henri-Charles Puech, and it is likely that his work, as well as that of Heidegger's student and Gnosticism scholar Hans Jonas, influenced Agamben's sense of the temporal experience that is proper to Gnosticism. Puech is also referred to in RG, 58.

10. This is a topic to which Agamben will return in *The Idea of Prose*, where he claims that it is in Aristotle's description of pleasure in the *Nicomachean Ethics* that the categories of potentiality and act are at their most "transparent" (see IP, 71 [51]). In one of the few asides in Agamben's encyclopedia entry on taste he refers to "the doctrine of pleasure—which is to say, of ethics [*la dottrina del piacere, cioè con l'etica*]" (G, 1020).

11. In a posthumously published draft for a preface to his *Materiali mitologici,* Furio Jesi employs a kindred image, writing of these titular "mythological materials" that they are "that which we dispose of today, those mythological materials stamped by the fiery clock which places *hic et nunc* over every supposed *once upon a time*" (Jesi 2001, 350, italics in original).

12. It is doubtless with this idea in mind that Agamben refers to Marx's idea of a classless society as being for Benjamin "a genuinely messianic idea" (P, 56 [48]).

13. For more on the idea of the messianic and the idea of the profane, see Chapters Nine and Ten.

14. For an important view on this complicated question, see Scholem's interview from 1976 in which he discusses Adorno's misunderstanding of Benjamin's refusal of dialectical mediation (see Scholem 1980, 21–23).

15. Benjamin places the expression "all factuality is already theory" in quotation marks because it is borrowed from a passage in which Goethe writes that "the highest achievement would be to grasp that all factuality is already theory."

16. Because Benjamin had not meant them for publication, he had not given them a title. The one that Adorno eventually chose was *Über den Begriff der Geschichte* (On the Concept of History), which became *Theses on the Philosophy of History* in English.

17. Sic: As a rule, Brecht did not capitalize substantives (as German grammar dictates) in his *Arbeitsjournal.*

18. More recently Agamben has explicitly linked Benjamin's idea with Foucault's claim that his historical work was written in the shadow cast by his theoretical investigation of the present (see CCC, 28).

19. In a similar vein, Agamben says of the images Warburg called *Pathosformeln* that they owe their "particular aura" to their "kairologic saturation [*saturazione cairologica*]" (N, 54). In an essay from 1992 he links Warburg's conception of the image to Benjamin's dialectical image—a parallel he returned to more than a decade later in a different essay on Warburg (see MWE, 54–55 [49]; and N, 58ff.). It should then come as no surprise that Agamben will say of both Warburg's *Pathosformel* and Benjamin's "dialectical image" that they are "charged with time [*caricate di tempo*]" (LDV; and N, 53ff.).

20. Alain Badiou, the author of a very different book on Paul, views Agamben's linking of Paul and Benjamin with skepticism, referring to it as a "paradoxical proximity" (see Badiou 2006, 584).

21. Describing the statue, Posidippus says he had his hair over his eyes but was bald behind because opportunity could be grasped as he approached but never once he had passed (see *Anth. Plan.* 4. 275 and *The Oxford Classical Dictionary* entry on *Kairos*).

22. Agamben also refers to the term's usage by the Stoics (see IH, 101 [107]). As for Benjamin's formula, Agamben sees in it an echo of Kafka's claim that "Judgment Day is the normal condition of history" (IH, 102 [108]; see also Kafka's claim that "the decisive moment in human development is perpetual [*immerwährend*]" (Kafka 1966, 39–40). In Adorno's letter to Horkheimer glossing Benjamin's fourteenth thesis he writes that it "is not without resemblance to the *kairos* of our Tillich" (see Benjamin GS, 7.774). Adorno has good reason to allude to a similarity between the two conceptions. The German theologian and philosopher Paul Tillich distinguished in his writings—such as the 1922 essay "Kairos"—between *chronos,* or chronological time, and *kairos,* a moment of truth when radical innovations could be effected. (Tillich believed at the time that Germany was at just such a moment.) Benjamin might, however, just as easily have borrowed the term from Paul, as Agamben claims, or from the Gnostics, and been influenced by Kierkegaard's idea of the "instant." It is telling in this connection that a recent selection of Benjamin's writings has been published under the title *Kairos* (2007).

23. Agamben's conception of Benjaminian temporality is radically different from the conception of a critic such as Michael André Bernstein, who feels that Benjamin contradicts himself in saying that "nothing that has ever happened should be regarded as lost for history," because for Bernstein such a view "requires an understanding of time as a succession of content-rich differences, each valid in its own right, rather than as an endless repetition of identically meaning-

less units suddenly punctuated and redeemed by the thunderclap of the cataclys-
mically significant crisis" (Bernstein 2000, 88).

CHAPTER 4

1. The first Italian edition of the work contained only thirty chapters. Those
added to the German, French, and English translations of the work, which were
incorporated into the second Italian edition (from 2002), are "The Idea of Study,"
"The Idea of Politics," and "The Idea of Language II." The English translation
gives as its source text the 1985 first Italian edition despite the fact that it contains
these three chapters not found in that edition.

2. The latter is falsely rendered in the English translation as "The Idea of
Universal Judgment."

3. The English translation's reproduction of this image is unfortunately of
poor quality and renders it almost unintelligible. The idiosyncratic translation
of its title as "Frenzied Love on a Snail" makes the task of understanding it still
more difficult.

4. This evocative image has had a long and rich life. One of the most influential Greek commentators on Aristotle, Alexander of Aphrodisias (second century A.D.), paraphrased it thus: "reason [is] like a tablet that has not been written upon"—and it was from this expression that Albertus Magnus and Thomas
Aquinas derived the celebrated term *tabula rasa*. Agamben refers to Aristotle's
image in his next book, *The Coming Community* (CC, 37 [34]). In a side note
to the history of this image, Curtius tells how in the twelfth century Baudri of
Bourgueil, "a pleasant poet who had a particular fondness for the scribal art,"
chose to outdo Ausonius, who had written an ode to paper, by dedicating poem
after poem to his wax tablet notebooks; in this he was a worthy inheritor to
Damascius (see Curtius 1993, 317).

5. Already in his first book, after examining Aristotle's distinction between
potentiality and entelechy, Agamben turns to the modern conceptions of "work-
in-progress" and "open work" in light of Aristotle's idea of potentiality (see
MWC, 66 [100]).

6. This description of language's material as woodlike seems to refer to the
fact that the Greek word for the original or first matter of the universe—*hyle*, the
same word that Aristotle employs when discussing first matter—derives from a
Greek word for *wood* (in the sense of "forest"), the Latin translation of which was
silva. (The Latin *materia* also shared this connotation, referring to wood not in
the sense of forest but as the usable wood of a tree.)

7. This preface is from the first French edition of *Infancy and History* (1989).
The English translation (1993) reproduces this preface but without anywhere noting that it was not part of the original 1978 Italian edition it gives as its source.

The preface was first published in Italian in the second expanded edition of *Infanzia e storia* in 2001.

8. That Agamben employs the Latin *experimentum* to indicate something that is both an *experiment* and an *experience* is attested to by his use of the term elsewhere. For the clearest instance of such—"an experience [*esperienza*], an *experimentum*..." see MWE, 9 [17].

9. On the relationship of this question of an experimental experience of language itself as it relates to the idea of a writer's *motivum* or vocation, see also Agamben's discussion of Dante: "in response to this intimate aptitude for jargon that every language possesses, [Dante] proposes not the remedy of a national language and grammar (as a long-standing falsification of his thought maintains) but instead a transformation of the experience of speech itself [*una trasformazione dell'esperienza stessa della parola*], which he called *volgare illustre*—a deliverance—not grammatical, but poetic and political—of jargons in the direction of the *factum loquendi*" (MWE, 69 [58], translation modified).

10. Had this been made clear, de Man's exchange with M. H. Abrams that followed the lecture (which is reproduced in *The Resistance to Theory*) would doubtless have advanced along clearer lines.

11. This affective scale is found throughout *Allegories of Reading, The Resistance to Theory,* and *Aesthetic Ideology,* as well as in more diffuse form in his earlier collection *Blindness and Insight.*

12. Just as in Greek *aporia* meant a perplexing difficulty—and it has been adopted into modern languages to denote such—the more rare *euporia* means a thing easily and smoothly done.

13. Agamben cites this remark with quotation marks in IH (15 [xiv]) and without them in both P (40 [27]) and PP (79).

14. Agamben's translator and student Daniel Heller-Roazen echoes these questions at the close of his *The Inner Touch* (2007): "That which cannot be represented as any single thing reveals itself, at the limit, in the barest of perceptions without object: in the mere sense 'that we are sensing' and in the simple thought 'that we are thinking'" (Heller-Roazen 2007, 299).

15. This letter is quoted (but without noting its source) by Agamben in both IH (4 [VII]) and P (54 [45]).

16. In his final (and unfinished) work, *Aesthetic Theory,* Adorno quotes this passage, claiming that this "elimination of the unsayable" is best understood with the "addition" that "the ontological asceticism of language is the only way to nevertheless say the unsayable" (Adorno GS, 7.304–7.305).

17. Agamben seems here to be also alluding to a number of other treatments of this theme by philosophers both ancient and modern. The reader may think, for instance, of Wittgenstein—not only of his celebrated final sentence in the *Tractatus,* but also of such private remarks as those he writes in a letter from 1917: "if

only you do not try to utter what is unutterable—then *nothing* gets lost. But the unutterable will be—unutterably—*contained* in what has been uttered!" (Letter to Paul Engelmann, April 4, 1917; cited in Monk 1990, 151, italics in original).

18. It should be recalled that one of the central goals of Agamben's *Language and Death* was the study of the Western philosophical tradition's linking of language with negativity, and that to this end he sought to locate an "original structure of negativity" (see LD, xii [5]).

19. This passage is also found verbatim in MWE, 85 [69–70].

20. Here we can best appreciate the insight and intelligence of Heller-Roazen's reference to Agamben's "most original philosophical project: *to conceive of the existence of language as the existence of potentiality*" (P, 13, italics in original).

21. Wall concludes that this idea of indirection renders "any formal presentation" of Agamben's thought impossible: "Any commentary on the writings of Lévinas, Blanchot, and Agamben will be difficult, because each writes in such a way that our power to read is neutralized and dispersed. Each of these thinkers writes in such a way that communication is interrupted, and any formal presentation of their thought, such as ours here, is ceaselessly postponed" (Wall 1999, 6).

22. This idea is also well reflected in Agamben's "Tradition of the Immemorial," published the same year as *The Idea of Prose*. The essay is composed of twelve sections, each of which is divided between a short reflection on tradition and its memorialization by Agamben, and one or more citations without quotation marks from authors ranging from Plato to Heidegger, Aristotle to Wittgenstein, Damascius to Nancy, Hölderlin to Celan (see P, 104ff. [147ff.]).

23. The clause "which *is* language" is not found in the English translation.

24. Dominick LaCapra claims that in Agamben's writing, "a sustained intricacy of formulation and an insistently paratactic or 'poetic' style in philosophy make it both difficult to understand him in a way that enables critical exchange and possible for a sympathetic (or perhaps extremely generous) reader (or over-writer) to gloss questionable passages in a quasi-theological manner that always displaces attention to other, less dubious passages, even if they are to be found in another work" (LaCapra 2007, 133–134). Agamben's esoteric—or indirect—manner of approaching the questions that are most important to him means that, of necessity, readers awaiting a transparent message will be disappointed—and nowhere so much as in *Idea of Prose*.

25. This remark provides the title for Alexander García Düttmann's introduction to the English translation of *Idea of Prose*. See Düttmann 1995, 3–25. Düttmann's analysis places special emphasis on the proximity of Agamben's views to those of not only Benjamin but also Adorno, as well as stressing the role of potentiality in Agamben's thinking.

26. This phrase is found verbatim in an essay entitled "Quattro glosse a Kafka" ("Four Glosses for Kafka") published in 1986 (see QGK, 43).

27. It bears noting that many of the citations that Benjamin used in his *Origin of German Tragic Drama* are not to be found where Benjamin locates them. On this curious point, see the editor's remarks in Benjamin GS, 1.978–1.981; and Voigt 2000, 826ff.

28. Agamben refers in *Stanzas* to "a vicious circle of authority and citation (the authority is the source of the citation but the citation is the source of authority), which renders impossible the birth of real authority in the modern world," and which he distinguishes from the practices of the Middle Ages (S, 74 [85]). Elsewhere Agamben attacks the cliquish citational practices of academics, focusing particularly on footnotes (see AA, xi–xii).

29. *Ein Stimmenimitator* is literally an imitator of voices, as well as an allusion to the title of a play by Thomas Bernhard, *Der Stimmenimitator* (1978).

30. He interrupted this project when Silvio Berlusconi's Mondadori-Mediaset corporation acquired the publishing house (Einaudi) for which he had been preparing the edition.

31. See IR; Missac 1983, 30ff.; and Benjamin GS, 7.526. Agamben's article announcing the discoveries is brief and formal, listing the discoveries and noting that they contained papers from Benjamin's youth, including a series of sonnets written after the death of his childhood friend Heinle, as well as a group of texts from the 1930s. In an interview conducted several years later, he noted that the two large folders he had unearthed had been placed with the private affairs of Bataille's late widow, and that "there have not failed to be . . . certain superfluous nationalistic and professorial jealousies" linked to this discovery (UIGA, 33). Paul Hegarty upbraids Agamben for wishing to distance Bataille and Benjamin, wrongly claiming that Agamben "ignor[ed] . . . Benjamin's entrusting his papers to Bataille when leaving for Spain" (Hegarty 2005, 242, n. 8).

32. The editors of the German edition return to the matter elsewhere, thanking Agamben for a photocopy of the theses, as well as expressing frustration that despite repeated requests he has refused to divulge where he discovered this and other manuscripts (see GS VII.782). Agamben ends his brief *Bibliothèque Nationale* article by announcing his discoveries of 1981 with the note, "Concerning another, more restricted, group of Benjamin's manuscripts that I have been able to recover (containing, among other items, the *Handexemplar* of Benjamin's *Über den Begriff der Geschichte*) I will give further details in the near future" (IR, 6). In an interview in which he discusses this discovery, he notes only that like his other discovery they were found in Paris, but "in different circumstances" from the folders from the National Library (UIGA, 33). Agamben reproduced a photograph of the second thesis from this *Handexemplar* in *The Time That Remains* (see TTR, 140 [130]).

33. Agamben's account is not, however, fully accurate. Apelles, the favorite painter of Alexander the Great and widely credited in antiquity as the greatest

painter of all time, lived at the end of the fourth century B.C. Most of what is known of him comes from Pliny's *Historia Naturalis* (see especially, for the anecdote in question, vol. 35, 181–183). The story that Agamben summarily recounts is as follows: Apelles comes to Rhodes to visit the painter Protogenes. Finding him not at home but a panel freshly prepared to be painted on in his studio, Apelles takes up a brush and makes a single, extremely fine line, which he then confides to a servant of Protogenes, asking that this line serve as his calling card. Protogenes, returning home, finely divides this fine line with one of his own, in a different (unnamed) color, and instructs his servant that in the event that the visitor comes again, he should be shown the panel. Apelles, returning some time later, finds Protogenes again not at home, and when he is shown his line divided, he divides it again with a third line, even finer, in a third (unnamed) color. Protogenes, returning home, recognizes the skill of Apelles, renounces any attempt to better it, and rushes to the port to greet Apelles. Agamben's account foreshortens the episode, leaving out the first visit, and the first line, of Apelles, as well Apelles and Protogenes' crossing paths (see TTR, 50–51 [52–53]). The panel in question was preserved and later displayed in the palace of the Caesars in Rome until perishing in a fire. No extant traces of Apelles' paintings exist. See also Gombrich 1976, 14–15; and Damisch 1995, 120–23.

34. The increasingly important role of Agamben's development of Benjamin's ideas can easily be seen in the representative work *Benjamin Handbuch: Leben, Werk, Wirkung* (Lindner 2006).

35. Heller-Roazen chose this remark for the title of his introduction to *Potentialities* and noted Benjamin's recurrent use of it in P, 275, n.1. In addition to the occurrences he notes there is an additional one in Benjamin's work—the epigraph to *Konvolut M* [*Der Flaneur*] of the *Arcades Project* (see GS, 5.524). Benjamin borrowed the phrase from Hofmannsthal's play *Der Tor und der Tod* ("Death and the Fool," 1894), the final lines of which are as follows (von Hofmannsthal 1894, 79–80):

> *DER TOD indem er kopfschüttelnd langsam abgeht*:
> *Wie wundervoll sind diese Wesen,*
> *Die, was nicht deutbar, dennoch deuten,*
> *Was nie geschrieben wurde, lesen,*
> *Verworrenes beherrschend binden*
> *Und Wege noch im Ewig-Dunkeln finden.*

CHAPTER 5

1. Wall finds that "the structure of Agamben's book is crazy, slightly drunk (even as the thinking in it is precise and delicate)" (1999, 121). He compares its chapters to "panels (like in comic books)" before noting that "we may describe the book as erudite, or as a philosophical serendipity, but that seems beside the point, for it is as if these panels came from elsewhere than one mind or one thinker" (121).

2. It bears noting that a year after Nancy's book appeared Agamben published an essay entitled "Bataille e il paradosso della sovranità," which discusses the ideas of community found in Bataille, Blanchot, and Nancy, as well as anticipating important elements of both *The Coming Community* and *Homo Sacer.*

3. In his entry on Agamben for the *Encyclopedia of Postmodernism,* David Clippinger (2001) writes, "Perhaps the most significant contribution by Agamben has been his meditation upon how the postmodern emphasis upon identity politics prompts a return to the centrality of ethics in any discussion of the social" (6).

4. As we will see, this same singular status of the example—lying both within and beyond that which it represents—corresponds precisely to the space of the sovereign in political theory and to the exception in legal theory as these are explored in *Homo Sacer* and *State of Exception.*

5. Another aspect of the theological question of the resurrected body is raised in *Profanations* (see PR, 29).

6. Agamben's discussion of the paradigmatic status of the Christian conception of limbo will remain a source of interest and a paradigm for the profane order he envisions. In *Profanations* he returns to this topic (see PR, 47). His interest in suspended figures is also found in "Nymphae," where he discusses the creatures of which Parcelsus speaks (such as nymphs), who in Agamben's paraphrase are "forever beyond the economy of salvation and redemption" (N, 62).

7. The degree to which Agamben juxtaposes Jewish and Christian theological motifs is rare, and has its most significant parallel in the work of Adorno.

8. The Latin title is retained in the English translation (but is mistranscribed as "Principium indivuationis").

9. Like its author, "Bartleby, the Scrivener: A Story of Wall-Street" is famously obscure. Melville published it anonymously in 1853 and, like his most famous novel, it knew next to no success during his lifetime. Aptly enough, no complete manuscript of the copyist's tale has survived—all that remains is a single page containing a brief passage copied out in Augusta Melville's hand. After copying out eleven lines of the story, she left off, perhaps frustrated by an ink blot that marred her clean copy. The sheet of paper survived in Melville's papers because she later reused it to copy out lists of addresses (see Melville 1987, 572–73).

10. Agamben correctly calls Bartleby not a scribe (*scriba*) but a scrivener (*scrivano*)—a distinction important here because a *scrivener* is not only a copyist but also a notary—and thereby a man of the law. Melville makes this amply clear by referring to him as a "law-copyist or scrivener" (Melville 1987, 13).

11. The two essays were published together in *Bartleby: La formula della creazione* (Agamben and Deleuze 1993). Deleuze's essay, "Bartleby, or the Formula," is translated in *Essays Critical and Clinical* (Deleuze 1997) and the original is found in *Critique et clinique* (Deleuze 1993). Alexander Cooke claims that "the arguments made by Deleuze and Agamben, which can be ultimately united under the concept of resistance, fail to account for an important element of that which they uncover in 'Bartleby, the Scrivener'" and that Cooke calls "the *materiality* of the law" (Cooke 2005, 80, emphases in original). In *Empire,* Negri and Hardt (2001, 204, 446, n. 1) write that Bartleby's preference "is the beginning of a liberatory politics, but it is still only a beginning." In light of Agamben's interest in the figure of Bartleby—above all from the mid-1980s to the mid-1990s—it is interesting to note that the sixth of the Harvard lectures that Calvino planned to give, and the only one he did not live to write, was to treat Bartleby. Calvino's daughter has noted of this lecture, "I know only that it was to refer to Herman Melville's Bartleby"(Calvino 1993, vi).

12. It should be recalled that Bartleby's refusal is not only a refusal to write. It is first copying that he would prefer not to do, but as the story progresses, the things he would prefer not to do become more vital—ending in his preference for not eating. The latter preference leads him in the war of attrition he has been waging with an unseen adversary to his preferring simply not to be. On a psychological level, it should be noted that Bartleby is given all the apathetic traits of a form of autism—as in his persistent "turning away" from his interlocutors and his preferring not to look them in the eyes to his final curling up to leave his life (Melville 1987, 44–45). In later works, such as *Remnants of Auschwitz,* the figure of autistic withdrawal is one that interests Agamben—most centrally the figure of the *Muselmann*—but there too it is not the psychological coordinates that he stresses.

13. Avicenna's distinctions are based on Aristotle's precedent (see *On the Soul* 412a9 and *Metaphysics* 1048a33–35).

14. From Leibniz's *Theodicy.* Agamben returns to this figure in the later Bartleby essay, as well as in an afterword to a French edition of *Stanzas* in 1994.

15. The extraordinarily reclusive Blanchot worked as a right-wing journalist and activist in the 1930s and made his only later public appearance (in support of the left) in May 1968. As concerns his privacy, Blanchot gave no interviews, and the two surviving photographs of him that have been published are emblematic: the first, dating from around 1925, shows him with tie, spats, and cane perched on the trunk of an automobile next to an equally young Lévinas and in the company

of another male friend and two ladies; the second, from 1985, is a grainy image of the aging writer alone in a supermarket parking lot.

16. The massacre in question took place on June 4, 1989, and is customarily referred to by that date. There were protests throughout May, but to refer to a "Chinese May" is to evoke above all the student protest of May 4, 1919. One reason for Agamben's reference appears to be the symmetry with the French protests of May 1968.

17. This is by no means a matter of general consensus, and whatever the paradigmatic value of the Tiananmen protests and massacre, the reaction of the government, however contemptible, is not a major anomaly—especially given the threats to communism taking place elsewhere in the world that year, as well as domestic issues such as high unemployment.

18. On a number of occasions Agamben credits acts of sovereign violence with a remarkable degree of intentionality and "lucidity." He uses virtually the same terms to describe this same event in an essay on Debord: "the Chinese leaders acted, from their point of view, with perfect lucidity" (MWE, 89 [73]). The clarity ascribed to such violence can also be seen in an essay from 1995 in which Agamben refers to the "lucid fury" with which "the German *Volk*" tried to forever eliminate the Jews from the body politic as the Jews represented an identity not bound to the state (see MWE, 34 [34]). In these cases the "lucidity" ascribed to acts of state-sponsored violence demands clarification. This is not the calculating lucidity of a brutal *Realpolitik,* but a deeper lucidity, an instinctive response on the part of representatives of the state to elements within it that they have difficulty disciplining, controlling, and punishing because those elements resist identification, localization, and subjection. In an article treating Agamben's *Remnants of Auschwitz,* David Bidussa credits Agamben with "a considerable philosophical sensibility" and a "rare capacity for reflecting on lexical and linguistic planes," but a "certain insufficiency on the analytical plane." He locates this insufficiency in crediting the Nazis with a "diabolical intelligence" in the treatment of their victims, whereas, in his view, it was far less "intelligence" than "ferocity" that was characteristic of the Nazis' actions (Bidussa 1998, 21, 22). Although this is true, it misses the thrust of Agamben's argument. Whether Agamben is right concerning the reality of such thoroughgoing or deep "lucidity" is of course another matter.

19. The English translation mistakenly renders *mondo abitabile* as "*un*inhabitable world."

20. Agamben first read Debord in the summer of 1968 (see UL, 17). In a section from *Stanzas* entitled "Eclipse of the Work," Agamben evokes the Situationists, and in the years thereafter he referred to Debord and his ideas with increasing regularity (S, 54 [63]). Not only do Debord's insights play a role in *The Coming Community, Homo Sacer,* and *Means Without End,* but they also feature

prominently in Agamben's recent books, *Profanations* and *Il Regno e la Gloria* (see especially RG, 10–11, 280).

21. This is an idea that is also found in an essay on Debord by Paolo Virno (from a collection entitled *I Situazionsti,* which begins with an essay by Agamben), who stresses that in Debord's society of the spectacle, "language presents itself at once as the area of conflict and as what is at stake" (Virno 1991, 26). For an analysis of the semantic range and relations of the term *spectacle* as it relates *in* to the terms *species, specter, speculum, speculation, species,* and even the Greek *eidos,* see PR, 61ff.

22. Agamben refers to the Shekinah in an essay on Benjamin from 1982 in connection with the idea of redemption, and he returns to it two years later in his discussion of the poetry of Paul Celan in the essay "The Just Do Not Feed On Light" from *The End of the Poem* (see P, 143 [213]).

23. The second instance is in the scholium to this chapter, the third is in MWE, 84 [68]. Agamben also refers to it in passing in BH, 17–18.

24. Elsewhere, Agamben, citing Hölderlin, says of a "free use of the proper" that it is "the most difficult task" (P, 204 [319]).

25. Although Agamben does not refer to Nietzsche in this connection, his expression echoes the latter's reference, in *Will to Power,* to nihilism as "this most uncanny of all guests [*dieses unheimlichsten aller Gäste*]." That Heidegger singles out and cites Nietzsche's epithet in a discussion of Ernst Jünger makes it all the more likely that Agamben was familiar with it and had it in mind (see Heidegger GA, 9.387).

26. The English translators mistranslate the term *extreme* here as "terminal."

27. Falsely dated as from 1995 in the English translation.

28. Heller-Roazen ends his introduction to *Potentialities* with a reference to this "coming community," which he describes as "without identity, defined by nothing other than its existence in language as irreducible, absolute potentiality" (P, 23).

29. After arguing that Derrida has misunderstood Kafka's parable on the law, Agamben turns to Derrida's misunderstanding of a text that is decisive for Agamben's own project: Benjamin's "For a Critique of Violence." Therein he notes Derrida's "peculiar misunderstanding" of what Benjamin calls "divine violence," which allows Derrida to compare it to the (Nazi) "Final Solution" (HS, 64 [73]). Like Geulen, both Mills and Marchart also see Derrida and Agamben first part theoretical ways at this point (see Mills 2004, 50–57; and Marchart 2007, 10). In her essay on undecidability in Derrida and Agamben, Elke Lachert (2007) does not trace this relation farther back than to *Homo Sacer.*

30. A more clear-cut philological reproach is also found in a much later text, "Friendship," in which Agamben recounts having discussed with Derrida, when the latter was writing the book that became *The Politics of Friendship,* the phrase

"oh friends, there are no friends" (*o philoi, oudeis philos*) from Diogenes Laertius' *Lives of the Philosophers,* which was to become the motto of Derrida's book. Agamben relates how his interest was piqued by their discussion and how he took it upon himself to trace this remark cited by, among many others, Montaigne and Nietzsche, back to its source, with the curious result that he found in Diogenes Laertius that the remark was the result of an error and that the original contains a different statement—one letter different—*oi* [an *iota* after the *omega*] *philoi, oudeis philos*: "he who has (many) friends, has no friend." That which Montaigne and Nietzsche cite is an error that had already been corrected by a seventeenth-century Swiss philologist, Isaac Casaubon, and that nevertheless continued to circulate (see F, 3). "Since I had immediately informed Derrida of the results of my research," Agamben writes, "I was astonished, when his book was published . . . not to find there any trace of the problem. If the motto—apocryphal according to modern philologists—appeared there in its original form, it was certainly not out of forgetfulness" but was "essential to the book's strategy" (F, 3). Agamben is wrong to be astonished, however, as there is indeed a clear trace of this problem in Derrida's book. Derrida raises the possibility that the version he uses of the remark may have resulted from "the bias of a copyist or a reader in a hurry" and thanks a group of "friends" among whom figures "Giorgio Agamben" (see Derrida 1994, 208 [234–35] and 225 [251]; see also Samuel Weber 2007, 1040–42). Both Weber and Wortham focus on questions of friendship, philosophy, and understanding as they are raised in Agamben's essay "Friendship" and in Derrida's *Politics of Friendship* (see Weber 2007 and Wortham 2007).

31. Agamben elaborates in that essay: "As phonology and structuralism have shown, metaphysics can do without the supremacy of the voice. . . . What is essential to the metaphysical project is that there be a *logos,* an interlacing of knowledge and speech; but it is of little importance whether this *logos* is located in the voice, in writing, or in an unconscious" (PS, 163).

32. As Attell has pointed out, this criticism rests on the debatable assumption that Derrida's deconstruction is to be understood as a surpassing of metaphysics after the fashion of Heidegger (see Attell 2006).

33. What is at issue here is of course nothing less than a definition of messianism. For a treatment of this question, see Chapter Ten.

34. Derrida's deconstruction is also compared to Foucault's archeology (as well as to Nietzsche's genealogy and Benjamin's dialectical image) in *Il Regno e la Gloria* (see RG, 16).

35. In a recent interview Agamben spoke of ways in which "pornography has made it impossible to distinguish sexuality as a public or a private matter" (PWP, 24). On the related level of the erotic word (as opposed to the erotic image), Agamben has shown a singular interest in the erotic poetics of the troubadors. The study, more broadly, of the latent and manifest eroticism of language is some-

thing that Agamben admired in the work of Lacan. (Agamben repeatedly singles out Lacan for his sharp-sighted analyses of the erotics of language—see, for one such instance, PS, 160). In an essay from 1979 Agamben describes how the Middle Ages often "assimilated sexual and grammatical rules, sexual perversions and grammatical violations"; the mysteriously titled essay "Corn" from *The End of the Poem* treats related matters (PS, "*La parola et il sapere,*" 156).

36. Cesare Casarino has written of "the elective affinity between pornography and communism" as a "political-philosophical conundrum that comes to haunt the writings of Giorgio Agamben," and he suggests, for his own part, what he calls a "pornocairology" as an element in its solution (see Casarino 2002, 120ff.).

37. Debord's strategic activities were not, of course, limited to his writings, and he went the further step of going underground and engaging in what he saw as guerilla revolutionary activity in Italy and Spain. To hone his strategic skills Debord also devoted a great deal of time and energy to the development of his Game of War (see Wark 2008).

38. The translational difficulty presented by the Italian word *potenza,* and by Debord's French term *puissance,* which corresponds to it, is also seen here. In English, the translator can choose either the blunt and forceful *power* or the at times abstract-sounding *potentiality,* but there is no ready term at his or her disposal that connotes a fusing of the two that is expressed by the French *puissance* and the Italian *potenza,* which is at the heart, for Agamben, of Debord's strategic effort.

39. Both men were early champions of Walser's work. In a touching turn of phrase, Benjamin once wrote of Walser's sentences, "Sie kommen in der Nacht, wo sie am schwärzesten ist, einer venezianischen, wenn man will, von dürftigen Lampions der Hoffnung erhellten, mit etwas Festglanz im Auge, aber verstört und zum Weinen traurig" (Benjamin GS, II.326). Agamben refers to Walser not only in *The Coming Community* but also in *Profanations* (see PR, 14). Anton Schütz (2000) asks, "Is Agamben's *homo sacer* his *homo Walser?*" (131). For more on Agamben's relation to Walser's writing, see Plug 2005. For an astoundingly apt commentary on Walser's art, see Mirra 2008.

40. Agamben also cites this remark (without quotation marks) in an essay from 1980 (see PP, 79).

CHAPTER 6

1. Speed and lightness play a central role in the Harvard lectures that Calvino lived to write but not to give (see Calvino 1993).

2. This essay is entitled "Comedy." In it Agamben traces how Dante abandoned his "tragic" project for a "comic" one with his *Divine Comedy.* He argues that Dante's choice of title and genre, contrary to what Boccaccio was to lead

many generations of readers to believe, had to do not with the "vulgar" language in which Dante chose to write, but, as Dante himself indicates in the letter to Cangrande, with the movement of the poem from "harsh" and "horrible" at its outset to "prosperous, desirable, and pleasant" at its end. "Insofar as it is a 'comedy,'" writes Agamben, "the poem is . . . an itinerary from guilt to innocence and not from innocence to guilt" (EP, 8 [12]).

3. It bears recalling, however, that animals were not infrequently brought to (ecclesiastical) trial during the Middle Ages, when cases are on record of rats, leeches, cocks, horses, sows, and other animals being brought to justice. See Réal 2006.

4. It bears noting that Agamben often returns to the terms *creature* and *new creature* in subsequent works. The "new creature" evoked at the end of Agamben's essay "Bartleby, or On Contingency" proves to be a citation without quotation marks from Paul's Second Letter to the Corinthians and is also evoked in *The Time That Remains.* As we will see in a later chapter, the term *creature* plays a central role in *The Open.*

5. This English translation by Cesare Casarino first appeared in Virno and Hardt, 1996. Casarino is cotranslator of Agamben's *Means Without End,* and his translation of this essay ("Form-of-Life") is reproduced therein.

6. Edmund Jephcott translates Benjamin's phrase not as "bare life" but as "mere life" (see Benjamin 1977b, 297). "The Critique of Violence" was composed alongside two other essays that have been lost—one tellingly entitled (for Agamben's interest in *Homo Sacer*) "Life and Violence [*Leben und Gewalt*]," which Benjamin noted in a letter of April 1920, was "written from my heart"; the second essay, "The True Politician [*Die wahre Politiker*]," contained or was to contain chapters (also suggestive of Agamben's later interests) bearing the titles "The Dismantling of Violence [*Abbau der Gewalt*]" and "Teleology Without End [*Teleologie ohne Endzweck*]" (see Benjamin GS, 2.943). Although Agamben does not refer to the background of this singular term's first appearance and the lost texts that mark it, there can be no doubt that he was aware of them.

7. Agamben returns to "the ambivalence of the term *sacer*" in *Il sacramento del linguaggio* (SL, 20). Ojakangas (2005a, 10) wrongly claims that "Agamben sees no ambivalence in the original meaning of the sacred."

8. Agamben noted in 1985 that in the face of the new attention to, honors for, and study of Arendt's work, he felt "a sense of irreparable delay, of a historical opportunity that had been missed" (UIGA, 33). Speaking more generally, Agamben has remarked that "the history of Italian culture is a history of missed opportunities" (AA, xxxiv).

9. Foucault's own development of those ideas can be traced to his earlier writings on *le grand enfermement* and to his "genealogical" analyses of how, in the modern era, states have come to concern themselves ever more intensively with

hitherto neglected or ignored aspects of the lives of their citizens—up to and including their biological existence. As Foucault showed in a series of studies from *The Birth of the Clinic* to *Discipline and Punish,* modern states have increasingly focussed their energies and attentions on the biological being, health, and hygiene of their citizens. Institutions such as the prison and the asylum offered Foucault privileged sites from which to observe the emergence of this biopolitical paradigm and the ways that modern individuals came to see themselves as, in more ways than one, subjects of the state.

10. This essay was originally published in a collective work alongside essays by Alain Badiou and Jean-Luc Nancy. In the book's preface, its editor laconically summarizes its rationale: "This book was born of a profound dissatisfaction—bordering on rage—with contemporary political discourse" (Zanardi 1993, 7).

11. In an essay from 2002 Agamben refers to the distinction between right and left as one that has "ceased to have any meaning" (NSIV, 118).

12. Elsewhere Agamben talks of Foucault's decision to leave law to the side in favor of what the latter considered more "concrete" matters (LDV).

13. The former term (archeology) is treated at various points in Agamben's recent writings, most prominently in the third and final chapter of *Signatura rerum,* entitled "Philosophical Archeology" (SG, 82–111). As its title indicates, "Archeolgia di un'archeologia" treats the topic at length (see especially AA, xviii–xxiv). Agamben's most recent work, *Il sacramento del linguaggio,* conceives of itself as a "philosophical archeoglogy of the idea of swearing oaths" (SL, 4). The latter term (genealogy), which Foucault famously borrowed from Nietzsche, also finds a variety of treatments in Agamben's work and even appears in the subtitle of Part 2.2 of *Homo Sacer: Toward a Theological Genealogy of Economy and Government.* Agamben notes at that book's outset, "This work . . . follows in the wake of Michel Foucault's research on the genealogy of government and governance while also seeking to understand why it was never completed" (RG, 9). On a critical note, Neal (2006) claims that "Agamben reads Foucault structurally rather than genealogically" (39). Relatedly, Ross (2008) finds that Agamben's "approach reverses Foucault's ascending methodology and leaves us to ask what the reasoning from extreme instances tells us about the hold of Agamben's analysis on the phenomena it wishes to decode" (6).

14. Patton argues that Foucault's analyses already contained these elements, albeit in somewhat indirect form (see Patton 2007, 214).

15. See also Žižek's remark in an interview from the following year: "For Agamben there is no place for the democratic project of renegotiating the limit that separates full citizens from homo sacer by gradually allowing their voices to be heard; rather, his point is that, in today's postpolitics, the very democratic public space is a mask concealing the fact that, ultimately, we are all *homo sacer*" (Žižek 2003, 494). In an interview conducted a year later, Žižek claimed that "Agamben's

basic insight is the following: it's not 'democracy will be abolished and we will return to some emergency state'; it's that we have two apparently opposed tendencies today. On the one hand, we have so-called biopolitics, that is to say, more and more our lives are controlled through state mechanisms. On the other hand, we have what right wingers usually refer to as a liberal, extreme narcissism, this 'culture of complaint' or 'culture of victimization'" (Žižek 2004, 83–84). Elsewhere Žižek has formulated his ideas on the *homines sacri* differently, writing that "today, as a term denoting exclusion, [*homo sacer*] can be seen to apply not only to terrorists, but also to those who are on the receiving end of humanitarian aid (Rwandans, Bosnians, Afghans), as well as to the Sans Papiers in France and the inhabitants of the favelas in Brazil or the African American ghettoes in the U.S. Concentration camps and humanitarian refugee camps are, paradoxically, the two faces, 'inhuman' and 'human,' of one sociological matrix" (Žižek 2002a, 1). In an essay from that same year, Noys also relates humanitarian interventions to Agamben's idea of "bare life" (see Noys 2002, 59).

16. In a footnote to "Giorgio Agamben and the Spatialities of the Camp: An Introduction," Ek remarks, "In preparation for this article, I reread *Homo Sacer* during a family vacation visiting family-oriented, heavily populated [Swedish] sun resorts and theme parks such as *Lådbilslandet* ('buggy land' or 'trolley land'). While my children Amanda and Alexander, happily unaware that they are also potential *homines sacri*, drove electrified trolleys for hours, my reading of Agamben became more intense and more clarifying" (Ek 2006, 379, n. 22).

17. Although Agamben nowhere refers to this essay, given that it was first published in a 1942 commemorative volume dedicated to the memory of Benjamin makes it certain that Agamben was familiar with it. For more on Agamben's relation to Adorno, see Chapters Four and Ten.

18. Although he offers no examples, LaCapra perhaps has in mind such statements as Derrida's *il n'y a pas d'hors-texte*, Barthes's "the death of the author," Lacan's "there are no sexual relations," or Monique Wittig's "a lesbian is not a woman." For a different view of this question, see William Flesch's remark that "the ease with which translation can yield mock-profundity has been a hazard for English readers of Blanchot, Lévinas, and Agamben (as perhaps has been the native ease with which French and Italian speakers may read them). The stylistic infelicity of the English language for their kind of writing has not infrequently tended to yield in their followers a kind of empty sloganeering, a claim to some knowledge different from the greet eerie clarity so essential to what they are saying" (Flesch 1999, ix-x).

19. This genealogical point is stressed in the first part of *Signatura rerum;* see especially 11–34.

20. See LDV; LKA, 16; SR, 18ff.

21. It bears noting that Negri's co-author for both *Labor of Dionysus* (1994) and *Empire* (2000), Michael Hardt, raises a different objection to this point in Agamben's work: "My hesitation with this view is that by posing the extreme case of the concentration camp as the heart of sovereignty it tends to obscure the daily violence of modern sovereignty in all its forms. It implies, in other words, that if we could do away with the camp then all the violence of sovereignty would also disappear" (Hardt and Dumm 2000, 14–15). Hardt continues: "The most significant difference between our projects, though, is that Agamben dwells on modern sovereignty whereas we claim that modern sovereignty has now come to an end and transformed into a new kind of sovereignty, what we call imperial sovereignty. Imperial sovereignty has nothing to do with the concentration camp. It no longer takes the form of a dialectic between Self and Other and does not function through any such absolute exclusion, but rules rather through mechanisms of differential inclusion, making hierarchies of hybrid identities. This description may not immediately give you the same sense of horror that you get from Auschwitz and the Nazi Lager, but imperial sovereignty is certainly just as brutal as modern sovereignty was, and it has its own subtle and not so subtle horrors" (15–16).

22. As concerns the question of determinism in Agamben's thought, Laclau is responding to an element that has perplexed even the most well-disposed of his readers. For more on this question, see Goisis 2007; Johns 2005; Khurana 2002, 2007; and Norris 2005.

23. Norris clearly has in mind the following remark from *Remnants of Auschwitz:* "Simply to deny the *Muselmann*'s humanity would be to accept the verdict of the SS and to repeat their gesture" (RA, 63 [57]).

24. Alongside Foucault's interesting books, Agamben clearly has in mind, among others, Marc Bloch's *Les Rois thaumaturges* (1924) and Ernst Kantorowicz's *The King's Two Bodies* (1957).

25. In a recent essay, Agamben speaks of the epistemological "civil war" raging between logic and analogy that he finds expertly treated in the work of Enzo Melandri, whose work he relates to Foucault (see AA).

26. Although this comparison may help Agamben's reader better understand the logical structure of his paradigms, it is far from clear that Kant's example helps his case. Agamben's account is perfectly accurate, and perceptive, but it also risks equating *aesthetic* categories with *epistemological* ones. For Agamben there is no rule that governs which things in a given ensemble can become paradigms, but comparing their selection to the ineffable perception of artistic beauty is not the most reassuring parallel for skeptical readers. An additional point of potential misunderstanding is that although Agamben presents his paradigms as a means to the end of understanding a given historical structure—or alternately, "our present situation"—works of art, following Kant, when they are perceived

as beautiful, are perceived as such independently of any considerations of use or end.

27. I discuss this idea in depth in Chapter Nine (devoted to Agamben's *State of Exception*).

28. Bruno Gullì (2007, 221) calls this chapter "philosophically speaking, the strongest and most philosophically interesting chapter of *Homo Sacer*," but he limits himself to summarizing Aristotle's conception of potentiality. Thomas Docherty's account (2002, 32) goes no farther, nor does Carlo Sini's (though it does add a Heideggerian gloss to Aristotle's ideas on potentiality as invoked by Agamben) (see Sini 1996, 493ff.). Colin McQuillan (2005) admirably engages with the responses of Negri, Žižek, and Butler on questions about the intersection of ethics, political theory, and an ontology of potentiality. Elise Guidoni (1998) approaches the question of potentiality not in the classically philosophical terms employed by Agamben but instead in terms of a psychoanalytically inflected theory of language. In a related vein, Kalliopi Nikolopoulou (2000) claims that "Agamben wishes to terminate the dialectic of potentiality and actuality," but does not ultimately clarify what sort of wish this is. Comparing Agamben to Freud, Nikolopoulou ultimately judges that "despite Agamben's preference for a non-psychological description of the struggle of human life against external power, *Homo Sacer* too is haunted by its own oedipal confrontations—in this case, with the Western political tradition it wishes to overcome in order to generate a new politics" (127, 131).

29. Somewhat more rarely, critics have taken up the question of Agamben's genealogy of the idea of *sacrality*, as has Jean-Phillipe Guinle (1997, vi–vii), who claims that Agamben does not sufficiently emphasize the properly Christian sacralisation of life—particularly in the cases of the figures of Augustine and Paul.

30. Virno's interest in Aristotle's categories of potentiality and actuality and their relation to political questions is seen at a number of points. See in particular Virno 1999. Agamben briefly distinguishes his vision of the potentiality of the past from Virno's in SR, 106.

31. Negri's 2002 republication of *Il potere costituente* contains responses to both Agamben's criticisms and those of Étienne Balibar. Negri brings together Agamben's reservations with Balibar's (very different) objections, noting that "constituent power . . . presents itself as a powerful singularity that cannot be reduced to the unrelenting repetitions of the Bergsonian creative and constitutive functions (as Balibar wants) or attracted to its domineering opposite, sovereignty, as Agamben wants (perhaps in search of an ontological alterity, bare life, which sounds like an utopian escape)" (Negri 2002, 10; cited and translated by Nielson 2004, 69). Nielson observes that "even in the introduction to the 2002 reissue of *Il potere costituente,* where Negri confronts the criticisms of *Homo Sacer* direct-

ly, there is a reluctance to engage patiently with Agamben's argument" (Nielson 2004, 69). Nielson compellingly argues that "Agamben and Negri, then, despite their incessant cross-referencing, read past each other" (71).

32. As is evidenced in a variety of works, Bataille is a decisive thinker for Agamben, but not in those realms and in association with those terms and topics with which he is most commonly linked. It is the idea of *désoeuvrement* that most interests Agamben, whereas Bataille's more famous conceptions of *eroticism* and *interior experience,* as well as his idea of the *sacred,* are ones that Agamben does not find particularly fruitful and, in the case of the latter, criticizes. For a treatment of the *sacred* as it arises in Agamben's work and that stresses its distance from Bataille's preoccupation with this same term, see Grottanelli 1996, 485–490. For Agamben's views on Bataille's idea of *sovereignty,* see BPS.

33. Connolly's own proposed solution is what he calls "renegotiating the ethos of sovereignty to mesh more smoothly with a culture of deep pluralism" (Connolly 2007, 28).

34. A list that Agamben's interpreters consistently update, from Žižek's (2002) inclusion of terrorists and recipients of humanitarian aid to Claudio Minca's (2006, 387) discussion of the case of the Brazilian electrician killed by the British police in the London Underground on July 22, 2005.

35. For a treatment of the at once "disturbing" and "provocative" proximity of Agamben's ideas of bare life and form-of-life, as well as how the one is a "counter-figure" for the other, see Khurana 2007, 32ff.

36. See also Agamben's remarks on the reappearance of concentration camps in the former Yugoslavia in the essay "What Is a Camp?" first published a year before *Homo Sacer* (see MWE, 44 [40–41]).

37. See Michael Dillon's claim that "Agamben takes Foucault's account of biopolitics away from history and relocates it in the center of . . . key determinants of political philosophy," as well as that "the key point of dispute with Agamben is then ontologisation versus historicisation" (Dillon 2005, 38, 42).

38. Agamben gives no examples here, but one might be found in the genealogy of sovereignty he traces in *Homo Sacer.* Another, more subtle historical shadow might be found in the link Agamben draws in a later installment of the *Homo Sacer* project between Foucault's discussion of punishment under the *Ancien régime* and Aquinas's treatment of the question of whether the blessed see and experience pity for the suffering of the damned (RG, 181–82). Agamben refers to Foucault's image of the shadow cast by the present onto the past again in CCC, 28.

39. Patton's description of the relationship between the two thinkers inclines in this direction. "In the end," he writes, "the difference between [Agamben's] approach and that of Foucault is not so much a matter of correction and completion as a choice between epochal concepts of biopolitics and bare life and a more

fine-grained, contextual, and historical analysis" (Patton 2007, 218). Malcom Bull claims that "although [Agamben] takes his examples and terminology from his recondite reading in legal history, his conceptualisation of the state of exception owes more to twentieth-century philosophy—to Benjamin, Derrida and Badiou—than to Roman law" (Bull 2004, 7). That Benjamin is a decisive influence in this matter is something about which Agamben could hardly be more explicit—although it is Benjamin's radical reformulation of Schmitt's conception that most intrigues Agamben, and compared to it, the roles played by Derrida and Badiou are minor. Whether Roman law and the guiding figure of the *homo sacer* are truly less important for Agamben's speculations is an open question (and a point that Bull does not argue so much as state).

CHAPTER 7

1. "Nobody / bears witness for the / witness."

2. See Adorno's remark that "the implausibility of [the Nazis'] actions made it easy to disbelieve . . . what no one wanted to believe" (Adorno 1974, 108 [138]). Michael Wood links Adorno's remarks with Levi's "war against memory," glossing their shared import as "This couldn't be happening, people thought. Even as it was happening, it couldn't be happening. And when it had happened, it couldn't have happened" (Wood 2005, 72).

3. Agamben recounts how, at the Italian publishing house Einaudi where Agamben also worked, Levi would express unease about being the author of works having nothing to do with his experience in the camps, but show a sort of grim satisfaction concerning the works that did testify to that experience. As Levi has said elsewhere, "I am at peace with myself because I bore witness" (see RA, 16–17 [14–15]).

4. From Coleridge's "The Rime of the Ancient Mariner," lines 582–85. Levi explicitly likens himself to the ancient mariner of Coleridge's rime elsewhere in his work (see 1997, 114).

5. The story of a member of one such *Sonderkommando* who survived an astonishing five such "selections" in Auschwitz from April 1942 to January 1945 is found in Filip Müller's *Eyewitness Auschwitz: Three Years in the Gas Chambers* (1979) and recorded by Claude Lanzmann in the film *Shoah* (1985).

6. In *Infancy and History,* Agamben stresses the difficulties of expressing experience *per se.* In an essay from 1996, he returns to the question, but this time employs the terminology of *witnessing,* referring to a "suspicion regarding our own witnessing" and to the sense that it seemed as if "nothing of what we have lived through during these years authorizes us to speak" (MWE, 121–22 [95]).

7. In a discussion of Agamben's relation to legal thought, Schütz (2000) sees a point of proximity with Foucault, claiming that Foucault's "*anti-juridisme* clearly determines his approach to history" (127). Concerning Paul, Guy Davenport

(1996) claims that before Paul's conversion (when he was a Pharisee named Saul) "he was something like an Eichmann when we first see him. . . . He was a zealot, a pedant in the law" (67). Paul may have been devoted to the law, but comparing him to Eichmann is surely misleading, and Agamben's vision of Paul's relation to the law is far more nuanced. Like Nietzsche before him, Davenport sees Paul preaching a gospel of deferral ("Paul relocated this return [of Christ] in historical time and made Christianity a preparation for the fullest life, rather than the fullest life itself" [1996, 70]), which is the opposite of the messianic message that Agamben finds therein.

8. Agamben refers to Celan in a number of works, from *Idea of Prose* to *The End of the Poem* to this one. Apparently unaware of this fact, Mesnard and Kahan (2001) find that Agamben is "strangely silent" concerning Celan (102).

9. Interned in Dachau and Buchenwald from 1938–39, Bruno Bettelheim was to base his analyses of infantile autism on the induced autism he viewed in such figures; he writes that "a description of prisoner behavior [in the camps] would amount to a catalogue of schizophrenic reactions" (Bettelehim 1967, 64).

10. Agamben appears to miss that this—Eichmann's neologism *kadavergehorsam,* "obedient like a corpe"—was in all probability a slip of his awkward tongue (he was a notoriously limited speaker—to the point that Arendt speculates that he might have suffered from some form of "aphasia"). *Kadergehorsam* is standard military parlance for obedience to a superior officer (*gehorsam,* obedient, to a *Kader,* someone of a higher rank). In Eichmann's case, those orders concerned the amassing of corpses might easily have become confounded in his clouded mind.

11. For more on this question see Scholium II to this chapter.

12. Adorno makes a similar point in a section of his *Negative Dialectics* entitled "After Auschwitz," where he argues that through "the murder of millions by administrative means . . . there is no longer any possibility that death might in some way be fitting to the experienced life of the individual" (Adorno GS, 6.355; see also 6.363ff.).

13. In this connection see also Palladino's (2003) discussion of "Agamben's apocalyptic vision and passive response" (330).

14. They also see Agamben's use of the *Muselmann* as part of the "common usage of the representative victim" employed by a vast array of authors and organizations with the side effect of "concealing an element of the real victimization and clouding an understanding of what took place" (Mesnard and Kahan 2001, 50). An opposite view is voiced by Humphreys (2006), who finds that "Agamben's refusal to examine the minutiae of legal and jurisprudential developments may instead enable him to focus squarely on the substrata of juridico-political evolution" (687).

15. Here the English translation renders *volere* in the sense of desiring ("want") rather than in the terms that Nietzsche employs and Agamben follows ("will").

16. LaCapra writes that "however one may respond to this understanding of shame as Agamben employs it (I think it diverts attention from social interaction and ethicopolitical issues), one may insist that the nonapplicability of values or norms with respect to the *Muselmann* would be primarily the responsibility of the perpetrators, and it is only from a questionably skewed perspective that the *Muselmann* could be invoked to invalidate them" (LaCapra 2007, 159).

17. Bat-Ami Bar On (2002) charges Agamben here with simply appropriating Arendt's views; LaCapra disputes this claim (see LaCapra 2004, 318).

18. Agamben does not discuss Freud in this context, but Freud's interpretation of original sin as well as his conception of subjectivity as unavoidably bound up with guilt and shame is clearly an important parallel.

19. Agamben displays this continued interest in the idea of *shame* by noting in *Profanations,* "that shame has a secret relation to glory is a profound messianic theme" (PR, 37).

20. The italics are those of the translator and do not appear in the Italian original.

21. Agamben focuses his discussion on one of Keats's letters on poetic creation—the same letter, in fact, studied by Maurice Blanchot in *Space of Literature.*

22. Agamben also examines this phenomenon in *The End of the Poem.* See also Heller-Roazen's relating of Agamben's *experimentum linguae* to Paul's denunciation of "speaking in tongues" (Heller-Roazen 2002, 92ff.).

23. In a separate article, Mesnard (2004), writing alone, invokes what he calls Agamben's "abstract aesthetics of disaster" (139).

24. J. M. Bernstein says of his ambivalent response to Agamben's book that "while I still find Agamben's analysis teasingly proximate to what needs to be said about Auschwitz, my continued reading has transformed my original sympathetic agreement first into repugnance, and then into frustrated anger and disappointment" (Bernstein 2004, 3). The source of his intense unease is the issue of "aestheticization" in that Bernstein finds that "witnessing in Agamben becomes, finally, an aesthetic act" (3). Roy Jay Schwartzman's judgment is similar; he sees Agamben's approach as ultimately "rhetorical": "although Agamben poses important questions about how to situate the Holocaust ethically and epistemologically, the outlines of a rhetorical approach to memory require further clarification" (Schwartzman 2001, 548).

25. In a French documentary from 1998 entitled *Maurice Blanchot* (directed by Hugo Santiago and produced by INA and France 3 for the series *Siècle d'écrivains*), Agamben chose precisely this remark to approach the life and work of Blanchot. Agamben's interest in Blanchot was evidenced as early as 1966 when

he referred to the "extremely pure posthumous space of Mallarmé which is the thought of Maurice Blanchot" (PB, 45). In an essay from 2003 Negri compares Agamben to Blanchot, claiming that during the period leading up to and including *Language and Death,* Agamben, like Blanchot before him, "traversed the linguistic world [*traversava il mondo linguistico*] in terms of critical ontology" (Negri 2003, 21).

26. In an essay on notions of *potentiality* and *contingency* written five years earlier, Agamben claimed that "our ethical tradition has often sought to avoid the problem of potentiality by reducing it to the terms of will and necessity," and it is this tendency that he is trying to counter here (P, 254).

27. Agamben also refers to this incident in *Signatura rerum,* 110. In an essay from 1966 Agamben relates a similar collapse into aphasia—that of Baudelaire in a church in Saint-Loup in Namur, Belgium (appropriately enough, Baudelaire's aphasia was not complete and he was able to utter a single word—the vulgar imprecation *Crénom*). A general tendency toward the silencing of speech—"the slow march of modern poetry . . . towards aphasia," as Agamben calls it—is the subject of that section of the essay (see PB, 46–47).

28. As we saw earlier, Agamben notes in an essay from 1975 that his work on Warburg was conceived "as the first of a series of portraits dedicated to exemplary personalities, each of which was to represent a human science" (P, 101 [144]). The portrait of Warburg was the only one Agamben completed. The only other portrait on which he began work was dedicated to Benveniste. In *Stanzas* Agamben says of Benveniste that he is "a linguist who has, in our opinion, effected a new 'situation' of the science of language" and that to him "we owe the most lucid perception of the inadequacy of the semiotic perspective (understood in the narrow sense) for an understanding of the linguistic phenomenon in its totality" (S, 186 [158]).

29. Agamben returns to this point in *Signatura rerum,* 63.

30. In a chapter entitled "The Author as Gesture" from *Profanations,* Agamben turns at greater length to this seminal essay (again as a counterpiece to another work by Foucault—in this case, his essay "What Is An Author?") (see PR, 71–73).

31. As Heller-Roazen has admirably shown, one of the tasks that Agamben inherited from Benjamin was the philological project of "reading that which was never written" (see Heller-Roazen 1999). In this same passage where Agamben is endeavoring to elaborate an idea of the archive, which he found important enough not only to put at the head of this culminating chapter but also to use as the subtitle of the work, he says that "between the obsessive memory of tradition, which knows only what has been said" and "the exaggerated thoughtlessness of oblivion, which cares only for what was never said, the archive is the unsaid or

sayable [*il non-detto o il dicibile*] inscribed in everything said by virtue of being enunciated" (RA, 144 [134]).

32. Geulen's account of this crucial element in Agamben's argumentation is rendered incoherent by her omission of one of these three terms. In her summary, "Latin disposes of two words" for *witness* in the sense that Italian and other European languages employ it: "Alongside of the *testis* who acts as a third party in a trial, there is also the *superstes* who him- or herself experienced some thing and bears witness to that experience. It is this aspect of witnessing that Agamben is here interested in" (2005, 114). Geulen omits the third Latin term for *witness,* the one that guides this section of the book—the one that, for Agamben, bridges the experience of the *author* (be it poet, chronicler, or other) and the *witness*: *auctor.*

33. Mills (2005) finds that "what is problematic here is that Agamben's concern with the ethical and ontological implications of the living being entering into the vacant place of the subject in enunciation means that he fails to consider the specifically sexed embodiment of the existent" (216–17).

34. Ultimately, however, Geulen avoids any firm statement about this work. The reason she gives is that she does not know what Agamben will attempt in the remaining volumes of the *Homo Sacer* project, as well as that "the discussion regarding Auschwitz is too complex and overdetermined so that even the necessary minimum might be said in such an introduction as this one" (2005, 118).

35. Throughout this section of the English translation, *il tutto*—even when included in the dialectical pair *il tutto et la parte*—is rendered not as "the whole" but as the somewhat cosmic-sounding "the all."

36. He begins the letter saying, "You will no doubt find me mad [*tu vas me trouver fou sans doute*]" and justifies his change of language by claiming that the difficulty he experienced in his current writing was such that he could not overcome it without what he, employing an elegant solecism, called "*cette façon d'alibi qu'est pour moi le français*"—"that aspect of an alibi that is for me French" (Benjamin 1966, 505).

37. Benjamin comments on this article in a letter to Gretel Adorno dated July 20, 1938 (see Benjamin GB, 6.138). The language of the article in question—from *Internationalen Literatur*—is slightly milder than Benjamin portrays it, limiting itself to saying that a French essay Benjamin wrote on Goethe ("L'angoisse mythique chez Goethe") represented "an attempt that would be a tribute to Heidegger [*ein Versuch, der Heidegger alle Ehre machen würde*]" (see Benjamin GB, 6.140).

38. Ryle's judgment was an oral one drawn from a conversation in 1960. For the vicissitudes of its citation see M. A. Bernstein 2000, 132.

39. Both Heidegger and Arendt were doubtless aware of Archilochus' famous remark, "The fox knows many things, but the hedgehog knows one thing deeply."

40. In addition to these coordinates, there is likely an additional reason that Arendt set her fable where she did. Agamben writes in *Means Without End*, "I remember in 1966 while participating in the seminar in Le Thor on Heraclitus, I asked Heidegger whether he had read Kafka. He answered that of the little he had read it was above all the short story 'Der Bau,' 'The Den,' that had made a lasting impression upon him" (MWE, 139 [108]). In Kafka's story, an animal (never precisely indicated) builds an impregnable burrow that reveals itself as an inescapable trap.

41. Reported in Arendt 1988, 237. The remark is not found in the manuscript for the lecture course to which Arendt is presumably referring—*Phänomenologische Interpretationen zu Aristoteles,* from the winter semester 1921–22 (published as vol. 61 of Heidegger's *Gesamtausgabe*). It bears noting that Arendt cites the remark not as an instance of Heidegger's indifference toward biography but as an instance of a thought and a life in which thinking was so "passionately" bound up with life that the two became indistinguishable from one another.

42. Letter to the author, November 10, 2004.

43. It is eminently possible that this remark is a paraphrase of one Hegel made. In critiquing Kant he announces, "No one knows, or even feels, that anything is a limit or a defect until he is at the same time above and beyond it" (Hegel 1975b, 91).

44. See Klossowski 1969. Though he does not evoke Klossowski in his multiple readings of Nietzsche's work, Agamben repeatedly refers to Klossowski in an essay from 1966, "Favola e fato," which ends with a quotation from Klossowski's novel *Le Baphomet* (see FF, 18 [21]). In his account of the rediscovery of lost manuscripts of Walter Benjamin, Agamben notes that it was thanks to an introduction from Klossowski to Bataille's widow that he was at last able in June of 1981 to examine the manuscripts in question (see IR, 4). As does Agamben, Klossowski sees questions of completion and potentiality at issue in Nietzsche's eternal recurrence: "Le remède de Zarathoustra: re-vouloir le *non-voulu* en tant qu'il desire assumer le fait accompli—donc le rendre *inaccompli,* en le revoulant d'*innombrables fois*" (1969, 105, italics in original).

45. In this book, Agamben's reading is essentially that of Heidegger's, in which eternal recurrence and will to power are shown to be integrally linked, as faces of the same coin, each presenting a world in the unending process of becoming. (At the end of the chapter Agamben explicitly stresses how fundamental Heidegger's reading of Nietzsche was for his own; see MWC, 127 [141]).

46. Agamben also cites this expression in yet another discussion of Nietzsche's eternal recurrence, his essay "Walter Benjamin and the Demonic: Happiness and Historical Redemption" (see P, 155 [229]).

47. We might note an ambivalence on Benjamin's part here given that he is also clearly sensitive to an element in Nietzsche's eternal recurrence that might constitute a critique of progress (see Benjamin AP, 115; GS, 5.173).

CHAPTER 8

1. See especially de Fontenay 1999.

2. After reflecting, during dissection, on the insides of animals and the multitudes of string-like elements to be pulled therein, Descartes likened animals to "machines" and it was from this experiment that his theory of *animaux-machines* came. In Part Five of the *Discourse on Method,* Descartes notes that we have signs that mean more than the tonalities of our voices, and that this "bears witness to the fact that not only do animals have less reason than do we, they have none." Despite this classificatory decision, Descartes was not what he has often been depicted as in popular representations (someone contemptuous toward animals). In fact, he was singularly fond of and attentive to "Monsieur Grat," his dog, looking carefully after the latter's health, priding himself on his puppies, and spending much time playing with him.

3. Like Benjamin before him, Agamben displays a remarkable interest in fables and children's stories. For an instance related to the themes of *The Open,* see the chapter in *Infancy and History* that treats stories in which speech is granted to animals, such as the Christian legend according to which animals—for a brief moment on Christmas night—are granted the power of speech (see IH, 127ff. [135ff.]).

4. In an early lecture course, Heidegger said of the experience of "wonder" that it was "the index of life's highest potentiality" (Heidegger GA, 56–57.115).

5. In his own consideration of "the open," Badiou (2006) acknowledges the centrality of Heidegger's contribution to the question but suggests that it be closely compared with Bergson's use of the term (see 583–584).

6. These lecture notes were published as volume 54 of Heidegger's complete works. The Italian edition of *The Open* wrongly lists this volume as the 44th ("XLIV") in the series. The English translation reproduces this bibliographical error.

7. Neither Heidegger nor Agamben seem aware that Rilke appears to have borrowed his enigmatic term from a specific source: the German writer Alfred Schuler. Schuler enjoyed a certain celebrity at the turn of the nineteenth century and belonged to the so-called Munich *Kosmiker*. In 1917–18, Rilke heard a lecture by Schuler and met him afterward. He was so fascinated by what Schuler had to say that he returned when the lecture series, entitled "The Eternal City," was repeated. The curious substantive "the open" is employed repeatedly by Schuler,

alongside the term "open" in its linguistic variants. In the life Schuler calls for (*offenen Leben*), "there is no religion because life as such is religious actuality." "In the open life there is no possession, no property" (Rilke 1996, 2.267). It is interesting to note that the political tone of Schuler's conceptions of "the open" are, if not always close to those that Rilke developed, close to those developed by Agamben.

8. The title is left in French in both the Italian original and the English translation—though in both the original and the translation it is misspelled.

9. The role of animals and the "becoming-animal" of man is fundamental for Deleuze's later philosophy and is on clear display in his works with Félix Guattari such as *Anti-Oedipus: Capitalism and Schizophrenia* (1972), *Kafka: Toward a Minor Literature* (1975), and *A Thousand Plateaus: Capitalism and Schizophrenia* (1980). Less obviously central is the question of the relation of man to animal in the philosophy of Derrida—at least until the recent publication of *L'animal que donc je suis* (2006).

10. See Matthew Calarco's work in this area—particularly the question he poses in relation to *The Open*: "Do animals have a place within a post-essentialist politics?" (Calarco 2007, 164). On a similar note, Janine Böckelmann's essay from that same year also approaches this question, paying particular attention to the reflections of Peter Singer (see Böckelmann 2007, 164).

11. Weaving a number of Benjamin's celebrated formulations into his review of the book, Uwe Justus Wenzel (2003) writes, "A weak messianic hope that the powerful machine might still come to a standstill is articulated in the images and interpretations of the book [*In den Interpretationen und Denkbildern artikuliert sich da und dort eine schwache messianische Hoffnung, die machtvolle Maschine möge doch noch zum Stillstand kommen*]" (59).

CHAPTER 9

1. Throughout his work Agamben translates Schmitt's formula as "state of exception [*stato di eccezione*]," although the less literal "state of emergency [*stato di emergenza*]" might also have applied. The only exception to this practice is a passage noted later.

2. In another essay published the same year as *State of Exception* Agamben employs the same distinction, comparing the set of laws (the so-called Moro law) instituted by the Italian government from 1978 to 1980 with the *Verordnung zum Schutz von Volk und Staat* of 1933. He is careful to stress that what is at issue is "a simple formal analogy" of legal structure—with, however, the distinction that although the German laws suspending certain civil liberties were in effect for thirteen years, the Italian ones have been in effect still longer (DBU, 79).

3. McQuillan (2005, 2) argues that Butler misunderstands Agamben's ideas of humanity, politics, and bare life in this work.

4. Agamben occasionally employs "state of emergency" to translate Benjamin's *Ausnahmezustand*. In his own translation of the eighth thesis, Agamben translates the first occurrence as "state of emergency" [*stato di emergenza*] and the second occurrence as "state of exception" [*stato di eccezione*] (SE, 57 [75]). Although there are idiomatic grounds for such a choice, it unfortunately occults Benjamin's provocative repetition of the term.

5. In addition to these items in Agamben's exoteric dossier is Schmitt's acknowledgement in a letter from 1973 that his *Der Leviathan in der Staatslehre des Thomas Hobbes* (1938) was "an attempt to answer Benjamin" (see SE, 53 [69], and Linder 2008, 66).

6. In a recent installment of the *Homo Sacer* project, *Il Regno e la Gloria* (*Homo Sacer 2.2*), Agamben follows a similar exchange—part exoteric and part esoteric—between Schmitt and German theologian Erik Peterson (see RG, 18ff.).

7. Both in this work and in an earlier essay where he discusses Benjamin's eighth thesis, Agamben underlines that this real state of exception is not to be taken for a "process of infinite deconstruction which maintains law in a spectral form of life" (SE, 64 [82], translation modified). See also *Potentialities*, 170ff. [265ff.], where Agamben, in his interpretation of the same thesis, opposed a messianic and revolutionary interruption to what he sees as the infinite process of deconstruction.

8. Virno's criticism of Agamben lays particular stress on the idea of biopolitics that Agamben developed from Foucault and on the contention that Agamben has neglected to take into account the economic underpinnings of such a conception.

9. In a review of the English translation of that work, Margaret Kohn (2006) echoes this idea and finds that Agamben writes at times in a "utopian-mystical mode." It bears noting that although Negri's response to *State of Exception* was mixed, it was ultimately positive. "This is a book vexing in its development and its dualisms," he wrote, "but extraordinary in its realization. It clarifies a point around which post-structuralist and post-modern philosophy has up until now turned, making of the biopolitical horizon a verifiable and practicable experience—a Copernican experience . . . " (Negri 2003, 21). For more on the relationship between the two thinkers, see Nielson 2004.

10. Understanding Benjamin's surprising exclamation is the task that Agamben set himself in an essay from 1987 entitled "Bataille e il paradosso della sovranità," which plays an important role in the evolution of the ideas that structure *The Coming Community*. Agamben's conclusion therein is that until we have understood the questions raised by Benjamin's remark—which, Agamben specifies, "we are still far from being able to do"—"the problem of a human community

free of presuppositions and no longer having sovereign subjects cannot even be posed" (BPS, 119).

11. For his part, Andrew Norris (2005) is in no such uncertainty and finds in *State of Exception* what he found in *Homo Sacer:* a "metaphysical destiny, for whom no-one can be blamed and which cannot be directly addressed or warded off" (45). This, he stresses, is a position that presents "disastrous implications" (Norris 2005, 45, n. 52). Fleur Johns (2005) reaches a similar conclusion, seeing that, as concerns the U.S. Military Order of November 2001, Agamben "characterizes the space of that decision . . . so as to suggest that its dynamics have been pre-codified and rendered 'permanent' by the onward march of history and language" (628).

12. In a parenthesis, Agamben paraphrase the Saussurian conception of *langue* as "a linguistic 'state of exception'" and thereby indicates the degree to which the concept is not limited to the rule or misrule of law but instead is applicable to all levels of philosophical and linguistic speculation (HS, 25 [30]).

13. As we saw earlier, Khurana (2007) suggests in a later essay that the "disturbing proximity" of disaster and salvation, of catastrophe and redemption—as well as a host of other figures in Agamben's work—should be understood not as a "political project" but as an "ethical turn," that what Agamben proposes is not a "political alternative" but an "ethical modification" (34–35). This would seem to alleviate many difficulties encountered in Agamben's political reflections, neutralizing questions of immediate and concrete political action in favor of a search for new modes through which to impose and understand value.

14. It is perhaps with such ideas in mind that Badiou refers to Agamben as a "Franciscan of ontology" (see Badiou 2006, 584).

15. Letter to the author from May 27, 2006.

16. It bears noting that Bataille's famous remarks on the Holocaust are also not mentioned in that work. Bataille wrote in "Le mal deans le platonisme at le sadisme" of how "the unleashing of the passions that raged in Buchenwald or in Auschwitz was conducted under the governance of reason," and he saw the Holocaust as, in part, rationality run amok (Bataille OC, 7.376). In an essay on Sartre, Bataille also claimed that "Auschwitz is the fact and sign of man [*Auschwitz est le fait, le signe de l'homme*]" (Bataille OC, 11.226). See Hegarty 2005, 229–30 for a discussion of these remarks.

17. Agamben perhaps has in mind the *metaphysical* watershed that Adorno made of Auschwitz, where the latter claims that "the capacity for metaphysics has been paralyzed because what happened [at Auschwitz] shattered any speculative metaphysical thought to be reconciled with experience" (Adorno GS, 6.354). He may equally well have in mind Adorno's declaration that "Auschwitz irrefutably demonstrated culture's failure," or that "all culture after Auschwitz, including its urgent critique, is garbage" (Adorno GS, 6.359).

18. See also *Il Regno e la Gloria* where Agamben discusses different conceptions of *secularization*—particularly the different usages of the term by Schmitt
and Weber, as well as the "strategic" implications of the idea (RG, 15ff.).

19. Ojakangas chose not to follow this distinction between *secularization* and
profanation, writing that in Agamben's reading of Paul—and more generally, in
Agamben's thought—"the messianic revolution is nothing but the original impetus of secularization—to the extent that secularization is understood as the process in which the law and politics descend from the isolated sacred sphere to the
common sphere of the profane" (Ojakangas 2005a, 25).

20. See also Fitzpatrick and Joyce (2007), who find that "Agamben's exception has the same components as Schmitt's but the composition of each is different" (67).

21. This exploration is first visible in "Bataille et il paradosso della sovranità"
(see especially 117–119) and is an abiding presence in the *Homo Sacer* series—most
notably in *Homo Sacer,* and in parts 2.1 and 2.2 of that project, *State of Exception*
and *Il Regno e la Gloria.*

22. It bears noting in this connection that, generally speaking, interest in
Schmitt's work is far greater in Italy than it is in the English-speaking world—
or even in Schmitt's native Germany. As a recent bibliography of Schmitt's work
makes amply clear, nowhere more than in Italy have Schmitt's writings been
translated and commented on (see de Benoist 2003).

CHAPTER 10

1. Morgenstern was, by his own account, less shaken by the Hitler-Stalin pact
because he was less surprised by it. (In an earlier letter to Scholem, he claims he
had indeed believed Stalin capable of the pact, but not Hitler; see Benjamin GS,
7.770–7.771).

2. In *Means Without End* Agamben refers in an aside to "the classless society
or the messianic kingdom," effectively equating the two ideas and thereby reiter-
ating Benjamin's assertion in the thesis Agamben himself rediscovered (MWE,
32–33 [32]).

3. In the first case, Agamben cites an abbreviated version of Benjamin's remark, and in the second case he refers to it as Benjamin's "*boutade*" about theology, with the claim that it could equally well apply to Caproni and his *Res amissa*
(see P, 58 [50]; and EP, 89 [92]).

4. The terms that Agamben employs, *Löschpapier* and *Tintenpapier,* clearly
denote the same sheet of blotting paper. The term that Benjamin employed was
Löschblatt.

5. On this matter Benjamin wrote to Scholem saying, "You are indeed right
to think that I do not want to fully displace a theological interpretation [of Kaf-

ka's work]—I practice, in fact, a form of it myself—I want only to displace the superficial and insolent interpretations that are coming out of Prague" (Benjamin 1966, 2.618).

6. In a letter from 1912 Benjamin wrote, "I am a Jew and so long as I live as a self-aware man I live as a self-aware Jew" (Benjamin GS, 2.837). This position did not change for him in the coming years. Whatever the vicissitudes in his sense of belonging to a Jewish community—particularly in the late 1920s as he became engaged in materialist and communist thought—Benjamin's sense of himself as a Jewish thinker seems to have remained essentially unchanged.

7. *Eingedenken* means "remembrance" in German, but is rarely used and, in Benjamin's hands, is given a decidedly theological cast. In Benjamin's wake it is a term that Adorno often employs. As concerns the theological tenor of Adorno's thought, it is interesting to note the change it underwent—in large part through his encounters with Benjamin. In 1930 Adorno spoke of the presence of theology in Benjamin's writing as the *"Blendwerk des Himmels"* (Letter from Adorno to Siegfried Kracauer from July 25, 1930; see Wiggershaus 1986, 109). A mere four years later, however, Adorno had changed his mind and was defending the role of theology in Benjamin's thought in debates with Horkheimer, praising the theological element in Benjamin's Kafka essay and his *Arcades Project*, and announcing for his own work "a restitution of theology" as part of a "radicalizing of the dialectic so as to include its glowing core [*Glutkern*]" (Letter to Benjamin August 2–4, 1935, in Adorno and Benjamin 1994, 139, 143).

8. In all probability this undated fragment was written in the early 1920s and is thus from the beginning of Benjamin's career. This date has been a matter of some dispute, however, among both Benjamin's friends and his editors. Scholem claims that the ideas expressed in this fragment are clearly of a piece with those with which Benjamin was occupied in the early 1920s, and that the fragment bears the unmistakable stamp of those years. Jacob Taubes—a philosopher who was intimately familiar with Benjamin's work, who did not always agree with Scholem, and who is an important thinker for Agamben—heartily concurs. Adorno, however, gives a much later date for the fragment. He claims that Benjamin read the text aloud to himself and his wife in San Remo in 1937 or 1938, calling it "the newest of the new" (see Benjamin SW, 3.306, n. 1). Benjamin's German editor, Rolf Tiedemann, found Scholem's testimony more compelling and dates the fragment to the early 1920s. The editors of the recent English edition of Benjamin's works, however, have followed Adorno in dating it to 1938 (see Benjamin SW, 3.306, n. 1).

9. The translation of *Unglück* as "misfortune" obscures Benjamin's clear opposition of *Unglück* (unhappiness) and *Glück* (happiness) in the passage.

10. In a singular insight, Jacob Taubes suggested that Benjamin's conception of the relation of happiness to transience in this fragment was a reformulation of

Nietzsche's idea of eternal recurrence—a conclusion that not only is conceptually compelling but would also help explain Benjamin's ambivalence and uncharacteristic nearsightedness concerning Nietzsche's thought experiment. Where Benjamin's thought diverges from Nietzsche's is in the question of *actual* recurrence. Nietzsche presents recurrence as a thought experiment, not as a cosmic hypothesis. But if one takes it as the latter, as did Benjamin, it can easily be seen as what Benjamin made of it—a punishment. It is in this sense that Agamben once wrote that "true lightness . . . is not the eternal return, but a never-return [*un non mai ritornare*]" (OGK, 42). Whether Nietzsche really conceived of anything other than a "never-return" (in his *Nietzsche and Philosophy,* Deleuze makes a compelling case that Nietzsche never was truly concerned with *actual* recurrence—as had, in far different fashion, Heidegger before him), what links the two conceptions (eternal return and never-return) is what Nietzsche called an "inverted Platonism." For more on this question, see Chapter Seven, Scholium III.

11.   See Agamben's remark that "the concept of messianic time . . . constitutes the theoretical nucleus of Benjamin's 'Theses'" (P, 160 [252]). On a related note, Agamben's interest in Paul is easier to grasp when we note that Paul spoke of a "time of the now" that was remarkably similar to Benjamin's "now-time." For Agamben, "Benjamin's messianism finds its canon [*il suo canone*] in Paul" (TTR, 144 [133], translation modified). What is more, he finds that Paul is "the purest representative of messianism" and says in a work that brings together Benjamin's final writings and Paul's writings that "this seminar proposes to restore Paul's *Letters* to their status as fundamental messianic texts of the West" (LDV; TTR, 9).

12.   It is interesting to note that an equation of *secular* with *profane* is also found in translations of Agamben's own writing. In the preface to *Stanzas* Agamben employs a citation without quotation marks from Benjamin, evoking an *illuminazione profana,* a "profane illumination," that the translator renders as "secular enlightenment," obscuring not only the veiled reference to Benjamin but also the sense behind it (see S, xvi [xii]).

13.   Agamben cites this passage in CC, 53 [45], although without noting its provenance. In an essay published two years later he repeats this practice (see P, 174 [270]).

14.   For a discussion of this passage in the context of Paul's idea of *vocation,* see TTR, 19ff. [25ff.].

CONCLUSION

1.   Brian Dillon (2002) writes of this passage that it expresses a "temporal paradox" such that "the written work can never coincide with itself in time" (2). As

I try to show here, this deconstructive emphasis on a temporal disjunction is but one of several aspects of what Agamben is trying to express.

2. Agamben cites this remark in "Bartleby, or On Contingency" and refers to it in passing in *Signatura rerum* (P, 267; SR, 106). He does not indicate its provenance, clearly assuming that his readers will recognize it as from the section of the *Arcades Project* that attempts to formulate a theory of historical knowledge.

3. Presumably translating from an earlier draft of this then unpublished essay, Heller-Roazen renders this passage as "the hardest and bitterest experience possible" (see P, 178).

4. In this connection we might recall Adorno's epochal claim that the only works that matter today "are the ones that are no longer works" (Adorno GS, 12.37).

5. This point is also amply reflected in Agamben's teaching. For a prominent instance, see Agamben's seminar given at the University of Venice in 2005 that bore the title "The Before and the After of the Work" and specified its aim as follows: "This course proposes to consider artistic activity starting not from the work itself but from that which precedes and follows it."

6. In the English translation the essay is falsely dated as from 1995.

7. The addition is nowhere noted in the new edition.

Bibliography

Adorno, Theodor Wiesengrund. *Gesammelte Schriften.* 20 vols. Herausgegeben von Rolf Tiedemann unter Mitwirkung von Gretel Adorno, Susan Buck-Morss, and Klaus Schultz. Frankfurt: Suhrkamp, 1973–1986. (Cited in text as Adorno GS.)

———. *Minima Moralia: Reflections from Damaged Life.* Trans. E.F.N. Jephcott. London: NLB, 1974. / *Minima Moralia: Reflexionen aus dem beschädigten Leben.* Frankfurt: Suhrkamp, 1985.

———. *Negative Dialectics.* Trans. E. B. Ashton. New York: Continuum Press, 1973.

Adorno, Theodor Wiesengrund, and Benjamin, Walter. *Briefwechsel.* Ed. Henri Lonitz. Frankfurt: Suhrkamp, 1994.

Adorno, Theodor Wiesengrund, and Bloch, Ernst. "Etwas fehlt: Über die Widersprüche der utopischen Sehnsucht." In Ernst Bloch, *Tendenz, Latenz, Utopie: Werkausgabe Ergänzungsband* (350–68). Frankfurt: Suhrkamp, 1985.

Agamben, Giorgio, and Deleuze, Gilles. *Bartleby: La formula della creazione.* Macerata: Quodlibet, 1993.

Allen, Jennifer. "Less Is More." *Artforum.* Online diary entry. April 14, 2005. Available at http://www.artforum.com/diary/archive=200504

Arendt, Hannah. *Between Past and Future: Eight Exercises in Political Thought.* New York: Viking Press, 1961.

———. *Denktagebuch.* Eds. Ursula Ludz and Ingeborg Nordmann. Munich and Zurich: Piper Verlag, 2002.

———. *Eichmann in Jerusalem: A Report on the Banality of Evil.* Rev. and Enlarged Ed. New York: Penguin Books, 1963.

———. "Introduction: Walter Benjamin, 1892–1940." In Walter Benjamin, *Illuminations* (1–58.). New York: Schocken, 1968.

———. "Martin Heidegger ist achtzig Jahre alt." *Antwort: Martin Heidegger im Gespräch.* Eds. Günther Neske and Emil Kettering (232–46). Pfullingen: Verlag Günther Neske, 1988. (First published in *Merkur,* 1969, 893–902)

———. *Men in Dark Times.* New York: Harcourt Brace, 1955.

————. *On Violence.* New York: Harcourt Brace Jovanovich, 1970.

Arendt, Hannah, and Jaspers, Karl. *Hannah Arendt / Karl Jaspers Briefwechsel 1926– 1969.* Eds. Lotte Köhler and Hans Saner. Munich: Piper, 1985.

Aristotle. *The Complete Works of Aristotle: The Revised Oxford Translation.* Ed. Jonathan Barnes. Princeton, NJ: Princeton University Press, 1984.

Artaud, Antonin. *Le théâtre et son double.* Paris: Gallimard, 1964.

Assmann, Jan. "Der Wille zum Jetzt." *Literaturen,* July / August 2006, 54–57.

Attell, Kevin. "An Esoteric Dossier: Agamben and Derrida." Unpublished conference paper presented at the Annual Conference of the International Association of Philosophy and Literature, Freiburg, Germany, June 6, 2006.

Badiou, Alain. *Logiques des mondes: L'être et l'évènement 2.* Paris: Seuil, 2006.

Bar On, Bat-Ami. *The Subject of Violence: Arendtean Exercises in Understanding* (Feminist Constructions). Lanham, MD: Rowman & Littlefield, 2002.

Bataille, Georges. *Oeuvres complètes.* 12 vols. Paris: Gallimard, 1970–88. (Cited in text as Bataille OC.)

Benedetti, Carla. *Pasolini contra Calvino.* Turin: Bollati Boringhieri, 1998.

Benjamin, Andrew, and Osborne, Peter, eds. *Walter Benjamin's Philosophy: Destruction and Experience.* London: Routledge, 1994.

Benjamin, Walter. *Kairos: Schriften zur Philosophie.* Selected and with afterword by Ralf Konersmann. Frankfurt: Suhrkamp, 2007.

————. *Briefe.* Herausgegeben und mit Anmerkungen versehen von Gersholm Scholem und Theodor W. Adorno. Frankfurt: Suhrkamp, 1966.

————. *Gesammelte Schriften.* 7 vols. Eds. Rolf Tiedemann and Herman Schweppenhäuser. Frankfurt: Suhrkamp Verlag, 1974–89. (Cited in text as Benjamin GS.)

————. *Gesammelte Briefe.* 6 vols. Eds. Christoph Gödde and Henri Lonitz. Frankfurt: Suhrkamp, 1995–2000. (Cited in text as Benjamin GB.)

————. *Selected Writings.* Eds. Marcus Bullock, Howard Eiland, Micahel W. Jennings, and Gary Smith. 4 vols. Cambridge, MA: Harvard University Press, 1996–2003. (Cited in text as Benjamin SW.)

————. *The Arcades Project.* 4 vols. Ed. Rold Tiedemann. Trans. Howard Eiland and Kevin McLaughlin. Cambridge, MA: Harvard University Press, 1999.

————. *The Origin of German Tragic Drama.* Trans. John Osborne. London: NLB, 1977a.

————. *Reflections: Essays, Aphorisms, Autobiographical Writings.* Ed. Peter Demetz. New York: Schocken, 1977b.

Bentham, Jeremy. "Panopticon; or, the Inspection House: Postscript: Part I." *The Works of Jeremy Bentham,* Vol. 4. London: Simpkin, Marshall, 1843.

Benveniste, Émile. *Problèmes de linguistique générale.* 2 vols. Paris: Gallimard, 1966–74.

Bergson, Henri. *La pensée et le mouvant.* Paris: PUF, 1998.

Bernstein, J. M. "Bare Life, Bearing Witness: Auschwitz and the Pornography of Horror." *Parallax,* 2004, 10 (1), 2–16.

Bernstein, Michael André. *Five Portraits: Modernity and the Imagination in Twentieth-Century German Writing.* Evanston, IL: Northwestern University Press, 2000.

Bettelheim, Bruno. *The Empty Fortress: Infantile Autism and the Birth of the Self.* New York: Free Press, 1967.

Bidussa, David. "Lo statuto della testimonianza." *Il Manifesto* (Rome), October 27, 1998, 21–22.

Binswanger, Daniel. "Prediger des Profanen." *Die Weltwoche* (Zurich), August 3, 2005, 5–6.

Blanchot, Maurice. *La communauté inavouable.* Paris: Minuit, 1983.

Boas, Franz. *Handbook of American Indian Languages.* Washington, DC: U.S. Government Printing Office, 1911.

Böckelmann, Janine. "Der Begriff des Lebens und die Perspektive des Ethischen." *Die gouvernementale Maschine: Zur politischen Philosophie Giorgio Agambens.* Eds. Janine Böckelmann and Frank Meier (131–48). Münster: Unrast, 2007.

Budd, Christopher. "*Homo Sacer.*" *Philosophers' Magazine,* 1999, 7, 55–56.

Bull, Malcolm. "States Don't Really Mind Their Citizens Dying (Provided They Don't All Do It at Once): They Just Don't Like Anyone Else to Kill Them." *London Review of Books,* 2004, 26 (24), 7–8.

Butler, Judith. *Precarious Life: The Powers of Mourning and Violence.* London and New York: Verso, 2004.

Calarco, Matthew. "Jamming the Anthropological Machine." *Giorgio Agamben: Sovereignty and Life.* Eds. Matthew Calarco and Steven DeCaroli (163–79). Stanford, CA: Stanford University Press, 2007.

Calarco, Matthew, and DeCaroli, Steven, Eds. *Giorgio Agamben: Sovereignty and Life.* Stanford, CA: Stanford University Press, 2007.

Calvino, Italo. *Lezioni americane: Sei propose per il prossimo millennio.* Milan: Oscar Mondadori, 1993.

Carson, Anne. *Decreation: Poetry, Essays, Opera.* New York: Knopf, 2005.

Casarino, Cesare. "Pornocairology: Or, the Communist Clinamen of Pornography." *Paragraph: A Journal of Modern Critical Theory,* 2002, 25 (2), 116–26.

Celan, Paul. *Collected Prose.* Trans. Rosmarie Waldrop. Manchester: Carcanet, 1986.

———. *Gesammelte Werke.* Ed. Beda Allemann and Stefan Reichard with Rolf Bücher. Frankfurt: Suhrkamp, 1983.

Char, René. *Feuillets d'Hypnos.* Paris: Gallimard, 1946.

Clippinger. David. "Giorgio Agamben." *Encyclopedia of Postmodernism.* Ed. Victor E. Taylor and Charles E. Winquist. London: Taylor & Francis, 2001.

Connolly, William E. "The Complexities of Sovereignty." *Giorgio Agamben: Sovereignty and Life.* Eds. Matthew Calarco and Steven DeCaroli (23–42). Stanford, CA: Stanford University Press, 2007.

Cooke, Alexander. "Resistance, Potentiality, and the Law: Deleuze and Agamben on 'Bartleby.'" *Angelaki: Journal of the Theoretical Humanities,* 2005, 10 (3), 79–89.

Culler, Jonathan. *Structuralist Poetics: Structuralism, Linguistics, and the Study of Literature.* Ithaca, NY: Cornell University Press, 1975.

Curtius, E. R. *Europäische Literatur und Lateinisches Mittelalter.* Elfte Auflage. Tübingen and Basel: Francke Verlag, 1993.

Damisch, Hubert. *Traité du trait.* Paris: Editions de la Réunion des Musées Nationaux, 1995.

Davenport, Guy. *The Hunter Gracchus, and Other Papers on Literature and Art.* Washington, DC: Counterpoint, 1996.

de Benoist, Alain. *Carl Schmitt: Bibliographie seiner Schriften und Korrespondenzen.* Berlin: Akademie Verlag, 2003.

de Boever, Arne. "Overhearing Bartleby: Agamben, Melville, and Inoperative Power." *Parrhesia,* 2006, 1, 142–62.

DeCaroli, Steven. "Boundary Stones: Giorgio Agamben and the Field of Sovereignty." *Giorgio Agamben: Sovereignty and Life.* Eds. Matthew Calarco and Steven DeCaroli (43–69). Stanford, CA: Stanford University Press, 2007.

de Fontenay, Elisabeth. *Le silence des bêtes: La philosophie à l'épreuve de l'animalité.* Paris: Fayard, 1999.

Deleuze, Gilles. *Critique et Clinique.* Paris: Editions du Minuit, 1993.

———. *Essays Critical and Clinical.* Trans. Daniel W. Smith and Michael A. Greco. Minneapolis: Minnesota University Press, 1997.

de Man, Paul. *Aesthetic Ideology.* Minneapolis: Minnesota University Press, 1996.

———. *The Resistance to Theory.* Minneapolis: Minnesota University Press, 1986.

———. *Allegories of Reading: Figural Language in Rousseau, Nietzsche, Rilke, and Proust.* New Haven, CT: Yale University Press, 1979.

Derrida, Jacques. *L'animal que donc je suis.* Paris: Galilée, 2006.

Dillon, Brian. "Introduction: In the Interim." *Paragraph: A Journal of Modern Critical Theory,* 2002, 25 (2), 1–15.

Dillon, Michael. "Cared to Death: The Biopoliticised Time of Your Life." *Foucault Studies,* 2005, 2, 37–46.

Docherty, Thomas. "Potential European Democracy." *Paragraph: A Journal of Modern Critical Theory,* 2002, 25 (2), 16–35.

Düttmann, Alexander García. "Integral Actuality." Trans. Kerstin Behnke. Introduction. *Idea of Prose.* Trans. Michael Sullivan and Sam Whitsitt (3–25). Albany: State University of New York Press, 1995.

———. "Never Before, Always Already: Notes on Agamben and the Category of Relation." *Angelaki: Journal of the Theoretical Humanities,* 2001, 6 (3), 3–6.

Eaglestone, Robert. "On Giorgio Agamben's Holocaust." *Paragraph: Journal of Modern Critical Theory,* 2002, 25 (2), 52–67.

Edkins, Jenny. "Whatever Politics." *Giorgio Agamben: Sovereignty and Life.* Eds. Matthew Calarco and Steven DeCaroli (70–91). Stanford, CA: Stanford University Press, 2007.

Ek, Richard. "Giorgio Agamben and the Spatialities of the Camp: An Introduction." *Geografiska Annaler: Series B, Human Geography,* 2006, 88 (4), 363–86.

Eliot, George. *Scenes of Clerical Life.* 2 vols. Edinburgh and London: Blackwell, 1858.

Emerson, Ralph Waldo. *The Collected Works of Ralph Waldo Emerson.* 7 vols. Eds. Robert E. Spiller, Alfred R. Ferguson, Joseph Slater, Jean Ferguson Carr, Wallace E. Williams, and Douglas Emory Wilson. Cambridge, MA: Harvard University Press, 1971–2008.

Fackenheim, Emil. *To Mend the World.* New York: Schocken, 1982.

Fédier, François. *Soixante-deux photographies de Martin Heidegger.* Paris: Gallimard, 1972.

Ferrari Bravo, Luciano. "Giorgio Agamben. *Homo Sacer.*" *Futuro anteriore,* 1996, 1, 167–172.

Fitzpatrick, Peter, and Joyce, Richard. "The Normality of the Exception in Democracy's Empire." *Journal of Law and Society,* 2007, 34 (1), 65–76.

Flesch, William. "Love's Characters." Foreword. *Radical Passivity: Lévinas, Blanchot, and Agamben.* Thomas Carl Wall (ix–xiv). Albany: SUNY Press, 1999.

Formenti, Carlo. "Immagini del forse." *Aut aut,* 1996, 271/272, 22–27.

Foucault, Michel. *Il faut défendre la société. Cours au Collège de France 1975–1976.* Paris: Gallimard/Seuil, 1997.

Franchi, Stefano. "Of the Synthetic and the Analytic." *Contretemps,* 2004, 5, 30–41.

Fraser, David. "Dead Men Walking: Law and Ethics After Giorgio Agamben's Auschwitz." *International Journal for the Semiotics of Law,* 12 (4), 1999, 397–417.

Galitz, Robert, and Reimers, Brita. "Vorwort." *Ekstatische Nymphe . . . trauernder Flußgott: Portrait eines Gelehrten.* Eds. Robert Galitz and Brita Reimers (8–12). Hamburg: Dölling und Galitz, 1995.

Geulen, Eva. *Giorgio Agamben zur Einführung.* Hamburg: Junius, 2005.

Goisis, Giuseppe. "*Stato di eccezione* di Giorgio Agamben: Alcune questioni." *DEP-Deportate, Esuli e Profughe,* February 2007, 282–285.

Gombrich, E. H. *Aby Warburg: An Intellectual Biography.* London: Warburg Institute, 1970.

———. *The Heritage of Apelles.* Ithaca, NY: Cornell University Press, 1976.

Guidoni, Elise. "Sur *Homo Sacer." Che vuoi? Revue de Psychanalyse.* Paris: Editions L'Harmattan, 1998, 10, 45–49.

Guinle, Jean-Phillipe. "*Homo sacer, le pouvoir souverain et la vie nue.* Giorgio Agamben." *Art Press,* 1997, 225, vi–vii.

Grottanelli, Cristiano. "Una variazione sul tema delle origini." *Iride* [Florence], 1996, 9, 485–90.

Gullì, Bruno. "The Ontology and Politics of Exception: Reflections on the Work of Giorgio Agamben." *Giorgio Agamben: Sovereignty and Life.* Eds. Matthew Calarco and Steven DeCaroli (219–40). Stanford, CA: Stanford University Press, 2007.

Habermas, Jürgen. "Walter Benjamin: Consciousness-Raising or Rescuing Critique." *On Walter Benjamin: Critical Essays and Recollections.* Ed. Gary Smith (91–128). Cambridge, MA: MIT Press, 1988.

Hamacher, Werner. *Entferntes Verstehen: Studien zu Philosophie und Literatur von Kant bis Celan.* Frankfurt: Suhrkamp, 1998.

Hanssen, Beatrice. *Walter Benjamin's Other History: Of Stones, Animals, Human Beings, and Angels.* Berkeley: University of California Press, 1998.

Hardt, Michael, and Dumm, Thomas. "Sovereignty, Multitudes, Absolute Democracy: A Discussion Between Michael Hardt and Thomas Dumm About Hardt and Negri's *Empire." Theory & Event,* 2000, 4 (3), 1–40.

———. "Introduction: Laboratory Italy." *Radical Thought in Italy: A Potential Politics.* Eds. Paolo Virno and Michael Hardt (1–10). Minneapolis: University of Minnesota Press, 1996.

Hartle, Johann Frederik. "Das unbestimmte Dritte. Giorgio Agambens Messianismus des Rechts." October 2004. Available at http://www.literaturkritik.de/public/rezension.php?rez_id=7435&ausgabe=200410

Haverkamp, Anselm. "*Richard II,* Bracton, and the End of Political Theology." *Law and Literature,* 2004, 16 (3), 313–26.

Hegarty, Paul. "Supposing the Impossibility of Silence and of Sound, of Voice." *Politics, Metaphysics, and Death: Essays on Giorgio Agamben's* Homo Sacer. Ed. Andrew Norris (222–47). Durham, NC: Duke University Press, 2005.

Hegel, Georg Wilhelm Friedrich. *Aesthetics: Lectures on Fine Art.* Trans. T. M. Knox, vol. 1. Oxford, UK: Clarendon Press, 1975a.

———. *Hegel's Logic; Being Part One of the Encyclopaedia of the Sciences.* Trans. W. Wallace. Oxford, UK: Oxford University Press, 1975b.

———. *Werke.* 20 vols. Frankfurt: Suhrkamp, 1970.

Heidegger, Martin. *Übungen für Anfänger: Schillers Briefe über die ästhetische Erziehung des Menschen.* Ed. Ulrich von Bülow with an essay by Odo Marquard. Marbach: Deutsche Schillergesellschaft, 2005.

———. *Being and Time.* Trans. Joan Stambaugh. Albany: SUNY, 1996.

———. *Basic Writings.* Rev., exp., ed., trans. David Farrell Krell. San Francisco: Harper and Row, 1993.

———. *Sein und Zeit.* Tübingen: Max Niemayer Verlag, 1993.

———. *Nietzsche. Volume II: The Eternal Recurrence of the Same.* Trans. David Farrell Krell. San Francisco: Harper and Row, 1984.

———. *Poetry, Language, Thought.* Trans. Albert Hofstadter. New York: Harper and Row, 1971.

———. *What Is Philosophy?* Trans. Jean T. Wilde and William Kluback. New York: Twayne, 1958.

———. *Was ist das—die Philosophie?* Pfullingen: G. Neske, 1956.

———. *Holzwege.* Frankfurt: Klostermann, 1950.

Heller-Roazen, Daniel. *Echolalias: On the Forgetting of Language.* New York: Zone Books, 2005.

———. "Speaking in Tongues." *Paragraph: Journal of Modern Critical Theory,* 2002, 2, 92–115.

———. *The Inner Touch: Archaeology of a Sensation.* New York: Zone Books, 2007.

———. "'To Read What Was Never Written.'" Editor's introduction. *Potentialities: Collected Essays in Philosophy.* Ed., trans., intro. Daniel Heller-Roazen (1–23). Stanford, CA: Stanford University Press, 1999.

Hölderlin, Friedrich. *Werke, Briefe, Dokumente.* Munich: Winkler-Verlag, 1969.

Hofmannsthal, Hugo von. *Sämtliche Werke. Kritische Ausgabe.* Vol. 3. Frankfurt: Fischer Verlag, 1982.

Humphreys, Stephen. "Legalizing Lawlessness: On Giorgio Agamben's *State of Exception.*" *European Journal of International Law,* 2006, 17 (3), 677–87.

Jäger, Lorenz. "Wie kann man für den Nicht-Menschen sprechen?" *Frankfurter Allgemeine Zeitung,* October 7, 2003, L 37.

Jarvis, Simon. "Sound Reasoning." *Times Literary Supplement,* April 7, 2000, 30.

Jesi, Furio. *Materiali mitologici: Mito e antropologia nella cultura mitteleuropea.* Nuova edizione a cura di Andrea Cavaletti. Turin: Einaudi, 2001.

Johns, Fleur. "Guantánamo Bay and the Annihilation of the Exception." *European Journal of International Law,* 2005, 16 (4), 613–35.

Kafka, Franz. *Hochzeitsvorbereitungen auf dem Lande.* Frankfurt: Fischer Verlag, 1966.

Kalyvas, Andreas. "The Sovereign Weaver: Beyond the Camp." *Politics, Metaphysics, and Death: Essays on Giorgio Agamben's* Homo Sacer. Ed. Andrew Norris (107–134). Durham, NC: Duke University Press, 2005.

Kant, Immanuel. *Critique of Judgment.* Trans. Werner S. Pluhar. Indianapolis: Hackett, 1987.

———. *Die drei Kritiken.* Bd. II. Ed. Alexander Ulfig. Cologne: Parkland Verlag, 1999.

Kaube, Jürgen. "Der mit den Duftstoffen tanzt." *Frankfurter Allgemeine Zeitung,* 2005, June 20, 41.

Khurana, Thomas. "Desaster und Versprechen. Eine irritierende Nähe im Werk Giorgio Agambens." *Die gouvernementale Maschine. Zur politischen Philosophie Giorgio Agambens.* Ed. Janine Böckelmann and Frank Meier (29–44). Münster: Unrast, 2007.

———. "Leben und sterben lassen. Giorgio Agambens Buch *Homo Sacer* und seine Rezeption." *Texte zur Kunst,* 2002, 12 (45), 122–27.

Klein, Robert. *La forme et l'intelligible.* Paris: Gallimard, 1970.

Klossowski, Pierre. *Nietzsche et le cercle vicieux.* Paris: Mercure de France, 1969.

Kohn, Margaret. "Bare Life and the Limits of Law." *Theory & Event,* 2006, 9 (2). Available at http://muse.jhu.edu/login?uri=/journals/tae/v009/9.2kohn.html

LaCapra, Dominick. Review of *The Subject of Violence: Arendtean Exercises in Understanding (Feminist Constructions)* by Bat-Ami Bar On. *Holocaust and Genocide Studies,* 2004, 18 (2), 315–18.

———. "Approaching Limit Events: Siting Agamben." *Giorgio Agamben: Sovereignty and Life.* Eds. Matthew Calarco and Steven DeCaroli (126–162). Stanford, CA: Stanford University Press, 2007. (First published in *Witnessing the Disaster: Essays on Representation and the Holocaust.* Eds. Michael Bernard-Donals and Richard Glejzer [263–304]. Madison: University of Wisconsin Press, 2003.)

Lachert, Elke. "Wege dorthin. Zum Problem der Unentscheidbarkeit bei Agamben und Derrida." *Die gouvernementale Maschine: Zur politischen Philosophie Giorgio Agambens.* Ed. Janine Böckelmann and Frank Meier (207–15). Münster: Unrast, 2007.

Laclau, Ernesto. "Bare Life or Social Indeterminacy?" *Giorgio Agamben: Sovereignty and Life.* Eds. Matthew Calarco and Steven DeCaroli (11–22.). Stanford, CA: Stanford University Press, 2007.

Lessing, Gotthold Ephraim. *Werke und Briefe in zwölf Bänden.* Ed. Wilfried Barner. Frankfurt: Deutscher Klassiker Verlag, 1985.

Levi, Primo. *Conversazioni e interviste.* Turin: Einaudi, 1997.

———. *I sommersi e i salvati.* Turin: Einaudi, 1986.

———. *Survival in Auschwitz: The Nazi Assault on Humanity.* Trans. Stuart Woolf. New York: Collier, 1961.

Levi, Neil, and Rothberg, Michael. "Auschwitz and the Remains of Theory: Toward an Ethics of the Borderland." *symploke,* 2004, 11 (1–2), 23–38.

Linder, Christian. *Der Bahnhof von Finnentrop: Eine Reise ins Carl Schmitt Land.* Berlin: Matthes & Seitz, 2008.

Lindner, Burkhardt (ed.). *Benjamin Handbuch: Leben, Werk, Wirkung.* Stuttgart: Metzler, 2006.

Marchart, Oliver. "Zwischen Moses und Messias. Zur politischen Differenz bei Agamben." *Die gouvernementale Maschine. Zur politischen Philosophie Giorgio Agambens.* Ed. Janine Böckelmann and Frank Meier (10–28). Münster: Unrast, 2007.

Marion, Esther. "The Nazi Genocide and the Writing of the Holocaust Aporia: Ethics and *Remnants of Auschwitz.*" *MLN,* 2006, 121 (4), 1009–24.

Mayer, Michael. "Ein Ausnahmezustand auf Dauer: Giorgio Agamben über die Idee einer 'Biopolitik.'" *Berliner Zeitung,* January 17, 1997, 21.

McQuillan, Colin. "The Political Life in Giorgio Agamben." *Kritikos: An International and Interdisciplinary Journal of Postmodern Cultural Sound, Text, and Image,* 2005, 2, 1–14.

Méchoulan, Eric. "Erudition et fétichisme." *La littérature en puissance. Autour de Giorgio Agamben.* Eds. Guillaume Asselin and Jean-François Bourgeault. Montreal: VLB, 2006.

Melville, Herman. *The Piazza Tales & Other Prose Pieces, 1839–1860.* Evanston, IL, and Chicago: Northwestern University Press and the Newberry Library, 1987.

Mesnard, Philippe. "The Political Philosophy of Giorgio Agamben: A Critical Evaluation." Trans. Cyrille Guiat. *Totalitarian Movements and Political Religions,* 2004, 5 (1), 139–57.

Mesnard, Philippe, and Kahan, Claudine. *Giorgio Agamben à l'épreuve d'Auschwitz.* Paris: Editions Kimé, 2001.

Mills, Catherine. "Linguistic Survival and Ethicality: Biopolitics, Subjectification, and Testimony in *Remnants of Auschwitz.*" *Politics, Metaphysics, and Death: Essays on Giorgio Agamben's* Homo Sacer. Ed. Andrew Norris (198–221). Durham and London: Duke University Press, 2005.

———. "Agamben's Messianic Politics: Biopolitics, Abandonment and Happy Life." *Contretemps,* 2004, 5, 42–62.

Minca, Claudio. "Giorgio Agamben and the New Biopolitical *Nomos.*" *Geografiska Annaler: Series B, Human Geography,* 2006, 88 (4), 387–403.

Mirra, Helen. "Index for *Der Räuber.*" *Cabinet,* 2008, 29, 7–10.

Missac, Pierre. "Walter Benjamin à la Bibliothèque Nationale." *Revue de la Bibliothèque Nationale,* 1983, 10, 30–43.

Monk, Ray. *Ludwig Wittgenstein: The Duty of Genius.* New York: Penguin, 1990.

Morris, Daniel. "Life, or Something Like It." *Bookforum,* Summer 2004, 1–7.

Müller-Doohm, Stefan. *Adorno: Eine Biographie.* Frankfurt: Suhrkamp, 2003.

Musil, Robert. *Der Mann ohne Eigenschaften.* 2 vols. Ed. Adolf Frisé. Frankfurt: Rowohlt, 1978.

Nancy, Jean-Luc. *La communauté désœuvrée*. Paris: C. Bourgois, 1986. / *The Inoperative Community*. Ed. Peter Connor. Minneapolis: Minnesota University Press, 1991.

Neal, Andrew W. "Foucault in Guantánamo: Towards an Archaeology of the Exception." *Security Dialogue*, 2006, 37 (1), 31–46.

Negri, Antonio. "Il frutto maturo della redenzione." *Il Manifesto* (Rome), July 26, 2003, 21.

———. *Il potere costituente*. Rome: Manifestolibri, 2002.

———. "Il mostro politico: Nuda vita e potenza." *Il desiderio del mostro: Dal circo al laboratorio alla politica*. Eds. Ubaldo Fadini, Antonio Negri, and Charles T. Wolfe. Rome: Manifesotlibri, 2001.

Negri, Antonio, and Hardt, Michael. *Empire*. Cambridge, MA: Harvard University Press, 2001.

Nielson, Brett. "*Potenza nuda?* Sovereignty, Biopolitics, Capitalism." *Contretemps* 5, December 2004, 63–78.

Nietzsche, Friedrich. *The Gay Science*. Trans. Josefine Nauckhoff and Adrian del Caro. Cambridge: Cambridge University Press, 2001.

———. *Thus Spoke Zarathustra: A Book for All and None*. Trans. Walter Kaufman. New York: Penguin Books, 1966.

Nikolopoulou, Kalliopi. "*Homo Sacer*." *SubStance*, 2000, 29 (3), 124–31.

Norris, Andrew. "The Exemplary Exception: Philosophical and Political Decisions in Giorgio Agamben's *Homo Sacer*." *Politics, Metaphysics, and Death. Essays on Giorgio Agamben's* Homo Sacer. Ed. Andrew Norris (262–83). Durham and London: Duke University Press, 2005.

Noys, Benjamin. "Time of Death." *Angelaki*, 2002, 7 (2), 51–59.

Ojakangas, Mika. "Impossible Dialogue on Bio-power: Agamben and Foucault." *Foucault Studies*, 2005a, 2, 5–28.

———. "The End of Bio-power? A Reply to My Critics." *Foucault Studies*, 2005b, 2, 47–53.

Ott, Hugo. *Martin Heidegger: A Political Life*. Trans. Allan Blunden. New York and London: HarperCollins, 1993.

———. *Martin Heidegger. Unterwegs zu seiner Biographie*. Frankfurt and New York: Campus Verlag, 1983.

Palladino, Paolo. "The Politics of Death: On Life After the 'End of History.'" *Journal for Cultural Research*, 2003, 7 (3), 321–35.

Passavant, Paul. "The Contradictory State of Giorgio Agamben." *Political Theory*, 2007, 35 (2), 147–74.

Patton, Paul. "Agamben and Foucault on Biopower and Biopolics." *Giorgio Agamben: Sovereignty and Life*. Eds. Matthew Calarco and Steven DeCaroli (203–18). Stanford, CA: Stanford University Press, 2007.

Plato. *The Collected Dialogues of Plato, Including the Letters.* Ed. Edith Hamilton and Huntington Cairns. New York: Pantheon Books, 1961.

Pliny. *Historia Naturalis.* Vol. 35. Trans. H. Rackam. Cambridge, MA: Harvard University Press, 1967.

Plug, Jan. "Shame: On the Language of Robert Walser." *MLN,* 2005, 120 (3), 654–84.

Pourciau, Sarah. "Bodily Negation: Carl Schmitt on the Meaning of Meaning." *MLN,* 2005, 120 (5), 1066–1090.

Rancière, Jacques. "Who Is the Subject of the Rights of Man?" *South Atlantic Quarterly,* 2004, 103 (2/3), 297–310.

Raulff, Ulrich. *Wilde Energien: Vier Versuche zu Aby Warburg.* Göttingen: Walllstein Verlag, 2003.

Réal, Jean. *Bêtes et juges.* Paris: Buchet Chastel, 2006.

Rilke, Rainer Maria. *Werke: Kommentierte Ausgabe in vier Bänden.* Eds. Manfred Engel, Ulrich Fülleborn, Horst Nalewski, and August Stahl. Frankfurt: Insel Verlag, 1996.

Robinson, Benjamin. "The Specialist on the Eichmann Precedent: Morality, Law, and Military Sovereignty." *Critical Inquiry,* 2003, 30 (1), 63–97.

Ross, Alison. "Introduction." *South Atlantic Quarterly,* 2008, 107 (1), Special Issue: "The Agamben Effect"), 1–13.

Safranski, Rüdiger. *Martin Heidegger: Between Good and Evil.* Trans. Ewald Osers. Cambridge, MA: Harvard University Press, 1998.

———. *Ein Meister aus Deutschland: Heidegger und seine Zeit.* Munich: Hanser, 1994.

Saxl, Fritz. "The History of Warburg's Library, 1886–1944." Ernst Gombrich, *Aby Warburg: An Intellectual Biography* (325–38). London: Warburg Institute and University of London, 1970.

Schickert, Katharina. *Der Schutz literarischer Urheberschaft im Rom der klassischen Antike.* Tübingen: Mohr Siebeck, 2005.

Schmitt, Carl. *Political Theology: Four Chapters on the Concept of Sovereignty.* Trans. George Schwab. Cambridge, MA: MIT Press, 1985.

———. *Politische Theologie. Vier Kapiteln zu Lehre von der Souveränität.* Munich: Duncker and Humboldt, 1922.

Scholem, Gershom. *Walter Benjamin und sein Engel: Vierzehn Aufsätze und kleine Beiträge.* Frankfurt: Suhrkamp, 1983.

———. *". . . und alles ist Kabbala": Gershom Scholem im Gespräch mit Jörg Drews.* Zweite, erweiterte Auflage. Munich: edition text+kritik, 1980.

———. *The Messianic Idea in Judaism.* Trans. Michael Meyer. New York: Schocken Books, 1972.

Schütz, Anton. "Thinking the Law with and Against Luhmann, Legendre, Agamben." *Law and Critique,* 2000, 11 (2), 107–36.

Schwartzman, Roy Jay. "Recovering the Lost Canon: Public Memory and the Holocaust." *Rhetoric & Public Affairs,* 2001, 4 (3), 542–83.

Sini, Carlo. "L'occultamento del politico e la crisi della democrazia." *Iride* (Florence), 1996, 9 (18), 490–94.

Stendhal. *De l'amour.* Texte établi, avec introduction et notes, par Henri Martineau. Paris: Garnier, 1959.

Stevens, Wallace. *Collected Poetry and Prose.* New York: Library of America, 1997.

Taubes, Jacob. *The Political Theology of Paul.* Trans. Dana Hollander. Stanford CA: Stanford University Press, 2004.

ten Bos, René. "Giorgio Agamben and the Community Without Identity." *The Sociological Review,* 2005, 53 (Supplement 1), 16–29.

Ternes, Bernd. "Die kommende Gemeinschafft und exzentrische Paradoxie." *Die gouvernementale Maschine. Zur politischen Philosophie Giorgio Agambens.* Ed. Janine Böckelmann and Frank Meier (114–30). Münster: Unrast, 2007.

Thrower, James. "Letter to the Editor." *Times Higher Education Supplement,* February 17, 1989, 12.

Thurschwell, Adam. "Cutting the Branches for Akiba: Agamben's Critique of Derrida." *Politics, Metaphysics, and Death: Essays on Giorgio Agamben's* Homo Sacer. Ed. Andrew Norris (173–197). Durham and London: Duke University Press, 2005.

Tronti, Mario. "The Strategy of Refusal." *Semiotext(e),* 1980, 3 (3), Special Issue: "Autonomia: Post-Political Politics," 28–34.

Vighi, Fabio. "Pasolini and Exclusion: Žižek, Agamben and the Modern Sub-proletariat." *Theory, Culture & Society,* 2003, 20 (5), 99–121.

Virno, Paolo. "General Intellect, Exodus, Multitude." *Archipélago,* 2002, 54. English translation available at http://www.generation-online.org/p/fpvirno2.htm

———. *Il ricordo del presente: Saggio sul tempo storico.* Turino: Bollati Borringhieri, 1999.

———. "Cultura e produzione sul palcoscenico." *I Situazionisti* (19–26.). Rome: Manifestolibri, 1991.

Virno, Paolo, and Hardt, Michael, eds. *A Potential Politics: Radical Thought in Italy.* Minneapolis: University of Minnesota Press, 1996.

Voigt, Manfred. "Zitat." *Benjamins Begriffe.* Eds. Michael Opitz and Erdmut Wizisla (826–850). Frankfurt: Suhrkamp, 2000.

Wall, Thomas Carl. *Radical Passivity: Lévinas, Blanchot, and Agamben.* Albany: SUNY Press, 1999.

Warburg, Aby. *Ausgewählte Schriften und Würdigungen.* Herausgegeben von Dieter Wuttke in Verbindung mit Carl Georg Heise. Baden-Baden: Verlag Valentin Koerner, 1979.

———. *Gesammelte Schriften.* Eds. Horst Bredekamp, Michael Diers, Kurt W. Forster, Nicholas Mann, Salvatore Settis, and Martin Warnke. Berlin: Akademie-Verlag, 1998.

Wark, McKenzie. "Game of War: Debord as Strategist." *Cabinet,* 2008, 29, 73–75.

Weber, Samuel. "'And When Is Now?' (On Some Limits of Perfect Intelligibility)." *MLN,* 2007, 122, 1028–49.

Weil, Simone. *Gravity and Grace.* Trans. A. Wills. Lincoln: University of Nebraska Press, 1997. / *La pesanteur et la grâce.* Paris: Plon, 1948.

Wenzel, Uwe Justus. "Die anthropologische Maschine: Giorgio Agamben über den Menschen und das Tier." *Neue Zürcher Zeitung,* 2003, 176 (2/3), 59.

Wiggershaus, Rolf. *Die Frankfurter Schule. Geschichte. Theoretische Entwicklung. Politische Bedeutung.* Munich: Hanser, 1986.

Wind, Edgar. *The Eloquence of Symbols: Studies in Humanist Art.* Ed. Jaynie Anderson. Oxford: Clarendon Press, 1983.

———. *Art and Anarchy.* London: Faber and Faber, 1963.

Wittgenstein, Ludwig. *Culture and Value.* Ed. G. H. von Wright with Heikki Nyman. Trans. Peter Winch. Chicago: University of Chicago Press, 1984.

———. *Philosophical Occasions: 1912–1951.* Indianapolis and Cambridge, UK: Hackett, 1983.

Wortham, Simon Morgan. "Law of Friendship: Agamben and Derrida." *New Formations: A Journal of Culture/Theory/Politics,* 2007, 62, 89–105.

Wood, Michael. *Literature and the Taste of Knowledge.* Cambridge, UK: Cambridge University Press, 2005.

Zanardi, Maurizio. "Premessa." *Politica,* Eds. Giorgio Agamben, Alain Badiou, Massimo De Carolis, Jean-Luc Nancy, Giuseppe Russo, Maurizio Zanardi (7–9). Naples: Edizioni Cronopio, 1993.

Ziarek, Ewa. "Evil and Testimony: Ethics 'After' Postmodernism." *Hypatia: Journal of Feminist Philosophy,* 2003, 18 (2), 197–205.

Žižek, Slavoj. "The Last Hegelian: An Interview with Slavoj Žižek." Interview with Eric Dean Rasmussen. *Minnesota Review,* 2004, 61/62, 79–94.

———. "Critical Response I: A Symptom—of What?" *Critical Inquiry,* 2003, 29 (3), 486–503.

———. "Are We In A War? Do We Have An Enemy?" *London Review of Books.* 2002a, 24 (10), 1–4.

———. *Welcome to the Desert of the Real.* New York: Verso, 2002b.

Index

207–26, 235, 243–46, 279, 286–88, 291–92, 297, 321, 333–34, 352, 419n34, 421–22n9, 422n12, 422n13, 422n14, 424n24, 426n37, 426n38, 426–27n39, 427n7, 430n30, 435n8
Fourcade, Dominique, 392n2
Franchi, Stefano, 10, 394n12
Fraser, David, 347
Freud, Sigmund, 64, 206, 425n28, 429n18

Galitz, Robert, 404n13
genealogy, idea of, 209, 215, 220, 321, 404n14, 419n34, 421–22n9, 422n13
Geulen, Eva, 10, 185, 187, 203, 297, 396n1, 402n1, 418n29, 431n32, 431n34
Ginzburg, Carlo, 72, 404n17
Goisis, Giuseppe, 349–50, 424n22
Gombrich, E. H., 72, 403n12, 414n33
Grandville, J. J., 405n19
Guantánamo Bay, 8, 337, 347, 351
Guattari, Félix, 299
Guidoni, Elise, 425n28
Guinle, Jean-Phillipe, 425n29
Gullì, Bruno, 425n28

Habermas, Jürgen, 17, 109, 237, 344
Hamacher, Werner, 49
Hanssen, Beatrice, 395–96n24
Hardt, Michael, 299, 394n16, 416n11, 424n21
Hartle, Johann Frederik, 348
Haverkamp, Anselm, 364
Hegarty, Paul, 413n31, 436n16
Hegel, Georg Wilhelm Friedrich, 19, 30–31, 34, 50, 66, 89–90, 96–97, 106–8, 118–19, 132, 141, 160–61, 273, 330–31, 360, 388, 392n2, 396n3, 398n10, 432n43
Heidegger, Martin, 1–4, 8–9, 24–25, 28–30, 34–45, 50–54, 57–58, 61–62, 66, 75–76, 91, 98–99, 102, 113, 121, 130–31, 137, 141, 160, 181, 186–87, 194, 198, 203, 225, 233–35, 237, 266–68, 278–79, 282–83, 303–12, 316–17, 319, 322, 325, 327–33, 336, 339, 350, 360,

364, 366, 387, 392n2, 392n3, 395n22, 395n23, 395n24, 396n2, 396n3, 398n7, 398n11, 399n15, 399n18, 401n28, 402n30, 406n25, 408n9, 412n22, 418n25, 419n32, 431n37, 431n39, 432n40, 432n41, 432n45, 433n4, 433n5, 433n6, 433n7, 439n10
Heller-Roazen, Daniel, xvii, 93, 202–3, 366, 393n5, 411n14, 412n20, 414n35, 418n28, 429n22, 430n31, 440n3
Heraclitus, 2, 174, 392n2, 432n40
Hilberg, Raul, 252, 271
historiography, 10, 15, 45, 71, 79, 99, 108–10, 117–18, 224, 240, 244, 281, 295, 297
Hoffmann, E. T. A., 405n19
Hofmannsthal, Hugo von, 414n35
Hölderlin, Friedrich, 31, 38–39, 42–43, 46, 66, 91, 181, 328, 399–400n18, 412n22, 418n24
Holocaust, 218, 247–97, 427n5, 429n24, 436n16. See also Shoah.
Horkheimer, Max, 42, 109, 241, 256, 409n22, 438n7
human rights, 201
Humphreys, Stephen, 347, 428n14

iconography, 10, 63, 69, 73, 122, 151, 404n17, 405n20
iconology, 63, 69, 73, 404n17
incompletion, idea of, 383–86
inoperative, inoperativeness, *inoperosità*, 7, 18–20, 24, 29, 157–58, 169, 189, 193, 330–34, 354, 357, 379, 388. See also *désoeuvrement*.
Ion of Chios, 116

Jäger, Lorenz, 297
Jakobson, Roman, 93, 399n17
Jarvis, Simon, 50, 68
Jaspers, Karl, 305–6
Jena Circle, 60, 75
Jesi, Furio, 402n3, 408n11
Joyce, Richard, 347, 437n20
Jünger, Ernst, 418n25
Justinian, Emperor, 122